M000313949

come expl

different perspectives on american politics

popular perspective

Do you know... that popular television shows, such as *24* and *The West Wing*, may have helped pave the way for the landmark election of an African-American President in 2008?

Turn to page 433

your perspective

Do you know... that a college sophomore played a significant role in securing passage of the Twenty-seventh Amendment to the U.S. Constitution?

Turn to page 49

AMERICAN GOVERNMENT

HISTORICAL, POPULAR AND GLOBAL PERSPECTIVES

SECOND EDITION

Kenneth Dautrich
Associate Professor of Public Policy
University of Connecticut

David A. Yalof
Associate Professor of Political Science
University of Connecticut

WADSWORTH
CENGAGE Learning™

Australia • Brazil • Japan • Korea • Mexico • Singapore • Spain • United Kingdom • United States

WADSWORTH
CENGAGE Learning

American Government: Historical, Popular and Global Perspectives, Second Edition

Kenneth Dautrich
David A. Yalof

Publisher: Suzanne Jeans

Executive Editor: Carolyn Merrill

Development Editor: Betty Slack

Associate Development Editor: Katherine Hayes

Editorial Assistant: Angela Hodge

Media Editor: Laura Hildebrand

Marketing Manager: Lydia LeStar

Marketing Coordinator: Josh Hendrick

Senior Marketing Communications Manager:
Heather Baxley

Associate Content Project Manager:
Sara Abbott

Art Director: Linda Helcher

Print Buyer: Fola Orekoya

Rights Acquisition Specialist, Image:
Amanda Groszko

Senior Rights Acquisition Specialist, Text:
Katie Huha

Production Service/Compositor:
Lachina Publishing Services

Text Designer: Nesbitt Design

Cover Designer: Rokusek Design

© 2012, 2009 Wadsworth, Cengage Learning

ALL RIGHTS RESERVED. No part of this work covered by the copyright herein may be reproduced, transmitted, stored, or used in any form or by any means graphic, electronic, or mechanical, including but not limited to photocopying, recording, scanning, digitizing, taping, Web distribution, information networks, or information storage and retrieval systems, except as permitted under Section 107 or 108 of the 1976 United States Copyright Act, without the prior written permission of the publisher.

For product information and technology assistance, contact us at
Cengage Learning Customer & Sales Support, 1-800-354-9706
For permission to use material from this text or product,
submit all requests online at **cengage.com/permissions**
Further permissions questions can be emailed to
permissionrequest@cengage.com

Library of Congress Control Number: 2010940279

Student Edition:
ISBN-13: 978-0-495-79815-6
ISBN-10: 0-495-79815-0

No Separate Policy Chapters Version:
ISBN-13: 978-0-495-91004-6
ISBN-10: 0-495-91004-X

Paper Edition:
ISBN-13: 978-0-495-91083-1
ISBN-10: 0-495-91083-X

Wadsworth
20 Channel Center Street
Boston, MA 02210
USA

Cengage Learning is a leading provider of customized learning solutions with office locations around the globe, including Singapore, the United Kingdom, Australia, Mexico, Brazil and Japan. Locate your local office at **international.cengage.com/region.**

Cengage Learning products are represented in Canada by Nelson Education, Ltd.

For your course and learning solutions, visit **www.cengage.com.**

Purchase any of our products at your local college store or at our preferred online store **www.cengagebrain.com.**

Printed in the United States of America
1 2 3 4 5 6 7 14 13 12 11 10

This book is dedicated to the next generation of responsible citizens who will inherit the American government; in particular, our students and our own children:

Allison, Benjamin, Jane, Kenny, and Rachel

Brief Contents

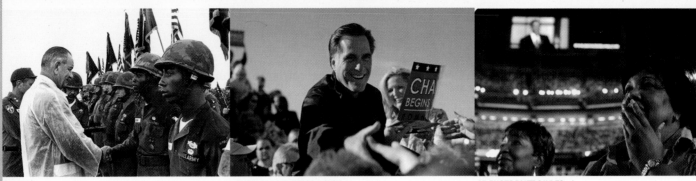

CORBIS   MIKE SEGAR/REUTERS/LANDOV   AP PHOTO/MATT SAYLES

1 FOUNDATIONS

2 INSTITUTIONS

3 POLITICAL BEHAVIOR

AP PHOTO/MICHAEL CAULFIELD

American Government: Historical, Popular and Global Perspectives

iv

Contents

AP PHOTO/RICK BOWMER

VISIONS OF AMERICA/JOE SOHM/PHOTODISC/GETTY IMAGES

ANNOTATED CONSTITUTION OF THE UNITED STATES OF AMERICA   C-1

© 2012 CENGAGE LEARNING

Chapter 2   The Founding and the Constitution

TAMI CHAPPELL/REUTERS/LANDOV

Chapter 4   Civil Liberties

Chapter 5   Civil Rights, Equality, and Social Movements

AP PHOTO/STEPHAN SAVOIA

PART 2

INSTITUTIONS

Chapter 6   Congress

Chapter 7   The Presidency

KEVIN LAMARQUE/REUTERS/LANDOV

Chapter 8 The Federal Bureaucracy

CHIP SOMODEVILLA/GETTY IMAGES

MARK WILSON/GETTY IMAGES NEWS/GETTY IMAGES

Chapter 9   The Judiciary

PART 3

POLITICAL BEHAVIOR

Chapter 10   Public Opinion

MANUEL BALCE CENETA/ASSOCIATED PRESS

Chapter 11 Interest Groups

JEFF GREENBERG/ALAMY

Chapter 12 The Media and Politics

ROCKTHEVOTE.COM

Chapter 14   Voting and Participation

CAROLYN KASTER/AP PHOTO

Chapter 13   Political Parties

JUSTIN SULLIVAN/GETTY IMAGES

Chapter 15   Campaigns and Elections

RHONA WISE/AFP/GETTY IMAGES

Special Features

American Government . . . In Historical Perspective

American Government . . . In Popular Perspective

American Government . . . In Global Perspective

Your Perspective... on American Government

 # CHECK the List

POLITICS InterActive!

An Introduction to American Government

This is a textbook about the American government, the success of which depends upon a responsible citizenry willing to ask tough questions of its leaders and demand reasonable answers in return. We live in an increasingly interconnected world; more than at any time in American history, the policies and actions of the U.S. government have an impact on the citizens of other nations, just as their governments' policies in turn have an impact on American citizens. Despite all the changes that have occurred over the course of the nation's history, the past is replete with examples from which we can learn. The challenge facing instructors of American government today is how to take adequate account of all these changes while never losing sight of the issues and events from the nation's past and their significance today.

We offer in this second edition of our textbook all the nuts and bolts of the U.S. government and how it works; but as with our first edition, we do not settle for mere surface descriptions and analysis of American government and politics. We also seek to educate students about American politics in ways that go beyond the essentials of government by placing current political issues and debates in perspective. By examining the current state of American politics from different angles, we hope to encourage students to think critically about the significance of certain persons, places, and events in American politics and consider all the different ways in which they might be viewed and interpreted. College students in recent years have been witness to historical shifts in American politics: Barack Obama's presidential campaign and the emergence of a more energetic and younger voting contingent as a force in the 2008 election; the unified resistance of moderate and conservative Republicans to most aspects of the Obama administration's agenda; the rise of the Tea Party movement and its criticism of both parties; the passage of landmark health care legislation and the political fallout of the Obama administration's legislative agenda on the 2010 elections. All of these events offer unprecedented opportunities for testing political theories and concepts against modern-day realities.

As educators, we never want to let students accept at face value these and other essential aspects of American politics—we thus offer alternative perspectives to help students think more critically about American government and politics. For example, we don't want students to assume that all victories in the American political system are equally important; we want them to realize that prevailing political circumstances exert a powerful influence on how different entities may define "victory." For example, some observers criticized Barack Obama and the Democrats for passing comprehensive health care legislation on the strength of a slim partisan majority; and yet when Lyndon Johnson, at the height of his party's political power in early 1965, was informed by an aide that the White House had just won passage of a desired piece of legislation by a wide margin, the president purportedly remarked: "How much more could we have gotten had we been willing to win by just one vote?" In similar fashion, some defeats may still advance the given cause, such as when losses generate attention or publicity for a previously unrecognized issue. For instance, the newly formed Republican Party's defeat in the 1856 presidential election set the stage for Abraham Lincoln's election as the first Republican president in 1860, and the eloquent dissents written by Supreme Court Justice Oliver Wendell Holmes in the 1920s pointed the way to the more liberal free speech doctrines embraced by a majority of Supreme Court justices in the 1960s.

Throughout the chapters of this textbook, we offer students of American government and politics the means by which to think critically about those topics. Blinded by what is in front of us now, we often ignore lessons from the past. American government and politics have changed dramatically in the more than two centuries of the nation's existence, yet certain issues persist. In this textbook we investigate America's political institutions and processes from a number of different viewpoints in an effort to take the full measure of American politics.

Different Perspectives on American Politics

We offer in these pages no polemic or theoretical argument about what American politics should look like or stand for, either now or in the years ahead. To the degree it's possible, we attempt to avoid normative judgments about American political institutions or individuals based on a particular ideological point of view—whether conservative or liberal, radical or moderate. Instead, we aim to provide a more measured view of government institutions and processes. We complement the text presentation of the essentials of American government with a focus on three perspectives, allowing students to view American government from a variety of different angles.

The Historical Perspective

The historical perspective places issues and problems of contemporary American politics within the context of past events and circumstances. Looking back provides important lessons applicable today. In examining the past we find that some of our new and "unprecedented" political controversies are neither new nor unprecedented. The faces may have changed and the policies may have been transformed, but the challenges the nation faces today are often newer versions of past dilemmas and problems.

Viewing American politics through the prism of history allows students to gain a greater appreciation for American government, both its flaws and its successes. Furthermore, placing American government in historical perspective facilitates an understanding of how the modern political system works. For example, the smoke-filled rooms of the nineteenth century in which political party bosses often selected political candidates threatened democracy and undermined accountability to the majority. Those smoke-filled rooms no longer exist today, as progressive reforms introduced in the early part of the twentieth century forced major political parties to use slightly more democratic means to choose candidates. Still, party bosses continue to exert considerable influence by determining where the party will allocate its resources. A thorough examination of past problems, issues, and conflicts does not negate the uniqueness of the current American condition, but it does offer a better understanding of contemporary issues. In some cases, studying the past assures us that the political process does work in a positive way; in other cases, it reminds us that we are not the first to face certain difficulties, and it suggests that we may want to seek more direction from the past about what works and what does not.

The Popular Perspective

The popular perspective offers yet another useful framework for examining political issues. At its core, American government is built upon the bedrock of popular consent. The U.S. Constitution itself and the institutions of government underscore the importance of the role of the people in American government. The biennial election of every member of the House of Representatives and the frequent elections of many state and local officials remind us that securing the popular will has been essential to our system from the beginning. The number and frequency of public opinion polls are further testament to the importance of the popular will. Popular culture also plays a role in influencing the popular perspective. Best-selling books, popular movies, and highly rated television shows all can have a lasting impact on the polity as well through their depiction of American politics . . . the good, the bad, and the ugly.

All these different sources offer a valuable perspective on where hot and not-so-hot political issues stand in the eyes of the public. As popular opinion on the war in Iraq shifted, Bush administration officials responsible for foreign policy were forced to make decisions and advise the president in a more complex (and increasingly hostile) political environment. Students need to take account of shifting political winds to understand why certain events transpired as they did. A popular perspective on American government promotes a deeper appreciation for the nuances of the American political system.

The Global Perspective

The global perspective offers viewpoints and opinions *about* U.S. government institutions and processes from the media, political elites, and the public in other parts of the world. (Though it may help foster some useful comparisons, this global perspective should not be confused with a strictly *comparative* analysis of political institutions and processes in different countries.) Over the years the nations of the world have become increasingly interconnected through communications advances (such as TV, satellite, and the Internet), the improved mobility of people (such as by more routine air travel), economic interdependencies (such as the North American Free Trade Agreement), and political changes (such as the creation of the United Nations after World War II). Now more than ever, American government affects and is affected by events, circumstances, and conflicts all over the world.

Though few would argue that the American government should develop policies based primarily on the views of others, awareness of how "outsiders" view the American government lends a valuable perspective to our understanding of the subject. Franklin Delano Roosevelt's controversial lend-lease agreement with Britain in 1940 (by which he "traded" war materials to Britain with little hope of repayment) angered many Democrats from his own party who wanted the United States to stay absolutely neutral in the conflict in Europe. FDR knew, however, that Western European hopes for victory in the war against the Nazis were fading, and he wanted to assure both the leaders and the citizens of Britain in particular that they were not alone. Almost sixty years later, many were surprised when in 2003 some of the long-time Western European allies of the United States refused to support American military operations in Iraq. American officials' awareness of how their actions are viewed in other parts of the world can only benefit decision makers as they guide the United States through the increasingly interconnected world of global politics.

The Perspectives

The three different perspectives described above offer students a broader view in which to enhance their understanding of American government and politics. Even more importantly, these perspectives provide the means for students to engage in critical thinking about American political issues—in effect, they allow students to challenge more effectively what they read and hear in the media and elsewhere. Does that television news anchor understand that the political rivalry he or she is discussing has roots in the early nineteenth century? Does knowing the history affect the significance of an event or change the way political officials should treat the issue? To what extent does that state legislature's controversial policy confront popular approval in its own state and region? Did officials know how the newly occupied nation might react, and did it craft its policies accordingly? These three perspectives are not just helpful—they may be critical to helping students see beyond the here and now.

That said, every student also views American politics through his or her own narrow prism. American military interventions abroad are one thing, but when the U.S. government actually drafts college-age student into the army—as occurred most recently during the Vietnam War—students may come to see the intervention with an entirely different eye. Similarly, the passage of landmark health care legislation means something entirely different for those students who can now remain longer on their family health care policies and thus put off worrying about obtaining their own health care insurance until much farther into the future. The textbook thus offers stu-

dents **"Your Perspective"** as a window into American politics that looks specifically at students' personal vantage points—with the understanding, of course, that students come from a wide range of backgrounds and experiences.

Organization of the Textbook

Part I Foundations

Part I ("Foundations," Chapters 1 through 5) of the textbook begins with a discussion of how three different perspectives on American politics can add to and help shape our understanding of American politics and the creation and evolution of its institutions and processes. In Chapter 1, after reviewing the forms and functions of government in general and highlighting fundamental aspects of American political culture, we pose a hypothetical question: Is American democracy on the decline? We then consider evidence that has been offered in recent years to support and contradict that controversial proposition, using an examination of historical perspectives in order to place contentions such as these in their proper contexts. Chapters 2 through 5 begin the textbook's consideration of the American political system with a discussion of the origins of the American government and the Constitution (Chapter 2), the federal system and the rights and liberties that derive from the Constitution (Chapter 3), and the Bill of Rights and subsequent amendments that guarantee equality (Chapters 4 and 5).

Part II Institutions

Part II ("Institutions," Chapters 6 through 9) considers the major institutions of government formed under the Constitution. Congress (Chapter 6), the executive branch (Chapter 7), and the judiciary (Chapter 9) were all established by the first three articles of the Constitution, though their appearance and functions today might surprise many of the founders who designed them. The bureaucracy (Chapter 8) is not specifically mentioned in the Constitution but it is an inevitable product of a government expected to tackle the problems of a nation that is home to a diverse population of over 300 million people.

Part III Political Behavior

In Part III ("Political Behavior," Chapters 10 through 15), we consider political behavior and its evolution. Interest groups (Chapter 11) and political parties (Chapter 13) are not modern phenomena; they were outgrowths of the American political system from the beginning. Public opinion (Chapter 10), the media (Chapter 12), voting (Chapter 14), and campaigns and elections (Chapter 15) receive extended attention in this part of the textbook.

New to the Second Edition

This revised second edition offers new features, updated coverage and updated features that will assist students as they grapple with the constantly shifting realities of American politics.

New features students will find most beneficial are:

- newly created **"Your perspective"** boxes for each chapter, which consider various aspects of American politics from the unique perspective of college students, and which take advantage of the experiences they bring to bear when studying American government;
- succinctly written **learning objectives** provided at the beginning of every chapter, and then repeated throughout each chapter at points in the text that directly address those objectives;

- **critical thinking questions** added at the end of many of the thematic boxes, which encourage students to think about the material in new and interesting ways, and which may be used to spark discussion of the material in class;
- a broader scope to the boxes on **popular perspectives**, which now includes discussion of how popular culture (including television shows, movies, bestselling books, etc.) interacts with American politics;
- and newly constituted **chapter summaries** presented in bullet-point format, which now directly parallel each chapter's learning objectives.

Updated Coverage

In recent years we have witnessed a significant transformation of the American political landscape. The collapse of the economy in late 2007 was followed a year later by Barack Obama's historic victory in the 2008 presidential election. The Obama administration's first two years in office proved especially contentious, as the President and his Democratic allies in Congress pushed through their legislative agenda against strong resistance from Republicans and newly formed outside groups such as the Tea Party. The bitterly contested November 2010 midterm elections were a product of this growing unrest.

The second edition features numerous new chapter-opening vignettes, boxes, tables and figures that emphasize these recent developments and should help bring students up to speed with new political realities.

Updated Features

- "Now and Then" vignettes at the beginning of Chapters 1 & 13, which consider the role that the Tea Party and other interest groups played in the November 2010 midterm elections; other new vignettes that consider such topics as historical parallels for constitutional amendments, incremental policymaking on social issues; the role that states play as "laboratories of democracy" for issues like universal health care; President Obama's methods of prosecuting the war on terror; President Bush's historic rise and fall in the polls; the role of a new medium (the Internet) in shaping policy; how president address economic crises; and more.
- New Popular Perspective boxes on Barack Obama's 2010 State of the Union Address; the role played by White House Web sites and other aspects of the "interactive presidency"; the way that criminal defense attorneys are portrayed heroically in movies; the role of blogs in shaping modern public opinion; television's embracing of women and racial minority presidents long before Barack Obama's historic victory; the use of campaign books by presidential wannabes hoping to get their message across to new audiences; the Oscar-award winning vice president, and more.
- New Historical Perspective boxes on Senators who switch their political parties; the role of sensationalism in driving media coverage; and the incorporation of civil liberties (including the Second Amendment right to bear arms) to be applied to state and local governments.
- New Global Perspective boxes addressing British perspectives on a new Supreme Court Justice who arose from poverty; Al Jazeera's perspective on Obama's war against terror; the German press's favorable coverage of the Obama campaign in 2008; China's reaction to Obama's fiscal stimulus plan; world perspectives on the Obama administration's new strategy for military intervention in Afghanistan; and Japan's reaction to the wealth and power of the New York City Mayor.

Special Instructional Features

We offer a number of recurring special instructional features designed to engage students' interest and provide pedagogical support to help them master chapter material. Several of the recurring features highlight the three perspectives that underlie the book's presentation.

Now & Then

Each chapter (except Chapter 1) begins with an opening vignette entitled **"Now & Then,"** in which some situation relevant to the chapter topic is presented. Many students with at least some exposure to American politics will be able to identify the more recent issue or event (i.e., "Now") to which the situation appears to refer. At the same time, however, the situation also refers to some event or issue in the past (i.e., "Then") that may not be so familiar to students. Those who correctly identified the more recent event may be surprised to learn that the situation presented also describes another event from the nation's past. The "Now & Then" opening vignette thus demonstrates that although people and circumstances may change dramatically, certain issues and problems persist. At the end of the chapter, the section entitled **"Now & Then: Making the Connection"** revisits the two examples from the beginning of the chapter, ties them together, and then connects them to major themes of the chapter as a whole.

Perspectives Features

Each chapter also includes four features that focus on the different perspectives (historical, popular, global, and your perspective). **American Government...in Historical Perspective** compares different moments in American history in which the same event or circumstance recurred, albeit with different actors and in somewhat different forms. **American Government...in Popular Perspective** offers evidence, ranging from public opinion polls to a review of popular culture, about where the American public stands on some issue relevant to the chapter. **American Government...in Global Perspective** presents material from other countries—perhaps a newspaper editorial, a quote from a foreign politician, or evidence from foreign public opinion polls—that offers outsiders' perspectives on some aspect of American politics. Finally, **Your Perspective...on American Government** provides material that relates the subject or topic at hand to students' own personal experiences.

Check the List

Late-night television host David Letterman is not the only one to offer "Top Ten" lists—such lists have become part of American culture, whether they feature the top ten movies of the year, the top ten political cartoons of the month, or the top forty songs of week. In each chapter of the textbook the **"Check the List"** feature presents a list (sometimes, but not always, a ranked list) of people, places, events, issues, and so on that addresses some aspect of American politics.

Study Aids and Resources

LEARNING OBJECTIVES
★ WHAT YOU WILL LEARN ★

Aids to facilitate study of the material include detailed **learning objectives** at the beginning of each chapter so students can know what will be expected of them at the outset, as well as a **chapter summary** of key points at the end of each chapter that specifically address the learning objectives laid out at the beginning. Additionally, within each chapter **key terms** are highlighted in boldface type and defined in the margins of the pages. These key terms are also listed at the end of the chapter, and the terms and definitions are repeated in a glossary at the end of the book. Also at the end of each chapter is a list of **resources**, both print and electronic, that students can explore on their own.

Politics InterActive!

The **Politics InterActive!** feature at the end of each chapter presents some contemporary political event or conflict related to the chapter content and instructs students to visit the Wadsworth Web site www.cengage.com/dautrich/americangovernment/2e accompanying this textbook to explore further Internet resources that offer historical, popular, and global perspectives on that same topic. These Internet resources encourage students' critical thinking and help them realize just how much their views of American politics may be shaped—or reshaped—by their exposure to alternate perspectives. The interactive exercise component of the Politics InterActive! feature then poses a similar issue and asks students to explore Internet resources that offer varying perspectives on that topic.

Many other textbooks subtly (and, in some cases, not so subtly) offer the authors' own "take" on American politics. Although some instructors may appreciate that more polemical approach, we aim to provide something different. Recognizing that students come to the introductory American government course from a variety of different backgrounds and with varying levels of understanding about American politics, we present all the nuts and bolts they need to understand the system in as straightforward and clear a manner as possible. But then we go a step further: To complement that foundation of basic information, we offer materials that present different perspectives on each topic. These different perspectives are intended to encourage students to engage in critical thinking about the political process as a whole.

The historical, popular, and global perspectives—as well as the material that address American politics from students' own perspectives—do not interfere with the description of essential foundations. If anything, they should spark students' interest in revisiting what they learned in high school, from the media, and elsewhere about American politics with a more discerning and critical eye. Perhaps many students will take this critical approach beyond the course itself and become actual participants in the process. If they do so with a more critical and skeptical eye, our democratic system can only benefit.

Supplements for Instructors

The Newsletter

Updated and e-mailed to professors four times per semester, these newsletters are written by the authors and use current events to provide lecture launchers, fast facts, and ways to view the news of the day through historical, popular, and global perspectives. They are archived and can be accessed via the instructor's companion site or the book's community site: http://www.cengagesites.com/academic/?site=1805.

PowerLecture™ with JoinIn™ and ExamView®

This DVD includes two sets of PowerPoint slides—a book specific and a media-enhanced set, a Test Bank in both Microsoft Word and ExamView formats, an Instructor Manual, JoinIn Clickers, and a Resource Integration Guide. The two types of PowerPoints are described below.

Interactive book-specific **PowerPoint**® lectures, a one-stop lecture and class preparation tool, makes it easy for you to assemble, edit, publish, and present book specific lectures for your course. You will have access to a set of PowerPoints with outlines specific to each chapter of *American Government: Historical, Popular, and Global Perspectives* as well as photos, figures, and tables found in the book.

The **media-enhanced PowerPoint**® slides for each chapter can be used on their own or easily integrated with the book-specific power point outlines. Audio and video clips depicting both historic and current day events; NEW animated learning modules illustrating key concepts; tables, statistical charts, and graphs; and photos from the book as well as outside sources are provided at the appropriate places in the chapter. You can also add your own materials—using both types of PowerPoints and your own material to create a powerful, personalized, classroom or online presentation.

A **test bank** in Microsoft® Word and ExamView® computerized testing offers a large array of well-crafted multiple-choice and essay questions, along with their answers and page references.

An **Instructor's Manual** includes learning objectives, chapter outlines, discussion questions, suggestions for stimulating class activities and projects, tips on integrating media into your class (including step-by-step instructions on how to create your own podcasts), suggested readings and Web resources, and a section specially designed to help teaching assistants and adjunct instructors.

JoinIn™ offers book-specific "clicker" questions that test and track student comprehension of key concepts. Political Polling questions simulate voting, engage students, foster dialogue on group behaviors and values, and add personal relevance; the results can be compared to national data, leading to lively discussions.

The **Resource Integration Guide** outlines the rich collection of resources available to instructors and students within the chapter-by-chapter framework of the book, suggesting how and when each supplement can be used to optimize learning.

Political Theatre 2.0 DVD

Bring politics home to students with Political Theatre 2.0, up to date through the 2008 election season. This is the second edition of this three-DVD series and includes video clips that show American political thought throughout the public sector. Clips include both classic and contemporary political advertisements, speeches, interviews and more. Available to adopters of Cengage textbooks, version 2.0 provides lots of added functionality with this updated edition.

JoinIn™ on TurningPoint for Political Theatre

For even more interaction, combine Political Theatre with the innovative teaching tool of a classroom response system through JoinIn™. Poll your students with questions created for you or create your own questions. Built within the Microsoft® PowerPoint® software, it's easy to integrate into your current lectures in conjunction with the "clicker" hardware of your choice.

The Wadsworth News Videos for American Government 2012 DVD

This collection of three- to six-minute video clips on relevant political issues serves as a great lecture or discussion launcher.

ABC Video: Speeches by President Barack Obama

DVD of nine famous speeches by President Barack Obama, from 2004 through his inauguration, including his speech at the 2004 Democratic National Convention; his 2008 speech on race, "A More Perfect Union"; and his 2009 inaugural address. Speeches are divided into short video segments for easy, time-efficient viewing. This instructor supplement also features critical-thinking questions and answers for each speech, designed to spark classroom discussion.

Online Resources

CourseMate The CourseMate for *American Government: Historical, Popular, and Global Perspectives* offers a variety of rich online learning resources designed to enhance the student experience. These resources include video activities, audio summaries, critical thinking activities, simulations, animated learning modules, interactive timelines, primary source activities, flashcards, learning objectives, glossaries, and crossword puzzles. Chapter resources are correlated with key chapter learning concepts, and users can browse or search for content in a variety of ways.

NewsNow, a new asset available on CourseMate, is a combination of weekly news stories from the Associated Press, videos, and images that bring current events to life for the student. For instructors, NewsNow includes an additional set of multimedia-rich PowerPoint slides posted each week to the password-protected area of the text's companion Web site. Instructors may use these slides to take a class poll or trigger a lively debate about the events that are shaping the world right now. And because this all-in-one presentation tool includes the text of the original newsfeed, along with videos, photos and discussion questions, no Internet connection is required!

How do you assess your students' engagement in your course? How do you know your students have read the material or viewed the resources you've assigned? How can you tell if your students are struggling with a concept? With CourseMate, you can use the included Engagement Tracker to assess student preparation and engagement. Use the tracking tools to see progress for the class as a whole or for individual students. Identify students at risk early in the course. Uncover which concepts are most difficult for your class. Monitor time on task. Keep your students engaged.

CourseMate also features an interactive eBook that has highlighting and search capabilities along with links to simulations, animated PowerPoints that illustrate concepts, Interactive Timelines, Videos, Primary Source Activities, Case Studies, Tutorial Quizzes and Flashcards.

Go to cengagebrain.com/shop/ISBN/0495798150 to access your Political Science CourseMate resources.

WebTutor™ on Blackboard or WebCT

Rich with content for your American government course, this Web-based teaching and learning tool includes course management, study/mastery, and communication tools. Use WebTutor™ to provide virtual office hours, post your syllabus, and track student progress with WebTutor's quizzing material. For students, WebTutor™ offers real-time access to interactive online tutorials and simulations, practice quizzes, and Web links—all correlated to *American Government: Historical, Popular, and Global Perspectives*.

Instructor Companion Web site

Instructors have access to the Instructor's Manual and PowerPoints, correlated by chapter.

Instructors also have access to the Instructor's Guide to YouTube, which shows American government instructors where on the Internet to find videos that can be used as learning tools in class. Organized by fifteen topics, the guide follows the sequence of an American government course and includes a preface with tips on how to use Internet videos in class.

American Government CourseReader: Politics in Context

American Government CourseReader: Politics in Context will enable instructors to create a customized reader. Using a database of hundreds of documents, readings, and videos, instructors can search by various criteria or browse the collection to preview and then select a customized collection to assign their students. The sources will be edited to an appropriate length and include pedagogical support—a head-note describing the document and critical-thinking and multiple-choice questions to verify that the student has read and understood the selection. Students will be able to take notes, highlight, and print content. The CourseReader allows the instructor to select exactly what students will be assigned with an easy-to-use interface and also provides an easily used assessment tool. The sources can be delivered online or in print format.

Aplia

Aplia is dedicated to improving students' learning by increasing their effort and engagement with your American Government course. Founded by an instructor for other instructors, Aplia offers students premium, automatically graded assignments. Aplia saves instructors valuable time they'd otherwise spend on routine grading while giving students an easy way to stay on top of coursework with regularly scheduled homework assignments.

Available through a Pin-code access, Aplia helps students learn the essential concepts of American Government and apply them to real life through the use of interactive coursework that strengthens their critical thinking and comprehensive reading skills. Organized by specific chapters of their textbook, students receive immediate, detailed explanations for every answer they input. Homework and class assignments help students come to class better prepared. Grades are automatically recorded in the instructor's Aplia gradebook. Aplia provides customer service that's quick, friendly, and knowledgeable. Aplia will be available with this book for Fall 2011. For more information, your local Cengage Wadsworth sales representative would be happy to assist you.

American Government and Aplia . . . a way to help students engage, prepare, and learn.

For Students, When Requested by Your Instructor

CourseMate The CourseMate for *American Government: Historical, Popular, and Global Perspectives* offers a variety of rich online learning resources designed to enhance the student experience. These resources include video activities, audio summaries, critical thinking activities, simulations, animated learning modules, interactive timelines, primary source activities, flashcards, learning objectives, glossaries, and crossword puzzles. All resources are correlated with key chapter learning concepts, and users can browse or search for content in a variety of ways.

Election 2010: An American Government Supplement

Written by John Clark and Brian Schaffner, this booklet addresses the 2010 congressional and gubernatorial races, with both real-time analysis and references.

The Obama Presidency—Year One Supplement

Much happens in the first year of a presidency, especially an historic one like that of Barack Obama. This full-color sixteen-page supplement by Kenneth Janda, Jeffrey Berry, and Jerry Goldman analyzes such issues as health care, the economy and the stimulus package, changes in the U.S. Supreme Court, and the effect Obama policy has had on global affairs.

Great Speeches Collection

Throughout the ages, great orators have stepped up to the podium and used their communication skills to persuade, inform, and inspire their audiences. Studying these speeches can provide tremendous insight into historical, political, and cultural events. The Great Speeches Collection includes the full text of over sixty memorable orations for you to incorporate into your course. Speeches can be collated in a printed reader to supplement your existing course materials or bound into a core textbook.

Latino American Politics

This thirty-two-page supplement by Fernando Pinon of San Antonio College uses real examples to detail politics related to Latino Americans.

PHOTO COURTESY OF THE AUTHORS

Kenneth J. Dautrich (Ph.D., Rutgers 1995) is an associate professor of public policy at the University of Connecticut in Storrs. He is also the founder and former director of the Center for Survey Research & Analysis at the University of Connecticut. Previously, Dr. Dautrich was a Research Fellow at the Media Studies Center in New York and has served as a senior faculty fellow at the Heldrich Center at Rutgers. His first book, *How the News Media Fail American Voters* (Columbia University Press, 1997), received scholarly praise in numerous political science circles. He also co-authored *The First Amendment and the Media in the Court of Public Opinion* (Cambridge University Press, 2002) and *The Future of the First Amendment* (Rowman & Littlefield, 2008). Dr. Dautrich's research and teaching focus on public opinion and American elections. For the past four years he has directed a set of national surveys on civic literacy in the American public and the role of higher education in advancing knowledge about American government. He is currently writing a book on findings from this project.

David A. Yalof (Ph.D., Johns Hopkins University 1997; J.D., University of Virginia 1991) is an associate professor of political science at the University of Connecticut. His first book, *Pursuit of Justices: Presidential Politics and the Selection of Supreme Court Nominees* (University of Chicago Press, 1999), was awarded the American Political Science Association's Richard E. Neustadt Award as the best book published on presidential studies in 1999. He is also the co-author of *The First Amendment and the Media in the Court of Public Opinion* (Cambridge University Press, 2002), *The Future of the First Amendment* (Rowman & Littlefield, 2008), and another textbook, *Constitutional Law: Civil Liberty and Individual Rights* (Foundation Press, 2007). Dr. Yalof has written extensively on issues in constitutional law and Supreme Court appointment politics—his work has been published in *Political Research Quarterly, Judicature, Constitutional Commentary*, and various other journals. He is currently nearing completion of a book-length manuscript about executive branch wrongdoing and the due process of law.

Acknowledgments

The second edition of *American Government: Historical, Popular, and Global Perspectives* is a product of the hard work of many, many people. First and foremost among them is our executive editor, Carolyn Merrill. At Cengage she has been the prime mover of this project. It is impossible to imagine pulling off a project like this without the management skills, temperament, and good humor that Carolyn provides. Tops among all of the great decisions Carolyn made was the hiring of Betty Slack as our development editor. In our minds, the team of Carolyn and Betty is a hard one to top.

Senior managers at Cengage also played a hands-on role in the development of this second edition, including Sean Wakely, P. J. Boardman, our publisher Suzanne Jeans, and Dan Silverburg. Their guidance and commitment to our book is, as always, greatly appreciated. We also extend our gratitude to the many other members of the Cengage staff we have come to depend upon in writing and producing this book and its supplemental materials: Katie Hayes, Lydia LeStar, Lindsey Richardson, Heather Baxley, Sara Abbott, Jeff Greene, Angela Hodge, Laura Hildebrand, Josh Allen, and Suzanne St. Clair. We would also like to extend a special note of thanks to Autumn Burger for her diligent work in the production process and Carly Bergey for her fine research in selecting pictures.

The many sales representatives at Cengage not only do a great job in getting the word out on our book, but they also have collected feedback from instructors and relayed it back to us. In many instances, our reps have provided their own guidance and feedback as well. Thankfully, all their efforts have helped improve the content of the book, and make it more responsive to the perspective of instructors who use it. Our hats are off to this terrific sales force. Mark, LeDawn, Houston, Sally, Nick, Laura, Davene . . . there are just too many of you to name. We are grateful for your many efforts.

Appreciation also goes to our colleagues at the University of Connecticut, especially those in the Department of Political Science and the Department of Public Policy, of which there are too many to list by name. Their patience, support, and advice in our writing of this second edition have not gone unnoticed; nor has the input we have received from our graduate students and undergraduate users of the text.

The many professionals, colleagues, and students who provide support and advice are not the only ones who influence the writing of a textbook. Our families must live with us through the writing and production cycles. Not only do they tolerate the fact that we often bring our work home, but they also give us strong motivation to get the job done. We cannot thank our better halves, Andrea and Mary Beth, enough. Our children, to whom this book is dedicated, are not shy about offering their ideas either. The book benefits from their youthful perspectives and advice.

Finally, there are many members of our profession and many practitioners in American politics who put in countless hours and intellectual energy aiding in the writing of this manuscript. Some participated in focus groups; others in informal conversations with us; and still others who spent much time marking up chapters. We are indebted to all those who have generously given time to this effort. A list of these contributors is found below. Please note, however, that any errors that remain are entirely our own.

We thank the reviewers who commented on drafts of the manuscript:

Reviewers of First Edition:

David Gray Adler
Idaho State University

Scott Ainsworth
University of Georgia

Noe Aguado
University of North Alabama

Dr. Lydia Andrade
University of the Incarnate Word

Yan Bai
Grand Rapids Community College

Christine M. Bailey
Ferris State University

Ross K. Baker
Rutgers University

Bethany Barratt
Roosevelt University

Timothy Barnett
Jacksonville State University

Brian Bearry
University of Texas–Dallas

William T. Bianco
Indiana University

David E. Birch
Tomball College

Scott E. Buchanan
Columbus State University

Jeffrey Bumgarner
Texas Christian University

Alexander M. Burton
South Texas College

Tom Caiazzo
East Georgia College

Douglas Camp Chaffey
Chatham College

Mark A. Cichock
University of Texas–Arlington

Stanley Clark
California State University–Bakersfield

Dewey M. Clayton
University of Louisville

Carolyn Cocca
SUNY–Old Westbury

Christopher A. Cooper
Western Carolina University

Kimberly Cowell-Meyers
American University

Brian Cravens
Montgomery College

Lane Crothers
Blinn College

Nicolas Damask
Scottsdale Community College

Andrew James Dowdle
University of Arkansas

LaVonne Downey
Roosevelt University

Dennis Driggers
California State University–Fresno

Anthony J. Eksterowicz
James Madison University

Charles Epp
University of Kansas

Matthew Eshbaugh-Soha
University of North Texas

Teri Fair
Suffolk University

Jeff Fox
Fort Lewis College

Brian Frederick
Northern Illinois University

Raymond Frey
Centenary College

Anthony Gabrielli
High Point University

G. David Gerson
North Carolina State

Joe Gershtenson
Eastern Kentucky University

Randy Glean
Midwestern State University

Timothy Gordinier
SUNY–Potsdam

Paul Goren
University of Minnesota–Twin Cities

Nathan Griffith
Belmont University

Joel Grossman
Johns Hopkins University

Willie Hamilton
Mount San Jacinto College

Thomas Haymes
Houston Community College, Northwest

Peter Heller
Manhattan College
John R. Hermann
Trinity University
Marjorie Hershey
Indiana University
Richard Himmelfarb
Hofstra University
Samuel Hoff
Delaware State University
Jennifer E. Horan
University of North Carolina–
Wilmington
Timothy Hoye
Texas Women's University
Lisa Huffstetler
University of Memphis
Charles F. Jacobs
St. Norbert College
W. Martin James
Henderson State University
Mark S. Jendrysik
University of North Dakota
Irina S. Khmelko
Georgia Southern University
Quentin Kidd
Christopher Newport University
Richard Kiefer
Waubonsee Community College
Kimi King
University of North Texas
Marvin P. King Jr.
University of Mississippi
Anders Michael Kinney
Calhoun Community College
Dina Krois
Lansing Community College
Paul Labedz
Valencia Community College
J. Celeste Lay
Tulane University
Nancy Lind
Illinois State University
Thomas H. Little
University of North Carolina–
Greensboro
Eduardo Magalhaes III
Simpson College
Gary Lee Malecha
University of Portland

Steven Marin
Victor Valley College
Wendy Martinek
SUNY–Binghamton
Tina Mavrikos-Adamou
Hofstra University
Scott D. McClurg
Southern Illinois University–
Carbondale
Eddie L. Meaders
University of North Texas
Scott Meinke
Bucknell University
Philip Meyer
University of North Carolina–
Chapel Hill
Mark C. Miller
Clark University
Richard Millsap
Texas Christian University,
University of Texas–Arlington
Craig Mulling
Prairie State College
Jason C. Newman
Consumnes River College
Patrick Novotny
Georgia Southern University
Anthony J. Nownes
University of Tennessee
Laura Olson
Clemson University
Richard Pacelle
Georgia Southern University
David Penna
Gallaudet University
Ronald Pettus
St. Charles Community College
John Queen
Glendale Community College
Donald R. Ranish
Antelope Valley College
Russell Renka
Southeast Missouri State
University
Heather Roberson
St. Petersburg College
J. Philip Rogers
San Antonio College
Donald Roy
Ferris State University

Martin Saiz
California State University–Northridge

Kay Scott
University of Central Florida, retired

T. M. Sell
Highline Community College

Ronald Seyb
Skidmore College

Youngtae Shin
University of Central Oklahoma

Rebecca L. Sims
South Georgia College

Fred Slocum
Minnesota State University–Mankato

John Speer
Houston Community College, Southwest

Mary Stegmeier
University of Virginia

Marcia B. Steinhauer
Rider University, retired

John P. Tuman
University of Nevada–Las Vegas

Brian Vargus
Indiana University at Purdue University, Indianapolis

John Vento
Antelope Valley College

Kevin Wagner
Florida Atlantic University

Adam L. Warber
Clemson University

Carl Anthony Wege
Coastal Georgia Community College

Paul Weizer
Fitchburg State College

Matt Wetstein
San Joaquin Delta College

Sharon G. Whitney
Tennessee Technological University

Kenneth C. Williams
Michigan State University

From the Advanced Placement community:

Karen Coston
Blacksburg High School (Blacksburg, VA)

Rebecca Small
Herndon High School (Herndon, VA)

Many thanks to those who attended focus groups:

Sharon Alter
Harper College

Lynn Brink
North Lake College

Randy Burnside
Southern Illinois University–Carbondale

Peggy Connally
North Central Texas College

Erwin Cornelius
McHenry County College

Renee Ann Cramer
Drake University

Rebecca Deen
University of Texas–Arlington

Louis DeSipio
University of California–Irvine

Victoria Farrar-Myers
University of Texas–Arlington

Susan Gluck Mezey
Loyola University–Chicago

Donna Guerin
Moraine Valley Community College

Ellen Lazarus
University of Texas–Arlington

Larry Martinez
California State University–Long Beach

Debra Moore
Southern Illinois University–Carbondale

Patrick Schmidt
Macalester College

Valerie Simms
Northeastern Illinois University, retired

Rorie Solberg
Oregon State University

Abigaile Van Horn
Purdue University

Richard Vollmer
Oklahoma City Community College

Molly Waite
Harper College

Charles Weston
Western Illinois University

David Wigg
St. Louis Community College

Laura M. Wood
Tarrant County College

Robert Wood
University of North Dakota
Mark Wrighton
Millikin University

Reviewers of Second Edition:

Mary Balchunis
LaSalle University
Murray Bessette
Morehead State University
Holly Brasher
University of Alabama at Birmingham
Robert Bromber
University of Maryland—University College
Steven Collins
Oklahoma State University—Oklahoma City
Thom Costa
Florida State College at Jacksonville
Lance Denning
Metropolitan State College of Denver
Sheng Ding
Bloomsburg University
Donald Gawronski
Maricopa Community College—Mesa Campus
Lauren Hall
Rochester Institute of Technology
M. Ahad Hayaud-Din
Brookhaven College
David Head
John Tyler Community College
Timothy Hoye
Texas Woman's University
Melody Huckaby
Cameron University

Terri Jett
Butler University
Gina Keel
SUNY Oneonta
Patricia Knol
Triton College
Christopher Latimer
SUNY Cortland
Randolph Lightfoot
Saint Petersburg College—Tarpon Springs
Gary Malecha
University of Portland
Roger Marietta
Darton College
Scott Meinke
Bucknell College
Jason Mycoff
University of Delaware
Chris Newman
Elgin Community College
Richard Pacelle
Georgia Southern University
Greg Rabb
Jamestown Community College
Cherry Rain
Redlands Community College
Mitzi Ramos
University of Illinois at Champaign
Susan Roomberg
University of Texas at San Antonio
David Ross
Stark State College of Technology
Sandy Self
Hardin-Simmons University
Patrick Shade
Edison Community College
Dari Sylvester
University of the Pacific
Roy Tate
Redlands Community College

AMERICAN GOVERNMENT

1 Perspectives on American Government

Introduction to Perspectives on American Government

* ★ Understand that issues and topics in American politics may be viewed from a variety of perspectives, including historical context, popular culture, views from others around the world, and views from college students

Forms and Functions of Government

* ★ Identify the philosophical underpinnings of the American political system through the exploration of important theories such as the "social contract" theory and the concept of the "natural law"
* ★ Compare and contrast democracy with other forms of government

American Government and Politics

* ★ Explain the importance of the value of popular sovereignty, and how that value is realized through "representative democracy" in the United States

American Political Culture

* ★ Define "political culture" and describe the unique combination of political beliefs and values that form the American political culture, including majority rule, liberty, limited government, diversity, individualism, and equality of economic opportunity.

Is American Democracy on the Decline?

* ★ Assess the health of American democracy and evaluate whether the American system is in decline by reviewing trends in voter turnout, negativity in politics, the influence of money in policy outcomes, and the integrity of election outcomes

Historical, Popular, and Global Perspectives

* ★ Appreciate that the American political system is best studied from a variety of perspectives, including historical, popular, and global

CourseMate

REUTERS/GARY HERSHOM/LANDOV

President-elect Barack Obama and Vice President-elect Joe Biden on the night of their victory in the 2008 presidential election.

AP PHOTO/J. SCOTT APPLEWHITE

Representative Nancy Pelosi and Senator Harry Reid (right) on the November 2006 evening of victories that cemented Pelosi's ascension to Speaker and Reid's becoming Senate majority leader.

TOM WILLIAMS/ROLL CALL VIA GETTY IMAGES

Representative John Boehner on election night 2010 gets teary-eyed as he realizes the GOP victory will make him Speaker of the House.

AP PHOTO/ED REINKE

Senator-elect Rand Paul (R-KY) was one of the victorious Tea Party-backed candidates in the 2010 midterm elections.

Placing the 2010 Midterm Elections into Perspective

The Republican Party achieved a major victory in the 2010 congressional elections by picking up more than 60 House seats and thus capturing a majority once again. The GOP also picked up 6 Senate seats, slicing the Democratic margin of control in that chamber from 18 to 6 Senate seats in all. The GOP shift, particularly in the House of Representatives, is significant. Between 1950 and 2008 partisan control of the House of Representatives switched only two times (1995 and 2007). The outcome of the 2010 races was also striking in the way it signaled a dramatic shift in voter preferences over a mere two-year period. When President Barack Obama took the oath of office in January 2009, he had the support of a Democratic-controlled Congress bolstered by successive election cycles that overwhelmingly favored his party. From the 2006 and 2008 election results, many political analysts felt that a permanent shift favoring the Democratic Party was underway. As it turned out, voters in 2010 quickly reversed course, sweeping Republicans into Congress and returning the American political system to a state of "divided government," with a Democrat in the White House and a comfortable majority of Republicans in the House of Representatives. What undercurrents of popular opinion could possibly produce such an abrupt change of course? Did 2010 mark a historically unprecedented midterm election outcome? How schizophrenic does the American electorate appear to the rest of the world, as the decisions made by the U.S. electorate may have significant implications on global policy? Finally, based on the conflicting outcome of the 2008 and 2010 elections, can anybody predict what lies ahead for the 2012 presidential election?

The Top Ten Largest Partisan Gains in House Elections since 1914*

The 2010 congressional elections produced what many considered historic gains by the Republican Party. In the modern era of congressional elections the GOP gains, while impressive, are by no means unprecedented. The 2010 GOP gains in the House are only the seventh highest total dating back to 1914.

Listed below are the top ten partisan seat gains in House elections since 1914.

Partisan gains in the House

	Year	Party	Gain
✔	1932	Democrats	+ 97
✔	1938	Republicans	+ 80
✔	1922	Democrats	+ 75
✔	1948	Democrats	+ 75
✔	1914	Republicans	+ 66
✔	1920	Republicans	+ 63 seats
✔	2010	Republicans	+61 seats **
✔	1946	Republicans	+ 56 seats
✔	1994	Republicans	+ 54 seats
✔	1930	Democrats	+ 53 seats

*1914 is selected as the starting point for this list because that was the first congressional election after House membership was capped at 435 and the first congressional election after the Constitution was amended to require the direct election of U.S. Senators by a state's population of voters.

**Figures are updated as of November 5, 2010.

Introduction to Perspectives on American Government

Historical Perspective

★ LO Understand that issues and topics in American politics may be viewed from a variety of perspectives, including historical context, popular culture, views from others around the world, and views from college students

At least two things are striking from the 2010 midterm election results. First, the GOP made important and significant gains that should empower the party in the policymaking process, at least through 2012. Second, the electorate abruptly reversed course from the direction it had steered American politics only two years earlier. How unprecedented are these outcomes of the 2010 midterms?

The 2010 GOP gains are by no means historically unprecedented. Since 1914 (see the "Check the List" box above), there have been numerous election cycles that ended with party shifts far greater than those of 2010. In seven elections for the Senate, the partisan gains actually reached into the double digits, and in four of the elections for the House over that same period, at least 75 seats shifted from one party to the other. American voters have never been shy about bringing change to Washington.

Nor has the electorate been reluctant to shift course quickly. Most recently, as the economy began to soften and the Iraqi war lingered in 2006, voters eliminated the GOP's 10-seat Senate margin entirely, and transferred partisan control of the House to the Democrats by a 35-seat margin. Two years later, with the economy in a tailspin, voters enhanced Democratic Party control by sending Barack Obama to the White House and increasing Democratic majorities in the Senate to 20 and in the House to 78. This zig to the Democrats clearly zagged back to the GOP in 2010. Before concluding that American voters have developed a schizophrenic voting disorder, however, a glance at history demonstrates that the electorate has zig-zagged over short periods of time in the past as well. In 1946, American voters awarded Republicans 56 new seats in the House and then just two years later sent the Republican Congress packing. Voters similarly zig-zagged in 1992 and 1994 when they first voted into office Democratic President Bill Clinton and a strong Democratic Congress, only to provide the GOP with congressional majorities just two years later. So while the results of 2010 have led some to wonder why the electorate is acting so erratically of late, a view from history shows that such behavior is no anomaly.

Popular Perspective

Understanding the opinions of American voters provides yet another perspective from which to examine the 2010 outcomes. Why would the dynamics of public opinion deliver the White House and strong majorities to the Democrats in 2008, only to punish the Democrats in 2010 with a new GOP House majority?

A review of public opinion from 2006 through 2010 reveals a consistent and salient set of findings: consumer confidence hit new all-time lows, most thought the country was headed in the wrong direction, and voters largely blamed government for the recession. Political scientists have long documented the dynamic nature of public opinion during elections, including the strong inclination of voters to hold the party in power accountable for a problematic economy. Under the theory of "retrospective voting," voters assess their own economic standing and accordingly either blame or reward the party in power. In 2008, most voters held a dim view of their economic prospects and thus were more likely to vote to "throw out the rascals"—in this case that meant jettisoning Republicans from the White House. Two years later, most Americans continued to take a dim view of the economy. While many heard and agreed with the 2008 Democratic theme of change, they did not see much tangible change at all. Finding themselves in the same place as they were in 2008, voters again expressed their frustration with government, this time punishing the Democratic majorities in Congress for failing to deliver. When examining the 2008 and 2010 elections from the popular perspective, it is not so surprising that voters opted in favor of several changes of course.

© 2012 CENGAGE LEARNING

Global Perspective

It is perhaps a truism today that what happens to America in the 21st century affects what happens in the rest of the world, and vice versa. New communications technologies, the growth in world trade, international travel, multinational corporations, immigration patterns, the common fear of weapons of mass destruction, and numerous environmental problems are just a few of the issues that have heightened the reciprocal impacts of what happens in America and what happens across the globe. Accordingly, understanding how the rest of world views what happens in America has implications for America itself. It is important to understand how other nations reacted to the 2010 midterm elections. This is what led Michael Schulman of *Time* magazine to write the following the day after the 2010 midterm elections:

> With all of this incessant talk about the decline of American global influence, we tend to forget that the U.S. is still by far the world's largest economy, and what happens in the U.S. matters to everyone, everywhere. That's why people from Beijing to Brasilia are watching the midterms with heightened interest. Shifts in U.S. policy, on issues such as trade, China, the budget, banking reform and so on, directly impact the global economy and attempts to reform it. And with the Republicans taking control of the House of Representatives . . . we're definitely in for a shift from the politics and policies of the first two years of the Obama presidency . . . (http://curiouscapitalist.blogs.time.com/2010/11/03/why-the-u-s-midterm-elections-are-bad-for-the-global-economy/#ixzz14FGZu61g)

In this book we examine the major topics and concepts in American government and politics. We attempt to answer sweeping questions about how American government works: How does public policy get made? Who are the major players and institutions that make laws? How do these major players achieve their position? How do disputes get settled? What is the role of the American people in governing? In this discussion, we draw on three perspectives to provide a deeper appreciation for American government and how it works. From a historical perspective, we view contemporary American government as a product of American history. From a popular perspective, we recognize the significant role that the American people play in influencing what government does. And from a global perspective, we examine how the rest of the world views American government and consider how those views might help shape policy. We also encourage you to develop your own perspectives on American government and to use those perspectives to make a difference.

Forms and Functions of Government

Government
The collection of public institutions in a nation that establish and enforce the rules by which the members of that nation must live.

Anarchy
A state of lawlessness and discord in the political system caused by lack of government.

Social contract
From the philosophy of Jean-Jacques Rousseau, an agreement people make with one another to form a government and abide by its rules and laws, and in return, the government promises to protect the people's rights and welfare and promote their best interests.

★ LO Compare and contrast democracy with other forms of government

Authority
The ability of public institutions and the officials within them to make laws, independent of the power to execute them.

Democracy
Form of government in which the people, either directly or through elected representatives, hold power and authority. The word *democracy* is derived from the Greek *demos kratos*, meaning "rule by the people."

★ LO Identify the philosophical underpinnings of the American political system through the exploration of important theories such as the "social contract" theory and the concept of the "natural law"

Government is the collection of public institutions in a nation that establish and enforce the rules by which the members of that nation must live. Even the most primitive of societies have found government to be necessary. Without government, society would be in a state of **anarchy**, a situation characterized by lawlessness and discord in the political system. Thomas Hobbes, a seventeenth-century British political philosopher, wrote that without government, life would be "solitary, poor, nasty, brutish and short."[1] Government is necessary to make the rules by which citizens must abide, promoting order, stability, and protection for the society. It exists in part to resolve conflicts that naturally arise when people live in communities. Elaborating on the role of government, Jean-Jacques Rousseau, an eighteenth-century French philosopher, posited that in fact a "social contract" exists.[2] A **social contract** is an agreement people make with one another to form a government and abide by its rules and laws. In return, the government promises to protect the people's rights and welfare and to promote their best interests.

A government's **authority** over its citizens refers to the ability of public institutions and the officials within them to make laws, independent of the power to execute them. People obey authority out of respect, whereas they obey power out of fear. There are a number of different forms of government with governing authority that can be found around the nations of the world. One such form—the form that will receive extended attention throughout this book—is **democracy**, defined as a government in which the people, either directly or through elected representatives, hold power and authority. The word democracy is derived from the Greek *demos kratos*, meaning "rule by the people."

By contrast, an **oligarchy** is a form of government in which a small exclusive class, which may or may not attempt to rule on behalf of the people as a whole, holds supreme power. In a **theocracy**, a particular religion or faith plays a dominant role in the government; Iran is just one example of a theocratic nation in the world today. A **monarchy** is a form of government in which one person, usually a member of a royal family or a royal designate, exercises supreme authority. The monarch may be a king, such as King Abdullah of Saudi Arabia, or a queen, like Queen Elizabeth II of Great Britain. In the past monarchies were quite common; today they are rarely practiced in the absolute sense. Although the United Kingdom continues to pay homage to its royalty, true political power rests in the Parliament, whose members are elected by the people.

Many of the nations in the world today have an **authoritarian** form of government in which one political party, group, or person maintains such complete control over the nation that it may refuse to recognize, and may even choose to suppress, all other political parties and interests. The nation of Iraq, before the American military intervention in 2003, was considered by most to be an authoritarian government under the dictatorial rule of Saddam Hussein. North Korea under Kim Jong-Il is an authoritarian government that still exists today.

An important characteristic of any government, whether democratic or not, is its power to exercise authority over people. **Power** is the capacity to get individuals to do something that they may not otherwise do, such as pay taxes, stop for red lights, or submit to a search before boarding an airplane. Without power, it would be very difficult for a government to enforce rules. The sustained power of any government largely rests on its legitimacy. **Legitimacy** is the extent to which the people (or the "governed") afford the government the authority and right to exercise power. The more that people subscribe to the goals of a government, and the greater the degree to which that government guarantees the people's welfare (for example, by supporting a strong economy or providing protection from foreign enemies), the higher will be the government's level of legitimacy. When the governed grant a high level of legitimacy to their government, the government wields its power to make and enforce rules more successfully.

American Government and Politics

★ LO

Explain the importance of the value of popular sovereignty, and how that value is realized through "representative democracy" in the United States

Politics is defined as the way in which the institutions of government are organized to make laws, rules, and policies, and how those institutions are influenced. More than seventy years ago, political scientist Harold Lasswell proposed a brief but very useful definition of politics as "who gets what, when and how." In American politics, the "who" includes actors within and outside the formal government such as citizens, elected officials, interest groups, and state and local governments. The "what" are the decisions the government makes and take the form of what government funds, the way it raises revenue, and the policies it produces and enforces. The "when" relates to setting priorities about what government does. The concerns and issues that government addresses differ in importance, and issues of greater importance tend to be addressed more quickly. Finally, the "how" refers to the way in which the government goes about its work, based on the political institutions that exist and the formal and informal procedures and rules that define the governing process. In describing American politics, this book provides answers to Lasswell's "who gets what, when and how?"

Government in the United States is especially complex. It is organized into multiple layers (national, state, and local); it encompasses a number of political institutions that share power—the executive (the president), the legislature (Congress), and the judiciary (the courts); and it provides countless methods for individuals and groups to influence the decisions made by those institutions. In this book, we will examine this complex organization of American government, describe the political institutions that exercise power, and explore the varied ways that people and groups exert influence. As we sort through this complexity of American government, we will seek to explain how and why the American political system has been able to endure the conflicts, both internal and external, that it has faced and currently faces. We will attempt to show how the American government is uniquely designed to stand up to its many challenges.[3]

Oligarchy
A form of government in which a small exclusive class, which may or may not attempt to rule on behalf of the people as a whole, holds supreme power.

Theocracy
A form of government in which a particular religion or faith plays a dominant role in the government.

Monarchy
A form of government in which one person, usually a member of a royal family or a royal designate, exercises supreme authority.

Authoritarianism
A form of government in which one political party, group, or person maintains such complete control over the nation that it may refuse to recognize and may even suppress all other political parties and interests.

Power
The ability to get individuals to do something that they may not otherwise do, such as pay taxes, stop for red lights, or submit to a search before boarding an airplane.

Legitimacy
The extent to which the people afford the government the authority and right to exercise power.

Politics
The way in which the institutions of government are organized to make laws, rules, and policies, and how those institutions are influenced.

TABLE 1.1 Governments in the United States

The government of the United States might be more correctly described as a system of governments. In addition to the federal government, there are fifty state governments and thousands of local governments. The 2002 edition of the *Statistical Abstract of the United States* listed these totals for the number of governments operating throughout the nation.

Government	Number
Federal	1
State	50
County	3,034
Municipal	19,429
School district	13,506
Township/Town	16,504
Special districts	35,052
Total	87,576

World Views on America

The Pew Global Attitudes Project conducted 24,000 interviews with people from around the world in 2008 and asked respondents whether they had a favorable or unfavorable view of America. This graph shows the percentage from each country who say they have a favorable view of America.

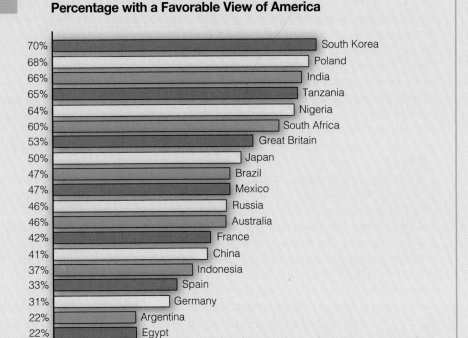

Percentage with a Favorable View of America

Country	Percentage
South Korea	70%
Poland	68%
India	66%
Tanzania	65%
Nigeria	64%
South Africa	60%
Great Britain	53%
Japan	50%
Brazil	47%
Mexico	47%
Russia	46%
Australia	46%
France	42%
China	41%
Indonesia	37%
Spain	33%
Germany	31%
Argentina	22%
Egypt	22%
Turkey	12%

Natural law

According to John Locke, the most fundamental type of law, which supersedes any law that is made by government. Citizens are born with certain natural rights (including life, liberty, and property) that derive from this law and that government cannot take away.

The strength and stability of the U.S. government is grounded in the high level of legitimacy it maintains with the American public. Americans may disagree vehemently with public officials, but rarely do they question their claim to authority. The Framers of the U.S. Constitution were keenly aware of the importance of the legitimacy of the system. They knew that if the government was to withstand the test of time, it must serve the people well. These ideas about legitimacy drew largely on the theories of the seventeenth-century British political philosopher John Locke (1632–1704).[4] Locke proposed that people are born with certain *natural rights*, which derive from **natural law**, the rules of conduct inherent in the relationship among human beings and thus more fundamental than any law that a governing authority might make. Government cannot violate these natural rights, which include life, liberty, and property. Therefore, government, or human law, must be based on the "consent of the governed." That is, citizens are responsible for choosing their government and its leaders. This theory loomed large in the mind of Thomas Jefferson as he drafted the Declaration of Independence to justify the American colonies' split with the British government: "All men . . . are endowed by their creator with certain unalienable rights . . . [and] whenever any form of government becomes destructive of these ends, it is the right of the people to alter or abolish it." A government maintains legitimacy as long as the governed are served well and as long as government respects the natural rights of individuals.

Drawing on this philosophy, the Framers drafted a Constitution that created a political system able to manage the inevitable conflicts that occur in any society. Mindful of Thomas Hobbes's notion that the essence of government is to manage naturally occurring conflicts, the Framers designed a government that encourages conflict and competition rather than attempts to repress it. As we shall see in the chapters that follow, the U.S. Constitution includes a number of mechanisms that allow naturally occurring conflict

Portrait of George Washington and the Constitution's drafters at the Constitutional Convention in 1787.

to play out in as productive a manner as possible. Mechanisms are also in place to resolve conflicts and arrive at consensus on issues. Those who disagree and come up on the short side of political battles are guaranteed rights and liberties nonetheless. Further, the rules by which conflicts are settled are predicated on fairness and proper procedures.

The significance of what the Framers of the Constitution accomplished cannot be overstated. They not only addressed the short-term problems challenging the new nation; they also drafted a blueprint for how government should go about dealing with problems and conflicts into the future. The U.S. Constitution has served as the cornerstone of an American political system that routinely attempts to tackle some of the thorniest problems imaginable. In Chapter 2 of this book, we examine the enduring principles and processes outlined in the Constitution.

The Constitution provides a way for the American government to navigate through the many problems and conflicts that have faced the nation, including severe economic depressions, two world wars, nuclear confrontations with the former Soviet Union, and persisting questions of equality. Through all these difficulties, the American government has endured. The foresight of the Framers to create a Constitution that possesses the flexibility to adapt to changing times has served as a basis for the United States' enduring democracy.

The preamble to the U.S. Constitution perhaps best summarizes the broad goals of American government:

> *We the People of the United States, in Order to form a more perfect Union, establish Justice, insure domestic Tranquility, provide for the common defense, promote the general Welfare, and secure the Blessings of Liberty to ourselves and our Posterity, do ordain and establish this Constitution for the United States of America.*

It is no accident that the first three words of the Constitution are "We the People." With this phrase the Framers acknowledged that the ultimate source of power rests with the people, a concept known as **popular sovereignty**. This "popular perspective" frames our understanding of how the American government works.

The U.S. Constitution provided for a form of **representative democracy**, under which regular elections are held to allow voters to choose those who govern on their behalf. In this sense, individual citizens do not directly make policies, rules, and other governing decisions (a system of government known as a **direct democracy**). Rather, representative democracy, also referred to as *indirect democracy* or a *republican* form

Popular sovereignty
The idea that the ultimate source of power in the nation is held by the people.

Representative democracy
A form of government designed by the U.S. Constitution whereby free, open, and regular elections are held to allow voters to choose those who govern on their behalf; it is also referred to as *indirect democracy* or a *republican* form of government.

Direct democracy
A system of government in which all citizens participate in making policy, rules, and governing decisions.

AMERICAN GOVERNMENT In Historical Perspective

Constitutional Amendments That Have Extended Voting Rights in the United States

In several states, approval of the new U.S. Constitution drafted in 1789 hinged on adding a bill of rights. Supporters of the Constitution agreed, and the first ten amendments, which compose the formal Bill of Rights, were added to the Constitution in 1791. Since then, the Constitution has been amended seventeen times. Six of these seventeen amendments extend Americans' voting rights, and no amendment has ever in any way restricted voting rights. Over the years, changes to the original Constitution have led to greater empowerment of the American people in determining the direction that government takes.

In 1870, the Fifteenth Amendment provided that the right to vote may not be denied on the basis of race.

In 1913, the Seventeenth Amendment changed the method of selection of U.S. senators from having state legislatures choose senators to having senators directly elected by the voters of a state.

In 1920, the Nineteenth Amendment provided voting rights to women by not allowing states to deny women the right to vote.

In 1961, the Twenty-third Amendment provided residents of the District Columbia with electoral votes in presidential elections.

In 1962, the Twenty-fourth Amendment prevented states from levying a tax on people in order for them to vote in federal elections. Some states used a poll tax to discourage poor people and African Americans from voting.

In 1971, the Twenty-sixth Amendment provided voting rights to those who are eighteen years of age by not allowing states to deny the franchise to those who have obtained this age.

of government, rests on the notion that consent of the governed is achieved through free, open, and regular elections of those who are given the responsibility of governing. An important source of the legitimacy of the U.S. government is the nation's commitment to representative democracy, which features the notion of majority rule. Majorities (more than 50 percent of the voters) and pluralities (the leading vote getters, whether or not they constitute absolute majorities) choose the winners of election contests, and so officeholders take their positions on the basis of who most voters prefer. If officeholders fall from public favor, they may be removed in subsequent elections.

Legitimacy is also enhanced by broad public support for the specific purposes of government stated in the preamble to the Constitution: to "insure domestic tranquility" (produce laws that maintain a peaceful and organized approach to living in the nation), to "provide for the common defense" (establish and maintain a military force to protect the nation from outside threats), to "promote the general welfare" (develop domestic policy programs to promote the welfare of the people), and to "secure the blessings of liberty" (guarantee basic freedoms,

"I agree to this Constitution, with all of its faults, if they are such: because I think a general government necessary for us, and there is no form of government but what may be a blessing to the people if well administered. I doubt too whether any convention we can obtain may be able to make a better constitution. For when you assemble a number of men to have the advantage of their joint wisdom, you inevitably assemble with those men all their prejudices, their passions, their errors of opinion, their local interests, and their selfish views. From such an assembly can a perfect production be expected? It therefore astonishes me . . . to find this system approaching so near to perfection."

—Benjamin Franklin (1788)

Part 1 Foundations

10

ARPL/HIP/THE IMAGE WORKS

such as the rights of free expression and the ownership of property, even to those in the minority). Though people may have different opinions on how to achieve these broad goals, few in the United States would disagree with the ideals as stated in the abstract, or with the broad outlines of our republican form of government. Problems arise when public officials stray so far from these goals that their actions are deemed illegitimate by a near, if not absolute, majority. Yet the political system as a whole has been able to maintain its legitimacy, even under such trying circumstances, because it has been flexible enough to eventually rid itself of those ineffective actors, whether through elections, impeachment, or some other means. The relatively high degree of legitimacy that is maintained in the United States has helped the American government persist under the U.S. Constitution through good times and bad since 1789.

American Political Culture

Political culture refers to the core values about the role of government and its operations and institutions that are widely held among citizens in a society. Political culture defines the essence of how a society thinks politically. It is transmitted from one generation to the next, and thus has an enduring influence on the politics of a nation. Every nation has a political culture, and the United States is no exception.

Whereas common ancestry characterizes the core of the political culture of many other nations, the United States has no common ancestry. Most other nations around the world, such as France, Britain, China, Japan, are bound by a common birth lineage that serves to define the cultural uniqueness of the nation. For example, the Russian people share common political values and beliefs as part of their ancestors' historical experiences with czars, and then later with the communist regime. Britain, despite being a democracy, retains a monarchy as a symbolic gesture toward its historical antecedents. In many nations rich with such common ethnic traditions, these routines often serve to underscore the political culture of the nation.

The United States has no such common ancestry to help define its political culture. Its land was first occupied by many different Native American tribes, and then settled by people from many different parts of the world. Most of the immigrants who settled the colonies were seeking a better life from the political or religious persecution they experienced in their native countries, or they were seeking better-improved economic opportunities for themselves or their families. As America continued to grow through the centuries, it attracted immigrants from around the world, anxious to find a better life. These circumstances had a profound influence on the core values that have become engrained in the American political culture. The ideas generated by democratic political philosophers such as Thomas Hobbes and John Locke also significantly contributed to American political culture. These ideas were used by the Founders to justify the Declaration of Independence and the U.S. Constitution, and they continue to underlie American political culture today.

The circumstances surrounding America's first and current immigrants, as well as the great ideas generated by enlightenment philosophers, form the core set of values that define the American political culture. One of these core values is **majority rule**. From its earliest times, the American nation has been committed to the notion that the "will of the people" ought to guide public policy, thus underscoring the importance of popular sovereignty in the thinking of the Founders. Majority rule is the way in which popular sovereignty is actually exercised. Rarely will all of the people agree all of the time; and so it is what the majority of people prefer that generally guides decision making. Early local governments, such as town governments in some of the New England colonies, relied on town meetings, where all citizens were invited to attend, discuss, and vote, to make governmental decisions. Elections for most local and state offices, and elections for the U.S. Congress, are all based on the idea that those who make and enforce laws are duly elected by majorities. A more recent aspect of U.S. commitment to majority rule is its heavy reliance on public opinion polling as a gauge to assessing the performance of elected leaders, and to ensure that leaders respect public preferences for certain policy positions.

★ LO
Define "political culture" and describe the unique combination of political beliefs and values that form the American political culture, including majority rule, liberty, limited government, diversity, individualism, and equality of economic opportunity

Political culture
The values and beliefs about government, its purpose, and its operations and institutions that are widely held among citizens in a society; it defines the essence of how a society thinks politically and is transmitted from one generation to the next.

Majority rule
The notion that the will of the majority should guide decisions made by American government.

While the preferences of the majority rule the day, another core value in the American political culture is minority rights. Those in the minority enjoy certain rights and liberties that cannot be taken away by government. The idea of the natural law (e.g., that people are "endowed by their creator with certain unalienable rights" that government cannot deny) is an important corollary to majority rule. The rights to speak freely, to choose a religion, or to decide not to practice religion at all, are among the many liberties that are protected by the U.S. Bill of Rights, and are widely endorsed by the American public.

These rights are intended to inspire debate on issues, to guarantee religious freedoms, to afford due process rights to those accused of crimes. The American political culture places a high value on individual liberty. The fact that many immigrants came to this country for the promise of greater freedom adds further credence to this proposition. Certainly there are some terrible black marks in American history that belie this claim. Among them are the perpetuation of slavery in the country up until the Civil War, the internment of Japanese Americans during World War II, and the treatment of early 1960s civil rights protesters in the South. Still, many Americans today view their nation as the world's "garden" of freedom and liberty, even if it has come to this status only slowly and sometimes with reluctance during its more than two centuries of existence.

Limited government
The value that promotes the idea that government power should be as restricted as possible.

Another core value in American political culture is the idea of **limited government**. Americans have generally supported the idea expressed by Thomas Jefferson that "the government that governs least governs best." From the days of the American Revolution, the colonists believed that the corruptive power of King George III and the British Parliament led to unfair treatment of the colonies. Suspicion of the government and those with power is firmly rooted in the psyche of American political culture. The "watchdog" function of the press, the separation of powers and the system of checks and balances among political institutions, and the rather negative connotation of the word "politics" all reflect an appreciation for limits and checks on those with authority. Corresponding to the value of limited government is the notion that communities and the private sector should take a role in helping fellow citizens. Problems that may be solved without government should be solved that way. The

TABLE 1.2 Daniel Elazar's Typology of American Political Culture

Many observers of American politics have used different approaches and typologies to describe American political culture. The late political scientist Daniel Elazar described three competing political subcultures, which he believed differentiated American political culture from that found in any other country in the world:*

Subculture	Description
Individualistic subculture	Is skeptical of authority, keeps government's role limited, and celebrates the United States' general reliance on the marketplace
Moralistic subculture	Has faith in the American government's capacity to advance the public interest and encourages citizens to participate in the noble cause of politics
Traditionalistic subculture	Maintains a more ambivalent attitude toward both government and the marketplace, believing that politicians must come from society's elite, whereas ordinary citizens are free to stand on the sidelines

According to Elazar, different subcultures can be found in different geographic areas, and sometimes within a single area itself. For example, he described the political subculture in Texas as part traditionalistic (as manifested in the long history of one-party dominance in state politics) and part individualistic (as seen in the state government's commitment to support for private business and its opposition to big government).

*See Daniel J. Elazar, *American Federalism: A View from the States* (New York: Thomas Y. Crowell, 1966).

French journalist Alexis de Tocqueville observed this tradition when he visited the United States in the early 1800s and credited the success of the American political system in part to citizens' strong interest in community and helping one another apart from government.[5]

Since the United States has no common ancestral or cultural bloodline, American political culture recognizes the value and strength derived from the diversity of its population—another important core value. At the base of the Statue of Liberty in New York harbor is inscribed the poem by Emma Lazarus beginning with the phrase "Bring me your huddled masses, yearning to be free." Until the U.S. government adopted a restrictive immigration policy in the early 1920s, those huddled masses arrived in waves from different parts of the world, as the United States became the chosen destination for those seeking a better life. Joining freed African American slaves who were originally brought here against their will were legions of Italians, Irish, Germans, and other immigrants from Europe and elsewhere. The United States today is one of the most racially and ethnically diverse nations in the world. Integrating these many peoples into a united nation has not come easy; in fact, resistance to the notion of a "melting pot" has been common. The nation has been wracked at times with racial and ethnic strife to a degree that more homogeneous countries can more easily avoid. Government officials occasionally exacerbate these tensions by promoting policies that discriminate against various groups, including Native Americans, African Americans, Asian Americans, and Hispanic Americans. No stranger to ethnic and racial tensions himself, the German dictator Adolph Hitler calculated that the diversity of the United States would eventually hamper its resistance against Germany's totalitarian aggression; in fact, American soldiers of different backgrounds, ethnicities, and religions fought in World War II. Much to Hitler's chagrin, U.S. diversity proved a source of strength, rather than weakness. Indeed, many Americans today believe that the heterogeneity of our society enhances the quality of our culture and helps guarantee the fairness of the government.

Barack Obama's bid for the presidency in 2008 represented a new chapter in the history of diversity as a value in American political culture.

AP PHOTO/RICK BOWMER

Americans also generally subscribe to the notion that individuals are primarily responsible for their lot in life—a value referred to as **individualism**. The seeds of this value were sown hundreds of years ago with the Puritans and their commitment to a strong work ethic that stressed that "what one sows determines what one reaps." In other words, hard work and intelligence should be rewarded. While the U.S. government has assumed some responsibility to provide a safety net for citizens who suffer economically, the American political culture, through its primary reliance on a capitalist economic system, free markets, and individual effort, is one that promotes individual initiative and responsibility. The value of individualism promotes another

Individualism
The value that individuals are primarily responsible for their own lot in life and that promotes and rewards individual initiative and responsibility. This value underlies America's reliance on a capitalist economy and free-market system.

core value—equality of opportunity, or the idea that the role of government is to set the stage for individuals to achieve on their own, and that everyone should be given the same opportunity to achieve success. Indeed, America has been an attractive place for highly motivated individuals from around the world to immigrate so that they might have a fair chance of achieving personal success. Many immigrants today, particularly from Asia and Latin America, are attracted to the United States for the opportunities to achieve individual success.

The United States has long set itself apart from those nations whose histories include traditions of a rigid class system of privileged aristocracies and oligarchies and peasants with few or no rights or freedoms. In the United States there is no formal recognition of a class system; nor is there a tradition of royalty, nobility, or monarchy. Indeed, Article I of the Constitution specifically prohibits both the federal government and the state governments from granting any title of nobility upon its citizens. Instead, American political culture values the so-called Horatio Alger myth. Alger was a popular writer in the late 1800s whose characters came from impoverished backgrounds but through pluck, determination, and hard work achieved huge success. Although this idealistic rags-to-riches notion often ignores the many harsh economic disparities that exist in the United States, it remains central to the American political culture. The stories of Benjamin Franklin and Abraham Lincoln exemplified this road to success, as do the more recent examples of Presidents Bill Clinton and Ronald Reagan, both of whom came from less than privileged circumstances to win the nation's highest political office and become leaders of the free world. Perhaps it is because of these success stories that so many Americans believe that they have boundless opportunities to better their lot on the basis of diligence and hard work.

These core values provide a window into American political culture. To be sure, there is plenty of room for disagreement as to how these values might be applied to specific situations, which we address in Chapter 10. In addition, these values are often in conflict. At the heart of the debate over affirmative action, for example, lies the value conflict pitting individualism against equality of opportunity. Those who oppose affirmative action in hiring claim that individuals should be evaluated exclusively based on who they are and what they can do rather than on their gender, race, or other demographic characteristic. Those supporting affirmative action claim that historical discrimination has led to a current job market that provides unequal opportunities for certain groups, such as racial minorities and women. While these values do not always solve problems and policy debates, they do lay the groundwork for how American politics goes about settling problems and debating issues.

Is American Democracy on the Decline?

★ LO Assess the health of American democracy and evaluate whether the American system is in decline by reviewing trends in voter turnout, negativity in politics, the influence of money in policy outcomes, and the integrity of election outcomes

The old saying that "those who ignore the problems of the past are destined to repeat them" holds as true in American politics as it does in any other context. Certainly new issues and problems may arise, requiring innovative new thinking to address them. But many other difficulties the United States faces can be effectively addressed by casting an eye on the distant or not-so-distant past. A historical view can help place modern dilemmas in proper perspective.

The Case for Decline

Some recent observers of American politics have suggested that the American political system is in decline. Are we currently witnessing a deterioration of democracy in the United States? Is the American political system in jeopardy? Are the problems that the American system of government faces today beyond repair? To try to answer these questions, let's first look at the factors some cite as contemporary indicators of the decline of American democracy.

- **Voter turnout.** Democratic theorists regard an active, participatory citizenry as a sign of a healthy, vibrant democracy. Thus many point to the half-century trend toward lower voter turnout as a sign of decline. In the 1960s, for example, the percentage of eligible voters who cast a ballot in presidential elections ranged from 62 percent to 65 percent, whereas the range since 1996 has been lower, from 51 percent to just over 60 percent. Ratification of the Twenty-sixth Amendment to the U.S. Constitution in 1971, which guaranteed eighteen-, nineteen-, and twenty-year-olds the constitutional right to vote, expanded the pool of eligible voters, but many of those younger voters have stayed away from the polls in disproportionate numbers, explaining at least in part this downturn in voter turnout. With a smaller percentage of people choosing to participate in elections, many have interpreted the decline as a sign of an ailing democracy.

- **Presidential selection.** For nearly one month after the 2000 presidential election, it remained unclear whether the next president would be Republican George W. Bush or Democrat Al Gore. The closeness of the race in the key state of Florida, along with controversies over how or whether to count certain ballots, left open the question of which candidate actually won the Electoral College vote. In the end, the U.S. Supreme Court indicated that there was insufficient time for a manual recount of Florida's paper ballots, thus effectively awarding Florida's twenty-five electoral votes to Bush, and with them, giving Bush the Electoral College victory. Confounding this outcome was the stark reality that Gore had received approximately half a million more popular votes in total than did Bush. Many regarded this situation as a true constitutional crisis, and called for the abolition of the Electoral College as a means of selecting the president on the basis that a president who takes office without having won the highest number of popular votes lacks the required legitimacy to govern. Four years later a similar electoral crisis was only narrowly averted. A swing of just 60,000 votes in Ohio would have given the Electoral College victory to Democrat John Kerry, even though he garnered several million fewer popular votes nationwide than did the Republican candidate, incumbent President George W. Bush.

- **Civil liberties protections.** The terrorist attacks of September 11, 2001, exposed a variety of security vulnerabilities in the United States. In response to these attacks, Congress passed and President Bush signed into law the USA Patriot Act, which gave the federal government increased authority to exercise wiretapping and other surveillance over citizens and to detain individuals deemed "suspicious." Rights advocates viewed this increased authority as a violation of the rights and liberties guaranteed to individuals by the Constitution, and indicative of how American society has become increasingly intolerant of the rights and freedoms of minorities. The willingness of the president and Congress to support laws that allow the government to jail individuals for an indefinite period of time, whether or not those individuals have been charged with a crime, suggests to critics of the USA Patriot Act that some of the core values upon which the American nation is built may now be under siege.

- **Money and politics.** In American politics today, most successful election campaigns require large amounts of money. Those who have the financial resources—corporations and wealthy individuals—provide the bulk of the financing. During the 2008 presidential primaries alone, candidates from both major political parties raised more than $1 billion. The winning congressional candidates in the 2006 elections for the House of Representatives and the Senate collectively raised nearly $750 million. Do these huge sums of money, most of which come from corporations and wealthy individuals, influence the behavior of those who win elections? If so, what does that indicate about the state of American democracy?

© 2012 CENGAGE LEARNING

■ **Negative politics.** Negative political advertising, partisan conflicts that degenerate into personal attacks, and exploitation of personal affairs into public spectacles seem to characterize a good deal of modern-day American politics. The inclination of political figures to "go negative," combined with the news media's taste for negative stories, has created a political atmosphere fraught with attacks, counterattacks and much partisan wrangling. From the Republican-driven impeachment of President Bill Clinton in 1998, to claims during the 2004 election that President George W. Bush had avoided serving in the Vietnam War, to the constant barrage of negative political ads throughout the 2006 midterm elections (such as the claim that Tennessee Senate candidate Harold Ford Jr. was a playboy), to the Republican attacks on Barack Obama comparing his celebrity status to that of Britney Spears and Paris Hilton, the measured and orderly democratic process envisioned by the Founders seems to have become much less deliberative and civil and much more strident and negative.

AP PHOTO/KNOBLOCK

One of the negative ads of the 2008 presidential campaign attacked Democratic candidate Barack Obama for his association with William Ayers, a cofounder of the Weather Underground, a radical 1960s anti-Vietnam War group that carried out bombings at the Capitol and the Pentagon. The Web video ad questioned Obama's judgment for his association with Ayers, seen here in a 1980 photo entering the Criminal Courts Building in Chicago. Ayers, labeled as a terrorist in the ad, is now a college professor, and he and Obama served together on the board of a school reform organization in the mid-1990s.

■ **"Red" state/"blue" state.** The Electoral College maps that the media used to follow the 2008 presidential election returns showed states that Democratic candidate Barack Obama won in blue, and states that Republican candidate John McCain won in red. Whereas the blue states were for the most part clustered in the northeastern United States, the northern Midwest, and the West Coast, the large land block between coasts and throughout the South was predominantly red, with few exceptions. The results of the 2000 and 2004 elections revealed an even sharper divide, with a sea of red extending from Nevada, Arizona, and Idaho in the west all the way to the southeast coast and Florida. (In the 2000 election, New Mexico offered a lone island of blue, while New Hampshire stood by itself as a red state in the Northeast.). It is perhaps no wonder that commentators, referring to this "blue versus red" division of the American public, argue that it represents an electorate widely divided not only along partisan lines, but also along cultural lines. These observers emphasize the divide between the socially moderate-to-liberal values of the Northeast and West Coast and the more conservative values embraced by the Great Plains states and the South.

These dilemmas in contemporary American politics have led some observers to conclude that American democracy is in sharp and deep decline. Yet even with the evidence provided, this may be a rather superficial examination of contemporary American government. If we examine these characteristics of American politics with the benefit of some historical perspective, it is possible to draw quite different conclusions,

Voter Turnout in U.S. Presidential Elections

The popular perspective of the American people finds multiple ways to influence the outcome of policy debates, including reporting poll results, working on campaigns, and donating time and/or money to political candidates and interest groups. But the most basic way in which the people affect policy is through voting. Prior to 1828, only a limited number of states held popular elections to help determine how a state's electoral votes would be allocated in a presidential election. Since then, most states have held popular elections for electors who in turn select the president. This figure shows the percentage of the eligible electorate that cast a vote in presidential elections since 1900.

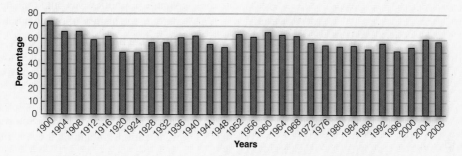

Source: From Harold W. Stanley and Richard G. Niemi, *Vital Statistics on American Politics* (CQ Press, 2006). ©2006 CQ Press, a division of Sage Publications.

which in turn suggest that our system of government is designed to allow conflict and controversy to be managed in a productive way. The system promotes clashes of ideas, sometimes characterized by personal animosity. The system also allows for multiple points of input from a large number of citizens and organized interests.

The Case against Decline

If we reexamine some of the criticisms of contemporary American politics with the benefit of historical perspective, we may reach far different conclusions about whether American democracy is now in a state of decline.

- **Voter turnout.** As shown in the figure above, there has been a general decline in voter turnout, from more than 60 percent in the 1950s to as low as 51 percent in some recent elections. A historical perspective reveals, however, that it has not been uncommon for only half—or even less than half—of voters to cast a ballot in a presidential election. In the elections of 1924 and 1928, turnout dropped below 50 percent. Even in the historically important election of 1932—the election that put Franklin Roosevelt's New Deal coalition into office—voter turnout was less than 60 percent. In the 1948 contest in which Democratic candidate Harry Truman came from far behind to defeat the Republican Thomas Dewey, turnout was a mere 53 percent. Thus by early-to mid-twentieth-century standards, a turnout rate of around 50 percent is not all that unusual. In fact, low voter turnout may even indicate the public's general contentment with the state of the union.

- **Presidential selection.** The confusion surrounding the outcome of the 2000 presidential contest was not unique to that presidential election. In fact, there have been other presidential election contests that either produced no clear winner in the Electoral College or produced an Electoral College winner different from the popular vote winner. The Framers of the Constitution may have even contemplated these possibilities, because they created a compromise that sought to give less populated states disproportionate influence over the outcome. In 1888, for example, Grover Cleveland won the popular vote but lost the Electoral College vote (and thus the presidency) to Benjamin Harrison. In 1876, Samuel Tilden won 51 percent of the popular vote but failed to capture a majority of electoral votes, and Rutherford B. Hayes became president as part of a brokered deal among political party elites. In the 1824 election, Andrew Jackson defeated John Quincy Adams by more than 10 percentage points of the popular votes cast; however, neither candidate won a majority of electoral votes, and the House of Representatives chose Adams as the new president. Even in one of the earliest presidential contests in 1800, the lack of an Electoral College majority was resolved by the House of Representatives awarding the presidency to Thomas Jefferson (it took more than thirty ballots for the House to arrive at this conclusion). What in 2000 seemed like a unique controversy in American politics was only the latest among many in the history of presidential elections.

A young woman participates in a protest of the controversial USA Patriot Act at Boston's historic Faneuil Hall in September 2003.

MARILYN HUMPHRIES/THE IMAGE WORKS

- **Civil liberties protections.** Under the terms of the USA Patriot Act, many individuals suspected of having connections with terrorist organizations have been detained by the U.S. government without being formally accused of having committed some specific crime. Some civil liberties organizations, including the American Civil Liberties Union (ACLU), claim the Patriot Act thus allows gross and unprecedented violation of individuals' due process rights. But there have been other instances in the nation's history when the government has curtailed individuals' rights. During the Civil War, President Abraham Lincoln closed down several newspapers and suspended the writ of habeas corpus, by which a prisoner can demand a trial or hearing before a judge so that the judge can determine whether the prisoner is being legally detained. Immediately after the Japanese attack on Pearl Harbor in 1941, the federal government ordered that more than 100,000 individuals be placed in internment camps; most of those interned were American citizens of Japanese ancestry. Thus although such actions may run counter to the American political culture, which places great value on individual liberties, allegations that the government has violated some of those liberties are nothing new in American politics, particularly when national security is severely threatened.

- **Money and politics.** There is no doubt that the bulk of money for political campaigns comes from corporations and wealthy Americans, and few would question that money greatly influences political campaigns. In addition, some of the most successful interest groups in the United States are funded by the wealthy. But this is by no means a new phenomenon in American politics either. Most of the Founders, all of whom were white males, were wealthy landowners. It has been reported that George Washington himself bought one and a half quarts of liquor for each vote he received in his first run for public office in 1758.[6] Just as today's large corporate contributors (such as Microsoft and IBM) and powerful interest groups (such as the American Medical Association and the American Trial Lawyers Association) enjoy disproportionately large influence over politics, so too did the so-called robber barons of the late nineteenth century, such as the financier J. Pierpont Morgan, the industrialist Andrew Carnegie, or the railroad magnate Cornelius Vanderbilt, wield considerable influence over the nation's politics.

- **Negative politics.** The negativity, combativeness, and personal conflict that characterize modern American politics—distasteful though these may be—are nothing new. Negativity and conflict are the product of the vigorous and spirited debate that occurs in a free and open democracy. One of the most negative political campaigns ever waged was the 1800 presidential battle between Thomas Jefferson and John Adams. During that campaign, Jefferson used partisan newspapers to launch a very negative campaign against Adams. The personal attacks that pervaded the impeachment hearings of President Bill Clinton in 1998 were no match for the character assassinations featured during the impeachment of President Andrew Johnson in 1868. And in neither of those cases could the personal attacks match the fatal wounding in 1804 of Alexander Hamilton by Aaron Burr in a duel over political differences that became personal. Nor is the general tone of negativity of the modern-day news media anything new. The intense partisanship of some of the nation's early newspapers, such as Ben Franklin's *Pennsylvania Gazette*, and the sensationalist "yellow journalism" of the late nineteenth century provide a good match for today's focus on negative news.

- **"Red" state/"blue" state.** The Electoral College vote totals of the 2000, 2004, and 2008 presidential elections may appear to depict an unprecedented new geographical divide among the nation's states. Yet nearly half of those states—twenty-three of the fifty—including a handful of states located in every region of the country, failed to give either presidential candidate as much as 55 percent of the popular vote, a signal that these were in fact not die-hard "red" or "blue" states as often portrayed by the media. In the 2006 congressional elections, Democratic Senate

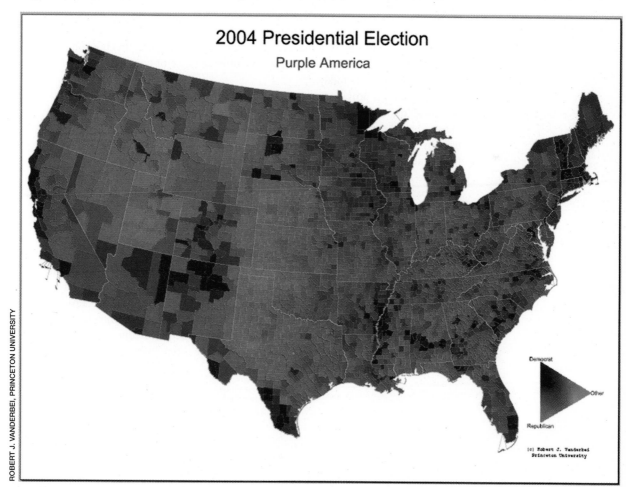

ROBERT J. VANDERBEI, PRINCETON UNIVERSITY

Discussion of the "blue vs. red" political divisions in America ignores the possibility that there may actually be a "purple America," as shown in this map from *Time* magazine. (Closely contested districts in 2004 are shown in purple; one-sided Republican districts are shown in red, and one-sided Democratic districts are shown in blue.)

victories in "red" Republican states such as Virginia and Montana helped put Democrats back in the majority not only in the House of Representatives but also in the Senate. Barack Obama moved Virginia, North Carolina, and Indiana into the Democratic column for the first time in decades. Moreover, in some states, such as Ohio, Florida, and Pennsylvania, divisions may be sharper than ever. As political scientist Morris Fiorina argued in his 2005 book, *Culture War? The Myth of a Polarized America*,[7] the percentage of American citizens who went to the polls at the beginning of the twenty-first century with a fairly set idea of how they would cast their votes was actually no greater than it had been a quarter century earlier, or even a full century earlier. Fiorina also discovered that geographic regions differ far less on such issues as abortion, gun control, or the role that religion should play in politics than the stereotypes of red state versus blue state would suggest. Reports of a sharp red–blue divide may be nothing more than a convenient story created by pundits and journalists to generate interest in news stories.

Historical, Popular, and Global Perspectives

History does not literally repeat itself. The specific people, circumstances, and events certainly change. But history can help us identify patterns, recurring problems, and trends in how the American political system functions and resolves conflicts. The preceding discussion of some of the contemporary arguments for why American democracy may be in a state of decline helps us frame current conditions. In doing so, we may gain a greater understanding of the challenges facing the nation today. Certainly, many contemporary challenges are no less daunting than problems the nation has encountered over the past two centuries. Throughout this book, a historical perspective on contemporary problems offers a sense of how the past might help us understand politics today.

As past events provide perspective on contemporary American politics, they also make quite clear the significant role that people play in influencing political outcomes and public policy. "The will of the people" is not just a rhetorical phrase used by politicians. Rather, it has guided American politics and government since the country's founding. Throughout this book, we employ a popular perspective to understand better how our system of government works. Citizens who actively participate in politics through voting, working on campaigns, contributing time and effort to interest group activities, participating in demonstrations, writing to elected officials and the op-ed pages, and running for office have an impact on public policy. In this book, consideration of the popular perspective allows us to see how the will of the people has an impact on American politics.

Finally, a look at American government would not be complete without some perspective on how the rest of the world views the United States. Through advanced technologies such as the Internet, satellites, and air travel, life in the modern world increasingly interconnects people from different nations. The governments of the globe, for better or for worse, are affected by this interconnectedness of the world's peoples. Throughout this book, a global perspective offers insights into how people around the world perceive American government.

"Isn't it sad that politics have become so negative these days?" Such is a common complaint about contemporary American politics in general, and political campaigns in particular. Poll after poll depicts how much Americans deplore negativity in campaigns, though that doesn't seem to deter its prevalence: in the 2008 presidential campaign, candidates were accused of being celebrities, liars, plagiarists, adulterers, and terrorist supporters. FactCheck.org, a Web site developed and maintained by the Annenberg School at the University of Pennsylvania, is an antidote to some of the negativity and misrepresentation of candidates' records. This Web site examines many of the negative claims that candidates launch against each other in political advertising and seeks to verify the claim or vilify the false accusation.

At www.cengage.com/dautrich/americangovernment/2e, find the Politics InterActive link for details and examples of negative campaigning in American politics. Consult as well the various links that relate to negativity in American politics in historical, popular, and global perspectives.

© 2012 CENGAGE LEARNING

NORTH WIND PICTURE ARCHIVES

HOOPER Sc.

The duel between Aaron Burr and Alexander Hamilton, which killed Hamilton, is perhaps one of the most famous and extreme instances of negativity in American politics.

Chapter Summary

★ Introduction to Perspectives on American Government

- Issues, topics, and controversies in American politics may be analyzed through a number of different perspectives. This book will encourage analyzing topics through three primary perspectives in particular: a historical perspective, a popular perspective, and a global perspective. Your own perspective will come to bear as well on the state of American politics.

★ Forms and Functions of Government

- The development of the American political system is grounded in the philosophy of John Locke and Jean-Jacques Rousseau, who argued that government is necessary and that it exists for the purpose of protecting the people that it serves. The "social contract" theory states that natural law gives people certain unalienable rights that government cannot take away, and that the people give government authority to rule, but the people can withdraw that authority if government does not serve the people's interests.

★ American Government and Politics

- Democracy includes at its core the idea of popular sovereignty. The United States practices a form of democracy known as "representative democracy," where the people indirectly rule by electing leaders who are responsible for making and carrying out policies and laws.

★ American Political Culture

- The political culture in America is reflected in the Constitution and the way in which the political system deals with and decides political debates. Among the core values guiding the American political culture are majority rule, liberty, limited government, diversity, individualism, and equality of economic opportunity.

★ Is American Democracy on the Decline?

- Although the current American government has been in place for more than 200 years, there have been questions raised about whether this political system is in a state of decline. Lower voter turnout, confusing election outcomes, negativity in politics, and the influence of money in policy outcomes have been offered as evidence of a decline. However, a review of historical patterns in American politics suggests that these seemingly contemporary problems are chronic, and the American political system has effectively dealt with these and many other problems.

★ Historical, Popular, and Global Perspectives

- Viewing American government from a historical perspective may enrich our understanding of how the political system works. History can help us identify patterns, recurring problems, and trends in how the American political system functions and resolves conflicts. Many contemporary challenges are no more significant than problems the nation has encountered over the past two centuries.

- Viewing American government from a popular perspective also informs our appreciation of the important role that citizens play in the political system. People play a large role in influencing political outcomes and public policy. The "will of the people" is not just a rhetorical phrase—it has guided American politics and government since the country's founding. Citizens who actively participate in politics through voting, working on campaigns, contributing time and effort to interest group activities, participating in demonstrations, writing to elected officials, authoring letters in op-ed pages, and running for office, all have an impact on public policy.

- Viewing American government from a global perspective has become increasingly important in a world that has become interconnected. Through advanced technologies such as the Internet, satellites, and air travel, life in the modern world increasingly interconnects people from different nations. The governments of the globe, for better or for worse, are affected by this interconnectedness of so many different peoples. A global perspective offers insights into how people around the world perceive American government.

CourseMate

Key Terms

Anarchy (p. 6)
Authoritarianism (p. 7)
Authority (p. 6)
Democracy (p. 6)
Direct democracy (p. 9)
Government (p. 6)
Individualism (p. 13)

Legitimacy (p. 7)
Limited government (p. 12)
Majority rule (p. 11)
Monarchy (p. 7)
Natural law (p. 8)
Oligarchy (p. 7)
Political culture (p. 11)

Politics (p. 7)
Popular sovereignty (p. 9)
Power (p. 7)
Representative democracy (p. 9)
Social contract (p. 6)
Theocracy (p. 7)

Resources

Important Books

Anderson, Terry H. *The Pursuit of Fairness: The History of Affirmative Action.* New York: Oxford University Press, 2004.

Fiorina, Morris. *Culture War? The Myth of a Polarizing America.* New York: Pearson Longman, 2005.

Gilliam, Howard. *Votes That Counted: How the Court Decided the 2000 Presidential Election.* Chicago: University of Chicago Press, 2001.

Greenberg, Stanley B. *The Two Americas: Our Current Political Deadlock and How to Break It.* New York: Thomas Dunne Books, 2004.

Putnam, Robert. *Bowling Alone.* New York: Simon and Schuster, 2000.

Internet Sources

www.nara.gov (the site for the National Archives; contains a wealth of information on documents relating to American culture)

www.whitehouse.gov (the official home page of the White House)

www.fjc.gov (the site for the Federal Justice Center, which provides detailed information on the federal judiciary)

www.house.gov (the site for the U.S. House of Representatives)

www.senate.gov (the site for the U.S. Senate)

2 The Founding and the Constitution

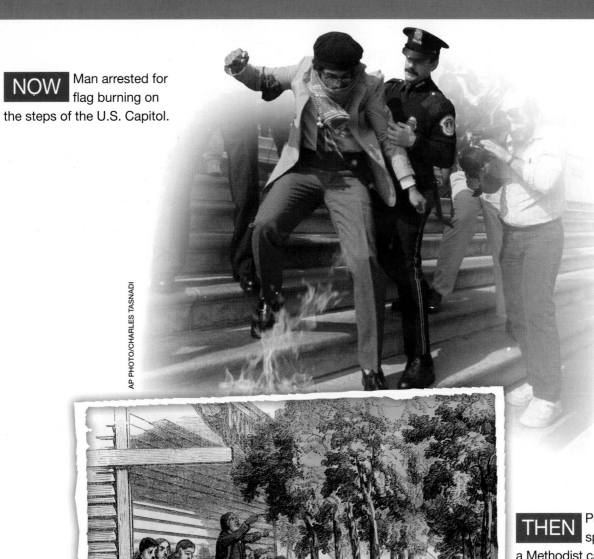

NOW Man arrested for flag burning on the steps of the U.S. Capitol.

AP PHOTO/CHARLES TASNADI

THEN Preacher speaking at a Methodist camp meeting in Eastham, Massachusetts, during the 1850s.

NORTH WIND / NORTH WIND PICTURE ARCHIVES

NOW &THEN

The Politics of the Amending Process

"Quote the Constitution . . . and if you don't like what it says, demand that it be changed." The latter political strategy rarely results in actual constitutional amendments, but it does offer considerable benefits for savvy politicians and special interests. Capitalizing on the perception that liberal elites were taking the country in an unwanted direction, several groups formed a movement to propose a constitutional amendment more consistent with their vision of the nation's values. The effort struck a chord, forcing legislators to take it seriously; yet the proposed amendment did not earn two-thirds support of both houses of Congress, and so it did not go forward to the states for ratification, Still, the groups' sustained effort found an audience with some of the nation's mainstream politicians, few of whom wished to offend a movement of followers so numerous and passionate. The arduous process of changing the Constitution produces few outright amendments, but nonetheless can provide political victories to those who advocate change.

LEARNING OBJECTIVES
★ WHAT YOU WILL LEARN ★

The Beginnings of a New Nation

* ★ Understand the origins and causes of the American Revolution
* ★ Describe the first national government under the Articles of Confederation, including its weaknesses and struggles

The Constitutional Convention

* ★ Compare and contrast the various plans for the new Constitution and the obstacles to agreement among the different colonies

The New Constitution

* ★ Understand how sovereign powers were divided in the new government

The Ratification Battle

* ★ Evaluate the advantages enjoyed by those seeking to ratify the new Constitution
* ★ Assess the role that the Federalist Papers played in ratification
* ★ Explain the origins of the Bill of Rights and its role in securing ratification

Changing the Constitution

* ★ Describe the process of amending the Constitution
* ★ Assess informal types of constitutional change, including different forms of constitutional interpretation

CourseMate

NOW & THEN

Senator Bob Dole (R-KS) speaks in Washington about the recently passed Flag Protection Act of 1989

The 27th Amendment

"The Congress and the States shall have power to prohibit the physical desecration of the Flag of the United States."

BETTMANN/CORBIS

NOW While efforts to protect the American flag date back to the late nineteenth century, they gained significant and widespread appeal in the 1960s, after Vietnam War protestors discovered the powerful reaction that flag burning could evoke. By the late 1980s, forty-eight of fifty states and the U.S. Congress had passed flag protection laws of some kind, only to see their efforts swept aside when the Supreme Court in 1989 held that all such laws unconstitutionally restricted free expression under the First Amendment. With polls indicating that a majority of Americans favored flag protection laws, specialized interests such as the Citizens Flag Alliance, an umbrella organization of veterans' and other groups, pressed Congress to propose a constitutional amendment that would make an exception to the First Amendment, allowing governments to ban flag desecration. These efforts gained considerable traction, and legislators attempted seven times to pass a flag burning amendment between 1990 and 2006. Though the initiative often garnered House approval, it was never able to generate two-thirds support in the U.S. Senate. To date, more than 3 million citizens have signed petitions asking Congress to pass the amendment, and nearly all state legislatures have passed resolutions urging the same. Legislators of every stripe will continue to oppose this effort only at their own electoral peril.

THEN The First Amendment proved to be a source of frustration in the nineteenth and early twentieth centuries as well, though the battle at that time was waged more on religious than patriotic grounds. During the Civil War a coalition of eleven Protestant denominations hailing from seven Northern states directed their anger at the Establishment Clause in the First Amendment to the Constitution, which prohibited Congress from making any law "respecting an establishment of religion." Calling themselves the "Christian Amendment Association," they believed the Civil War was God's punishment for omitting God from the Constitution, and they sought to alter the wording of the Preamble to acknowledge God and profess the idea that civil governments derive their legitimacy from God in general, and from Jesus in particular. As the movement gained momentum, it renamed itself the National Reform Association (NRA) and earned the active support of important senators, including John Sherman of Ohio, B. Gratz Brown of Missouri, and the eminent Charles Sumner of Massachusetts. Indeed, the NRA even found an audience with President Abraham Lincoln in February 1864. Despite consideration from Congress in 1864, 1874, 1896, and 1910, the amendment was never able to secure formal passage. Given how quickly the movement had gained popularity, few members of Congress were willing to denounce the cause publicly. That is still a far cry from seeing the amendment proposed and ratified, as the NRA learned repeatedly during the latter part of the nineteenth century.

LIBRARY OF CONGRESS

Senator Charles Sumner (R-MA), a key supporter of efforts to pass the so-called Christian amendment.

ebraska Senator Ben Nelson once wrote that amending the Constitution "is a delicate endeavor and should be done only on the basis of the most clear and convincing evidence that a proposed amendment is necessary." Certainly the numbers back Nelson up: of the thousands of constitutional amendments discussed, an average of just one amendment every thirteen years has been ratified since 1791, and that event normally occurs only after years (if not decades) of frustrations and failures. Aware of the odds against them, interest groups often take up the cause of amending the constitution for political reasons: a push to alter the U.S. Constitution can fire up the passions of many Americans; it also enables groups to gauge the support of legislators by holding their feet to the fire. In the case of the "Christian amendment" and the "flag desecration amendment," those efforts went a step further, gaining an audience for their respective supporters before some of Washington, DC's most powerful politicians. Still, no one could have rightfully expected this two-centuries-old document to bend so quickly in either case. To most Americans the document's success is due largely to its capacity to endure and survive in much the same form for over two centuries.

The Beginnings of a New Nation

Throughout the seventeenth and early eighteenth centuries, thousands of people, many of them British subjects, migrated to North America. Many came in search of greater economic opportunities; others fled to escape religious persecution and sought freedom to worship as they pleased. Slowly, a culture dedicated to the protection of social and civil rights began to take shape in the colonies.

The political structures that governed the colonies up through the early 1760s roughly paralleled those of England during the same period: (1) royal governors served as substitutes for the king in each individual colony; (2) a governor's council in each colony served as a mini House of Lords, with the most influential men in the colony serving effectively as a high court; and (3) the general assembly in each colony was elected directly by the qualified voters in each colony and served essentially as a House of Commons, passing ordinances and regulations that would govern the colony. Up until the middle of the eighteenth century, the colonies' diverse histories and economies had provided little incentive for them to join together to meet shared goals. In fact, Great Britain feared other European powers attempting to encroach on their American holdings far more than they feared any form of uprising on the part of the colonists.

The French and Indian War that was waged in the colonies from 1754 through 1763 was a significant turning point in British-colonial relations.[1] For nearly a decade the French, from their base in Canada, fought the British in the colonies for control of the North American empire. Both nations were interested in rights to the territory that extended west of the colonial settlements along the Atlantic seaboard and over the Appalachian Mountains into the Ohio Valley. Britain defeated France, and under the terms of the Treaty of Paris (1763), which settled the war, all territory from the Arctic Ocean to the Gulf of Mexico between the Atlantic Ocean and the Mississippi River (except for New Orleans, which was ceded to Spain, an ally of Britain during the war) was awarded to Britain. But along with the acquisition of all this new territory came a staggering debt of approximately 130 million pounds. Administering its huge new North American empire would be a costly undertaking for Britain.

British Actions

Following the war, Britain imposed upon its colonies a series of regulatory measures intended to make the colonists help pay the war debts and share the costs of governing the empire. To prevent colonists from ruining the prosperous British fur trade, the Proclamation of 1763 restricted them to the eastern side of the Appalachian chain,

TOPHAM/THE IMAGE WORKS

angering those interested in settling, cultivating, and trading in this new region. The Sugar Act (1764) was the first law passed by Parliament for the specific purpose of raising money in the colonies for the crown. (Other regulatory acts passed earlier had been enacted for the purpose of controlling trade.) The Sugar Act (1) increased the duties on sugar; (2) placed new import duties on textiles, coffee, indigo, wines, and other goods; and (3) doubled the duties on foreign goods shipped from England to the colonies. The Stamp Act (1765) required the payment of a tax on the purchase of all newspapers, pamphlets, almanacs, and commercial and legal documents in the colonies. Both acts drew outrage from colonists, who argued that Parliament could not tax those who were not formally represented in its chambers. Throughout late 1765 and early 1766, angry colonists protested the Stamp Act by attacking stamp agents who attempted to collect the tax, destroying the stamps, and boycotting British goods. When English merchants complained bitterly about the loss of revenue they were suffering as a result of these colonial protests, Parliament repealed the Stamp Act in March 1766.[2]

Patrick Henry, a leading revolutionary who coined the phrase "Give me liberty or give me death," speaking before the Virginia House of Burgesses in 1775.

Colonial Responses

As a result of the Stamp Act fiasco, positions on the state of British rule were articulated both in the colonies and in Parliament. Following the lead of the Virginia assembly, which sponsored the Virginia Resolves that had declared the principle of "no taxation without representation," an intercolonial Stamp Act Congress met in New York City in 1765. This first congressional body in America issued a Declaration of Rights and Grievances that acknowledged allegiance to the Crown, but reiterated the right to not be taxed without consent. Meanwhile, the British

Understand the origins and causes of the American Revolution ★ LO

29

Top Ten Most Important Founders?

Jim Allison, an independent researcher from Virginia Beach, Virginia, recently tried to identify those Founders who most influenced the early republic. Rejecting traditional forms of subjective or impressionistic analysis, Allison invented his own ranking system, which allotted to each Founder a specific number of points for participation in selected activities. For example, he awarded two points for signing the Declaration of Independence, two points for attending the Constitutional Convention, one point for authoring documents that had an impact on state government, and so on. The ranking system can be found at http://members.tripod.com/~candst/tnppage/quote1.htm. Allison's system has its flaws; most notably, it awards to each person the same number of points for participating in an activity, even though some obviously had more influence on the outcome of these activities than others. Thus the appearance of James Madison at the top of the list seems reasonable, whereas Thomas Jefferson's low ranking (19th) may be explained in part by his absence from America (he was in France) during both the Constitutional Convention and subsequent congressional debates over the Bill of Rights. Perhaps what is most surprising about Allison's list is the absence of such well-known figures as George Washington, Benjamin Franklin, and John Adams.

Who would you list as the ten most important founding fathers? The list of Allison's top ten is as follows:

Founder	Points	State
✔ James Madison, key drafter of Constitution, author of some Federalist Papers, congressional sponsor of Bill of Rights, fourth President of the United States	364	VA
✔ Roger Sherman, author of the Great Compromise that saved the Constitutional Convention	295	CT
✔ James Wilson, played a leading role at the Constitutional Convention, one of the first Supreme Court justices	276	PA
✔ Rufus King, delegate to Constitutional Convention, early 18th-century candidate for president, vice president	272	MA
✔ Elbridge Gerry, delegate to Constitutional Convention, American commissioner to Paris, vice president	214	MA
✔ Edmund Randolph, proposed Virginia Plan at the Constitutional Convention, first U.S. Attorney General, Second Secretary of State	154	VA
✔ George Mason, key revolutionary statesman, opposed the Great Compromise, fought for federal Bill of Rights	131	VA
✔ Alexander Hamilton, author of Federalist Papers, Secretary of Treasury, inspired creation of national bank	125	NY
✔ Gouverneur Morris, led floor debates at Constitutional Convention, prepared final draft of Constitution	119	PA
✔ John Rutledge, member of Continental Congress, delegate to the Constitutional Convention, associate justice of the Supreme Court, nominee for Chief Justice	112	SC

Parliament—on the same day that it repealed the Stamp Act—passed into law the Declaratory Act, asserting that the king and Parliament had "full power and authority" to enact laws binding on the colonies "in all cases whatsoever."

Despite the colonists' protests, Parliament continued to pass legislation designed to raise revenue from the colonies. The Townshend Acts, passed in 1767, imposed duties on various items, including tea, imported into the colonies and created a Board of Customs Commissioners to enforce the acts and collect the duties. When the colonists protested by boycotting British goods, in 1770 Parliament repealed all the duties except that on tea. The Tea Act, enacted in 1773, was passed to help the financially troubled British East India Company by relaxing export duties and allowing the company to sell its tea directly in the colonies. These advantages allowed the company to undersell colonial merchants. Angry colonists saw the act as a trick to lure Americans into buying the cheaper tea and thus ruining American tea sellers. On December 16, 1773, colonists disguised as Mohawk Indians boarded ships in Boston Harbor, and threw overboard their cargoes of tea. Outraged by this defiant Boston Tea Party, Parliament in 1774 passed the Intolerable Acts (known in the colonies as the Coercive Acts), designed to punish the rebellious colonists. The acts closed the port of Boston, revised the Massachusetts colonial government, and required the colonists to provide food and housing for British troops stationed in the colonies.

The colonists had had enough. In September 1774, fifty-six leaders from twelve colonies (there were no delegates from Georgia) met in Philadelphia to plan a united response to Parliament's actions. This First Continental Congress denounced British policy and organized a boycott of British goods. Although the Congress did not advocate outright independence from England, it did encourage the colonial militias to arm themselves and began to collect and store weapons in an arsenal in Concord, Massachusetts. The British governor general of Massachusetts ordered British troops to seize and destroy the weapons. On their way to Concord, the troops met a small force of colonial militiamen at Lexington. Shots were exchanged, but the militiamen were soon routed and the British troops marched on to Concord. There they encountered a much larger group of colonial militia. Shots again were fired, and this time the British retreated. The American Revolution had begun.

After the skirmishes at Lexington and Concord in early 1775, a Second Continental Congress met in May of that year, this time with all thirteen colonies represented. This Congress established a continental army and appointed George Washington as its commander in chief, initiating the process that resulted in independence for the colonies and the formation of a new nation, the United States of America.[3]

The Decision for Independence

Despite the events of the early 1770s, many leading colonists continued to hold out hope that some settlement could be reached between the colonies and Britain. The tide turned irrevocably in early 1776, when one of the most influential publications of this period, *Common Sense*, first appeared. In it, Thomas Paine attacked King George III as responsible for the provocations against the colonies, and converted many wavering Americans to the cause of independence.[4]

On June 7, 1776, Richard Henry Lee, a delegate to the Second Continental Congress from Virginia, proposed a resolution stating that "these United Colonies are, and of right ought to be, free and independent States." Of course the Congress needed a formal document both to state their list of grievances and to articulate their new intention to seek independence. The Congress thus appointed a committee to draft a document that would meet those objectives.

The committee, consisting of Thomas Jefferson, John Adams, Roger Sherman, Robert Livingston, and Benjamin Franklin, appointed Jefferson to compose the document. At first, Jefferson may have seemed an unlikely choice to produce such a declaration. The thirty-three-year-old lawyer and delegate to the Continental Congresses of 1775 and 1776 had played a relatively minor role in those bodies' deliberations. But according to historian David McCullough, Adams initially believed that the

© 2012 CENGAGE LEARNING

The Declaration of Independence.

Declaration of Independence

Formal document listing colonists' grievances and articulating the colonists' intention to seek independence; formally adopted by the Second Continental Congress on July 4, 1776.

★ LO — Describe the first national government under the Articles of Confederation, including its weaknesses and struggles

Articles of Confederation

The document creating a "league of friendship" governing the thirteen states during and immediately after the war for independence; hampered by the limited power they vested in the legislature to collect revenue or regulate commerce, the Articles eventually proved unworkable for the new nation.

document was really just a symbolic "side show," and quickly justified the choice of Jefferson over himself as follows: "Reason first: you are a Virginian and a Virginian ought to appear at the head of this business. Reason second: I am obnoxious, suspected and unpopular. You are very much otherwise. Reason third: You can write ten times better than I can." Later, Adams fumed for decades over the larger-than-life reputation Jefferson gained on the basis of authoring the nation's first great political document.[5]

The committee submitted its draft to Congress on July 2, 1776; after making some changes, Congress formally adopted the document on July 4. The **Declaration of Independence** restated John Locke's theory of natural rights and the social contract between government and the governed.[6] Locke had argued that although citizens sacrifice certain rights when they consent to be governed as part of a social contract, they retain other inalienable rights. In the Declaration, Jefferson reiterated this argument with the riveting sentence: "We hold these truths to be self-evident, that all men are created equal, that they are endowed by their Creator with certain inalienable rights, that among these are life, liberty and the pursuit of happiness." Jefferson went on to state that whenever government fails in its duty to secure such rights, the people have the right to "alter" or "abolish" it and institute a new one. Through the centuries, America's political leaders have consistently invoked the Declaration of Independence as perhaps the truest written embodiment of the American Revolution. Before independence could become a reality, however, the colonists had to fight and win a war with Great Britain.

The First National Government: The Articles of Confederation

The colonies also needed some sort of plan of government to direct the war effort. The Second Continental Congress drew up the **Articles of Confederation**, a written statement of rules and principles to guide the first continent-wide government in the colonies during the war and beyond. Although the document was initially adopted by Congress in 1777, it was not formally ratified by all thirteen states until 1781. The Articles of Confederation created a "league of friendship" among the states, but the states remained sovereign and independent with the power and authority to rule the colonists' daily lives. The sole body of the new national government was the Congress, in which each state had one vote. The Congress enjoyed only limited authority to govern the colonies: it could wage war and make peace, coin money, make treaties and alliances with other nations, operate a postal service, and manage relations with the Native Americans.[7] But Congress had no power to raise troops, regulate commerce, or levy taxes, which left it dependent on state legislatures to raise and support armies or provide other services. Congress's inability to raise funds significantly hampered the efforts of George Washington and the Continental Army during the war against Britain. Although Congress employed a "requisition system" in the 1780s, which essentially asked that states voluntarily meet contribution quotas to the federal government, the system proved ineffective. New Jersey, for example, consistently refused to pay such requisitions. Reflecting the colonists' distrust of a strong centralized government, the Articles made no provision for a chief executive who could enforce Congress's laws.

JEFFREY SYLVESTER/TAXI/GETTY IMAGES

TABLE 2.1 The Articles of Confederation and the U.S. Constitution: Key Features

Articles of Confederation Provisions	Problems Generated	1787 Federal Constitution
Unicameral (one-house) Congress with each state having one vote, regardless of population	Gave smaller, less populated states disproportionate power in lawmaking	Bicameral (two-house) legislature with one house apportioned by population (House of Representatives) and second house (Senate) apportioned equally among states (two senators from each state)
Approval by nine of thirteen states required for most legislative matters	Restricted lawmaking by simple majorities, halting the legislative process in most cases	Approval of simple majority (one-half plus one) of both houses required for most legislation
No separate executive or judiciary	Legislative abuses went unchecked	Three separate branches of government: legislative, executive, and judicial
Congress did not have the power to regulate foreign or interstate commerce	States negotiated separately among themselves and with foreign powers on commercial matters, to the detriment of the overall economy	Congress given power to regulate interstate and foreign commerce
Congress did not have the power to levy or collect taxes	Suffering from the economic depression and saddled with their own war debts, states furnished only a small portion of the money sought by Congress	Congress given power to levy and collect taxes
Congress did not have power to raise an army	Once the war with Britain had ended, states were reluctant to provide any support for an army	Congress given power to raise and support armies
Amendments to articles required unanimous approval of state legislatures	Articles were practically immune from modification, and thus inflexible to meet changing demands of a new nation	Amendments to Constitution require two-thirds vote of both houses of Congress, ratification by three fourths of states

The limited powers of the central government posed many problems, but changing the Articles of Confederation to meet the needs of the new nation was no easy task. The Articles could be amended only by the assent of all thirteen state legislatures, a provision that made change of any kind nearly impossible. Wealthy property owners and colonial merchants were frustrated with the Articles for various reasons. Because Congress lacked the power to regulate interstate and foreign commerce, it was exceedingly difficult to obtain commercial concessions from other nations. Quarrels among states disrupted interstate commerce and travel. Finally, a few state governments (most notably, Pennsylvania) had come to be dominated by radical movements that further threatened the property rights of many wealthy, landowning colonists.

These difficulties did not disappear when the war ended with the Americans' victory in 1783. Instead, an economic depression, partially caused by the loss of trade with Great Britain and the West Indies, aggravated the problems facing the new nation. In January 1785, an alarmed Congress appointed a committee to consider amendments to the Articles. Although the committee called for expanded congressional powers to enter commercial treaties with other nations, no action was taken. Further proposals to revise the Articles by creating federal courts and strengthening the system of soliciting contributions from states were never even submitted to the states for approval; congressional leaders apparently despaired of ever winning the unanimous approval of the state legislatures needed to create such changes.

Then in September 1786, nine states accepted invitations to attend a convention in Annapolis, Maryland, to discuss interstate commerce. Yet when the Annapolis Convention opened on September 11, delegates from only five states (New York, New Jersey, Delaware, Pennsylvania, and Virginia) attended. A committee led by Alexander Hamilton, a leading force at the Annapolis meeting, issued a report calling upon all thirteen states to attend a convention in Philadelphia the following May to discuss all matters necessary "to render the constitution of the federal government adequate to the exigencies of the Union." At the time, few knew whether this proposal would attract more interest than had previous calls for a new government.

NORTH WIND/NORTH WIND PICTURE ARCHIVES

Daniel Shays leads a rebellion of farmers to a Massachusetts courthouse in 1786 to protest the state legislature's inaction.

Events in Massachusetts in 1786–1787 proved a turning point in the creation of momentum for a new form of government. A Revolutionary war veteran, Daniel Shays, was also one of many debt-ridden farmers in Massachusetts, where creditors controlled the state government. Shays and his men rebelled against the state courts' foreclosing on the farmers' mortgages for failure to pay debts and state taxes.[8] When the state legislature failed to resolve the farmers' grievances, Shays's rebels stormed two courthouses and a federal arsenal.[9] Eventually the state militia put down the insurrection, known as **Shays's Rebellion**, but the message was clear: a weak and unresponsive government carried with it the danger of disorder and violence. In February 1787, Congress endorsed the call for a convention to serve the purpose of

Shays's Rebellion
Armed uprising by debt-ridden Massachusetts farmers frustrated with the state government.

drafting amendments to the Articles of Confederation, and by May eleven states had acted to name delegates to the convention to be held in Philadelphia.

The Constitutional Convention

The **Constitutional Convention** convened on May 25, 1787, with twenty-nine delegates from nine states in attendance. Over the next four months fifty-five delegates from twelve states would participate. Fiercely resistant to any centralized power, Rhode Island sent no delegates. Some heroes of the American Revolution like Patrick Henry refused appointments due to their opposition to the feelings of nationalism that had spurred the convention to be held in the first place. Meanwhile, lending authority to the proceedings were such well-known American figures as George Washington, Alexander Hamilton, and Benjamin Franklin. (The thirty-six-year-old James Madison of Virginia was only beginning to establish a reputation for himself when he arrived in Philadelphia; meanwhile, John Adams and Thomas Jefferson were both on diplomatic assignment in Europe.)

Portrait of George Washington, circa 1775. Washington was elected president of the Constitutional convention in Philadelphia.

The delegates, who unanimously selected Washington to preside over the convention, were united by at least four common concerns: (1) the United States was being treated with contempt by other nations, and foreign trade had suffered as a consequence; (2) the economic radicalism of Shays's Rebellion might spread in the absence of a stronger central government; (3) the Native Americans had responded to encroachment on their lands by threatening frontiersmen and land speculators, and the national government had been ill-equipped to provide citizens with protection; and (4) the postwar economic depression had worsened, and the national government was powerless to take any action to address it.[10] Of course, on many other matters the delegates differed. Those from bigger, more heavily populated states such as Virginia and Pennsylvania wanted a central government that reflected their larger population bases, whereas those from smaller states like Georgia and Delaware hoped to maintain the one-state, one-vote principle of the Articles.

Plans and Compromises

It quickly became evident that a convention originally called to discuss amendments to the Articles of Confederation would be undertaking a more drastic overhaul of the American system of government. Members of the Virginia delegation got the ball rolling when they introduced the **Virginia Plan**, also known as the "large states plan," which proposed a national government consisting of three branches—a legislature, an executive, and a judiciary. The legislature would consist of two houses, with membership in each house proportional to each state's population. The people would elect members of one house, and the members of that house would then choose members of the second house. The legislature would have the power to choose a chief executive and members of the judiciary and authority to legislate in "all cases to which the states are incompetent" or when the "harmony of the United States" demands it. Finally, the legislature would have power to veto any state law. Under the plan, the only real check on the legislature would be a Council of Revision, consisting of the executive and several members of the judiciary, which could veto the legislature's acts.

To counter the Virginia Plan, delegates from less populous states proposed the **New Jersey Plan**, which called for a one-house legislature in which each state, regardless of size, would have equal representation. The New Jersey Plan also provided for a national judiciary and an executive committee chosen by the legislature; expanded the powers of Congress to include the power to levy taxes and regulate foreign and interstate commerce; and asserted that the Constitution and national

Constitutional Convention
Meeting of delegates from twelve states in Philadelphia during the summer of 1787, at which was drafted an entirely new system to govern the United States.

★ LO
Compare and contrast the various plans for the new Constitution and the obstacles to agreement among the different colonies

Virginia Plan
A proposal known also as the "large states plan" that empowered three separate branches of government, including a legislature with membership proportional to population.

New Jersey Plan
A proposal known also as the "small states plan" that would have retained the Articles of Confederation principle of a legislature where states enjoyed equal representation.

laws would become the "supreme law of the United States." Both the Virginia and New Jersey plans rejected a model of government in which the executive would be given extensive authority.

By July 2, 1787, disagreements over the design of the legislature and the issue of representation had brought the convention to a near dead end. The delegates then agreed to submit the matter to a smaller committee in the hope that it might craft some form of compromise.

The product of that committee's deliberations was a set of compromises, termed the **Great Compromise** by historians. (Formally proposed by delegate Roger Sherman of Connecticut, the agreement is also known as the Connecticut Compromise.) Its critical features included (1) a bicameral (two-house) legislature with an upper house or "Senate" in which the states would have equal power with two representatives from each state, and a lower House of Representatives in which membership would be apportioned on the basis of population; and (2) the guarantee that all revenue bills would originate in the lower house. The convention delegates settled as well on granting Congress the authority to regulate interstate and foreign commerce by a simple majority vote, but requiring that treaties be approved by a two-thirds vote of the upper house. The Great Compromise was eventually approved by a narrow 5–4 margin of the state delegations. Connecticut, New Jersey, Delaware, Maryland, and North Carolina approved; Pennsylvania, Virginia, South Carolina, and Georgia opposed; New York and New Hampshire were absent, and the Massachusetts delegation was deadlocked. Thus a vote margin of just one state paved the way for the creation of a new federal government.

Great Compromise

A proposal also known as the "Connecticut Compromise" that provided for a bicameral legislature featuring an upper house based on equal representation among the states and a lower house whose membership was based on each state's population; approved by a 5–4 vote of the state delegations.

TABLE 2.2 The Virginia Plan, the New Jersey Plan, and the Great Compromise

The Virginia Plan	The New Jersey Plan	The Great Compromise
Introduced on May 29, 1787, by Edmund Randolph of Virginia; favored initially by delegates from Virginia, Pennsylvania, Massachusetts	Introduced on June 15, 1787, by William Paterson of New Jersey; favored initially by delegates from New Jersey, New York, Connecticut, Maryland, Delaware	Introduced by Roger Sherman of Connecticut; approved at the convention by a narrow 5–4 vote on July 16, 1787
Bicameral legislature with one house elected by the people and second house chosen by the first	Unicameral legislature elected by the people	Bicameral legislature with one house elected by the people and second house chosen by state legislatures
All representatives and senators apportioned by population	Equal representation among states	Members of one house (representatives) apportioned by population (five slaves counted as three free men); members of second house (senators) apportioned equally among states
Singular executive chosen by the legislature	Plural executive chosen by the legislature	Singular executive chosen by the "Electoral College" (Electors appointed by state legislatures choose President; if no one receives majority, House chooses President)
Congress can legislate wherever "states are incompetent" or to preserve "harmony of the United States"	Congress has power to tax and regulate commerce	Congress has power to tax only in proportion to representation in the lower House; all appropriation bills must originate in lower house

Compromise also resolved disagreement over the nature of the executive. Although rejecting the New Jersey Plan's call for a plural executive—in which officials would have exercised executive power through a multi-person council—the delegates split on whether the executive should be elected by members of Congress or directly by the people. The agreement reached called for the president (and vice president) to be elected by an electoral college. Because the number of electors equaled that of the number of representatives and senators from each state, this system gave disproportionately greater influence to smaller states. As chief executive, the president would have the power to veto acts of Congress, make treaties and appointments with the consent of the Senate, and serve as commander-in-chief of the nation's armed forces.

The Slavery Issue

The issue of representation collided with another thorny issue looming over the convention proceedings—the issue of slavery. Four Southern states—Maryland, Virginia, North Carolina, and South Carolina—had slave populations of more than a hundred thousand each. Meanwhile, two New England states, Maine and Massachusetts, had already banned slavery and another four Northern states—Vermont, New Hampshire, Rhode Island, and Connecticut—had a combined total of just four thousand slaves within their borders. The steady march of abolition in the North was matched by a Southern slave population that had been doubling every two decades. The convention delegates who advocated a new form of government were wary of the role slavery would play in this new nation, but they were even more wary of offending Southern sentiments to the point that consensus at the convention would be endangered.

Some delegates from the Northern states that had already voted in favor of banning slavery sought a similar emancipation of slaves in all the colonies by constitutional edict. Southerners hoping to protect their plantation economy, which depended on slave labor, wanted to prevent future Congresses from interfering with the institution of slavery and the importation of slaves. Moreover, even among Northerners there was disagreement on how emancipation should proceed: some favored outright freedom, whereas others argued for some form of colonization of the slaves, which would in effect ship them back to Africa. Many delegates feared that any extended discussion of slavery at the convention would become so divisive that it might bring the entire gathering to a standstill.

Southern delegates also wanted slaves to be counted equally with free people in determining the apportionment of representatives; Northerners opposed such a scheme for representation because it would give the Southern states more power, but did want slaves counted equally for purposes of apportioning taxes among the

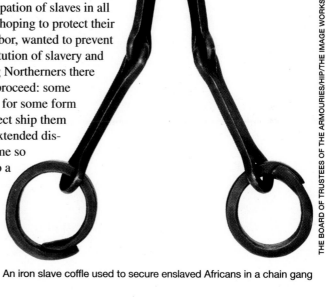

THE BOARD OF TRUSTEES OF THE ARMOURIES/HIP/THE IMAGE WORKS

An iron slave coffle used to secure enslaved Africans in a chain gang

states. In an effort to forestall the convention's collapse, the delegates crafted a series of compromises that amounted to misdirection, and in some instances outright silence on the issue of slavery.[11] By the agreement known as the **Three-Fifths Compromise**, five slaves would be counted as the equivalent of three "free persons" for purposes of taxes *and* representation. Delegates from Southern states also feared that a Congress dominated by representatives from more populous Northern states might take action against the slave trade. Most Northerners continued to favor gradual emancipation. Once again, neither side got exactly what it wanted. The Constitution said nothing about either preserving or outlawing slavery. Indeed, the only specific

Three-Fifths Compromise

A compromise proposal in which five slaves would be counted as the equivalent of three free people for purposes of taxes and representation.

provision about slavery was a time limit on legislation banning slave importation: Congress was forbidden from doing so for at least twenty years. In 1807, however, with the slave population steadily outgrowing demand, many Southerners allied with opponents of the slave trade to ban the importation of slaves. Not until the Civil War decades later would the conflict over slavery be finally resolved.

On September 17, 1787, after four months of compromises and negotiations, the twelve state delegations present approved the final draft of the Constitution. By the terms of Article VII of the document, the Constitution was to become operative once ratified by nine of the thirteen states.

The New Constitution

★ LO   Understand how sovereign powers were divided in the new government

As a consequence of the many compromises in the draft Constitution, few of the delegates were pleased with every aspect of the new document. Even James Madison, later heralded as the "Father of the Constitution" for his many contributions as a spokesman at the convention, had furiously opposed the Great Compromise; he hinted at one point that a majority of the states might be willing to form a union outside the convention if the compromise were ever approved, and he convinced the Virginia delegation to vote "no" when it came up for a formal vote.

FIGURE 2.1 Concentration of Slavery (by County) circa 1790

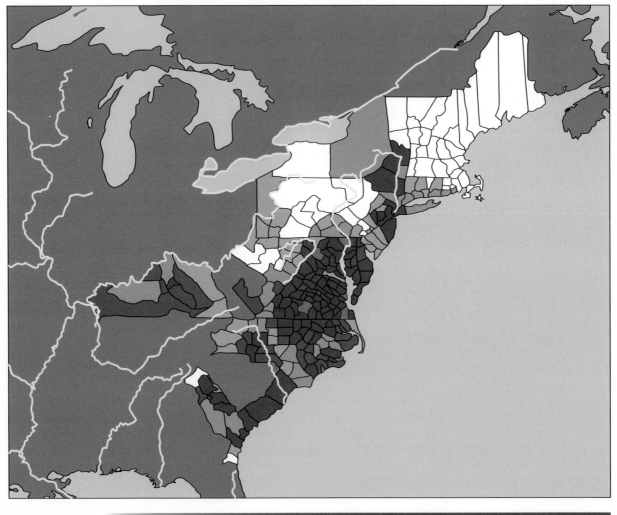

Number of Slaves

0	25.317	50.634

Source: From the Web site for the "GIS for History" project at the University of Illinois at Chicago, http://gis.uchicago.edu/data.htm

AMERICAN GOVERNMENT In Global Perspective

One Canadian's View of the Founders' Approach to Immigration

The increasingly contentious debate in the United States over illegal immigration has inspired some modern-day American politicians to cite America's historical roots as a shelter for the world's oppressed as justification for a more open approach to immigration. Observing this debate from his own vantage point north of the border, Canadian newspaper columnist Hartley Steward of the *Toronto Sun* offered his own perspective on the Founders and how their unique and unprecedented attitudes toward immigration are encapsulated in the words of poet Emma Lazarus inscribed at the base of the Statue of Liberty: "Give me your tired, your poor, your huddled masses yearning to breathe free. . . ." Reflecting on these words, Steward notes:

You understand, this is no simple welcome-to-America greeting. This is an achingly beautiful articulation of one of the most noble notions of national purpose ever in history. . . . At a time when most of the xenophobic world guarded its borders jealously, fearing anything unfamiliar or foreign, America's founding fathers conceived their new nation as a home for the weary and dispossessed. At a time when democracy could still be considered a new idea and freedom mostly a dream, America had freedom beyond imagining, hope and dignity seldom found anywhere.

Source: "Mexico: Oil Depletion and Illegal U.S. Immigration," *World Press Review*, April 25, 2006 (http://www.worldpress.org).

Nonetheless, the central desire of most of the delegates to craft a new government framework did lead them to consensus on a set of guiding principles that are evident throughout the document. The following principles continue to guide politicians, lawyers, and scholars today as they study the many ambiguous provisions of the Constitution:

- Recognizing that calls for fairer representation of colonists' interests lay at the heart of the Declaration of Independence, popular sovereignty was a guiding principle behind the new Constitution. The document's preamble beginning with "We the People" signified the coming together of people, not states, for the purposes of creating a new government. Under the Constitution, no law could be passed without the approval of the House of Representatives, a "people's house" composed of members apportioned by population and subject to reelection every two years. Of even greater significance, the delegates agreed that all revenue measures must originate in the House, an explicit affirmation of the principle that there would be "no taxation without representation."

- The delegates recognized the need for a **separation of powers**. The Founders drew upon the ideas of the French political philosopher Baron de Montesquieu, who had argued that when legislative, executive, and judicial power are not exercised by the same institution, power cannot be so easily abused. Mindful of the British model in which Parliament combined legislative and executive authority, the drafters of the Constitution assigned specific responsibilities and powers to each branch of the government—Congress (the legislative power), the president (the executive power), and the Supreme Court (the judicial power). In the new government, individuals were generally prohibited from serving in more than one branch of government at the same time. The vice president's role as president of the Senate was a notable exception to this rule.

- While establishing separate institutions, the drafters of the Constitution also created a system of **checks and balances** to require that the branches of government would have to work together to formulate policy. This system of "separate institutions sharing power" helped ensure that no one interest or faction could easily dominate

Separation of powers
The principle that each branch of government enjoys separate and independent powers and areas of responsibility.

Checks and balances
A system of limits imposed by the Constitution that gives each branch of government the limited right to change or cancel the acts of other branches.

Chapter 2 The Founding and the Constitution

FIGURE 2.2 Checks and Balances in the U.S. Constitution

CHECKS BY JUDICIARY

Checks on Congress
✓Federal judicial power extends to all cases arising under the laws of the United States (Art. III, § 2, Cl. 1) **(subsequently interpreted to include power to invalidate unconstitutional laws passed by Congress)**

Checks on Executive
✓Federal judicial power extends to all cases or controversies to which the U.S. government is a party (Art. III, § 2, Cl. 1) **(subsequently interpreted to include power to invalidate unconstitutional acts by president)**

✓Chief justice shall preside over Senate impeachment trials of the president (Art. I, § 3, Cl. 6)

CHECKS BY EXECUTIVE

Checks on Congress
✓Presidential power to sign or veto bills (Art I, § 7, Cl. 2)

✓In alternate role as president of Senate, vice president of United States can cast votes to break ties in a divided Senate (Art. I, § 3, Cl. 4)

✓President can bypass Senate temporarily by filling vacancies during Senate recess that expire at end of next Senate session (Art. II, § 2, Cl. 3)

✓President may "on extraordinary occasions" convene or adjourn either or both houses of Congress (Art. II, § 3)

✓President must "take care" that congressional laws are faithfully executed (Art. II, § 3)

Checks on Judiciary
✓President nominates and (with Senate advice and consent) appoints Supreme Court justices (Art. II, § 2, Cl. 2)

CHECKS BY CONGRESS

Checks on Executive
✓Impeachment by House (Art. I, § 2, Cl. 5) and removal by Senate (Art. I, § 3, Cl. 6) of president, vice president, and all civil officers of the United States (Art. II, § 4)

✓Congressional override of presidential vetoes by two-thirds vote of both houses (Art. I, § 7, Cl. 2)

✓Senate must approve all treaties by two-thirds vote (Art. II, § 2, Cl. 2)

✓House selection of president and Senate selection of vice president in event there is no Electoral College majority (Art. II, § 1, Cl. 3, Twelfth Amendment)

✓Senate advice and consent required for appointment of "Officers of the United States" (Art. II, § 2, Cl. 2)

Checks on Judiciary
✓Senate advice and consent required for appointment of Supreme Court Justices (Art. II, § 2, Cl. 2)

✓Impeachment by House (Art. I, § 2, Cl. 5) and removal by Senate (Art. I, § 3, Cl. 6) of Supreme Court justices

✓Congress can make exceptions to appellate jurisdiction of the Supreme Court (Art. III, § 2, Cl. 2)

the government. Through the exercise of presidential vetoes, Senate advice and consent, and judicial interpretations and other tools, each institution would have an opportunity to contend for influence.

■ Dividing sovereign powers between the states and the federal government—a system later termed *federalism*—is also a defining characteristic of the government framework, established by the Constitution. Rather than entrusting all powers to a centralized government and essentially reducing the states to mere geographical subdivisions of the nation, the convention delegates divided powers between two levels of government: the states and the federal government. The distinction drawn between local concerns—controlled by state governments—and national concerns—controlled by the federal government—was as confusing then as it is today. But the delegates determined that such a division was necessary if they hoped to achieve any consensus. It would be politically impossible to convince the states to become mere geographic subdivisions of a larger political whole.

■ Although united by the belief that the national government needed to be strengthened, the framers of the Constitution were products of a revolutionary generation that had seen governmental power abused. Thus, they were committed to a government of limited or **enumerated powers**. The Constitution spelled out the powers of the new federal government in detail, and it was assumed that the government's authority did not extend beyond those powers. By rejecting a government of unlimited discretionary power, James Madison argued, individual rights, including those "inalienable rights" cited in the Declaration of Independence, would be protected from the arbitrary exercise of authority.

Enumerated powers
Express powers explicitly granted by the Constitution such as the taxing power specifically granted to Congress.

- Finally, some delegates believed that the new Constitution should be a "living" document; that is, it should have some measure of flexibility in order to meet the changing demands placed on it over time. Perhaps the most frustrating aspect of the Articles of Confederation was the near impossibility of any sort of modification: because any change to the Articles required the unanimous consent of the states, even the most popular reform proposals stood little chance of being implemented. Thus, the Framers decided that the new Constitution would go into effect when it had been ratified by nine of thirteen states. Furthermore, once ratified, the Constitution could be amended by a two-thirds vote of each house of Congress (subject to subsequent ratification by three fourths of the state legislatures).

VISIONS OF AMERICA/JOE SOHM/PHOTODISC/GETTY IMAGES

Benjamin Franklin at the time of the Constitutional Convention—statue, Franklin Institute, Philadelphia.

The Ratification Battle

Federalists versus Anti-Federalists

Once Congress submitted the Constitution to the states for approval, battle lines were formed between the **Federalists**, who supported ratification of the new document, and the **Anti-Federalists**, who opposed it. From the outset, the Federalists enjoyed a number of structural and tactical advantages in this conflict:

- **Nonunanimous consent.** The rules of ratification for the new Constitution, requiring approval of just nine of the thirteen states, were meant to ease the process of adopting the new document. The delegates understood that once the Constitution had been approved, it would be difficult for even the most stubborn of state holdouts to exist as an independent nation surrounded by this formidable new national entity, the United States of America.

- **Special "ratifying conventions."** The delegates realized that whatever form the new constitution might take, state legislatures would have the most to lose from an abandonment of the Articles. Thus they decided that the Constitution would be sent for ratification not to state legislatures, but instead to special state ratifying conventions that would be more likely to approve it.

- **The rule of secrecy.** The Constitutional Convention's agreed-upon rule of secrecy, which forbade publication or discussion of the day-to-day proceedings of the convention, followed the precedent established in colonial assemblies and the First Continental Congress, where it was thought that members might speak more freely and openly if their remarks were not subject to daily scrutiny by the public at large. In the fall of 1787, the rule of secrecy also gave the Federalists on the inside a distinct advantage over outside opponents, who had little knowledge of the new document's provisions until publicized. Because the number of convention delegates who supported the new Constitution far exceeded the number of delegates opposed, the rule of secrecy gave the Federalists a distinct advantage. As it turned out, five state ratifying conventions approved the Constitution within four months of the convention's formal conclusion, just as Anti-Federalist forces were collecting their strength for the battle ahead.

- **Conventions held in the winter limited rural participation.** Winter was approaching just as the fight over the new Constitution was being launched. This timing gave the Federalists another advantage, especially in the critical ratification battlegrounds of Massachusetts, New Hampshire, and New York. It would be difficult for rural dwellers—mostly poor farmers resistant to a strong central government and thus opposed to the new Constitution—to attend the ratification conventions if they were held in the dead of winter. Supporters of the Constitution

Evaluate the advantages enjoyed by those seeking to ratify the new Constitution

★ LO

Federalists
Those who supported ratification of the proposed Constitution of the United States between 1787 and 1789.

Anti-Federalists
Those who opposed ratification of the proposed Constitution of the United States.

successfully pressed for the ratifying conventions to be held as soon as possible. And of the six states that held such conventions over the winter, all voted to ratify by substantial margins.

The Federalist Papers

★ LO Assess the role that the Federalist Papers played in ratification

Between the fall of 1787 and the summer of 1788, the Federalists launched an aggressive media campaign that was unusually well organized for its time. James Madison, Alexander Hamilton, and John Jay wrote seventy-seven essays explaining and defending the new Constitution and urging its ratification. Signed under the name "Publius," the essays were printed in New York newspapers and magazines. These essays—along with eight others by the same men—were then collected, printed, and published in book form under the title *The Federalist*.[12] The essays allayed fears and extolled the benefits of the new Constitution by emphasizing the inadequacy of the Articles of Confederation and the need for a strong government. Today these essays are considered classic works of political philosophy. The following are among the most frequently cited Federalist Papers:

ROGER VIOLLET/THE IMAGE WORKS

Portrait of James Madison, the "Father of the Constitution."

Federalist Papers

A series of articles authored by Alexander Hamilton, James Madison, and John Jay, which argued in favor of ratifying the proposed Constitution of the United States; the Federalist Papers outlined the philosophy and motivation of the document.

- **Federalist No. 10.** In Madison's first offering in the **Federalist Papers**, he analyzes the nature, causes, and effects of *factions*, by which he meant groups of people motivated by a common economic and/or political interest. Noting that such factions are both the product and price of liberty, Madison argued that by extending the sphere in which they can act, "you make it less probable that a majority of the whole will have a common motive to invade the rights of other citizens." Political theorists often cite Federalist No. 10 as justification for pluralist theory—the idea that competition among groups for power produces the best approximation of overall public good.

- **Federalist No. 15.** Hamilton launched his attack on the Articles of Confederation in this essay. Specifically, he pointed to the practical impossibility of engaging in concerted action when each of the thirteen states retained virtual power to govern.

- **Federalist No. 46.** In this essay, Madison defended the system of federalism set up by the new Constitution. He contended that the system allowed the states sufficient capacity to resist the "ambitious encroachments of the federal government."

- **Federalist No. 51.** In perhaps the most influential of the essays, Madison described how the new Constitution would prevent the government from abusing its citizens. His argument is that the "multiplicity of interests" that influence so many different parts of the government would guarantee the security of individual rights. Because the federal system of government divides the government into so many parts (federal versus state; legislative versus executive versus judicial branches; and so on), "the rights of the individual, or of the minority, will be in little danger from interested combinations of the majority."

- **Federalist No. 69.** Hamilton in this essay defined the "real character of the executive," which, unlike the King of Great Britain, is accountable to the other branches of government and to the people.

- **Federalist No. 70.** In this essay, Hamilton presented his views on executive power, which had tempered considerably since the convention when he advocated an executive for life. Still, Hamilton argued for a unitary, one-person executive to play a critical role as a check on the legislative process (that is, by exercising vetoes), as well as in the process of negotiating treaties and conducting war. According to Hamilton, "energy in the executive is a leading character in the definition of good government"; by contrast, "the species of security" sought for by those who advocate a plural executive is "unattainable."

In late 1787 and early 1788, Anti-Federalists countered the Federalist Papers with a media campaign of their own.[13] In letters written under the pseudonyms

AMERICAN GOVERNMENT In Historical Perspective

The Continuing Call to the *Federalist Papers*

The *Federalist Papers* had a significant impact on the birth of the new nation. The essays argued persuasively that the Articles of Confederation were inadequate. Many scholars today attribute the narrow margin in favor of ratification of the Constitution at New York's ratification convention to the sophisticated media campaign waged by the Federalists, especially through the Federalist Papers.

In 1905, the Supreme Court's controversial decision in *Lochner v. New York*, which invalidated a New York State health regulation restricting the hours that bakers could be exposed to flour dust, set off a furious political debate about the role government should play in a newly industrialized society. Advocates on both sides of the debate repeatedly cited the *Federalist Papers* to bolster their arguments. Those who supported government regulation argued that it was not the job of courts to disagree with the decisions of legislatures on such public interest issues; even if factions and interest groups had produced such legislation, they cited Federalist No. 10 to justify the proposition that the corrupting spirit of "factions" distinguished democracy from true republics. Opponents of government regulations countered that Madison's preference for more factions was simply his way of reaching toward an ideal politics in which all these factions would cancel themselves out—by contrast, they argued that factions remained heavily influential in state legislatures. In support of the Court's ruling, they cited Federalist No. 78 in which Hamilton argued that "the independence of the judges may be an essential safeguard against the effects of occasional ill humors in the society." Only a sudden switch by the Supreme Court to stop interfering with industrial regulations in 1937 saved the nation from a constitutional crisis fueled in part by dramatically contrasting readings of the *Federalist Papers*.

In 1996, President Bill Clinton (a Democrat) signed a welfare reform bill that slashed federal welfare spending, reduced welfare benefits, and shifted major responsibilities for welfare programs from the federal government to state governments. To defend the president's actions against incensed Democratic Party leaders like Senator Patrick Moynihan (D-NY), who feared the bill unfairly turned the government's back on the poor, the White House dug into the *Federalist Papers* for its defense. In Federalist No. 51, James Madison defended the Constitution against charges that it unduly transferred excessive powers to the new government: "A double security arises to the rights of people . . . the different governments will control each other, at the same time that each will be controlled by itself." The White House argued that shifting major welfare responsibilities to the states represented a sharing of the duties and responsibilities of government that was consistent with the intentions of the Founders.

JOYCE NALTCHAYAN/AFP/GETTY IMAGES

President Bill Clinton listens to former welfare mother Rhonda Costa in 1998. Two years earlier, Clinton signed a major welfare bill that shifted primary responsibilities for overseeing welfare to the fifty state governments.

"Brutus" and "The Federal Farmer" and published by newspapers throughout the colonies, the Anti-Federalists claimed that they were invoking a cause more consistent with that of the revolution—the cause of freedom from government tyranny. For them, the new national government's power to impose internal taxes on the states amounted to a revival of the British system of internal taxation. Perhaps the Anti-Federalists' most effective criticism was that the Constitution lacked a bill of rights that explicitly protected citizens' individual rights. They rejected Madison's contention in Federalist No. 51 that limitations on the central government provided those protections.

TABLE 2.3 Ratifying the Constitution

State	Vote	Date of Ratification
Delaware	30–0	December 7, 1787
Pennsylvania	43–23	December 12, 1787
New Jersey	38–0	December 18, 1787
Georgia	25–0	January 2, 1788
Connecticut	128–40	January 9, 1788
Massachusetts	187–168	February 16, 1788
Maryland	63–11	April 26, 1788
South Carolina	149–73	May 23, 1788
New Hampshire	57–46	June 21, 1788
Virginia	89–79	June 25, 1788
New York	30–27	June 26, 1788
North Carolina*	194–77	November 21, 1789
Rhode Island	34–32	May 29, 1790

* Despite strong Federalist sentiment at the convention, North Carolina withheld its vote in 1788 until a Bill of Rights was formally introduced. The submission by Congress of twelve proposed amendments to the states on September 25, 1789, led North Carolina to hold a second ratifying convention the following November.

Ratification ultimately succeeded, but by a somewhat narrow margin. Of the first five states to ratify, four (Delaware, New Jersey, Georgia, and Connecticut) did so with little or no opposition, whereas Pennsylvania did so only after a bitter conflict at its ratifying convention. Massachusetts became the sixth state to ratify when proponents of the Constitution swung the convention narrowly in their favor only by promising to push for a bill of rights after ratification. By June, three more states (Maryland, South Carolina, and New Hampshire) had voted to ratify, providing the critical threshold of nine states required under the Constitution. Still, the Federalists worried that without ratification by the major states of New York and Virginia, the new union would not succeed.

Opposition in Virginia was formidable, with Patrick Henry leading the Anti-Federalist forces against James Madison and the Federalists.[14] Eventually Madison gained the upper hand with an assist from George Washington, whose eminent stature helped capture numerous votes for the Federalists. Madison also promised to support adding a bill of rights to the new Constitution. Then, Alexander Hamilton and John Jay capitalized on the positive news from Virginia to secure victory at the New York ratifying convention. With more than the required nine states—including the crucial states of New York and Virginia—the Congress did not wait for the votes from North Carolina or Rhode Island; on July 2, 1788, it appointed a committee to prepare for the new government.

A Bill of Rights

★ LO Explain the origins of the Bill of Rights and its role in securing ratification

Seven of the state constitutions created during the Revolutionary War featured a statement of individual rights in some form. The Virginia Declaration of Rights of 1776, for example, had borrowed (from John Locke) its grounding of individual rights in a conception of natural law and social contract: "All men are by nature equally free and independent, and have certain inherent rights, of which, when they enter into a state of society, they cannot, by any compact, deprive or divest their posterity." Later, during the battle over ratification, five state ratifying conventions had stressed the need for amendments to the Constitution in the form of a bill of rights, which would expressly protect fundamental rights against encroachment by the national government.[15]

Still, not all the Federalists saw the need for a federal bill of rights. Madison, for one, believed a bill of rights was unnecessary because the central government held only those powers enumerated in the Constitution. He explained: "The rights in question are reserved by the manner in which the federal powers are granted . . . the limited powers of the federal government and the jealousy of the subordinate governments afford a security which has not existed in the case of the state governments, and exists in no other." Madison was also concerned about the dangers of trying to enumerate all important rights: "There is great reason to fear that a positive declaration of some of the most essential rights could not be obtained," leaving some essential rights omitted for the future. Hamilton underscored this sentiment in Federalist No. 84, arguing that such a list of rights might invite governmental attempts to exercise power over those rights not included in the list.

Among the most ardent supporters of adding a bill of rights to the Constitution was Thomas Jefferson, who warned about the dangers of abuses of power.[16] From his distant vantage point in France, where he continued to serve as an American minister, Jefferson was in the dark about the new constitution until November 1787. Then, in a December 20, 1787, letter to his friend and political protégé from Virginia, James Madison, Jefferson wrote: "A bill of rights is what the people are entitled to against every government on earth, general or particular, and what no just government should refuse, or rest on inference." Although recognizing Madison's fears of omissions as legitimate, Jefferson continued to argue the point. In a subsequent letter dated March 15, 1789, Jefferson argued that "half a loaf is better than no bread. If we cannot secure all our rights, let us secure what we can."

In the end Jefferson's arguments prevailed, and Madison (by this time a congressman from Virginia) became a principal sponsor of a bill of rights in the first Congress. Introducing the bill in the House of Representatives, he declared: "They will be an impenetrable bulwark against every assumption of power in the legislative or executive." On September 9, 1789, the House of Representatives voted to submit a list of twelve **amendments** to the states; ten of these were ratified by the required nine states by December 15, 1791, and compose today's **Bill of Rights**.

Among the rights protected by the Bill of Rights are the rights of free religious exercise, free speech, free press, and assembly (First Amendment); rights against search and seizure without a warrant stating "probable cause" (Fourth Amendment); and rights of due process and no self-incrimination (Fifth Amendment). The two amendments not ratified in 1791 did not relate to individual rights at all. They were (1) a prohibition on salary increases for legislators taking effect prior to the next congressional election (in 1992—more than two hundred years later—this became the Twenty-seventh Amendment); and (2) a provision defining the rules for determining the number of members of the House of Representatives.

Changing the Constitution

The Formal Amendment Process

Though political circumstances dictated that the Bill of Rights be passed in a relatively speedy fashion, future proposed amendments would not have it so easy. In crafting the rules for amending the new constitution, the Framers sought to balance two competing interests: (1) the need to protect the Constitution from short-lived or temporary passions by making amendments exceedingly difficult to pass; and (2) sufficient flexibility to allow for amendments to be added when the needs of the nation demanded change. Their determination to strike such a balance was shaped by their experience in dealing with the Articles of Confederation, whose "unanimous consent of states" rule had left them immune from even the most necessary of reforms.

© 2012 CENGAGE LEARNING

Amendments
Modifications or additions to the U.S. Constitution passed in accordance with the amendment procedures laid out in Article V.

Bill of Rights
The first ten amendments to the U.S. Constitution, which protect various rights of the people against the new federal government.

Describe the process of amending the Constitution ★ LO

FIGURE 2.3 How an Amendment Gets Proposed and Ratified

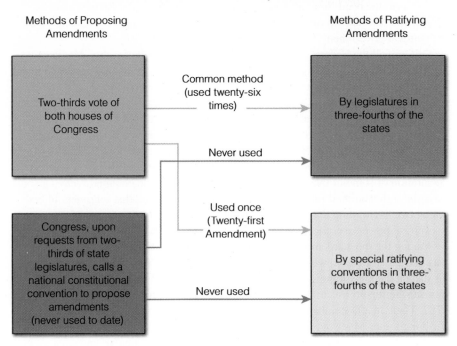

Article V of the Constitution specifies two ways in which amendments can be proposed and two methods of ratification. Congress may propose an amendment by a two-thirds vote of both houses; alternatively, two thirds of the state legislatures may apply to Congress to call a special national convention for proposing amendments. Amendments take effect when ratified either by a vote of three fourths of the state legislatures or by special ratifying conventions held in three fourths of the states. To date, all twenty-seven amendments (including the Bill of Rights) have been proposed by Congress, and all but one (the Twenty-first) have been ratified by the state legislatures.

No national convention has ever been called for the purpose of proposing amendments. Indeed, the closest the states have ever come to applying to Congress for such an event occurred in 1967, when thirty-three states (just one short of the required number) petitioned Congress to call a convention that would propose an amendment reversing the 1964 Supreme Court ruling requiring that both houses of each state legislature be apportioned according to population. Given the ambiguity of Article V, numerous questions have been raised about the form such a convention would take. How would delegates be chosen? When Congress proposed the Twenty-first Amendment, it left it to each state to determine the manner in which delegates to the ratifying conventions would be chosen. How would the convention be run? Could a convention go beyond the limitations placed on it by Congress? What would happen if a convention went far afield and proposed an entirely new constitution, just as the convention in 1787 did? Congress has to date refused to pass laws dictating the terms of future conventions, in part because it has not wanted to encourage such an event.[17]

Critics of the amendment process charge that it is undemocratic, as today just thirteen of the fifty states can block amendments desired by a large majority. Additionally, amendments, especially those ratified by special conventions, may be adopted even if they lack widespread popular support.

TABLE 2.4 Amendments, Date of Ratification, Length of Ratification Process

Amendment	Subject of Amendment	Date Proposed	Date Ratified	Length
Bill of Rights				
First	Free speech, press, religion, assembly	Sept. 25, 1789	Dec. 15, 1791	2+ years
Second	Right to bear arms			
Third	No quartering of troops in homes			
Fourth	No unreasonable searches/seizures			
Fifth	Right to due process, grand jury, no double jeopardy, self-incrimination			
Sixth	Right to speedy & public trial, counsel			
Seventh	Right to trial by jury in civil cases			
Eighth	No excessive bail, fines, cruel/unusual punishment			
Ninth	Rights not enumerated retained by people			
Tenth	Powers not delegated to Congress or prohibited to states belong to states or people			
Subsequent Amendments				
Eleventh	No federal cases between state, citizen of other state	March 5, 1794	Jan. 8, 1798	3+ years
Twelfth	Modification of electoral college rules	Dec. 12, 1803	July 16, 1787	9+ months
Thirteenth	Ban on slavery	Feb. 1, 1865	Dec. 18, 1865	10+ months
Fourteenth	States can't deprive right to due process, equal protection, privileges & immunities	June 16, 1866	July 28, 1868	2+ years
Fifteenth	Right to vote can't be denied by race	Feb. 27, 1869	March 30, 1870	1+ years
Sixteenth	Congress can levy individual income taxes	July 12, 1909	Feb. 25, 1913	3+ years
Seventeenth	Direct election of senators	May 16, 1912	May 31, 1913	1+ years
Eighteenth	Prohibition of liquors	Dec. 18, 1917	Jan. 29, 1919	1+ years
Nineteenth	Women's right to vote	June 4, 1919	Aug. 26, 1920	1+ years
Twentieth	Dates for inauguration, Congress's session	March 2, 1932	Feb. 6, 1933	11+ months
Twenty-first	Repeal of prohibition	Feb. 20, 1933	Dec. 5, 1933	9+ months
Twenty-second	Presidential term limits	March 24, 1947	Feb. 26, 1951	3+ years
Twenty-third	D.C. residents' vote for president	June 16, 1960	March 29, 1961	9+ months
Twenty-fourth	Ban on poll taxes	Aug. 27, 1962	Jan. 23, 1964	1+ years
Twenty-fifth	Appointment of new vice president, presidential incompetence	July 6, 1965	Feb. 10, 1967	1+ years
Twenty-sixth	Eighteen-year-olds' right to vote	March 23, 1971	July 1, 1971	3+ months
Twenty-seventh	Congressional pay raises effective only after election	Sept. 25, 1789	May 7, 1992	202+ years

Although twenty-seven amendments have been ratified since 1789, only seventeen of those were ratified after 1791. More than 5,000 amendments have been introduced in Congress since that time, but only thirty-three have been formally proposed by Congress. Among the proposed amendments not ratified have been

- An amendment that would withdraw citizenship from any person who has accepted a title of nobility or who has received (without the consent of Congress) an office or salary from a foreign power (proposed in 1810)

- An amendment proposed on the eve of the Civil War in 1861 that would have prohibited further interference by the federal government with slavery in any state

- An amendment that would have prohibited labor by young children (proposed in 1924)

MICHAEL KLEINFELD/UPI/LANDOV

The Equal Rights Amendment (ERA) proposed by Congress in 1972 also came up short during the ratification process, after years of effort to secure its passage. Although the courts have consistently held that ratification of an amendment must take place within a "reasonable time," it has been left up to Congress to determine what constitutes a reasonable time. When drafting the proposed Eighteenth Amendment in 1917, Congress placed into the text of the amendment a seven-year limit on ratification and continued to do so with subsequent amendments it proposed up until 1960. That year, when Congress proposed the Twenty-third Amendment giving residents of the District of Columbia the right to vote in presidential elections, it began the practice of setting time limits in the resolution accompanying submission of the amendment to Congress, rather than in the formal part of the amendment. As a consequence, when it appeared that the ERA would not be ratified, proponents of the amendment managed to get the ratification period extended to June 30, 1982 (an additional three years and three months beyond the original deadline), by a majority vote of both houses. Despite the extension, however, the proposed amendment died when it failed to win the approval of more than thirty-five state legislatures, three short of the thirty-eight necessary for passage. The "reasonable time" requirement for ratification of an amendment reached an extreme with the Twenty-seventh Amendment (forbidding congressional pay raises from taking effect until an intervening election in the House of Representatives has occurred). Originally proposed in 1789 as part of the Bill of Rights, it was finally ratified in 1992, just over 202 years later. (See the "Your Perspective" box for more detailed discussion of what occurred).

Demonstrators (including Rep. Carolyn Maloney (D-NY), at the podium) urging reintroduction of the ERA as an amendment to the Constitution.

★ LO   Assess informal types of constitutional change, including different forms of constitutional interpretation

Informal Processes of Change

After the Constitution and Bill of Rights were ratified, there remained the difficult task of interpreting those documents for use by the different branches of government. Among the framers, Alexander Hamilton was perhaps most attuned to the danger that Anti-Federalists and other opponents of the new Constitution might attempt to overturn the convention's carefully crafted compromises so many years later by judicial fiat. Certainly most of the Constitution's provisions were vague enough that they allowed discretion for maneuvering by the generation that interprets them—but how much discretion was justified in the process of constitutional interpretation?

As it turned out, the Supreme Court under Chief Justice John Marshall was the first to put its own lasting imprint on the Constitution. Marshall, who hailed from Virginia, served as the Chief Justice of the United States[18] from 1801 until his death in 1835.

One Student's Term Paper Proves That the Constitution Is Indeed a "Living Document"

College students may be forgiven for assuming that classroom assignments that invite them to propose constitutional amendments are strictly theoretical exercises. Yet in the case of one University of Texas student, such an assignment on constitutional change became much more than theoretical. Gregory Watson chose as the topic for his research a long-forgotten amendment to forbid congressional pay raises from taking effect until an intervening election in the House of Representatives had occurred. Originally proposed in 1789 as part of the Bill of Rights, the amendment was finally ratified 203 years later, thanks largely to Watson. The sophomore had discovered the amendment while doing research for a paper on American government. Watson's final paper—in which he argued that the amendment was still viable for ratification—garnered a mere "C" from his professor. But Watson continued his quest to secure ratification of the amendment. Tapping into the resentment of citizens over various instances in which members of Congress had quietly passed pay raises for themselves without calling attention to their actions, Watson joined forces with several state lawmakers to get the required number of states to ratify the provision. Their efforts succeeded, and the Twenty-seventh Amendment was eventually ratified in May 1992. Although Watson's grade from a decade earlier remained unchanged, he at least had the satisfaction of knowing that he had made history . . . literally.

Greg Watson, whose efforts helped to ratify the Twenty-seventh Amendment in 1992.

For Critical Thinking and Discussion

1. What amendments to the Constitution would you like to see implemented?

2. Would you be willing to sacrifice your own time, energy, and resources to organize interest group activities on an amendment's behalf?

Marshall believed in a **loose construction** (or interpretation) of the Constitution, meaning that under his leadership, many of the Constitution's provisions enjoyed broad and quite open-ended meanings. Thus, for example, Article I, Section 8, Clause 18 empowered Congress "to make all laws which shall be necessary and proper for carrying into execution" any of the powers specifically listed in the Constitution. Marshall's loose construction of that provision gave the federal government considerable implied powers (those not explicitly stated) to regulate the economy. For example, in the 1819 case of *McCulloch v. Maryland*,[19] Marshall's court ruled that Congress had the power to create a national bank, even though the Constitution said nothing explicitly about such a power. The Court determined that a national bank was "necessary and proper" to assist in regulating commerce or raising armies. This philosophy of loose constitutional interpretation underlies the concept of a "living Constitution," one that is adaptable to changing times and conditions.

Thomas Jefferson, James Madison, and many others viewed the powers of the central government more narrowly. They favored a **strict construction**, arguing that the government possessed only those powers explicitly stated in the Constitution. Thus, although Article I, Section 8, Clause 3 gave Congress the power to regulate interstate commerce, it could not do so by creating a national bank or utilizing

Loose construction

Constitutional interpretation that gives constitutional provisions broad and open-ended meanings.

Strict construction

Constitutional interpretation that limits the government to only those powers explicitly stated in the Constitution.

ZIGY KALUZNY. ALL RIGHTS RESERVED.

Chapter 2   The Founding and the Constitution

AMERICAN GOVERNMENT In Popular Perspective

The State of the Union Address

On January 27, 2010, President Barack Obama faced a rocky moment in his young presidency: the economy remained stagnant, his administration's hallmark health care initiative was in peril, and polls showed that his approval rating had dipped below 50 percent for the first time since he took office. Even members of his own Democratic Party were complaining that President Obama had lost sight of the needs of ordinary Americans. And yet for a brief period that evening little of that seemed to matter, as members of Congress of every political stripe, along with the nation's Supreme Court justices, Cabinet members, and others among Washington's political elite, jammed into the Capitol's House chamber to hear Obama speak. What was the occasion? Obama was giving his first State of the Union address, a yearly right of passage for every modern president. For the ninety or so minutes that Obama spoke, even his most staunch foes in Congress sat quietly and listened, along with millions of television viewers in the United States and around the world.

Article III, Section 3 of the U.S. Constitution requires that the president "from time to time give to Congress information of the State of the Union." George Washington personally delivered the first State of the Union address, on January 8, 1790, but Thomas Jefferson discontinued the practice, opting instead to send his written address to Congress. Woodrow Wilson reestablished the in-person practice in 1913, and with rare exceptions every president since then has delivered the address personally.

For modern presidents, the State of the Union address offers the chief executive a rare moment when competing politicians defer to him on a mostly unfiltered stage. Though applause for the president is often political in tone (the Republicans in the chamber, for example, refused to applaud when Obama mentioned his administration's controversial stimulus package), most presidents pepper their addresses with patriotic items that will generate applause throughout the chamber. In the case of Obama's 2010 address, 48 million Americans watched on one of the eleven major TV and cable networks that carried the speech live. Since 1997 the addresses have also been available live on the World Wide Web.

For Critical Thinking and Discussion

1. Should the networks continue to preempt normal programming to cover the president's State of the Union address live? Now that the speech is broadcast on the Internet and elsewhere, is this type of wall-to-wall coverage necessary?

2. Given the increased polarization of the two major political parties in Washington, should the president use his State of the Union address to build bridges to the opposition, or to announce new (and potentially controversial) policies? What would you like to see the president emphasize in his State of the Union address?

3. Currently the opposition party is afforded a brief "response to the State of the Union address" delivered by one of its leaders live on all the networks. Would you prefer a more direct give-and-take (i.e., a debate) between party leaders? Or is our current tradition of "dueling addresses" sufficient?

AP PHOTO/CHARLES DHARAPAK

50

any other means not specifically mentioned in the Constitution. They supported a "fixed" constitution, one that could be changed only by the formal amendment process, not by congressional action or judicial ruling.

The tension between advocates of strict and loose constructions of the Constitution continues to this day. Robert Bork, a former Yale law professor and failed Supreme Court nominee, argues that overly loose interpretations of the Constitution are outside the court's proper task. In particular, Bork says, the Supreme Court has "simply abandoned" the Constitution by refusing to enforce limits on the subjects that come within congressional reach.[20] In accordance with this philosophy, the more conservative Supreme Court of the late 1990s struck down federal statutes regulating guns in the schools and domestic violence, on the theory that such regulations were not grounded in any specifically enumerated power of Congress, such as the power to regulate interstate commerce.

This strict-construction approach contrasts markedly with the approach advocated by Professors Lawrence Tribe[21] and John Hart Ely,[22] as well as Supreme Court Justice William Brennan, who argued for a loose or more flexible interpretation of the Constitution. Advocates of a loose construction view the document as evolving with the times. In the 1960s and 1970s, the Supreme Court utilized a loose-construction approach to interpret congressional power more broadly to include the power to create civil rights legislation and federal criminal laws.

With so few amendments proposed and ratified during the nation's history, students of American politics may wonder how a Constitution written in 1787 has developed to meet the needs of a changing nation. In truth, an informal constitutional convention occurs on a frequent basis in the American political system. Congress, the president, and the courts engage in constitutional interpretation every day through their respective activities, both official and unofficial. Thus the Constitution has not been a straitjacket at all—rather, its elegant vagueness has opened it up to a variety of interpretations.

Much of the rise in presidential power during the twentieth century occurred in the absence of any formal amendments conferring new powers on the chief executive; the president of the United States reacted to circumstances facing the executive office by assuming greater authority over foreign and domestic policy making, and the other branches of government have allowed the president considerable latitude to do so. With its ruling in *Marbury v. Madison* (1803),[23] the Supreme Court asserted its right of judicial review, that is, its authority to review acts of Congress for their constitutionality and void those that the Court determines are contrary to the Constitution. As part of its decision in *McCulloch v. Maryland* (1819), the Court ruled that when state and federal powers collide, federal powers take precedence. With some notable exceptions, the other branches of the federal government and state courts have more or less acquiesced to such exercises of power.

NOW & THEN

Making the Connection

When state legislatures in 1791 ratified the Bill of Rights, citizens must have marveled at the flexibility of the new Constitution. After all, it had been amended ten times in just two years! And yet the Constitution has proven remarkably resistant to change since then, incorporating only seventeen additional amendments over the next 220 years. How has the federal Constitution survived so long, and in nearly the same exact form as the original? It is the cornerstone of a political system that encourages discussion, debate, and in some cases outright conflict over the meaning of its provisions, while only occasionally being subject to formal change. In short, the Constitution is forever bending, but it only rarely "breaks." And thanks to the Union's victory over the Confederacy in the Civil War, it has never been permanently broken.

Two amendments pressed by interest groups nearly a century apart—the "Christian amendment" favored by the National Reform Association beginning in the 1860s, and the "flag desecration amendment" favored by the Citizens' Flag Alliance since the 1990s—made considerable headway in their respective eras. Proposed in Congress on multiple occasions, each gained enough momentum to force even mainstream politicians to take them seriously. Congress never formally submitted either amendment for ratification by the state legislatures, as the threshold requirement of two-thirds support from both houses proved too high to overcome. Still, supporters of each movement were energized by the pursuit, and its leaders were encouraged by the positive support they generated. The constitutional amendment process is supposed to be arduous—how else could the nation's political system ensure that its provisions not be treated like simple statutes? Instead they are treated like scripture—the higher law found in a document that so many deem sacred.

© 2012 CENGAGE LEARNING

Many provisions in the U.S. Constitution are conveniently vague, affording politicians of different parties and ideologies the chance to interpret the document as they wish. What about constitutional provisions that are extremely specific and less susceptible to interpretation? So long as the two major parties are in agreement, even those provisions may offer few constitutional obstacles. Consider the dilemma facing Senator Hillary Clinton of New York after her appointment as the nation's sixty-seventh secretary of state. By executive order issued in January 2008, the salary of the secretary of state increased from $186,600 to $191,300 per year. What's the problem? Article I, Section 6 of the Constitution reads as follows:

> *No Senator or Representative shall, during the Time for which he was elected, be appointed to any civil office under the authority of the United States . . . the Emoluments whereof shall have been increased during such time. . . .*

Did the Constitution bar Hillary Clinton from accepting the post of secretary of state? John F. O'Connor, who has studied the clause in detail,* believes that "it is beyond dispute" that Senator Clinton was ineligible under the clause to be appointed as secretary of state. When President Obama selected Senator Ken Salazar of Colorado to be his secretary of the interior, the same issue resurfaced.

Secretary of State Hillary Clinton greets Indian Foreign Minister S. M. Krishna.

Members of Congress, both Republicans and Democrats, quickly resolved the situation by means of the so-called Saxbe fix, named after Senator William Saxbe, who was appointed as attorney general by President Richard Nixon in 1973. In Saxbe's case, Congress reduced the attorney general's salary to pre-1969 levels by legislation and subsequently approved his appointment. In a similar fashion, Congress in December 2008 passed (and President George W. Bush signed) legislation cancelling all salary increases made during Hillary Clinton's Senate term.

Several constitutional scholars (including O'Connor) and at least one public interest organization (Judicial Watch) believe the so-called Saxbe fix is unconstitutional. Yet no lawsuit to date has survived. Assuming that both political parties and their leaders in Congress have consented, who is personally aggrieved enough by the Saxbe fix to sue? More important, who are the victims of this effort to circumvent plain constitutional language? In an ironic twist, the real victim may be Hillary Clinton herself, who as secretary of state was forced to accept a lower salary than that of her predecessor, Condoleezza Rice.

Former Attorney General William Saxbe.

*See John F. O'Connor, "The Emoluments Clause: An Anti-Federalist Intruder in a Federalist Constitution," *Hofstra Law Review* 24 (1995): 89–178.

Chapter 2 The Founding and the Constitution

Chapter Summary

★ The Beginnings of a New Nation

- Britain's victory in the French and Indian War put the British Empire into significant debt. Following the war, Britain imposed numerous regulatory measures on the colonies that were intended to raise money; those measures generated outrage, protests, and eventually outright resistance from the colonists.

- After a series of military skirmishes, the Second Continental Congress in 1776 authorized the drafting of a Declaration of Independence listing the colonists' grievances and justifying its call for independence based on John Locke's theory of natural rights and the social contract.

- The Articles of Confederation created a "league of friendship" among the thirteen states by vesting them with equal authority in the central government during and immediately after America's successful war for independence. Under the Articles, the central government also possessed only limited powers to raise revenue and regulate commerce.

- Congress's inability to raise funds hampered the U.S. government's war effort and its economic relations with foreign nations.

★ The Constitutional Convention

- A constitutional convention consisting of delegates from twelve states convened in the summer of 1787 in an attempt to revise the Articles. The delegates immediately began to consider the "Virginia Plan," which proposed to overhaul the Articles by empowering a new government with three separate branches and the power to raise revenue.

- The Virginia Plan favored large and more populous states by allotting membership in its proposed legislature based on each state's population; delegates from less populous states countered with the "New Jersey Plan," based on the principle of equal representation of the states. The Constitutional Convention eventually resolved the conflict by accepting the so-called Great Compromise, which proposed a bicameral legislature with a House of Representatives apportioned by population, and a Senate that allots equal power to each of the states.

- With the issue of slavery dividing Northern and Southern states, the convention sidestepped the issue by settling on the "Three-Fifths Compromise" (counting five slaves as three people for purposes of taxes and representation) and by deferring a ban on slave importation for at least twenty years.

★ The New Constitution

- The new Constitution combined features of popular sovereignty, separation of powers, and checks and balances with a commitment to a system of "federalism," which divides sovereignty between state and federal governments.

★ The Ratification Battle

- The battle over ratification was waged between Federalists (who supported the new Constitution) and Anti-Federalists (who opposed it).

- The Federalists' carefully crafted media campaign, which included publication of the Federalist Papers justifying various provisions of the new Constitution, helped ensure its ratification.

- Several state ratifying conventions insisted that the new government add a bill of rights to the Constitution; James Madison, the "father of the Constitution," was initially reluctant to propose such a bill for fear that it might omit important rights, but eventually sponsored a new Bill of Rights in the first Congress.

★ Changing the Constitution

- Article V of the Constitution makes it exceedingly difficult to amend the Constitution. Since the Bill of Rights was ratified in 1791, only seventeen additional amendments have been ratified.

- The Supreme Court under Chief Justice John Marshall favored a loose construction of several constitutional provisions, giving the federal government considerable implied powers; Thomas Jefferson and Jeffersonian Republicans favored a stricter construction of the Constitution's provisions.

CourseMate

Key Terms

Amendments (p. 45)
Anti-Federalists (p. 41)
Articles of Confederation (p. 32)
Bill of Rights (p. 45)
Checks and balances (p. 39)
Constitutional Convention
(p. 35)

Declaration of Independence
(p. 32)
Enumerated powers (p. 40)
Federalist Papers (p. 42)
Federalists (p. 41)
Great Compromise (p. 36)
Loose construction (p. 49)

New Jersey Plan (p. 35)
Separation of powers (p. 39)
Shays's Rebellion (p. 34)
Strict construction (p. 49)
Three-Fifths Compromise
(p. 37)
Virginia Plan (p. 35)

Resources

Important Books

Amar, Akhil Reed. *America's Constitution: A Biography*. New York: Random House, 2006.

Bailyn, Bernard. *The Ideological Origins of the American Revolution*. Cambridge, MA: Harvard University Press, 1967.

Beard, Charles S. *An Economic Interpretation of the Constitution*. New York: Macmillan, 1941.

Federalist Papers, various editions, including paperback version edited by Isaac Kramnick. New York: Penguin Press, 1987.

McDonald, Forrest. *Novus Ordo Seclorum*. Lawrence: University Press of Kansas, 1985.

Maier, Pauline. *American Scripture: Making the Declaration of Independence*. New York: Alfred A. Knopf, 1997.

Rakove, Jack N. *Original Meanings: Politics and Ideas in the Making of the Constitution*. New York: Alfred A. Knopf, 1996.

Wood, Gordon S. *The Creation of the American Republic*. Chapel Hill: University of North Carolina Press, 1998.

Wood, Gordon S. *The Radicalism of the American Revolution*. New York: Alfred A. Knopf, 1991.

Internet Sources

http://lcweb2.loc.gov/ammem/bdsds/bdsdhome.html (Library of Congress exhibit on documents from the Continental Congress and the Constitutional Convention)

http://www.constitution.org/dfc/dfc-0000.htm (the debates of the Constitutional Convention of 1787)

http://www.archives.gov/exhibits/ (exhibit hall of the National Archives and Records Administration on the charters of freedom: Declaration of Independence, U.S. Constitution, Bill of Rights, and so on)

Annotated Constitution
of the United States
# of America

The Constitution of the United States of America

We the people of the United States, in order to form a more perfect union, establish justice, insure domestic tranquility, provide for the common defense, promote the general welfare, and secure the blessings of liberty to ourselves and our posterity, do ordain and establish this Constitution for the United States of America.

As a statement containing the essential reasons for drafting the Constitution and the purposes of the new central government, the Preamble theoretically does not confer any actual power on government. Nevertheless, on numerous occasions the Supreme Court has cited the preamble to illustrate the origin, scope, and purposes of the Constitution, as well as to help discern the meaning of certain constitutional provisions that follow it. Most notably in McCulloch v. Maryland (1819), Chief Justice John Marshall quoted from the Preamble at length to confirm that the Constitution comes directly from the people, and not from the states.

Article I

Section 1. All legislative powers herein granted shall be vested in a Congress of the United States, which shall consist of a Senate and House of Representatives.

The placement of provisions for congressional power in Article I confirms what the Founders undoubtedly assumed to be true: that Congress would be the preeminent branch of the new central government. Section 1 established two important principles. First, by specifying "powers herein granted" it declared that the national government is one of enumerated powers. Despite the broadening of powers implied by the necessary and proper clause of Section 8, this statement of Section 1 still means that Congress theoretically cannot do whatever it wants to do. Rather, it must ground its exercise of power (whether explicitly stated or implied) in a specific provision of Article I. Second, Section 1 established the principle of bicameralism—the presence of two separate but equally powerful legislative bodies as a further safeguard against government tyranny.

Section 2. The House of Representatives shall be composed of members chosen every second year by the people of the several states, and the electors in each state shall have the qualifications requisite for electors of the most numerous branch of the state legislature.

No person shall be a Representative who shall not have attained to the age of twenty five years, and been seven years a citizen of the United States, and who shall not, when elected, be an inhabitant of that state in which he shall be chosen.

Representatives and direct taxes shall be apportioned among the several states which may be included within this union, according to their respective numbers, which shall be determined by adding to the whole number of free persons, including those bound to service for a term of years, and excluding Indians not taxed, three fifths of all other Persons. The actual Enumeration shall be made within three years after the first meeting of the Congress of the United States, and within every subsequent term of ten years, in such manner as they shall by law direct. The number of Representatives shall not exceed one for every thirty thousand, but each state shall have at least one Representative; and until such enumeration shall be made, the state of New Hampshire shall be entitled to chuse three, Massachusetts eight, Rhode Island and Providence Plantations one, Connecticut five, New York six, New Jersey four, Pennsylvania eight, Delaware one, Maryland six, Virginia ten, North Carolina five, South Carolina five, and Georgia three.

When vacancies happen in the Representation from any state, the executive authority thereof shall issue writs of election to fill such vacancies.

The House of Representatives shall choose their speaker and other officers; and shall have the sole power of impeachment.

> *Section 2 of Article I establishes a House of Representatives as the lower House of the Congress. The membership of the U.S. House of Representatives is apportioned according to each state's population; the so-called Three-Fifths Compromise (only three fifths of the population of slaves would be counted for enumeration purposes) helped resolve an impasse at the Convention between Southern states, who wanted slaves to count as more, and Northern states, who wanted them to count as less. Although the number of House members has grown with the population, since 1911 it has been fixed by statute at 435. As constituted, the House is as powerful as the U.S. Senate, and in one respect is even more powerful: the House has the sole power to originate revenue bills. Section 2 also lays out the two-year term rule and qualifications for each House member, as well as providing procedures for apportionment and filling vacancies. Finally, it authorizes the House to choose top officials, including the Speaker.*

Section 3. The Senate of the United States shall be composed of two Senators from each state, chosen by the legislature thereof, for six years; and each Senator shall have one vote.

Immediately after they shall be assembled in consequence of the first election, they shall be divided as equally as may be into three classes. The seats of the Senators of the first class shall be vacated at the expiration of the second year, of the second class at the expiration of the fourth year, and the third class at the expiration of the sixth year, so that one third may be chosen every second year; and if vacancies happen by resignation, or otherwise, during the recess of the legislature of any state, the executive thereof may make temporary appointments until the next meeting of the legislature, which shall then fill such vacancies.

No person shall be a Senator who shall not have attained to the age of thirty years, and been nine years a citizen of the United States and who shall not, when elected, be an inhabitant of that state for which he shall be chosen.

The Vice President of the United States shall be President of the Senate, but shall have no vote, unless they be equally divided.

The Senate shall choose their other officers, and also a President pro tempore, in the absence of the Vice President, or when he shall exercise the office of President of the United States.

The Senate shall have the sole power to try all impeachments. When sitting for that purpose, they shall be on oath or affirmation. When the President of the United States is tried, the Chief Justice shall preside: And no person shall be convicted without the concurrence of two thirds of the members present.

Judgment in cases of impeachment shall not extend further than to removal from office, and disqualification to hold and enjoy any office of honor, trust or profit under the United States: but the party convicted shall nevertheless be liable and subject to indictment, trial, judgment and punishment, according to law.

> *Just as Section 2 does for the House of Representative, Section 3 establishes various powers and procedures for the U.S. Senate. Individual senators may be more powerful than their counterparts in the House because of the longer length of their terms (six years) and because there are far fewer members in the body; however, there is no constitutional basis for the claim that the Senate is a superior chamber. Although the vice president theoretically presides over the Senate as its president, and the president pro tempore serves in the vice president's absence, in actual practice the president pro tempore usually deputizes a more junior senator to preside over most Senate business. The provisions of Clause 1 and Clause 2 that state legislatures choose senators have been overturned by the Seventeenth Amendment, which now provides that senators are chosen by popular election.*

Section 4. The times, places and manner of holding elections for Senators and Representatives, shall be prescribed in each state by the legislature thereof; but the Congress may at any time by law make or alter such regulations, except as to the places of choosing Senators.

The Congress shall assemble at least once in every year, and such meeting shall be on the first Monday in December, unless they shall by law appoint a different day.

> *According to Article I, Section 4, states can regulate the time, place, and manner of all federal elections, but Congress can still establish a single uniform date for elections (and it has done so on the first Tuesday following the first Monday in November).*

Section 5. Each House shall be the judge of the elections, returns and qualifications of its own members, and a majority of each shall constitute a quorum to do business; but a smaller number may adjourn from day to day, and may be authorized to compel the attendance of absent members, in such manner, and under such penalties as each House may provide.

Each House may determine the rules of its proceedings, punish its members for disorderly behavior, and, with the concurrence of two thirds, expel a member.

Each House shall keep a journal of its proceedings, and from time to time publish the same, excepting such parts as may in their judgment require secrecy; and the yeas and nays of the members of either House on any question shall, at the desire of one fifth of those present, be entered on the journal.

Neither House, during the session of Congress, shall, without the consent of the other, adjourn for more than three days, nor to any other place than that in which the two Houses shall be sitting.

Section 6. The Senators and Representatives shall receive a compensation for their services, to be ascertained by law, and paid out of the treasury of the United States. They shall in all cases, except treason, felony and breach of the peace, be privileged from arrest during their attendance at the session of their respective Houses, and in going to and returning from the same; and for any speech or debate in either House, they shall not be questioned in any other place.

No Senator or Representative shall, during the time for which he was elected, be appointed to any civil office under the authority of the United States, which shall have been created, or the emoluments whereof shall have been increased during such time: and no person holding any office under the United States, shall be a member of either House during his continuance in office.

> *Article I, Section 6 extends to members of Congress various immu-*
> *nities. The speech and debate clause of Section 6 prevents House*
> *members or senators from being sued for slander during congres-*
> *sional debates, committee hearings, or most other official con-*
> *gressional business. In deference to the principle of separation*
> *of powers, Clause 2 ensures that members of Congress cannot*
> *hold another civil office while retaining their legislative seats.*

Section 7. All bills for raising revenue shall originate in the House of Representatives; but the Senate may propose or concur with amendments as on other Bills.

Every bill which shall have passed the House of Representatives and the Senate, shall, before it become a law, be presented to the President of the United States; if he approve he shall sign it, but if not he shall return it, with his objections to that House in which it shall have originated, who shall enter the objections at large on their journal, and proceed to reconsider it. If after such reconsideration two thirds of that House shall agree to pass the bill, it shall be sent, together with the objections, to the other House, by which it shall likewise be reconsidered, and if approved by two thirds of that House, it shall become a law. But in all such cases the votes of both Houses shall be determined by yeas and nays, and the names of the persons voting for and against the bill shall be entered on the journal of each House respectively. If any bill shall not be returned by the President within ten days (Sundays excepted) after it shall have been presented to him, the same shall be a law, in like manner as if he had signed it, unless the Congress by their adjournment prevent its return, in which case it shall not be a law.

Every order, resolution, or vote to which the concurrence of the Senate and House of Representatives may be necessary (except on a question of adjournment) shall be presented to the President of the United States; and before the same shall take effect, shall be approved by him, or being disapproved by him, shall be repassed by two thirds of the Senate and House of Representatives, according to the rules and limitations prescribed in the case of a bill.

> *Article I, Section 7 is often referred to as the presentment clause. It estab-*
> *lishes the procedures by which Congress presents bills to the president*
> *for approval; it also lays out the process by which the president may*
> *veto legislation, either by refusing to sign it and sending it back, or by*
> *keeping the bill for a period of ten days without signing it while Con-*
> *gress has adjourned in the interim (referred to as a pocket veto). In 1996,*
> *Congress passed the Line Item Veto Act, which allowed the president*
> *to veto specific expenditures at the time of signing; the Supreme Court*
> *declared the Line Item Veto Act unconstitutional in* Clinton v. City of
> New York *(1998) because it gave the president the power to repeal parts*
> *of duly enacted statutes in a manner different from the "finely wrought*
> *and exhaustively considered procedure" described in this section.*

Section 8. The Congress shall have power to lay and collect taxes, duties, imposts and excises, to pay the debts and provide for the common defense and general welfare of the United States; but all duties, imposts and excises shall be uniform throughout the United States;

To borrow money on the credit of the United States;

To regulate commerce with foreign nations, and among the several states, and with the Indian tribes;

To establish a uniform rule of naturalization, and uniform laws on the subject of bankruptcies throughout the United States;

To coin money, regulate the value thereof, and of foreign coin, and fix the standard of weights and measures;

To provide for the punishment of counterfeiting the securities and current coin of the United States;

To establish post offices and post roads;

To promote the progress of science and useful arts, by securing for limited times to authors and inventors the exclusive right to their respective writings and discoveries;

To constitute tribunals inferior to the Supreme Court;

To define and punish piracies and felonies committed on the high seas, and offenses against the law of nations;

To declare war, grant letters of marque and reprisal, and make rules concerning captures on land and water;

To raise and support armies, but no appropriation of money to that use shall be for a longer term than two years;

To provide and maintain a navy;

To make rules for the government and regulation of the land and naval forces;

To provide for calling forth the militia to execute the laws of the union, suppress insurrections and repel invasions;

To provide for organizing, arming, and disciplining, the militia, and for governing such part of them as may be employed in the service of the United States, reserving to the states respectively, the appointment of the officers, and the authority of training the militia according to the discipline prescribed by Congress;

To exercise exclusive legislation in all cases whatsoever, over such District (not exceeding ten miles square) as may, by cession of particular states, and the acceptance of Congress, become the seat of the government of the United States, and to exercise like authority over all places purchased by the consent of the legislature of the state in which the same shall be, for the erection of forts, magazines, arsenals, dockyards, and other needful buildings;—And

To make all laws which shall be necessary and proper for carrying into execution the foregoing powers, and all other powers vested by this Constitution in the government of the United States, or in any department or officer thereof.

Article I, Section 8 may be the most heavily cited clause in the original Constitution, as it lays out all the enumerated powers of Congress. The 18th clause listed, the necessary and proper clause, was the source of significant controversy in the early republic. In McCulloch v. Maryland (1819), Chief Justice John Marshall interpreted the clause as essentially aiding Congress in carrying out its expressed powers. Combining the powers granted by the 18th clause with other powers allows Congress to exercise implied powers not explicitly listed in the Constitution, so long as those powers offer a theoretical means of achieving the enumerated powers. Thus Congress successfully incorporated a bank of the United States because it was deemed necessary and proper to achieve the power to coin money and regulate its value (Clause 5), as well as other powers. Similarly, Congress chartered a railroad company as a necessary means of promoting commerce (Clause 3) and waging war (Clauses 11–14). No wonder the necessary and proper clause has also been called the elastic clause: it gives Congress the power to enact laws on almost any subject it desires. The power to regulate interstate commerce under Clause 3 has been especially useful in this regard. Citing the commerce clause, Congress since 1937 has regulated minimum wages of state employees, outlawed loan sharking, and passed numerous civil rights laws, among other legislation. The only current limits to that practice were outlined by the Supreme Court in United States v. Lopez *(1995) and* United States v. Morrison *(2000)—the law in question must regulate activities that are at least directly economic in nature.*

Section 9. The migration or importation of such persons as any of the states now existing shall think proper to admit, shall not be prohibited by the Congress prior to the year one thousand eight hundred and eight, but a tax or duty may be imposed on such importation, not exceeding ten dollars for each person.

The privilege of the writ of habeas corpus shall not be suspended, unless when in cases of rebellion or invasion the public safety may require it.

No bill of attainder or ex post facto Law shall be passed.

No capitation, or other direct, tax shall be laid, unless in proportion to the census or enumeration herein before directed to be taken.

No tax or duty shall be laid on articles exported from any state.

No preference shall be given by any regulation of commerce or revenue to the ports of one state over those of another: nor shall vessels bound to, or from, one state, be obliged to enter, clear or pay duties in another.

No money shall be drawn from the treasury, but in consequence of appropriations made by law; and a regular statement and account of receipts and expenditures of all public money shall be published from time to time.

No title of nobility shall be granted by the United States: and no person holding any office of profit or trust under them, shall, without the consent of the Congress, accept of any present, emolument, office, or title, of any kind whatever, from any king, prince, or foreign state.

> *Section 9 places some explicit limits on congressional power, including restrictions on the power to ban the import of slaves (at least through 1808), the power to bestow titles of nobility, and the power to lay direct taxes not apportioned to the states' populations. This last restriction was effectively removed by ratification of the Sixteenth Amendment in 1913. It also prohibits Congress from issuing bills of attainder (legislative acts that inflict punishment without a judicial trial) or from passing ex post facto laws (criminal laws that apply retroactively to acts committed in the past).*

Section 10. No state shall enter into any treaty, alliance, or confederation; grant letters of marque and reprisal; coin money; emit bills of credit; make anything but gold and silver coin a tender in payment of debts; pass any bill of attainder, ex post facto law, or law impairing the obligation of contracts, or grant any title of nobility.

No state shall, without the consent of the Congress, lay any imposts or duties on imports or exports, except what may be absolutely necessary for executing its inspection laws: and the net produce of all duties and imposts, laid by any state on imports or exports, shall be for the use of the treasury of the United States; and all such laws shall be subject to the revision and control of the Congress.

No state shall, without the consent of Congress, lay any duty of tonnage, keep troops, or ships of war in time of peace, enter into any agreement or compact with another state, or with a foreign power, or engage in war, unless actually invaded, or in such imminent danger as will not admit of delay.

> *The final section of Article I limits states from exercising powers reserved exclusively to the federal government. Most controversial of these clauses was the contracts clause, which prohibits states from*

impairing the obligation of contracts. Added to the Constitution largely to prevent state laws that undermined the collection of valid debts, it was later used to protect certain franchises or special privileges that corporations had received from state legislatures. Thus the Supreme Court held in Trustees of Dartmouth College v. Woodward *(1819) that the charter given to Dartmouth by a colonial legislature in 1769 could not be changed without Dartmouth's consent. State legislatures complained that the contracts clause unduly restricted their ability to legislate; thus, the Supreme Court over the course of two centuries has narrowed the meaning of the clause to allow states greater freedom to operate, relying on the theory that such contracts are by implication the laws of the state and thus may be modified by the state. The Court has also upheld state bankruptcy laws when the laws are applied to debts incurred after passage of the law.*

Article II

Section 1. The executive power shall be vested in a President of the United States of America. He shall hold his office during the term of four years, and, together with the Vice President, chosen for the same term, be elected, as follows:

Each state shall appoint, in such manner as the Legislature thereof may direct, a number of electors, equal to the whole number of Senators and Representatives to which the State may be entitled in the Congress: but no Senator or Representative, or person holding an office of trust or profit under the United States, shall be appointed an elector.

The electors shall meet in their respective states, and vote by ballot for two persons, of whom one at least shall not be an inhabitant of the same state with themselves. And they shall make a list of all the persons voted for, and of the number of votes for each; which list they shall sign and certify, and transmit sealed to the seat of the government of the United States, directed to the President of the Senate. The President of the Senate shall, in the presence of the Senate and House of Representatives, open all the certificates, and the votes shall then be counted. The person having the greatest number of votes shall be the President, if such number be a majority of the whole number of electors appointed; and if there be more than one who have such majority, and have an equal number of votes, then the House of Representatives shall immediately choose by ballot one of them for President; and if no person have a majority, then from the five highest on the list the said House shall in like manner choose the President. But in choosing the President, the votes shall be taken by States, the representation from each state having one vote; A quorum for this purpose shall consist of a member or members from two thirds of the states, and a majority of all the states shall be necessary to a choice. In every case, after the choice of the President, the person having the greatest number of votes of the electors shall be the Vice President. But if there should remain two or more who have equal votes, the Senate shall choose from them by ballot the Vice President.

The Congress may determine the time of choosing the electors, and the day on which they shall give their votes; which day shall be the same throughout the United States.

No person except a natural born citizen, or a citizen of the United States, at the time of the adoption of this Constitution, shall be eligible to the office of President; neither shall any person be eligible to that office who shall not have attained to the age of thirty five years, and been fourteen Years a resident within the United States.

In case of the removal of the President from office, or of his death, resignation, or inability to discharge the powers and duties of the said office, the same shall devolve on the Vice President, and the Congress may by law provide for the case of removal, death, resignation or inability, both of the President and Vice President, declaring what officer shall then act as President, and such officer shall act accordingly, until the disability be removed, or a President shall be elected.

The President shall, at stated times, receive for his services, a compensation, which shall neither be increased nor diminished during the period for which he shall have been elected, and he shall not receive within that period any other emolument from the United States, or any of them.

Before he enter on the execution of his office, he shall take the following oath or affirmation:—'I do solemnly swear (or affirm) that I will faithfully execute the office of President of the United States, and will to the best of my ability, preserve, protect and defend the Constitution of the United States.'

> *Article II, Section 1 lays out the manner by which the president and vice president are selected, the qualifications for those two offices, and the means for removal and succession. (Clause 2 on presidential elections has been replaced by the Twelfth Amendment.) Section 1 begins with the vague declaration that the "executive power shall be vested in a president of the United States of America." Does this clause serve as a source of independent power for the chief executive? Beginning in the twentieth century, the Supreme Court has held that the president possesses broad "inherent powers" to exercise certain powers not specifically enumerated in the Constitution. These vast executive powers included, for example, Franklin Roosevelt's various executive agreements extending the scope of the federal government during the 1930s. On the other hand, the Supreme Court ruled in Youngstown Sheet and Tune Co. v. Sawyer (1951) that a president's inherent powers did not include President Truman's attempt to seize the steel mills to avert a strike without congressional approval; similarly, in United States v. Nixon (1974) the Court held that the chief executive's inherent powers did not encompass President Richard Nixon's refusal to turn over important documents in a criminal matter.*

Section 2. The President shall be commander in chief of the Army and Navy of the United States, and of the militia of the several states, when called into the actual service of the United States; he may require the opinion, in writing, of the principal officer in each of the executive departments, upon any subject relating to the duties of their respective offices, and he shall have power to grant reprieves and pardons for offenses against the United States, except in cases of impeachment.

He shall have power, by and with the advice and consent of the Senate, to make treaties, provided two thirds of the Senators present concur; and he shall nominate, and by and with the advice and consent of the Senate, shall appoint ambassadors, other public ministers and consuls, judges of the Supreme Court, and all other officers of the United States, whose appointments are not herein otherwise provided for, and which shall be established by law: but the Congress may by law vest the appointment of such inferior officers, as they think proper, in the President alone, in the courts of law, or in the heads of departments.

The President shall have power to fill up all vacancies that may happen during the recess of the Senate, by granting commissions which shall expire at the end of their next session.

> *Article II, Section 2 is striking for how few express powers are granted to the president, as compared to the long list of powers granted to Congress in Article I, Section 8. In the twentieth century the powers granted to the president expanded to create a far more powerful*

presidency than the Founders envisioned. Thus, invoking their power as commander-in-chief, modern presidents have deployed troops around the world in military battles even without a formal declaration of war by Congress. Recent presidents have occasionally terminated treaties without the consent of the Senate. Presidents have also asserted the power to terminate officers of the United States without cause. The combined Supreme Court precedents of Myers v. United States *(1926) and* Humphrey's Executor v. United States *(1935) authorize them to do so in the case of purely executive officers, but not in the case of independent agency heads.*

Section 3. He shall from time to time give to the Congress information of the state of the union, and recommend to their consideration such measures as he shall judge necessary and expedient; he may, on extraordinary occasions, convene both Houses, or either of them, and in case of disagreement between them, with respect to the time of adjournment, he may adjourn them to such time as he shall think proper; he shall receive ambassadors and other public ministers; he shall take care that the laws be faithfully executed, and shall commission all the officers of the United States.

Article II, Section 3 lists numerous presidential responsibilities, including the obligation to give a report on the "state of the union" to Congress (today this occurs in the form of a yearly address), and the duty to "take care that laws be faithfully executed." Citing this latter phrase, presidents have asserted the power to impound money appropriated by Congress, and to suspend the writ of habeas corpus. Though reluctant to afford the chief executive such unbridled authority the Supreme Court has upheld nearly all efforts by the president to call upon the military to assist in faithfully executing the law. President Eisenhower, for example, exercised this power when he used federal troops to enforce desegregation decrees in Arkansas and Mississippi in the late 1950s.

Section 4. The President, Vice President and all civil officers of the United States, shall be removed from office on impeachment for, and conviction of, treason, bribery, or other high crimes and misdemeanors.

Article II, Section 4 lays out the process of impeachment and conviction of civil officers, but the phrase "high crimes and misdemeanors" is vague and subject to conflicting interpretations. Regardless, the House of Representatives has asserted its authority to decide on its own how to define the term. Only two chief executives have ever been formally impeached under this section: Andrew Johnson in 1868, and Bill Clinton in 1998. However, in both cases, the U.S. Senate failed to provide the required two-thirds vote necessary for conviction.

Article III

Section 1. The judicial power of the United States, shall be vested in one Supreme Court, and in such inferior courts as the Congress may from time to time ordain and establish. The judges, both of the supreme and inferior courts, shall hold their offices during good behaviour, and shall, at stated times, receive for their services, a compensation, which shall not be diminished during their continuance in office.
Section 2. The judicial power shall extend to all cases, in law and equity, arising

under this Constitution, the laws of the United States, and treaties made, or which shall be made, under their authority;—to all cases affecting ambassadors, other public ministers and consuls;—to all cases of admiralty and maritime jurisdiction;—to controversies to which the United States shall be a party;—to controversies between two or more states;—between a state and citizens of another state;—between citizens of different states;—between citizens of the same state claiming lands under grants of different states, and between a state, or the citizens thereof, and foreign states, citizens or subjects.

In all cases affecting ambassadors, other public ministers and consuls, and those in which a state shall be party, the Supreme Court shall have original jurisdiction. In all the other cases before mentioned, the Supreme Court shall have appellate jurisdiction, both as to law and fact, with such exceptions, and under such regulations as the Congress shall make.

The trial of all crimes, except in cases of impeachment, shall be by jury; and such trial shall be held in the state where the said crimes shall have been committed; but when not committed within any state, the trial shall be at such place or places as the Congress may by law have directed.

Section 3. Treason against the United States, shall consist only in levying war against them, or in adhering to their enemies, giving them aid and comfort. No person shall be convicted of treason unless on the testimony of two witnesses to the same overt act, or on confession in open court.

The Congress shall have power to declare the punishment of treason, but no attainder of treason shall work corruption of blood, or forfeiture except during the life of the person attainted.

> *Article III establishes a U.S. Supreme Court, spells out the terms of office of its members, and lists the various cases to which its judicial power extends. Just as important, it provides the basis for a more elaborate judicial system featuring numerous levels of courts, which Congress may establish at its discretion. Note how vague and general this Article is compared to Articles I and II: only one court (the Supreme Court) is specifically mentioned, and there are no provisions that specify the size or composition of the court. Congress subsequently established that federal judges on the courts of appeals and the district courts, like justices of the Supreme Court, are appointed by the president and confirmed by the Senate. They too serve for indefinite terms on good behavior, which provides the equivalent of life tenure to federal judges on those three levels of courts. Article III does not specifically grant the Supreme Court the power of judicial review, that is, the power to review the actions of other branches for their constitutionality. The Supreme Court seized that power for itself in Marbury v. Madison (1803), and it remains a fundamental precept of the federal judicial system today.*

Article IV

Section 1. Full faith and credit shall be given in each state to the public acts, records, and judicial proceedings of every other state. And the Congress may by general laws prescribe the manner in which such acts, records, and proceedings shall be proved, and the effect thereof.

Section 2. The citizens of each state shall be entitled to all privileges and immunities of citizens in the several states.

A person charged in any state with treason, felony, or other crime, who shall flee from justice, and be found in another state, shall on demand of the executive authority of the state from which he fled, be delivered up, to be removed to the state having jurisdiction of the crime.

No person held to service or labor in one state, under the laws thereof, escaping into another, shall, in consequence of any law or regulation therein, be discharged from such service or labor, but shall be delivered up on claim of the party to whom such service or labor may be due.

Section 3. New states may be admitted by the Congress into this union; but no new states shall be formed or erected within the jurisdiction of any other state; nor any state be formed by the junction of two or more states, or parts of states, without the consent of the legislatures of the states concerned as well as of the Congress.

The Congress shall have power to dispose of and make all needful rules and regulations respecting the territory or other property belonging to the United States; and nothing in this Constitution shall be so construed as to prejudice any claims of the United States, or of any particular state.

Section 4. The United States shall guarantee to every state in this union a republican form of government, and shall protect each of them against invasion; and on application of the legislature, or of the executive (when the legislature cannot be convened) against domestic violence.

Article IV describes the responsibilities states have to one another under the Constitution, and the obligations of the federal government to the states. It also provides the procedures for admitting new states to the union (no state has been admitted since the entry of Alaska and Hawaii in 1959). In recent years, the most controversial aspect of Article IV has been the full faith and credit clause of Section 1, which theoretically binds states to respect the public acts and proceedings of other states, including the granting of drivers' licenses and child custody rulings. Does the full faith and credit clause apply as well to the institution of same-sex marriage? The federal government and various states have sought to evade the recognition of gay marriages sanctioned elsewhere through legislation, including the Defense of Marriage Act of 1996. (At the time of this writing, five states have sanctioned the practice by a vote of their respective legislatures; three others recognize same-sex marriage under certain conditions, but do not actually grant same-sex marriage licenses.)

The ambiguous privileges and immunities clause of Article IV, Section 2 requires that states not discriminate against citizens of other states in favor of its own citizens, although the Supreme Court has allowed states to establish more favorable terms for in-state residents when distributing certain recreational rights such as amateur fishing licenses or permits to use state parks; taxes on commuters, by contrast, may be unconstitutional if they penalize out-of-state residents who work or do business in the state. The requirement in Section 4 that the United States guarantee to every state a republican form of government was invoked in the 1840s when President John Tyler threatened the use of federal troops after a rebellion occurred in Rhode Island. Today that provision is obscure and little-used.

Article V

The Congress, whenever two thirds of both houses shall deem it necessary, shall propose amendments to this Constitution, or, on the application of the legislatures of two thirds of the several states, shall call a convention for proposing amendments, which, in either case, shall be valid to all intents and purposes, as part of this Constitution, when ratified by the legislatures of three fourths of the several states, or by conventions in three fourths thereof, as the one or the other mode of ratification may be proposed by the Congress; provided that no amendment which may be made prior to the year one thousand eight hundred and eight shall in any manner affect the first and fourth clauses in the ninth section of the first article; and that no state, without its consent, shall be deprived of its equal suffrage in the Senate.

Article V spells out the process for amending the Constitution. By far the most common form of constitutional amendment has been by congressional proposal, with state legislatures ratifying the proposal. Twenty-six of the twenty-seven amendments have been adopted in this way. The sole exception was the Twenty-first Amendment, which was ratified by specially chosen state ratifying conventions to assure that farmer-dominated state legislatures would not undermine the effort to repeal Prohibition. The procedure by which the requisite number of state legislatures (two thirds) apply to Congress to call a convention for proposing amendments has never been used. Article V does not provide a deadline for considering proposed amendments, although Congress has the power to set such deadlines in the language of the proposed amendment. Congress did not do so in the case of the Twenty-seventh Amendment, which received the approval of the required three fourths of states necessary for ratification in 1992—fully 203 years after the amendment was first proposed.

Article VI

All debts contracted and engagements entered into, before the adoption of this Constitution, shall be as valid against the United States under this Constitution, as under the Confederation.

This Constitution, and the laws of the United States which shall be made in pursuance thereof; and all treaties made, or which shall be made, under the authority of the United States, shall be the supreme law of the land; and the judges in every state shall be bound thereby, anything in the Constitution or laws of any State to the contrary notwithstanding.

The Senators and Representatives before mentioned, and the members of the several state legislatures, and all executive and judicial officers, both of the United States and of the several states, shall be bound by oath or affirmation, to support this Constitution; but no religious test shall ever be required as a qualification to any office or public trust under the United States.

Article VI establishes that the Constitution, laws, and treaties are to be the supreme law of the land. In interpreting this supremacy clause, the U.S. Supreme Court has countenanced little resistance. Thus the Supreme Court has consistently struck down attempts by states to control federal institutions, and it has reminded state governments that even state constitutions are subordinate to federal statutes. Even more important, in Cooper v. Aaron *(1957) the U.S. Supreme Court stated in no uncertain terms that its own rulings are to be treated as if they are the words of the Constitution itself, heading off attempts by some state governments to resist Supreme Court rulings on desegregation by offering their own interpretations of the federal Constitution as authority.*

Article VII

The ratification of the conventions of nine states, shall be sufficient for the establishment of this Constitution between the states so ratifying the same. Done in convention by the unanimous consent of the states present the seventeenth day of September in the year of our Lord one thousand seven hundred and eighty seven and of the independence of the United States of America the twelfth. In witness whereof We have hereunto subscribed our Names,

G. Washington—Presidt. and deputy from Virginia

New Hampshire
John Langdon
Nicholas Gilman
Massachusetts
Nathaniel Gorham
Rufus King

Connecticut
Wm. Saml. Johnson
Roger Sherman

New York
Alexander Hamilton

New Jersey
Wil. Livingston
David Brearly
Wm. Paterson
Jona. Dayton

Pennsylvania
B. Franklin
Thomas Mifflin

Robt. Morris
Geo. Clymer
Thos. FitzSimons
Jared Ingersoll
James Wilson
Gouv Morris

Delaware
Geo. Read
Gunning Bedford jun
John Dickinson
Richard Bassett
Jaco. Broom

Maryland
James McHenry
Dan of St Thos. Jenifer
Danl Carroll

Virginia
John Blair—
James Madison Jr.

North Carolina
Wm. Blount
Richd. Dobbs Spaight
Hu Williamson

South Carolina
J. Rutledge
Charles Cotesworth
   Pinckney
Charles Pinckney
Pierce Butler

Georgia
William Few
Abr Baldwin

Amendments to the Constitution of the United States

The Bill of Rights, ratified in 1791, consists of the first ten amendments to the Constitution. Since that time, seventeen additional amendments have been ratified by the states. Originally the Bill of Rights applied only to the federal government and not to the state governments; however, through a process known as incorporation, the Supreme Court has ruled that the Fourteenth Amendment (adopted in 1868) made most of the provisions found in the Bill of Rights applicable to the states as well. Subsequent amendments have extended the franchise, established (and repealed) Prohibition, and clarified important procedures that the federal government must follow.

Amendment I (1791)

Congress shall make no law respecting an establishment of religion, or prohibiting the free exercise thereof; or abridging the freedom of speech, or of the press; or the right of the people peaceably to assemble, and to petition the government for a redress of grievances.

Although many provisions of the original Bill of Rights are based on aspects of English law, the extensive guarantees found in the First Amendment have no true English equivalent. The First Amendment offered one of the first written guarantees of religious freedom, and it formed the basis for extensive free speech and free press protection as well. Yet its unqualified language notwithstanding, the First Amendment has never conveyed absolute freedom to Americans. Whether it was the Alien and Sedition Acts of 1798, the aggressive application of the Espionage Act during World War I, or the "red scare" of the late 1940s, government has often found ways to evade the First Amendment, especially during times of crisis. The Supreme Court has also specifically exempted obscenity, libel, fighting words, and incitement from free speech protections. Nor has the separate and independent provision for the freedom of the press been interpreted to give members of the press any more protection than is afforded to ordinary citizens. Finally, as noted above, although the first word of the amendment implies that its protections apply only against actions of the federal government, today the First Amendment offers protection against the state governments as well.

Amendment II (1791)

A well regulated militia, being necessary to the security of a free state, the right of the people to keep and bear arms, shall not be infringed.

The Second Amendment originated as a compromise in the debate between those who feared mob rule by the people, and those committed to give the people everything they need to fight governmental tyranny. In 2008, the U.S. Supreme Court ruled for the first time that certain gun control laws may violate an individual's Second Amendment right to "bear arms." Two years later it went a step further, applying those protections against all 50 states governments and their subdivisions. See District of Columbia v. Heller, *554 U.S. ____ (2008);* McDonald v. Chicago, *561 U.S. ___ (2010).*

Amendment III (1791)

No soldier shall, in time of peace be quartered in any house, without the consent of the owner, nor in time of war, but in a manner to be prescribed by law.

The Third Amendment has been all but lost to history. The Quartering Act, which required the American colonists to provide shelter and supplies for British troops, was one of the grievances that provoked the Declaration of Independence and ultimately the Revolution. Many colonists resented having to house British soldiers in private homes. The Third Amendment aimed to protect private citizens from such intrusions.

Amendment IV (1791)

The right of the people to be secure in their persons, houses, papers, and effects, against unreasonable searches and seizures, shall not be violated, and no warrants shall issue, but upon probable cause, supported by oath or affirmation, and particularly describing the place to be searched, and the persons or things to be seized.

Like the First Amendment, the Fourth Amendment is a uniquely American right. It arose out of colonists' anger over the warrantless searches and so-called General Warrants by which British authorities would conduct raids of colonists' homes virtually at their own discretion. The Fourth Amendment guarantees that with certain carefully specified exceptions (consent of the owner, urgent circumstances, etc.), government authorities can conduct searches only when they possess a reasonably specific warrant demonstrating probable cause. Enforcement of the Fourth Amendment occurs primarily through application of the controversial exclusionary rule, which excludes from trial all evidence seized in violation of a defendant's constitutional rights.

Amendment V (1791)

No person shall be held to answer for a capital, or otherwise infamous crime, unless on a presentment or indictment of a grand jury, except in cases arising in the land or naval forces, or in the militia, when in actual service in time of war or public danger; nor shall any person be subject for the same offense to be twice put in jeopardy of life or limb; nor shall be compelled in any criminal case to be a witness against himself, nor be deprived of life, liberty, or property, without due process of law; nor shall private property be taken for public use, without just compensation.

The Fifth Amendment is a collection of various rights, most of which are important primarily to those accused of a crime. Those who "take the Fifth" under oath are normally invoking the privilege against self-incrimination; under current precedents they can invoke that privilege in other contexts as well, such as whenever they are being questioned by police or other authorities. The grand jury requirement has never been incorporated to apply against state governments. The requirement against double jeopardy prevents defendants who have been acquitted from being retried for the same offense by the same government. The due process clause of the Fifth Amendment was later duplicated in the Fourteenth Amendment and applied to states as well. Finally, the takings clause limits the traditional power of eminent domain by requiring that the government must pay compensation whenever it takes private property for public use.

Amendment VI (1791)

In all criminal prosecutions, the accused shall enjoy the right to a speedy and public trial, by an impartial jury of the state and district wherein the crime shall have been committed, which district shall have been previously ascertained by law, and to be informed of the nature and cause of the accusation; to be confronted with the witnesses against him; to have compulsory process for obtaining witnesses in his favor, and to have the assistance of counsel for his defense.

> *The Sixth Amendment offers the accused numerous constitutional protections. The need for a speedy and public trial dates back to concerns raised by imprisoned enemies of the British crown who were detained indefinitely and without notice. The right to a jury trial—considered a sacred aspect of the American political culture—is not all-encompassing either: it applies only to nonpetty offenses (punishable by more than six months of prison).*

Amendment VII (1791)

In suits at common law, where the value in controversy shall exceed twenty dollars, the right of trial by jury shall be preserved, and no fact tried by a jury, shall be otherwise reexamined in any court of the United States, than according to the rules of the common law.

> *The Seventh Amendment is the only amendment in the Bill of Rights that focuses on elements of civil trials exclusively. It preserves the distinction the English system draws between courts of common law (in which juries grant monetary relief) and courts of equity (in which a judge grants nonmonetary relief, such as an injunction).*

Amendment VIII (1791)

Excessive bail shall not be required, nor excessive fines imposed, nor cruel and unusual punishments inflicted.

> *The Eighth Amendment offers protections that come directly from the English Bill of Rights. The prohibition against excessive bail was established to prevent judges from keeping the accused indefinitely imprisoned while waiting for trials on minor offenses; it has subsequently been interpreted to allow judges to deny bail in instances where the charges are sufficiently serious, or where preventative detention is warranted for the safety of the community. The prohibition against cruel and unusual punishment forbids some punishments entirely (drawing and quartering, burning alive, and other forms of torture), while forbidding other punishments only when they are excessive compared to the crime. Aside from the four-year period from 1972 through 1976, the Supreme Court has consistently held that with proper safeguards, capital punishment is not cruel and unusual punishment. However, consistent with this clause it may not be imposed for rape or crimes lesser than murder, and it may not be imposed against the mentally retarded or against juvenile offenders.*

Amendment IX (1791)

The enumeration in the Constitution, of certain rights, shall not be construed to deny or disparage others retained by the people.

The Ninth Amendment has been nicknamed the Madison Amendment in deference to James Madison's general concerns about the Bill of Rights. During debates over ratification of the Constitution, Anti-Federalists called for a bill of rights to protect the people against a potentially abusive new central government. In correspondence with Thomas Jefferson, Madison expressed the fear that by listing exceptions to congressional powers, such a bill of rights would effectively deny the existence of rights that did not happen to appear on the list. Eventually, as a member of the House of Representatives in the First Congress, Madison sponsored passage of the Bill of Rights, but he included this amendment as a way to ensure that the listing of certain rights did not mean that other rights were denied. As interpreted, the Ninth Amendment has not had much impact on the constitutional landscape. Likened by some to an "inkblot," it has been most commonly viewed not as a source of rights, but rather as a loose guideline on how to interpret the Constitution.

Amendment X (1791)

The powers not delegated to the United States by the Constitution, nor prohibited by it to the states, are reserved to the states respectively, or to the people.

The Tenth Amendment lays out in explicit terms that the federal government is limited only to the powers granted to it in the Constitution. For most of the twentieth century, the Supreme Court regarded this amendment largely as a redundant truism, adding little to the Constitution as it was originally ratified. Yet since the early 1990s the Supreme Court has began to put teeth into the amendment, interpreting it as a prohibition on attempts by Congress to force states to participate in federal programs.

Amendment XI (1798)

The judicial power of the United States shall not be construed to extend to any suit in law or equity, commenced or prosecuted against one of the United States by citizens of another state, or by citizens or subjects of any foreign state.

The Eleventh Amendment was ratified to modify the Supreme Court's controversial decision in Chisholm v. Georgia *(1793), which upheld the authority of federal courts to hear lawsuits brought by citizens of one state against another state. The Supreme Court has ruled that the Eleventh Amendment provide states with some form of sovereign immunity, which means that it generally protects states from civil or criminal prosecution. The Supreme Court has also determined that under the Eleventh Amendment, a state cannot be sued by one of its own citizens.*

Amendment XII (1804)

The electors shall meet in their respective states and vote by ballot for President and Vice-President, one of whom, at least, shall not be an inhabitant of the same state with themselves; they shall name in their ballots the person voted for as President, and in distinct ballots the person voted for as Vice-President, and they shall make distinct lists of all persons voted for as President, and of all persons voted for as Vice-President, and of the number of votes for each, which lists they shall sign and certify, and transmit sealed to the seat of the government of the United States, directed to the President of the Senate;—The President of the Senate shall, in the presence of the Senate and House of Representatives, open all the certificates and the votes shall then be counted;—the person having the greatest number of votes for President, shall be the President, if such number be a majority of the whole number of electors appointed; and if no person have such majority, then from the persons having the highest numbers not exceeding three on the list of those voted for as President, the House of Representatives shall choose immediately, by ballot, the President. But in choosing the President, the votes shall be taken by states, the representation from each state having one vote; a quorum for this purpose shall consist of a member or members from two-thirds of the states, and a majority of all the states shall be necessary to a choice. And if the House of Representatives shall not choose a President whenever the right of choice shall devolve upon them, before the fourth day of March next following, then the Vice-President shall act as President, as in the case of the death or other constitutional disability of the President. The person having the greatest number of votes as Vice-President, shall be the Vice-President, if such number be a majority of the whole number of electors appointed, and if no person have a majority, then from the two highest numbers on the list, the Senate shall choose the Vice-President; a quorum for the purpose shall consist of two-thirds of the whole number of Senators, and a majority of the whole number shall be necessary to a choice. But no person constitutionally ineligible to the office of President shall be eligible to that of Vice-President of the United States.

The Twelfth Amendment altered the Constitution's original procedures for holding presidential elections. Under Article II, the winner of a majority of Electoral College votes would become president, and the runner-up would become vice president. The election of 1800 exposed the peculiarity that if every member of the Electoral College voted for both members of a party ticket, each member of the most popular ticket would receive the same number of votes, resulting in a deadlock. The Twelfth Amendment cured that flaw by requiring electors to cast separate votes for president and vice president, and by ensuring that if a deadlock occurred anyway and the House of Representatives failed to choose a president, then the candidate who received the highest number of votes on the vice presidential ballot would act as president (thus all vice presidents must be constitutionally eligible to serve as president).

Amendment XIII (1865)

Section 1. Neither slavery nor involuntary servitude, except as a punishment for crime whereof the party shall have been duly convicted, shall exist within the United States, or any place subject to their jurisdiction.

Section 2. Congress shall have power to enforce this article by appropriate legislation.

The Thirteenth Amendment was the first of the three Civil War Amendments. It officially prohibited slavery in all states, and with certain exceptions (such as in the case of convicts) involuntary servitude. Immediately prior to its ratification in December 1865, slavery remained legal in only two states, Kentucky and Delaware. (Slavery in the former confederate states had been outlawed by the Emancipation Proclamation of 1863.)

Amendment XIV (1868)

Section 1. All persons born or naturalized in the United States, and subject to the jurisdiction thereof, are citizens of the United States and of the state wherein they reside.

No state shall make or enforce any law which shall abridge the privileges or immunities of citizens of the United States; nor shall any state deprive any person of life, liberty, or property, without due process of law; nor deny to any person within its jurisdiction the equal protection of the laws.

Section 2. Representatives shall be apportioned among the several states according to their respective numbers, counting the whole number of persons in each state, excluding Indians not taxed. But when the right to vote at any election for the choice of electors for President and Vice President of the United States, Representatives in Congress, the executive and judicial officers of a state, or the members of the legislature thereof, is denied to any of the male inhabitants of such state, being twenty-one years of age, and citizens of the United States, or in any way abridged, except for participation in rebellion, or other crime, the basis of representation therein shall be reduced in the proportion which the number of such male citizens shall bear to the whole number of male citizens twenty-one years of age in such state.

Section 3. No person shall be a Senator or Representative in Congress, or elector of President and Vice President, or hold any office, civil or military, under the United States, or under any state, who, having previously taken an oath, as a member of Congress, or as an officer of the United States, or as a member of any state legislature, or as an executive or judicial officer of any state, to support the Constitution of the United States, shall have engaged in insurrection or rebellion against the same, or given aid or comfort to the enemies thereof. But Congress may by a vote of two-thirds of each House, remove such disability.

Section 4. The validity of the public debt of the United States, authorized by law, including debts incurred for payment of pensions and bounties for services in suppressing insurrection or rebellion, shall not be questioned. But neither the United States nor any state shall assume or pay any debt or obligation incurred in aid of insurrection or rebellion against the United States, or any claim for the loss or emancipation of any slave; but all such debts, obligations and claims shall be held illegal and void.

Section 5. The Congress shall have power to enforce, by appropriate legislation, the provisions of this article.

The Fourteenth Amendment was ratified in an attempt to secure rights for freed slaves by broadening the definition of national citizenship and offering all persons equal protection of the law as well as due process of law from state governments. In the Slaughterhouse Cases (1873), the Supreme Court held that the privileges and immunities of national citizenship are actually quite limited: they include visiting the seat of government, petitioning Congress, using the nation's navigable waters, and other narrow privileges. By contrast, the equal protection clause provided the basis during the twentieth century for dismantling legally enforced segregation in Brown v. Board of Education (1954) and other cases. It also has been used to extend equal protection to groups other than African Americans, including women and other ethnic minorities. Of equal significance, the Supreme Court has also interpreted the equal protection clause to require states to apportion their congressional districts and state legislative seats on a "one-person, one-vote" basis.

The due process clause has been interpreted to provide procedural safeguards before the government deprives a person of life, liberty, or property. More controversially, in the early part of the twentieth century the Supreme Court in Lochner v. New York (1905) interpreted the clause as providing substantive protection to private contracts and other economic agreements. In later rulings the clause sparked considerable controversy when the Court used it as the basis for protecting substantive privacy rights not explicitly spelled out in the Constitution, such as that of a woman's right to an abortion (in the Court's 1973 Roe v. Wade *decision), and of homosexual sodomy (in its 2003 ruling in* Lawrence v. Texas*).*

Amendment XV (1870)

Section 1. The right of citizens of the United States to vote shall not be denied or abridged by the United States or by any state on account of race, color, or previous condition of servitude.

Section 2. The Congress shall have power to enforce this article by appropriate legislation.

The Fifteenth Amendment was ratified in order to enfranchise all the former male slaves. (As was the case with all women, former female slaves would have to wait for passage of the Nineteenth Amendment to gain the franchise.) Unfortunately, the promise of the franchise was subsequently undermined in many states by the proliferation of rigorous voter qualification laws, including literacy tests and poll taxes. Not until passage of the Voting Rights Act of 1965 and the elimination of poll taxes did the franchise become a reality for African American voters in many parts of the South.

Amendment XVI (1913)

The Congress shall have power to lay and collect taxes on incomes, from whatever source derived, without apportionment among the several states, and without regard to any census of enumeration.

The Sixteenth Amendment was ratified in response to the Supreme Court's controversial decision in Pollack v. Farmer's Loan & Trust Co. *(1895), which held that a tax on incomes derived from property was a "direct tax." Prior to the Pollack case, income taxes had been considered "indirect" taxes, and thus well within the powers given to Congress by the Constitution. "Direct taxes," by contrast, could be imposed only if they were apportioned among the states according to each state's population (Article I, Section 9). The effect of the Pollack decision was to make an income tax all but impractical; the Sixteenth Amendment remedied the situation by placing income taxes back in the category of "indirect taxes."*

Amendment XVII (1913)

The Senate of the United States shall be composed of two Senators from each state, elected by the people thereof, for six years; and each Senator shall have one vote. The electors in each state shall have the qualifications requisite for electors of the most numerous branch of the state legislatures.

When vacancies happen in the representation of any state in the Senate, the executive authority of such state shall issue writs of election to fill such vacancies: Provided, that the legislature of any state may empower the executive thereof to make temporary appointments until the people fill the vacancies by election as the legislature may direct.

This amendment shall not be so construed as to affect the election or term of any Senator chosen before it becomes valid as part of the Constitution.

The Seventeenth Amendment changed the method by which U.S. senators were elected, overturning the provisions in Article I, Section 3. The amendment was the culmination of an extended effort of Progressive Era reformers at the beginning of the twentieth century, who frequently targeted institutions marked by economic privilege and corrupt politics. Eventually they demanded that U.S. senators should be more responsive to the public will—the best way to accomplish that goal was to require that senators should be chosen by popular election, rather than by state legislatures. Prior to the amendment's ratification, many states had already amended their primary laws to allow a popular vote for party nominees, and a handful of states had bound their respective legislatures to select the candidate who received the highest number of popular votes in the general election. The Seventeenth Amendment soon followed, receiving the approval of the required number of states (three fourths) less than a year after it was first introduced.

Amendment XVIII (1919)

Section 1. After one year from the ratification of this article the manufacture, sale, or transportation of intoxicating liquors within, the importation thereof into, or the exportation thereof from the United States and all territory subject to the jurisdiction thereof for beverage purposes is hereby prohibited.

Section 2. The Congress and the several states shall have concurrent power to enforce this article by appropriate legislation.

Section 3. This article shall be inoperative unless it shall have been ratified as an amendment to the Constitution by the legislatures of the several states, as provided in the Constitution, within seven years from the date of the submission hereof to the states by the Congress.

The Eighteenth Amendment slipped into the Constitution on the strength of efforts by the Anti-Saloon League and other groups who believed that intoxicating liquors were harmful and sinful. The amendment was proposed immediately after the end of World War I, and the Prohibition era began a year after its formal ratification on January 16, 1919.

Amendment XIX (1920)

The right of citizens of the United States to vote shall not be denied or abridged by the United States or by any state on account of sex.

Congress shall have power to enforce this article by appropriate legislation.

The Nineteenth Amendment was a reform spurred by the Progressive movement. Although women had been fighting for their right to vote since before the Civil War, the drive for woman suffrage started achieving success only with the entry of Western states such as Wyoming, which extended the right to vote to women upon its admission to the Union in 1890. (Five other Western states followed suit in subsequent decades.) By concentrating their efforts on a federal constitutional amendment guaranteeing women the right to vote, woman suffrage activists brought immediate pressure to bear on Congress and the president to support the movement. With momentum clearly on its side, the Nineteenth Amendment was ratified less than fifteen months after it was first proposed.

Amendment XX (1933)

Section 1. The terms of the President and Vice President shall end at noon on the 20th day of January, and the terms of Senators and Representatives at noon on the 3d day of

January, of the years in which such terms would have ended if this article had not been ratified; and the terms of their successors shall then begin.

Section 2. The Congress shall assemble at least once in every year, and such meeting shall begin at noon on the 3d day of January, unless they shall by law appoint a different day.

Section 3. If, at the time fixed for the beginning of the term of the President, the President elect shall have died, the Vice President elect shall become President. If a President shall not have been chosen before the time fixed for the beginning of his term, or if the President elect shall have failed to qualify, then the Vice President elect shall act as President until a President shall have qualified; and the Congress may by law provide for the case wherein neither a President elect nor a Vice President elect shall have qualified, declaring who shall then act as President, or the manner in which one who is to act shall be selected, and such person shall act accordingly until a President or Vice President shall have qualified.

Section 4. The Congress may by law provide for the case of the death of any of the persons from whom the House of Representatives may choose a President whenever the right of choice shall have devolved upon them, and for the case of the death of any of the persons from whom the Senate may choose a Vice President whenever the right of choice shall have devolved upon them.

Section 5. Sections 1 and 2 shall take effect on the 15th day of October following the ratification of this article.

Section 6. This article shall be inoperative unless it shall have been ratified as an amendment to the Constitution by the legislatures of three-fourths of the several states within seven years from the date of its submission.

The Twentieth Amendment brought an end to the excessively long period of time between the November election and the March inauguration of a new president. Given advances in transportation and communications systems over the previous century, such a delay in the president taking office—with the outgoing president reluctant to act even during times of crisis—could no longer be justified. The amendment also limited Congress's lame duck sessions that followed the November elections: newly elected members of Congress could now begin their service to constituents in early January, rather than waiting thirteen months until the following December. Finally, the amendment authorized Congress to provide for a line of succession in the event that neither a president-elect nor a vice president–elect qualified to serve by the January 20th date.

Amendment XXI (1933)

Section 1. The eighteenth article of amendment to the Constitution of the United States is hereby repealed.

Section 2. The transportation or importation into any state, territory, or possession of the United States for delivery or use therein of intoxicating liquors, in violation of the laws thereof, is hereby prohibited.

Section 3. This article shall be inoperative unless it shall have been ratified as an amendment to the Constitution by conventions in the several states, as provided in the Constitution, within seven years from the date of the submission hereof to the states by the Congress.

The Twenty-first Amendment repealed Prohibition. The enforcement of the Eighteenth Amendment had proven too difficult and expensive, as thousands of illegal sources arose to meet the continuing public demand for alcohol. Crime gangs involved in the

*illegal liquor trade spread violence and bloodshed throughout
the nation, which pressured politicians to end Prohibition. Finally,
when both political parties came out in favor of repeal during the 1932 election, Prohibition's days were clearly numbered.
After the Twenty-first Amendment was ratified on December 5,
1933, states would thereafter have the exclusive power to prevent
the import and use of liquor in their respective jurisdictions.*

Amendment XXII (1951)

Section 1. No person shall be elected to the office of the President more than twice,
and no person who has held the office of President, or acted as President, for more
than two years of a term to which some other person was elected President shall be
elected to the office of the President more than once. But this article shall not apply
to any person holding the office of President when this article was proposed by the
Congress, and shall not prevent any person who may be holding the office of President, or acting as President, during the term within which this article becomes operative from holding the office of President or acting as President during the remainder
of such term.

Section 2. This article shall be inoperative unless it shall have been ratified as an
amendment to the Constitution by the legislatures of three-fourths of the several states
within seven years from the date of its submission to the states by the Congress.

*Franklin Roosevelt's election to a record fourth term as president in
1944 sent politicians clamoring for a means of restoring the unwritten two-term tradition originally established by George Washington.
Within two years of FDR's death, Congress proposed the Twenty-second
Amendment, and it was adopted soon thereafter. In addition to setting a limit on the number of terms (two) to which a president may
be elected, the amendment also sets a maximum of ten years less
one day for a president to serve in the event he or she also succeeds
to a part of another president's term. The amendment was worded
so as not to apply to the then-sitting president, Harry S Truman, but
it has applied to Dwight Eisenhower and all other presidents since.*

Amendment XXIII (1961)

Section 1. The District constituting the seat of government of the United States shall
appoint in such manner as the Congress may direct:

A number of electors of President and Vice President equal to the whole number
of Senators and Representatives in Congress to which the District would be entitled
if it were a state, but in no event more than the least populous state; they shall be
in addition to those appointed by the states, but they shall be considered, for the
purposes of the election of President and Vice President, to be electors appointed by
a state; and they shall meet in the District and perform such duties as provided by the
twelfth article of amendment.

Section 2. The Congress shall have power to enforce this article by appropriate
legislation.

*The Twenty-third Amendment cured the anomaly of U.S. citizens
being denied the right to vote for federal officials (including president of the United States) so long as they remained permanent
residents of the District of Columbia. Since ratification of the amendment in 1961, DC residents have been entitled to vote for presidential and vice-presidential candidates, but the amendment did*

*not authorize residents of DC to elect members to either branch
of Congress. Nor did it provide DC residents with home rule or the
power to run their own local government. Since 1973 Congress has
authorized the DC government to be run primarily by locally elected
officials, subject to the oversight and supervision of Congress.*

Amendment XXIV (1964)

Section 1. The right of citizens of the United States to vote in any primary or other election for President or Vice President, for electors for President or Vice President, or for Senator or Representative in Congress, shall not be denied or abridged by the United States or any state by reason of failure to pay any poll tax or other tax.
Section 2. The Congress shall have power to enforce this article by appropriate legislation.

> *The Twenty-fourth Amendment eliminated yet another vestige of
> legally enforced racism in the South and elsewhere. Many states had
> already eliminated the requirement that voters pay a tax before vot-
> ing, a restriction that created an undue hardship on lower economic
> classes, including disproportionate numbers of racial minorities. Still,
> as late as 1964, five states (Alabama, Arkansas, Mississippi, Texas, and
> Virginia) continued to tie a poll tax to the voting privilege. In 1966 the
> Supreme Court ruled in* Harper v. Board of Education *that poll taxes
> also violated the equal protection clause of the Fourteenth Amendment.*

Amendment XXV (1967)

Section 1. In case of the removal of the President from office or of his death or resignation, the Vice President shall become President.
Section 2. Whenever there is a vacancy in the office of the Vice President, the President shall nominate a Vice President who shall take office upon confirmation by a majority vote of both Houses of Congress.
Section 3. Whenever the President transmits to the President pro tempore of the Senate and the Speaker of the House of Representatives his written declaration that he is unable to discharge the powers and duties of his office, and until he transmits to them a written declaration to the contrary, such powers and duties shall be discharged by the Vice President as Acting President.
Section 4. Whenever the Vice President and a majority of either the principal officers of the executive departments or of such other body as Congress may by law provide, transmit to the President pro tempore of the Senate and the Speaker of the House of Representatives their written declaration that the President is unable to discharge the powers and duties of his office, the Vice President shall immediately assume the powers and duties of the office as Acting President.

Thereafter, when the President transmits to the President pro tempore of the Senate and the Speaker of the House of Representatives his written declaration that no inability exists, he shall resume the powers and duties of his office unless the Vice President and a majority of either the principal officers of the executive department or of such other body as Congress may by law provide, transmit within four days to the President pro tempore of the Senate and the Speaker of the House of Representatives their written declaration that the President is unable to discharge the powers and duties of his office. Thereupon Congress shall decide the issue, assembling within forty-eight hours for that purpose if not in session. If the Congress, within twenty-one days after receipt of the latter written declaration, or, if Congress is not in session, within twenty-one days after Congress is required to assemble, determines by two-thirds vote of both Houses that the President is unable to discharge the powers and duties of his office, the Vice President shall continue to discharge the same as Acting President; otherwise, the President shall resume the powers and duties of his office.

The Twenty-fifth Amendment clarified several ambiguous aspects of presidential succession. At the outset, it formalized an unwritten precedent first established by John Tyler, who succeeded to the presidency upon the death of William Henry Harrison in 1841: If the office of president becomes vacant because of the president's death or resignation, the vice president becomes president and assumes all powers and duties of the office. If the vice presidency is vacant, the amendment establishes new procedures for filling the position between elections: the president nominates a successor, to be confirmed by a majority vote of both houses of Congress. Since its adoption in 1967, two vice presidents have been selected in this manner: Gerald Ford in 1973, and Nelson Rockefeller in 1974. When Gerald Ford succeeded to the presidency upon the resignation of Richard Nixon in 1974, he became the first—and to date, the only—president in American history to hold that office without being formally elected to either the presidency or the vice presidency.

The amendment also addresses the vexing problem of presidential disabilities. In the early twentieth century, Woodrow Wilson was an invalid for more than a year of his presidency; in the 1950s, Dwight Eisenhower suffered a stroke once during each of his two terms in office. The Twenty-fifth Amendment addresses the problem of presidential disability by providing procedures for the president to temporarily discharge the duties and powers of the office to the officer next in line (normally the vice president), who then becomes "acting president." This has happened only twice: in 1985, when Vice President George H. W. Bush received a transmission of power temporarily while President Ronald Reagan underwent a minor medical procedure; and in 2002, when President George W. Bush temporarily transferred his powers to Vice President Dick Cheney while he underwent a colonoscopy. The amendment further authorizes the vice president and certain members of the executive branch to declare the president disabled or incapacitated, subject (within twenty-seven days) to Congress upholding the finding of incapacity. This final provision has never been invoked.

Amendment XXVI (1971)

Section 1. The right of citizens of the United States, who are 18 years of age or older, to vote, shall not be denied or abridged by the United States or any state on account of age.

Section 2. The Congress shall have the power to enforce this article by appropriate legislation.

The Twenty-sixth Amendment extended suffrage to those age eighteen and older. At the time of its passage, soldiers under the age of twenty-one were fighting in Vietnam, creating intense pressure on Congress and state legislatures to extend the vote to all those who were old enough to fight. The amendment does not apply to the denial of rights other than voting to those who are between eighteen and twenty-one years of age. Thus the National Minimum Drinking Age

Act of 1984 obliges states to establish a twenty-one-year-old drinking age or risk the loss of federal highway funds. Additionally, Utah and Alaska have established nineteen as the minimum age for tobacco use.

Amendment XXVII (1992)

No law, varying the compensation for the services of the Senators and Representatives, shall take effect, until an election of Representatives shall have intervened.

The Twenty-seventh Amendment was intended to serve as a restraint on the power of Congress to raise its own pay—it may only do so if the raise takes effect after a subsequent general election. Although the Supreme Court has never ruled on the issue, lower courts have held that this amendment does not prevent Congress from receiving cost of living adjustments immediately.

3 Federalism

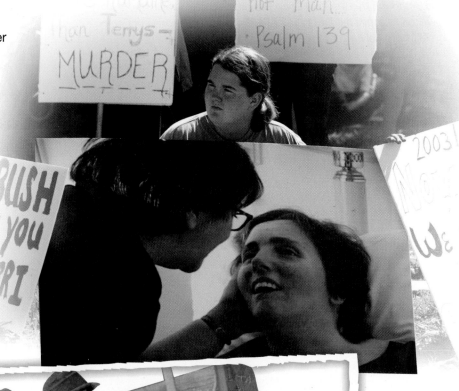

NOW A protester (above) expresses her feelings about the case of Terri Schiavo (below).

MATT MAY/STRINGER/GETTY IMAGES

THEN Children working in a factory at the turn of the 20th century, before the advent of child labor laws.

LEWIS WICKES HINE/BETTMANN/CORBIS

NOW &THEN

Dueling Sovereign Powers in the United States

? *At the time of the nation's founding, worries about an excessively powerful central government threatening the states' sovereignty nearly brought a halt to the American experiment before it had even begun. Now it seemed like some of the Founders' worst fears were being realized, as Congress was attempting to interfere in a matter that until then had been under the strict control of state authorities. State officials were actually divided on the issue in question; some were shocked by the federal intrusion, whereas others welcomed federal assistance in dealing with such a difficult matter. Yet for those who favored federal influence, there was no basis either in tradition or in the words of the Constitution to support such unprecedented infringement in what appeared to be a strictly state matter. Ultimately, the courts stepped in to reassert state control over the issue, and the central government saw its hopes for influence frustrated, at least for the time being. Still, local officials had been put on notice that when Congress disagrees with a state action, that body will not stand by silently and defer without a struggle.*

LEARNING OBJECTIVES
★ WHAT YOU WILL LEARN ★

What Is Federalism?

* ★ Define federalism and assess the nature of sovereignty in a federal system
* ★ Compare federalism to other systems of government, including confederations and unitary systems of government
* ★ Understand how the Constitution differentiates between federal government powers, state government powers, and concurrent powers
* ★ Recognize the powers accorded to Congress under Article I, including the necessary and proper clause
* ★ Explain the significance of the supremacy clause, the preemption doctrine, and the full faith and credit clause of Article IV in dividing sovereignty between the federal and state governments

The History of American Federalism

* ★ Define the five eras of American federalism
* ★ Assess the role played by the Supreme Court in articulating the various doctrines and frameworks that determined the relationship between the state and federal governments during the five eras of American federalism
* ★ Distinguish between different forms of federalism (layer cake federalism versus marble cake federalism) in the modern era

Why Federalism? Advantages and Disadvantages

* ★ Recognize the advantages of a system that serves a diverse array of interests
* ★ Understand the disadvantages of federalism in terms of fairness and accountability

Current Problems in American Federalism

* ★ Describe some of the abuses under federalism, including the use of unfunded mandates and the underfunding of urban centers

NOW & THEN

MATT MAY/STRINGER/GETTY IMAGES

NOW It was a matter of family law, a subject traditionally controlled by state authorities. On March 31, 2005, forty-one-year-old Terri Schiavo died in a Florida hospice. Thirteen days earlier her feeding tube had been removed by court order. Schiavo first went into respiratory and cardiac arrest in 1990; temporarily denied oxygen to her brain, she fell into a short-lived coma. Although she emerged from the coma after two and a half months, Terri Schiavo would live for the next fifteen years in a persistent vegetative state, exhibiting no awareness of her environment. In 1998, Schiavo's husband and legal guardian, Michael Schiavo, petitioned to remove his wife's feeding tube on the grounds that there was no longer any hope for his wife's recovery. His petition thrust him into a protracted legal dispute with his wife's parents. Michael claimed that his wife would never have wanted to be kept alive if she were in a vegetative state; Terri's parents disagreed, and they sought a series of stays against removal of any apparatus necessary to keep their daughter alive.

On September 17, 2003, after five years of hearings, trials, and back-and-forth court orders, a Florida state judge ordered the removal of the feeding tube; less than a month later, the order was executed. Just days after the tube was removed, Florida Governor Jeb Bush ordered the tube to be reinserted in accordance with a new Florida law recently passed to give him that authority. Consistent with their earlier orders, the Florida courts struck down the law as unconstitutional and ordered the tube to be removed; the court's removal order was eventually reinstated on March 18, 2005. Yet at this point the unthinkable happened: federal authorities chose to insert themselves into the state proceedings. On March 21, 2005, President George W. Bush signed newly enacted legislation from Congress that transferred the case over to federal courts for what he hoped would be a different resolution. Unfortunately for Terri Schiavo's parents, this extra layer of federal court review proved no more fruitful, as the U.S. Court of Appeals for the Eleventh Circuit refused to overturn the state court decision. Thus on March 31, 2005, Terri Schiavo died. In the final analysis, the decision over who had the power to determine the medical fate of a patient remained with the state judiciary, Congress's efforts notwithstanding.

THEN   The Terri Schiavo case was not the first instance in which the U.S. Congress intervened in a state matter when there was no legal precedent to do so. At the beginning of the twentieth century, many reformers were growing increasingly concerned about the abuses of child labor. By some accounts as many as two million children, often as young as five or six years old, were working long hours in brutal conditions for barely any compensation. In response, state legislatures around the country began passing laws limiting or banning the use of child labor. The result was a patchwork quilt of state regulations, varying in their effectiveness. Reformers in Congress became frustrated with the slow pace of reform at the state level; they wanted uniform standards imposed immediately to prohibit child labor across the nation. But a string of judicial precedents dating back one hundred years cautioned that states alone had the constitutional power to regulate the manufacturing process. Congress then tried a back-door approach to the problem by deploying its power to regulate interstate commerce under the Constitution: in 1916 it passed the Keating-Owen Child Labor Act, which banned the interstate transport of all goods made by children under age fourteen. Some state legislatures were stunned at this aggressive exercise of federal authority. But with its ruling in the case of *Hammer v. Dagenhart* (1918), the U.S. Supreme Court struck down the federal child labor law as unconstitutional. Consistent with its precedents, the Court held that Congress could not ban certain goods from entering interstate commerce, even if its intention in doing so was to regulate manufacturing.

Nineteen years later the Supreme Court—spurred in part by the harshness of the Great Depression and by the appointment of justices more disposed to defer to Congress—gave its approval to federal laws that regulated manufacturing, including new child labor laws. In the end Congress did have its say over the issue. Unfortunately for those who demanded a national solution to the problem of child labor law, conflict between federal and state sovereigns—interpreted by the Supreme Court to prohibit federal intervention in 1918—hamstrung the federal government for the better part of two decades.

LEWIS WICKES HINE/BETTMANN/CORBIS

O nly once in the nation's history have state–federal tensions ignited an all-out military conflict among the parties: the U.S. Civil War of 1861–1865. There have been countless other incidents, however, when the tensions inherent in a system of dual sovereigns have given rise to conflicts between the federal government and state authority. In addition to the Terri Schiavo case in early 2005 and the battle over child labor laws in the early part of the twentieth century, other examples of such conflicts in the not-so-distant past include the protests by many Arizona state officials against a national movement to honor Martin Luther King Jr. with a federal holiday, the movement by Georgians to hoist a state flag with the controversial confederate symbol, and the efforts by Florida state officials to hinder federal attempts to return a young emigrant named Elian Gonzalez to his father's custody in Cuba. In all such instances, tempers eventually cooled and the crisis passed. Passed, but not soon forgotten.

★ LO Define federalism and assess the nature of sovereignty in a federal system

Federalism

The doctrine underlying a system of government in which power is divided between a central government and constituent political subunits.

Sovereignty

The supreme political power of a government to regulate its affairs without outside interference.

What Is Federalism?

The term *federal* comes from the Latin *foedus*, which means a covenant, or an agreement linking different entities. A federal (or federated) system of government is one in which power is divided between a central authority and constituent political subunits. Both types of government are linked in order to provide for the pursuit of common ends; at the same time, each government maintains its own integrity. **Federalism** is the doctrine underlying such a system. It generally requires the existence of a central government tier and at least one major subnational tier of governments (usually referred to as "states" or "provinces"). Each tier is then assigned its own significant government powers. For a system of federalism to maintain itself, it must sustain this division of powers by whatever means possible, including—but not limited to—a resort to the courts to define the proper bounds of authority.

Perhaps the greatest challenge facing any federalist system is the task of determining **sovereignty**, defined as the supreme political power of a government to regulate its affairs without outside interference. In a system based on federalism, sovereignty resides not just in the central government, but also within each of the subunits or federated states, which in the case of the United States are the individual fifty states. Yet how can there be two separate sovereign governments sharing power over the exact same territory? The distribution of national and local responsibilities to more than one sovereign power depends on how the terms *national* and *local* are defined. These definitions are important, for a government based on federalism must both achieve national unity for certain overarching purposes and also preserve local governments' autonomy so they can respond to diverse subsets of citizens.

Related to these issues are complex questions concerning the nature of national citizenship. American federalism rests on the principle that two separate sovereigns—the state government and the federal government—both exert authority over the individual. But can an individual citizen really be subject to two separate sovereign governments at the same time? U.S. citizens have official status as citizens both of the state where they reside and of the nation as a whole. Many take pride in *both* associations. What remains unclear are the obligations and duties that dual citizenship requires. Is national citizenship every citizen's primary form of identification? To which sovereign government is the citizen obligated when the nation and individual states are in conflict? Although these conceptual difficulties tend to be unique to a federal system, there are other forms of government that involve multiple governments or tiers of government, and these alternative forms have significant problems of their own.

FIGURE 3.1 Comparing Systems of Government

The three figures below illustrate the most common configurations for (1) federal systems of government, (2) unitary systems of government, and (3) confederate systems of government. The directions of the arrows indicate the relationship that exists between the different forms of government. Note the two-way arrows found in the federal system.

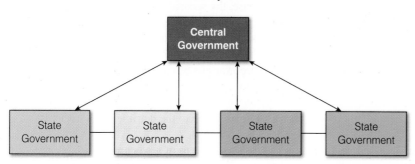

Federal System

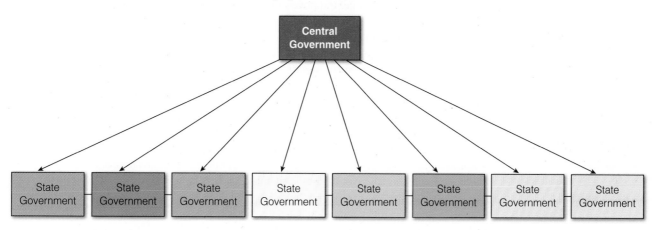

Unitary System of Government

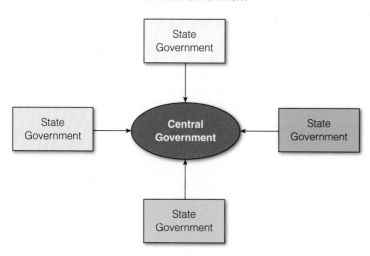

Confederate Government

Comparing Federalism to Other Systems of Government

★ LO Compare federalism to other systems of government, including confederations and unitary systems of government

Confederation

A system of government (or "league") in which two or more independent states unite to achieve certain specified common aims.

Unitary system of government

A system of government in which the constituent states are strictly subordinated to the goals of the central government as a whole.

A federal system of government can be thought of as existing on a continuum of different forms of government. At one end of the continuum is a **confederation** (or "confederacy"), defined as a league of two or more independent states that unite to achieve certain specified common aims. Those aims may be quite limited, as is often the case with offensive or defensive military alliances. For example, the Articles of Confederation, which prescribed the rules of government for the newly independent colonies until 1788, featured thirteen states entering into "a firm league of friendship with each other, for their common defense, the security of their liberties, and their mutual and general welfare." Recently the European Community, a collection of European nations united in a commercial alliance, has acquired its own status as a type of confederation.[1] Similarly, the United Nations is a league of countries from around the world that work together to enforce various provisions of international law. Although a confederation may be a useful arrangement to achieve some aims, it can result in political chaos, as when separate member countries bound only by limited rules strike out on their own at critical times, often to the detriment of the larger confederation.

At the other end of the continuum is a **unitary system of government**, which subordinates the independent aims of constituent states (if any even exist) to the goals of the central whole. Although individual states within such a government may enjoy some form of representation in the central legislature (such as through the election of state senators) and may even assert their own systems of municipal law, sovereignty rests in the central government alone, with states exerting authority over citizens only through the larger government entity. Of the Western industrialized nations, Great Britain and France come closest to this unitary government ideal, with their provinces and subunits having little or no power independent of the national government. Problems with a unitary system of government often arise from the tendency toward *hypercentralism*, that is, the more or less complete reliance on the central government and the extinguishing of individual state differences. Such a system often hampers local officials from responding to the particular needs of their varying constituencies.

As Figure 3.1 shows, a federal system of government sits in the middle of this continuum, granting its member states significant power but still subordinating them to the national government in critical instances. James Madison believed this federal system was the preferred "middle ground" of government types. At least twenty countries today, including Canada, Germany, Australia, and Switzerland, may be characterized as federal systems. It is the United States' brand of federalism, however—first established with the ratification of the Constitution in 1788—that represents the most significant breakthrough in the evolution of this government type among modern nation-states.

Government Powers in a Federal System

★ LO Understand how the Constitution differentiates between federal government powers, state government powers, and concurrent powers

Reserved powers

Those powers expressly retained by the state governments under the Constitution.

Concurrent powers

Those powers shared by the federal and state governments under the Constitution.

Under the U.S. Constitution, the national government of the United States was formed to serve a community of thirteen states, and each state delegated to the new central government significant powers while retaining full powers within its own constitutionally designated sphere of authority. The Framers of this new government relied on no overarching philosophy or political theory in designing this federalist form of government; federalism was simply a political compromise calculated to build consensus among them. The powers delegated to Congress under Article I of the Constitution are called enumerated powers. The powers retained by the states are **reserved powers**. And the powers shared by the federal and state governments are generally referred to as **concurrent powers** (see Table 3.1).

Article I, Section 8 enumerates the specific powers held by the national legislature. Among these are economic powers such as the authority to levy and collect taxes, borrow money, coin money, and regulate interstate commerce and bankruptcies; military powers such as the authority to provide for the common defense,

TABLE 3.1 The Powers of the Federal and State Governments under the Constitution

Federal Government Powers (Enumerated Powers)	State Government Powers (Reserved Powers)	Concurrent Powers (Shared Powers)
Borrow money on U.S. credit	Regulate intrastate commerce	Spend money for general welfare
Regulate foreign commerce	Regulate state militias	Regulate interstate commerce
Regulate commerce with Indian nations	Conduct elections/qualify voters	Establish bankruptcy laws
Conduct foreign affairs	Regulate safety/health/morals	Lay and collect taxes
Coin money/punish counterfeiting	Ratify amendments	Charter/regulate banks
Establish courts inferior to Supreme Court		Establish courts
Establish post offices		Establish highways
Establish patent/copyright laws		Take private property for public purposes (with compensation)
Define/punish high-seas offenses		
Declare war		
Raise and support armies, navies		
Call forth militias		
Govern District of Columbia matters		
Admit new states to union		
Establish rules of naturalization		

declare war, raise and support armies and navies, and regulate the militia; and legislative powers such as the authority to establish regulations governing immigration and naturalization. Congress also enjoys the prerogative to make laws that are "necessary and proper" to carry out these foregoing powers.[2]

On its face, the Constitution appears to draw clear and explicit lines between the powers afforded the state and national governments. In brief, the national government is to assume responsibility for great matters of national importance, including the protection of national economic interests, relations with other countries, and the military security of the United States. All local and/or internal matters—including the health, safety, and welfare of citizens—were to be to the province of state governments. Indeed, in a delayed victory for states' rights advocates who had opposed the new Constitution, the Tenth Amendment restates this fundamental division of powers: that any specific power not assigned to the federal government by the Constitution may be exercised by the states, unless the Constitution prohibits the states from exercising that power.

The Framers of the Constitution believed that Congress should legislate only within its enumerated powers under Article I; in their view the **necessary and proper clause** (later referred to as the elastic clause) was *not* to be used as an instrument to expand federal legislative authority unnecessarily. Yet within a few years, competing views of the necessary and proper clause would arise, giving the national government far more discretion in determining how to carry out its enumerated powers.

★ LO

Recognize the powers accorded to Congress under Article I, including the necessary and proper clause

Necessary and proper clause

The clause in Article I, Section 8 of the Constitution that affords Congress the power to make laws that serve as a means to achieving its expressly delegated powers.

Supremacy clause

The provision in Article VI, Clause 2 of the Constitution that provides that the Constitution and federal laws override any conflicting provisions in state constitutions or state laws.

Comparing Views of Federal, State, and Local Government

Surveys conducted by the Pew Research Center for the People and the Press monitor Americans' views of the performance of federal, state, and local governments. As the figure below demonstrates, Americans hold their local and state governments in fairly high esteem. However, positive views of the federal government in 2009 were relatively low by recent standards. Only 42 percent of people said they held a favorable view of the federal government, which is down significantly from 2002, when 64 percent held a favorable opinion. By contrast, 50 percent held favorable views of their state governments and 60 percent held favorable views of their local governments in 2009.

The public's favorable opinion of the federal government in 2002 (favorable opinions outnumbered unfavorable opinions that year by 64 percent to 27 percent) was a product of the rally-around-the-flag sentiment generated in the months following the terrorist attacks of September 11, 2001. In most years since 2000, state and local governments have fared much better than the federal government in the eyes of the public.

Now, I'd like your opinion of some organizations and institutions. . . . is your overall opinion of (the federal government/your state government/your local government) very favorable, mostly favorable, mostly unfavorable, or very unfavorable?

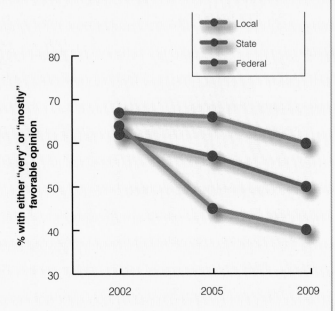

Source: Pew Research Center for the People and the Press, http://people-press.org/report/534/government-favorability

The Supremacy Clause

Overlaying this explicit system of enumerated powers for Congress and reserved powers for the states is the **supremacy clause** of Article VI, which provides that the Constitution and the laws passed by Congress shall be "the supreme law of the land," overriding any conflicting provisions in state constitutions or state laws. The supremacy clause gives special weight to the federal Constitution by ensuring that it cannot be interpreted differently from state to state. In the landmark case of **Martin v. Hunter's Lessee (1819)**,[3] the U.S. Supreme Court rejected the Virginia Supreme Court's attempt to interpret the federal Constitution in a way that conflicted with the U.S. Supreme Court's own rulings. Accordingly, each state legislature and state judiciary not only must abide by the terms of the federal Constitution; it must also abide by the interpretation of those terms laid out by the U.S. Supreme Court.

The language of the supremacy clause also gives rise to the doctrine of preemption. When Congress exercises power granted to it under Article I, the federal law it creates may supersede state laws, in effect "preempting" state authority. In practice, when a federal law clearly bars state action, the doctrine of **preemption** is relatively uncontroversial. For example, when the federal government acted to regulate the commercial advertising of tobacco products, it essentially "occupied the field," and all state rules governing tobacco advertising immediately gave way to the new federal standard. But when Congress enacts a law that does not clearly articulate its intentions with regard to state laws, a court may have to decide whether the doctrine

Martin v. Hunter's Lessee (1819)
The Supreme Court case that established that state governments and state courts must abide by the U.S. Supreme Court's interpretation of the federal Constitution.

Preemption
The constitutional doctrine that holds that when Congress acts affirmatively in the exercise of its own granted power, federal laws supersede all state laws on the matter.

The Real-life Benefits of Attending College Close to Home

Many high school seniors dream of attending colleges or universities in distant and exotic locations, far from the watchful eyes of parents or guardians who may be footing the bill. Did you ever dream of attending the University of Hawaii . . . or perhaps the Florida Keys Community College?

While admission standards to such schools may or may not pose an obstacle, the bigger issue may be financial. State legislatures try to attract in-state students by offering lower-cost in-state tuition: They know that those students will often stay in the state after graduation and secure good jobs, contributing to the state's economy. For example, if you live in Wisconsin and you want to go to the University of Rhode Island, your college

tuition in 2008 would have cost you $23,038. But if you were from Rhode Island, it would only cost you $8,184. UCLA offers perhaps the biggest home-state discount in the country: $26,658 per year for out-of-staters, as compared to just $7,038 in tuition for California residents.

For Critical Thinking and Discussion

1. Did you consider attending (or are you currently attending) a school far from your own home state?
2. As a high school senior, did you know about the significant disparities in tuition charged by some public universities to students from other states?
3. Should states be allowed to discriminate against out-of-state applicants?

---

of preemption applies, subject to later court review. In addition, Congress's lack of action within its enumerated powers opens the door to limited state regulations. For example, a state government can enact transportation regulations affecting truck drivers in the state so long as Congress has not passed any similar laws and the state law does not burden interstate commerce.

Relations between the States

A federalist system must not only manage relations between the state governments and the federal government, it must also arbitrate disagreements among member states. A feature of American federalism in this regard is the requirement that individual states must respect the civil laws of all other states, as guaranteed by the **full faith and credit clause** of Article IV, Section 1 of the Constitution. This clause provides that each state abide by the decisions of other state and local governments, including their judicial proceedings. This clause acts to assure stability in commercial and personal relations that extend beyond one state's borders. For example, contracts duly entered into in California under the laws of that state cannot simply be ignored or invalidated by the courts in Arizona or any other state. Similarly, when an unhappy married couple meets the legal requirements of divorce in one state and ends their marriage, they are not required to meet new divorce requirements in other states, as the divorce decree of one state must be recognized as valid by every other state.

In recent years, the proliferation of more controversial family law provisions, such as gay marriage laws, has placed considerable strain on the full faith and credit clause of Article IV. Vermont in 2000 was the first state to sanction so-called civil unions between same-sex partners; a handful of states eventually followed suit in authorizing these types of domestic partnerships. Then, on November 18, 2003, Massachusetts became the first state in the nation to provide for same-sex marriages by decree of its Supreme Judicial Court.[4] Since then at least four other states (New Hampshire, Connecticut, Iowa, and Vermont) and the District of Columbia have legalized marriages for same-sex couples;[5] at the time of this writing, federal courts were busy considering whether a California Constitutional provision banning same-sex marriage violates the Equal Protection Clause; meanwhile, three other states (New York, Rhode Island, and Maryland) recognize same-sex marriages performed

★ LO

Explain the significance of the supremacy clause, the preemption doctrine, and the full faith and credit clause of Article IV in dividing sovereignty between the federal and state governments

Full faith and credit clause

The provision in Article IV, Section 1 of the Constitution that forces states to abide by the official acts and proceedings of all other states.

in other states while not actually granting same-sex marriage licenses. Unlike civil unions, full-fledged gay marriage laws allow same-sex couples to gain formal state recognition on an equal plane with everyone else under the traditionally accepted institution of "marriage." Opponents of same-sex marriage contend that equating same-sex and opposite-sex marriage in this way changes the meaning of marriage and its traditions.

Even though the full faith and credit clause has traditionally required states to respect the public proceedings of every other state, many state legislatures have attempted to prevent same-sex couples from asserting their newfound status as married couples. At least thirty states have passed laws denying recognition to same-sex marriages. Legislatures in most other states, including some of those that have sanctioned civil unions, considered but ultimately failed to pass laws of their own that would have denied legal recognition to such out-of-state, same-sex marriages. In denying this recognition, these states enjoy the support of Congress, which in 1996 passed the Defense of Marriage Act, authorizing any state to deny a "marriage-like" relationship between persons of the same sex, even when such unions are recognized by another state. As a further sign of the heated feelings generated over this issue, voters in thirty states between 1998 and 2008 approved referenda preventing gay marriages in their own states. Ultimately, the U.S. Supreme Court may have to determine whether the Defense of Marriage Act and similar laws at the state level evade the full faith and credit clause of the Constitution.

Gay marriage ceremony in Massachusetts.

Another clause that provides for the equal treatment of out-of state citizens is the privileges and immunities clause of Article IV. Through this clause, which guarantees that the citizens of each state are "entitled to all Privileges and Immunities of Citizens in the several States," the Constitution protects the rights of every citizen to travel through other states, to reside in any state, and to participate in trade, agriculture, and professional pursuits in any state.[6] Some states have tried to limit bar memberships to in-state residents, or to impose hefty commuter taxes on out-of-staters who cross state lines each day for work. Such legislative efforts potentially conflict with the privileges and immunities clause. Article IV also provides that the criminal laws of individual states must be respected across state lines. When a criminal in one state escapes to another state, he or she is normally "extradited" or handed over to the original state either to stand trial or to complete a previously imposed sentence.

Ellis Island.

Article III, Section 2 of the Constitution gives the U.S. Supreme Court the authority to decide disputes between states. Although such jurisdiction is rarely exercised, the Court has taken its responsibility to arbitrate state conflicts seriously on those occasions when it has been asked to do so. So when officials in New York and New Jersey were battling in the late 1990s over which of those two states could claim sovereign authority over Ellis Island, the site where millions of immigrants to the United States were initially processed, the Supreme Court authorized a fact-finding investigation on the issue. Presented with the evidence of that investigation, the Court ruled that Ellis Island lay within the state boundaries of New Jersey—news no doubt to the millions of immigrants who thought they had disembarked in New York.[7] The Framers of the Constitution believed it was critically important that the highest federal court enjoy the power to arbitrate disputes between state governments, a key component of American federalism.

The History of American Federalism

In the more than two centuries that have passed since the ratification of the Constitution, different conceptions of federalism have prevailed during different eras. Some of these shifting patterns in state–federal relations were inevitable given the changing state of the nation and the increasingly important role it would play in world politics. The dominance of a global economy in the late twentieth and early twenty-first centuries, changing patterns in population growth, and technological developments in communication and transportation all spurred wholesale reexamination of the nature of federal and state governmental functions. Various government figures— presidents, Supreme Court justices, and members of Congress—have also played a role in shaping the nature of federalism. The flexibility of the federalist system has allowed it to adapt to changing circumstances.

Although a clear delineation of periods may oversimplify history, scholars have identified at least five eras of American federalism: (1) state-centered federalism, 1789–1819; (2) national supremacy period, 1819–1837; (3) dual federalism,

★ LO

Define the five eras of American federalism

CHECK the List

State Legislatures Staffed with Professionals

America's federalist system relies on state and local governments to perform many functions on behalf of citizens. State legislatures are a key engine in the process, passing laws and overseeing state agencies charged with implementing those laws. Unfortunately, state legislatures are not all equally equipped to meet the many challenges of modern governance; in fact, their memberships vary widely in their professionalism and time spent on the job. Some large states like California employ legislators and staffs all year long, whereas smaller state legislatures are often in session just three months or less per year. Below is a list of the ten states that have full-time, well-staffed, well-paid legislatures in session for almost ten months per year or longer. (Note that Texas, one of the more populous states in the union, does not appear on this list.)

✔ California

✔ Florida

✔ Illinois

✔ Massachusetts

✔ Michigan

✔ New Jersey

✔ New York

✔ Ohio

✔ Pennsylvania

✔ Wisconsin

1837–1937; (4) cooperative federalism, 1937–1990; and (5) the "new federalism," 1990–present. Each of these periods is defined by some shift in the power relationship between the national and state governments.

State-Centered Federalism, 1789–1819

The Framers' vision of federalism was relatively clear at the time the Constitution was ratified: other than in those policy areas clearly identified in Article I as subject to the national government's control (the military, foreign affairs, creation of currency, and so on), state governments would have full sovereignty over all other matters. Indeed, it is tough to imagine the Constitution being ratified by the requisite number of states had it called for any further subordination of traditional state authority. And with some notable exceptions, the national government's reach was exceedingly limited during the first thirty years of the Constitution's history.[8] At the urging of Treasury Secretary Alexander Hamilton, the Washington administration cautiously undertook some first steps in nationwide economic planning when it chartered the first National Bank of the United States and the federal government assumed all the debts of the state governments. Nevertheless, during this earliest period of federalism states remained the principal authority for American citizens. For the most part, each state managed its own affairs, often with little interference from the federal government.

President Thomas Jefferson took office in 1801 on the strength of a campaign in which his party, the Democratic-Republicans, offered to curtail the national government's occasional excesses, such as its passage of the Alien and Sedition Acts of 1798, which (among other things) punished individuals who criticized the national government. Jefferson articulated his own "principled distaste" for centralized authority. Notwithstanding his administration's authorization of funds to purchase the Louisiana Territory from France for $15 million, thereby doubling the size of the United States and speeding westward development, federal government functions during Jefferson's administration were usually linked to enumerated national powers. State governments exercised a nearly exclusive role in the administration of education, family and criminal law, civil and property rights, elections, and labor relations during this same period.

National Supremacy Period, 1819–1837

Just before leaving office in 1801, President John Adams installed as chief justice of the United States a fellow nationalist, John Marshall of Virginia. That appointment may have been the most significant act of Adams's presidency; although the Federalists would never again occupy the White House or control Congress, the national government–oriented party would influence American politics through Chief Justice Marshall for the next three decades.

Marshall's **national supremacy doctrine** of federalism is most evident in the Supreme Court decision in ***McCulloch v. Maryland*** **(1819)**,[9] which concerned the National Bank of the United States. As secretary of the treasury during the Washington administration, Alexander Hamilton successfully pushed for Congress to charter the first bank of the United States in 1792, arguing that such an institution would help provide for a sound national currency and a national system of credit. Thomas Jefferson, then secretary of state, and James Madison opposed the bank, believing that the Constitution gave Congress no authority to charter such a bank. Consequently when the bank's twenty-year charter expired, the Jeffersonian Republican-controlled Congress declined to recharter it. Recognizing that the lack of a national bank had hindered American efforts to obtain needed financial resources throughout the War of 1812, many in the Democratic-Republican Party, including Madison, who was now president, swallowed their pride and supported the chartering of a second national bank in 1816.

The bank still remained unpopular in many states where state-chartered banks were forced to compete (often unsuccessfully) with local branches of the National

National supremacy doctrine

Chief Justice John Marshall's interpretation of federalism as holding that states have extremely limited sovereign authority, whereas Congress is supreme within its own sphere of constitutional authority.

★ LO   Assess the role played by the Supreme Court in articulating the various doctrines and frameworks that determined the relationship between the state and federal governments during the five eras of American federalism

McCulloch v. Maryland (1819)

The Supreme Court case that established that Congress enjoys broad and extensive authority to make all laws that are "necessary and proper" to carry out its constitutionally delegated powers.

Bank for business and influence. The Maryland legislature passed a law that levied taxes on the notes of all banks—including the Baltimore branch of the National Bank—that were not chartered by the state. When James W. McCulloch, the cashier for the National Bank's Baltimore branch, refused to pay the tax, Maryland sued and won in its own state courts, setting up a monumental showdown on the future of the bank in the U.S. Supreme Court.

Writing for a unanimous 7–0 Supreme Court on March 6, 1819, Chief Justice John Marshall upheld the constitutionality of the bank. According to Marshall, the necessary and proper clause of the Constitution gave Congress the power to do nearly anything it wanted, so long as it was a means to exercising their expressly delegated powers, which included the power to borrow money and regulate inter-state commerce. The Maryland tax amounted to an unconstitutional interference with national supremacy. "The power to tax involves the power to destroy," the Court declared. Marshall used the occasion of the Court's ruling to articulate a broad vision of the national government's power, asserting that the national government could exercise its powers flexibly to meet the unexpected problems of changing national times. "This . . . is . . . a constitution we are expounding," Marshall noted, "intended to endure for ages to come, and consequently, to be adapted to the various crises of human affairs." According to Marshall, the Constitution altered the position of the states; no longer were they sovereign entities on a par with the federal govern-ment. Within the sphere of its own powers, Congress was supreme.

Marshall's Court also refuted the power of state courts to interpret and apply the Constitution in ways that conflicted with the Supreme Court's own interpretations. Thus the Constitution assumed its status as the uniform governing law of all the states. To Marshall, the Court's duty was not to preserve state sovereignty, but rather "to protect national power against state encroachments." Consistent with this view, the Marshall Court routinely interpreted Congress's legislative authority quite broadly. In **Gibbons v. Ogden (1824)**,[10] for example, the Court invalidated a monopoly granted by the New York legislature covering the operation of steamboats in New York waters, because the New York monopoly was in conflict with a federal license.

The national supremacy doctrine articulated by Marshall was not without its critics. State politicians accused the Court of ignoring the sovereign power of the states. Some national politicians were no less sympathetic. As president, Andrew Jackson opposed the National Bank and all internal improvements (such as the building of roads or canals) ordered by Congress as unconstitutional. He even vetoed a rechartering of the bank in 1832. Yet, at the same time, he also applied Marshall's national supremacy doctrine in defending the Tariff of 1828. After Congress passed a highly protection-ist tariff over the objections of Southern free-trade adherents, the South Carolina legislature adopted a series of resolutions negating the tariff on the theory that state sovereignty allowed each state to nullify any law passed by Congress that the state deemed unconstitutional. (New Englanders had used that same argument during the War of 1812 when a convention of the region's states met in Hartford, Connecticut, in early 1815 and endorsed the right of states to interpose themselves against "dangerous infractions" of the Constitution by the federal government.) In response to the action by South Carolina, President Jackson declared that such a nullification was an "impractical absurdity" and rejected the right of individual states to refuse to obey federal laws. A call by South Carolina Senator John Calhoun and others for a "general convention of the states" to reconsider state–federal relations, including possible secession from the Union, elicited enthusiasm from numerous Southern states, but eventually the nullification crisis

Gibbons v. Ogden (1824)

The Supreme Court case that held that under the Constitu-tion, a federal license to oper-ate steamboats overrides a state-granted monopoly of New York water rights.

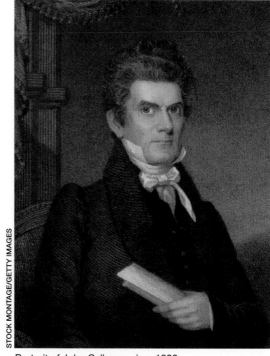

STOCK MONTAGE/GETTY IMAGES

Portrait of John Calhoun, circa 1830.

passed when Congress approved a compromise tariff that progressively lowered rates until they reached the same level they had been at in 1816.[11]

Dual Federalism, 1837–1937

Marshall's successor as chief justice, Roger B. Taney of Maryland (1836–1864), dedicated much of his twenty-eight-year tenure on the Court to rearticulating a vision of federalism more consistent with that of the Framers. Significantly, Taney did not overturn decisions of the Marshall Court asserting the authority of the Supreme Court over state judiciaries to interpret the Constitution, nor did he deny the broad power to regulate interstate commerce that Marshall had announced in *Gibbons v. Ogden*. The Taney Court was not a radical champion of state sovereignty. But Taney did abandon the more sweeping aspects of the national supremacy doctrine, which had heralded the federal government as "superior" to state governments. Instead, he maintained that the Constitution was a "compact of sovereign states," with the powers reserved to the states by the Tenth Amendment serving as a limit on congressional power. In a series of cases in the 1840s and 1850s, the Taney Court raised the status of state involvement in contract and corporate affairs. For example, in *Cooley v. Board of Wardens of the Port of Philadelphia* (1852),[12] the Court upheld a Pennsylvania statute imposing a fee on vessels that passed through the port of Philadelphia because the fee went into a fund for the relief of pilots and pilots' widows, and was thus deemed a "local subject." Even though the fee affected interstate and international commerce to a degree, the nature of the subject matter counseled against a rigid interpretation that favored national supremacy.

Although slavery was a crucial component of the fight between the Union and the Confederacy, the Civil War was at its core a struggle about the relationship between the states and the federal government. The Union's victory undermined dual federalism's "compact of states" premise by rejecting the authority of states to leave the compact. Then, in a series of cases handed down after the Civil War, a newly constituted Supreme Court acknowledged national power and congressional authority to set the terms for readmitting former Confederate states into the Union. This power was considered an outgrowth of Congress's exclusive and unquestioned authority not only to regulate the territories of the United States, but also to oversee the admission of new states to the Union. With twenty-four of the fifty states joining the Union between 1836 and 1912 (see Figure 3.2), admission to statehood was an important function of the federal government during this period.

FIGURE 3.2 Admission of States to the Union

Under **dual federalism**, however, the states did retain considerable authority to regulate economic affairs that were not directly within the "stream of commerce" between two or more states, including matters concerning the manufacturing of products and the health and safety of factory workers. Ignoring *McCulloch v. Maryland*, the Supreme Court refused to give Congress the discretionary authority it enjoyed during the era of the national supremacy doctrine. Regulatory legislation passed by Congress, such as the child labor laws referenced in the opening section of this chapter, was set aside as unconstitutional. Once again the Court had greatly diminished the scope of the necessary and proper clause. Despite the onset of the Industrial Revolution, Congress was eventually rendered helpless to regulate the abuses of some businesses. Later, in the 1930s, the Court struck down a series of New Deal laws implementing pension and retirement systems for workers and regulating industrial relations.[13] In this way, dual federalism prevented Congress from addressing the hardships brought on by the Great Depression.

Dual federalism
The doctrine of federalism that holds that state authority acts as a limit on congressional power under the Constitution.

Cooperative Federalism, 1937–1990

Faced with judicial opposition to New Deal policies regulating the workplace, retirement policies, and other subjects traditionally ceded to the states, President Franklin D. Roosevelt (FDR) and his supporters grew increasingly frustrated. To them, the economic hardships of the Great Depression demanded an activist federal government, and a conservative Supreme Court now stood in the way. FDR and his allies in Congress proposed expanding the size of the Supreme Court from nine to fifteen, which would allow Roosevelt to "pack" the Supreme Court with advocates of a broader vision of federal legislative power.[14] The proposed "court-packing plan" became unnecessary, however. As public frustration with the Court was mounting, one member of the Court in 1937 (Justice Owen Roberts) suddenly did an about-face, abandoning dual federalist principles in favor of a more expansive view of congressional authority. A shift in just one vote had a significant impact; a shift in two votes on the Supreme Court meant that nearly all federal legislation would now survive high-court scrutiny. Once Roosevelt was able to add his own judicial appointees to the mix, the Court as a whole was ready to support unprecedented exercises of congressional power.

Social scientists speak of the post–New Deal period as marking a shift from **layer cake federalism**, in which the authority of state and federal governments is distinct and more easily delineated, to a system of **marble cake federalism**, in which state and federal authority are intertwined in an inseparable mixture. This new era, later labeled as the period of **cooperative federalism**, in some ways harkened back to the national supremacy doctrine articulated by John Marshall. Congress once again became the judge of its own powers, including those powers implied under the necessary and proper clause. Congress could, for example, restrict the activities of labor unions, criminalize loan sharking, or enact any policy under the theory that it may be "necessary and proper" to exercise enumerated powers such as the power to regulate interstate commerce. The limits on congressional power under so-called cooperative federalism were thus quite small: so long as some link to commerce could be offered, for example, no matter how tenuous such a link might be, Congress remained free to exert its authority over the states. When Congress passed civil rights laws in 1964 under the premise that racial discrimination in restaurants and hotels "burdened" interstate commerce, the Supreme Court barely batted an eye at what was in fact an extremely broad reading of congressional authority.[15]

Cooperative federalism, however, can be distinguished from Marshall's doctrine of national superiority. Whenever concurrent legislative power is exercised, Congress can act in one of three ways:

1. Preempt the states altogether and assert exclusive control over the subject matter

2. Leave the states to act on their own

3. Provide that the operation of its own law depends on or is qualified by existing state laws

Distinguish between different forms of federalism (layer cake federalism versus marble cake federalism) in the modern era ★ LO

Layer cake federalism
Description of federalism as maintaining that the authority of state and federal governments exists in distinct and separate spheres.

Marble cake federalism
Description of federalism as intertwining state and federal authority in an inseparable mixture.

Cooperative federalism
The doctrine of federalism that affords Congress nearly unlimited authority to exercise its powers through means that often coerce states into administering and/or enforcing federal policies.

This last category provides an opening in state–federal relationships that even Marshall could not have anticipated: the possibility that the federal government might actually enlist state officials and other state actors to implement federal policies.

The positive aspects of cooperative federalism are obvious. The expansion of the central government beginning in the 1930s into the $2.5 trillion per year behemoth that it is today means that federal officials now have huge sums of money at their disposal. Individual states can benefit from this pool of funds whenever the federal government passes on some of its revenues directly to the states to initiate and administer programs. **Grants-in-aid** from the federal government to the states have been used to fund state educational initiatives, build roads, and provide unemployment relief, among other programs that fulfill purposes expressly approved by Congress and/or its federal regulatory agencies. Federal grants also help balance the economic inequities that arise because states have vastly different tax bases. Occasionally the federal government has transformed grants-in-aid, which are allocated only for specific programs or policies, into **block grants**, which a state or local government may use at its discretion for more generalized programs.

Grants-in-aid
Grants from the federal government to states that allow state governments to pursue specific federal policies, such as highway construction.

Block grants
Grants from the federal government to the states that may be used at the discretion of states to pursue more generalized aims.

FIGURE 3.3 Comparing Federal Expenditures to State Expenditures

The system of federalism dictates that the federal government, not the states, must provide national defense. By contrast, state expenditures focus on educational expenses, criminal justice, and social services in particular. Although different systems of categorization make budget comparisons among governments difficult, a glimpse of the budgets of the federal government and two state governments provides some interesting insights as to where your tax dollars are going . . . or not going.

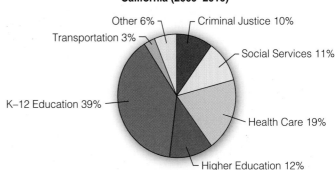

California (2009–2010)

Other 6% — Criminal Justice 10%
Transportation 3% —
Social Services 11%
K–12 Education 39% —
Health Care 19%
Higher Education 12%

Source: State of California Legislative Analyst's Office (www.lao.ca.gov)

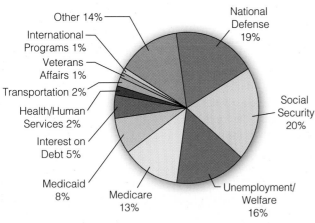

Federal Spending-FY2010

Other 14% —
National Defense 19%
International Programs 1% —
Veterans Affairs 1% —
Transportation 2% —
Health/Human Services 2% —
Social Security 20%
Interest on Debt 5% —
Medicaid 8%
Medicare 13%
Unemployment/ Welfare 16%

Source: Office of Management and Budget

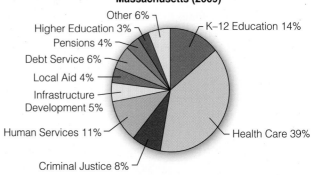

Massachusetts (2009)

Other 6% —
Higher Education 3% —
K–12 Education 14%
Pensions 4% —
Debt Service 6% —
Local Aid 4% —
Infrastructure Development 5% —
Human Services 11% —
Health Care 39%
Criminal Justice 8% —

Source: Massachusetts Budget and Policy Center (www.massbudget.org)

The collaboration between state governments and the federal government in the era of cooperative federalism also carried some negative implications for state sovereignty. Federal government officials increasingly insisted that federal appropriations to the states be accompanied by various conditions. Often these consisted of "protective conditions," designed to ensure that the state would administer its program consistent with the objectives of Congress. For example, Congress required that states receiving educational assistance meet federal requirements for educating handicapped children, including the creation of individualized education programs for special needs students. On occasion, however, Congress has imposed coercive burdens on states that increasingly rely on such federal assistance. In 1984, for example, Congress passed the National Minimum Drinking Age Amendment, which withheld 5 percent of federal highway funds from any state "in which the purchase or public possession of any alcoholic beverage by a person who is less than 21 years of age" is lawful. The purpose of the law was to decrease the number of serious automobile accidents among those aged eighteen to twenty—statistics showed that this group was responsible for a high percentage of accidents on the nation's highways.

All the states but one rushed to comply with the directive. South Dakota permitted individuals aged nineteen or older to purchase beer containing 3.2 percent alcohol, and the state legislature did not want to modify that law. The state then sued to keep its highway funds, asserting that the law was "coercive" and exceeded Congress's constitutional powers of taxation and spending. By a 7–2 decision, the Supreme Court rejected South Dakota's claim. "The spending power is of course not unlimited," Justice Sandra Day O'Connor wrote for the majority, as "in some circumstances the financial inducement offered by Congress might be so coercive as to pass the point at which 'pressure turns into compulsion.'" But the Court determined that such was not the case in that instance. "All South Dakota would lose if she adheres to her chosen course as to a suitable minimum drinking age is 5% of the funds . . . the argument as to coercion is shown to be more rhetoric than fact." With its highway funds threatened, the South Dakota legislature voted to raise the drinking age in the state.

Although the conditions imposed by the National Minimum Drinking Age Amendment essentially coerced state governments to pass laws at the behest of the federal government, the Supreme Court generally approved of such tactics. Yet when Ronald Reagan was elected president in 1980, he openly trumpeted federal initiatives to return policymaking authority to the states. In his first State of the Union Address in early 1981, Reagan proposed to terminate the federal role in welfare and return to the states forty-three other major federal grant programs.

The voluntary transfer of power by the central government to state or local governments is known as "devolution."[16] If Reagan's proposals had been fully implemented, such a large-scale devolution of federal programs would have returned federal–state relations to the version of federalism that existed before the New Deal. As it turned out, however, strong resistance from the Democratic-controlled House led to the defeat of many of Reagan's devolution initiatives. Nonetheless, Reagan administration rhetoric emphasizing federal deregulation and increased state responsibilities set the stage for more sweeping reforms to be implemented in the years ahead.

1981 *New Yorker* cartoon depicting President Ronald Reagan's plans to return some federal programs to the states.

"Sorry, but all my power's been turned back to the states."

© THE NEW YORKER COLLECTION 1981 LEE LORENZ FROM CARTOONBANK.COM. ALL RIGHTS RESERVED.

The "New Federalism," 1990–Present

Scholars assessing the state of federalism since 1990 have failed to reach a consensus on the proper label for characterizing what appears to be a counterthrust favoring states' rights in certain areas. This new era of federal–state relations has been marked by a resuscitation of state authority, helped by a Supreme Court which, since the early 1990s, has been far more attentive to protecting states' rights. The changed composition of the Court accounts for this shift. Between 1991 and 2005, four Reagan appointees to the Court (Chief Justice Rehnquist and Associate Justices Antonin Scalia, Sandra Day O'Connor, and Anthony Kennedy) and one of George H. W. Bush's appointees (Associate Justice Clarence Thomas) generally favored states' rights in federalism disputes.[17] (President George W. Bush's appointments of Chief Justice John Roberts and Associate Justice Samuel Alito to the Supreme Court did little to reverse this trend.) The modern Court's decisions on federalism fit into a number of different categories.

This radioactive waste plant in New Mexico was built by the state with strong monetary incentives from the federal government.

First, although the Supreme Court has continued to allow Congress to place conditions on federal appropriations to the states, it put a stop to coercive conditions that leave the states with no discretion to form their own policies. Faced with the difficult challenge of encouraging states to build radioactive-waste dumps within their own borders, Congress in the mid to late 1980s passed a series of laws that created monetary and other forms of incentives for states to assume that responsibility. Even more extreme, Congress warned that states that shirked their responsibility on the matter might be forced to assume legal ownership of the waste from private companies, and thereafter incur all the legal liability that would arise from its hazards. In *New York v. United States* (1992), the Supreme Court ruled that this final provision crossed the line, and was unconstitutionally coercive.[18] Recent Supreme Court decisions have also prevented Congress from requiring state officials to implement or carry out federal policies; when the Brady Bill required that local sheriffs conduct background checks of gun purchasers, the Supreme Court in *Printz v. United States* (1997) struck down that provision as unconstitutional.[19]

Second, since the mid-1990s, Congress's virtually unlimited authority to regulate interstate commerce has been scaled back somewhat. In *United States v. Lopez* (1995), the Supreme Court declared that Congress could not ban guns in school zones.[20] Whereas during the cooperative federalism era Congress regulated all manner of criminal and social activities, the present-day Supreme Court has more strenuously insisted that Congress show a clear connection with commerce when exercising its power to regulate interstate commerce, for example. Then, in 1997, Congress ran into more obstacles when it enacted a law entitling sexual assault victims to sue their perpetrators in federal court. Once again, the Supreme Court stood firm for state sovereignty, ruling in *United States v. Morrison* (2000) that the law was unconstitutional, on the grounds that domestic abuse had only a slight connection to commerce.[21]

Third, a series of recent Supreme Court decisions has scaled back the doctrine of preemption, at least as applied to Congress's regulation of state governmental workers and employees. In *Alden v. Maine* (1999), the Supreme Court refused Congress the authority to allow private citizens to sue state governments for damages when they fail to pay minimum wages required under federal law.[22] A year later, the Supreme Court issued a similar ruling, disallowing private lawsuits against state governments that violated federal age discrimination laws.

Meanwhile a Supreme Court increasingly intent on protecting states' rights has given new teeth to the Eleventh Amendment, which bars citizens of one state from bringing suit against another state in federal court. As a result of Court decisions,

JOE RAEDLE/GETTY IMAGES

AMERICAN GOVERNMENT In Historical Perspective

When Must the Federal Government Put State Governments in Their Place?

Citizens of the United States are also citizens of one of the fifty states. Policies in the states are by no means uniform. Notwithstanding some of the uniform testing requirements imposed by federal "No Child Left Behind" legislation, educational policy differs widely from state to state. So too will an individual accused of a crime find one state's criminal justice system far more onerous and difficult than another. The federal government (which includes federal courts) has occasionally stepped in to smooth out those differences, much to the chagrin of states that prefer to maintain their own unique identity on specific issues. Sometimes uniformity is favored as a matter of good policy; at other times it may be mandated by the Constitution itself. This delicate balancing act between state interests and the need to maintain states' unique political and cultural identities has never been easy to maintain.

In 1850, Congress debated a legislative compromise at a time when Northern and Southern Senators were growing increasingly anxious about the future course of slavery in the United States. Though Southern legislators recognized the right of Northern states to forbid slavery, they rejected all efforts to undermine Southern laws that allowed the practice. Especially controversial were "personal liberty laws" passed by Northern states, which mandated a jury trial before fugitive slaves could be moved. (Northern juries often refused to convict those indicted under runaway slave laws). Other states forbade the use of local jails or the assistance of state officials in the arrest or return of such fugitives. Eventually Congress passed the Fugitive Slave Act of 1850 to redress the conflict: now federal marshals could be held liable for not enforcing runaway slave laws, and former slaves could not request jury trials. In this instance Congress did not mandate uniform laws on slavery; it did, however, bring Northern states into line with the clear expectations of Southern states. A fugitive slave act could shift legal requirements, but it proved to have little effect on Northern sentiments. The Northerners'

refusal to assist with runaway slaves proved one of many factors that precipitated the outbreak of the Civil War a decade later.

In 1963, uniformity in the treatment of criminal defendants was squarely at issue before the U.S. Supreme Court. By late 1962, close to half of the states were automatically providing indigent defendants a right to counsel whenever jail time was a possibility. In fact, just prior to the landmark Supreme Court case of *Gideon v. Wainwright* (1963), twenty-two of those states urged the Court to adopt this right as a federal standard. By contrast, many states (including Florida) provided such counsel only on a case-by-case basis—if an indigent defendant seemed competent enough to try his or her own case, judges usually insisted that he or she do so. Could such a patchwork of protections stand under the Sixth Amendment? "No," said the Supreme Court, which in *Gideon* effectively nationalized the requirement that counsel be provided to indigent defendants. Following the landmark decision, the mid-to-late 1960s witnessed the creation of public defenders programs across the country.

In 2010, the U.S. Supreme Court once again inserted itself into a social and cultural debate where individual feelings tend to run high. This time the issue was gun control. In 2007 the Court ruled that the Second Amendment protects an individual's right to possess a firearm for public use. Its ruling was limited, however, to federal restrictions on firearms (in that case it was a DC law); the Supreme Court did not address whether the Second Amendment applied to state laws as well under the process known as *incorporation*. (Incorporation is discussed in detail in Chapter 4). Certainly the possession of firearms has different implications for residents of the South Bronx than it does for residents of rural farmland in Wyoming. Does the Fourteenth Amendment hold all governments accountable to the protections afforded by the Second Amendment? The Supreme Court's answer was "yes." On June 28, 2010, the Court held in *McDonald v. Chicago* that the Second Amendment right to bear arms applies to all 50 states as well as the District of Columbia.

many plaintiffs are now restricted from bringing lawsuits in federal court against public employers; instead, plaintiffs must bring suit in state courts.[23]

Of course Supreme Court decisions are not solely responsible for the resurrection of state sovereignty that has occurred over the past decade and a half. Political

Free trade between the United States and Latin American countries is theoretically the province of the federal government. Reality tends to be a bit more complicated. In 2003, talks began among thirty-four countries in the Americas to propose an extension of the North American Free Trade Agreement (NAFTA) to countries in Central America and South America as well. The location of this proposed Free Trade Area of America (FTAA) headquarters caused a bit of controversy, however. The city of Miami, Florida, believed it would be a shoo-in for the headquarters, and the Florida state government—with so much to gain from the FTAA—tried mightily to secure Miami as the headquarters. The U.S. government, concerned about the massive anti-corporatization and anti-globalization protests that had taken place at the FTAA negotiations held in Miami and elsewhere, generally steered clear of these lobbying efforts. The federal government was apparently concerned not just about the possibility of violence; it also wanted to stay neutral in a contest among Florida, Georgia, and other states and cities vying to be the FTAA headquarters.

Where does this leave Latin American countries concerned that the U.S. government's "neutrality" about the headquarters site creates a vacuum that may slow down, if not outright derail, the process? Simon Romero, a *New York Times* journalist who currently lives and works in Caracas, Venezuela, tried to capture the Latin American perspective on this competition being waged between the states of Georgia and Florida (His article was reprinted in the *Latin-American Post*) :

If it seems like Mr. [Jorge] Arrizurieta [a Florida-born Cuban-American working on behalf of his home state] is maintaining a busy traveling schedule, his counterpart in Atlanta, José Ignacio González, is just as frenzied . . . Mr. González and Mr. Arrizurieta crossed paths as they met with the president of Uruguay, Jorge Batlle, and other government representatives on the same day in late August in Montevideo, the Uruguayan capital. Though they did not see each other, they heard of each other's movements from the officials they were meeting with, both men said. . . . Mr. Batlle later endorsed Miami's bid, becoming the first government leader in the region to publicly

developments have also altered the character of American federalism in important ways. Many of President Reagan's federalism initiatives met with limited success in a Democratic-controlled House of Representatives. For example, his own Republican Party's platforms in the 1980s called for the abolition of the Department of Education; yet that controversial proposal proved a nonstarter in the Congress. Still, his administration managed to push through deregulation initiatives in a number of partially preempted programs, and it relaxed federal oversight of state performance to a considerable degree. In addition, six years after Reagan left office, Republicans took control of both the House and the Senate for the first time since the early 1950s. In 1994, Newt Gingrich (R-GA), then House Minority Whip, and 366 other Republican candidates for Congress rallied around the "Contract with America," a series of initiatives they promised to introduce in the first one hundred days of the 104th Congress. (Republicans would maintain control of at least one and usually both houses of Congress for more than a decade, up until the Democratic sweep of both houses in 2006.)

Republican leaders hoped to institute major changes in the nature of the relationship that existed between the federal government and state

AP PHOTO/JOHN DURICKA, FILE

Then-House Minority Whip Newt Gingrich addressing Republican Congressional candidates during the 1994 election campaign. The "Contract with America" was credited in part with helping the Republicans take back the Congress in November 1994 and with making Gingrich the first Republican Speaker of the House in forty years.

side with any city, even though it is ultimately the Uruguayan trade minister who will put forward his position in a consensus process involving negotiators from throughout the region. . . .

Mr. González, the [Georgia] envoy, has taken a different approach from Mr. Arrizurieta's by declining to discuss the negative attributes of his competitors in favor of promoting Atlanta's advantages. "Initially," he said in an interview, "Atlanta might not seem like the most obvious choice but we bring the most to the table economically, culturally and historically[.]" . . . Atlanta, buoyed by support from local and state political leaders, appears to be doing fairly well in increasing visibility for its bid. Earlier this month, for example, ministers from five Andean countries—Bolivia, Ecuador, Colombia, Peru and Venezuela—met in Atlanta to discuss preparations for next month's talks in Miami. While in Georgia, they dined with former President Jimmy Carter and met with executives from large Atlanta companies. . . .

"We're the indisputable gateway to the Americas," Mr. Arrizurieta said, adding that he bristled upon seeing that exact phrase, "Gateway to the Americas," as part of an extensive advertising insert purchased by Atlanta recently in the magazine Latin Trade to win support for its bid. "That really got to me," Mr. Arrizurieta said.

© 2012 CENGAGE LEARNING

Source: Simon Romero, "Miami Caught in Free Trade Quandary," *New York Times*, October 28, 2003.

and local governments. With the Republican takeover of Congress complete after the 1994 midterm elections, newly elected Speaker of the House Gingrich and other House leaders introduced legislation in early 1995 that would have required states to reduce the level of benefits paid to welfare recipients specified as "undeserving." The targets included mothers who gave birth to more children while they were already on welfare, and mothers who had refused to determine paternity. The 104th Congress also proposed budget resolutions in May 1995 that would have created a new series of block grants to states; consolidated or eliminated hundreds of federal programs, agencies, and commissions; and abolished three federal departments—the Departments of Energy, Education, and Commerce.

In the end, that Congress passed few revolutionary new laws. A standoff between President Bill Clinton, who refused to sign the budget resolutions, and Congress, which threatened to close down the government unless the president gave way, led to government shutdowns in November 1995 and January 1996; eventually, on April 26, 1996, Clinton signed a budget bill that cut federal domestic discretionary spending for the first time in three decades. Yet the bill did not achieve anything close to the revolution that the leaders of the 104th Congress had hoped for. Devolution of programs to the states has instead evolved far more gradually, through legislation like the Personal Responsibility and Work Opportunity Reconciliation Act of 1996, which capped federal block grants to states for welfare aid. States have been encouraged by the law to create their own, cost-efficient welfare benefits programs. But the states' rights movement stopped significantly short of the vaunted "devolution revolution" promised by Republican House leaders when they first took control in 1995.

Why Federalism?
Advantages and Disadvantages

Supporters of federalism point to several advantages offered by this form of government, and opponents of federalism counter with arguments of their own concerning the disadvantages of this form of government.

Advantages of Federalism

★ LO Recognize the advantages of a system that serves a diverse array of interests

Supporters of federalism cite among the specific advantages of this form of government that it is more likely to accommodate the needs of a diverse citizenry, to strengthen liberty by dividing powers between levels of government, to encourage experimentation, and to respond to change.

- **Accommodation of diversity.** If a unitary system of government threatens to treat citizens of different states as interchangeable parts for purposes of quick and easy administration, federalism acts as an important counterbalance to this trend. A citizen of the United States can also take pride in being a citizen of Texas or some other state with a clearly defined culture or character. State and local politicians can perhaps respond to the specific demands or needs of its citizens better than a central government can. The culture of a state may be reflected in that state's handgun control laws, its rules on the distribution of alcohol, or its laws concerning abortion, prostitution, the use of land, and many other issues that tend to receive differing levels of support across America.

Like this Texan, many citizens take pride in their home states.

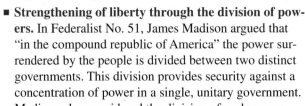

- **Strengthening of liberty through the division of powers.** In Federalist No. 51, James Madison argued that "in the compound republic of America" the power surrendered by the people is divided between two distinct governments. This division provides security against a concentration of power in a single, unitary government. Madison also considered the division of such power "essential to the preservation of liberty," because it becomes harder for a corrupt agreement between these two separate governments to last for long—in the unlikely event that one entire government turns corrupt, the other government would still be available to check that government's abuses. Thus the existence of two distinct levels of government, combined with the separation of executive, legislative, and judicial powers within each of those governments, offers individuals considerable protection. Accordingly, Madison argued that "a double security arises to the rights of the people."

  Throughout American history, Madison's prophecy has often proven true, as state governments have rallied against federal government abuses of the rights of the people, and vice versa. For example, the Kentucky and Virginia resolutions drafted by legislatures of those states in the late 1790s negated the power of the federal government to pass federal laws restricting seditious speech and the free movement of aliens.[24] The respective roles of these governments in protecting liberty were reversed 160 years later, when the federal government sent federal troops to Arkansas to protect the rights of African American citizens to attend public schools in the segregated South. "Liberty through government" thus became a principle of the civil rights movement, aided by the rivalry between two sovereign governments.

- **Encouragement of laboratories of democracy.** In 1932, Supreme Court Justice Louis Brandeis made famous a metaphor for creative federalism when he wrote that "a single courageous state may, if its citizens choose, serve as a laboratory, and try social and economic experiments without risk to the rest of the country."[25] This notion of states serving as "laboratories of democracy" is encouraged by a federalist system that gives the states authority to craft policies at the outset, while at the same time affording the central government authority to implement polices that prove successful throughout the nation. During the 1930s, FDR borrowed from the experience of various states in crafting many New Deal policies. In 1993, the Brady Bill passed by Congress drew heavily on successful state gun control provisions that established waiting periods for handgun purchases. The flip side of such successes is also significant: state policies that proved to be failures discourage broad-based applications by the federal government. For example, given that California's deregulation of utilities helped bring about an energy crisis in that state in early 2001, it seems unlikely that other states or the federal government will seek similar forms of deregulation anytime soon.

- **Adaptability to changing circumstances.** Some areas of policymaking clearly lie within the purview of the central government: foreign affairs, the development of a strong military, and the resolution of conflicts between states lead the list. By way of comparison, state and local governments maintain relatively strong control over public education in the state and local communities. Similarly, over the past decade responsibility for social welfare policies has rested primarily with state governments. In these and other policy areas, state and local control affords considerably more flexibility to officials wrestling with various ways of addressing policy problems. Changing circumstances, such as a sudden influx of students in a state's K–12 educational programs or a migration of welfare recipients to a state, may require a quick and flexible response from government. Federal control over such issues may ensure the benefits of uniformity, but the cost is some loss of flexibility. State control provides the opportunity for legislative reform over a bureaucracy that may be far more manageable in its size.

FRANK CEZUS/GETTY IMAGES

An interstate highway beset with construction. Many states must rely heavily on federal construction funds to help them maintain roads and highways.

Disadvantages of Federalism

Opponents of federalism present arguments of their own concerning the disadvantages of this form of government. Chief among their objections to a federalist system are the unfairness caused by economic disparities among the states, questions about government accountability for many public programs that are inherent with competing sovereigns, and the system's heavy reliance on the courts to define the nature of federalism.

- **Fiscal disparities among the states.** States differ markedly in the wealth of their citizens, and thus in the taxable resources available to them for programs. According to the U.S. Department of Commerce's Bureau of Economic Analysis, Connecticut's citizens in 2007 boasted a per capita personal income of $54,117, nearly twice that of citizens in Mississippi ($28,845).[26] Because of these fiscal differences, the amount that states have to spend on governmental programs varies widely. Furthermore, when the central government defers to state entities in the governing process, such as when it requires states to fund their own welfare programs, wide fiscal inequalities among states (and localities) may mean disparate—and inequitable—programs for citizens in different states. Advocates of social equity and justice routinely complain about this consequence of federalism. Although federal financing of state developmental projects or other state programs relieves some of these inequities, the current trend toward reducing state dependency on the federal government promises more, not less, equity in the distribution of government benefits across states.

- **Lack of accountability.** Numerous government programs fall under the exclusive authority of neither the state nor the federal governments; both may act, either may act, or, in some cases, neither may act. At least in the abstract, federalism creates

Understand the disadvantages of federalism in terms of fairness and accountability

★ LO

President Barack Obama meets with state and local officials in Grand Isle, Louisiana, to discuss efforts to cap the 2010 oil spill in the Gulf of Mexico.

the prospect of multiple levels of government vying for the opportunity to address economic or social problems. In practice, however, the federal and state governments often play a game of "chicken," each hoping the other will act first and assume greater economic responsibility, and perhaps accountability for failures. In an era when public frustration with rising taxes discourages government spending, this "blame game" may go on for years, with both sides accusing the other of shirking its responsibilities to the public. During the 1990s, for example, many state governments eliminated benefits for the needy and imposed stricter requirements on those seeking welfare. State legislatures facing growing budget deficits hoped to "push" the poverty problem onto other states by passing laws that encouraged poor people to move to states with more liberal benefits programs. During this same period Congress passed welfare legislation in 1996 that transferred welfare responsibilities back to states. Critics charge that this arrangement of shared accountability quickly transforms into a lack of accountability, with neither government accepting responsibility for dealing with problems.

■ **Undue reliance on courts to define the rules of federalism.** Because of the ambiguities inherent within a federalist system, courts play a far greater role in defining this form of government than in defining other forms. Because the federalist system is grounded in a political compromise, the rules are unclear; the limits of governmental power fit into no neat or simple formula. Judicial decision making is a mainstay of most federalist systems because it is necessary; without judicial rulings, it may be difficult if not impossible to balance the competing goals of national and subnational governments. This continued reliance on courts to make these weighty decisions exacts a price, however. Unlike legislators or high-level executives who must court public support to be elected, most judges are appointed and thus never need to directly curry the public's favor. When the courts fail to acknowledge public opinion, as the Supreme Court did when it struck down extremely popular measures to fight the Great Depression in the 1930s, a democratic system such as ours may find the delicate balance of powers tipping too far in favor of the unelected branches of government.

■ **The pros and cons of federalism.** Those who favor expanding states' rights and responsibilities can cite a number of advantages that accrue with a healthy brand of federalism, while those who doubt the capacity of state governments to address complex modern problems are just as passionate when citing its various disadvantages. Debates over the merits of federalism are likely to continue well into the future, as political actors at every level of government stake a claim in difficult public policy problems that have few clear solutions.

Current Problems in American Federalism

Describe some of the abuses under federalism, including the use of unfunded mandates and the underfunding of urban centers ★ LO

Beginning in the 1980s, the national Republican Party identified itself closely with the states' rights movement. In seeking to decrease the size of government programs at the national level, President Ronald Reagan and congressional Republicans invited state governments to assume greater responsibilities for their own citizens. Unfortunately, it was never made clear where the money to support such state programs would come from. As state governments continue to shoulder greater responsibilities for some programs, the issue of funding has moved front and center in the debate over federalism.

Unfunded Mandates

Unfunded mandates are directives from the federal government to the states requiring them to perform regulatory tasks at their own expense. By placing conditions on federal grants to states, and then threatening to withdraw those funds if the states don't meet the conditions, the federal government can impose a whole range of such mandates on states seeking their share of federal funds. Even in the 1980s, when the trend was toward deregulation and devolution, Congress continued to place coercive requirements on states that received grants-in-aid. Laws were passed mandating national standards on a host of subjects such as transportation, school and work safety, and environmental hazards. According to social scientist Timothy Conlan, the number of major new intergovernmental regulatory provisions enacted during the 1980s surpassed that of any previous period.[27] States complained that many of these regulations posed considerable economic hardships on their budgets, without any compensatory economic support from the federal government. For example, compliance with federal environmental requirements imposed since 1970 cost all state and local governments combined more than $19 billion per year by the end of the 1980s.

Unfunded mandate

A directive from the federal government to the states requiring that they perform certain functions, with no accompanying funds to support those functions.

One of the legislative successes claimed by Republicans under the Contract with America was the Unfunded Mandates Reform Act, which President Clinton signed into law in the spring of 1995. On its face, the law made it harder for Congress to impose mandates on the states without accompanying funds for implementation—the law allowed individual members of Congress to block consideration of such mandates unless the requirement for funding was waived by Congress as a whole. Federal agencies were also prevented from carrying out mandates that were unfunded (or underfunded) without the direct consent of Congress. Such mandates have continued in the years since the act was passed, as Congress has continued to enact legislation providing directives to states. As it turned out, the Unfunded Mandates Act could do little to counter the federal legislative zeal for ordering states to carry out initiatives at their own cost.

A public school in Camden, New Jersey, that first opened in 1887.

The Growing Crisis in Big Cities

The inequities arising in a federal system that relies heavily on each state to fund many of its own social programs have created a crisis in many large cities in the United States. Big-city government programs can be expensive, and the needs of poor urban populations (for social and economic services, for example) often outstrip the city's tax base. Education is a particular concern: big-city education has always been more expensive to deliver than education in the

A modern public high school in the wealthy suburb of Hudson, Ohio.

suburbs and rural towns because of high land prices, the higher salaries needed to retain teachers in big-city schools, and the high costs of school safety and other problems that are most commonly associated with inner-city education.

The structure of the American federalist system does not benefit urban cities to the degree that their high populations would seem to require. Congress—which includes members from all states and congressional districts—is reluctant to pass laws that exclude nonurban areas. Moreover, states with small populations enjoy disproportionately greater influence in the Senate, where they can stymie legislation aimed at assisting big cities. State aid to big cities increased during the cooperative federalism era, with grants to cities quadrupling between the late 1950s and the late 1970s. However, as the national government scaled back its financial support to states, cities, which benefited disproportionately during the 1960s and 1970s, have started to suffer.

Making the Connection

The pride citizens take in their home state connections is inevitable in a republic that celebrates state identities through its formal institutions and structures. The Constitution of the United States guarantees that each state (from California, the most heavily populated, to the least populated states of Delaware, Wyoming, and Alaska) is represented by exactly two members of the U.S. Senate, through which all federal legislation must pass. The presidential election in 2000 came down to the vote count of one state (Florida), whose state-specific and county-specific rules, regulations, and practices figured prominently in the final outcome. Citizens continue to face a dizzying variety of rules and regulations when they move from one state to another. Sometimes the different rules governing citizens in two different states are more akin to the rules that govern different countries. Indeed, citizens of western New York State crossing by car into Canada often suffer far less culture shock than when they deplane in Texas, Louisiana, or another southern state.

State politicians often push the envelope on the legitimate bounds of state authority, both to win popularity among the state's citizens and to protect what they consider the state's best political interests. In recent years some states—New York and Pennsylvania, for example—have sought to impose "commuter taxes" on people who live in other states but work in their respective states. In an extreme case of state government action, Massachusetts, to protest human rights violations in the country of Burma (Myanmar) and to encourage reform in the nation's domestic policies, attempted to apply indirect economic pressure against Burma by prohibiting the state and its agents from purchasing goods or services from anyone doing business with the Union of Myanmar.

Are these modern federalism disputes any different from disputes over the reach of federal authority at other times in the nation's history? When Congress attempted to legislate against child labor in the early part of the twentieth century, it ran squarely into a tradition of federalism—enforced by a conservative Supreme Court—that prohibited the federal government from regulating business matters that occurred entirely within the manufacturing stage. When congressional leadership intervened in the Terri Schiavo case nearly a century later, it was once again rebuffed for entering into the kind of political thicket that has divided federal and state lawmakers throughout American history. In all such cases, advocates of state authority must stand strong against federal government's enhanced authority, or they risk being swept aside in the process. The United States of America has not always been the "obedient states" of America, but it is hard to imagine that the Founders would have intended the states to act otherwise.

The federal government's Marijuana Tax Act of 1937 effectively prohibited the use of cannabis as a prescription drug in the United States. Cannabis is the chemical in marijuana plants that provides the mind-altering effects which made it so popular as a recreational drug, and thus led to the 1937 law. However, cannabis has also been used for centuries for medicinal purposes. In fact, prior to the discovery of aspirin, cannabis was the most common drug used to treat headaches and other types of pain in the 19th century. The 1937 law was inspired by nonmedical uses of the drug, although it had the effect of banning it for medical purposes as well. At the time the federal law was passed, many in the medical community, including the American Medical Association, opposed restricting its use for medical purposes.

Marijuana joints can be prescribed to patients suffering extreme pain.

Today, the use of cannabis for medicinal purposes has become a controversial issue, debated throughout the American federal system. A number of states, including California, have recently passed laws that allow the use of cannabis for medical purposes. In 2002, Angel Raich, a Californian, was using home-grown marijuana prescribed by her physician, who had determined that without it, Raich's high level of pain could endanger her life. Federal agents from the Drug Enforcement Administration seized and destroyed the marijuana plants that Raich was using. Raich sued, claiming that her rights were violated and that the federal government could not rely on the commerce clause to trump California law in this instance. In *Gonzales v. Raich* (2005),* the U.S. Supreme Court ruled in favor of the federal government, holding that Congress indeed has the authority under the commerce clause to regulate activities such as marijuana use that have a substantial impact on interstate commerce.

At www.cengage.com/dautrich/americangovernment/2e, find the Politics Inter-Active link for details on why the use of cannabis in medical treatment remains a point of controversy in federal–state relations. Additionally, learn how the National Organization for the Reform of Marijuana Laws (NORML) works with states and policymakers advocating states' rights to allow the use of the drug for medicinal purposes. Consult as well the various links that relate to the "medical marijuana controversy" in historical, popular, and global perspective.

*545 U.S. 1 (2005).

Chapter Summary

★ SUMMARIZING WHAT YOU HAVE LEARNED ★

★ What Is Federalism?

- The American system of federalism links the central government in Washington, DC, to all fifty state governments. Sovereignty (the power of a government to regulate its affairs) resides concurrently in both the central government and the state governments.

- Federal systems of government can be distinguished from confederations (a simple alliance of independent states) or unitary systems of government (in which subunits such as states subordinate their aims to those of the central government).

- The Framers of the Constitution assigned to the national government matters of great national importance (including foreign and military affairs) and assigned to the states all local and internal matters, including those relating to the health, safety, and welfare of citizens.

- The supremacy clause of Article VI provides that the Constitution and all federal laws override conflicting provisions in state constitutions or state laws.

- The full faith and credit clause of Article IV requires that states respect each other's acts and official proceedings. Notwithstanding this clause, some states have attempted to prevent same-sex married couples from asserting their status as married couples across state lines.

★ The History of American Federalism

- Beginning in 1819, the Supreme Court under Chief Justice John Marshall substituted the Framers' vision of federalism (state-centered federalism) with its own national supremacy doctrine, which held that (1) states possess extremely limited sovereignty and (2) Congress was supreme within the sphere of its own constitutional powers.

- In *McCulloch v. Maryland* (1819), Chief Justice Marshall applied the national supremacy doctrine to uphold the authority of Congress to create a national bank even though the Constitution did not explicitly authorize Congress to do so; congressional authority arose from a broader interpretation of the necessary and proper clause in Article I, Section 8.

- Beginning in 1837, a system of "dual federalism," in which state authority under the Constitution served as a limit on congressional power, reigned for nearly a century until the New Deal period of the 1930s.

- The economic hardships of the Great Depression led to an activist federal government; facing these realities, the Supreme Court eventually abandoned its dual federalism principles in favor of a more expansive view of congressional authority.

- The era of "cooperative federalism" (1937–1990) barely limited Congress in the exercise of its powers. Through grants-in-aid and block grants, the federal government has placed huge sums of money at the disposal of states.

- Critics of cooperative federalism note that by attaching conditions to these funds, the federal government often coerces states and state officials to administer federal laws. The National Minimum Drinking Age Amendment, for example, required states to increase their drinking age to twenty-one or risk losing national highway funds.

- The rhetoric of the Reagan administration emphasized federal deregulation and increased state responsibilities; Reagan's Supreme Court appointees helped usher in a period of "new federalism" (1990–present) in which state sovereignty has once again been resuscitated to prevent certain forms of congressional coercion.

★ Why Federalism? Advantages and Disadvantages

- Federalism carries with it many advantages, including the accommodation of diverse interests in a large republic, the increased protection of individual liberty, and the encouragement of states to serve as "laboratories of democracy" where they might try out new policies. Because of their smaller size, state and local governments are also more flexible in adapting to changing circumstances.

- There are also disadvantages to a federalist system, including the problems caused by significant fiscal disparities among the states, the potential lack of accountability of officials to oversee certain undesirable programs, and the heavy reliance of federalism on unelected courts to define its boundaries and perimeters.

- Today the American system of federalism continues to impose significant financial burdens on states. Unfunded mandates from Congress require states to perform certain regulatory tasks at their own expense; the needs of the urban poor in big cities often outstrip city tax bases, and in recent years the federal government has scaled back its support of states and cities.

CourseMate

Key Terms

Block grants (p. 72)
Concurrent powers (p. 62)
Confederation (p. 62)
Cooperative federalism (p. 71)
Dual federalism (p. 71)
Federalism (p. 60)
Full faith and credit clause (p. 65)
Gibbons v. Ogden (1824) (p. 69)

Grants-in-aid (p. 72)
Layer cake federalism (p. 71)
Marble cake federalism (p. 71)
Martin v. Hunter's Lessee (1819) (p. 64)
McCulloch v. Maryland (1819) (p. 68)
National supremacy doctrine (p. 68)

Necessary and proper clause (p. 63)
Preemption (p. 64)
Reserved powers (p. 62)
Sovereignty (p. 60)
Supremacy clause (p. 63)
Unfunded mandate (p.81)
Unitary system of government (p. 62)

Resources

Important Books

Conlan, Timothy. *From New Federalism to Devolution: Twenty-five Years of Intergovernmental Reform.* Washington, DC: Brookings Institution Press, 1998.

Elazar, Daniel J. *Exploring Federalism.* Tuscaloosa: University of Alabama Press, 1987.

Noonan, John T. *Narrowing the Nation's Power: The Supreme Court Sides with the States.* Berkeley: University of California Press, 2002.

Peterson, Paul. *The Price of Federalism.* New York: 20th Century Fund, 1995.

Purcell, Edward A. *Originalism, Federalism and the American Constitutional Enterprise: A Historical Inquiry.* New Haven: Yale University Press, 2007.

Walker, David. *The Rebirth of Federalism: Slouching Toward Washington.* New York: Chatham House, 2000.

Internet Sources

http://www.loc.gov/law/help/guide/states.php (Library of Congress Web Page that offers an excellent resource for accessing state laws and constitutions, legislative Web sites, state executive branch laws, and state judicial rulings, as well as legal guides and other state sources).

http://www.statenews.org/ (Web site produced by the Council of State Governments with information about state issues and federalism)

http://www.nascio.org (National Association of State Information Resource Executives Web site)

4 Civil Liberties

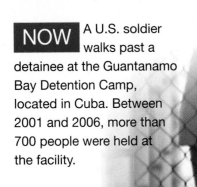

NOW A U.S. soldier walks past a detainee at the Guantanamo Bay Detention Camp, located in Cuba. Between 2001 and 2006, more than 700 people were held at the facility.

BRENNAN LINSLEY, POOL/AP PHOTO

THEN An alien suspected of having "treasonable leanings" is arrested in accordance with the Alien Act of 1798.

MULTIEDUCATOR, INC.

NOW & THEN

LEARNING OBJECTIVES
★ WHAT YOU WILL LEARN ★

The Bill of Rights: Origins and Evolution

* ★ Compare civil rights to civil liberties; describe the different categories of rights
* ★ Understand the origin of the Bill of Rights and the process of nationalizing those rights though the process of incorporation

Freedom of Religion and the Establishment Clause

* ★ Comprehend the free exercise clause and the rules for granting exemptions
* ★ Identify the rules governing the separation of church and state; recognize the tests for upholding government accommodations of religion

Free Expression Rights

* ★ Appreciate the theories that justify giving heightened protection to expression rights
* ★ Understand the scope of free speech rights, free press rights, and symbolic speech; learn the rules for exempting from protection lesser value speech, including libel and obscenity

The Second Amendment Right to Bear Arms

* ★ Identify the scope of the right to bear arms and the constitutional limits on gun control laws

The Rights of the Criminally Accused

* ★ Understand the scope of Fourth Amendment rights and the privacy issues raised by technology
* ★ Understand the rules against double jeopardy and the privilege against self-incrimination
* ★ Recognize the rights granted under the Sixth and Eighth Amendments

The Modern Right to Privacy

* ★ Understand the right of abortion and its scope under *Roe v. Wade*, and then later under *Planned Parenthood v. Casey*
* ★ Become familiar with the privacy rights that apply to government restrictions on sodomy and euthanasia

Civil Liberties during Wartime

Although Congress had made no formal declaration of war, calls for some form of military intervention remained fierce. Enemies from the other side of the world continued to pose a threat to the United States of America and its security. The nation enjoyed the natural protection of two large oceans and had long tried to steer clear of disputes among warring entities abroad that did not directly threaten U.S. interests. But the United States was now fighting an undeclared war, and the first-term president was determined not to be seen as weak. Congress had already approved far-reaching measures to deal with noncitizens who were perceived as threats. Due process rights for aliens were restricted, if not outright discarded. Though pressured by some to scale back these initiatives, the president and his administration left most of the measures intact. At least for the time being, civil liberties would be forced to take a backseat to national security interests, as they often do when a new president is trying to prove his bona fides as a protector of the nation's security.

CourseMate

NOW & THEN

BRENNAN LINSLEY, POOL/AP PHOTO

NOW Certainly many aspects of the scenario just described apply to the "war on terrorism" inherited by President Barack Obama when he took over the White House from President George W. Bush in January 2009. The Bush administration launched wars in Afghanistan and Iraq in the years following the September 11, 2001, terrorist attacks. Congress enacted the USA Patriot Act, authorizing the president to take numerous steps to prosecute the war, including giving the federal government broad new powers to detain suspects without hearings at the Guantanamo Military Base ("Gitmo") in Cuba and elsewhere. The law targeted aliens in particular, allowing authorities to hold noncitizens suspected of terrorism for seven days without charging them, and utilized a system of military tribunals with limited due process protections. When Barack Obama campaigned for the presidency in 2008, he promised to scale back many of these Bush-era measures. Yet as president, Obama quickly discovered the dangers of rolling back those measures in the absence of clear guarantees that national security would not be compromised. The new president announced plans to close Gitmo, but was soon thwarted in his efforts to do so by Congress. He halted the use of torture against suspected terrorists, but his administration continued the practice of indefinitely holding prisoners deemed "unlawful combatants," denying them habeas corpus rights. Nearly a decade after 9/11, the state of civil liberties in the United States was still fundamentally different than it had been before the terrorist attacks, even with President Obama in office.

THEN The difficult task of balancing civil liberties and national security interests during wartime is nothing new to American politics. The scenario described above also harkens back to 1798, when the federal government led by first-term President John Adams was gearing up for hostilities against the French dictator Napoleon Bonaparte. Napoleon's forces had already captured Rome and invaded Switzerland and Egypt earlier that year, and now Napoleon's aides intimated to American diplomats that a war against the United States might be next. Congress passed twenty acts to help consolidate the national defense against France and prepare for the possibility of invasion. The most controversial of these acts were the Alien Act, which authorized the president to deport from the United States all aliens suspected of "treasonable or secret" inclinations; the Alien Enemies Act, which allowed the president during wartime to arrest aliens subject to an enemy power; and the Sedition Act, which criminalized the publication of materials that brought the U.S. government into "disrepute." According to Adams biographer David McCullough, the second president was a reluctant partner in the controversial measures, which he neither asked for nor encouraged.[1] Angered by the treatment of his administration's diplomats and fearful of being viewed as weak on foreign policy, Adams did not oppose their passage, and he eventually signed them into law. And while he did not issue even one deportation order during his presidency, a handful of Republican editors were jailed for violating the Sedition Act. Such was the dilemma faced by an emotional president torn between the need to appear strong to outsiders, and his desire to abide by real constitutional limits.

MULTIEDUCATOR, INC.

n many other nations, restrictions on individual rights—especially during times of tension and upheaval—fail to solicit much intense resistance even from the political opposition. But the founding of the United States rested on a call for protecting the inalienable rights of all people, and the Bill of Rights, added to the U.S. Constitution in 1791, stands as a beacon against the potential tyranny of the majority. That was not always the case: the Bill of Rights has gathered true muscle only during the past seventy-five years. The challenge for so many is how to most effectively recognize the rights that are available to them. That challenge may be especially difficult during times of war, when individual rights come under the greatest threat, although perhaps with all the best intentions.

In this chapter we take up the subject of **civil liberties**—those specific individual rights that cannot be taken away by government and are guaranteed by the Constitution, such as the freedom of expression and the right of protection against self-incrimination. These individual rights, which are subject to formal interpretation from the courts and informal interpretation by those charged with their enforcement, are usually found either in the Bill of Rights or in subsequent amendments to the Constitution. Here we will focus primarily on the provision of rights guaranteed by the First, Second, and Fourth Amendments, and certain provisions within the Fifth, Sixth, Eighth, and Fourteenth Amendments.

Civil liberties may be distinguished from "civil rights" (sometimes called *equal rights*), a more modern term that refers specifically to the rights that members of various groups (racial, ethnic, sexual, and so on) have to equal treatment by government under the law and equal access to society's opportunities. This chapter deals with civil liberties, whereas Chapter 5 deals with civil rights.

The Bill of Rights: Origins and Evolution

What are rights? Strictly speaking, they are powers or privileges to which individuals are entitled. The central question is: where do rights come from, and are they absolute? *Natural rights*, which are based on the natural laws of human society, exist even in the absence of a formal government. Because natural rights theoretically transcend government entities, no authority can legitimately take them away. As Thomas Jefferson so eloquently stated in the Declaration of Independence, human beings are endowed with certain rights that are "inalienable," which means they cannot be denied by government.

Positive rights, by comparison, are granted by government authority and can usually be shaped and modified by that authority according to certain rules. An indigent person's right to a lawyer paid by the state in felony cases, for example, is a positive right. The term *liberty* refers to a right received from a higher authority, such as a government. As they articulated the basis for a new government, many of the Framers grappled with these and other terms in the nation's founding documents.

It is sometimes easy to forget that, as U.S. Supreme Court Justice Antonin Scalia once stated, individual rights are only "the fruits, rather than the roots, of the Constitutional tree."[2] The Constitution of the United States was intended to provide individuals with protection by guaranteeing a framework of limited government based on a theory of enumerated powers—the central government was allowed to exercise only those powers delegated to it by the Constitution. As James Madison wrote in Federalist No. 14, "the general government is not to be charged with the whole power of making and administering laws . . . its jurisdiction is limited to *certain enumerated objects*."[3] Thus by Madison's logic, separate provisions for the protection of individual rights were unnecessary; protection for those rights was inherent in the nature of limited government with enumerated powers. Because the government possessed no explicit power to infringe on those rights in the first place, they should never be in danger.

Yet Madison's logic ran up against an early American tradition that called for the explicit delineation of individual rights. The Declaration of Independence not only

Civil liberties

Those specific individual rights that are guaranteed by the Constitution and cannot be denied to citizens by government. Most of these rights are in the first ten amendments to the Constitution, known as the Bill of Rights.

Compare civil rights to civil liberties; describe the different categories of rights

formally recognized that certain "unalienable rights" exist; it also stated that when a government created by "the consent of the governed" fails to protect those rights, the people have the right to "alter or abolish such government." At the time of the founding, individual rights were considered an important element of America's political culture, because they embodied the principles that justified the American Revolution. Many of the former colonists wanted those rights clearly spelled out, lest there be any doubt of their significance to the new nation.

When the U.S. Constitution was created in 1787, most state governments already maintained a bill of rights to protect citizens against government encroachment. As the final draft of the Constitution was being debated at ratification conventions in the states, it became evident to the Constitution's supporters that its approval was going to require the inclusion of a more formal bill of rights to protect citizens against the federal government. George Mason and Patrick Henry of Virginia cast votes against ratification, in part because the Constitution lacked a formal statement of rights. Thomas Jefferson was also an early proponent of a bill of rights. To Madison's fears that such a declaration of rights could never be comprehensive, and thus might leave out something important, Jefferson replied: "Half a loaf is better than no bread."[4]

Eventually it was Madison who framed the list of rights that the first Congress proposed in 1789—ten amendments to the Constitution in all were ratified by the required three fourths of state legislatures. These are normally regarded as the Bill of Rights. While the first eight amendments guarantee specific rights, the Ninth and Tenth Amendments offer more general statements describing divisions of power between the federal and state governments under the Constitution.

The provisions listed in the Bill of Rights enjoyed little influence in late eighteenth-and early nineteenth-century America, because they were understood to be restrictions on the federal government only. The Supreme Court confirmed as much in the case of *Barron v. Baltimore* (1833),[5] which pitted a wharf owner against the city of Baltimore. City officials had lowered the water level around the wharves, causing him a significant economic loss. The wharf owner thus sued the city under the Fifth Amendment's "taking clause," which stated that no private property could be taken from an individual for public use without just compensation. But the Supreme Court dismissed the suit because at that time only the federal government could be held up to the standards of the Bill of Rights. In light of the dominant role state governments played in regulating individuals' daily lives during most of this period, the *Barron v. Baltimore* decision essentially reduced the Bill of Rights to paper guarantees that only occasionally provided protection for ordinary citizens.

ELIZA SNOW/ISTOCKPHOTO.COM

That all changed in the twentieth century, as the Supreme Court grew increasingly willing to protect individuals against intrusive state actions. Their instrument for doing so was the Fourteenth Amendment (ratified in 1868), which provided that no *state* could "deprive any person of life, liberty or property without due process of law." The Fourteenth Amendment had been passed immediately after the Civil War to protect freed slaves from discriminatory state laws. Yet at the beginning of the twentieth century and increasingly throughout the century, the Supreme Court by a process known as **incorporation** (or "nationalization") demonstrated a new willingness to hold state governments accountable to the Bill of Rights by utilizing the Fourteenth Amendment's vague requirement that states respect "due process." Specifically, the Court carefully considered

★ LO

Understand the origin of the Bill of Rights and the process of nationalizing those rights though the process of incorporation

Incorporation
The process by which the U.S. Supreme Court used the due process clause of the Fourteenth Amendment to make most of the individual rights guaranteed by the Bill of Rights also applicable to the states. Incorporation provided that state and local governments, as well as the federal government, could not deny these rights to citizens.

TABLE 4.1 Incorporating the Bill of Rights to Apply to the States

Provision (Amendment)	Year	Case
Protection from government taking property without just compensation (Fifth)	1897	*Chicago, Burl. & Quincy Rwy. v. Chicago*
Freedom of speech (First)	1925	*Gitlow v. New York*
Freedom of the press (First)	1931	*Near v. Minnesota*
Right to assistance of counsel in capital cases (Sixth)	1932	*Powell v. Alabama*
Freedom of assembly (First)	1937	*Delaware v. Van Arsdall*
Free exercise of religion (First)	1940	*Cantwell v. Connecticut*
Protection from establishment of religion (First)	1947	*Everson v. Board of Education*
Right to public trial (Sixth)	1948	*In re Oliver*
Right against unreasonable search and seizure (Fourth)	1949	*Wolf v. Colorado*
Exclusionary rule (Fourth & Fifth)	1961	*Mapp v. Ohio*
Protection against cruel and unusual punishment (Eighth)	1962	*Robinson v. California*
Right to paid counsel for indigents in felony cases (Sixth)	1963	*Gideon v. Wainwright*
Right against self-incrimination (Fifth)	1964	*Malloy v. Hogan*
Right to confront witnesses (Sixth)	1965	*Pointer v. Texas*
Right to an impartial jury (Sixth)	1966	*Parker v. Gladden*
Right to compulsory process to obtain witnesses (Sixth)	1967	*Washington v. Texas*
Right to speedy trial (Sixth)	1967	*Klopfer v. North Carolina*
Right to jury in nonpetty criminal cases (Sixth)	1968	*Duncan v. Louisiana*
Right against double jeopardy (Fifth)	1969	*Benton v. Maryland*
Right to keep and bear arms (Second)	2010	*McDonald v. Chicago*

individual clauses from the Bill of Rights, and if the right was deemed fundamental enough, the Court held that no state could legitimately ignore the right without depriving an individual of the right to "life, liberty and property, without due process of law." By this incorporation process, states were required to live up to the dictates of the First Amendment free speech clause beginning in 1925, the Fourth Amendment right against unreasonable searches and seizures beginning in 1961, and the Sixth Amendment right to a speedy trial beginning in 1967. (See Table 4.1.) Slowly but surely the provisions of the Bill of Rights were incorporated by the Fourteenth Amendment to apply to state governments as well as to the federal government.

By 1969, nearly every provision of the Bill of Rights had been applied to state governments through the incorporation doctrine. At present, however, there are still several provisions of the Bill of Rights that theoretically provide protection against the federal government only:

- The Third Amendment safeguard against the involuntary quartering of troops
- The Fifth Amendment requirement that defendants be indicted by a grand jury
- The Seventh Amendment guarantee of a trial by jury in civil cases
- The Eighth Amendment prohibition against excessive bail and fines

Virtually all other provisions contained within the first eight amendments of the Constitution are considered applicable to all state governments and to all local governments within the states in exactly the same manner as they are applicable to the federal government.

Freedom of Religion and the Establishment Clause

THE FIRST AMENDMENT: Congress shall make no law respecting an establishment of religion, or prohibiting the free exercise thereof....

Although the first words of the Bill of Rights speak to the freedom of religion, the actual rights guaranteeing religious freedom did not become widespread until the latter half of the twentieth century. In early America, Protestantism played a highly influential role in public life, and the First Amendment was intended to provide a limited barrier against its influence. In 1802, Thomas Jefferson described the First Amendment as erecting a "wall of separation" between church and state,[6] but that metaphor captured his hopes more than the reality of the time. Although there existed no official church of the United States, government aid to religion—in particular to certain Protestant sects—stood little chance of being overturned by a court on constitutional grounds. And for much of American history, minority religious groups such as Mormons, Jehovah's Witnesses, and the Amish were forced to change or abandon some of their religious practices whenever public policy conflicted with them. By the 1940s, however, American public life had grown increasingly secular, and application of the First Amendment's guarantees of freedom of religion was transformed. Even today the interest in accommodating religion continues to run up against the desire to create a "wall of separation" emphasizing government neutrality.

The Free Exercise of Religion

The **free exercise clause** of the First Amendment bans government laws that prohibit the free exercise of religion. Debate over the clause has largely focused on whether government laws can force adherents of a certain religion to engage in activities that are prohibited by their religious beliefs or prevent them from performing acts that are compelled by their religious beliefs. During the heart of World War II, the Supreme Court in *West Virginia v. Barnette* (1943)[7] ordered school officials to reinstate the children of Jehovah's Witnesses who had been suspended for refusing to salute the American flag in their public school classrooms. Yet although those children could claim legitimate religious objections to the law (the Jehovah's Witnesses' creed forbids them from saluting any "graven image"), they also could claim more generally the right of free expression—those who disagreed with the U.S. government were free to withhold displays of public support for the nation's symbol. It remained for the Court in subsequent years to sort out what rights of religious freedom might exist under the free exercise clause.

Seventh Day Adventists and the Refusal to Work. In the landmark case of *Sherbert v. Verner* (1963),[8] the Supreme Court ordered the State of South Carolina to pay unemployment benefits to a Seventh-Day Adventist who refused to work on Saturdays. Even though the state's unemployment laws required that she make herself available for work on Saturday, the Court refused to apply that law to this worker because Saturday was the Seventh-Day Adventists' sabbath. Although the state could provide legitimate reasons for refusing to pay her benefits (guarding the unemployment insurance fund against running low, for example), the Supreme Court declared that only a *compelling state interest* could justify denying her such an exception on the basis of religion. What interest counts as "compelling"? Although no precise definition is available, the Court has held that administrative convenience is not compelling; rather, the Court must be convinced that the government program (whether the draft, Social Security, unemployment benefits, and so on) would be significantly undermined by religious exemptions in order to say that the government's interest is compelling.

Comprehend ★ LO
the free exercise clause and the rules for granting exemptions

Free exercise clause
The religious freedom clause in the First Amendment that denies government the ability to prohibit the free exercise of religion. Debate over the clause has largely focused on whether government laws can force adherents of a certain religion to engage in activities that are prohibited by their religious beliefs or prevent them from performing acts that are compelled by their religious beliefs.

The Amish at work moving haystacks. In 1972 the Supreme Court ruled that Amish children could not be forced to attend school after the eighth grade, as it would undermine the religion's emphasis on "community welfare" and "learning by doing."

The Amish and Mandatory School Attendance. Continuing to accept exemptions for religious reasons, the Supreme Court in *Wisconsin v. Yoder* (1972)[9] held that members of the Amish religion were not required to send their children to school after the eighth grade. Even though Wisconsin law compelled high school attendance, the Court ruled that the enforcement of that law would undermine Amish religious principles, which include the value of "learning through doing" and support for "community welfare" over all other interests.

The Mormons and Polygamy Laws. Up until the late nineteenth century, a central tenet of the Mormon Church, also called the Church of Jesus Christ of Latter-Day Saints, required some of its adherents to practice polygamy—the act of having multiple spouses "when circumstances would permit." During the 1870s, many Mormons were prosecuted under a federal antibigamy statute that applied to federal territories, including the new Utah territory where many Mormons had settled. George Reynolds, secretary of one of the founders of the Mormon Church in America as well as the founder of Brigham Young University, brought suit in 1878, challenging the law as destructive to the Mormon Church, and thus a violation of the free exercise clause of the First Amendment.

The Supreme Court, in a unanimous decision, rejected Reynolds's argument that the First Amendment protects plural marriage. According to the Court, religious practices that impair the "public interest" do not receive constitutional protection; such practices were to be distinguished from religious "beliefs," which the government had no power to regulate. *Reynolds v. United States*[10] remains the law today, and polygamy is now banned in all fifty states. Additionally, since 1890 the Mormon Church has formally renounced the practice of polygamy by its members.

Illegal Drug Use and the Smith Case. In 1990, the Supreme Court adopted a new approach to the free exercise of religion, one that dramatically diminished the

AP PHOTO/AMY SANCETTA

likelihood that future religious exemptions might be granted. Two Native Americans were dismissed from their jobs as drug rehabilitation counselors when it was discovered that they had ingested the illegal drug peyote as part of their tribe's religious rituals. Because their drug use violated the Oregon criminal code, the two men were subsequently denied unemployment compensation. The Supreme Court ruled in *Employment Division v. Smith* (1990)[11] that the state's legitimate interest in maintaining its unemployment insurance fund at a high level outweighed the Native Americans' religious rights and thus that it could deny the two men unemployment benefits. State governments may choose to accommodate otherwise illegal acts done in pursuit of religious beliefs, but they are not *required* to do so.[12]

Today *Smith* remains the rule for judicial interpretation of free exercise cases: instead of being forced to show a *compelling* government interest (which is extremely hard to do), a government interested in applying its neutral laws over religious objections may do so based on any *legitimate state interest* it might claim. What is a legitimate state interest? The bar here is quite low; only an arbitrary or irrational objective by government will fail the test of legitimacy. The Religious Freedom Restoration Act passed by Congress in 1993 attempted to reverse the Court's holding in *Smith* and revert to the more liberal rules established in the *Sherbert* and *Yoder* decisions. However, the Supreme Court invalidated the religious freedom law in 1997. The Supreme Court—and not the Congress—holds the lever of power in the debate over religious exemptions. And, at least for the time being, that means the courts generally will not grant such exemptions.

The Establishment Clause

Even more controversial than the debate over religious exemptions from public policies has been the battle over what role religion may play in American public life under the **establishment clause**, which prohibits the government from enacting laws "respecting an establishment of religion." Most Americans take it for granted that during the holiday season they will see Christmas decorations prominently displayed in government buildings, in front of the town hall, and in public squares. But what about nativity scenes? Menorahs? The Ten Commandments? What types of religious activities and symbols are considered acceptable in public places, and which ones run afoul of the First Amendment, whose prohibition of government "respecting an establishment of religion" has been interpreted to mean creating a "wall of separation" between church and state?

Modern debates over the proper role religion may play under the establishment clause generally divide advocates into two camps. Those who advocate a strict dividing line between church and state support a principle of "separation," which holds that government should have no involvement whatsoever with religious practices, although religion remains free to flourish privately on its own, with its own resources.[13] Opponents of strict separation argue instead for the principle of "accommodation," which holds that government neutrality toward religion requires only that it treat all religions equally. Government should be free to aid and subsidize religious activities as long as it does so fairly across different religions, and aids comparable nonreligious activities as well. In recent decades, the Supreme Court has moved from a position of especially strict separation to one that shifts back and forth between principles of separation and accommodation.

Historically Accepted Practices. Certain religious practices have been a part of political and public life for generations, and the Supreme Court has generally allowed such activities to continue. Congress opens each legislative session with a prayer from a clergy member, chaplains serve in religious capacities with the U.S. armed forces, and U.S. currency proclaims "In God We Trust." Even the Supreme Court opens every court session to a marshal's bellowing pronouncement: "God save this honorable court!" All of these are considered acceptable practices, products of the American historical tradition. But not all religious displays on public property will be automatically deemed as "historically accepted practices." On occasion, the

Identify the rules governing the separation of church and state; recognize the tests for upholding government accommodations of religion

★ LO

Establishment clause
The clause in the First Amendment that prohibits government from enacting any law "respecting an establishment of religion." Separationist interpretations of this clause affirm that government should not support any religious activity. Accommodationists say that support for a religion is legal provided that all religions are equally supported.

Court has ordered the removal of nativity scenes and other religious displays during Christmastime.

In Kentucky, versions of the Ten Commandments were posted on the walls of several county courthouses. In Texas, a six-foot-high monolith inscribed with the Ten Commandments sits among numerous other monuments and historical markers outside the state capitol building commemorating the "people, ideals, and events that compose Texan identity." Do these public displays of the Ten Commandments, which feature such statements as "Thou shalt have no other gods before me" and "Thou shalt not take the name of the Lord thy God in vain," violate the establishment clause of the First Amendment?

In a set of cases handed down in 2005, the Supreme Court ordered the Kentucky courthouses to remove their displays, but allowed the Texas display to remain standing. In explaining its different approach to these cases, the Court ruled that even though the Ten Commandments are inherently religious, their placement in a monument outside the state capitol is an essentially "passive" act, whereas their placement within the courthouse had been motivated by a desire on the part of legislators to advance religion. Of course the members of the U.S. Supreme Court need not be reminded that a frieze in their own courtroom depicts Moses holding tablets exhibiting a portion of the secularly phrased Commandments in the company of seventeen other lawgivers. Perhaps the Court believes that there is little risk that such a depiction of Moses would strike an observer as evidence of the federal government violating religious neutrality.

Religious Prayers in Public School Classrooms. The public school classroom has always been viewed as a unique context in which to assess claims that the government has violated the establishment clause. Judges and politicians alike assume that students—particularly elementary school students—have not yet formed firm beliefs about religion and thus may be susceptible to even subtle forms of religious coercion. Public officials interested in promoting religion in society as a whole have focused on the school as a place to encourage religious practices; as a consequence, school policies touching on the subject of religion have undergone serious scrutiny in the courts.

In 1962, the Supreme Court in *Engel v. Vitale*[14] invalidated the New York public schools' policy of having each class recite a specified nondenominational religious prayer each day. That prayer, which proclaimed in nondenominational terms, "Almighty God, we acknowledge our dependence upon thee," was held to be a violation of the First Amendment's prohibition against the establishment of religion. In *Abington School District v. Schempp* (1963)[15] the Court refused to allow spiritual Bible readings in public

A Ten Commandments monument is moved outside the Alabama Judicial Building in Montgomery, 2003.

TAMI CHAPPELL/
REUTERS/LANDOV

school classrooms, and in *Wallace v. Jaffree* (1985)[16] it outlawed "moments of silence" authorized by a government officials to encourage religious prayer during those moments. The Court held that in neither of those instances was the government acting with a "secular purpose"—one not grounded in a desire to "advance religion." These decisions are especially difficult to enforce, as the closed nature of most public school classrooms allows prayer to escape the notice of those seeking to enforce these landmark decisions. And it remains unclear whether the general ban on religious prayer in public schools extends to the teaching of the Ten Commandments, among other issues.

Despite these seemingly clear rulings against school prayer, some teachers continue to lead students in prayer in public school classrooms across the country. Defiance has become widespread in some instances, forcing one court in Alabama to forbid prayer in schools throughout the state fully thirty-five years after *Engel v. Vitale* invalidated the practice. Anecdotal evidence of violations continue to mount as well: in one highly publicized case, officials in DeKalb County, Georgia, helped lead a religious revival at a public high school in admitted disobedience of the Supreme Court. Defiance persists in part because public schools are so rarely challenged in court for their violations. Community sentiment has also played an influential role in squelching potential litigation, as dissenting parents quickly realize that only continued and expensive litigation over many years will bring a defiant school into line.

© 2012 CENGAGE LEARNING

Financial Aid and the *Lemon* Test. During the last several decades, government officials seeking to promote religion as part of the educational process have expanded the variety and scope of their efforts. Many initiatives have occurred in public schools—provisions for school prayer recitations, released time programs (allowing students to visit religious schools for instruction during normal school hours), and the teaching of subjects with religious content, such as creationism. Efforts to provide religious private schools that teach students full-time with public funds have met with some recent success. In 2000, the Supreme Court approved of a program to provide government-funded computers and other teaching aids to certain parochial schools. Two years later, the Court in *Zelman v. Simmons-Harris* (2002)[17] upheld a system of private school vouchers, whereby parents are given coupons that can be used to pay tuition at private schools, including parochial schools. Such programs continue to be a source of heated policy debate between proponents of separation and accommodation.

Since 1971, issues involving the separation of church and state have often been governed by the ***Lemon* test** articulated by the Supreme Court in the landmark decision of *Lemon v. Kurtzman* (1971).[18] Under the test, government aid to public or private schools is considered unconstitutional if it fails to meet three separate criteria: "First, the statute must have a secular [that is, not religious] purpose; second, its principal or primary effect must be one that neither advances nor inhibits religion; finally, the statute must not foster 'an excessive government entanglement with religion.'" The test has been criticized by many, including a number of the Supreme Court justices, who assert that its requirements are so stringent that literally all deliberate government accommodation of religion is presumptively invalid. The Court has never renounced the test, and it continues to play a role in the consideration of various types of financial aid.

Prayers at Graduation Ceremonies and Football Games. In recent years, some school officials have attempted to facilitate student prayers in school contexts outside of the classroom. Those efforts have met with little success. In *Lee v. Weisman* (1992),[19] the Supreme Court ordered a Providence, Rhode Island, middle school to stop its practice of permitting prayers to be read at the school's graduation ceremony, even though attendance was voluntary. Eight years later, in *Santa Fe v. Doe* (2000),[20] the Court ruled that a student-led prayer before a football game at a Texas public high school violated the separation of church and state. The Court believed

Lemon test

The legal test that determines if a government statute aiding public or private schools is an unconstitutional violation of the establishment clause. The statute is unconstitutional if the statute has no secular purpose, if its principal or primary effect advances or inhibits religion, or if it fosters "an excessive government entanglement with religion."

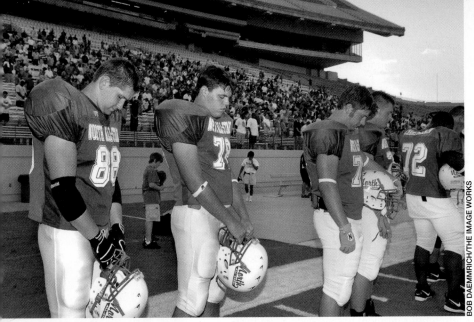
Group prayer before a high school football game in Austin, Texas.

that both practices forced all of those present to participate in an act of religious worship. In addition, these practices could have been interpreted as state endorsements of prayer, which is unconstitutional.

The debate over the role religion should play in American public life remains a highly charged topic. Public schools especially will continue to be a focus of intense interest, as the proponents of a greater role for religion seek ever more creative ways to combine the educational process with efforts at spirituality and religious participation.

★ LO Appreciate the theories that justify giving heightened protection to expression rights

Free Expression Rights

THE FIRST AMENDMENT: Congress shall make no law . . . abridging the freedom of speech, or of the press. . . .

Among the many civil liberties guaranteed by the Bill of Rights, the First Amendment rights of free speech and press enjoy especially revered status. That wasn't always the case. The Sedition Act of the late 1790s egregiously restricted speech that negatively reflected on the Federalists who were in power; during the Civil War, the Lincoln administration took harsh action against those who sought to undermine the Union's cause. Today, nearly all politicians openly celebrate rights of free expression, at least in the abstract. For many, these rights of free expression serve as a cornerstone for all other individual rights, facilitating the more effective realization of such freedoms as the right to vote and participate in the democratic process.

What accounts for the lofty status of free expression rights in the American political system? Several theories have been offered to justify this high level of respect:

- **"The marketplace of ideas,"** a phrase coined by Supreme Court Justice Oliver Wendell Holmes in 1919, is a metaphor for the premise that the best test of truth is the free trade of ideas; only through such free exchange and presentation of all arguments, valid and invalid, can the truth prevail. To ensure a robust "marketplace of ideas," government restrictions on speech must be kept to a minimum.

- **Self-governance** is another frequently cited justification for protecting free expression. Speech is considered essential to representative government, because it provides the mechanism by which citizens deliberate on important issues of public policy. Free speech also serves as a means for ordinary citizens to check the abuse of power by public officials.

- **Self-fulfillment.** Some philosophers have emphasized the importance of free speech and expression as a means of achieving individual self-fulfillment. The human capacity to create ideas and express oneself is thus considered central to human existence; government restrictions on free speech invariably threaten that human capacity. Such a justification of free speech rights extends as well to the protection of music, pictures, and other forms of artistic expression.

- **A "safety valve."** Free speech also serves a critical role in encouraging adaptability and flexibility according to the changing circumstances in society. If the suppression of free speech forces citizens to adopt more extreme means of enacting change such as violence, the promotion of free speech provides an essential mechanism for balancing the need for order with cries for reform.

BOB DAEMMRICH/THE IMAGE WORKS

Each of the above justifications for free speech protection may be subject to legitimate criticisms as well. But for better or worse, the First Amendment's protection of free expression today enjoys a special status in our constitutional system, even though that was not always the case.

Free Speech during the Early Twentieth Century: The Clear and Present Danger Test

The modern status of free expression rights is a far cry from the low level of protection the First Amendment afforded to free speech nearly a century ago. Many of the early cases pitting dissenting speakers against the government came before the Court when tensions were great—first during wartime, then at the height of the Cold War when fears of communist infiltration in American society gripped many ordinary Americans. In neither instance did free speech fare well.

The Supreme Court gave birth to the "clear and present danger" test in *Schenck v. United States* (1919).[21] In 1917, with the United States readying for active participation in World War I, Charles Schenck, a general secretary for the American Socialist Party, was tried and convicted for distributing leaflets arguing that the military draft was immoral. Although the pamphlet posed little danger of interfering with the draft, the Supreme Court refused to release Schenck from jail. Writing the majority opinion for a unanimous court, Justice Oliver Wendell Holmes stated that there was in fact "a clear and present danger" that the pamphlet could bring about the damage being claimed by the government.

In practice, the clear and present danger test soon became a hammer on speakers' rights rather than a shield against government suppression. Under the doctrine, members of the Socialist and Communist parties were tried and punished for participating in organizational meetings or declaring allegiance to their party's principles. Justice Holmes was clearly alarmed by the legacy his *Schenck* decision had wrought; in subsequent decisions he modified his earlier view by insisting that the present danger must relate to an "immediate evil" and a specific action. But Holmes was now in the minority, and there was little he could do to stop the momentum. During the late 1940s and early 1950s, when the fear of communism in the United States was reaching a fever pitch, members of the Communist Party were convicted for their advocacy of sedition. In *Dennis v. United States* (1951),[22] the Supreme Court gave a measure of credibility to this red scare when it upheld the convictions of numerous communist defendants for "teaching and advocating the overthrow and destruction of the Government of the United States."

The Warren Court and the Rise of the "Preferred Freedoms" Doctrine

By the late 1950s, fears of subversion and communist infiltration in the United States were beginning to subside. However, it was the ascension of former California Governor Earl Warren to the position of chief justice of the United States in 1953 that eventually changed the Court's free speech doctrine from one that offered little protection to dissenting speakers into one that protected even the most unpopular speakers against suppression by the majority. The Warren Court brought about this change by embracing a doctrine first articulated by Justice Harlan Fiske Stone in 1938. In a footnote to the otherwise unnotable case of *United States v. Carolene Products* (1938),[23] Justice Stone declared that various civil liberties guaranteed in the Bill of Rights, including the right of free expression, enjoyed a "preferred position" in constitutional law. Stone's explicit support for this preferred freedoms doctrine did not take immediate hold. Yet in the 1960s, when new social tensions such as the battle over civil rights and resistance to the Vietnam War threatened to wreak havoc on civil liberties, the Warren Court issued several key decisions that shattered any possibility the government might be able to suppress the exercise of free speech rights under the Constitution, as it had in the earlier part of the century.

★ LO

Understand the scope of free speech rights, free press rights, and symbolic speech; learn the rules for exempting from protection lesser value speech, including libel and obscenity

AMERICAN GOVERNMENT In Global Perspective

The Leading Middle East Network Weighs in on "Gitmo"

The U.S. government has leased the Guantanamo Bay Naval Base, located on the Southeastern shore of Cuba, since the Cuban-American Treaty of 1903. Beginning in 2002, the naval base became home to a military prison for "unlawful combatants" in the war on terrorism who do not receive protection under the Geneva conventions. Amnesty International and the United Nations—believing the prison to be the source of fundamental rights abuses—have requested that the facility be shut down. President Obama issued an executive order to that effect on January 22, 2009, but his order was thwarted by Congress, which has forbidden the transfer of detainees to other facilities in the United States.

Al Jazeera is an Arabic satellite television network headquartered in Doha, Qatar. It has caused controversy in the Arab world due to its willingness to air competing views. Half a year into Obama's presidency, Al Jazeera provided a voice to the legal charity Reprieve concerning the Gitmo debate:

When Obama became president [ ] and said he would close the prison, 34-year-old Ayman al-Shurafa was still being held on the US naval base but should have been one of the first detainees to leave. Although he had admitted to attending a training camp in Afghanistan, the Pentagon assessed that he posed no threat and should be released. But in the strange world of Guantanamo Bay, degrees of innocence and guilt are

only part of the story. Al-Shurafa's case helps to explain why, six months after ordering the closure of Guantanamo Bay, Obama has made so little tangible progress to this end—only 11 of the 242 prisoners he inherited from the Bush administration have been released during his tenure.

In the midst of the political and diplomatic wrangling over Guantanamo's closure, it is easy to forget that at the centre of this story are 229 human beings. Cori Crider, an attorney from the UK-based legal charity Reprieve, says many of the prisoners are losing faith in Obama's promises. "Many of them thought the new administration might finally be the light at the end of their tunnel, but most of them have started to lose hope again," she says. Just last month one of the Yemeni prisoners, Mohammad al-Hanashi, could take no more and committed suicide. It was a stark reminder that every day Guantanamo Bay remains open increases the human cost of a system built on an inherent contradiction— that even if you are found innocent, you are still treated as if you were guilty.

Source: Aljazeera.net, July 22, 2009.

In 1969, the Supreme Court in *Brandenburg v. Ohio* (1969)[24] abandoned the clear and present danger test and replaced it with a test that was much more protective of free speech. A Ku Klux Klan rally in Cincinnati, Ohio, featured numerous figures in white hoods uttering phrases that demeaned African Americans and Jews. The principal speaker had argued that some form of vengeance be taken against both groups. The group's leader was convicted under a law criminalizing the advocacy of violence. The Supreme Court overturned his conviction. In the process, it declared a new "imminent danger" test for such speech: first, is the speech "directed to inciting or producing imminent lawless action" and second, is the advocacy *likely* to produce such action? Few of the speakers jailed in the previous half century for seditious speech could have been convicted under this new standard.[25]

The preferred freedoms doctrine also offered protection to those exercising their rights of free expression in other contexts—to writers and publishers, filmmakers and protesters. Indeed, it provided a foundation for the protection of such modern activities as the dissemination of information on the Internet. Even speakers and publishers of certain categories of speech that have not traditionally enjoyed First Amendment protection—obscenity and libel, for example—soon discovered that the preferred freedoms doctrine provided protection for their activities.

The Freedom of the Press, Libel Laws, and Prior Restraints

Freedom of the press enjoys a long and storied tradition in the United States. Well before the American Revolution or the drafting of the Constitution, the trial of newspaper publisher John Peter Zenger in 1734 on charges of libel laid the foundation for robust press freedoms. **Libel** is the crime of printing or disseminating false statements that harm someone. Zenger was accused of attacking the corrupt administration of New York's colonial governor in his weekly newspaper. When he was acquitted on the basis of his lawyer's argument that he had printed true facts, Zenger's case helped to establish the legal principle that truth would serve as a defense to any libel action. In the late 1790s, after many Republican editors and publishers had been jailed under the highly controversial Sedition Act, public distaste for the act helped to catapult Thomas Jefferson and his Republican Party into power in the election of 1800.

Libel
Printing or disseminating false statements that harm someone.

Despite the general recognition of the importance of the press, newspapers traditionally enjoyed few special privileges under the law. Specifically, individuals whose reputations were harmed were free to bring libel suits against newspapers and other publications without any implications for the First Amendment. That all changed in 1964 with the landmark decision of *New York Times v. Sullivan*.[26] A Montgomery, Alabama, police commissioner sued the *New York Times* in March 1960 for an advertisement the newspaper had published. The ad—charging the existence of "an unprecedented wave of terror" against blacks in Montgomery—had been signed by several black clergymen. In its description of events that had transpired, the ad also contained some minor inaccuracies. Although the police commissioner was unable to prove that he had suffered any actual economic harm, he still sought a $500,000 judgment against the *Times*. But the Supreme Court refused to allow the official to claim damages, and in the process articulated a much more stringent test to be met by public officials suing for libel: they must prove that the newspapers had published false facts with malice (bad intentions) or reckless disregard for the truth (they ignored clear evidence of contrary facts).[27]

In subsequent years, the *New York Times v. Sullivan* decision has applied to public figures as well as public officials; today a libel lawsuit brought by any famous person—whether it's the president of the United States, Tiger Woods, or Julia Roberts—must prove that the newspaper or magazine in question not only printed false facts, but did so either with "malicious intent" or in "reckless disregard" for the truth. Of course, an important question remains: Who is a public figure? This was the question raised in the case of Richard Jewell, a security guard suspected of setting off a bomb in Centennial Park in Atlanta, Georgia, during the 1996 Summer Olympics. Two people died in the explosion. Jewell was initially portrayed as a hero for his role in discovering the bomb, alerting authorities, and evacuating bystanders from the immediate vicinity. But when Jewell's status changed from hero to suspect, the resulting media coverage of the criminal investigation caused Jewell and his family considerable anguish. Although the investigation ultimately cleared Jewell of any involvement in the bombing, his reputation had been harmed enough that he decided to sue the *Atlanta Journal-Constitution*, which had rushed to judgment against him.

Jewell's entire lawsuit rested on the premise that he was (and continued to be) a private figure. Unlike public figures who had to prove the libeling newspaper had demonstrated a "reckless disregard for the truth," private figures seeking monetary damages need only show that the newspaper was "negligent." Immediately following the bomb explosion, but before he became a suspect, Jewell granted one photo shoot and ten interviews to the media, including *Larry King Live* and the *Today* show. During the course of these interviews, Jewell repeatedly stated that he had spotted a suspicious bag after a group of rowdy, college-age men had left the park, and announced that he had matched one of the men to a composite sketch. These interviews proved Jewell's undoing, as both a trial judge and the Georgia Court of Appeals ruled that his media activities meant he had "voluntarily assumed a position of influence in the controversy," and thus was a public figure for purposes of his lawsuit. Jewell never received any monetary relief from the *Atlanta Journal-Constitution*.

Prior restraint
The government's requirement that material be approved by government before it can be published.

Whereas libel laws punish publications after the fact, a **prior restraint** imposes a limit on publication *before* the material has actually been published. Securing a prior restraint is very difficult for government to accomplish. In the *Pentagon Papers Case* (1971),[28] the Supreme Court refused the U.S. government's request to stop the *Washington Post* and the *New York Times* from publishing a classified study of U.S. decision making about the Vietnam War. The courts have made it very difficult for government to implement a prior restraint of expression. In only the rarest of cases, such as the publication of information about troop movements during wartime, has government been able to block the publication of a story.

Obscenity and Pornography

Despite the exalted status free expression rights enjoy under the Constitution, obscenity has long been recognized as an exception to the rule. Even through the so-called sexual revolution of the 1960s and 1970s, the Supreme Court continued to adhere to the premise that truly obscene speech—words or publications that tend to violate accepted standards of decency by their very lewdness—may under certain circumstances be regulated. When asked how he would define obscene pornography, Justice Potter Stewart in 1964 uttered his now celebrated phrase: "I can't define it, but I know it when I see it." Stewart's statement captures the often confusing state of obscenity law in the United States. The First Amendment does not allow governments simply to ban all sexually explicit materials. But what types of materials can be banned? Is all pornography to be considered "obscene"?

Poster advertising *Lady Chatterley's Lover*. The film was based on a book that was the target of a New York state ban during the 1950s.

In *Miller v. California* (1973),[29] the Supreme Court created the modern legal test for determining what sexually explicit materials may be legitimately subject to regulation under the Constitution. According to the Court, a work is obscene if *all* of these three conditions are met:

1. The average person applying contemporary community standards would think that the work (taken as a whole) appeals to the "prurient" (that is, lustful) interest.

2. The works depicts sexual conduct in a patently offensive way.

3. The work taken as a whole lacks "serious literary, artistic, political or scientific value."

This third condition has come to be known as the **SLAPS test** (derived from taking the first letter of each word in the quoted phrase). In theory, adherence to the SLAPS test allows a jury to apply its own conception of "contemporary community standards" and thus ban relatively innocent sexual materials. In practice, however, courts have found very few materials able to survive the SLAPS test (after all, who is to say what possesses "artistic value"?). None of the above rules apply to child pornography, which enjoys no First Amendment protection whatsoever under the Constitution.

The rise of the Internet as a medium of communication in recent years has caused even more confusion as to what types of obscenity and/or pornography can be regulated. In *Reno v. ACLU* (1997)[30] the Supreme Court invalidated a federal law passed to protect minors from "indecent" and "patently offensive" communications on the Internet. The Court feared that in denying minors access to potentially harmful speech, the law had suppressed a large amount of speech that adults have a constitutional right to receive. Still, the question of how to restrict sexually explicit speech on the Internet will remain an issue for years to come.

SLAPS test
A standard that courts established to determine if material is obscene based in part on whether the material has serious literary, artistic, political, or scientific value. If it does, then the material is not obscene.

Symbolic Speech and the Flag-Burning Controversy

When school officials in Des Moines, Iowa, suspended two students for wearing black armbands in protest of the Vietnam War in the 1960s, they claimed they were not restricting free speech rights at all—rather, the students were engaging in conduct that could be regulated by authorities.[31] The Supreme Court in 1969 disagreed and the students were vindicated;[32] but the line between speech and conduct remains difficult to draw. Protesters often engage in disruptive activities that make powerful statements about important issues of public policy. They may camp out in public parks overnight to bring attention to the plight of the homeless, or burn their draft cards as a statement of opposition to a war. Are such forms of **symbolic speech** protected by the First Amendment?

Symbolic speech
Nonspoken forms of speech that might be protected by the First Amendment, such as flag burning, wearing armbands at school to protest a war, or camping out in public parks to protest the plight of the homeless.

In 1968, the Supreme Court in *United States v. O'Brien*[33] refused to allow a Vietnam War protester to burn his draft card in violation of federal law. That case introduced three criteria for determining whether the regulation of symbolic speech may be justified:

1. The government interest must be valid and important.

2. The interest must be unrelated to the suppression of free speech.

3. The restriction should be no greater than is essential to the furtherance of that interest.

In *United States v. O'Brien*, the key was motive: the Court believed the government actions were motivated by the need to

HULTON ARCHIVE/GETTY IMAGES

Antiwar demonstrators burn their draft cards on the steps of the Pentagon during the Vietnam War.

Crossing the Bounds of Contemporary Tastes

With regard to obscenity, the First Amendment has often provided a measure of protection against attempts by communities to impose the majority's tastes on the minority. As social mores have evolved—and the bounds of tastelessness have been stretched—the courts have required governmental entities to go beyond oversimplified pleas for decency and good taste in their efforts to regulate sexually explicit material. At the same time, courts remain unwilling to ban any and all forms of regulating obscenity. As a consequence, court rulings attempt to find the fine line between tasteless speech and social mores.

In the late 1950s, a New York State licensing agency denied a movie company a license to show the film *Lady Chatterley's Lover* in the state. Although the movie's depiction of sexuality would be considered tame even by 1950s standards, the film focused at its core on an adulterous relationship, accompanied by the suggestion that adultery may be "right and desirable" for certain people under certain circumstances. The state banned *Lady Chatterley's Lover*

as an "immoral film" that portrayed sexual immorality as "desirable, acceptable or proper." But in 1959, the Supreme Court reversed the licensing decision as a violation of free speech rights. At the same time, the Court distinguished the mere concept or idea of "sexual immorality" from "obscenity" or "pornography," both of which could still be regulated under certain circumstances.

In 1973, during a midafternoon weekday broadcast on contemporary attitudes toward the use of language, a New York City radio station aired satirist comedian George Carlin's twelve-minute monologue titled "Filthy Words." Immediately before the broadcast, the station had advised listeners that it would include sensitive language that might be offensive to some. In the monologue, Carlin provided his thoughts about "the words you can't say on the public airwaves, um, the ones you definitely wouldn't say ever," especially the "original seven dirty words." Carlin then repeated the outlawed words in a variety of colloquialisms. When the Federal Communications Commission (FCC) threatened to impose formal sanctions on the radio station, the station sued. In 1978, the Supreme Court narrowly upheld the FCC's authority to impose sanctions. The Court took pains to say that in this particular case, context was all-important: "Broadcasting is uniquely accessible to

operate a military registration system during wartime, rather than simply to suppress the ideas and message of this particular protester. Similarly, protesters do not have the right to violate federal park service rules and sleep in parks after closing—those rules were established for one reason: to prevent damage to public property. By contrast, students were granted the constitutional right to wear black armbands in school to protest the Vietnam War—their "conduct" was considered the equivalent of "pure speech," and school officials' arguments about the maintenance of order and discipline were given little credibility.

The constitutionality of flag burning has been a source of considerable debate in recent years. To many the American flag is a symbol of nationhood and national unity, and thus must be preserved at all costs. For that very reason, protesters seeking to attract publicity for their ideas have burned or desecrated the flag in public places. The Supreme Court ended the legal debate over flag burning with its decision in *Texas v. Johnson* (1989).[34] In 1984, Gregory Lee Johnson was arrested and convicted for "desecrating a venerated object" at a political demonstration in Dallas, the site of the Republican National Convention. Johnson had been leading a protest against the Reagan administration; he eventually set an American flag on fire, after which he and the other protesters chanted: "America, the red, white and blue, we spit on you." But the Supreme Court threw out Johnson's conviction because the "government may not prohibit the expression of an idea simply because society finds the idea itself offensive or disagreeable."[35]

GETTY IMAGES

Controversial disc jockey Howard Stern.

children, even those too young to read." At the same time, the Court hinted that occasional expletives, including even those in Carlin's monologue, might never justify a full criminal prosecution or some more serious sanction.

In 2004, Howard Stern signed a five-year contract with Sirius Satellite Radio, a medium free from regulations imposed by the FCC. Stern, self-nicknamed "the King of All Media," regularly describes in graphic detail oral, anal, and other forms of sex during his morning radio show at a time when children may be part of the listening audience. The decision to move to satellite was motivated by business and free speech concerns. Back in 1996 the Infinity network paid over $1.7 million to the FCC to clear more than a hundred indecency claims made against the Howard Stern radio show. Nearly a decade later, Stern accused FCC Chairman Michael Powell of crusading against his radio show by levying huge fines, though never allowing him a day in court to determine if the show was obscene. Since moving to satellite the fines have stopped, though Stern has revealed that he has begun to feel "creatively dead inside." Can Howard Stern survive without the daily rigors of walking on the edge?

Despite the Supreme Court's apparent resolution of the matter, heated feelings on both sides of the flag-burning issue have kept it alive. After an initial attempt by Congress to pass flag-burning legislation failed to withstand judicial scrutiny in 1990, some members of Congress proposed passage of an amendment to the Constitution that would make flag burning unconstitutional. Although that proposed amendment has on several occasions achieved the necessary level of support in the House of Representatives, the U.S. Senate has so far failed to approve it, thus preventing it from being promulgated to state legislatures for ratification.

Hate Speech Codes

Since the 1970s, communities have sought to prevent speakers who preach hatred for certain groups—whether racial, religious, or some other classification—from exercising their rights of free speech in certain specified neighborhoods or other places where the perceived harms may be great. Such efforts have not always passed constitutional muster. In one instance during the late 1970s, the courts refused to deny neo-Nazis the right to march in a parade in Skokie, Illinois, home to a large number of Holocaust victims.[36] By contrast, efforts to ban cross burning and other controversial forms of expression have sometimes been upheld. In *Virginia v. Black* (2003)[37] the U.S. Supreme Court ruled that the state of Virginia could prohibit cross burning with the "intent to intimidate any person or group," because the law applied

AMERICAN GOVERNMENT In Popular Perspective

Varying Levels of Support for the First Amendment

A recent comprehensive national study of American adults, high school students, teachers, and principals revealed the depth of support that exists for First Amendment free expression rights. The study, analyzed in a 2008 book, found that students are less likely than adults to think that people should be allowed to express unpopular opinions or that newspapers should be allowed to publish freely without government approval of stories. The study also revealed that when it comes to situations more relevant to students' own lives and concerns, students agree at higher rates than adults that certain forms of expression should be allowed (for example, musicians singing songs with

offensive lyrics or student newspapers reporting controversial issues without administrative approval).

For Critical Thinking and Discussion

1. Why do you think students are less tolerant of civil liberties exercised by professional editors and publishers than they are of their own free press rights? Why aren't the two rights connected?

2. Do you agree that musicians' use of controversial lyrics deserves full constitutional protection? Explain.

3. Print newspapers are on the decline, while Internet newspapers are on the rise. Do you think those different types of publications should be treated the same for First Amendment purposes? Why or why not?

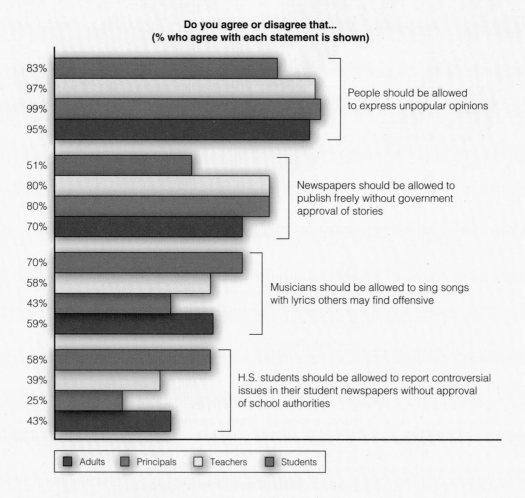

Do you agree or disagree that...
(% who agree with each statement is shown)

	People should be allowed to express unpopular opinions
Adults	83%
Principals	97%
Teachers	99%
Students	95%

	Newspapers should be allowed to publish freely without government approval of stories
Adults	51%
Principals	80%
Teachers	80%
Students	70%

	Musicians should be allowed to sing songs with lyrics others may find offensive
Adults	70%
Principals	58%
Teachers	43%
Students	59%

	H.S. students should be allowed to report controversial issues in their student newspapers without approval of school authorities
Adults	58%
Principals	39%
Teachers	25%
Students	43%

Legend: ■ Adults ■ Principals ☐ Teachers ■ Students

Source: Kenneth Dautrich, David Yalof, and Mark Hugo Lopez, *The Future of the First Amendment* (Lanham, MD: Rowman & Littlefield, 2008).

106

only to intimidation and not to cross burning in general. The law also applied to all groups, not just racial or ethnic groups.

It is a considerable challenge for school officials to restrict hate speech by students at public colleges and universities, even when that speech proves disruptive to the school's mission of providing a constructive environment for learning.[38] In 1988, the University of Michigan passed a regulation subjecting individuals to discipline for "behavior, verbal or physical" that stigmatized or victimized an individual on the basis of race, ethnicity, religion, sex, or a host of other criteria. Stanford University similarly attempted to prohibit "discriminatory harassment," which was defined to include speech intended to stigmatize or insult on the basis of sex, race, and so on. Lower courts invalidated both of these "hate speech codes" on grounds that they violated the First Amendment.

The Second Amendment Right to Bear Arms

★ LO
Identify the scope of the right to bear arms and the constitutional limits on gun control laws

THE SECOND AMENDMENT: A well regulated militia, being necessary to the security of a free State, the right of the people to keep and bear Arms, shall not be infringed.

The Second Amendment "right to keep and bear arms" remains something of a puzzle for Americans. On one hand, the second part of the amendment appears to trumpet the "people's" right to own firearms at their discretion, and has taken its place as a central tenet in the platforms of interest groups such as the National Rifle Association (NRA), which opposes nearly all government attempts to restrict gun ownership. On the other hand, the first part of the amendment speaks directly of a "well-regulated militia," and implies that some relationship must exist between the private gun owner's rights and more formal state activities. The U.S. Supreme Court finally weighed in on the subject in 2008. In *District of Columbia v. Heller* (2008),[39] the Supreme Court by a 5–4 vote held that the Second Amendment forbids the government from banning all forms of handgun possession in the home for purposes of immediate self-defense.

In *McDonald v. Chicago* (2010),[40] the Supreme Court went a step further, ruling that the right to bear arms is incorporated by the due process clause of the Fourteenth Amendment, and thus applies to all 50 states as well. However, this Second Amendment right is not absolute: the Court in *Heller* noted that government can still regulate the commercial sale of handguns; it can also prohibit their possession by felons and the mentally ill, or in sensitive places such as school buildings.

Second Amendment considerations aside, Congress has been reluctant to regulate gun ownership—only rarely are the sponsors of gun control able to overcome fierce lobbying efforts by the NRA and others in opposition. Advocates of gun control scored some success following the attempted assassination of President Ronald Reagan in 1981. Reagan was wounded in the attempt, as was James Brady, his press secretary. Although the president fully recovered from his injuries in a matter of weeks, Brady sustained serious head injuries because a bullet tore into his temple and lodged in the base of his brain. He ultimately experienced a partial recovery, though he permanently lost the use of his left arm and left leg and suffers from slurred speech.

GABRIEL BOUYS/AFP/GETTY IMAGES

A man buying a handgun at a gun shop in California. The 2008 Supreme Court decision in *District of Columbia v. Heller* held that the Second Amendment protects a person's right to own a handgun.

In 1985 Brady and his wife, Sarah, became spokespersons for gun control measures. Their efforts resulted in the Brady Handgun Violence Prevention Act, signed by President Clinton in 1993. The "Brady Law" required a five-day waiting period and a background check on handgun purchases from licensed firearms dealers to ensure that felons, drug users, fugitives, and other specified categories of individuals not be permitted to purchase guns. The NRA avoided any direct court challenges to the law on Second Amendment grounds, hammering instead at more peripheral aspects of the law, such as the requirement that local sheriffs conduct these checks as part of a federal regulatory scheme. In 1997, the Supreme Court struck down this aspect of the Brady Law as a violation of federalism, although leaving the substance of the law in place. Congress has also attempted to restrict the carrying of firearms near schools, even though some of these efforts have been invalidated by the Supreme Court on the grounds that the federal government cannot commandeer the states to enforce federal legislation.

★ LO   Understand the scope of Fourth Amendment rights and the privacy issues raised by technology

Bill of attainder

An act of a legislature declaring a person (or group) guilty of some crime, and then carrying out punishment without a trial. The Constitution denies Congress the ability to issue a bill of attainder.

Ex post facto laws

A law that punishes someone for doing something in the past, at a time when the act was not illegal. The Constitution denies government the ability to write laws ex post facto.

The Rights of the Criminally Accused

A few rights for the accused may be found in the language of the original Constitution. Article I prohibits Congress from passing a **bill of attainder**, which is an act of a legislature declaring a person (or group) guilty of some crime and then carrying out punishment without a trial. It also prohibits **ex post facto laws**, which are new criminal laws retroactively applied to those who engaged in activities when they were not yet illegal. But the vast majority of constitutional rights for those accused of crimes are contained in the Fourth, Fifth, Sixth, and Eighth Amendments to the Constitution. Despite the seemingly explicit protections found in those four amendments, accused individuals enjoyed only limited substantive protection from arbitrary violations of criminal due process for better than a century and a half of this nation's history, as they protected defendants primarily only against intrusions by the federal government.

Much of that changed in the 1960s with a number of decisions handed down by the Warren Court. During that period the Supreme Court applied many of the provisions of the Bill of Rights against state governments by incorporating most of the protections given accused persons in the federal judicial system. In addition, the Warren Court gave increased substance to these rights, holding government officials accountable under the Bill of Rights for their actions at highway road stops, during the interrogation of witnesses at the police station, and elsewhere.[41] Even the right to counsel was broadened to extend to far more of those accused of committing crimes. During the late 1980s and 1990s under Chief Justice William Rehnquist, the Court scaled back some of these protections. Nevertheless, defendants forced to weave their way through the criminal justice system today still enjoy numerous rights protections that were not guaranteed before the Warren Court era.

Fourth Amendment Rights

> *THE FOURTH AMENDMENT: The right of the people to be secure in their persons, houses, papers and effects, against unreasonable searches and seizures, shall not be violated, and no Warrants shall issue, but upon probable cause. . . .*

The right of citizens to be free from unreasonable searches and seizures has a long history in America. Before the American Revolution, colonists loudly protested English abuses of the power to inspect merchants' goods through the use of an unlimited "general warrant." Although the Fourth Amendment had been in place for nearly two centuries, the Warren Court modernized the rules governing police searches with its decision in *Katz v. United States* (1967).[42] The Court's ruling created the **Katz test**, which requires that the government attain a warrant demonstrating "probable cause" for any investigative activity that violates a person's reasonable expectation of

Katz test

The legal standard that requires the government to attain a warrant demonstrating "probable cause" for any "search" that violates a person's actual and reasonable expectation of privacy.

Shedding Fourth Amendment Rights at the Schoolhouse Door

Justice Abe Fortas once wrote that "students do not . . . shed their constitutional rights when they enter the schoolhouse door." His comment held true in *Tinker v. Des Moines* (1967), when the Court upheld the rights of students to wear black armbands in protest of the Vietnam War. Yet the Court has not been so kind to students in subsequent civil liberties cases. This has been especially true in the schoolhouse itself, where Fourth Amendment rights may be implicated. When the state's power to search and seize conflicts with student claims of privacy, all the advantages lie with the state.

The leading Supreme Court case addressing students' Fourth Amendment rights is *New Jersey v. TLO* (1985), involving the search of a high school student for contraband after she was caught smoking. The assistant vice principal's subsequent search of her purse without a warrant revealed drug paraphernalia and marijuana. The U.S. Supreme Court held that the search was constitutional so long as it was "deemed reasonable given the circumstances." Since the student was caught and taken directly to the office, it was considered "reasonable" to assume the purse contained some evidence of wrongdoing.

MIKAEL KARLSSON/ALAMY

For Critical Thinking and Discussion

1. Do you think the rights of college students on your campus should be equivalent to the rights adults enjoy in the workplace, or should they be equivalent to the more limited rights of high school students?

2. Is the location of the search relevant?

3. Should college students enjoy the same rights against unreasonable searches and seizures in their dorm rooms as they enjoy elsewhere on campus?

4. Should private colleges and universities have greater power to search students than public colleges or universities? Why or why not?

---

privacy, whether or not the person is at home. A **warrant** is a document issued by a judge or magistrate that allows law enforcement to search or seize items at a home, business, or anywhere else that might be specified.

Perhaps the most controversial aspect of the Fourth Amendment is the mechanism by which it is enforced. Although no specific provision for enforcing civil liberties is provided in the amendment, since its 1961 decision in *Mapp v. Ohio*,[43] the Supreme Court has demanded that the states adhere to the **exclusionary rule**, by which all evidence obtained by police in violation of the Bill of Rights must be "excluded" from admission in a court of law, where it might have assisted in convicting those who have been accused of committing crimes. Complaints about the exclusionary rule focus on its most likely beneficiaries: those who are guilty of committing some wrongdoing. They are the ones with the most potential evidence against them and thus have the most to gain from such exclusion. Detractors also complain about the "injustice" of the rule—whenever evidence is thrown out because of a warrantless search by police, "the criminal is to go free because the constable has blundered." Defenders of the rule counter that without a means of excluding such evidence, the government could violate the rights of guilty and innocent individuals alike by conducting the equivalent of fishing expeditions.

Warrant
A document issued by a judge or magistrate that allows law enforcement to search or seize items at a home, business, or anywhere else that might be specified.

Exclusionary rule
The legal rule requiring that all evidence illegally obtained by police in violation of the Bill of Rights must be "excluded" from admission in a court of law, where it might have assisted in convicting those accused of committing crimes.

Good faith exception

An exception to the exclusionary rule that states if a search warrant is invalid through no fault of the police, evidence obtained under that warrant may still be admitted into court.

Since the 1960s, the Court has modified application of the exclusionary rule somewhat, although it has refused to back down from its central requirements. The most significant of these modifications is the **good faith exception** to the rule, which was first instituted in 1984: if a search warrant is invalid through no fault of the police (for example, the judge puts the wrong date on the warrant), evidence obtained under that warrant may still be admitted into court. Police may also under certain circumstances conduct warrantless searches of a defendant's premises. The allowable circumstances for a warrantless search include (1) the search is incidental to a lawful arrest; (2) the defendant has given consent to be searched; (3) the police are in "hot pursuit" of the defendant; and (4) the evidence is in "plain view" of police standing in a place where they have the legal right to be. Police may also briefly stop individuals driving in their cars, or conduct a "pat down" of suspicious individuals for weapons—in neither case is a warrant required. Nevertheless, police should conduct such warrantless searches with caution, as the good faith exception may be relied on only when conducting searches under the authority of a warrant.

Advances in technology and new innovations in police work have invited new types of Fourth Amendment civil liberties claims, and a potential reinterpretation of those rights by the U.S. Supreme Court. The testing of defendants for drug or alcohol use through breathalyzer tests and the taking of blood samples may require the police to jump through a series of procedural hoops imposed on them by the state, but no warrant is generally required in either instance when the defendant is in the legitimate custody of the police. Similarly, the DNA testing of defendants has provided a significant breakthrough in the prosecution of difficult cases that lack eyewitnesses or other "hard" evidence of the crime. The use of thermal imaging scans, which expand police investigative tactics from afar, has also been tested in the courts. A thermal imaging scan detects infrared radiation, which then converts radiation into images based on relative warmth, operating somewhat like a video camera showing heat images. In the mid-1990s, police forces began to employ the device to detect the presence of indoor halide lights used to grow marijuana plants inside large buildings; police are able to conduct these scans from vehicles parked across the street from the buildings in question. Do such scans violate a person's reasonable expectation of privacy? "Yes," said the Supreme Court, in a narrow 5–4

A thermal imaging instrument used by police to detect intense heat emissions. The Supreme Court banned its use without a warrant in 2001.

AP PHOTO/GARY TRAMONTINA

decision handed down in 2001:[44] "Where the Government uses a device that is not in general public use, to explore details of the home that would previously have been unknowable without physical intrusion, the surveillance is a 'search' and is presumptively unreasonable without a warrant."

Recently, some communities have posted cameras at stoplights that produce photographic evidence of traffic violations. Other communities have installed cameras on street corners in busy areas. When used in conjunction with computer databanks of convicted criminals, these cameras can provide surveillance capable of instantly detecting the presence of such figures on the street. Officials in Tampa, Florida, have recently turned to closed-circuit television systems to assist police departments in performing surveillance. Specifically, face recognition software programmed to identify certain wanted individuals has been employed on the streets of Tampa as well as in certain airports; an extensive network of cameras deployed throughout those areas can theoretically identify the faces of wanted individuals, and alert authorities quickly and efficiently of their presence.

Reviews of this technology have so far been mixed: Critics complain that the system often makes false matches in the same way that humans so often are mistaken. Civil libertarians further complain that the use of surveillance cameras in general violates many citizens' privacy rights, which they believe extend beyond the privacy of their own homes. Tampa abandoned the face recognition system in April 2001, but other cities continue to rely on closed-circuit cameras in general as a means of detecting crime—or if possible, preventing it from taking place.

To date, none of these modern police tactics have been successfully challenged on Fourth Amendment grounds. But as the use of these techniques is broadened—perhaps to facilitate racial profiling or other controversial forms of police investigation—it is certain that legal challenges will be waged.

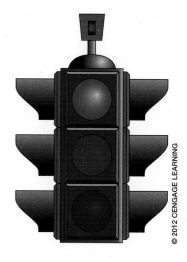

© 2012 CENGAGE LEARNING

Fifth Amendment Rights

THE FIFTH AMENDMENT: No person shall be held to answer for a capital, or otherwise infamous crime, unless on a presentment or indictment of a grand jury . . . nor shall any person be subject for the same offense to be twice put in jeopardy of life or limb; nor shall be compelled in any criminal case to be a witness against himself. . . .

Under the Fifth Amendment, the accused enjoy an assortment of rights that may prove crucial to their defense. The requirement that a grand jury, a jury that meets to decide whether the evidence is sufficient to justify a prosecutor's request that a case go to trial, be convened for serious crimes is theoretically significant; it forces prosecutors to convince an initial jury that a defendant should rightfully be forced to go to trial. (Grand juries do not decide on a defendant's guilt or innocence.) In practice, however, the grand jury requirement is rarely much of an obstacle to a skilled prosecutor, who can selectively present evidence to the jury members outside the view of the defendant or the defendant's lawyer. Moreover, because the grand jury requirement was never incorporated, it applies only to federal prosecutors in federal court.[45] The **double jeopardy clause** is a source of much greater protection for defendants: it provides that no defendant may be tried twice for the same crime. Prosecutors must weigh carefully their probability of success at trial and bring forth all the relevant resources at their disposal. If the jury acquits the defendant, the prosecutor cannot try the defendant again. Still, the double jeopardy clause does not stop an altogether different government from retrying the defendant for violating that government's own laws. This occurred in the high-profile case of several white Los Angeles police officers who were accused in 1991 of beating Rodney King, an African American motorist whom they had stopped for a traffic violation. The acquittal of the police set off a series of race riots in Los Angeles. Later, federal charges were brought against the police for violating King's civil rights. At the federal trial, the officers were convicted.

★ LO
Understand the rules against double jeopardy and the privilege against self-incrimination

Double jeopardy clause
The constitutional protection that those accused of a crime cannot be tried twice for the same crime.

DAVID R. FRAZIER/THE IMAGE WORKS

"You have the right to remain silent. Anything you say will be used against you in a court of law. You have the right to an attorney during interrogation; if you cannot afford an attorney, one will be appointed to you."

—*Miranda* warning,
Miranda v. Arizona

Miranda warning
The U.S. Supreme Court's requirement that an individual who is arrested must be read a statement that explains the person's right to remain silent and the right to an attorney.

Another provision of the Fifth Amendment is the so-called self-incrimination clause, which prevents individuals from being compelled to testify against themselves. Although originally interpreted to provide protection for defendants only in the courtroom, the self-incrimination clause today offers substantial protection to defendants being questioned by police at the station house or elsewhere. Certainly the clause protects defendants from being coerced or tortured into confessing to crimes. But the Warren Court truly changed this area of the law in the now famous case of *Miranda v. Arizona* (1966).[46] In that ruling, the Supreme Court announced the requirement that a **Miranda warning** be read to all defendants in custody before they are questioned by police.

Ernesto Miranda was convicted of the March 1963 kidnapping and rape of an eighteen-year-old girl in Phoenix, Arizona. Soon after the crime, the police picked up Miranda, who fit the description of the girl's attacker. Officers immediately took him into an interrogation room and told him (falsely) that he had been positively identified by his victim. After two hours of questioning, Miranda confessed. At trial, the defense counsel prodded one of the detectives into admitting that Miranda had never been given the opportunity to seek advice from an attorney prior to his interrogation. Miranda was nevertheless convicted and sentenced to forty to sixty years in prison. On appeal, the U.S. Supreme Court in 1966 set aside Miranda's conviction. Chief Justice Warren wrote: "Prior to any questioning, the person must be warned that he has a right to remain silent, that any statement he does make may be used as evidence against him, and that he has a right to the presence of an attorney, either retained or appointed. . . ."

Miranda was retried, this time without his confession being introduced into evidence at the trial, and again convicted. Although his original confession could not be used, a former girlfriend testified that Miranda had told her about the kidnapping and rape. After Miranda was paroled in 1972, he spent time in and out of prison before being stabbed fatally in a bar at the age of thirty-four. Thanks to police drama shows and movies, the *Miranda* warnings are better known to citizens today than are any other constitutional protections: police must routinely tell suspects being questioned that they have the right to remain silent and the right to a court-appointed attorney, and confirm that the suspects understand these rights. Perhaps that's why a more conservative Supreme Court conceded in the case of *United States v. Dickerson* (2000) that *Miranda* has become so "embedded in routine police practice" that the warnings have become "part of our national culture." Thus a failure to read the list of *Miranda* rights to witnesses may still result in any subsequent confession to the police being thrown out of court by virtue of the exclusionary rule.[47]

Sixth Amendment Rights

THE SIXTH AMENDMENT: In all criminal prosecutions, the accused shall . . . have the Assistance of Counsel for his defense.

Images of beleaguered and confused defendants trying desperately to defend themselves against experienced and well-seasoned prosecutors are now mostly a thing of the past. In 1963, the Supreme Court in *Gideon v. Wainwright*[48] ordered a new trial for an indigent defendant who had been ordered by the State of Florida to defend himself in a criminal trial, even though he possessed no legal training. Under prevailing Sixth Amendment standards today, no indigent criminal defendant can be sentenced to jail unless the defendant has been provided with a lawyer at no cost. This constitutional right to the assistance of counsel even extends beyond the trial: a court-appointed lawyer must assist the defendant in preparing the case and in all other hearings and meetings before trial. Some critics of the criminal justice system cite the disparity that often exists between the quality of court-appointed counsel and of paid counsel for well-off defendants. Nevertheless, public defenders' offices have been established all over the country in response to the requirement that indigent defendants be provided with lawyers.

Eighth Amendment Rights

THE EIGHTH AMENDMENT: Excessive bail shall not be required, nor excessive fines imposed, nor cruel and unusual punishments inflicted.

The Eighth Amendment deals in a limited way with defendants being held for trial: according to its language, **bail**, which is an amount of money paid to the court as security against a defendant's freedom before trial, may not be excessive. In practice, that provision applies only when bail is proper in the first place; many high-risk defendants are held either to prevent flight or to ensure that they do not cause more harm while on release. In those instances, bail may be denied altogether without any violation of the Constitution.

★ LO

Recognize the rights granted under the Sixth and Eighth Amendments

Bail
An amount of money determined by a judge that the accused must pay to a court as security against his or her freedom before trial.

Far more significant are the concluding words of the Eighth Amendment with respect to "cruel and unusual punishment." No government may impose a cruel and unusual punishment on an individual, but there remains heated debate over what is "cruel and unusual." Traditionally, the clause prohibited only those punishments that even the drafters of the Bill of Rights would have disapproved of—drawing and quartering, beheading, and other forms of extreme torture. In recent times, the Court has added to the mix the requirement of "proportionality," in which serious punishments may not be imposed for relatively minor offenses. Thus, for instance, the Court struck down imprisonment for the controversial offense of "being addicted to the use of narcotics" on the ground that the state was punishing someone for an illness.

The Supreme Court has never held the death penalty to be inherently cruel and unusual. Most modern lawsuits by prisoners on "death row" focus on the manner by which the death sentence has been imposed. Any judge or jury that imposes capital punishment must have the opportunity to consider mitigating circumstances that might generate some sympathy for the accused. Nor can a jury impose a death sentence at the same time that it finds the defendant guilty; the defendant's lawyers must be given a chance to argue against imposition of the death penalty without also having to prove the defendant is innocent. Finally, certain defendants may not receive the death penalty. In 2002, the Court in *Atkins v. Virginia* ruled executions impermissible in the case of mentally retarded defendants.[49] Then in 2005, the Court also ruled executions impermissible for defendants who committed their crimes while under the age of eighteen.

Critics of the system claim that so many death penalty cases are held up on appeal that bad luck and misfortune are inevitable in the process.[50] Furthermore, advances in DNA testing technology have revealed that some prisoners on death row were innocent of the crime for which they had been sentenced to death. Even in the face of unrelenting popular support for the death penalty, governors in Illinois and Maryland recently announced a "moratorium" on executions in their respective states, to be continued as long as the process by which death sentences are determined remains so riddled with errors.

The Modern Right to Privacy

© 2012 CENGAGE LEARNING

"...Nor cruel and unusual punishment inflicted."

★ LO Understand the right of abortion and its scope under *Roe v. Wade*, and then later under *Planned Parenthood v. Casey*

Perhaps no single constitutional right garnered more controversial attention during the second half of the twentieth century than the right to have an abortion. Unlike all the other rights mentioned so far in this chapter, however, neither the specific right to abortion, nor the more general right to privacy, are explicitly referred to in the Constitution or in the amendments to the Constitution. The right to privacy is thus often referred to as an unwritten or "unenumerated" right. The Ninth Amendment counsels against dismissing such rights offhand. It reads: "The enumeration in the Constitution of certain rights, shall not be construed to deny or disparage others retained by the people." In other words, the fact that other rights such as freedom of speech are written down in the Bill of Rights does not mean that the Constitution doesn't also recognize certain unwritten rights.

The recognition of unstated rights in the Constitution raises difficult questions, such as how to justify recognizing certain unenumerated rights but not others. In 1965, the Supreme Court stepped into this controversy with its decision in *Griswold v. Connecticut*,[51] when it invalidated an 1879 Connecticut law prohibiting the dissemination of information about and the sale of contraceptives. Seven of the nine justices ruled that although the right to birth control is not explicitly mentioned in the Constitution, several provisions of the Bill of Rights (the First, Third, Fourth, and Fifth) and the Fourteenth Amendment, taken together, suggest that these provisions create a "zone of privacy" that includes within it the right to decide whether or not to bear a child. Although the Supreme Court's methods were considered highly speculative, widespread acceptance of birth control devices allowed the Supreme Court to avoid controversy in the years following the decision.[52]

Three "Might Have Beens" on the Road to the Rights Revolution

In his *Book of Legal Lists* (1997), the late scholar Bernard Schwartz identified what he termed "The Ten Greatest Supreme Court 'Might Have Beens.'" Of those ten, three would have had a direct impact on the rights revolution, which enjoyed unprecedented encouragement from the Supreme Court during the 1960s and 1970s.

✔ **Earl Warren might never have joined the Court.** President Eisenhower did not want to name California Governor Earl Warren, who had no judicial experience whatsoever, to be the next chief justice of the U.S. Supreme Court. But he had promised Warren the "first available Supreme Court vacancy" to earn his support at the 1952 Republican convention, and when sixty-three-year-old Chief Justice Fred Vinson died unexpectedly in 1953, Warren insisted that President Eisenhower live up to his promise. Warren's subsequent leadership of the Supreme Court gave birth to the rights revolution of the 1960s.

✔ **The first draft of *Roe v. Wade* might have been the final.** Justice Harry Blackmun's first draft of a majority opinion in this famous case was unremarkable, avoiding altogether the critical issue of whether a pregnant woman had an absolute right to an abortion. Rather, the draft actually supported state substantive power over abortion, but ruled that the laws presented to the Court (those in Texas and Georgia) were too "vague" to be constitutional. Had that draft been handed down as the official Court opinion, the "subsequent schism that has been a major factor in American life" might well have been postponed or avoided. But Chief Justice Warren Burger ordered reargument in the case, and Blackmun's later draft became the controversial law of the land.

✔ **The justices in *Mapp v. Ohio* might have taken separate elevators.** Called the most radical decision of its time, the 1961 *Mapp* decision ensured that in every state of the country, whenever the police blunder, the criminal goes free and society pays the price. But the decision truly came out of nowhere—the briefs and arguments in the Supreme Court were all devoted to the First Amendment issue of whether Ohio's law barring obscene material (which the police found in Mapp's possession) was constitutional. The Court's discussion of the case at conference even proceeded that way. But in the elevator after leaving the conference room, three justices decided this would be a good case to use to overrule the exclusionary rule, and they found two more allies within the next few days, including Justice Tom Clark, who agreed to reverse his position on the exclusionary rule. "I was shocked," wrote Justice Potter Stewart later about the events that had transpired. As Bernard Schwartz notes, had the elevator meeting and Clark's switch not occurred, "the Warren Court's most important criminal law holding would have been stillborn."

Source: Bernard Schwartz, *A Book of Legal Lists* (New York: Oxford University Press, 1997). Reprinted by the permission of Oxford University Press.

No such sidestepping of heated controversy was possible in 1973, when the Supreme Court formally recognized the constitutional right to abortion in *Roe v. Wade*.[53] By the early 1970s, nearly fifteen states had passed liberal abortion laws, but lawyers for Norma McCorvey (she used the pseudonym of "Jane Roe" for purposes of her lawsuit) argued that the decision to end a pregnancy was a constitutional right that *all fifty states* must adhere to. McCorvey herself had been unable to secure a legal abortion in Texas and so eventually gave birth and put her baby up for adoption. The Supreme Court agreed to take her case and rule on the general constitutionality of abortion restrictions.

In ruling in McCorvey's favor, the Supreme Court affirmed that the Constitution recognizes a right to privacy in general—and thus a right to abortion more specifically—even though neither of those rights is ever spelled out explicitly. Such a right is not absolute throughout the term of the pregnancy, however. The author of the opinion, Justice Harry Blackmun, divided the pregnancy into three stages as part of a highly controversial *trimester framework*. During the first trimester, a woman's right to end her pregnancy is absolute. During the second trimester the right is nearly absolute, although the government has the right to restrict abortions that might pose threats to a woman's health. Finally, in the third trimester (when the fetus is potentially viable), the state government is allowed to impose any abortion restrictions on the mother, so long as they do not limit efforts to protect the life or health of the mother.[54]

The number of legal abortions that occurred in the United States rose dramatically in the years immediately following *Roe v. Wade*. The decision also unleashed a fury of controversy from antiabortion interest groups and conservative lawmakers. The election of Ronald Reagan to the presidency in 1980 and his reelection in 1984 set the stage for *Roe v. Wade*'s weakening; as a candidate for high office, Reagan had specifically targeted *Roe v. Wade* as a case of illegitimate judicial activism and had promised to nominate Supreme Court justices who would overturn the controversial decision. Reagan's more conservative Supreme Court appointments began to make their presence known during the late 1980s, when increasingly severe restrictions on abortion were upheld by the Court.

In 1992, the Supreme Court overhauled *Roe v. Wade*'s controversial trimester framework in *Planned Parenthood v. Casey*.[55] Although the Court did not specifically overturn *Roe*, the justices replaced the trimester framework with a less stringent *undue burden test*: does the restriction at issue—regardless of what trimester it affects—*unduly burden* a woman's right to privacy under the Constitution? One example of this new constitutional test at work can be found in the Court's approach to state-mandated twenty-four-hour waiting periods for abortion. Under *Roe v. Wade*, the requirement that a woman wait for an abortion in either of the first two trimesters would have been unconstitutional. Yet in *Casey*, the Court held that such a waiting period does not unduly burden the woman's right to privacy. Other regulations that have been upheld under the *Casey* framework include the requirement that minors seek permission from a parent or a court before having an abortion, and the requirement that women seeking abortions be provided information about the specific medical effects an abortion will have on the fetus.

Not all abortion restrictions are allowed under this new framework. In *Casey*, the Supreme Court invalidated a requirement that women notify their spouses of their intention to have abortions. Yet many more provisions restricting abortion have been upheld since 1992 under the less restrictive *Casey* doctrine. In *Gonzales v. Carhart* (2007),[56] the Supreme Court upheld the Partial Birth Abortion Act of 2003, which effectively banned the use of the "intact dilation and extraction" abortion procedure, most often performed during the second trimester of pregnancy.

Once the unwritten right to privacy became a reality in constitutional law, it seemed inevitable that citizens might try to claim other unwritten rights implicating

★ LO Become familiar with the privacy rights that apply to government restrictions on sodomy and euthanasia

privacy in the same fashion. Although most efforts to expand the right to privacy beyond abortion and birth control have met with limited success, the Court has not always shut the door on these claims. In 1986, the Court held that a Georgia law that criminalized acts of sodomy by homosexuals was constitutional. Seventeen years later in the case of *Lawrence v. Texas*,[57] the Court reversed itself, holding that a Texas law making it a crime for two people of the same sex to engage in certain types of intimate sexual conduct did in fact violate the individual's right to due process.

The highly visible prosecutions of Dr. Jack Kevorkian for helping terminally ill patients end their lives has brought added attention to the issue of physician-assisted suicide in recent years. On April 13, 1999, Kevorkian, a retired pathologist, was sentenced to jail in Michigan for helping a terminally ill man die by direct injection, a form of voluntary euthanasia. Kevorkian, labeled by many of his opponents as "Dr. Death," had already acknowledged publicly that he had helped at least ninety other people to die by assisted suicide in Michigan between 1990 and 1997. Indeed, when enforcement authorities in Michigan initially refused to charge Kevorkian with killing his most recent patient, he took a tape of the incident to CBS television and aired it on the widely watched news program *60 Minutes*. On the program, Kevorkian challenged the state to act: three days later he got his wish.

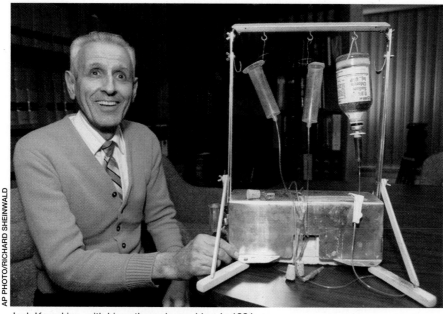

AP PHOTO/RICHARD SHEINWALD

Jack Kevorkian, with his euthanasia machine, in 1991.

Questions remain about Kevorkian's tactics—do terminally ill patients have the right to end their life, and if so, can a licensed physician assist them in doing so? Although the Court has been willing to recognize a right of terminally ill patients to end their medical treatment, it has steadfastly refused to extend that privilege to the active termination of one's life. In 1997, the Supreme Court held that no such constitutional right exists, although the justices were significantly divided as to the specific reasons why that is so. But the Court also indicated that states are free to legalize physician-assisted suicide. Since then, only one state (Oregon) has enacted an assisted suicide law. As for Kevorkian, after serving eight years of his prison sentence for second-degree murder, he was granted parole and released from prison on June 1, 2007.

NOW & THEN

Making the Connection

Passionate debates over constitutional rights are hardly a new phenomenon. With a tradition of robust press protections in America dating back to John Peter Zenger's acquittal in the early eighteenth century, the Sedition Act of 1798 stood little chance of long-term success; America's policy of openness to immigrants from abroad similarly doomed the Alien Act passed that same year. (Both acts were repealed just three years after their passage.) As a candidate, Barack Obama attacked the George W. Bush administration for violating the rights of the accused in prosecuting the war on terror; yet once he became president, he left many of his predecessor's more controversial measures in place, and he failed to effectively modify a handful of others. Where necessary, Obama vigorously defended those initiatives as necessary for national security. Although the actions of the Adams and Obama administrations could be loosely defined as "wartime measures," not all Americans are equally willing to compromise the Bill of Rights in pursuit of a greater cause. John Adams suffered the public's wrath at the polls in 1800; if President Obama fails to protect the nation from further terrorist attacks, he too may suffer the same fate. Ultimately a balancing act is required between the interests of national security and the integrity of these constitutional rights. Not all presidents are able to strike that balance with the same degree of political success.

Notwithstanding the enduring value conflict between national security and individual liberty, it is quite clear that during the past half century the Bill of Rights has been transformed from a set of mostly paper guarantees with only limited impact on the daily lives of Americans into a truly formidable arsenal of rights that have revolutionized government practices in the public square, at police stations, and in the nation's criminal courts. Certainly the Warren Court of the 1960s was responsible for much of this transformation. But the seeds of change were planted much earlier, first through ratification of the Fourteenth Amendment to protect individuals against state intrusion on their rights, and then later, when Justice Harlan Fiske Stone offered a theory of preferred freedoms in 1938 that trumpeted the freedom of speech and other rights that gave citizens their voice in the democratic process. Chief Justice Warren took Justice Stone up on this offer nearly a quarter of a century later, and the rights revolution was subsequently born.

In recent decades, the Supreme Court has attempted to return some authority to state governments to manage their own affairs. It has also scaled back some of the more controversial Warren Court decisions. In particular, the Rehnquist Court loosened many of the restrictions on government imposed by the two religious clauses of the First Amendment, the establishment clause and the free exercise clause; it also diluted a woman's right to abortion under *Roe v. Wade* in the 1990s. At the same time, many of the sweeping changes introduced by the Warren Court have been left untouched. And some constitutional protections have even been broadened in the past fifteen years—the right to free speech, for example, now encompasses the right to burn a flag as a statement of political protest.

The death penalty is the ultimate punishment for those convicted of crimes—it cannot be reversed once carried out, and it effectively trumps the exercise of all other rights. And yet capital punishment remains a staple of the American criminal justice system, sustained by public opinion polls that have long shown a clear majority of Americans in its favor. An ABC News survey in July 2006 found 65 percent in favor of capital punishment, consistent with many other polls taken in recent years. Moreover, according to a Gallup poll from two months earlier, nearly half the American public thinks the death penalty isn't imposed frequently enough, and fully 60 percent believe it is applied fairly in its current form. Since 1976, the Supreme Court has consistently held that with proper safeguards, the application of the death penalty to competent adults does not violate the Eighth Amendment's prohibition against "cruel and unusual punishment."

AP PHOTO/MICHAEL CONROY

What may seem surprising to many is the degree to which Americans' support for the death penalty defies worldwide trends, which have moved consistently in the opposite direction since World War II. By 1977, sixteen countries had become "abolitionist" regarding the death penalty; by 2010, ninety-five countries worldwide had abolished capital punishment for all offenses, including all but one European country (Belarus is the exception), many Pacific area states (including Australia and New Zealand), and Canada. In 2009, just eighteen countries carried out executions, with the United States ranking fifth (52 executions), behind only China, Iran, Iraq, and Saudi Arabia. To a nation that prides itself as a beacon of light for freedom, this seems like unusual company. And yet the movement to abolish the death penalty in the United States has not made much headway in recent years. Supporters of capital punishment argue that it deters crime and prevents recidivism. Opponents counter that it does not deter criminals more than life imprisonment, risks the execution of the wrongfully convicted, and discriminates against minorities.

At www.cengage.com/dautrich/americangovernment/2e, find the Politics InterActive link for details on the current state of the death penalty in the United States, the factors that have contributed to its continued support, relevant statistical information, and death penalty studies. Consult as well the various links that help place the current debate over the death penalty into historical, popular, and global perspectives.

Chapter Summary

★ The Bill of Rights: Origins and Evolution

- Civil liberties are those specific individual rights guaranteed by the Constitution that government cannot deny to citizens. Most of these rights are found in the Bill of Rights.

- The original Constitution did not include a bill of rights, and the way the Framers guaranteed ratification of the Constitution was to promise that the first Congress would take up as its first task the passage of these amendments.

- Civil liberties are subject to formal interpretation by the courts and informal interpretation by those charged with their enforcement. The courts' interpretation of these rights has evolved greatly over the past two centuries. Originally, these rights were protected from intrusion by the federal government, not necessarily by state or local government.

- Beginning in the mid-twentieth century, the U.S. Supreme Court, through a process known as incorporation, used the Fourteenth Amendment's Due Process Clause to require state and local governments to uphold most of these protections as well.

★ Freedom of Religion and the Establishment Clause

- The free exercise clause bans government laws that prohibit the free exercise of religion. Debate over the clause has largely focused on whether government can force adherents of a certain religion to engage in activities that are prohibited by their religious beliefs or prevent them from performing acts that are compelled by their religious beliefs.

- The establishment clause prohibits the government from enacting any law "respecting an establishment of religion." In recent decades, the Supreme Court has moved from a position of especially strict separation to one that shifts back and forth between principles of separation and accommodation.

★ Free Expression Rights

- The First Amendment rights of free speech and press enjoy especially revered status in the United States because free expression promotes the marketplace of ideas, acts as a watchdog on government, and advances the capacity for individuals to create ideas and improve society.

- The press is afforded a great deal of latitude because the courts have made libel suits very difficult to prosecute, and only under very few conditions may government issue a prior restraint on the publication of a story. Speech is not just the spoken word—it also includes such things as flag burning, referred to as symbolic speech, which also enjoys a high level of protection from the courts.

★ The Second Amendment Right to Bear Arms

- The Constitution protects the right of individuals to possess a firearm; still, the government retains the power to enact a broad range of firearms laws, including reasonable restrictions on possession by felons, or in sensitive places like schools or government buildings.

★ The Rights of the Criminally Accused

- The right of citizens to be free from unreasonable searches and seizures has a long history in America, and is the subject of the Fourth Amendment. Although there are some exceptions to the exclusion of evidence based on a warrantless search, the basic notion that probable cause is a requirement for a warrant and that a warrant is necessary for a search holds true.

- Modern technologies have given the police and investigators new methods of search and surveillance. Some of these modern police tactics have been successfully challenged on Fourth Amendment grounds. But as the use of these techniques is broadened—perhaps to facilitate racial profiling or other controversial forms of police investigation—it is certain that legal challenges will be waged.

- Additional rights of the accused are articulated in the Fifth Amendment, including the double jeopardy clause, the grand jury requirement, and the self-incrimination clause. The U.S. Supreme Court has ruled that police must read the "*Miranda* warnings" to anyone who is arrested, which indicates not only the right to remain silent, but also the right to an attorney—a right protected by the Sixth Amendment. Failure to read the *Miranda* rights may lead to a confession being excluded as evidence at trial.

- The Ninth Amendment indicates that just because an individual right is not explicitly spelled out does not mean that the right is not protected. Two such high-profile rights are the subject of much national debate: the right to privacy and the right to die. The former served as the basis for *Roe v. Wade*—the case that first established abortion rights under the Constitution.

- A more recent conservative Supreme Court (since the decision in *Planned Parenthood v. Casey*) has allowed the states to place more restrictions on abortion rights of late.

- Although the Court has been willing to recognize the right of terminally ill patients to end their medical treatment, it has steadfastly refused to extend that privilege to the active termination of one's life. The Supreme Court has also recognized the rights of gays and lesbians to sexual privacy.

CourseMate

Key Terms

Bail (p. 113)	Exclusionary rule (p. 109)	Libel (p. 101)
Bill of attainder (p. 108)	Free exercise clause (p. 93)	*Miranda* warning (p. 112)
Civil liberties (p. 90)	Good faith exception (p. 110)	Prior restraint (p. 102)
Double jeopardy clause (p. 111)	Incorporation (p. 91)	SLAPS test (p. 103)
Establishment clause (p. 95)	*Katz* test (p. 108)	Symbolic speech (p. 103)
Ex post facto laws (p. 108)	*Lemon* test (p. 97)	Warrant (p. 109)

Resources

Important Books

Amar, Akhil Reed. *The Constitution and Criminal Procedure.* New Haven, CT: Yale University Press, 1997.

Brigham, John. *The Constitution of Interests: Beyond the Politics of Rights.* New York: New York University Press, 1996.

Graber, Mark. *Transforming Free Speech.* Berkeley: University of California Press, 1991.

Lewis, Anthony. *Gideon's Trumpet.* New York: Vintage, 1989.

Lewis, Anthony. *Make No Law: The Sullivan Case and the First Amendment.* New York: Vintage, 1991.

O'Connor, Karen. *No Neutral Ground? Abortion Politics in the Age of Absolutes.* Boulder, CO: Westview Press, 1996.

Ravitch, Frank. *School Prayer and Discrimination.* Boston: Northeastern University Press, 1999.

Stone, Geoffrey. *Perilous Times.* New York: W. W. Norton, 2004.

Internet Sources

http://www.aclu.org (the home page of the American Civil Liberties Union; features coverage of a wide range of developments in civil liberties, as well as links to resources and other relevant Web sites)

http://www.fac.org/ (the Web site of the First Amendment Center, which works to preserve and protect First Amendment freedoms in America through information and education)

http://www.eff.org/ (the Web site of the Electronic Frontier Foundation, founded to protect rights and promote freedom on the electronic frontier, including the Internet)

 **NOW** Shannon Faulkner at The Citadel in 1995.

AP PHOTO/WADE SPEES, POOL

THEN Autherine Lucy at the University of Alabama in 1956.

BETTMANN/CORBIS

NOW & THEN

Slow Going for a Pioneer in Equal Rights

? *After fighting a landmark legal battle with the help of civil rights groups, she had finally secured the right to attend this famous southern institution of higher education. The Fourteenth Amendment, the courts had ruled, prohibited the school from excluding her. Bracing for the worst, she expected resentment and hostility from fellow students once she arrived on campus. The torments and continuous taunting were worse than she anticipated. After receiving numerous death threats, she needed an armed escort to accompany her to classes. Soon the isolation proved unbearable, and in less than a week this landmark experiment in equal rights had reached its premature conclusion. While detractors cheered, the woman packed her bags and left the school she had fought so long and hard to enter. Although equal rights did not prevail at that moment in time, her overall cause was not lost—within a few years many other students like her would successfully enter that same institution under more favorable conditions, and many of them would go on to graduate. Although her efforts to strike a blow at the backward traditions of the institution had failed for her personally, those efforts had not been in vain.*

LEARNING OBJECTIVES
★ WHAT YOU WILL LEARN ★

Types of Equality

* ★ Define the three types of equality: political, social, and economic
* ★ Define civil rights and describe its role as a source of conflict among various groups

The Struggle for Equality: Approaches and Tactics

* ★ List the means groups employ to pursue equality within and outside the system

The African American Struggle for Equality and Civil Rights

* ★ Review the history of racial discrimination against African Americans
* ★ Explain the role courts played in initially denying African Americans full equality, and then granting that equality in *Brown v. Board*
* ★ Understand the Court-created framework of equality and the challenges it presented
* ★ Trace the civil rights movement's history
* ★ Describe civil rights and voting rights laws
* ★ Appreciate more recent battles waged over affirmative action and racial profiling

The Women's Movement and Gender Equality

* ★ Understand the history of women's rights from women's suffrage up through the present
* ★ Evaluate the role of the courts in upholding challenges to gender discrimination in the 1970s
* ★ Understand Title IX's effect on women's rights

Other Struggles for Equality

* ★ Examine the struggles for equality waged by other racial, religious, and ethnic groups including Native Americans, Asian Americans, Muslims, and Hispanic Americans
* ★ Recognize the struggles of older Americans, Americans with disabilities, and gays and lesbians

CourseMate

NOW & THEN

MIC SMITH/AFP/
GETTY IMAGES

NOW In 1995, Shannon Faulkner became a modern-day pioneer in equal rights. The institution Faulkner challenged was The Citadel in Charleston, South Carolina. The Citadel was a 152-year-old male-only military academy that prided itself on producing "citizen-soldiers," men uniquely prepared for leadership in military service and in civilian life. Faulkner had been accepted to The Citadel in 1993 after submitting an application that had failed to reveal her gender. When the school found out Faulkner was a woman, it immediately withdrew her acceptance, sparking a lawsuit filed on her behalf. Eventually a federal district court ordered The Citadel to admit Faulkner in 1995 on the grounds that no public school could discriminate on the basis of sex. She moved into the barracks on August 12, 1995, accompanied by federal marshals because she had received so many death threats. Although Faulkner began "hell week" with the rest of her classmates, the emotional toll of the death threats and her isolation—combined with the physical toll of intense physical training—eventually proved too much for her. After only a day of training she was admitted to the infirmary with heat-related symptoms, and on her fifth day at The Citadel Faulkner dropped out of the school. When the news of her withdrawal got out, the male cadets let out a roar of celebration around campus. But their "victory" was short-lived: taking advantage of the court order that Faulkner had secured, four more women enrolled at The Citadel the following year. The Citadel finally graduated its first female cadet (Nancy Mace) in 1999; since then over 200 women have successfully navigated The Citadel's grueling program to become full-fledged graduates of the institution.

THEN Faulkner was hardly the first pioneer to face such trying circumstances at an institution of education steeped in tradition. The scenario also describes the experience of Autherine Lucy, the first African American student to win admission to the University of Alabama. On June 29, 1955, lawyers from the National Association for the Advancement of Colored People (NAACP) secured a court order restraining the university from rejecting Lucy's application on the basis of race; seven months later, on February 3, 1956, the twenty-six-year-old Lucy enrolled as a graduate student in library science at the university's main campus in Tuscaloosa. That's when her personal nightmare began. Immediately upon her arrival she faced mobs of students yelling "Kill her! Kill her!" wherever she walked on campus. She needed a police escort to get her to class and protect her in the classroom, where she could hear crowds chanting epithets at her from outside. Just three days after Lucy enrolled, the university's board suspended her, defending its action as necessary "for her safety and that of other students." Although the NAACP's attempts to overturn Lucy's suspension were unsuccessful, within a decade many more African American students would follow in her footsteps, using a series of court orders to force the integration of the University of Alabama. The battle Autherine Lucy waged against University of Alabama officials was played out over and over again at other educational institutions in the late 1950s and early 1960s as part of a civil rights movement that brought national and international attention to issues of racial discrimination and inequality.

BETTMANN/CORBIS

Chapter 5 Civil Rights, Equality, and Social Movements

ust as Autherine Lucy challenged the white-only traditions of the South, Shannon Faulkner dared to rock the foundations of a well-entrenched male-only institution. Neither of these two women was able to stay in her school long enough to see the institution transformed. Both women, however, made significant contributions to the cause of equal rights. Traditions die hard, and those who battle such institutions in the name of equality must prepare themselves for slow going. Even when court opinions and legislation have transformed the political landscape in favor of equality, social and cultural landscapes often remain products of a stubborn past.

CHECK the List

The Eleven Largest Political Demonstrations Ever Held in Washington, DC

Demonstration	Date	Number of People
✔ March for Women's Lives (favoring abortion and reproductive rights)	April 24, 2004	1,150,000
✔ Vietnam Moratorium Rally	November 15, 1969	600,000
✔ Vietnam "Out Now" rally	April 24, 1971	500,000
✔ National Organization for Women March for Women's Lives	April 5, 1992	500,000
✔ Million Man March	October 16, 1995	400,000
✔ March on Washington II	August 20, 1983	300,000
✔ Pro-Choice Rally	April 9, 1989	300,000
✔ Lesbian and Gay Rights Rally	April 25, 1993	300,000
✔ Solidarity Day Labor Rally	September 19, 1981	260,000
✔ Solidarity Day for Labor	August 31, 1991	250,000
✔ March on Washington	August 28, 1963	250,000

List does not include routine events such as presidential inaugurations or Fourth of July festivities.

Types of Equality

In the abstract, the word *equality* sits alongside terms such as *liberty*, *freedom*, and *justice* as lofty values that underlie American political culture. Unfortunately, when it comes to settling on a formal definition of equality, no consensus exists. "All men are created equal," Thomas Jefferson wrote in the Declaration of Independence of 1776. But Jefferson never intended that document to extend to African American slaves, at least not in the short run. When Abraham Lincoln warned in 1859 that "those who deny freedom to others, deserve it not for themselves," the future president of the United States did not consider the lot of women in American society, who at that time enjoyed no freedom to vote or own property, among other rights. As with any other abstract ideal, we must fully define *equality* in order to understand all that it encompasses.

References to different types of equality tend to appear again and again in discussions of American politics:

Political equality generally refers to a condition in which members of different groups possess substantially the same rights to participate actively in the political system. These rights include voting, running for office, and formally petitioning the government for redress of grievances. In a democracy, the rights to free speech, to free press, and (at least arguably) to a quality education may also be considered necessary elements of political quality, as those who are denied such rights often are less able to exercise influence over the political process in any meaningful way. In the years immediately following the Civil War, some moderates in Congress argued that if freed slaves were simply given formal political equality, other benefits and privileges would inevitably follow. Reality quickly proved otherwise, as even African Americans in the North who were able to exercise their right to vote were generally unable to influence the political process.

Social equality extends beyond the granting of political rights; it refers additionally to equality and fair treatment within the various institutions in society, both public and private, that serve the public at large. Social equality calls for a sameness of treatment in stores, theaters, restaurants, hotels, and public transportation facilities among many other operations open to the public. Jim Crow laws passed in the South during the late nineteenth century segregated many of these institutions, thus denying social equality to African Americans.

Economic equality remains the most controversial form of equality—indeed, its very mention often touches off heated debate among political officials. To some, society's responsibility to promote economic equality requires only that it provide equality of economic "opportunity," by which different groups enjoy substantially the same rights to enter contracts, purchase and sell property, and otherwise compete for resources in society. To others, economic equality extends beyond equality of economic opportunity to something approaching an "equality of results." Whichever meaning one gives to the term, economic equality has been exceedingly difficult to achieve. Although the government has introduced a graduated income tax and other resource-leveling measures during the past century to improve economic opportunities for the poor, large variances in the quality of education afforded to different groups continue to render economic equality an elusive ideal.

The term **civil rights** has traditionally referred to those positive rights, whether political, social, or economic, conferred by the government on individuals or groups that had previously been denied them. What type of equality does the guarantee of civil rights promote? Immediately after the Civil War, civil rights legislation that would have provided for extensive social equality (equal accommodations in hotels, restaurants, trains, and other public facilities) was struck down as unconstitutional by the U.S. Supreme Court. As a result, the package of civil rights granted to freed slaves included only limited political rights, including the right to vote. In the late 1950s and 1960s, renewed efforts to guarantee equality in all areas of American life led to the civil rights movement.[1]

★ LO Define the three types of equality: political, social, and economic

★ LO Define civil rights and describe its role as a source of conflict among different groups in American history.

Political equality
A condition in which members of different groups possess substantially the same rights to participate actively in the political system. In the United States, these rights include voting, running for office, petitioning the government for redress of grievances, free speech, free press, and the access to an education.

Social equality
Equality and fair treatment of all groups within the various institutions in society, both public and private, that serve the public at large, including in stores, theaters, restaurants, hotels, and public transportation facilities among many other operations open to the public.

Economic equality
May be defined as providing all groups the equality of opportunity for economic success, or as the equality of results. In the United States, the latter has been the more common understanding of economic opportunity.

Civil rights
Those positive rights, whether political, social, or economic, conferred by the government on individuals or groups.

Many civil rights battles in American history have been waged by African Americans, but other ethnic groups, women, the physically disabled, the aged, and homosexuals have also sought the political, social, and economic equality denied them. The Constitution of the United States and the amendments to it have provided a framework for these groups to use to win equality. As a result, the meaning of civil rights has been significantly expanded both in the scope of its protection and in the variety of groups who seek its guarantees.

★ LO List the means groups have employed to pursue equality within and outside the system

The Struggle for Equality: Approaches and Tactics

The methods and tactics various groups use to achieve equality have evolved since the end of the Civil War. Initially, the battle over what constituted the most effective means of fostering change—at least in the context of challenging racial discrimination against African Americans—pitted two competing philosophies against each other. Booker T. Washington, who founded Tuskegee Normal and Industrial Institute (today Tuskegee University) in Alabama in 1881, advocated a philosophy of *accommodation*, which promoted vocational education for African Americans and opposed confrontation with the mostly white power structure in place in post–Civil War America. Washington urged his fellow African Americans to accept existing conditions, even to the point of tolerating racial segregation and all but surrendering the newly won right to vote. According to his philosophy, only by engaging in law-abiding practices and standing by their former white oppressors would African Americans become prepared for the exercise of the franchise. Washington's philosophy of accommodation fit comfortably within the dominant conservative political and economic structure of his time. Although some critics charged him with accepting second-class citizenship for his race, Washington was perhaps the most powerful and influential figure in African American affairs until his death in 1915.[2]

Washington's passive approach contrasted with the philosophy of *agitation*, which challenged racial discrimination and injustice through various forms of political activity. Among Washington's contemporaries, the most widely recognized proponent of this alternative approach was W. E. B. Du Bois. At the beginning of the twentieth century, Du Bois and his associates proposed a specific platform of legal, political, and social reforms to achieve social, economic, and political equality for

Members of the Congressional Black Caucus at the August 2008 Democratic National Convention in Denver, Colorado.

PAUL J. RICHARDS/AFP/GETTY IMAGES

African Americans.[3] Their demands included the unfettered right to vote and an immediate end to all segregation. Agitation eventually replaced accommodation as the dominant mode by which African Americans and other groups sought equality in twentieth-century America. New debates emerged, however, over what would be the most effective means and methods for achieving these reforms. Tactics that various groups have used to seek their civil rights include

- **Working within the political system.** Some groups have used the political process to implement reforms to end discrimination. In recent decades, for example, African Americans have used their substantial power as a voting bloc to influence the outcome of some elections. Various groups have expanded their influence more directly over public policies and programs by lobbying and petitioning government officials; in some cases members of these groups have been elected to high public office, giving them a place at the table of political power.

- **Litigation.** When the political arena fails to provide adequate remedies to discrimination, a lawsuit brought before a court may afford a better opportunity for success. Founded in 1909 for the purpose of ensuring the political, educational, social, and economic equality of rights of all Americans, the NAACP focused its efforts on legal challenges to discrimination and segregation because the political arena had offered inadequate remedies. Civil rights legislation in particular had proven ineffective, with southern state legislatures either ignoring or circumventing the laws. The NAACP won a string of legal battles that gradually broke down racial barriers in education and elsewhere. These efforts culminated with the U.S. Supreme Court's decision in **Brown v. Board of Education (1954)**,[4] which ordered desegregation of public schools. In subsequent years women's groups, disabled people, and other victims of discrimination have similarly turned to the courts for remedies to discriminatory practices.

- **Legal boycott.** The organized refusal to buy, sell, or use certain goods or to perform certain services has long been a tool in economic battles waged between employers and unions. Adopting this tactic for use in the war on racial discrimination, African American citizens of Montgomery, Alabama, refused to ride the city's buses for more than a year in the mid-1950s; their efforts drained the city's public transportation budget and ultimately forced city officials to desegregate the bus system. In 2003, women's rights organizations discouraged some companies from sponsoring the Masters Golf Tournament held at the all-male Augusta National Golf Club in Augusta, Georgia.

- **Civil disobedience.** Sometimes citizens resort to passive resistance to what they see as an unjust government policy or law by openly refusing to obey it. Such a tactic may result in arrests, fines, or even jail time for those who practice it. Still, civil disobedience may also call attention to a group's plight in an especially effective way. The Reverend Martin Luther King Jr., who had studied the methods used by Mohandas Gandhi of India and other nonviolent protestors, applied these methods to the civil rights movement in the American South.

Brown v. Board of Education **(1954)**
The 1954 U.S. Supreme Court decision that declared school segregation to be unconstitutional.

The African American Struggle for Equality and Civil Rights

Review the history of racial discrimination against African Americans ★ LO

Colonists who supported the American Revolution trumpeted the notion of equality as a means of justifying their war with England. Yet when the U.S. Constitution was drafted in 1787, the document said nothing about such a call to equality, nor did the Bill of Rights (ratified in 1791) guarantee to all citizens "equal protection of the law." The period following the Revolution offered equality primarily to property-owning white men. Nowhere did Jefferson's call for equality, as stated in the Declaration of Independence, seem more hollow than in the area of racial discrimination. Throughout the North, African Americans were denied the right to vote and numerous other economic and social privileges enjoyed by white citizens. And in the South, the institution of slavery thrived for more than a half century after the Constitution was ratified.

Racial Discrimination: From Slavery to Reconstruction

The organized antislavery movement in the United States began in the late eighteenth century as an effort to eradicate slavery through progressive elimination. Advocates of gradual emancipation believed that by preventing the extension of slavery to new areas and relocating emancipated slaves to areas outside the United States, slavery would eventually die out. Opposed to gradual emancipation were the abolitionists, who sought the immediate emancipation of all slaves. A leader of the abolitionist movement was William Lloyd Garrison, who founded the antislavery periodical, *The Liberator*, in 1831. It is noteworthy, however, that even extreme abolitionists such as Garrison believed that the "fatal characteristic" of slavery was that it denied African Americans the basic legal rights to own property, enter into contracts, or testify in court. Many abolitionists at the time did *not* believe that emancipation automatically entitled freed slaves to the right to vote or serve on juries. Even among some of the most ardent advocates of equality before the Civil War, a sharp distinction was often drawn between economic rights—which they felt African Americans were entitled to—and basic political rights including suffrage, which were somehow not viewed as natural entitlements.

Neither conception of civil rights for slaves gained much favor in the South, where the economy of the plantation system depended on slave labor. The Southerners' approach to racial equality was perhaps best summed up by Chief Justice Roger Taney of Maryland, who in the landmark Supreme Court case of *Dred Scott v. Sandford* (1857)[5] wrote that blacks were "so far inferior that they had no rights which the white man was bound to respect." The initial rhetoric surrounding the outbreak of the Civil War in 1861 focused on issues such as states' rights and territorial expansion in addition to slavery. The Emancipation Proclamation issued by President Lincoln in 1863 declared the freedom of all slaves in states fighting the Union and allowed blacks to enlist in the Union Army. By the end of the struggle in 1865, the war was essentially transformed into a battle over the end of the institution of slavery.

With the Union victory in the Civil War, the complete emancipation of African Americans after the war was a foregone conclusion. Former slaves were able to legally marry, worship as they wished, and migrate to different parts of the country. But the years following the Civil War—normally referred to as the Reconstruction Era (1865–1877) in American history—proved a mixed blessing for the newly freed slaves.[6] The **Civil War Amendments** to the Constitution did grant African Americans the rights of citizenship. The Thirteenth Amendment (ratified in 1865) banished slavery from all states and U.S. territories. The Fourteenth Amendment (ratified in 1868) granted full U.S. and state citizenship to all people born or naturalized in the United States and guaranteed to each person "the equal protection of the laws." Finally, the Fifteenth Amendment (1870) forbade the denial or abridgement of the right to vote by any government on account of race. The Republican-controlled Congress hoped that these three amendments would institutionalize freedom for the former slaves and protect their rights from being undermined by future generations.

During the Reconstruction era, many freed slaves were successful in getting on ballots in the former Confederate states—in all, twenty-two African Americans were elected to the House and one (Hiram Revels of Mississippi) was elected to the Senate during the latter part of the nineteenth century. African American participation in Congress tailed off at the beginning of the twentieth century, however, because restrictions on the franchise curtailed the political viability of most black candidates. No African American served in either house of Congress for most of the first three

DRED SCOTT SUBJECT OF THE DECISION OF THE SUPREME COURT OF THE UNITED STATES IN 1857, WHICH DENIED CITIZENSHIP TO THE NEGRO AND BECAME ONE OF THE EVENTS THAT RESULTED IN THE CIVIL WAR

BASED ON DIVINE/BREEN/FREDRICKSON/
WILLIAMS, *AMERICA PAST AND PRESENT*,
SIXTH EDITION, © 2002 ADDISON-WESLEY
EDUCATIONAL PUBLISHERS.

Civil War Amendments

The Thirteenth Amendment (ratified in 1865) banished slavery from all states and U.S. territories. The Fourteenth Amendment (ratified in 1868) granted full U.S. and state citizenship to all people born or naturalized in the United States and guaranteed to each person "the equal protection of the laws." The Fifteenth Amendment (1870) forbade the denial or abridgement of the right to vote by any government on account of race.

decades of the twentieth century, and just four served in the House up to 1954. After George Henry White (R-NC) left Congress in 1901, no African American was elected from a southern state again until 1973, when Barbara Jordan (D-TX) and Andrew Young (D-GA) were elected to serve in the Ninety-third Congress.

Although African Americans achieved some gains during Reconstruction, the Reconstruction-era generation posed the greatest threat to those civil rights victories. The Fourteenth Amendment had been proposed in part to negate the infamous *Black Codes* passed by the Southern states, which denied African Americans numerous economic and social rights. However, in *The Slaughterhouse Cases* (1873),[7] a conservative U.S. Supreme Court narrowly defined the scope of rights protected by the Fourteenth Amendment, holding that the great body of civil rights still lay under the protection of state governments, not the U.S. Constitution. The Civil Rights Act of 1875 attempted to ensure the social and political rights of freed slaves by, among other provisions, prohibiting discrimination in public accommodations. The Supreme Court invalidated the act in *The Civil Rights Cases* (1883),[8] ruling that whereas the Constitution prohibits the states from discriminating by race against certain civil rights, it does not protect the invasion of such civil rights by private individuals unaided by state authority. Therefore, privately owned restaurants and hotels could freely discriminate on the basis of race without violating the Constitution.

This judicial gutting of federal civil rights guarantees opened the way for numerous abuses of freed slaves once the federal government's military occupation of the South ended in 1877. Although the Fifteenth Amendment had given African American men the right to vote, the Southern states imposed new barriers to disenfranchise the former slaves. They levied *poll taxes*, which a voter had to pay before being allowed to vote; they required potential voters to pass *literacy tests*; they demanded some form of property-owning and residency documentation; they issued a grandfather clause requirement, which stated that to be eligible to vote one's grandfather had to have voted; and they restricted blacks from participating in crucial party primaries. Discrimination against African Americans in all areas of public life soon became the norm. Terrorist groups like the Ku Klux Klan intimidated or threatened African Americans to keep them under control, sometimes backing up their threats with beatings, arson, or murder. White vigilante groups resorted to lynching in an effort to restore white supremacy and deny blacks their rights. Post–Civil War blacks might no longer be slaves, but they could hardly be considered fully equal citizens under the law.

Racial Segregation and Barriers to Equality

In the period immediately following the Civil War, some African Americans were able to use public accommodations as long as they could afford to pay for them. By the turn of the twentieth century, however, growing racial tensions, exacerbated by urbanization and industrialization, led to racial segregation throughout America. The Southern states enacted **Jim Crow laws**, which required segregation of blacks and whites in public schools, railroads, buses, restaurants, hotels, theaters, and other public facilities. The laws excluded blacks from militias and denied them certain education and welfare services. When Homer Plessy (described in court filings as being "seven-eights Caucasian and one-eight African blood") was arrested on a Louisiana train for refusing to leave a seat in a coach section designated for whites, he challenged the Louisiana law requiring segregated railroad cars, arguing that the law violated the equal protection clause of the Fourteenth Amendment. In *Plessy v. Ferguson* (1896),[9] the Supreme Court upheld the Louisiana law on the theory that as long as the accommodations between the racially segregated cars were equal, the equal protection clause was not violated. The Court's ruling established the constitutionality of racial segregation according to the *separate but equal* doctrine. To the argument that such an enforced separation of the two races stamps the colored race

Jim Crow laws
Laws used by some southern states that required segregation of blacks and whites in public schools, railroads, buses, restaurants, hotels, theaters, and other public facilities. The laws excluded blacks from militias and denied them certain education and welfare services.

Plessy v. Ferguson (1896)
The Supreme Court case that upheld a Louisiana segregation law on the theory that as long as the accommodations between the racially segregated facilities were equal, the equal protection clause was not violated. The Court's ruling effectively established the constitutionality of racial segregation and the notion of "separate but equal."

with a "badge of inferiority," the Supreme Court replied matter-of-factly: "If this be so, it is not by reason of anything found in the act, but solely because the colored race *chooses* to put that construction upon it."

African American leaders responded to the spread of segregation in different ways. Initially, Booker T. Washington's accommodationist philosophy prevailed. W. E. B. Du Bois, by contrast, advocated direct and militant challenges to segregation. Perhaps the greatest breakthrough against segregation occurred through the legal arm of the organization that Du Bois helped found: the NAACP. Beginning in the late 1930s, NAACP lawyers Charles Houston and Thurgood Marshall began attacking the legal basis for segregation in the courts.[10] They won their first battles against state-mandated segregation in institutions of higher education, as the Supreme Court in 1950 recognized that separate accommodations in law schools and colleges had failed to meet the essential requirements of equality mandated by the Fourteenth Amendment (see Table 5.1).

The NAACP's incremental approach to eliminating segregation in education reached its climax in 1954, with the Supreme Court's landmark decision in *Brown v. Board of Education*. Chief Justice Earl Warren, writing for a unanimous Court, held that racial segregation in any facet of public education constituted a denial of equal protection by the laws. Recognizing the psychological harms of segregation on African American children, the Court declared that segregated schools were "inherently unequal."

★ **LO** Explain the role courts played in initially denying African Americans full equality, and then granting that equality in *Brown v. Board*

TABLE 5.1 Tracking the NAACP's Legal Assault on Racially Segregated Education

U.S. Supreme Court Case	Description
Missouri ex. rel. Gaines v. Canada (1938)	Invalidated the exclusion of black students from the University of Missouri's School of Law absent some other provision for their legal training.
Sipuel v. Bd. of Regents of Univ. of Okla. (1948)	Rejected Oklahoma's attempt to create a separate law school for blacks by roping off a section of the state capitol for black law students and assigning three law teachers to them; such a form of separation failed to comply with the constitutional requirement of "equality."
Sweatt v. Painter (1950)	Invalidated Texas's attempt to create an alternative to the University of Texas law school for blacks, because any such alternative would be inherently different in the reputation of its faculty, the experience of its administration, the position and influence of its alumni, its standing in the community, and so on.
McLaurin v. Okla. State Regents (1950)	Rejected as "unequal" Oklahoma's attempt to provide graduate education to a black student by making him sit in a classroom surrounded by a railing marked "reserved for colored," assigning him a segregated desk in the library, and requiring him to sit separately from whites in the cafeteria.
Brown v. Board of Education (1954)	Rejected the "separate but equal" doctrine altogether, declaring that in the field of public education, "separate educational facilities are inherently unequal."
Cooper v. Aaron (1957)	Condemned the attempts of the Little Rock, Arkansas, school board to postpone desegregation efforts, ruling that no scheme of racial discrimination against black schoolchildren can stand if "there is state participation through any arrangement, management, funds, or property."

The *Brown* decision also confirmed that in all future cases related to racial (and ethnic) discrimination, the Court would apply a standard of **strict scrutiny**, a level of judicial review that requires the government to prove that the racial classification of the law or practice in question is "narrowly tailored" to meet a "compelling state interest." What precisely does this mean? At a minimum, there should be no less-restrictive alternative means available for achieving the government's objectives, and those objectives should stand among the most necessary that may be pursued by any government. Many legal scholars and judges say the strict scrutiny standard tends to invalidate nearly all government laws and programs. In the years following *Brown*, the courts would apply the standard of strict scrutiny in decisions on segregated public swimming pools, police forces, and laws banning interracial marriages.

A year after handing down the *Brown* decision, the Supreme Court declared that its implementation should proceed "with all deliberate speed." Despite that decree, many local school boards resisted desegregation. The school board of Little Rock, Arkansas, adopted a plan for "phased integration" over a ten-year period, spurring more lawsuits to speed up the process. Undeterred, Arkansas Governor Orval Faubus declared that no "*Brown* decisions" enjoyed "the force of law" in his state. In one famous instance, he placed soldiers of the Arkansas National Guard at Little Rock's Central High School to stop African American students from entering the school.

Strict scrutiny
A legal standard set in *Brown v. Board of Education* for cases related to racial discrimination that tends to invalidate almost all state laws that segregate racial groups.

★ LO
Understand the Court-created framework of equality and the challenges it presented

African American students are escorted through the doors of Little Rock's Central High School by the U.S. National Guard on September 25, 1957.

Governor Ross Barnett of Mississippi refused to comply with court desegregation orders on so many occasions that a federal court held him in contempt and committed him "to the custody of the Attorney General of the United States." Alabama Governor George Wallace blocked a University of Alabama doorway, refusing to allow black students to pass through in 1963. As discussed in the chapter opening, Autherine Lucy was turned back in her attempt to remain a student at the University of Alabama. One hundred members of Congress signed a "Southern Manifesto" declaring their intention to use "all lawful means" to reverse the *Brown* decision. On several occasions, the Supreme Court was forced to reassert its authority over state governments. In *Cooper v. Aaron* (1957),[11] for example, the Court held that the rights of African

American students could "neither be nullified openly and directly by state legislatures or state executive officials . . . by evasive schemes for segregation."

Despite the Supreme Court's increasingly clear edicts against segregation, many school districts in the South and North continued to drag their feet.[12] Significant and widespread change would not occur until after passage of civil rights legislation in the mid-1960s, which gave the executive branch of the government increased power to enforce school desegregation in local districts. Additionally, a sudden influx of federal money into local schools gave extra bite to court desegregation decrees. As scholar Gerald Rosenberg remarked: "Put simply, courts could hold up federal funds." Many school districts in the Deep South where less than half of all blacks were being educated alongside whites as late as 1967 were almost fully integrated by 1971.

In urban areas where whites and blacks lived largely apart, strict adherence to a neighborhood school system meant indefinitely perpetuating a racially unmixed setting; thus massive court-ordered "busing" in the late 1960s and 1970s became a controversial feature of efforts to integrate these schools. Many such court orders were issued in both northern and southern cities, as the Supreme Court required communities to cease both *de jure discrimination* (segregation sanctioned by the law), which was found mostly in the South, and *de facto discrimination* (segregation in reality, such as that which occurs when different racial groups voluntarily choose to live in different neighborhoods or attend different schools), which was found in both the North and the South. Yet busing was a remedy limited to a single metropolitan area, and comprehensive efforts to integrate schools were further hindered by white flight to suburbia, which left inner-city school districts in many large northern cities predominantly black and Hispanic. Today, fully 70 percent of the nation's African American students attend schools that are predominantly black. Thus more than fifty years after the *Brown* decision, de facto discrimination in public education remains a reality in many parts of America.

The Beginnings of the Civil Rights Movement

Although *Brown* signaled the end of state-sponsored segregation, the Supreme Court took pains to note that its holding applied only to discriminatory acts by the government. The extension of civil rights protections to all public accommodations did not occur until the civil rights movement began to gather momentum in the late 1950s and early 1960s. In December 1955, Rosa Parks, an African American seamstress in Montgomery, Alabama, was arrested for refusing to give up her seat at the front of a city bus. Her arrest sparked a racial boycott of the city's bus system. Leading the boycott was Martin Luther King Jr., pastor of the Dexter Avenue Baptist Church. King's eloquent speeches and his methods of nonviolent civil disobedience brought national attention to the boycott. King had been introduced to these tactics of nonviolent protest when he was a student at Crozer Theological Seminary in Chester, Pennsylvania, and studied the pacifist philosophy of Mohandas Gandhi of India, whose

MICHAEL EVANS/HULTON ARCHIVE/CONTRIBUTOR/GETTY IMAGES

In 1948, a nineteen-year-old student named Martin Luther King Jr. was first introduced to the pacifist philosophy of Mohandas Gandhi. By seeking a nonviolent confrontation with the segregation laws, King's followers practiced Gandhi's philosophy in a way that sent shock waves throughout the South and eventually the entire nation. King would continue to preach Gandhi's call for nonviolent protest up until his assassination in 1968.

unshakable belief in nonviolent protest and religious toler-
ance helped secure independence for his country from Great
Britain.

In 1957, King and other African American ministers in the
South formed the Southern Christian Leadership Conference
(SCLC), which encouraged Ghandian practices of nonviolent
civil disobedience as a way to gain equal rights for blacks
and spur white politicians into action. African American and
white college students in numerous cities across the South
eventually became the engine for pressing such change. One
early tactic the students used was the sit-in. On February 1,
1960, four freshmen from the black North Carolina A&T College in Greensboro sat down at a whites-only lunch counter
and refused to move after being denied service. The next day
more students—black and white—joined them. Angry mobs
harassed the students verbally and physically. Committed
to nonviolence, the students endured the abuse. The episode
brought considerable publicity to the civil rights movement.
In 1961, interracial groups of students sponsored "Freedom
Rides," traveling together from Washington, DC, to the South
to test court decisions prohibiting segregation on interstate
buses and in bus terminals; many within the groups of interstate travelers of mixed races were beaten when their buses
arrived in Alabama. Eventually President John F. Kennedy
was forced to nationalize the Alabama police to help assure
the freedom riders safe passage.

FOX PHOTOS/STRINGER/HULTON ARCHIVE/GETTY IMAGES

Mohandas Gandhi of India, whose unshakable belief in
nonviolent protest helped secure independence of his
country from Great Britain.

Birmingham 1963: The Turning Point of the Civil Rights Movement

The civil rights movement's strategy of nonviolent civil disobedience reached a climax between 1963 and 1965.[13] The year 1963 will long be remembered as the "Year
of Birmingham." Tension was growing between King's SCLC and new civil rights
groups that favored more radical and militant action, including the use of violence.

BETTMANN/CORBIS

In 1963, firefighters in
Birmingham, Alabama,
sprayed civil rights demonstrators with fire hoses.

Civil Rights Act of 1964

The federal law that banned racial discrimination in all public accommodations, including those that were privately owned; prohibited discrimination by employers and created the Equal Employment Opportunity Commission to investigate complaints of discrimination; and denied public funds to schools that continued to discriminate on the basis of race.

Voting Rights Act of 1965

The federal law that invalidated literacy tests and property requirements and required select states and cities to apply for permission to the Justice Department to change their voting laws. As a consequence, millions of African Americans were effectively reenfranchised in the South.

Civil Rights Act of 1968

The federal law that banned race discrimination in housing and made interference with a citizen's civil rights a federal crime.

Twenty-fourth Amendment

A 1964 constitutional amendment that banned poll taxes in federal elections.

Looking for a site where nonviolent demonstrations might succeed and draw national attention to the civil rights movement, King and his followers settled on Birmingham, Alabama. Birmingham was an obvious target, for several reasons. First, as an industrial city (unlike most southern cities), it had a sizable concentration of workers. Also, during the 1930s and 1940s, the labor movement had introduced to the city a tradition of organized protest unusual throughout most of the South. And finally, the city was a stronghold of segregation; city leaders included the notoriously racist Public Safety Commissioner Eugene "Bull" Connor, who ruthlessly enforced segregation laws throughout the city.

In Birmingham, King led other demonstrators in a nonviolent march downtown, where he was arrested and placed in solitary confinement. While confined, he wrote his famous "Letter from Birmingham City Jail," addressed to the white Alabama clergymen who had criticized King's campaign. In the letter, King explained his philosophy and defended his strategy of nonviolent protest. Despite King's arrest, the demonstration in Birmingham continued. The marchers, including more than a thousand black schoolchildren, were met by attack dogs, cattle prods, and fire hoses. Pictures of children being attacked flashed across the nation's television sets and the violence was covered by newspapers and magazines across the world. The nation would be forever aroused by these events; the civil rights movement had finally been transformed into a truly national cause.

Birmingham businessmen, fearing damage to their downtown stores, hastened negotiations with King and his fellow civil rights leaders. An accord was eventually reached on May 10, 1963, with merchants agreeing to desegregate lunch counters and hire more black workers for clerical and sales positions. Yet the agreement did not bring peace to Birmingham: On the night of May 11, a Ku Klux Klan rally outside the city was followed by the explosion of bombs at the motel where King was staying. Riots erupted and some stores were set ablaze. This time, however, the federal government got involved; President Kennedy dispatched soldiers to Fort McClellan, thirty miles outside of Birmingham. Nevertheless, in September a bombing at the city's Sixteenth Street Baptist Church killed four African American schoolgirls.

The events in Birmingham were neither the last of the civil rights demonstrations nor did they mark the end of violence in response to those activities. In August 1963, more than 250,000 people participated in the March on Washington where King delivered his memorable "I Have a Dream" speech from the steps of the Lincoln Memorial. In 1964, the murder of three civil rights workers and a local NAACP leader in Mississippi revealed the depth of continuing opposition to racial equality. In 1965, King and other civil rights leaders organized a march from Selma, Alabama, to the state capital in Montgomery to bring attention to harsh political realities in the South, where African Americans had been denied the right to vote by illegitimate tests and in some instances outright intimidation.

President Lyndon Johnson and the U.S. Congress were eventually prodded into action. Johnson signed into law the **Civil Rights Act of 1964**, which banned racial discrimination in all public accommodations, including those that were privately owned; it also prohibited discrimination by employers and created the Equal Employment Opportunity Commission to investigate complaints of discrimination; and it denied public funds to schools that continued to discriminate on the basis of race.[14] The **Voting Rights Act of 1965**, enacted the following year, invalidated literacy tests and property requirements and required that certain states and cities with a history of voting discrimination obtain pre-approval from the Justice Department for all future changes to their voting laws. As a consequence, millions of African Americans were effectively reenfranchised in the South.

The **Civil Rights Act of 1968** banned race discrimination in housing and made interference with a citizen's civil rights a federal crime. Even the state legislatures played a role in this civil rights transformation by ratifying the **Twenty-fourth Amendment** in 1964, which banned poll taxes in federal elections.

TABLE 5.2 The Effect of the Voting Rights Act on Registration Rates in the South

The following table compares black voter registration rates with white voter registration rates in seven Southern states in 1965 and 1988. All numbers are percentage rates.

State	March 1965			November 1988		
	Black	White	Gap	Black	White	Gap
Alabama	19.3	69.2	49.9	68.4	75.0	6.6
Georgia	27.4	62.6	35.2	56.8	63.9	7.1
Louisiana	31.6	80.5	48.9	77.1	75.1	-2.0
Mississippi	6.7	69.9	63.2	74.2	80.5	6.3
North Carolina	46.8	96.8	50.0	58.2	65.6	7.4
South Carolina	37.3	75.7	38.4	56.7	61.8	5.1
Virginia	38.3	61.1	22.8	63.8	68.5	4.7

Source: The U.S. Commission on Civil Rights, 1975.

The focus of the civil rights movement began to shift in the mid to late 1960s with the rise of "black nationalism," which was grounded in the belief that African Americans could not effectively work within the confines of a racist political system to produce effective change. Malcolm X, a leading advocate of black nationalism, sought to turn the characteristic of being black-skinned into a source of strength, and he urged African Americans to shun white culture and the values promoted by white society. He and other black nationalists criticized the civil rights leaders who advocated integration into white society rather than building separate black institutions. Following the assassination of Martin Luther King Jr. in 1968, the influence of black nationalism in the civil rights movement reached its peak during the late 1960s and early 1970s. Epitomizing a revolutionary vision of society that replaced the strategy of nonviolence with confrontational tactics, the Black Panther Party became a controversial militant presence in some cities.

Although the Black Panther Party had all but faded as a significant entity by 1972, black separatist organizations continue to maintain a strong presence. For example, the Nation of Islam (Black Muslims), led by Louis Farrakhan, preaches class consciousness and the concept of black self-rule. In 1995, Farrakhan's Nation of Islam led the Million Man March in Washington, DC, which far outdrew the 1963 March on Washington. This Million Man March garnered international attention for Farrakhan's movement. Four years later, African American women held their own million women march.

Barack Obama's historic election as the first African American president in U.S. history may have fundamentally changed how many African Americans perceive their national government. Still, African Americans as a whole face immense challenges in making their voices heard in other institutions on the national political scene. Obama left a Senate chamber in November 2008 in which he had been the only African American then serving, and where he was just the third popularly elected African American senator to serve since Reconstruction. (His replacement as junior senator from Illinois, Roland Burris, also an African American, was appointed to the position.) African Americans enjoyed a bit more success in the other house of Congress, as forty-two African Americans (9.5 percent) served in the House of Representatives during the 111th Congress. Finally, African Americans have been mostly absent from the highest levels of state government: In 2006, Deval Patrick of Massachusetts became only the second popularly elected African American governor in history.

Barack Obama takes the oath of office as President of the United States on January 20, 2009.

CHIP SOMODEVILLA/GETTY IMAGES

★ LO Appreciate more recent battles waged over affirmative action and racial profiling

Affirmative action

Programs, laws, or practices designed to remedy past discriminatory hiring practices, government contracting, and school admissions.

Continuing Struggles over Racial Equality

Two contemporary and hotly debated topics related to racial equality are affirmative action and racial profiling.

Affirmative Action. Some observers have called the civil rights movement a "Second Reconstruction," because it eliminated most of the vestiges of racial discrimination and segregation from the books. But would this successful legal revolution translate into real change? Various civil rights leaders in the 1970s and 1980s shifted their focus to affirmative action as a means of promoting African American gains in education and the workplace. **Affirmative action** programs are generally laws or practices designed to remedy past discriminatory hiring practices, government contracting, and school admissions. The women's movement too has benefited from affirmative action programs in the workplace and elsewhere. Although "quotas" (specifically defined numerical goals for hiring or admitting members of certain groups) have been used in the past, more often such programs involve giving some form of preferential treatment, whether by adding points to a mathematical score due to a person's status as a member of a particular racial group, or by creating economic or other incentives for administrative bodies to increase the diversity of their incoming workforce and/or educational institutions.

Proponents of affirmative action argue that past discriminatory practices have deprived certain racial groups and women of opportunities to get the skills or experiences they need to compete for jobs or college admissions on an equal footing with those who have not experienced such discrimination. The issue of affirmative action reached the U.S. Supreme Court in the case of *Regents of the University of California v. Bakke* (1978).[15] In 1973, Alan Bakke, one of 2,664 applicants for one hundred seats at the University of California–Davis Medical School, interviewed with one of the school's officials, Dr. Theodore West. At that time, West told Bakke that he was a "very desirable applicant to the medical school." Thus Bakke was quite surprised when he was denied admission. Bakke in fact was rejected not once but twice for admission: in 1973 and again in 1974. In both instances, sixteen applicants with lower grade point averages and MCAT (Medical College Admission Test) scores than Bakke's were admitted to the school under a special minority admissions program. Bakke challenged the program as a violation of the Fourteenth Amendment's equal protection clause. In previous years, the courts had dismissed most lawsuits because they were quickly rendered "moot," a legal term that indicates that circumstances have removed the practical significance of deciding the case. (By attending some other school, those unsuccessful applicants had essentially prevented their cases from ever being decided.) But Bakke was determined to go to University of California–Davis Medical School and thus his case eventually reached the U.S. Supreme Court.

In deciding the case, the Supreme Court ruled that a university could take into account race and ethnicity when making decisions about the admission of students, as long as it did not utilize specifically assigned numerical goals. To the Court, no constitutional infirmity exists where "race or ethnic background is simply one element—to be weighed fairly against other elements—in the selection process." In his majority opinion, Justice Lewis Powell also heralded the benefits of a diverse student body, noting that students with particular racial backgrounds may bring to a school "experiences, outlooks and ideas that enrich the training of its student body."[16]

Five years after he was first denied admission, Bakke got what he wanted: on June 28, 1978, the U.S. Supreme Court directed that he be admitted to the university's medical school. Opponents of affirmative action thought they had received the victory they were looking for; after all, the Court held that the university could not use fixed racial quotas in this instance. But schools and universities took refuge in the Court's statements favoring the consideration of racial criteria more generally, and in the quarter century that followed, countless schools of higher education utilized race-conscious admissions programs. Thus although Alan Bakke won his personal battle for admission, the war over affirmative action would continue to be waged in the years that followed.

Opponents of affirmative action complain that such programs punish white applicants who played no role at all in the original discriminatory practices. They also claim that a racial divide that currently exists in this country may be exacerbated by affirmative action, because members of racial groups who benefit from such programs may be stigmatized by the perception that they are not fully deserving. Finally, affirmative action programs are explicit racial classifications, and thus may be thought to violate the principle of a "color-blind Constitution" that was celebrated by the Supreme Court's decision in *Brown v. Board of Education*.

A string of Supreme Court decisions in the late 1980s and 1990s have effectively brought an end to explicit affirmative action programs in public employment and contracting. The final nail in the coffin for affirmative action in contracting may have been the Court's decision in *Adarand v. Peña* (1995),[17] which held that any racial classification may be considered unconstitutional unless it meets the test of strict scrutiny: that it must be "narrowly tailored" to further a "compelling governmental interest," a standard that has proved nearly impossible for the government to meet. In fact, no affirmative action employment plan has been upheld as constitutional since the early 1990s.

By contrast, affirmative action in education remains steeped in controversy; the confusion over what is legal in this context was only partially resolved by two

University of Michigan cases in 2003 that essentially reaffirmed *Bakke*'s finding that diversity constitutes a "compelling state interest" under certain circumstances. In *Grutter v. Bollinger* (2003),[18] the Court upheld the university's law school admission program because it only considered race as a positive factor in a review process where all individual applications were carefully reviewed and analyzed on their own merits. Yet that same day in *Gratz v. Bollinger* (2003),[19] the Supreme Court struck down the same university's undergraduate admissions program because instead of providing such careful, individualized review, it automatically awarded twenty points to all students from underrepresented groups, greatly enhancing their chances of being admitted. The Court declared that such a blanket award of benefits was not "narrowly tailored" enough to promote diversity.

In an attempt to balance the interests of having a diverse student body with frequently heard criticisms of affirmative action, state governments in Texas, Florida, and California have enacted alternative programs that would guarantee a place at the state's top universities for every student who finishes in the upper tier (normally the top 5 or 10 percent) of his or her high school class. Given that racial minorities tend to predominate at high schools both in the inner city and in especially poor rural neighborhoods in the South, these percentage plans tend to guarantee seats at major state universities to minority students who would otherwise have been denied admission. Critics of the plans charge that they capitalize on patterns of segregation in housing and geography.

Racial inequality remains a fact of life in twenty-first-century America. According to a 2000 U.S. Census Bureau report, the mean and median income of African American workers is just 64 percent that of similarly situated non-Hispanic whites, and the mean net wealth of African Americans is 17 percent of what it is for non-Hispanic whites.[20] Meanwhile, the *Journal of Blacks in Higher Education* recently reported that almost 37 percent of non-Hispanic white Americans age thirty to thirty-four hold at least a bachelor's degree, as compared to just 21 percent of all African Americans in that same age group.[21]

Racial Profiling. Statistics pertaining to the criminal justice system also testify to continuing racial inequality and racial tensions. For instance, although African American youth at the end of the twentieth century represented just 15 percent of the nation's total youth population, they made up 26 percent of the youth arrested, 31 percent of the youth referred to juvenile court, and 44 percent of the youth detained by the police.[22] African American males in particular compose a disproportionate number of those

Students at the University of Michigan rally in support of affirmative action. In 2003 the U.S. Supreme Court upheld the use of affirmative action by the University of Michigan's Law School but struck down the affirmative action program utilized in undergraduate admissions.

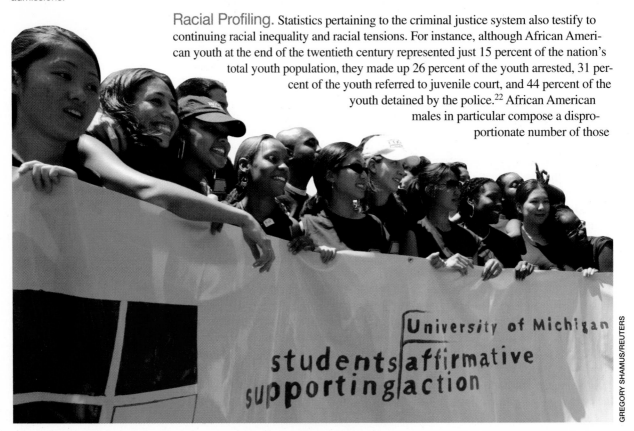

students affirmative supporting action

University of Michigan

GREGORY SHAMUS/REUTERS

SCOTT OLSON/GETTY IMAGES

A policeman interviews several teenagers on a street corner in Tucson, Arizona. The state's controversial new immigration law would allow officers to check any person's immigration status while in the process of enforcing other laws.

imprisoned. Critics of the system charge that it is racially biased, especially in how it metes out capital punishment. A study conducted by social scientist David Baldus in the early 1990s concluded that the victim's race was a significant factor in predicting which convicted murderers receive the death penalty. Specifically, killers of whites were 4.3 times more likely to be sentenced to death than killers of African Americans.

Racial discrimination may also characterize the initial phases of gathering information about a crime. For example, some law enforcement officials admit to using **racial profiling**—the practice of taking race into account when investigating crimes. African Americans may be stopped, questioned, and even held in custody not because there is specific evidence that links them to a particular crime, but because they fit a "profile" of the perpetrator that includes the characteristic of race.

Even in the wake of the civil rights revolution of the 1960s, little objection was raised against the practice, provided that it was done for purposes of "bona fide law enforcement" and not racial harassment, and so long as race was one of several factors that police officers considered when investigating crimes. But racial profiling became a source of considerable controversy in the 1990s. During the spring of 1999, victims of the New Jersey State Police force's allegedly overaggressive racial profiling testified at hearings held by the Black and Latino caucus of the state's legislature. President Bill Clinton publicly condemned racial profiling as a "morally indefensible, deeply corrosive practice." Finally, in March 2003, New Jersey became the first state in the nation to enact an antiprofiling law, which made any profiling by police punishable by five years in prison and a $15,000 fine. Yet by the end of that decade a majority of states still had not banned racial profiling as a law enforcement practice. In June 2003, President George W. Bush issued a directive that banned racial profiling by federal law enforcement agencies, though critics complained about both the law's exception for the use of racial profiling in "national security" investigations and the lack of enforcement mechanisms provided.

Are criticisms of racial profiling exaggerated? Statistics overwhelmingly confirm that African American young men commit a disproportionate share of street crime in the United States. Thus not all racial profiling may be driven by prejudice against African Americans—civil rights leader Jesse Jackson admitted in 1993 that he was less fearful of white strangers than black strangers on dark streets, if only because

Racial profiling
The law enforcement practice of taking race into account when identifying possible suspects of crimes.

Securing a Piece of the Franchise

The belief that "all men are created equal" has become part of the American ideology. Yet reality hasn't always kept up with theory. In the early years of the republic, the eligible electorate consisted primarily of white, male property owners. For everyone else, the road to suffrage remained fraught with legal and political struggles.

In 1841, the state of Rhode Island became the last of the United States to liberalize suffrage requirements so that even white males with little or no property enjoyed the right to vote. During the late 1820s and 1830s, the Whig Party had resisted suffrage for all white males, trumpeting the principle of a "hierarchical society" in which voting was treated as a privilege rather than an entitlement. But the rival Democratic Party, worried less about civic virtue and more about government tyranny, called for universal white male suffrage to put electoral pressure on the Whigs. The Democrats converted state after state to their cause. Rhode Island's requirement that a man outright own land worth $134 in order to vote seemed increasingly restrictive once the Rhode Island economy shifted from the emphasis on agriculture to industry. Only after the state held a constitutional convention in 1841, and then a special gubernatorial election that same year, did Rhode Island join the rest of the union in championing suffrage for all white males.

In 1920, following decades of intense struggles dating back even before the Civil War, the requisite number of states finally ratified the Nineteenth Amendment, granting women the right to vote. Meeting in 1848 in Seneca Falls, New York, some three hundred male and female reformers issued a Declaration of Sentiments (modeled on the Declaration of Independence), which included a demand for the right of women to vote. As the movement for women's suffrage grew, it encountered especially well-organized resistance from the liquor industry (which feared female support for prohibition) and the textile industry (which feared female support for restrictions on child labor). The sudden triumph of progressive reforms at the turn of the century, which helped to clean up industrial workplace abuses, made the women's suffrage movement seem less radical by comparison. In 1916, both the Republicans and the Democrats embraced female enfranchisement, and four years later, it became a constitutional reality.

In 1965, the newly passed Voting Rights Act established a foundation for the mass registration of African Americans throughout the South. Their realization of the right to vote should not have had to wait so long; the Fifteenth Amendment, ratified in 1870, had formally guaranteed the right to vote to all U.S. citizens regardless of race. But racial intimidation at the polls, the use of poll taxes and literacy requirements, and the manipulation of election laws by local registrars all combined to render the right to vote for African Americans a hollow promise at best. Only when the civil rights movement started making significant headway in the late 1950s did national politicians begin seriously to reconsider the issue of voting rights. The key moment in this struggle came in March 1965, when police in Alabama assaulted marchers making their way from Selma to Montgomery. President Lyndon B. Johnson then demanded passage of an effective voting rights act, and in August 1965 Congress passed and Johnson signed into law the Voting Rights Act. The new act, combined with ratification of the Twenty-fourth Amendment in 1964, which prohibited poll taxes, spelled the effective end to nearly a century of systematic disenfranchisement.

statistically speaking, he stands a greater risk of being robbed by a black person than a white person. At the same time, defenders of racial profiling (as one of many factors in the investigative process) tend to minimize the extent to which the practice adds to the sense of resentment of law enforcement felt by rich and poor blacks alike. No court has ever banned the practice outright. Moreover, even if a court did take such a bold action, it would be difficult to disprove an officer's claim that nonracial factors were in fact the primary consideration in his or her decision-making process.

Controversies surrounding affirmative action and racial profiling highlight a vexing challenge in modern society. Even if all vestiges of formal racial classifications

under the law are eliminated, calculations of racial differences inevitably enter into the subjective judgments of those in positions of authority. Thus for all the successful challenges launched against the racist legal and political structures that prevailed in American society during much of the twentieth century, the greater challenge of winning over the "hearts and minds" of individuals still remains.

The Women's Movement and Gender Equality

Understand the history of women's rights from women's suffrage up through the present ★ LO

The process by which women achieved their own degree of equality during the course of the 20th century took a circuitous route. In the early part of the twentieth century, women's rights leaders linked their calls for equality to other social movements of the same period, including those calling for child labor laws and increased literacy for immigrants. Initially, the women's rights movement pressed for protective laws, arguing that such legislation was necessary because of women's otherwise inferior legal status. For example, in *Muller v. Oregon* (1908),[23] the Supreme Court upheld an Oregon law that prohibited women laundry workers from being required to work more than ten hours a day; similar laws applied to male workers had been invalidated as beyond the government's authority. Yet the reason for the holding could hardly have cheered advocates of women's equality: according to the Court, "a woman's physical structure and the performance of maternal functions place her at a disadvantage in the struggle for subsistence."

Women's Suffrage and the Equal Rights Amendment

After ratification of the Nineteenth Amendment in 1920 guaranteed women the right to vote, women's rights groups began to alter their strategy for pursuing gender equality through the courts. In attempting to expand women's legal rights, these groups now argued that men and women should be treated equally. Their efforts met with only limited success at first. Although the NAACP achieved a string of successful challenges to racial discrimination in the 1940s and 1950s, the Supreme Court refused to view gender discrimination as similarly deserving of suspect scrutiny. In *Goesaert v. Cleary* (1948),[24] the Court upheld a Michigan law that banned women from tending bar unless they were the daughter or wife of the bar owner. Thirteen years later, the Court accepted as legitimate a Florida law that gave only women the right to excuse themselves from jury duty. In both cases, the Court continued to accept sex-role stereotypes of women as weak, and as dedicated above all else to taking care of the children at home. As the Court pointed out in *Hoyt v. Florida* (1961), "despite the enlightened emancipation of women from the restrictions and protections of bygone years . . . woman is still regarded as the center of home and family life."[25]

© 2012 CENGAGE LEARNING

The women's rights movement did not achieve any significant breakthroughs in this regard until the early 1970s. Although the National Women's Party had first proposed an equal rights amendment to the Constitution in 1923 and in nearly every session of Congress since then, the amendment never got very far. In 1966, the newly formed National Organization for Women (NOW) became a new and forceful advocate for the Equal Rights Amendment and other equal rights in education, employment, and political opportunities for women. NOW and other women's groups vigorously pressed for passage of the Equal Rights Amendment, which stated simply that "equality of rights under the law shall not be denied or abridged by the United States or any state on account of sex." In 1972, Congress passed the amendment and sent it to the state legislatures for ratification. Even after the deadline for ratification was extended to June 1982, the amendment failed to achieve the approval of the three fourths of state legislatures necessary for passage, falling just three states shy.

International Perceptions of Women as Leaders

A 2007 Pew Global Attitudes survey conducted in forty-six countries around the world queried respondents about gender and the qualities of leadership. Specifically, the surveys asked people whether they thought men or women made better leaders. The table below shows how people from the forty-six nations responded. In the United States, three quarters of those surveyed said that men and women were equally qualified, whereas 16 percent said men were better qualified and 6 percent said women were better qualified. Opinions about gender equality in leadership are similar in Canada, Central and South American nations, and western European countries. As the table shows, however, most eastern European, Middle Eastern, Asian, and African nations strongly favor male leadership.

PAUL J. RICHARDS/AFP/GETTY IMAGES

Secretary of State Hillary Clinton meeting with the President of Haiti, René Préval.

Which Sex Generally Makes Better Political Leaders?

	Men %	Women %	Both equally %		Men %	Women %	Both equally %
U.S.	16	6	75	Egypt	38	15	43
Canada	10	8	80	Turkey	34	10	51
Chile	26	5	66	Lebanon	34	11	53
Argentina	17	9	68	Israel	30	14	53
Mexico	12	9	76	Morocco	21	5	65
Venezuela	11	6	82	Pakistan	54	8	32
Brazil	10	15	73	Bangladesh	52	8	41
Peru	9	7	83	Indonesia	43	3	52
Bolivia	8	6	85	Malaysia	43	4	52
France	15	4	81	China	28	4	64
Italy	12	11	74	South Korea	25	5	68
Germany	11	8	80	India	19	17	62
Britain	9	6	83	Japan	16	4	77
Spain	7	8	83	Mali	65	6	29
Sweden	3	6	90	Ethiopia	51	3	45
Russia	40	7	44	Nigeria	48	6	45
Ukraine	34	7	52	Ghana	42	14	43
Bulgaria	30	9	52	Senegal	36	15	48
Poland	23	10	65	Ivory Coast	31	9	60
Slovakia	15	9	76	South Africa	28	11	61
Czech Rep.	14	11	73	Kenya	27	10	62
Palest. Ter.	64	17	16	Uganda	27	6	65
Kuwait	62	4	33	Tanzania	17	8	74
Jordan	49	6	42				

Source: Juliana Manasce Horowitz, *How the World Rates Women as Leaders*, Dec. 5, 2007, Pew Global Attitudes Project (http://pewresearch.org/pubs/650/women-leaders).

Although the Equal Rights Amendment failed, women have recently achieved some noteworthy victories in politics. For example, women made political history in 2003, when Democrat Nancy Pelosi of California was elected minority leader in the House, the first woman ever to hold that high a position in either branch of Congress. When Democrats won control of Congress after the 2006 midterm elections, Pelosi was elected Speaker of the House, again the first woman to hold that exalted position. Pelosi's ascension to such high congressional leadership positions contrasts with the way women in Congress were often relegated to lesser committees and non-influential positions in the past. When the 111th Congress began in 2009, there were seventy-six women serving in the U.S. House of Representatives and seventeen in the U.S. Senate.

Legal Challenges to Gender Discrimination

★ LO
Evaluate the role of the courts in upholding challenges to gender discrimination

Ironically, some attributed the failure of the Equal Rights Amendment to other legal developments that may have rendered it unnecessary. The American Civil Liberties Union (ACLU), an organization traditionally dedicated to protecting the First Amendment rights of political dissidents and labor unions, turned its attention to women's rights in the late 1960s. Led in court by board member Ruth Bader Ginsburg (who was later appointed by President Clinton to the U.S. Supreme Court), the ACLU brought suit on behalf of women who charged that they had been victims of gender discrimination. Although the Court refused to accord gender discrimination the strict scrutiny normally reserved for racial discrimination, the ACLU achieved several victories in cases brought before the Supreme Court. In *Reed v. Reed* (1971),[26] the Court invalidated an Idaho law that gave males preference over females as administrators of estates. In *Frontiero v. Richardson* (1973),[27] the Court struck down a federal law requiring only female members of the armed forces to show proof that they contributed more than 50 percent to the income of their household in order to receive certain fringe benefits. And in the landmark case of *Craig v. Boren* (1976),[28] the Court invalidated an Oklahoma law that prohibited the sale of 3.2 percent beer to males under the age of twenty-one and to women under the age of eighteen.

Since *Craig*, the Supreme Court has applied *intermediate scrutiny* in all gender discrimination cases, a standard requiring the government to show that the gender classification is "substantially related to an important state interest." This level of scrutiny is less than that of strict scrutiny, which tends to invalidate all racial classifications. But under intermediate scrutiny, *nearly* all laws that discriminate against women will be invalidated. That fact alone distinguishes intermediate scrutiny from *rational basis (or "minimum") scrutiny*, which asks only whether the law is "rationally related to a legitimate state interest"—a question to which courts can readily answer "yes" in nearly every instance.

In fact, in the modern era the Court has upheld only a handful of gender classifications as constitutional. For example, in 1981 the Court upheld a challenge to federal laws that required selective military service registration for males, but not for females. That same year the Court upheld a statutory rape law in California that punished men for having sex with underage females, although not vice versa. In each of those two instances, perceptions of real and relevant differences between men and women persuaded the Court to allow the discrimination to stand.

The highest-profile lawsuits charging gender discrimination targeted two all-male southern military academies, The Citadel in Charleston, South Carolina, and the Virginia Military Institute (VMI) in Lexington, Virginia. Both were classified as state institutions because they accepted significant funds from their respective states' budgets; thus each was hard-pressed to continue excluding women in violation of the Fourteenth Amendment's equal protection clause. Shannon Faulkner's frustrating experience as the first female cadet at The Citadel paved the way for future women to apply and be accepted to the institution in subsequent years. In an attempt to fend off gender integration of its own student body, VMI contracted with nearby Mary Baldwin College to create a parallel military program for women called the Virginia Women's Institute for Leadership (VWIL). But in 1996, the Supreme Court ruled that VWIL did not approximate VMI in terms of student body, faculty, course offerings, facilities, or opportunities for its alumni and ordered VMI to accept women. The issue of "separate but equal" that was resolved by the Supreme Court for racial classifications in 1954 was still being litigated for gender classifications well into the 1990s.

As with race discrimination, discrimination against women has been mostly eliminated in the formal sense. **Title IX** of the Federal Educational Amendments of 1972 prohibited the exclusion of women from an educational program or activity receiving financial assistance from the federal government. Courts have interpreted those provisions to force colleges and universities to provide as many athletic teams for women as they do for men. Title VII of the Civil Rights Act of 1964 extended to women's protection against discrimination in private and public businesses alike. Armed with equal rights to education and to entry in the workforce, women have made considerable occupational gains during the twentieth century.

Women have also benefited from affirmative action programs, especially in the workplace and in admission to professional and trade schools. To rectify long traditions of excluding women from certain occupations, scores of businesses and firms have aggressively recruited women. The period of most striking change occurred over the two decades between 1970 and 1990, when the proportion of women physicians doubled from 7.6 percent to 16.9 percent, and the percentage of women lawyers and judges nearly quadrupled from 5.8 percent to 22.7 percent. The percentage of women who are engineers rose over that same period from 1.3 percent to 8.6 percent. Still, complaints remain that in some occupations women continue to be clustered in low-paying positions. Thus women still compose only 3 percent of the nation's firefighters, 8 percent of state and local police officers, 1.9 percent of construction workers, 11.8 percent of college presidents, and 3 to 5 percent of senior-level positions in major companies. Some observers contend that a "glass ceiling" exists in many businesses, whereby women are prevented from receiving raises and promotions due them because of the subjective biases of their male bosses.

The securing of formal equality under the law and the proliferation of affirmative action programs have not always translated into actual equal opportunities to succeed. Women today continue to earn less than men in comparable positions—calls for "equal pay for equal work" have not always generated substantive changes in the pay structures of private companies or even the government. When women's salaries are compared with those of equally qualified men, the differences remain dramatic. Although Congress passed the Equal Pay Act in 1963 to ensure that women would be paid the same as men for work that is "substantially equal" (that is, almost identical unless the pay difference is based on seniority, experience, or other legitimate factors), in the year 2000 a woman on average still earned only 81 cents for every dollar a man received.

A recent study conducted by the AFL-CIO revealed the salary discrepancies by gender for several different occupations:

- Female lawyers' median weekly earnings are nearly $500 less than those of male attorneys.

- Female clericals receive about $100 a week less than male clericals.

- Female doctors' median earnings are nearly $500 less each week than male doctors.

- Although 95 percent of nurses are women, they earn $100 less each week on average than the 5 percent of nurses who are men.

- Women elementary school teachers receive $70 less a week than men.

- Waitresses' weekly earnings are about $50 less than waiters' earnings.

Title IX

The section of the Federal Educational Amendments Law of 1972 that prohibits the exclusion of women from an educational program or activity receiving financial assistance from the federal government. Courts have interpreted those provisions to force colleges and universities to provide as many athletic teams for women as they do for men.

★ LO   Understand Title IX's effect on women's rights.

Title IX Brings Gender Equality—and Controversy—to a Campus Near You

Every March on college campuses all across the country, many students get caught up in March Madness—the NCAA men's basketball tournament that crowns the sport's annual champion. In April, another event occurs that has become a serious business at many schools as well: the NCAA women's basketball tournament. Women have been crowned as NCAA champions since 1982; before that, between 1972 and 1982, women's college basketball championships were held by the Association for Intercollegiate Athletics for Women. Women who have won the NCAA championship may not realize that they owe some form of debt not just to the parents who supported them and the coaches

University of Tennessee women's basketball coach Pat Summit giving instructions to one of her players. Thanks to Title IX, colleges and universities have been forced to provide as many sports teams for women as they do for male athletes.

who coached them, but also to the late Rep. Patsy Mink (D-HI), the first Asian American woman elected to Congress. In 1972 Representative Mink authored the Title IX Amendment to the Higher Education Act, which banned gender discrimination in any "education program or activity" receiving federal assistance. Though Mink's law made no explicit mention of intercollegiate athletics, that is where the law has had its most prominent impact to date.

The implications of Title IX are profound: courts have interpreted the statute to require gender equality in roster sizes for men's and women's athletic teams in general, as well as to require comparable budgets for recruiting, scholarships, coaches' salaries, and other expenses. The law has not been without controversy: some schools have eliminated successful men's athletic teams to bring the percentage of women's athletic scholarships up to par. Critics complain that men's football and basketball teams are normally the only sports teams that bring in revenue, and so they should be judged independently of all the other sports. Regardless, colleges and universities have fallen into line in the past thirty years; so much so in fact, that in 2006 the Western Kentucky University Board of Regents ordered the upgrading of its football team (from Division 1-AA to 1-A), ostensibly because its share of female scholarship athletes had become disproportionately large.

For Critical Thinking and Discussion

1. Is the intense focus of colleges and universities on gender equality in their collegiate sports programs justified?

2. Would you favor the elimination of a successful men's sports team at your own institution on the basis of an imbalance in male and female scholarship athletes on campus?

3. Do you participate in other aspects of college life such as school-sponsored clubs or the school band where gender inequality exists in some form? Does the intense focus of Title IX enforcement on sports teams in particular tend to obscure gender discrimination where it exists elsewhere on campus?

Sexual harassment, normally in the form of unwelcome sexual advances by superiors, continues to pose a threat to working women in America. Since the mid-1980s the Supreme Court has considered such harassment—which includes any and all actions that create a hostile working environment such as putting up provocative posters, making lewd comments, and so forth—to be a form of sexual discrimination actionable under Title VII of the 1964 Civil Rights Act. Still, many such sexual advances in the workplace continue despite the law, either because women remain unclear about the bounds of permissible conduct or because they fear reprisals for reporting the legal violations of superiors. Indeed, more than four in ten women employed in federal agencies say they have experienced some form of harassment.[29] For all the legal equality that is now afforded to women, discrimination continues on a level that falls under the radar screen of the legal and judicial process.

Other Struggles for Equality

★ LO   Examine the struggles for equality waged by other racial, religious, and ethnic groups including Native Americans, Asian Americans, Muslims, and Hispanic Americans

The political and legal systems in the United States directed increased attention during the late nineteenth and twentieth centuries to the plights of African Americans and women. The hardships suffered by these two groups inspired the passage of five constitutional amendments in all (the three Civil War Amendments, the Nineteenth Amendment granting women the right to vote, and the Twenty-fourth Amendment banning poll taxes) as well as many federal and state antidiscrimination laws. But both these groups' continuous quests for equal privileges under the law compose only part of the equal rights landscape. American history is replete with accounts of discrimination against other underrepresented groups as well. In recent years, these additional groups have begun to see their own claims to fairness and equal treatment recognized and vindicated within the American political system.

Native Americans

One of the nation's most unfortunate tales of mistreatment concerns Native Americans. For much of the eighteenth and nineteenth centuries, vast numbers of white Americans migrated west, pursuing what they viewed as their manifest destiny to settle across the continent. Consequently, millions of Native Americans were herded onto reservations according to a removal policy backed by the federal government. By a federal law passed in 1871, the government no longer agreed to recognize Native American tribes or nations as independent powers capable of entering treaties with the United States—all future tribal affairs were to be managed by the federal government without tribal consent. With passage of the Dawes Severalty Act in 1887, the U.S. government divided tribal lands still in existence among individual Indians who renounced their tribal holdings, further undermining tribal cultures and structures.

Although certain Native American tribes received piecemeal U.S. citizenship beginning in the 1850s and the Dawes Act granted citizenship to those who ceded their tribal holdings, the class of Native Americans as a whole was not admitted to full citizenship until 1924, nearly sixty years after freed slaves had been afforded that same privilege. The federal government's attempt to undo the tribal structure did not produce widespread assimilation of Indians into American society as proponents of the

Native Americans protest federal policies by temporarily occupying Alcatraz Island in San Francisco Bay.

AP PHOTO

Dawes Act intended; many chose to remain on reservations in an attempt to protect their culture from outside influences. Beginning in the middle of the twentieth century, some Native Americans turned to activism to protest their mistreatment by government authorities. From November 1969 until June 1971, seventy-eight members of one tribe occupied Alcatraz Island in San Francisco Bay, demanding that it be made available as a cultural center to the tribes. Members of the American Indian Movement (AIM), an organization founded in 1968 to promote civil rights for Native Americans, occupied the Washington, DC, offices of the Bureau of Indian Affairs in 1972, demanding that they receive the rights and privileges that had been promised them under the original treaties entered into by the federal government. This activism drew public attention to Native American causes and spurred action by Congress, which formally terminated its policy of assimilation and began to recognize the autonomy of Native American tribes to administer federal programs on their own lands. In the past quarter century, the U.S. government has settled millions of dollars in legal claims pressed by Native American tribes and has returned nearly half a million acres of land to the Navajo and Hopi tribes alone.

Asian Americans

Immigrants from East Asia—especially Japan and China—supplied much of the labor building U.S. railroads in the nineteenth century. Even so, many were excluded from labor unions and denied other civil rights. The government has enacted several immigration acts specifically designed to limit or prevent Asian immigration. For example, the Chinese Exclusion Act passed in 1882 prohibited Chinese laborers from immigrating and denied U.S. citizenship to Chinese living in the United States. The 1907 Gentleman's Agreement with Japan prohibited the immigration of Japanese laborers. The National Origins Act of 1924 banned all Asians from further immigration to the United States.

Discrimination was especially rampant on the West Coast, where many Asian American populations were concentrated. Asian children were segregated into separate public schools in San Francisco, and the state of California restricted Japanese immigrants' rights to own farmland. Perhaps the most notorious incident of discrimination against Asian Americans occurred in 1942, when the U.S. government in response to the Japanese bombing of Pearl Harbor forcibly relocated 110,000 Japanese Americans to inland internment camps and seized their property. The Supreme Court upheld the internment policy in 1944, perpetuating an especially egregious brand of racial discrimination committed against legal residents of the country, including more than sixty thousand legal U.S. citizens. National security concerns used to justify the policy at that time have been exposed in later decades as baseless claims.

In the post–World War II period, Asian Americans enjoyed increased economic prosperity and made significant civil rights gains as well. The ban on Asian immigration was officially lifted in 1952, and provisions of federal law encouraging the immigration of professionals helped attract to the United States large numbers of educated and highly skilled Asian professionals. The end of the Vietnam War in 1975 brought a great influx of immigrants from Vietnam, Laos, and Cambodia to the United States. With increasing numbers of immigrants from South Korea and the Philippines, the Asian American population today stands at approximately 4 percent of the American population as a whole.

Muslim Americans

The events of September 11, 2001, had a profound impact on America's foreign policy priorities and its approach to international terrorism. Those events have also taken a toll on citizens' perceptions of Muslim Americans, a group already set apart by its members' distinct religious practices and forms of dress. When plans for an Islamic community center and mosque to be built near the site of "Ground Zero" were revealed in early

2010, anger directed at Muslim-Americans suddenly found a new cause. Polls showed a clear majority of Americans opposed to the project, even though most of those surveyed also recognized that the Muslim group had a legal right to build there. Politicians of all stripes, including Sarah Palin and Senate Majority Leader Harry Reid (D-NV), were quick to oppose the proposal, knowing that such opposition would offer them immediate political benefits.

The stereotype that associates the Islamic religion with terrorism is hardly applicable to the vast majority who practice the faith, but post–September 11 initiatives sanctioned by Congress under the USA Patriot Act targeted many Muslim Americans for questioning, and in some cases temporary detention. Of course African Americans have long suffered from racial profiling in criminal law enforcement, but the level and degree to which Muslim Americans have been singled out has created a special source of worry for civil rights groups.

Hispanic Americans

Hispanic Americans are defined as those of Spanish-speaking descent. A majority descended from Mexicans who were living in the Southwest when it became part of the United States in the 1840s. Even after immigration laws were tightened in the 1890s, hundreds of thousands of Mexicans continued to enter the United States illegally, drawn by opportunities in farming, mining, and other industries. Segregation of Mexican students from white students began in California in 1885 and continued through the 1950s; beginning in the 1960s, many Mexican Americans moved from rural areas to cities. Public schools in California, Texas, and elsewhere were forced to assimilate this growing population, including the children of illegal aliens, into overcrowded school districts.

Today with more than fourteen hundred miles of border in common between the two nations, the United States and Mexico continue to be at odds over some important issues, including immigration. Meanwhile, more than 35 million people of Hispanic descent currently live in the United States, forming the nation's largest language minority. Cubans, Puerto Ricans, and numerous immigrants and refugees from other Central American countries contribute to the ranks of Hispanic Americans today. Some of the Cubans who left their native land hailed from privileged socioeconomic conditions; fleeing Castro's communistic agenda, their move to the United States was at least in part an effort to save their standard of living. Still, most immigrants from Hispanic countries such as Mexico and Cuba come from adverse economic circumstances in those nations. The crime linked to Mexican immigration in particular may be directly related to the impoverished conditions many of them live under in the United States.

Of course discrimination against Hispanics also contributes to the overall disproportionate levels of poverty and unemployment in this group. Unlike African Americans, Hispanics were never legally barred from the polls, and in New Mexico and California they have been a large and influential minority for several decades. And yet despite the large number of Hispanic Americans, the group's political power has yet to have its due influence on public policy, perhaps because many Hispanics are not yet citizens, and thus do not have the right to vote. Still, the appointment of Judge Sonia Sotomayor as the first Hispanic to the U.S. Supreme Court in 2009 was a source of pride among American Hispanic community.

As governor of Texas in the late 1990s before becoming president, George W. Bush regarded the Hispanic community as a potential source of growth within the more conservative Republican Party. Yet in the 2006 midterm elections, exit polls showed Hispanics voting in favor of the Democrats by a wide margin, helping them defeat many Republican incumbents. And in the 2008 presidential election, Hispanics voted for the Democratic ticket by a margin of more than two-to-one. As the fastest growing ethnic minority in the country, Hispanic Americans should see their political clout increase even more in the coming years.

Older Americans

Today approximately 13 percent of Americans are over the age of sixty-five, compared with just 4 percent of Americans who were at that age at the beginning of the twentieth century. With their increased numbers has come increased political power; older Americans are among the most politically active of all citizens, and groups such as AARP (formerly the American Association of Retired Persons), with more than 40 million members on its rolls, have become especially influential players on the political scene. This increased influence has been used to counteract incidents of age discrimination in the workplace and elsewhere. The Age Discrimination in Employment Act, passed in 1967 and broadened in 1986, makes it unlawful to hire or fire a person on the basis of age. Older Americans have also been at the forefront of lobbying efforts to protect Social Security trust funds and to ensure the continuation of cost-of-living adjustments to their payments. Ironically, older Americans' success at wielding influence within the political system has given credence to the suggestion that age classifications do not require suspect scrutiny by courts; at least in this instance, the political system appears to protect the civil rights of this particular subset of Americans.

Individuals with Disabilities

As with age classifications, discrimination against Americans with physical and mental disabilities has never received heightened scrutiny from the courts. Misperceptions about the nature of certain disabilities have on occasion led to discriminatory treatment of individuals with disabilities. In the 1920s, some states passed laws authorizing the sterilization of institutionalized "mental defectives"—Justice Oliver Wendell Holmes callously dismissed all legal challenges to such laws with the statement that "three generations of imbeciles are enough." Today, thanks to significant technological

Activists for the rights of individuals with disabilities at a rally advocating broader enforcement of the Americans with Disabilities Act of 1990.

and medical advances, a more enlightened social understanding, and a more sophisticated approach to educating citizens about the nature of these limitations, millions of Americans with disabilities have been mainstreamed into society, attending school, going to work, and living otherwise normal lives. The Americans with Disabilities Act of 1990 established a national commitment to such mainstreaming efforts and extended to those with disabilities protection from discrimination in employment and public accommodations comparable to that afforded women and racial minorities under the 1964 Civil Rights Act.

Gays and Lesbians

Of all the groups that have claimed to be discriminated in the United States, homosexuals stand among the least successful in having their claims to equal treatment vindicated under the law. Gays and lesbians have traditionally suffered discrimination in society, whether from those whose religions frown on homosexuality in general or from those who are simply uncomfortable with this lifestyle. In the period immediately following World War II, a movement for gay rights emerged with generally integrationist goals, encouraging homosexuals to conform to most existing social standards. Gays and lesbians assumed a more activist quest for equality beginning in the late 1960s, marching for "gay power," urging reluctant gays to "out" themselves by openly admitting their sexual orientation, and interrupting government meetings to draw attention to their cause of equal treatment and nondiscrimination. Although homosexual activists made some advances, no significant antidiscrimination legislation followed. Some communities reacted by passing laws that prohibited the granting of "any special rights or privileges" to homosexuals. The Supreme Court in *Romer v. Evans* (1996)[30] struck down such a provision of the Colorado Constitution in 1996. Perhaps the biggest court victory of all for gays and lesbians occurred in 2003, when the Supreme Court in *Lawrence v. Texas* struck down a Texas law that forbade same-sex partners from engaging in certain types of intimate relations. Despite these victories, the Supreme Court has still never recognized homosexuals as a protected class on a par with women or African Americans.

Gay-marriage supporters at a Seattle rally in March 2006.

AP PHOTO/SCOTT COHEN

The issue of homosexuals in the military first drew intense national attention when Army Colonel Margarethe Cammermeyer was discharged from the armed forces in June 1992 when, during a routine security clearance interview, she acknowledged that she was a lesbian. Cammermeyer hinged her hopes for restatement on a promise made to her by candidate Bill Clinton during his successful presidential campaign that fall. At one campaign stop, Clinton reportedly told the twenty-seven-year Army veteran and winner of a bronze star in Vietnam that he "absolutely" would carry out his promise to end the ban against homosexuals in the military. Yet what Clinton the candidate viewed as a "simple civil rights issue" became much more complicated for Clinton the president. Even before his inauguration, Republicans in Congress made clear that they had the votes to reverse any executive order Clinton might issue to allow gays in the military. The Senate Armed Services Committee Chairman, Sam Nunn (D–GA), became infuriated when the new administration began communicating with the Joint Chiefs of Staff while ignoring and taking for granted the support of Senate Democrats. Quickly the president began to backtrack on his promise: at his first televised news conference two weeks into his presidency, he indicated he might go along with a supposed compromise that would segregate gays within the military. The ultimate compromise reached was a "don't ask, don't tell" policy that would allow gays still in the closet to stay in the military, so long as they never publicized their status. In his 2010 State of the Union Address, President Barack Obama indicated that he plans to work with Congress and

Recognizing the Legitimacy of Same-Sex Marriage

When New Hampshire in June 2009 became the sixth state in the union to formally legalize same-sex marriage, many interpreted the event as just the most recent sign of a trend in favor of increased rights for gays and lesbians. Yet there are counterindications to that trend in the majority of other states that have rejected measures such as civil rights laws that could afford "special rights" or "special status" to homosexuals, as well as the far more controversial institution of same-sex marriage. At the time this book went to press, five states (Massachusetts, Connecticut, Iowa, New Hampshire, and Vermont) and the District of Columbia still perform marriages for same-sex couples (Maine repealed its previous law while California's ban on same-sex marriages was still under review in the courts), while voters in thirty states have approved referenda to ban same-sex marriage.

In 1996, the Defense of Marriage Act—which attempts to ensure that each state retain the option of deciding whether or not to recognize same-sex marriage—was passed overwhelmingly by Congress (85–14 in the House and 342–67 in the Senate) before being signed into law by President Bill Clinton, considered a supporter of gay rights in other contexts. Eight years later, the issue of whether states must recognize same-sex marriages sanctioned in other states was thrown into the spotlight once again when eleven states voted on ballot measures that either defined marriage as between a man and a woman (three states), refused to recognize same-sex civil unions or domestic partnerships from other states (eight states) or banned all such civil unions outright. All these ballot measures were held at the same time as the November 2004 presidential election. And all eleven states passed the measures, with eight of the eleven ballot measures receiving at least two-thirds public support, and four measures topping the 75 percent mark (see the figure below). Then, on Election Day 2008, voters in Arizona and Florida joined Californians in passing measures to ban same-sex marriage in their respective states as well. Gay rights advocates know that so long as these measures retain their overwhelming popularity, an uphill fight for their cause remains.

November 2, 2004: Same-Sex Ballot Measures

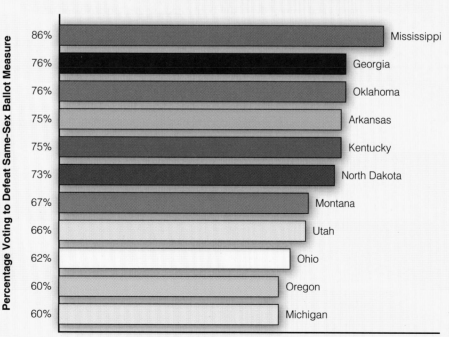

the military to repeal the "don't ask, don't tell" rule. Still, to many critics this promise should have become reality long ago. Though some European countries have actively recruited gays and lesbians for military service, the U.S. military continues to formally oppose open homosexuality in the armed services.

Meanwhile, antigay violence continues. The 1998 murder of college student Matthew Shepard brought new calls for hate crime legislation directed at such criminal activity. Despite suffering countless setbacks, gays and lesbians continue to enjoy a significant presence in the political system, forging alliances with more liberal administrations and even electing some openly gay politicians. The attention paid to the Log Cabin Republicans—members of that party who actively promote gay and lesbian rights—provides some indication that homosexuals represent a political force in America today that cannot be so easily ignored.

Making the Connection

A form of the civil rights movement continues to be waged in modern-day courts and legislatures. Despite all the gains of the past, battles are still being taken up by racial, ethnic, and religious groups, as well as by other traditionally disadvantaged groups, to attain equal rights under the law. Just as Autherine Lucy walked a lonely path to achieve admission for African Americans at the University of Alabama in the 1950s, Shannon Faulkner walked a similar path to achieve admission for female applicants at the all-male Citadel in the 1990s. Both Lucy and Faulkner quickly learned that formal recognition of their rights would not suffice to transform many people's minds and hearts. But their actions provided a foundation for future aspirants to build on their accomplishments and present those stubborn minds with alternative perspectives on equality.

Today, groups such as Native Americans, gays and lesbians, and Muslim Americans walk this path as well, seeking recognition of rights traditionally denied to them by authorities acting on behalf of "the political majority." For every one or two steps they take forward, they are just as likely to take one other step backward. The hearts and minds of the majority are not so easily transformed. Fortunately, the openness of the American political system encourages some form of dialogue between the majority and underrepresented groups, and it shows no sign of stifling that dialogue anytime soon.

POLITICS InterActive!

Even in Congress, a Muslim Braces for Discrimination

The midterm congressional elections of 2006 resulted in a Democratic Party sweep of both houses of Congress. Lost at first in the headlines about the elections was a smaller event that occurred during that same election season: Keith Maurice Ellison, an American lawyer and politician running as a Democrat and member of the Farmer-Labor Party, became the first African American elected to the House from Minnesota when he won the right to represent Minnesota's fifth congressional district. Yet Ellison's race was not as much an issue as his religion: he was also the first Muslim elected to the federal government in American history and became only the fourth elected Muslim official in the United States as of December 2006. Of course all this occurred during a period when the federal government's war on terrorism has raised questions within the general public about the loyalty of Muslim Americans, the vast majority of whom have done nothing illegal or even suspicious.

Ellison's religion made national news when he was first elected. Yet media coverage of Ellison went through the roof when words of intolerance were directed at him by one of his future colleagues, Congressman Virgil Goode (R-VA). After his victory, Ellison indicated that he planned to use the Koran for his unofficial swearing-in ceremony. This led Goode to send a letter to constituents in which he wrote the following:

> I do not subscribe to using the Koran in any way. The Muslim Representative from Minnesota was elected by the voters of that district and if American citizens don't wake up and adopt the Virgil Goode position on immigration, there will likely be many more Muslims elected to office and demanding the use of the Koran.

Ellison criticized Goode about the letter, noting that he was not an immigrant and that Goode does not understand Islam. He has also offered to meet with Goode to discuss the matter. Rather than defusing the issue, Goode went on to state publicly that he was in favor of decreasing legal immigration to the United States, and that he hoped to eliminate diversity immigration visas, which go to applicants from countries that do not normally provide many individuals to the United States. Goode argued that such visas might allow people "not from European countries" or from "some terrorist states" to enter America.

On www.cengage.com/dautrich/americangovernment/2e, find the "Politics Inter-Active" link for details about Ellison's political and religious background, as well as statistics about religious diversity in the current and past congresses. Consult these and other links that relate to religious diversity in American government institutions, and incidents of current discrimination directed against Muslim Americans, including those who are U.S. citizens.

ROGER L. WOLLENBERG/UPI/LANDOV

Congressman-elect Keith Ellison, being sworn in to the House of Representatives in January 2007.

Chapter 5 Civil Rights, Equality, and Social Movements

Chapter Summary

★ **Types of Equality**

- References to equality in discussions of American politics often refer to one of three types: political equality, economic equality, and social equality.

- Civil rights are those political, social, or economic rights conferred by the government to individuals in groups that had previously been denied those rights. The battle for civil rights in American history has focused primarily on African Americans and other ethnic groups (Hispanics, Asian Americans, Native Americans, Muslim Americans), women, older Americans, individuals with physical disabilities, and gays and lesbians.

★ **The Struggle for Equality: Approaches and Tactics**

- The tactics used by groups seeking to achieve civil rights include working within the existing rules and political process, litigation, boycotts, and civil disobedience.

★ **The African American Struggle for Equality and Civil Rights**

- The long and hard-fought African American struggle for equality included heated debate as early as the Constitutional Convention. The Civil War and the amendments that passed in its aftermath (Thirteenth, Fourteenth, and Fifteenth) ended slavery, granted citizenship to former slaves, guaranteed all Americans "equal protection under the laws," and denied states the ability to prevent voting rights on the basis of race.

- Despite these amendments, states have used many means to prevent African Americans from obtaining political, social, and economic equality, including black codes, literacy tests, poll taxes, and Jim Crow laws. A number of U.S. Supreme Court decisions, along with congressional legislation and constitutional amendments, have served to bring America closer to the goal of equality for African Americans.

- The *Brown v. Board of Education* decision of 1954 eliminated the "separate but equal" doctrine. The movement toward civil rights to minority groups in all public accommodations began in the later 1950s and emerged as a major force under the leadership of Martin Luther King Jr. and his use of nonviolent civil disobedience tactics.

- King's legacy was memorialized through sweeping civil rights legislation including the Civil Rights Act of 1964 (which banned racial discrimination in all public places), the Voting Rights Act of 1965 (which effectively reenfranchised millions of African Americans by eliminating the literacy test and property requirements for voting), and the Civil Rights Act of 1968 (which prohibited discrimination in housing and made it a federal crime to deny individuals their civil rights).

- Two contemporary issues relating to civil rights are affirmative action and racial profiling. The courts have struck down many affirmative action programs, but many states continue to try to find ways for government to level the playing field in hiring and college admissions.

★ **The Women's Movement and Gender Equality**

- The seeds were sown for the movement for gender equality in the early twentieth century with the ratification of the Nineteenth Amendment, guaranteeing women the right to vote.

- Not until the formation of the National Organization for Women (NOW) and its emergence as a significant political force did women's equality capture national attention.

★ **Other Struggles for Equality**

- Some of the most heated contemporary debates over equality relate to discrimination against Muslim Americans (and how to protect their civil rights in the post-9/11 era), Hispanic Americans and immigration policy, and the rights of gays and lesbians, particularly as they relate to marriage.

CourseMate

Key Terms

Affirmative action (p. 138)

Brown v. Board of Education (1954) (p. 129)

Civil rights (p. 127)

Civil Rights Act of 1964 (p. 136)

Civil Rights Act of 1968 (p. 136)

Civil War Amendments (p. 130)

Economic equality (p. 127)

Jim Crow laws (p. 131)

Plessy v. Ferguson (1896) (p. 131)

Political equality (p. 127)

Racial profiling (p. 141)

Social equality (p. 127)

Strict scrutiny (p. 133)

Title IX (p. 146)

Twenty-fourth Amendment (p. 136)

Voting Rights Act of 1965 (p. 136)

Resources

Important Books

Bowen, William, and Derek Bok. *The Shape of the River.* Princeton, NJ: Princeton University Press, 2000.

Branch, Taylor. *Parting the Waters: America in the King Years, 1954–1963.* New York: Simon & Schuster, 1988.

Gerstmann, Evan. *The Constitutional Underclass: Gays, Lesbians, and the Failure of Class-Based Equal Protection.* Chicago: University of Chicago Press, 1999.

Hochschild, Jennifer. *The New American Dilemma: Liberal Democracy and School Desegregation.* New Haven, CT: Yale University Press, 1984.

Kluger, Richard. *Simple Justice.* New York: Vintage Books, 1975.

Washington, Booker T. *Up from Slavery.* New York: Airmont Publishing, 1967.

Woodward, C. Vann. *The Strange Career of Jim Crow.* New York: Oxford University Press, 1955.

Internet Sources

http://www.civilrights.org (the official site of the Leadership Conference on Civil and Human Rights, which is made up of more than 200 civil rights organizations from around the country; up-to-date civil rights news and information can be found here)

http://www.naacp.org (the National Association for the Advancement of Colored People's home page; contents include information about the organization, its programs, and its activities, as well various links to other sites of interest)

http://www.feminist.org (the Feminist Majority Foundation site, which features coverage of global feminist news, issue highlights, links to issues about women in sports, and so on)

http://www.hrc.org (the Web site of the Human Rights Campaign, which works on behalf of lesbian, bisexual, gay, and transgender equal rights; features extensive coverage of issues related to gay and lesbian interests, including a comprehensive review of legislation in all fifty states)

6 Congress

NOW Senator Patrick Leahy (D-VT), Chairman of the Senate Judiciary Committee.

AP PHOTO/TOBY TALBOT

THEN Senator Henry Cabot Lodge (R-MA), Chairman of the Senate Foreign Relations Committee from 1919 to 1924.

HISTORICAL/CORBIS

NOW & THEN

The U.S. Senate Plays the Role of Disloyal Opposition

? *Once a regal and powerful lawmaking body, the United States Senate—like so many other institutions in Washington, DC—had learned to defer to the reality of the modern presidency. An elite group of ambitious politicians advocating their own independent political agendas proved little match for a president determined to make strategic use of the bully pulpit. When the president reached a bit too far in a policy area where the Senate had traditionally exercised significant control, something unexpected happened: the U.S. Senate pushed back. Suddenly the president had to deal with a revitalized institution prepared to stymie the president's objectives by exercising its own considerable tools of political power, including the power wielded by Senate committee chairs to control committee procedures and the ever-present threat of a filibuster. Just when the political system appeared to be under the president's thumb, the upper house of Congress served notice that it remained a vibrant and stubborn obstacle to efforts at presidential steamrolling . . . at least when it wanted to be.*

LEARNING OBJECTIVES
★ WHAT YOU WILL LEARN ★

Article I and the Creation of Congress

★ Assess the role of the U.S. Congress as the legislative branch of government, and how that role has evolved over time

The Structure and Organization of Congress

★ Understand the structure and powers of Congress as defined by Article I of the Constitution

★ Appreciate the role that political parties play in the leadership of Congress

★ Identify key leadership positions and their functions in Congress

★ Explain reapportionment and redistricting

The Committee System

★ Compare and contrast the different types of committees found in Congress

How a Bill Becomes a Law

★ Describe the various steps necessary for a bill to become a law

Oversight and Personnel Functions of Congress

★ Explain why Congress often delegates its lawmaking authority to regulatory agencies

★ Learn the role of the Senate in confirming presidential appointments

★ Describe the congressional procedures for impeachment and removal of executive and judicial officers

Constituent Service: Helping People Back Home

★ Assess the "casework" functions of members of Congress in assisting constituents, educating them on policy issues, and performing other services on their behalf

NOW & THEN

AP PHOTO/
TOBY TALBOT

NOW President George W. Bush arrived in office in January 2001 with both houses of Congress under his own Republican Party's control. That changed on May 24, 2001, when Senator Jim Jeffords (R-VT) announced that he was leaving the party to become an independent, but would caucus with the Democrats. Jeffords's decision swung control of the Senate to the Democrats by a narrow 51–49 margin. Democratic control of the Senate would have negative implications for many aspects of George W. Bush's agenda, but it would have perhaps the most devastating and immediate effect on his plans to pack the federal courts with ideologically conservative judges—those who, in the words of Senator Charles Schumer (D-NY), lay outside the "judicial mainstream." Notwithstanding the "advice and consent" provisions of the Constitution, with his judicial nominations President Bush paid little heed to senatorial courtesy, the traditional practice of respecting the wishes of the nominee's home-state senators. In response, the new chair of the Senate Judiciary Committee, Senator Patrick Leahy (D-VT), announced that some of Bush's judicial nominees would be denied an up-and-down vote in his committee; by exercising this prerogative against the most conservative nominees, the Democrats prevented those nominations from being passed to the full Senate, where a handful of more conservative Democrats might give Bush's nominees the margin for victory. Even after Republicans recaptured the Senate in 2002, ending the committee bottleneck, those controversial nominations that made it to the floor of the full Senate now faced a second obstacle: the threat of a filibuster. That tool of the Senate minority, which stops Senate business based on the vote of just forty-one senators, had rarely been used against judicial nomination in the past. Now, it would serve as a central threat in the Democratic senators' war on judicial nominations: If President Bush did not agree to withdraw his most controversial judicial nominees, Senate Democrats would continue to tie up many of his less controversial choices as well. President Bush was eventually forced to adjust to this new reality, as moderate senators from both parties brokered a deal in the spring of 2005 to allow some, but not all, of the president's controversial nominees through to confirmation.

THEN   Nearly a century earlier, another president ran head-first into an emboldened U.S. Senate whose leaders were equally unwilling to defer to the chief executive on issues where its power and authority were constitutionally grounded. Article II, Section 2 of the Constitution affords the Senate a clear role in overseeing treaties—the president can make treaties, but only "by and with the advice and consent of the Senate" and only so long as "two thirds of the Senators present concur." The first sitting president to travel to Europe, Woodrow Wilson participated in the 1919 peace negotiations after World War I, and he worked tirelessly to incorporate a proposed League of Nations (the precursor to the modern United Nations) into the Treaty of Versailles, the treaty that ended the war. But Wilson, a Democrat, was not willing to seek advice from the Senate, especially after control of both houses of Congress went to the Republicans after the 1918 midterm elections. The new Senate Majority Leader, Senator Henry Cabot Lodge (R-MA), was especially irked by Wilson's refusal to afford senators any kind of voice in the treaty negotiations; he and his Republican colleagues already detested Wilson, and they now feared that U.S. membership in the League of Nations would tie the hands of future Congresses over whether to enter international conflicts. Lodge's official "reservations" to the treaty would have allowed passage of the agreement only so long as the U.S. Congress maintained its full autonomy to act at its discretion in the future. As a member of the Senate Foreign Relations Committee, Lodge slowed the treaty approval process down to a trickle: he took two weeks to read aloud every page of the 268-page treaty and then solicited testimony from scores of witnesses. The treaty would win approval only if Wilson accepted the "reservations," a path that he refused to take. Wilson was awarded the Nobel Peace Prize in 1919, but the League of Nations itself was formed without U.S. participation, and Wilson left office several months later. He never adjusted to the reality of a Senate willing to stand up to the twentieth-century presidency and reject his peace treaty. Biographer Robert Caro put the battle this way: "Woodrow Wilson was defeated by a body he considered both unrepresentative and oligarchical. He was right . . . [b]ut it had the power."

HISTORICAL/CORBIS

While lower court judicial nominations and international peace treaties were two very different issues debated at markedly different moments in the nation's history, the characteristics of Senate resistance in opposing the president proved remarkably similar in each instance. Senators with considerable power in their branch of government dug in, used Senate committee and floor procedures to their own benefit, and then let the slow pace of the Senate work its will to frustrate the chief executive. The separation of powers—a provision that gives Congress a significant role—was never designed to run quickly, and in both cases described here, that pattern of slow movement was readily apparent. This chapter discusses the complex organization, structure, and processes of both houses of Congress that underlie the often slow and difficult manner in which this important institution does its work. It shows how particular members achieve disproportionate power and influence in the legislative process and offers the rationale for why Congress plays such a central role in dealing with issues of paramount importance to the nation.

DOUG MILLS/THE NEW YORK TIMES/ REDUX PICTURES

Senator Carl Levin (D-MI) grills executives from Goldman-Sachs during an April 2010 committee investigation of the firm's investment practices prior to the collapse of the financial industry. Seated next to Levin is Senator Susan Collins (R-ME).

★ LO   Assess the role of the U.S. Congress as the legislative branch of government, and how that role has evolved over time

Article I and the Creation of Congress

Article I of the U.S. Constitution created Congress; and the fact that it came first was no accident. James Madison, the Father of the Constitution, referred to Congress as the "first branch of government," and as a graduate student, Woodrow Wilson (later the twenty-eighth president of the United States) wrote in his book *Congressional Government* (1885) that "anyone who is unfamiliar with what Congress actually does and how it does it . . . is very far from a knowledge of the constitutional system under which we live."[1] As the legislative branch of the federal government, Congress has ultimate authority for enacting new laws. Because this authority is central to any system of government, the Founders took considerable debate and care in building this first branch.

There was little question that a congress of some type would be the central institution in the new political system—a congress had been a central feature in all attempts to organize the states up through and including the Constitutional Convention of 1787. The Albany Congress of 1754 was the first attempt to unite the colonies—at the time for common defense against the French in the pending French and Indian War. The Albany Plan of Union called for the colonies to organize through the vehicle of a "congress." The first official government of the United States, created under the Articles of Confederation, again used a congress

NEW YORK TIMES CO./GETTY IMAGES

In 1916, Jeannette Rankin, a Republican from Montana, became the first woman elected to Congress. After one term in the House, she ran for the Senate and lost. She was reelected to the House in 1940. An ardent pacifist, she was the only member to vote against American entry into both World War I and World War II.

as its organizing principle. It is not surprising, then, that Article I, Section 1 of the U.S. Constitution states: "All legislative powers herein granted shall be vested in a Congress of the United States."

The Founders engaged in plenty of debate, negotiation, and compromise in defining the powers, functions, and structure of the U.S. Congress. The complexity of this institution continues today. Congress is filled with paradoxes. On one hand, it is a highly democratic institution in which senators and representatives are selected in free and open elections; on the other hand, Congress often is responsive to an exceedingly narrow set of specialized interests. Citizens and journalists frequently criticize the institution as being too slow to act responsively; yet voters return more than nine in ten of their elected members to office. At times, such as in the weeks following the terrorist attacks of September 11, 2001, Congress can show enthusiasm for tackling large issues expeditiously: within days of the attacks it passed the USA Patriot Act, which featured numerous antiterrorism measures. At other times, it seems to avoid taking positions on important issues, such as campaign finance reform and abortion rights.

NORTH WIND/NORTH WIND PICTURE ARCHIVES—ALL RIGHTS RESERVED.

Joseph Rainey of South Carolina was the first African American elected to Congress. He took office in 1870 and was reelected four times.

Most significantly, Congress is the branch of the U.S. government that ensures representation of the people through the direct election of members of the House and in more recent times, of members of the Senate as well. Through its 535 members, Congress provides representation of many groups throughout the country, such as women, African Americans, Native Americans, and Hispanics.

Bicameral legislature
A legislature composed of two separate chambers.

The Structure and Organization of Congress

A fundamental characteristic of Congress is that it is organized into two separate chambers, the Senate and the House of Representatives, and is thus termed a **bicameral legislature**. At the time the U.S. Constitution was written, ten of the thirteen states featured this type of legislature. Creating a bicameral legislature enabled the Founders to reach a compromise between two factions at the Constitutional Convention—those who represented large states and wanted congressional representation according to population, and those from small states who favored the model of the Articles of Confederation: that each state, regardless of population, would be equally represented in Congress. The "Great Compromise" reached by the convention delegates allowed for equal state representation in the Senate, and representation based on population in the House. These two chambers have shared lawmaking responsibilities since 1789.[2]

This nearly equal sharing of legislative power between the two chambers is significant. Many other nations in the world have bicameral legislatures, but the two legislative houses are rarely equal in power and usually do not share power. In the British Parliament, for example, the House of Lords has little power and serves a mostly symbolic function in that nation's politics, whereas the House of Commons wields the most authoritative power. Legislatures in other nations, such as Canada, France, Germany, Israel, and Japan, are also heavily dominated by one house. By contrast, in the U.S. Congress, the Senate and House are coequal chambers, each enjoying about as much power as the other. Similar to the United States, the national legislatures in Italy and Mexico include two houses with nearly equal power. Many nations have *unicameral* legislatures that consist of only one body, such as the 275-member legislature elected to govern the democracy established in Iraq in 2005.

Bicameralism has important implications for the legislative process in American politics—passing new laws is difficult because the two chambers, constructed so differently, must come to absolute agreement before a new law is enacted. The slowness that so often characterizes lawmaking in Congress is, in part, a product of this reality. The sharing of power and the "checks" that each chamber has on the other are no mistake. Indeed, the Founders intentionally built a Congress that would move slowly and carefully in the adoption of new laws, a process that, although often characterized as gridlock, ensures that change is well contemplated before it is adopted.

The House of Representatives: The "People's House"

The Founders intended the House of Representatives to be the "people's house," or the institution through which ordinary people would be represented in government. At the time the Constitution was adopted, the only federal officials directly elected by the people were members of the House of Representatives. Senators were chosen by state legislatures; the president and vice president were selected by electors in the Electoral College; and judges, ambassadors, and high-ranking officials in the executive branch were nominated by the president and approved by the Senate. In Federalist No. 51, James Madison admonished, "As it is essential to liberty that the government in general should have a common interest with the people, so it is particularly essential that the branch of it under consideration [the House] should have an immediate dependence on, and an intimate sympathy with, the people."[3] The House of Representatives thus directly connects voter sentiment with popular representation.

To ensure that members of the House would be accountable to voters, Article I, Section 2 sets the term of a House member at two years, keeping members constantly attentive to the currents of public opinion. Indeed, because of their relatively brief term of office, members of the House are typically consumed with concerns about winning reelection. This preoccupation has been well documented by scholars such as Thomas Mann, who argues that incumbent House members are in campaign mode most of the time, feeling "unsafe at any margin" of victory.[4]

Article I also ensures that the House of Representatives reflects the popular will by requiring that the number of representatives from each state be proportional to each state's population. States are not equally represented in the House of Representatives; rather, the population of each state is proportionately represented, at least to a large degree. This means that a more populous state has greater representation than a less populous one. The state of California, for example, now has fifty-three seats in the House of Representatives, compared to Wyoming, which has only one.

The first Congress in 1789 included sixty-five members, consistent with the Article I requirement that the number of House members should not exceed one for every thirty thousand people in a state. As the nation grew in both the number of states and number of people, the number of members of the House of Representatives also grew. If the thirty thousand people to one representative ratio persisted to today, there would be nearly ten thousand members of the House of Representatives! By the mid-1800s, Congress began enlarging the population size of a congressional district to keep the membership of the House from getting too large. Public Law 62-5, passed in 1911 to take effect in 1913, capped the total number of House seats at 435.[5]

Today there are still 435 **congressional districts**, each represented by one House member. The number of people who are represented in a congressional district is tied to a number that changes after every census. Since fixing the number of seats at 435, Congress has struggled to find an equitable way to allocate House seats to the states—a process known as **reapportionment**.

Several U.S. Supreme Court decisions in the early 1960s[6] established the basic principle that guides the process of reapportionment after every census—the "one man, one vote" principle. According to this principle, the population size of congressional districts must be as equal as possible. Currently, that amounts to roughly 650,000 people per district. The requirement that each state maintain at least one House district causes some variance among the population sizes of each district. The single congressional district for Wyoming, for example, has a population of about 500,000 because that is the number of people who live in that state. Consequently, Wyoming's population is proportionately "overrepresented," compared to most other congressional districts. Because congressional districts cannot cross state boundaries, the population size of congressional districts across states also varies. Yet once congressional districts are officially allocated to states based on the U.S. census, the size of each district within a state must be as close to equal as possible.

The Constitution requires that a new census of the population be taken every ten years, which is used to reapportion seats in the House of Representatives to each state. The states are then responsible for **redistricting** congressional boundary lines to achieve equal representation in each of the congressional districts; that is, redrawing congressional district lines to achieve the "one man, one vote" principle within the borders of the state.

In addition to equalizing the size of congressional districts, parties in each state try to optimize the partisan characteristics of each district to their advantage. This drawing of district boundaries to favor one party over the other is referred to as **gerrymandering**, a term named for Elbridge Gerry, who was a signer of the Declaration of Independence, a Massachusetts delegate to the Constitutional Convention, a U.S. congressman, governor of Massachusetts, and vice president under James Madison. While governor, he endorsed legislation that redrew districts in Massachusetts, resulting in huge advantages for his political party, the Democratic-Republicans. The map of one of the new districts took on an odd shape, that of a salamander. Gerry's political opponents, the Federalists, dubbed the plan the "gerrymander plan." The political fallout for Gerry was significant—he lost his next bid for governor. But the legacy of gerrymandering continues. Every decade or so, parties in states with more than one House member must ultimately negotiate a

Congressional district
A geographic region (either a state itself or a region located entirely within one state) whose residents select one member to represent it in the House of Representatives.

Reapportionment
The allocation of a fixed number of House seats to the states.

Redistricting
The act of redrawing congressional boundaries to achieve equal representation in each of the congressional districts.

Gerrymandering
The drawing of House district boundaries to the benefit of one political party over another. The term is named for Elbridge Gerry, a Massachusetts delegate to the Constitutional Convention, who (as governor) redrew districts in this fashion to favor the Democratic-Republicans.

AMERICAN GOVERNMENT In Popular Perspective

Compared to its perceptions of the other institutions in American society, the American public expresses lower levels of confidence in Congress. The figure below shows the Gallup Poll's 2008 survey on confidence levels in a variety of institutions. As the chart shows, confidence in Congress ranks the lowest.

An important book on the topic of public confidence in Congress is *Congress as Public Enemy* by John Hibbing and Elizabeth Theiss-Morse (New York: Cambridge University Press, 1995). The authors argue that the openness of Congress to public scrutiny is responsible for its lower confidence ratings. Despite the low regard for Congress as an institution, Americans have a much higher opinion of the particular members who represent them in Congress. When national polls ask people to rate their own senator and representative, the average ratings tend to be twenty points higher than those that people give to the rating of the institution as a whole.* Why do people "love their congressperson, but hate Congress?" Individual members' visibility in their home states and districts and the constituent services provided to those they represent tend to promote favorable ratings. In contrast, news about the institution tends to revolve around conflict, debate, and gridlock in the legislative process.

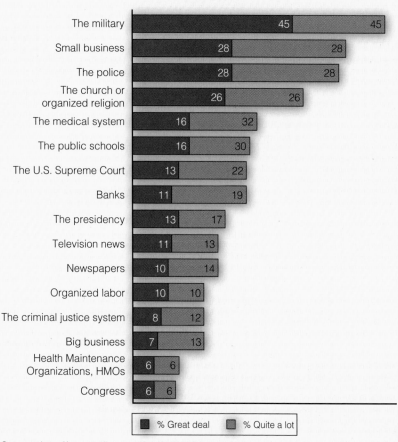

Confidence in institutions

Institution	% Great deal	% Quite a lot
The military	45	45
Small business	28	28
The police	28	28
The church or organized religion	26	26
The medical system	16	32
The public schools	16	30
The U.S. Supreme Court	13	22
Banks	11	19
The presidency	13	17
Television news	11	13
Newspapers	10	14
Organized labor	10	10
The criminal justice system	8	12
Big business	7	13
Health Maintenance Organizations, HMOs	6	6
Congress	6	6

Source: http://www.gallup.com/poll/108142/confidence-congress-lowest-ever-any-us-institution.aspx

* *Public Perspective* magazine, 1998.

redistricting plan based on gerrymandered district boundaries that each party hopes will optimize its electoral successes.

Article I requires that all members of the House of Representatives be at least twenty-five years of age, have been a U.S. citizen for a minimum of seven years, and live in the state (though not necessarily the congressional district) from which they are elected. These requirements are somewhat less restrictive than those for the Senate (see below)—another indication of the Founders' intention to give the people a greater role in deciding on who members of the House should be.

The Senate: A Stabilizing Factor

Whereas the Founders wanted to make the House of Representatives highly responsive to the people, their idea for the Senate was quite different. The Senate was to represent the states—with each state having two senators, thus being equally represented. As adopted, the Constitution specified that senators were to be elected not by the people of the state, but by the state legislatures, another way to recognize states' importance. Not until passage of the Seventeenth Amendment to the Constitution in 1913 were senators elected directly by the people of the state they represented.

The Founders were also concerned that the "people's house" might be too prone to radical changes in membership resulting from swift changes in popular opinion. James Madison in particular regarded the U.S. Senate as "a necessary fence against this danger,"[7] able to resist fast changes in federal legislation because it was less accessible to the people. In fact, during the first five years of our constitutional government, the U.S. Senate met in closed session. By sharing legislative power with the House of Representatives, the Senate, a slower, more deliberative body, would be the mechanism for protecting against the potential tyranny of the masses. Thus the creation of new laws would be forced to proceed at a more thoughtful pace.

The Constitution sets the term of a U.S. senator at six years, three times the length of that for a House member. The Founders staggered the terms of senators. Every two years, only one-third of the seats in the Senate are up for reelection, as compared to all of the seats in the House. So although in theory all of the seats in the House can change every other year, the Senate may change only by a maximum of thirty-four seats every two years and is thus less prone to drastic changes in membership.

The qualifications for becoming a U.S. senator are also tighter. The minimum age is thirty, five years older than in the House, with the idea being that older people were less likely to endorse radical change. Also, a U.S. senator must have been a citizen for at least nine years (rather than seven for the House) and be a resident of the state that he or she represents.

Article I requires that there be two senators from each state. The total number of senators grew from twenty-six in 1789 to one hundred in 1959, the year Alaska and Hawaii became the forty-ninth and fiftieth states, respectively, to join the union. Although the size of the Senate has grown, it still remains small, at least relative to the size of the House of Representatives. The smaller size of the Senate is often cited as the primary reason why debate in the Senate tends to be more civil and camaraderie between individuals more important.

Leadership in Congress

Unlike the executive branch of American government, which is headed by the president, no one person or office leads Congress as a whole. Leadership is distinct in the Senate and the House of Representatives. Though both chambers must work together to pass new laws, each chamber maintains its own leadership structure to work on bills, pass laws, and conduct its other business. Cooperation between the House and Senate is necessary to accomplish legislation.

The principal factor driving leadership in each chamber is the political party system, which, interestingly, is not mentioned in the U.S. Constitution.[8] The two-party system in America typically generates a majority of members from one of the two major parties, in both the Senate and House of Representatives. Since 1851, the majority party in each house has been either the Democratic Party or the Republican Party. Members of the party that has the majority of seats constitute the **majority caucus**, whereas those who are members of the party with a minority of seats constitute the **minority caucus**. The majority caucus in the House and the majority

© 2012 CENGAGE LEARNING

★ LO

Appreciate the role that political parties play in the leadership of Congress

Majority caucus
The members of the party that has the majority of seats in a particular chamber.

Minority caucus
The members of the party that has a minority of seats in a particular chamber.

caucus in the Senate use their respective majorities to elect leaders and maintain control of their chamber. The larger the party's majority, and the more discipline and unity among party members, the stronger the power of the majority party's leadership ability.

Over the past thirty years, party control of the Senate has changed hands quite a few times. The 1980 elections gave Republicans control of the Senate for the first time since 1954, and they held at least a narrow margin of control up until the 1986 elections, when Democrats won back a majority. The 1994 elections swept the Republicans once again back into the majority, and they maintained control over that body until 2001, when Vermont Senator James Jeffords's switch from lifelong Republican to independent threw a 50–50 split chamber back into Democratic hands. The Republicans regained control after the 2002 midterm elections, but then forfeited it once again in 2007, when fifty-one senators caucused with the Democrats and placed them back in control. As a result of the 2008 elections, the Democratic majority widened its margin to a filibuster-proof 60–40 margin in the Senate. Subsequently, the January 2010 special election in Massachusetts to fill the seat of deceased Democratic Senator Ted Kennedy was won by Republican Scott Brown, reducing the large Democratic margin to a near-filibuster proof majority.

In the midterm elections of 2010, however, the GOP scored a number of victories in the Senate. While the Democrats retained control of the upper chamber, their margin of control was slashed significantly, increasing the prospect for more filibusters in the 112th Congress.

By contrast, the House of Representatives has enjoyed a bit more stability, undergoing fewer changes in party control of the majority caucus since 1954. Up through 1994, the Democratic Party had maintained a seemingly iron grip of control over the House. Finally after forty years, the 1994 elections transformed a Democratic majority to a Republican majority. The Republicans continued to dominate the House until the 2006 midterm elections, at which point the Democrats once again regained leadership of the people's chamber and then increased their majority as a result of the 2008 elections. Democratic control of the House, however, proved short lived. In 2010, the GOP won back more than 60 House seats from the Democrats and reestablished a Republican majority that promised to make life difficult for the White House in 2011 and beyond.

Leadership in the House of Representatives

The only guidance the Constitution offers regarding House leadership is contained in Article I, Section 2: "The House of Representatives shall choose their Speaker and other officers." The **Speaker of the House** is the title given to the leader of this chamber. Every two years, when a new Congress takes office, the full House of Representatives votes to determine who the Speaker will be from among its 435 members. In practice, the selection of Speaker is made by the political party in the House that holds the majority of seats. Members in the majority caucus meet prior to the vote for Speaker and agree on their leader, who receives virtually all the votes from the majority party members, thus guaranteeing that the majority party will occupy the Speaker of the House post.

As presiding officer, the Speaker of the House is the most powerful member of the House of Representatives, though that was not always so. Throughout the first century of the American political system, the Speaker acted mostly as procedural leader, or presiding officer, of the House, and had little more power than committee chairs. However, with the accession of Joe Cannon to Speaker in 1903, this post became much more powerful. Cannon, a Republican from Illinois, served in the House for more than fifty years and was Speaker from 1903 to 1911. As Speaker, Cannon used the House Rules Committee to amass a tremendous amount of power.[9] Known as "Uncle Joe," he arbitrarily recognized who could speak in the House chamber and required that any measure passing the Rules Committee would have to be personally approved by him. Cannon also made a practice of filling important committee posts with those who were loyal to him. A coalition of Democrats and insurgent

Speaker of the House
The leader of the House of Representatives, responsible for assigning new bills to committees, recognizing members to speak in the House chamber, and assigning chairs of committees.

Republicans eventually unseated Cannon, but Uncle Joe permanently changed the visibility and power of the Speaker position.

The Speaker remains powerful today for a variety of reasons. First, as the person responsible for assigning new bills to committees, the Speaker can delay the assignment of a bill or assign it to a committee that is either friendly or hostile to its contents, a power that gives the Speaker control over much of the House agenda. Second, the Speaker has the ability to recognize members to speak in the House chamber. Because an important part of the legislative process involves members debating bills on the House floor, the Speaker's authority over this process is significant.

Third, the Speaker is the ultimate arbiter and interpreter of House rules. The ability to cast final judgment on a rule of order can make or break a piece of legislation. For example, Republican Speaker Newt Gingrich's decision in 1998 to assign impeachment authority over President Bill Clinton to the House Judiciary Committee rather than to a select committee on impeachment was significant. Gingrich may have surmised that the makeup of the existing Judiciary Committee was inclined toward impeachment. Indeed, the Judiciary Committee ultimately recommended the impeachment of Clinton to the full House. Fourth, the Speaker appoints members to serve on special committees, including conference committees, which iron out differences between similar bills passed in the House and Senate. The Speaker's influence is thus felt in the final changes made to a bill before Congress completes work on it. Fifth, the Speaker plays an influential role in assigning members to particular permanent committees. Some committees, as we will see later in this chapter, are more important than others. Being on the Speaker's "good side" can help in getting a good committee assignment. In addition, the Speaker hand-picks the nine members of the all-important Rules Committee. Finally, the Speaker has ultimate authority to schedule votes in the full House on a bill, an authority that allows the Speaker to speed the process or delay it, using timing to either improve or subvert a bill's chances of being passed.

Partisan control of the House is the key factor regarding how that body is organized to do its work. Because the party that holds a majority of seats selects the Speaker, the majority party controls the legislative agenda through members serving in other leadership posts, including chairs of committees. In 2007, Nancy Pelosi, a Democrat from California, became the first woman in American history to hold a top leadership position in one of the three branches of government. Pelosi was chosen as speaker-elect by the House Democratic caucus when it convened in mid-November 2006; she assumed the formal constitutional title of Speaker of the House during the first week of January 2007. Pelosi would relinquish the Speaker's office in 2011, after the GOP won back its majority.

CHIP SOMODEVILLA/GETTY IMAGES

After the Democrats won control of the House of Representatives in the 2006 elections, the new Congress elected Nancy Pelosi as the first woman Speaker of the House. Pictured above, Pelosi takes the gavel from Republican John Boehner in her historic first day on the job as Speaker on January 4, 2007. Four years later in January 2011, Pelosi would hand the Speaker's gavel back to Boehner as the GOP won control of the House.

Rep. John Boehner (R-OH) making a tearful address on election night in November 2010, after he learned that the GOP would control the House, and that he would likely become the next Speaker.

JIM LO SCALZO/EPA/CORBIS

To promote partisan leadership, the majority caucus in the House votes for a House **majority leader**, and the minority caucus for a House **minority leader**. These leaders oversee the development of their party platforms and are responsible for achieving party coherence in voting. Other important party leadership positions in the House are the House minority and majority **whips**. Whips report to their respective party leaders in the House and are primarily responsible for counting up the partisan votes on bills—that is, they contact members of their party caucus and try to convince them to vote the way their party leadership wants them to vote. The whips spend much of their time on the floor of the House, on the phone, or in the offices of their party colleagues, counting votes and urging their members to vote the party line on bills.

Majority leader

In the Senate, the controlling party's main spokesperson who leads his or her party in proposing new laws and crafting the party's platform. The Senate majority leader also enjoys the power to make committee assignments. In the House, the majority leader is the controlling party's second in command, who helps the Speaker to oversee the development of the party platform.

Minority leader

The leader of the minority party in each chamber.

Whip (majority and minority)

Member of Congress elected by his or her party to count potential votes and promote party unity in voting.

The GOP House leadership campaigned on "A Pledge to America" to rein in federal spending and reduce the size of government. This campaign helped the GOP cement victories in the 2010 congressional elections.

AP PHOTO/J. SCOTT APPLEWHITE

AMERICAN GOVERNMENT In Historical Perspective

Important Tie-breaking Votes Cast by Vice Presidents in the Senate

The Constitution specifies only two formal functions for the vice president of the United States: to be the presiding officer of the U.S. Senate and to cast a vote in Senate in the event (and only in the event) of a tie. A number of tiebreaking votes by vice presidents have been quite consequential.

In 1790, Vice President John Adams's second tie-breaking vote in the Senate was responsible for moving the capital of the United States from New York City to Washington, DC. The decision to find a permanent capital for the new country was a divisive issue. New York City was the early temporary home of the capital, but southerners feared that the location of the national capital in the North would give that region an unfair advantage on important regional issues, such as slavery and urban development, at the expense of farmers and rural areas. In the House, a deal had already been struck to support moving the capital to a plot of land on the Potomac River bordering Virginia and Maryland. A move by several senators to block the move by supporting a bill that would keep the capital in New York resulted in a 13–13 tie. Adams's tie-breaking vote in favor of moving the capital paved the way for passage of a new bill to move the capital to Philadelphia for ten years, while the land that would become Washington, DC, was prepared to be the nation's capital.

In 1881, on March 18 the Senate met to begin its session by selecting a slate of committee leaders and members. For twenty years, the Senate had been controlled by the Republicans, making such votes quite predictable. But in the 1880 elections, Americans sent thirty-six Republicans and thirty-six Democrats to the U.S. Senate, along with two independents. The Senate vote on this day would determine whether the Democrats or the Republicans would control the Senate and thus hold the power to confirm or deny Republican President Garfield's patronage appointments. The initial vote was 37–37, giving Republican Vice President Chester Arthur the all-important deciding vote. Arthur's tie-breaking vote allowed the Senate Republicans to ward off a significant Democratic threat to their power.

In 1993, newly elected President Bill Clinton placed at the cornerstone of his new presidency a budget proposal that included tax increases and new federal spending to stimulate a sluggish economy. Much was riding on this budget proposal, as Clinton had won the election of 1992 over George H. W. Bush based on his criticism of Bush's lack of concern for bringing the nation out of economic recession (made famous by the Clinton campaign slogan "It's the economy, stupid"). Clinton argued that the budget plan was essential not only to economic recovery, but ultimately to eliminating the federal budget deficit. Though passed by the House of Representatives, the vote in the Senate ended in a 50–50 tie, setting the stage for Vice President Al Gore to cast the deciding vote to pass the budget. A most remarkable economic development of the 1990s was, in fact, the elimination of federal deficits.

Leadership in the Senate

The Constitution prescribes that the presiding officer of the Senate is the vice president of the United States. In this capacity, the vice president also holds the title of president of the Senate. Unlike the Speaker of the House, who is necessarily a member of the House of Representatives, the president of the Senate is not a member of the Senate. The president of the Senate cannot engage in debate on the floor of the Senate and has no legislative duties in the Senate, with one notable exception: to cast a vote in the Senate in the event of a tie. John Adams, the first vice president of the United States, was the most frequent tiebreaker in U.S. history, casting a vote twenty-one times in the Senate.

In practice, the vice president rarely shows up on the Senate floor to preside over its session. The presiding officer, in the absence of the vice president, is the **president pro tempore** (*pro tempore* is Latin, meaning "for the time being"). By custom, the official president pro tempore is the senator in the majority caucus who has served the longest number of consecutive years in the Senate. Again, however, in practice the president pro tempore rarely exercises the authority to preside over the Senate. With

President pro tempore
In the absence of the vice president, the senator who presides over the Senate session. By tradition, this is usually the senator from the majority caucus who has served the longest number of consecutive years in the Senate.

Pictured above is the leadership of the Senate, beginning in the 110th Congress, which started its work in January 2007. Pictured with their Senate colleagues are Minority Leader Mitch McConnell (R-KY), left, and Majority Leader Harry Reid (D-NV).

fewer rules and a greater culture of respect to fellow members than in the House, the presiding officer of the Senate serves what is largely a ceremonial role.

Leadership in the Senate is principally a function of partisanship, with the majority and minority caucuses organizing through leadership posts similar to those of the House of Representatives. As in the House, the majority party exercises tremendous power by controlling the agenda and mobilizing majority votes on important issues for the party. The majority caucus elects a Senate majority leader, and the minority caucus a Senate minority leader. These leaders are the main party spokespersons in the Senate, lead their party caucuses in proposing new laws, and are the chief architects of their party's platform. As leader of the majority, the Senate majority leader enjoys special power in making assignments to leadership of committees.

As in the House, the Senate majority and minority leaders are supported by whips, majority and minority. The whips in the Senate serve the same function as those in the House—they keep track of how caucus members are planning to vote on upcoming bills, and they communicate the positions of party leaders on upcoming legislative votes.

Leaders in the Senate generally have far less power than their counterparts in the House. The smaller number of senators requires less discipline in membership, and the culture of the Senate includes a greater amount of deference from one senator to another. Because there are fewer rules and formal procedures in the Senate, leaders and rule-making members have less power to control debate in that body.

★ LO   Compare and contrast the different types of committees found in Congress

The Committee System

The work of a member of Congress can be classified into four categories: (1) running for reelection, (2) serving constituents, (3) working on legislation, and (4) providing oversight of federal agencies. Working on legislation involves two activities—working on bills in committees and voting on proposed bills.[10] The bulk of work on legislation consists of what members do in committees, which includes generating ideas for new laws, debating the merits of those ideas, holding hearings, conducting investigations, listening to the testimony of experts, offering modifications and additions to proposed bills, and giving important advice to all House and Senate members regarding how they should vote on a new bill. Committee work also is the means through which members fulfill their role of oversight of federal agencies. Voting, on the other hand, is a rather simple and straightforward process. Members show up on the House or Senate floor and cast a vote of either "aye," "nay" or "present," indicating their support for, opposition to, or abstention from voting on a proposed piece of legislation.

Every year about ten thousand bills are introduced into Congress. A **bill** is a formally proposed piece of legislation, and many bills are long, complex documents with much legal and technical information. It is not practical to assume that each senator and House member reads and digests every bill that is introduced. As a way to manage the workload, both chambers of Congress rely heavily on a committee system. In both the House and Senate, each member is assigned to a few committees and becomes an expert in the subject area of the committee. Most of members' legislative work revolves around the committees to which they are assigned.

Congressional committees also include subcommittees, providing for even more specialization and division of labor. Currently there are more than 100 subcommittees in the House alone. Each of the subcommittees is also assigned a chair, so many members in the majority party of the House are chairs of either a committee or subcommittee. In the Senate, with fewer members, all members of the majority are usually the chair of at least one committee or subcommittee. A House member sits on an average of five different committees, whereas a senator sits on an average of seven committees.

What makes the committee system so powerful a force in legislation? It is the deference that most members give to the work of their colleagues in committees. Recognizing specialized knowledge, respecting the need for division of labor, and protecting one's own authority in the committees in which one serves all lead senators and House members to vote on the basis of a committee's recommendation on a bill.

Types of Committees in Congress

There are four general types of congressional committees: standing committees, select committees, conference committees, and joint committees.

Standing committees are permanent committees that exist in both the House and Senate. Most standing committees focus on a particular substantive area of public policy, such as transportation, labor, foreign affairs, and the federal budget. A few focus on procedural matters of the House and Senate, such as the House Rules Committee and the Senate Rules and Administration Committee. The most significant power of the standing committee is that of **reporting legislation**—which means that the full House or Senate cannot vote on a bill unless the committee votes to approve it first. No other type of congressional committee has the power to report legislation. Table 6.2 lists the standing committees of the House and Senate.

Standing committees have been the heart and soul of congressional organization since the very early 1800s. Just like today, standing committees then were divided into substantive policy areas and had plenty of authority to determine the future of a bill within its jurisdiction. For example, in 1802 the House of Representatives established the Ways and Means Committee to set policies for America's federal tax system. Any bill dealing with changes in the tax system had to pass through this committee, as it still does today. The House Ways and Means Committee remains the primary author of tax bills, including the tax cuts approved by Congress and signed into law by President Bush in 2001 and 2003.

Though most standing committees focus on a substantive area of public policy, such areas of focus are often broad and complex. In order to further divide labor and provide for even greater levels of specialization, most standing committees include subcommittees. For example, the House Transportation and Infrastructure Committee includes the following subcommittees: Aviation; Coast Guard and Marine Transportation; Economic Development, Public Buildings, Hazardous Materials, and Pipeline Transportation; Ground Transportation; Oversight, Investigations, and Emergency Management; and Water Resources and Environment.

Bill
A proposed law presented for consideration to a legislative body.

Standing committee
A permanent committee that exists in both the House and Senate; most standing committees focus on a particular substantive area of public policy, such as transportation, labor, foreign affairs, and the federal budget.

Reporting legislation
The exclusive power of standing committees to forward legislation to the full House or Senate. Neither chamber can vote on a bill unless the committee votes to approve it first.

TABLE 6.1 The Standing Committees in Congress

Committees in the House	Committees in the Senate
Agriculture	Agriculture, Nutrition, and Forestry
Appropriations	Appropriations
Armed Services	Armed Services
Budgets	Banking, Housing, and Urban Affairs
Education and Labor	Budget
Energy and Commerce	Commerce, Science, and Transportation
Financial Services	Energy and Natural Resources
Homeland Security	Environment and Public Works
House Administration	Homeland Security and Governmental Affairs
Intelligence*	Finance
Judiciary	Foreign Relations
Natural Resources	Health, Education, Labor, and Pensions
Oversight and Government Reform	Judiciary
Rules	Rules and Administration
Science and Technology	Small Business and Entrepreneurship
Small Business	Veterans Affairs
Standards of Official Conduct	
Transportation and Infrastructure	
Veterans Affairs	
Ways and Means	

*Technically a "permanent select committee."

Before the House of Representatives or the Senate can vote on any bill, it must first be approved by a majority of members on the committee. A number of factors can affect a committee's consideration of a bill, which can seriously slow down the process of a bill becoming law and create a sense of "legislative gridlock." When a committee gets a new bill, the chair usually directs the bill to a subcommittee. The subcommittee discusses the bill, holds hearings, and makes changes, additions, or deletions to the bill. Usually, after a successful subcommittee vote, the bill moves back to the full committee, where additional debate and hearings might occur. Only after a successful committee vote is the bill ready to be considered by the full House and/or Senate. This process occurs in both the House and the Senate. There are, therefore, many opportunities for standing committees to slow the policymaking process, or bring it to a grinding halt.

A second general type of committee in Congress is the **select committee**, a special committee established to examine a particular issue of concern. Select committees do not have the power to report legislation, and they are not permanent. Once their work on a particular issue of the day is complete, the select committee is dissolved. Select committees are often formed to deal with a particularly serious

Select committee

A committee established by a resolution in either the House or the Senate for a specific purpose and, usually, for a limited time.

national problem—a problem for which legislation may not be considered but rather a recommendation might be made. Recently, for example, select committees have been established to investigate the problem of illegal immigration and the national drug problem. House or Senate leaders may choose a select committee to deal with an issue for political reasons as well. If leaders suspect that a standing committee might have trouble reporting a bill to the full chamber, they might appoint a select committee, which does not have reporting power.

A third type of committee found in Congress is the **conference committee**. As described earlier in this chapter, the House and Senate are equal players in the legislative process. This means that both chambers debate, hold hearings on, comment on, and vote on individual pieces of legislation. A bill, then, is considered, modified, and voted on by both the House and Senate. Assuming that a bill survives both chambers and passes, it is likely that the changes made to the bill during the standing committee process will differ between the House and Senate. Conference committees consist of both House members and senators, who work together to iron out differences in the House and Senate versions of a bill.

A fourth type of committee is the **joint committee**, which consists of members from both chambers. Joint committees do not propose legislation and have no reporting power, but rather are investigative in nature, focusing on issues of general concern, such as oversight of programs that are administered by the executive branch of the federal government. Unlike select committees, which are temporary and focus on a narrower topic, joint committees are typically permanent and focus on broader policy areas. An example is Congress's Joint Economic Committee. This committee keeps tabs on the performance of the nation's economy and provides oversight to the Federal Reserve Board, the unit that, among other things, has authority to adjust the federal prime interest rate.

Conference committee

A joint committee of Congress appointed by the House of Representatives and the Senate to resolve differences on a particular bill.

Joint committee

A committee composed of members of both the House and the Senate that is investigative in nature.

Leadership of Congressional Committees

Although there are a handful of broad leadership positions such as "presiding officers" and "party leaders" in the House and Senate, the vast majority of leaders are the chairs of the many committees and subcommittees in the two chambers. The power of the majority caucus is fully felt in the committee and subcommittee chairs, as all chairs are members of the majority caucus. Committees are where Congress gets most of its work done, and the chairs of committees have a great deal of power in determining what gets done and when it gets done.[11]

For example, the chairs decide how much time, if any, to spend on a new bill; they choose the people who will testify before the committee; and they allot the time to be spent on testimony and committee discussion. House and Senate leaders choose committee chairs from members of the majority caucus, a selection generally based on seniority and party allegiance. For each committee, the majority party's ranking, or senior, member is typically the person who becomes the committee chair, although the Speaker of the House ultimately determines the chairs for House committees and the Senate majority leader does the same for Senate committees.[12] Though seniority remains important, congressional reforms in 1974 and 1994 have somewhat reduced the power of seniority in the determination of committee chairs. More recently, the selection of chairs and the chairs' adherence to party leadership has provided a strong basis for party influence in congressional leadership.

Partisan Nature of the Committee System

The large number of standing committees and subcommittees, along with the significant power of the committee given its expertise in the policy area, disperses legislative power. It is in the interest of the majority party, however, to control what bills are given priority, how bills are written, and what bills get passed. Thus, the primary organizational characteristic of most committees in Congress is partisanship. To

The Five Members of Congress You Should Draft for Your "Fantasy Team"

Fantasy sports leagues have grown increasingly popular over the past twenty-five years. In the most common fantasy team form, groups of friends meet just before a pro sport league's opening day to draft players; then, as the season progresses, they follow their players' statistics, make trades, and compile scores as part of an ongoing competition. Today there are fantasy leagues for every sport: baseball, football, basketball, hockey, even Formula One auto racing. Few people were surprised therefore when political junkie Andrew Lee and several of his fellow students at California's Claremont McKenna College developed an online fantasy Congress game back in 2005.

The game Lee developed requires players (called "citizens") to draft members of the U.S.

House, and then keep track of their participation within the actual U.S. Congress. A member of Congress can earn five points for introducing a bill or amendment, and more points for successfully pushing a bill through the legislative process. Points are also earned for voting participation, for being a maverick (voting against your party), and for being mentioned in the media. Of course the most powerful members of Congress often exert their authority behind the scenes, where their actions cannot always be assessed by simple measures such as those listed above. Which members rank highest in the Fantasy Congress? Based on number of bills sponsored and cosponsored in the first session of the 111th Congress, these were the five highest ranked members:

Rep. Rosa DeLauro

Rep. Earl Pomeroy

✔ 1. Rep. Earl Pomeroy (D-ND)

✔ 2. Rep. Howard Berman (D-CA)

✔ 3. Rep. Rosa DeLauro (D-CT)

✔ 4. Rep. Anna Eshoo (D-CA)

✔ 5. Rep. Christopher Van Hollen (D-MD)

SCOTT J. FERRELL/CONGRESSIONAL
QUARTERLY/GETTY IMAGES

SCOTT J. FERRELL/CONGRESSIONAL
QUARTERLY/ALAMY

Source: govtrack.us/congress/repstats.xpd. Scores are computed based on the number of bills sponsored by the member and cosponsored by another member of Congress divided by the number of bills sponsored by the other member of Congress and cosponsored by the member. (The higher the number, the more times others are cosponsoring the member's bills without the member returning the favor.)

control the committee agenda and the committee votes, the majority caucus ensures that all committees have a majority of members of their party.[13] Furthermore, the chair of each committee is from the majority caucus. In addition, the majority caucus typically reserves a "supermajority" of seats on the most powerful committees, such as the Rules and Appropriations Committees.

Congressional Staffing

The 435 House members and 100 senators are supported by a large professional staff, many of whom are young, recent college graduates. Staffers perform a variety of support functions related to the roles of members of Congress. They conduct background research on bills, help generate new ideas for bills, provide services to constituents, and aid in the oversight of executive agencies. There are three categories of congressional staff.

First is the member's **personal staff**. Members of Congress are given a budget to support a group of staffers to assist them. They typically have a staff in their Washington, DC, office and one in their home district office. The personal staffers serve a number of legislative support functions, including tracking bills that the member has introduced and conducting research on ideas for new bills. They also work with the local media in the member's home district, answering journalists' questions and providing information on the member's legislative activities. Perhaps the personal staffers' most important responsibility is responding to constituents in the district. House and Senate members receive many kinds of communications from constituents, ranging from requests for information about bills and explanations of why they voted a particular way, to letters expressing opinions on various issues and requests for speaking engagements. The personal staffers are responsible for dealing with these myriad constituent inquiries.

Another form of support for members of Congress comes in the form of **congressional agencies**. The volume of legislative work has grown substantially over the years, as has the complexity of the federal budget and the policy issues that Congress deals with. One way that Congress has dealt with problems of growth and complexity has been to delegate authority to executive agencies of government, a consequence of which was that Congress began to lose control of the ability to keep tabs on what those agencies were doing. The explosion of budget deficits in the 1970s and suspicions about the administration that were inspired by the Watergate scandal also left Congress feeling that it lacked necessary information for effective monitoring of executive agencies under presidential control. Through the 1970s, Congress relied on budget data from the Office of Management and Budget (OMB), which reports to the president. Congress suspected that the budget figures produced by OMB were compiled with an eye toward supporting the president's point of view. In response, in 1974 Congress created a new congressional agency, the Congressional Budget Office (CBO), to monitor the nation's economic situation and provide objective projections of the national budget. It reports directly to Congress. With the CBO, Congress no longer needs to depend exclusively on the executive branch to gather economic data and produce information to help Congress oversee the budget process.

At the same time, Congress also substantially expanded the size and funding of the Government Accountability Office (GAO; formerly called the General Accounting Office) and the Congressional Research Service (CRS). Congress uses the GAO to monitor executive agency expenditures. Essentially, the GAO audits the spending of federal organizations to find and remove any abuses. The CRS is Congress's information and statistical data archive. It provides members with information they might need in preparation for writing a bill, conducting a hearing or investigation, or making a speech. Other important agencies of Congress include the Library of Congress,

Congressional personal staff
A group of workers who assist an individual member of Congress in performing his or her responsibilities.

AP PHOTO/RUSTY KENNEDY

Congressman Patrick Murphy (D-PA) is congratulated by his wife (immediate left) and staff after his reelection victory in 2006. Murphy lost his reelection bid in the GOP landslide of 2010.

Congressional agencies
Government bodies formed by and relied on by Congress to support members of Congress in performing their functions.

The Library of Congress, Washington, DC.

THOMAS MICHAEL CORCORAN/PHOTOEDIT

which acts both as the de facto national library of the United States as well as a research arm for congressional members; and the Government Printing Office, which prints and provides access to documents produced by and for all three branches of the federal government.

A third type of staffing resource at Congress's disposal is the congressional committee staff. Each standing committee of Congress employs a professional staff, many of whom are policy or legal experts in the policy area of the committee.

★ **LO** Describe the various steps necessary for a bill to become a law

How a Bill Becomes a Law

It is not easy for a bill to become a law. Though most work on bills occurs in committees, there are numerous other points at which a bill might be "killed." The Speaker of the House, the Senate majority leader, and the president all have means at their disposal to kill a bill. There are other points, as well, when bills might be stopped dead in their tracks. Not surprisingly, of the 10,000 or so bills introduced annually in Congress, only about 500 to 1,000 end up becoming law. And rarely does a bill, as originally introduced, become law without significant revision in the process. An important book on the process of a bill becoming law by is *The Dance of Legislation*, by Eric Redman.[14] As the title suggests, the lawmaking process involves many people and much politicking; the process is difficult and often follows no regular or consistent path. The steps to a bill becoming law are also highly influenced by partisan politics, lobbyists and special interests, public opinion, and powerful voices in and out of government. Even though the actual dance of legislation typically follows no neat pattern or order, we describe here the general way in which a bill becomes a law.

FIGURE 6.1 The Steps in a Bill Becoming a Law

CONGRESS

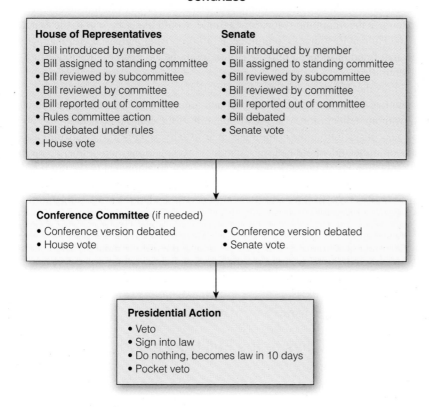

House of Representatives
- Bill introduced by member
- Bill assigned to standing committee
- Bill reviewed by subcommittee
- Bill reviewed by committee
- Bill reported out of committee
- Rules committee action
- Bill debated under rules
- House vote

Senate
- Bill introduced by member
- Bill assigned to standing committee
- Bill reviewed by subcommittee
- Bill reviewed by committee
- Bill reported out of committee
- Bill debated
- Senate vote

Conference Committee (if needed)
- Conference version debated
- House vote
- Conference version debated
- Senate vote

Presidential Action
- Veto
- Sign into law
- Do nothing, becomes law in 10 days
- Pocket veto

Step 1: A Bill Is Introduced

With the exception of tax or revenue proposals, which must originate in the House of Representatives, a bill can be first introduced into either the Senate or the House. The revenue exception, as stipulated in the Constitution, is a product of the American colonial experience with England, and the famous cry "no taxation without representation." Because the House provides popular representation, and representation is the philosophical basis undergirding taxation, the Founders gave the House sole authority to originate tax and revenue bills.

Whereas the Constitution requires that only a House member or a senator can introduce a bill, the ideas for new bills come from a variety of sources. Many come from the president of the United States or someone in the president's office or executive branch of government. Others come from lobbyists. Because House members and senators depend on lobbyists for information, and lobbyists represent groups who support candidates for congressional office, those with access to members are an important source of ideas for new legislation. Business leaders, educators, journalists, and regular constituents may also generate ideas for new bills. The next step for those with a suggestion for a new law is to find a sponsor in the House or Senate to introduce the idea in the form of a bill.

Whether the idea for a law comes directly from a member of Congress or from some other source, the first official step in the process is for the sponsoring member to submit the bill to the House or Senate clerk, who issues a unique number to the bill. The clerk in the House sends the bill to the Speaker of the House; the Senate clerk forwards the bill to the Senate majority leader.

AP PHOTO/GERALD HERBERT

FDIC Chair Sheila Blair, Assistant Treasury Secretary Neel Kashlari, and Assistant HUD Secretary Brian Montgomery attend an October 2008 hearing of the Senate Banking Committee, which was meeting to address the U.S. financial crisis.

Step 2: The Bill Is Sent to a Standing Committee for Action

The next step in the process requires the bill to be assigned to the standing committee that has policy jurisdiction over the topic the bill addresses. A bill introduced in the Senate to raise the minimum wage, for example, would likely be sent to the Senate Labor and Human Resources Committee; a bill proposing increased criminal penalties for mail fraud introduced into the House might be assigned to the House Judiciary Committee.

Most bills die during their initial consideration by the committee. In some cases, the committee chair simply sits on the bill and ignores it. In other cases the full committee, without deliberation, votes to kill the bill. If the committee decides to give the bill serious consideration, the committee chair usually assigns it to a subcommittee. The subcommittee may hold hearings, conduct investigations, and deliberate on the merits of the bill. Often the subcommittee will make amendments to the bill before sending it back to the full committee.

When a bill is back in full committee, the recommendations of the subcommittee may be accepted, rejected, or further revised. The full committee may conduct additional hearings, call more witnesses and experts to testify, and debate the bill. At the end of this process, a "markup," or final version of the bill is prepared. The markup is the proposed legislation on which the full committee will vote. If a majority of committee members vote against the bill, the bill goes no further, so here is another point in the process where a bill might be stopped. If a majority of committee members vote in favor of the bill, it moves forward in the process.

Step 3: The Bill Goes to the Full House and Senate for Consideration

At this next stage, the full House or Senate debates the bill and proposes amendments. The start of this process differs between the House and Senate. In the House, a bill that makes it through the committee is immediately assigned to the House **Rules Committee**. The Rules Committee decides when the bill will be debated, the amount of time that will be allotted for debate, and the extent to which amendments may be added from the floor of the House. The ability to control the timing and amount of time for debate is significant, thus making this committee one of the most important ones in the House. The ability to control the amendment process is even more powerful. If the Rules Committee issues a **closed rule**, House members are severely limited in their ability to amend the bill. An **open rule** order, on the other hand, permits amendments to the bill.

In the Senate, there are no rules set up ahead of time for debate. The Senate majority leader decides when to bring a bill to the floor. But, in theory, there are no limits on the amount of time the bill will be debated, and all senators are given the courtesy of speaking on any bill, if they so wish. The fact that the Senate includes far fewer members than the House allows for less structured debate. With no rules about how long a senator might speak, there is a possibility that a minority of senators—or even one senator—might try to block a bill from passage by refusing to end discussion, a process known as a **filibuster**.[15]

In 1917, a group of senators successfully filibustered to thwart a bill that would have armed American ships in anticipation of the nation's entry into World War I. In response to this event, the Senate adopted a **cloture** rule, which permitted the Senate to end debate and force a vote on a bill by approval of a two-thirds vote. The Senate left a loophole in place, however: if any senator, once properly recognized, refuses to concede the floor, he or she can exercise the equivalent of a one-person filibuster for as long as his or her voice will hold out. Accordingly, in 1957 South Carolina Senator Strom Thurmond spoke for more than twenty-four hours in an attempt to block the Senate from passing civil rights legislation. For many years, Senate filibusters successfully blocked legislation supported by a majority of senators. Then in 1975, the Senate modified the cloture requirement, so that currently a less stringent three-fifths vote of the Senate (sixty out of one hundred senators) is required to end debate.

Rules Committee
A committee in the House of Representatives that determines the rules by which bills will come to the floor, be debated, and so on.

Closed rule
A rule of procedure adopted by the House Rules Committee that severely limits the ability of members of Congress to amend a bill.

Open rule
A rule of procedure adopted by the House Rules Committee that permits amendments to a bill.

Filibuster
The action by a single senator or a minority of senators to block a bill from passage by refusing to end discussion.

Cloture
A Senate debate procedure that permits that body to end debate and force a vote on a bill by a vote of sixty senators.

In the 111th Congress, Senate Republicans increasingly resorted to the use of a filibuster in their attempts to block the Democratic majority from passing legislation endorsed by the Obama administration. At the end of 2009, the House and Senate each passed a version of the Obama administration's health care reform legislation. Yet final passage was initially thwarted by a threatened filibuster in the Senate after the election of Senator Scott Brown (R-MA) in February 2010 gave the Republicans the necessary forty-one votes to defeat cloture on a party-line vote. (Ultimately the Obama administration pressed successfully for House passage of the original Senate version, which did not require a revote by the Senate in 2010). In all, Senate Republicans made use of the filibuster more than 100 times during the 111th Congress.

At the end of the debate and amendment process, the House and Senate take a vote on the proposed bill. Passage of a bill must achieve a majority of votes (half of all present for voting, plus one) from members on the floor. A majority of votes must be achieved in both the Senate and House for the bill to survive to the next step in the legislative process.

How any one member of the House or Senate makes the decision to vote "aye" or "nay" on a given proposed bill differs from one bill to another, and from one member to another. But there are six common explanations, which vary in importance, depending on the situation:

1. **Personal opinion and judgment.** Many members of Congress have strong personal opinions and convictions on issues, and cast their votes on bills on the basis of those opinions. Rep. Henry Waxman (D-CA), for example, is an ardent environmentalist and consistently votes this position on environmental bills. Similarly, Rep. Chris Smith's (R-NJ) pro-life stance on abortion leads him to vote that position on bills.

2. **Constituent opinion.** Members of Congress want to be liked by their constituents, and most want to be reelected. In voting on particular bills, members often use results of polls, editorial commentary in local media, and letters written to them by their constituents to help them make up their minds in voting on a particular bill.

3. **Interest groups and lobbying.** As a way of achieving their goals, interest groups exert influence on congressional voting in a number of ways, including making contributions to congressional campaigns and hiring lobbyists to provide arguments to members regarding why they should vote a particular way on a bill. So members use both information provided by lobbyists to aid in their voting, and the campaign support from interest groups to prompt how they will vote.

4. **Political parties.** The party of a member often conveys quite a bit about their political positions and ideology, with Democrats tending to be more liberal on social and economic issues, and Republicans tending to be more conservative on these issues. So party membership is an important cue. In addition, the leadership of each party is organized to influence party members to vote the "party line" on bills. Members voting with their party tend to be rewarded with better committee assignments and greater campaign funding, thus making party a very important factor in voting on legislation.

5. **The president.** Presidents are the focus of national attention and have, as President Teddy Roosevelt once said, a "bully pulpit" to make their case and influence others, including members of Congress. Presidents are quite influential in directing congressional members of their own party how to vote, but often exert influence on members of the opposition party as well. Particularly in times of international crisis, presidents can effectively make appeals to put partisanship aside and convince members to vote in the interests of the country.

6. **Logrolling.** Members often enter into an agreement with other members to vote a certain way on one bill in exchange for a favorable vote on another bill. This process is known as **logrolling**. Members vote on thousands of bills every term. Giving up a vote on less important bills in exchange for favorable votes on more important bills is a common practice, and one that often guides congressional voting behavior.

Logrolling

The trading of influence or votes among legislators to achieve passage of projects that are of interest to one another.

© 2012 CENGAGE LEARNING

Step 4: Conference Committee Action

Often the version of a bill that passes the Senate differs from that passed by the House. To iron out any differences between Senate and House bills, Congress has two options. The first and most common route is to work out the differences informally. Of course the ability to do this depends on the extent of differences in the two versions of the bill and the closeness of the votes in committee and in the full chambers. When the versions are not far apart in content and when the margins of approval are large, informal discussions between House and Senate leaders and committee chairs are usually sufficient to strike a deal. When the prospects for informal agreement are less likely, then House and Senate leaders select a conference committee to work out the kinks. The conference committee consists of House and Senate members—usually drawn from the standing committees that worked on the bills.

President Obama signs the health care reform bill into law at the White House in March 2010.

Step 5: Presidential Action

Veto

The constitutional procedure by which the president refuses to approve a bill or joint resolution and thus prevents its enactment into law.

Overriding a veto

The power of the Congress to enact legislation despite a president's veto of that legislation; requires a two-thirds vote of both houses of Congress.

Pocket veto

The indirect veto of a bill received by the president within ten days of the adjournment of Congress, effected by the president's retaining the bill unsigned until Congress adjourns.

The president plays both an informal and a formal role in the passage of new laws. The president's informal role is to develop new ideas for laws and urge members of Congress to introduce them. The president also lobbies Congress, attempting to persuade members to support or oppose certain bills. The president's strong presence in the American political system, along with attention from the national media, offers the president a unique platform to lobby on behalf of or against certain legislation.

The formal constitutional role that the president plays in legislation is the fifth step in the process by which a bill becomes law. Once both chambers of Congress have agreed to a bill, the bill is sent to the president for action. The president has three options for dealing with the congressionally approved bill. First, the president can sign the bill, which officially makes it new law. Second, the president can **veto** (or refuse assent to) the bill, which stops the bill from becoming law. If the bill is vetoed, Congress has one more opportunity to pass the bill, by **overriding** the presidential veto. This requires a two-thirds vote in favor of passage in both the Senate and the House, a margin substantially more difficult to achieve than the simple majority vote required prior to a presidential veto. Third, the president can decide not to act on a bill (that is, neither sign it nor veto it), in which case the bill automatically becomes law after it has sat on the president's desk for ten days. If Congress passes a bill and sends it to the president within ten days of the end of a congressional session and the president does not act on the bill, then the bill does not become law, a process known as a **pocket veto**.

World Views of the United States

In March 2010, the House and Senate both held hearings to investigate the image of the United States around the world. The Foreign Relations committees in both houses called upon international relations and public opinions experts to provide their perspectives on what people from around the world thought of the United States, and how these views are changing. Andrew Kohut, the president of the Pew Research Center, presented findings to the House Foreign Relations Committee from the Pew Global Attitudes Project. The project features surveys in fifty-seven countries conducted over the past decade. A "U.S. Favorability Rating" is a standard question used in these surveys. The table below shows the U.S. Favorability Rating around the world, as reported to the Foreign Relations Committee.

U.S. Favorability Rating

	1999/ 2000 %	2002 %	2003 %	2005 %	2006 %	2007 %	2008 %	2009 %
U.S.	--	--	--	83	76	80	84	88
Canada	71	72	63	59	--	55	--	68
Britain	83	75	70	55	56	51	53	69
France	62	62	42	43	39	39	42	75
Germany	78	60	45	42	37	30	31	64
Spain	50	--	38	41	23	34	33	58
Poland	86	79	--	62	--	61	68	67
Russia	37	61	37	52	43	41	46	44
Turkey	52	30	15	23	12	9	12	14
Egypt	--	--	--	--	30	21	22	27
Jordan	--	25	1	21	15	20	19	25
Lebanon	--	36	27	42	--	47	51	55
Palest. ter.	--	--	*	--	--	13	--	15
Israel	--	--	78	--	--	78	--	71
China	--	--	--	42	47	34	41	47
India	--	66	--	71	56	59	66	76
Indonesia	75	61	15	38	30	29	37	63
Japan	77	72	--	--	63	61	50	59
Pakistan	23	10	13	23	27	15	19	16
S. Korea	58	52	46	--	--	58	70	78
Argentina	50	34	--	--	--	16	22	38
Brazil	56	51	35	--	--	44	47	61
Mexico	68	64	--	--	--	56	47	69
Kenya	94	80	--	--	--	87	--	90
Nigeria	46	76	61	--	62	70	64	79

Source: The Pew Research Center for the People and the Press, Pew Global Attitudes Project, http://pewglobal.org/2009/07/23/confidence-in-obama-lifts-us-image-around-the-world. 1999/2000 survey trends provided by the Office of Research, U.S. Department of State.

Oversight and Personnel Functions of Congress

In addition to creating new laws, Congress performs four other important constitutional functions: oversight of federal agencies, confirmation of top federal executives and judges, approval of treaties, and impeachment of top federal executives and federal judges.

Congressional Oversight

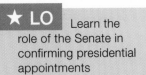

★ LO Explain why Congress often delegates its lawmaking authority to regulatory agencies

Congress's principal responsibility is to enact new laws to deal with national problems and concerns. But given the complexity of many issues (nuclear and toxic waste disposal, creating new sources of energy, promoting the role of high technology, and enhancing the performance of a multitrillion-dollar economy that has become highly integrated in the global economy, to name just a few), Congress often lacks the scientific and technological expertise needed to enact laws. In addition, for political reasons, sometimes Congress prefers not to deal with issues on its own, but rather to "pass the buck" to a bureaucratic agency. Defining the limits of genetic cloning is one such political hot potato. Whether the reason is technical capability or politics, Congress often delegates more specific legislative authority to the executive branch, which has the resources and expertise to make more highly technical policy decisions. The delegation of congressional power to the executive branch has become more frequent as our society has become more complex.

This delegation of authority, however, is not carried out blindly or without accountability. When Congress delegates its authority, it generally monitors the activities of agencies and administrators who are given this power through congressional oversight. One agency to which Congress has delegated considerable authority is the Federal Reserve Board (known as "the Fed"). Established by the Federal Reserve Act of 1913, the Fed has authority over credit rates and lending activities of the nation's banks. Congress created the agency because it recognized that specialized monitoring of the economy and the technical expertise of economists were necessary to make decisions about credit rates and lending activities in order to maintain a viable economy. The act gave the Fed the authority to adjust the supply of money to banks and to shift money from where there is too much to where there is too little. The Fed also has the power to take means to ensure that banks do not overextend themselves in lending so that a sudden economic scare will not cause a sudden run on banks for money. For nearly 100 years, Congress has given this agency the power to set important monetary policy for the nation. But Congress retains its authority to exercise oversight of the Fed. The Joint Economic Committee in Congress carefully monitors the Fed's performance and regularly holds hearings to inquire about its policies and decisions. In addition, newly appointed members of the Federal Reserve Board must be approved by Congress.

In his book on Congress titled *Congress: The Keystone of the Washington Establishment*,[16] political scientist Morris Fiorina notes other important reasons for congressional delegation of power to executive agencies, including garnering political rewards while shifting blame to the executive branch, enabling Congress to blame federal agencies for failing to fulfill legislative intent, and taking credit for problem solving by holding oversight and investigative hearings.

Confirmation of Presidential Nominations and Approval of Treaties

★ LO Learn the role of the Senate in confirming presidential appointments

The U.S. Senate plays a pivotal role in the selection of cabinet officers, other agency and executive branch heads, federal judges, and foreign ambassadors. The president nominates individuals for these posts, but the Senate must consent to the nomination with a majority vote in favor of the candidate. This function is one performed solely by the U.S. Senate, and not the House of Representatives.

At the beginning of a new presidential administration, the U.S. Senate is typically quite busy reviewing the president's nominations for high executive office

An Internship as a Steppingstone

Many college students interested in politics and public policy seek internships with Congress during the summer. Such an experience allows them to see firsthand how Congress works, gain valuable experience, and prepare for a possible job with the federal government. In early 2010, the job search Web site Monster.com estimated that job opportunities in the federal government would grow from 2.1 million to 2.5 million by end of 2012. Building one's resume with an internship in Congress can help to jump-start a successful career in public service.

The dozens of committees in Congress all have spots for college interns, as do large congressional agencies such as the General Accounting Office, the Congressional Budget Office, and the Library of Congress. In addition, all 535 members of Congress maintain offices in Washington, DC, as well as in their home state or district. Interns are commonly found helping with casework in many of these offices. Moreover, the partisan leadership offices, such as the majority and minority leaders and whips, frequently staff college interns to help them do their work, as do the Democratic and GOP House and Senate campaign committees. Many senators and representatives first got introduced to Congress through an internship that they themselves had. At a minimum, an internship with Congress provides a great resume item when applying for a full-time position in some part of the federal government.

A recent group of interns who work with the Congressional Hispanic Caucus

If you are interested in a congressional internship, there are a number of ways to get one. You can contact the office of a member of the House or Senate directly and inquire about future openings. You can visit the internship coordinator at your college or in your university's political science department and ask what might be available and how to apply. Or you can click on the following Web sites for information about ongoing internship opportunities:

- http://dc.about.com/od/jobs/a/Internships.htm
- http://www.twc.edu
- http://www.cbo.gov/employment/intern.cfm

positions.[17] Although the Senate usually endorses most nominees, there have been a number of high-profile instances when the Senate has been unwilling to confirm the nominee, typically occurring during eras of divided government when the political party of the president is different from the majority party in the Senate.

When there is a vacancy on the U.S. Supreme Court, a situation that often draws considerable interest from both the press and the public, the president nominates a new justice, whom the Senate also must confirm with a majority vote. Conflict between the Senate and the president over Supreme Court nominees goes all the way back to the first U.S. president, George Washington, and his choice of John Rutledge for chief justice of the Supreme Court. Although Rutledge appeared eminently qualified for the post (he was associate justice on the Supreme Court from 1789 to 1791 and chief justice of the South Carolina Court of Common Pleas from 1791 to 1795), he had openly criticized the highly controversial Jay Treaty with Britain (backed by Washington and the Federalists), which reneged on the terms of America's 1778 treaty with France. Rutledge's criticism was directed as much at its chief negotiator, John Jay, as at the treaty itself, which reassured Britain of American neutrality. Apparently, Rutledge still harbored a grudge against Jay, who had edged him out to become the nation's first chief justice in 1789. Although Washington stood behind his nominee and gave him a temporary recess appointment as chief justice, Federalist senators argued that confirmation of Rutledge would be an extreme embarrassment to their party and denounced him publicly. One called him a character "not very far above mediocrity." On December 15, 1795, the Senate rejected Rutledge's nomination by a 14–10 vote.

A more recent example of Senate opposition to a Supreme Court nominee occurred in the case of Clarence Thomas, nominated for the Court by President George H. W. Bush in 1991. The Democrat-controlled Senate opposed Thomas, an African American who held conservative views on numerous issues. Thomas's problems mounted further when One of his former employees at the Equal Employment Opportunity Commission, Anita Hill, testified that he had sexually harassed her while he was her boss. Thomas ultimately won confirmation by a close 52–48 vote and currently sits on the Supreme Court.

Under certain circumstances, Congress may also become involved in the selection of president and vice president of the United States. When no candidate receives a majority of electoral votes, the House of Representatives chooses the president and the Senate chooses the vice president. This has happened three times in the history of the nation—in 1801 when the House chose Thomas Jefferson as president, in 1825 when the House chose John Quincy Adams, and in 1877 when the House appointed a commission to resolve the controversial 1876 election (it chose Rutherford B. Hayes).

In the event of a vacancy in the vice presidency, the Twenty-fifth Amendment to the Constitution stipulates that the president's nomination of an individual to fill that position is subject to the approval of both the House and Senate by majority vote. This has happened twice since adoption of that amendment: in 1973 when Vice President Spiro Agnew resigned and Nixon's nomination of Gerald Ford was quickly approved, and in 1974 when Ford became president due to Nixon's resignation and Congress approved Ford's nomination of Nelson Rockefeller as vice president.

Finally, the Senate has the power to approve treaties that the president negotiates with foreign countries. The Constitution stipulates that approval of a treaty requires the consent of two thirds of the Senate. Even though the standard for treaty approval is much higher than a simple majority, most treaties do obtain the necessary two-thirds approval. Perhaps the most important rejection concerned the Treaty of Versailles following World War I. The relatively low number of rejected treaties may be due to presidents' reluctance to negotiate treaties that they are not reasonably certain will pass. President Woodrow Wilson's failure to consult with the Senate and consider their objections to the Treaty of Versailles led to the treaty's twice being rejected by the Senate, once in 1919 and again in 1920. More recently, the House has also played an important role in approving treaties because most of them involve financial issues that require the approval of that chamber.

Impeachment and Removal of Federal Judges and High Executives

★ LO Describe the congressional procedures for impeachment and removal of executive and judicial officers

Congress also has the authority to impeach and remove federal judges, cabinet officers, the president, the vice president, and other civil officers. The removal process requires an impeachment action from the House and a trial in the Senate. Only two presidents (Andrew Johnson in 1867 and Bill Clinton in 1998) have been impeached, and neither was actually removed from office.

Impeachment is the formal process by which the House brings charges against federal officials. A judge, president, or executive official who is "impeached" by the House is not removed; he or she is charged with an offense. In this sense, the House acts as an initial forum that makes the decision about whether a trial is warranted. An impeachment occurs by a majority vote in the House of Representatives. An official may be impeached by the House on more than one charge, each of which is referred to as an article of impeachment.

Assuming the House passes at least one article of impeachment, the official must then stand trial in the Senate. The prosecutors in the trial are members of the House of Representatives and are referred to as House "managers." Selected by the House leadership, the House managers present the case for removal to the full Senate. If the defendant is the president, the chief justice of the U.S. Supreme Court presides over the trial; otherwise the vice president of the United States (who is president of the Senate) or the president pro tempore of the Senate presides. Other than in the impeachment of a president or vice president, the Senate in recent times has usually designated a committee to receive evidence and question the witnesses. The impeached official provides lawyers in his or her own defense. A two-thirds vote of the full Senate is required for removal of an official.

Constituent Service: Helping People Back Home

Assess the "casework" functions of members of Congress in assisting constituents, educating them on policy issues, and performing other services on their behalf

★ LO

Much of what has been discussed thus far in this chapter pertains to what members of Congress do in Washington. As the people's representatives, members are sent to Washington to develop new laws and deliberate on important issues. They are expected to safeguard the nation's security, act as watchdogs against fraud, and ensure that judges and high-ranking executive officers are qualified for office. An integral part of the way members serve their constituents is by reflecting the opinions and input of those whom they represent while carrying out these legislative functions.

However, the service of members of Congress does not stop with the work they do in Washington. Often constituents will call upon a House member or senator to provide information about federal programs, to render assistance in getting benefits from federal programs, or to prepare a talk or visit with a community group to educate them about the political system or on a specific legislative or policy topic. Members are often asked by officials in state or local government to facilitate federal help for a local or state issue. The direct assistance that a member provides to a constituent, community group, or a local or state official is referred to as **casework**. A now classic book by Richard F. Fenno Jr., titled *Home Style: House Members in Their Districts*, provides a rich description of this role played by members of Congress.[18]

Casework is important for a number of reasons. First is its electoral importance to members of Congress. Casework raises the visibility of members in their home state or district, which reflects positively on how well the member is regarded and gives members an advantage over their opponents in elections. More than nine in ten House and Senate members who run for reelection are returned to office, and effectively managing casework is an important reason for this high return rate.

It has also become an implicit responsibility of members to help their constituents navigate the complex federal bureaucracy. Federal programs are varied and complex, and constituents are often overwhelmed in their efforts to obtain the benefits for which they are eligible. For example, under the Workforce Development Act, the federal government has programs that provide assistance to "displaced workers," defined as those who have lost their jobs due to technological or broad trends in the workplace. Many workers in the manufacturing industry in the United States have lost their jobs over the past decade as the national economy has shifted away from manufacturing and toward technology and information services. A variety of programs are available for these displaced workers to help them obtain training in new skills necessary to adapt to the new workforce. Finding these programs is often difficult, and members provide information to connect constituents with available programs.

Third, casework provides a direct connection between members and their constituents. Casework requires members to keep in touch with those whom they represent. Giving a speech to a local Rotary club or League of Women Voters meeting, showing up to "cut the ribbon" at an opening of a new local school building or park, and coming to speak to a group of students or employees all provide face time between

Casework
The direct assistance that a member of Congress provides to a constituent, community group, or a local or state official.

AP PHOTO/KELLEY MCCALL

Missouri Congressmen Russ Carnahan (left) and Rodney Hubbard (right), both Democrats, visit with some constituents back home.

the members and their constituents. The experiences that members have and the type of work they do in Washington can shelter them from the real-life concerns of their constituents back home. Casework provides a constant reminder of the needs and interests of those whom members represent.

Another aspect of constituent service involves what is known as "pork-barrel" politics. The federal budget includes a great deal of money for local projects, such as parks, dams, or road improvements. Members secure federal funds to support these projects in their states and districts through what is often referred to as **pork-barrel legislation**. The pork-barrel reference is based on the idea that members are "bringing home the bacon." Members use their influence on congressional committees and leadership positions to add amendments to bills that authorize pork-barrel spending on projects back home. Though many observers of the political system decry the unfairness of pork-barrel legislation, it has been an important aspect of constituent service since the beginning of our political system and promises to remain so in the future.

Pork-barrel legislation
A government project or appropriation that yields jobs or other benefits to a specific locale and patronage opportunities to its political representative.

Making the Connection

This chapter began with examples of Senate resistance in two issue areas at two very different points in American history—the approval of the League of Nations provisions of the Treaty of Versailles following World War I, and lower court judicial nominations in the first decade of the twenty-first century. In both instances, the Senate moved at a glacier pace, frustrating an impatient president at every turn. When Senate leaders offered the president compromises that might speed up the process, he was reluctant to give up any of what he viewed as "executive prerogative" and so the stalemates continued. Putting these two instances of Senate resistance in the context of the information presented in this chapter, what conclusions can we draw about the way the Congress as a whole, and the Senate in particular, tend to work?

First, and most apparent, when Congress is dealing with major problems or issues of the day, the process of creating new laws, approving new treaties and approving presidential appointments can be very slow indeed—many observers use the word "gridlock" to describe congressional inaction. Congress's actions are slow and deliberate; there are many points at which the process may be halted, and many actors with the capacity to hinder progress. Second, the compromises necessary to achieve success in Congress rarely prove entirely satisfactory to everyone involved. In the case of the Treaty of Versailles, Senator Henry Cabot Lodge's reservations to the treaty, which rejected any advance U.S. obligation to enter international conflicts to defend the autonomy of another country, were considered unacceptable to President Wilson, and so the Senate rejected the treaty and U.S. membership in the League of Nations. In the case of George W. Bush's judicial nominations, Senate Democratic leaders proposed to speed up the nomination process for some nominees only if his more controversial nominees were withdrawn.

Both these conflicts also highlight the power and significance of individual actors in the legislative process. Strong individuals such as Senator Henry Cabot Lodge and Senator Patrick Leahy dominated the debate over these issues. Congress is not simply two houses of 535 individuals who vote, with a majority obtaining victory. Those in leadership positions can exert a disproportionate influence on the process. Those with special communication skills enjoy more power, as do those who are highly informed on a particular issue. The better part of a century separated Senate debate and action on the treaty of Versailles and President Bush's judicial nominations. However, in both instances the same principles guided Senate activity and worked to produce similar approaches to resisting the chief executive.

Replacing Members of the U.S. Senate: Special Elections or Gubernatorial Appointment?

On August 25, 2009, Democratic Senator Ted Kennedy of Massachusetts passed away after a Senate career that spanned nearly half a century. His death created a vacancy in the U.S. Senate and reduced the Democratic majority from 60 to 59, thus allowing Senate Republicans to filibuster the Obama administration's health care reform legislation. The temporary replacement of a Senate seat is a matter determined by state law. In Massachusetts, the law in 2009 required a special election to be held between 145 and 160 days of the vacancy arising. In 2004 the Democratic majority in the Massachusetts State legislature withdrew the authority of then-governor Republican Mitt Romney to fill a Senate seat vacancy, anticipating that presidential candidate John Kerry, a Democratic senator from Massachusetts, might win the 2004 election. (As it turned out, he lost.) Senator Kennedy strongly encouraged the Democrats in the state's legislature to override Governor Romney's veto of that change, and they did. Ironically, in 2009 the vacancy created by Kennedy's death now threatened to hold up or even kill the federal health care reform legislation that Kennedy himself had championed.

Seven days before his death, Senator Kennedy was again lobbying the Democrats in the Massachusetts legislature. Now with Democrat Deval Patrick as governor and the fate of health care reform in question, Kennedy urged yet another change in the law: allowing the governor to make a temporary appointment prior to the special election for Senate seat vacancies. On September 22, 2009, the Massachusetts legislature posthumously approved Kennedy's request, paving the way for Patrick to appoint long-time Kennedy aide Paul Kirk as interim senator, thus temporarily protecting the Democrats' veto-proof majority until the January 19, 2010, special election. Republican Scott Brown eventually won that special election, and his election eliminated the veto-proof majority once again.

The political circumstances surrounding the actions of the Massachusetts legislature in 2004 and 2009 raise questions about how vacated Senate seats get filled. Changes in the Massachusetts laws are not the only examples of political gamesmanship in state legislatures. What is the best process for filling vacated seats in the Senate—special elections or gubernatorial appointments, or a hybrid approach such as the one adopted by Massachusetts in 2009? As a result of the 2004 and 2009 actions by the Massachusetts legislature, some have called for an amendment to the U.S. Constitution standardizing the manner in which interim vacancies get filled, thus removing political considerations from the process. Do you think that the Constitution should or should not be amended for this purpose?

On www.cengage.com/dautrich/americangovernment/2e, find the Politics Inter-Active link for details on filling vacated Senate seats. Consult the various links that relate to the process of filling vacated Senate seats across the fifty states, as well as historical, popular, and global perspectives on the topic.

MATTHEW HEALEY/UPI/LANDOV

Newly elected U.S. Senator Scott Brown (R-MA) celebrates his victory in the January 19, 2010, special election.

Chapter Summary

★ Article I and the Creation of Congress

- Congress, the legislative branch of the government, was the central institution in America's new political system at the beginning of the republic. Congress consists of two houses, a "people's house" apportioned by population (the House of Representatives), and a Senate in which the states, regardless of population, have equal representation.

- To ensure the principle of "one person, one vote" in the House, the population of congressional districts must be made as equal as possible based on the results of a federal census conducted every ten years. Parties try to maximize their advantage in the House of Representatives by "gerrymandering," which means that they draw district boundaries in order to favor their party on Election Day.

★ The Structure and Organization of Congress

- The relative strength of political party membership determines leadership in each legislative chamber. The Constitution designates that the leader of the House carry the title Speaker of the House. The Speaker is responsible for assigning new bills to committees and recognizing members to speak in the House chamber. The Constitution also prescribes that the vice president is to be the presiding officer of the Senate. Unlike the Speaker, the president of the Senate can vote only to break ties. When the vice president is absent from the Senate chamber (as is quite often the case), the presiding officer is the president pro tempore ("for the time being").

★ The Committee System

- There are four types of congressional committees: standing committees (permanent), select committees (established to look at a particular issue for a limited time), conference committees (reconcile differences between House and Senate versions of a bill), and joint committees (includes members from both houses, investigative in nature). Most members defer to committee recommendations on a bill.

★ How a Bill Becomes a Law

- The lawmaking process is often slow, and bills that survive frequently receive significant revisions along the way. After a bill is introduced by a member of Congress, it is usually sent to a committee for consideration (often in the form of hearings) and possible action. If the bill is endorsed by a majority of the committee, it then goes to the full House and Senate for consideration. Finally, if it is endorsed by a majority of each chamber, a conference committee reconciles differences in versions between the chambers, and then after a vote on the bill's final version, it goes to the president for signature.

- If the president vetoes the final bill, Congress can override the presidential veto by a two-thirds vote of both houses of Congress.

★ Oversight and Personnel Functions of Congress

- Congress delegates considerable legislative authority to the executive branch, whether because it lacks the expertise of bureaucrats or because it wishes to shift blame for policies to the executive branch. Still, Congress may exercise oversight to ensure that the implementation of laws and regulations is consistent with national problems and concerns.

- The U.S. Senate plays an important role in consenting to the president's selection of cabinet officers, other executive branch officials, and judges. Senate confirmation of Supreme Court nominees in particular has been the subject of considerable controversy.

- If a majority in the House of Representative impeaches a president, federal judge, or other executive official, the official must stand trial in the Senate. A two-thirds vote of the full Senate is required for the removal of an official from office.

★ Constituent Service: Helping People Back Home

- Members of Congress play an important role doing casework for local constituents, whether by assisting them in getting federal benefits, educating them on policy issues, or performing some other service on their behalf. Casework provides a direct connection between members and their constituents.

CourseMate

Key Terms

Bicameral legislature (p. 164)

Bill (p. 173)

Casework (p. 187)

Closed rule (p. 180)

Cloture (p. 180)

Conference committee (p. 175)

Congressional agencies (p. 177)

Congressional district (p. 165)

Congressional personal staff (p. 177)

Filibuster (p. 180)

Gerrymandering (p. 165)

Joint committee (p. 175)

Logrolling (p. 181)

Majority caucus (p. 167)

Majority leader (p. 170)

Minority caucus (p. 167)

Minority leader (p. 170)

Open rule (p. 180)

Overriding a veto (p. 182)

Pocket veto (p. 182)

Pork-barrel legislation (p. 188)

President pro tempore (p. 171)

Reapportionment (p. 165)

Redistricting (p. 165)

Reporting legislation (p. 173)

Rules Committee (p. 180)

Select committee (p. 174)

Speaker of the House (p. 168)

Standing committee (p. 173)

Veto (p. 182)

Whip (majority and minority) (p. 170)

Resources

Reference Works

Barone, Michael, and Richard E. Cohen, eds. *The Almanac of American Politics*. Washington, DC: The National Journal, 2010. The *Almanac* is published biannually with each new Congress and contains in-depth profiles of the 535 members of Congress along with the states and congressional districts that they represent.

The *Congressional Record* is the official proceeding of Congress. It contains a record of all the proceedings of the House and Senate.

Important Books

Davidson, Roger H., Walter J. Oleszek, and Frances E. Lee. *Congress and Its Members*. Washington, DC: CQ Press, 2007.

Fenno, Richard F., and Richard F. Fenno, Jr. *Congressmen in Committees*. Boston: Little, Brown, 1973.

Fenno, Richard F., Jr. *Home Style: House Members in Their Districts*. Boston: Little, Brown, 1978.

Fiorina, Morris. *Congress: Keystone of the Washington Establishment*. New Haven, CT: Yale University Press, 1979.

Hibbing, John R., and Elizabeth Theiss-Morse. *Congress as Public Enemy: Public Attitudes Toward American Political Institutions*. New York: Cambridge University Press, 1995.

Mayhew, David R. *Congress: The Electoral Connection*, 2nd ed. New Haven, CT: Yale University Press, 2004.

Smith, Stephen S., Jason M. Roberts, and Ryan J. Vander Wielen. *The American Congress*. New York: Cambridge University Press, 2007.

Internet Sources

http://www.thomas.gov (offers links to the *Congressional Record*, which provides the text of bills, floor debate, committee hearings, and reports)

http://www.whitehouse.gov (offers links to the official pages of the Senate and the House of Representatives; the site also provides links to the pages of all 535 members and to congressional agencies

7 The Presidency

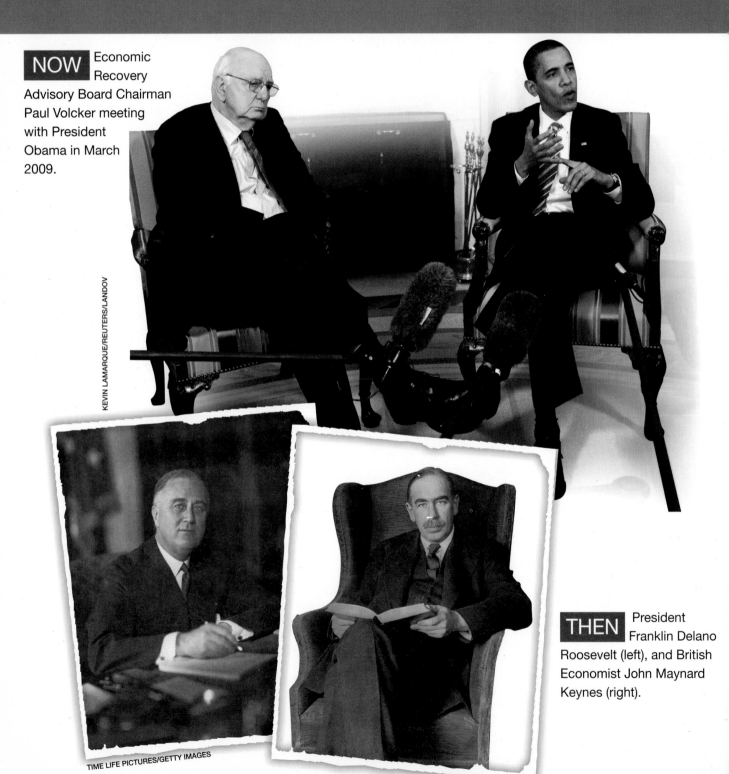

NOW Economic Recovery Advisory Board Chairman Paul Volcker meeting with President Obama in March 2009.

KEVIN LAMARQUE/REUTERS/LANDOV

TIME LIFE PICTURES/GETTY IMAGES

THEN President Franklin Delano Roosevelt (left), and British Economist John Maynard Keynes (right).

BETTMANN/CORBIS

NOW & THEN

A Leader's Determination to Stick to His Principles during a Severe Economic Crisis

? *The president of the United States was no economist, so he kept economists close by to help him make sense of detailed economic data. He understood that economic forces could make or break his administration. He also knew that the United States was facing a financial crisis of epic proportions, and achieving a recovery would require forceful action. Keynesian economic theory—named after its founder, the British economist John Maynard Keynes—justified what the president had in mind: using massive financial government investments to stimulate the economy and increase private economic activity. The president hoped that active public sector spending would provide the spark for economic recovery. His administration sponsored comprehensive legislation in line with this philosophy, and Congress followed the president's lead. Not everyone in Washington agreed with the president's approach: his policy choice would explode the deficit, and some economists believed to do so was dangerous given the difficult economic times. But the president had been elected to deal with the crisis, and as the nation's chief legislator and crisis manager, he alone would take the lead in choosing the road to recovery.*

LEARNING OBJECTIVES
★ WHAT YOU WILL LEARN ★

Where Do Presidents Come From? Presidential Comings and Goings

- ★ Analyze the past traits of presidents; assess the requirements for holding the position
- ★ Understand the process by which presidents may be impeached and removed from office; know the order of presidential succession

The Evolution of the American Presidency

- ★ Trace the evolution of the presidency from "chief clerk" in the late 18th and 19th centuries to eventual political dominance
- ★ Understand how the modern presidency has persevered in the recent era of divisiveness

Express Powers and Responsibilities of the President

- ★ Recognize the formal powers vested in the president under Article II of the Constitution
- ★ Explain how presidents use the veto, appointment and removal, and the pardon
- ★ Define the powers and limits of the president as commander in chief

Implied Powers and Responsibilities of the President

- ★ Recognize the implied powers of the presidency not spelled out in the Constitution including those exercised as the nation's crisis manager and political party leader
- ★ Explain how presidents exercise power through executive orders and agreements

Presidential Resources

- ★ Describe the other individuals and offices in the executive branch that contribute to the modern presidency

Important Presidential Relationships

- ★ Recognize how the power of the presidency is enhanced by communications with the public, the Congress, and the media

CourseMate

NOW & THEN

CHARLES OMMANNEY/
CONTOUR BY GETTY
IMAGES

NOW Though John Maynard Keynes had been dead for over sixty years, his economic theories were alive and well in the Obama administration during the early months of 2009. Since the 1980s, many economists had argued that the United States was in a "post-Keynesian world" where manipulating interest rates (instead of massive government spending) offered the best chance of staving off serious economic recessions. Then came December 16, 2008, the day the Federal Reserve tried to stabilize an economy in crisis by lowering the interest rate to 0 percent; the economy only continued to worsen in the weeks that followed.

After huddling with his top economic advisors, newly elected President Obama in February 2009 threw his administration's weight behind a quintessentially Keynesian solution: a $787 billion fiscal stimulus plan. The American people looked to Obama as the nation's chief legislator and crisis manager for a recovery plan, and Obama in turn pressed successfully for the American Recovery and Reinvestment Act (ARRA) of 2009. The new act expanded unemployment benefits, increased government spending in education, health care, and energy, and invested over $100 billion in transportation and other infrastructure . A year later, several independent macroeconomic firms, including Moody's and IHS Global Insight, estimated that the stimulus had saved or created 1.6 to 1.8 million jobs. On the other hand, the Congressional Budget Office conceded that the ARRA had increased the deficit by $200 billion for 2009 alone. By favoring the Keynesian route to recovery, Barack Obama cast his nation's lot with a British economist who had spearheaded a revolution in economic thinking more than seventy-five years earlier.

THEN   John Maynard Keynes was nearly fifty years old and at the height of his prestige as an economic theorist when Franklin D. Roosevelt took office as president of the United States in March 1933. FDR had remained open-minded about how his administration should tackle the Great Depression: during his first year in office he offered many different legislative solutions, and all offered hope, but little in the way of tangible improvements to the underlying economy. On a visit to the White House in 1934, Keynes urged the president to forget about the steep deficit that arose when tax revenues dried up during the Great Depression and instead engage in massive government spending to create jobs, build the nation's infrastructure, and assist struggling industries. These suggestions squared with FDR's deeply held belief that the government needed to be active and aggressive, rather than passive, about the economy. The Roosevelt administration eventually relied on these tools of fiscal policy to pass laws aimed at increasing productivity: the Public Works Administration increased its outlays in 1934, eventually spending over $3 billion to fund more than 35,000 public works projects. In the spring of 1938, FDR launched a $5 billion spending program in an effort to increase mass purchasing power in his second term. As chief legislator and crisis manager, FDR enjoyed considerable deference in taking this road. In doing so he ignored the protests of his own Treasury Department officials, who had advocated greater fiscal responsibility by tightening the government's belt. Of course they were right in one respect: the deficit quickly mushroomed, and only the onset of World War II curbed the out-of-control budget shortfalls that resulted. But no one questioned FDR's duty to point the direction to recovery.

TIME LIFE PICTURES/GETTY IMAGES

BETTMANN/CORBIS

P residents Roosevelt and Obama arrived at the White House more than seventy-five years apart, but they both faced serious economic crises, and the nation looked to both men for solutions. The Constitution vests in Congress the power to pass laws, and it says nothing about special rules that govern during a crisis, whether military, economic, or otherwise. Yet in the modern era, it is practically impossible for a Congress of 535 members to provide decisive leadership, and when the nation's economy has run out of gas, a "wait and see" approach is not likely to gain much approval. In this environment, the president must step to the forefront and use the formidable powers as chief legislator and crisis manager to command the nation's attention, direct its spirits, and act decisively. Competing economic theories may point down different paths, and so the president must sort through the evidence and choose a solution. Of course he may end up on the wrong side of history as a result of his difficult choices: The roads to recovery chosen by Herbert Hoover and Jimmy Carter, for example, failed to achieve much, and both men lost their bids for reelection. FDR and Barack Obama knew the stakes. But both recognized that a refusal to lead might be the greatest failing of all.

Where Do Presidents Come From? Presidential Comings and Goings

What career experiences have provided the most effective launching pads for the forty-three individuals who have attained the presidency? Many vice presidents have gone on to become president, including most recently George H. W. Bush, vice president under Ronald Reagan, who in 1988 won election to the White House in his own right. Yet that form of promotion is actually quite rare. Although five of the last thirteen vice presidents have become president, only Bush won election as a sitting vice president. In fact, in the 132-year period between Vice President Martin Van Buren's presidential victory in 1836 and former Vice President Richard Nixon's election in 1968, every vice president who rose to the presidency did so (at least initially) only as a consequence of the president's untimely death in office.

Although the U.S. Senate has been aptly described as a body of one hundred individuals who all think they should be president, only sixteen senators have gone on to the White House, including Senator Barack Obama, who won election as president in 2008. By comparison, nineteen governors and nineteen members of the House of Representatives have served as president. Three presidents—William Henry Harrison, John Tyler, and Andrew Johnson—actually served in all three of those jobs. Another nine presidents formerly served in another president's Cabinet, although none have held that distinction since Herbert Hoover, who was commerce secretary before he was elected president in 1928. The military has also been something of a breeding ground for presidents: twenty-nine had some military experience, and twelve served as generals. Fully twenty-seven of the forty-three chief executives have been lawyers, but the cohort of presidents also includes among its ranks a mining engineer (Hoover), a peanut farmer (Carter), a baseball team executive (George W. Bush), and even a hat salesman (Truman).

As a formal matter, the adage that "anyone can grow up to be president" is not literally true. Article II of the Constitution imposes three prerequisites on those who aspire to the Oval Office. Every president must be (1) a "natural born" citizen, (2) thirty-five years of age or older, and (3) a resident within the United States for at least fourteen years. Although the Constitution poses no other formal obstacles to the presidency, as a practical matter the first forty-three individual holders of the office have tended to fall into several clearly identifiable categories. All but one of these chief executives have been white males (Barack Obama is the lone African American president) between the ages of forty-two and seventy-seven. All were born Christians, and nearly all identified themselves as Protestants at one point or another in their lifetimes. (John Kennedy was Catholic; Lyndon Johnson was mostly nonobservant in his adulthood.) Twenty-four were firstborn males in their families, and all but nine attended college (since 1897, every president except Harry Truman received some form of higher education). Some states have served as birthplaces for

Changing images of FDR, seen here in 1932, 1936, 1940, and 1944.

a disproportionate share of presidents, including Virginia (eight), Ohio (seven), Massachusetts (four), and New York (four). Although presidents are not royalty and none are entitled to serve for life, on several occasions birthright has played a role in helping an individual reach the Oval Office. Twenty-six presidents have been related to other presidents; these relationships encompass two father–son combinations (John and John Quincy Adams; and George H. W. and George W. Bush), a grandfather–grandson combination (William Henry Harrison and Benjamin Harrison), and cousins (James Madison and Zachary Taylor were second cousins; Theodore Roosevelt and Franklin Roosevelt were fifth cousins).

When George Washington, after serving two terms as the nation's first president, declined to run again, he established an unwritten two-term precedent. No president challenged that precedent until Franklin Roosevelt sought a third term in 1940. FDR's successful election to four consecutive terms (he won in 1932, 1936, 1940, and then again in 1944) led to passage of the **Twenty-second Amendment** in 1951, which restricts any one person from being elected to the presidency "more than twice," or from acting as president for longer than two and a half terms. Four chief executives were assassinated while in office, and four others died of natural causes while still serving as president including Franklin Roosevelt, who died in 1945, only a few months into his unprecedented fourth term.

The constitutional means of removing a president from office is by **impeachment** and subsequent conviction. Article II, Section 4 of the U.S. Constitution provides that the president may be removed from office upon impeachment by a majority vote of the House and conviction by two thirds of the Senate of "Treason, Bribery, or other high Crimes and Misdemeanors." Just what type of offense qualifies as a "high crime and misdemeanor"? It's difficult to say. Just two presidents, Andrew Johnson and Bill Clinton, have ever been impeached under these provisions, and both were impeached for primarily political reasons: Johnson was charged with illegally firing a Cabinet member, pardoning traitors, and impeding ratification of the Fourteenth

Military hero William Henry Harrison won election to the presidency in 1840. Yet for all of his strengths as a war hero, he was ultimately a victim of his own stubbornness. Inauguration Day, March 4, 1841, was one of the coldest and most blustery days of the year in Washington, DC. Harrison refused to wear a hat and coat, and his nearly two-hour inaugural address was one of the longest in history. One month later Harrison died of pneumonia, probably contracted during his inaugural speech. He was the first president to die in office, but perhaps the last not to bundle up warmly for his inauguration day celebration.

NORTH WIND/NORTH WIND PICTURE ARCHIVES — ALL RIGHTS RESERVED.

★ **LO**

Understand the process by which presidents may be impeached and removed from office; know the order of presidential succession

Twenty-second Amendment
Passed in 1951, this constitutional amendment restricts any one person from being elected to the presidency "more than twice," or from acting as president for longer than two and a half terms.

Impeachment
The first step in a two-step process outlined in Article II, Section 4 of the U.S. Constitution to remove a president or other high official from office. The House of Representatives, by majority vote, may impeach if the official has committed "treason, bribery, or other high crimes or misdemeanors." The second step requires a conviction in the Senate by a two-thirds vote.

Chapter 7 The Presidency

Presidential Sex Scandals

In 1802, rumors that President Thomas Jefferson had secretly fathered children by his slave Sally Hemings were published by one of Jefferson's political rivals, James Callender. Hemings herself was the daughter of Jefferson's father-in-law and another female slave. Such personal attacks were not unusual in the early politics of the republic, and historians dismissed the rumors as scurrilous for the better part of two centuries. Finally in 1998, the British journal *Nature* published the results of DNA tests that suggested Jefferson was the "probable father" of at least one of Sally Hemings's descendants. Recent reunion celebrations that included both the descendants of Jefferson and descendants of Sally Hemings may have put this issue to rest once and for all.

In 1922, President Warren Harding entertained a mistress, Nan Britton, in the White House. Three years earlier, while Harding was still a U.S. senator, Britton gave birth to Harding's child. The Republican Party effectively buried evidence of the relationship during the 1920 presidential campaign, but once elected Harding resumed the relationship. Four years after Harding's death in 1923, Britton wrote a tell-all bestseller disclosing details of her relationship with the president, including intimate acts performed in an anteroom near the White House.

Between 1995 and 1997, President Bill Clinton had a series of sexual encounters with White House intern Monica Lewinsky. The affair became public when an independent counsel investigating Clinton's activities with respect to another alleged affair came across evidence of his affair with Lewinsky. Clinton was ultimately impeached for lying to a grand jury and obstructing justice with respect to the Monica Lewinsky affair. The Senate eventually acquitted him of both charges, but the scandal would occupy the Clinton presidency for more than a year.

Amendment; Clinton was accused of lying to a grand jury about his sexual relationship with an intern and for obstructing justice. Both men were acquitted on all charges by the U.S. Senate and served out their respective terms.

The only president to resign was Richard Nixon, who was accused of obstructing justice in the now infamous Watergate scandal. Nixon left office less than halfway through his second term in 1974 under the looming threat of impeachment. In practice, unpopular presidents are usually turned out of office not by removal, but by a failed reelection. In recent times, three sitting presidents (Gerald Ford, Jimmy Carter, and George H. W. Bush) lost reelection bids; Lyndon Johnson chose not to run for reelection in 1968 when frustration with his unpopular Vietnam War policy undermined his prospects for victory in the November election.

When President John Adams was defeated for reelection in 1800 and turned over the White House to arch-rival Thomas Jefferson, he helped establish a precedent of peaceful transition between chief executives that has held firm to this day, despite the hostile feelings that sometimes exist between successive presidents. In the case of the president's removal by death, resignation, or inability to serve, the Constitution requires that the powers and duties of the president "devolve" on the vice president. When William Henry Harrison died barely a month after becoming president in 1841, Vice President John Tyler took over all the powers, duties, and responsibilities of the presidency, rejecting any notion that he was simply there to serve as a more limited "acting president" until the next election. Since Tyler, seven vice presidents have become chief executive in this manner, including most recently Lyndon Johnson, who assumed office after John Kennedy was assassinated in November 1963. Of the last six vice presidents thrust unexpectedly into office, four—Theodore Roosevelt, Calvin Coolidge, Harry Truman, and Lyndon Johnson—eventually secured election as presidents in their own right.

The Evolution of the American Presidency

The U.S. Constitution places as many limitations on the office of the presidency as it grants the president specific powers and duties. Wary of the excessive authority wielded by the king of England, most of the Founders rejected Alexander Hamilton's radical suggestion that the president should be elected for life; instead, the Founders designed a chief executive who would be powerful enough to respond quickly when necessary, but also would be limited by lack of lawmaking power and the need to gain congressional approval for most long-term commitments, whether foreign or domestic.

The presidency has evolved over the past two centuries not so much because of any constitutional expansion of the chief executive's powers, but rather through practice, tradition, and the personal energy of some presidents. The changing dynamics of policymaking in the United States from a mostly local focus to a national phenomenon has given presidents the opportunity to exert unprecedented influence over the process, and many have done exactly that. In many ways, the growth of power of the presidency has paralleled the growth of the United States.

The President as "Chief Clerk" of the United States, 1789–1836

The earliest presidents established the office as a forceful power in the national government. Still, even the most popular presidents of the period were careful to avoid interfering with the clear legislative prerogatives of Congress. Several played a major role in helping steer America away from or toward war, despite the inclinations of Congress. But the truly dominant chief executive would not emerge until many years later.

When George Washington, the immensely popular former general of the Continental Army, agreed to be nominated as the nation's first president, widespread public confidence in his abilities helped secure immediate respect for this new office. Serving as the first chief executive from 1789 to 1797, Washington established various precedents that helped preserve a republican form of government in the nation's infancy. Washington rejected entrapments of royalty such as being referred to as "Your Majesty," preferring instead to be called "Mr. President." As a practical matter, Washington consulted constantly with the other branches—at one point he even asked the Supreme Court for an advisory opinion about his own interpretations of a foreign treaty. (The Court declined his invitation for comment.) Washington also established the executive's influential role in crafting public policy, siding with his Secretary of Treasury Alexander Hamilton's plans for industrialization and the creation of a national bank, and striving to maintain an isolationist foreign policy. Often serving as a mediator between differing positions in his administration, Washington rejected the less interventionist, farmer-friendly policies favored by his secretary of state, Thomas Jefferson.[1] For better or worse, most subsequent presidents would be forced to work within the framework of a divided party system that originated as an intramural fight within the Washington administration.

During the four decades after Washington's retirement, most presidents served more as chief "clerks" than chief "executives," doing Congress's bidding and performing mostly administrative duties on behalf of the federal government. Upon winning the presidency in 1800, Thomas Jefferson (1801–1809)[2] put into practice his own theory that "government is best which governs least." Accordingly, the Jefferson administration abolished many judgeships, trimmed government economic planning efforts, and scaled back the armed forces. The one crucial exception to such downsizing occurred in the area of land acquisition: Jefferson arranged for the purchase of the vast Louisiana territory from France, more than doubling the physical size of the country.

A presidency characterized by limited executive powers soon confronted unexpected challenges. When tensions between Great Britain and the United States erupted into the War of 1812, President James Madison (1809–1817) found himself hampered both by the small size of the federal army and by the lack of a powerful

Trace the evolution of the presidency from "chief clerk" in the late 18th and 19th centuries to its eventual political dominance

★ LO

© 2012 CENGAGE LEARNING

national bank capable of funding the government's prosecution of the war. This war with Britain revealed the limited powers of the president to influence national matters without strong institutional resources at his disposal. Madison's successor, James Monroe (1817–1825), exercised most of his influence in foreign affairs. Monroe's Secretary of State John Quincy Adams, who himself was president from 1825 to 1829, helped craft the "Monroe Doctrine," which declared that the United States would thereafter regard as an "unfriendly act" any attempt by a European nation to increase its possession or otherwise intervene on the American continent.

Portrait of General Andrew Jackson, later the seventh president of the United States.

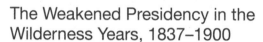

Meanwhile, Congress led the way in domestic matters, crafting key compromises over slavery and paying off much of the public debt incurred during the War of 1812.

Andrew Jackson, who served as president from 1829 to 1837, remade the presidency into an office of tremendous political power. The military hero of the Battle of New Orleans in 1815, Jackson came to the White House as a political outsider but with overwhelming popular support. Capitalizing on this resource, Jackson wielded presidential power in a way that few of his predecessors had, dismissing hundreds of officeholders, forcing out cabinet members who angered him, using his constitutionally authorized power to veto Congress's bill to recharter the Second National Bank of the United States, and introducing the so-called spoils system of doling out federal offices to individuals as rewards for political service.[3]

The Weakened Presidency in the Wilderness Years, 1837–1900

Andrew Jackson raised the profile and authority of the presidency to unprecedented heights, but its ascendancy was largely a product of his own popularity and energetic personality. The pre–Civil War presidents who followed Jackson also proved to be much weaker. The model of president as chief clerk seemed once again alive and well.

Perhaps the only effective president during this antebellum period was James K. Polk (1845–1849), who presided over a period of incredible westward expansion. Polk exercised his powers as commander in chief to instigate a successful war with Mexico over the Texas territory; his foreign relations successes included the acquisitions of the California and Arizona territories after the Mexican-American War, and the Oregon territory (including the current-day states of Oregon and Washington) from the British.[4] More typical were Presidents Franklin Pierce and James Buchanan during the 1850s; the failures of both to address growing sectional tensions over slavery left pro-slavery and abolitionist interests alike bitterly frustrated.

The presidency of Abraham Lincoln (1861–1865) thrived due to a rare combination of factors. Frequently underestimated as a great political mind, Lincoln was confronted with the single greatest threat in the history of the republic—the secession of eleven southern states and the great battle between North and South to restore the Union. Although Lincoln proceeded carefully in his prosecution of the war against the South for fear of alienating crucial border states, those acts he did undertake were bold and unprecedented. At the outset of the war in April 1861, with Congress not even in session, Lincoln proclaimed a blockade of southern ports and called on the northern states to provide 75,000 soldiers for battle. He (at least in one court's opinion[5]) unconstitutionally suspended the writ of habeas corpus, by which anyone arrested is to be brought before a judge or court to determine if there is sufficient reason to hold the person for trial. Suspending the writ allowed Lincoln to hold some criminal defendants indefinitely. The president also spent freely from the U.S.

MARY EVANS PICTURE LIBRARY/THE IMAGE WORKS

LIBRARY OF CONGRESS/GETTY IMAGES

President Abraham Lincoln delivering the Gettysburg Address in 1863.

Treasury without congressional approval. Although Congress ultimately ratified all his actions after the fact, Lincoln's bold exercise of authority essentially reinterpreted Article II into a source of executive authority during emergencies.

Following Lincoln's assassination in April 1865, Congress, dominated at that time by radical Republicans determined to punish the former Confederate states, quickly reasserted its control over the nation's agenda. For the remainder of the century, Congress would determine domestic policy. Indeed, after the former Civil War hero Ulysses Grant left office in 1877, no sitting president won election to a second term until William McKinley accomplished the feat in 1900.

The Birth of the Modern Presidency and Its Rise to Dominance, 1901–1945

The beginning of the twentieth century marked the onset of a new era for the American presidency. In an increasingly global and interconnected world, the power of the presidency grew disproportionately. By the time two world wars had concluded, the presidency had emerged as the premier institution in American politics.

In the fall of 1901, William McKinley was assassinated during the first year of his second term, thrusting into office his young and ebullient vice president, forty-two-year-old Theodore Roosevelt. Roosevelt's presidency (1901–1909) ushered in a new era of presidential authority. He injected a forceful energy and enthusiasm into the office, using his position as "a bully pulpit" (Roosevelt's own words). As one observer noted, "He wanted to be the bride at every wedding; the corpse at every funeral." Unlike many of his predecessors, Roosevelt was willing to gamble political capital on bold assertions of presidential power: his efforts to break up corporate monopolies were narrowly upheld by the Supreme Court and forced Congress to enact new anti-trust legislation. Roosevelt, through the creative use of executive orders, increased the

AMERICAN GOVERNMENT In Global Perspective

A Nominee with African Roots, as Viewed by a Writer in Kenya

In securing the Democratic nomination for the presidency in 2008, Barack Obama became the first major party nominee with direct roots to Africa, as his father was from Kenya. One foreign journalist asked: How might that connection affect Obama's policy on U.S.–African relations as president of the United States? John Harbeson wrote as follows in the August 16, 2008, edition of the *Daily Nation*, an English-language newspaper serving the East African countries of Kenya and Nairobi:

> *Obama needs to align himself as both a "black" politician and an exemplar of post-black politics, keeping alive the civil rights agenda while crowning the success of the civil rights generation by merging it with the agendas of mainstream liberal American politics. But what has all this to do with African politics? The connection is between building on the achievements of the civil rights generation in America and those of the generation that has spearheaded African political liberation from colonial rule.*
>
> *Neither agenda has been completed. America has made real civil rights progress over the past half-century, and African nationalism has largely expelled colonial political oppression over the same period. But affirmative action in the US*

is still needed, and Nepad (New Partnership for Africa's Development) has in many ways only just begun. So here's the question, common to both the American and African contexts.

> *How possible, indeed how legitimate and politically viable, will it be for Obama to continue the civil rights agenda while crowning its success by moving beyond it, and for post-independence generations of African leaders to maintain continuity with the political liberation agenda while building on its successes to embrace new and wider issues? There are many parallels between Obama's challenge and analogous challenges for Africa's political leaders. . . .*

Senator Barack Obama of Illinois in the attire of a Somali Elder during a visit to Kenya, the homeland of his father.

Source: John Harbeson, "Obama's Dreams and the African Agenda," *Daily Nation*, August 16, 2008 (http://www.nation.co.ke/News/world/-/1068/457288/-/rx0emi/-/index.html; accessed on August 19, 2008).

acreage of national parks fivefold. When Roosevelt became president, foreign affairs were assuming an ever more significant place in the nation's list of priorities. In less than two full terms in office, Roosevelt encouraged a Panamanian revolution, initiated the building of the Panama Canal, won a Nobel Peace Prize for mediating war settlements between Japan and Russia, and sent the nation's naval fleet around the world as a demonstration of American military authority.[6] The first president to travel to foreign lands, Roosevelt expanded the Monroe Doctrine by advancing the "Roosevelt Corollary," which declared that the United States would serve as a police power to maintain stability in the Western Hemisphere by opposing any European interference in the affairs of Latin American nations. In foreign affairs, where force of personality is so important, Congress proved little match for this charismatic president.

As president from 1913 to 1921, Woodrow Wilson achieved some significant successes and suffered some great failures: his aggressive industrial reform agenda marked a successful first term in office; during his second term he eventually led the

United States into World War I and received accolades at the Paris Peace Conference following the war. But Wilson's hopes for a stable international order based on a system of collective security ultimately confronted political reality, as Senate leaders whom Wilson had excluded from the peace talks rejected U.S. membership in the League of Nations. Still, Wilson's presidency illustrated just how much more powerful the presidency had become since the mid-nineteenth century. In the early part of the twentieth century, the president began to dominate the political landscape.

MUSEE DE LA VILLE DE PARIS, MUSEE CARNAVALET, PARIS, FRANCE/ARCHIVES CHARMET/THE BRIDGEMAN ART LIBRARY INTERNATIONAL

Parade on the Rue Royale in front of Maxim's during the visit of President Woodrow Wilson to Paris in 1919.

The onset of the Great Depression during Herbert Hoover's presidency (1929–1933) and the looming threat of a second world war in the late 1930s called for a new and innovative approach to the office. Franklin Delano Roosevelt placed his own indelible stamp on the nation by transforming the presidency into an institution marked by permanent bureaucracies and well-established repositories of power. FDR tackled the Great Depression with **New Deal** policies that tied the economic fate of millions of Americans to the fate of the American government: a social security program of old-age insurance and unemployment insurance would provide income for the elderly and the jobless; the government would guarantee deposit accounts in commercial banks through the Federal Deposit Insurance Corporation (FDIC); and the government would provide federal jobs to the unemployed to perform various public works. Roosevelt communicated extensively with the American people through the media—millions listened to his "fireside chats" on the radio. By restoring public confidence with his energetic support for New Deal programs, FDR redefined the presidency as a source of national leadership. Future presidents would enjoy significant resources of power simply by taking the helms of the formidable institution FDR established.

Like Theodore Roosevelt and Woodrow Wilson, FDR felt especially at home in foreign affairs. Although adhering to popular sentiment that the United States should maintain strict neutrality in foreign wars, in the early days of World War II, Roosevelt met with British royalty and the British prime minister as a show of support, initiated a "lend-lease" policy by which Britain could purchase war supplies from the United States as long as it paid cash and transported the supplies in its own ships, and traded Britain fifty destroyers in exchange for rights to build military bases on British possessions in the Western Hemisphere—all without the consent of Congress. When America did enter the war in 1941 after the attack on Pearl Harbor, presidential power was put on full display. FDR met personally with British and Soviet leaders to craft military plans; then, near the end of the war, the Allied leaders carved Europe and the Middle East into "spheres of influence" that would establish an American presence across the Atlantic Ocean for decades. With the president playing a dominant role in both national and world affairs, the imperial presidency that took root at the beginning of the twentieth century came to fruition by the close of World War II.

New Deal

An set of aggressive federal domestic policies proposed by President Franklin Roosevelt in the 1930s and passed by Congress as a response to the Great Depression; it ultimately transformed the presidency into an institution marked by permanent bureaucracies and well-established repositories of power.

The Ten Greatest Presidents of All Time

More than half a century ago, historian Arthur M. Schlesinger Jr. began the process of polling historians to rank the presidents of the United States. Recent surveys continue to borrow heavily from Schlesinger's original methodology. In 2009, the C-SPAN Survey of Presidential Leadership ranked the opinions of presidential historians and "professional observers of the presidency." Another poll of presidential scholars was conducted by *The Wall Street Journal* in 2005, with support from the Federalist Society. Interestingly, the results vary. Among the most significant differences: Ronald Reagan was ranked at No. 6 in the *Wall Street Journal* poll but barely broke the top ten in the C-SPAN poll; Woodrow Wilson and John Kennedy landed in the top ten of the C-SPAN poll but were ranked eleventh and fifteenth, respectively, in the *Wall Street Journal* poll. While Washington, Lincoln, and Franklin D. Roosevelt usually top most lists, presidential scholars substantially disagree on how to complete the list of greatest presidents.

C-SPAN Survey—2009 Top 10	Wall Street Journal Poll—2005 Top 10
1. Lincoln	1. Washington
2. Washington	2. Lincoln
3. Roosevelt, F.	3. Roosevelt, F.
4. Roosevelt, T.	4. Jefferson
5. Truman	5. Roosevelt, T.
6. Kennedy	6. Reagan
7. Jefferson	7. Truman
8. Eisenhower	8. Eisenhower
9. Wilson	9. Polk
10. Reagan	10. Jackson

The Imperial Presidency Comes Under Attack, 1945–1980

By the end of World War II, the presidency had emerged as a very powerful office. FDR's fireside chats on the radio linked average Americans to the occupier of the White House in a fashion that was unimagined by the Founders. In the late 1940s, television became a central influence in American life, and presidents honed their skills with this new medium to further nurture their relationship with the public.

Now recognized as powerful chief executives, those who followed in the footsteps of FDR confronted a new and unprecedented threat to American national security: the presence of a second world military superpower—the Soviet Union. With presidential authority greatest in the area of national security, waging the Cold War that began in the late 1940s consumed much of these presidents' energies. Harry Truman, FDR's immediate successor, proclaimed the "Truman Doctrine" in foreign policy, by which the United States pledged military and economic aid to any nation threatened by communism or the Soviet Union. Like Truman, Presidents Eisenhower and

Kennedy also focused their administrations' energies on containing the Soviet communist threat. As long as the Soviet Union challenged American interests, the presidency would remain the focus of attention in the American political system.

Not until the presidency of Lyndon Johnson (1963–1969) was a president able to enact a sweeping domestic agenda similar to FDR's New Deal. Johnson's **Great Society** program featured more than sixty reform measures, including increases in federal aid to education, the enactment of Medicare and Medicaid, and a voting rights act for African Americans. But Johnson's domestic policy success was offset by his failures in foreign policy. Exercising his authority as commander in chief, Johnson sent more than half a million troops to Vietnam to fight an increasingly unpopular war. The failure to stop the Communists from taking over South Vietnam was laid squarely at the feet of Johnson, just as earlier foreign policy successes had been credited to his predecessors.

The presidents who followed Johnson came under increasing attack in the 1970s. Richard Nixon achieved foreign policy success by improving America's relationship with the Soviet Union and China, but in 1974 he became the first president in history to resign from office before the end of his term when the Watergate scandal enveloped his presidency. Jimmy Carter's presidency (1977–1981) was beset with hardships, as the nation's economy faltered in the 1970s. Carter's failure to resolve an Iranian revolution that included the taking of fifty American hostages further cemented his image as an inept commander in chief. Carter thus became the first elected president since 1932 to lose a reelection bid. By the end of the 1970s, the modern presidency created by Theodore Roosevelt and brought to new heights by Franklin Delano Roosevelt found itself increasingly under attack from an emboldened Congress and a frustrated public.

Redefining the Presidency in an Era of Divisiveness, 1981–2008

The election of Ronald Reagan to the White House in 1980 marked the return of the chief executive as an unmatched force over American politics. No president in the twentieth century (save perhaps FDR) could match Reagan's prowess as a "great communicator"; by speaking directly to the American people in terms they could understand, Reagan bypassed Congress and enjoyed early victories with passage of an economic program marked by tax cuts, decreased social spending, and a marked increase in defense spending. Reagan's legislative success was all the more remarkable given that he was working with a divided-party government. The Democrats controlled the House of Representatives in every year of Reagan's presidency; his legislative success thus contrasted favorably with that of previous presidents who had struggled to get legislation passed by a Congress controlled by the opposite party. In foreign policy, Reagan's aggressive program of military buildup combined with his own hard-line position against the Soviet Union is credited with helping bring about the fall of Communist regimes in eastern Europe, the breakup of the USSR, and thus victory in the Cold War. In addition, Reagan's immense popularity allowed him to weather numerous crises and scandals in a way that few of his predecessors had.

Reagan's successors also faced the reality of divided-party government at different points in their respective presidencies. George H. W. Bush took the lead in foreign policy, overseeing the dismantling of the Soviet Union and forging international alliances prior to mounting a successful war against Iraqi aggression in Kuwait. However, by compromising with the opposition Democrats on tax legislation, he frustrated some of his more conservative constituencies and undermined his efforts at reelection. Bill Clinton became the first Democratic president in a half century to serve two full terms. Clinton appealed to moderates largely by in effect borrowing central elements of the opposition party's domestic program—His three main legislative successes (free-trade agreements, budget cutting, and welfare reform) were all programs that had been more closely associated with Republicans than Democrats at the time Clinton took office in the early 1990s.

Great Society

A set of aggressive federal domestic policies proposed by President Lyndon Johnson and passed by Congress in the 1960s that further enhanced the role of the presidency.

ASSOCIATED PRESS

President Lyndon Baines Johnson.

Understand how the modern presidency has persevered in the recent era of divisiveness ★ LO

Another "Tweet" from the Commander in Chief: The Interactive Presidency of Barack Obama

In the age of the Internet, most private companies and government agencies maintain a Web site. The White House is no different. The George W. Bush administration's White House Web site featured extensive videos and links to speeches and addresses by the forty-third president. (See the photo of the Bush White House home page immediately below.) What the Bush White House Web site lacked, however, was more cutting-edge interactive features: there was a simple tool that allowed visitors to "ask the White House" a question, and a "White House interactive" feature with officials answering basic questions from students, but little more.

Enter the Obama administration and its brand new state-of-the-art Web site at www.whitehouse.gov (see bottom of box). The site hosts no less than eleven substantive blogs, all archived and indexed by category; a tool that allows the visitor to receive e-mail updates on the latest White House news and events; live streams of the president and his top aides speaking from around the world; and archived podcasts available on nearly any subject imaginable. This site also offers visitors the chance to stay connected to presidential events by Twitter, Facebook, mySpace, Flickr, and a number of other social networking sites. President Obama also maintains his own personal website at www.barackobama .com—as of August 1, 2010, the president's daily (and sometimes hourly) "tweets" were followed by nearly 5 million people around the world. In fact, that same day twittaholic.com's statistical algorithm ranked President Obama as the fifth most popular Twitter user in the United States, trailing behind only Ashton Kutcher, Britney Spears, Ellen DeGeneres, and Lady Gaga.

For Critical Thinking and Discussion

1. What types of information would you expect to find on www.whitehouse.gov that is not available on other media Web sites or other Internet sites that follow the presidency?

2. What advantages does a modern president have in the ability to communicate with a younger generation of citizens?

3. Do the political views of a Web surfer affect his or her willingness to visit the White House Web site? Why or why not?

The White House Web page posted on the final day of George W. Bush's presidency

The more interactive White House Web site used by the Obama administration, here pictured from March 29, 2009.

THE U.S. NATIONAL ARCHIVES AND RECORDS ADMINISTRATION

MLADEN ANTONOV/AFP/GETTY IMAGES

After securing a controversial election victory in 2000, Republican President George W. Bush focused his efforts at the outset on passing numerous economic reforms. During Bush's first six months in office, his administration secured passage of a tax cuts package and the "No Child Left Behind" education bill, which favored greater accountability of school performance through testing of students. With the Congress narrowly split between the two parties, each of those bills required a degree of bipartisan support.

In the aftermath of the terrorist attacks of September 11, 2001, Bush moved quickly to position his administration as the eminent world leader in an emerging "war on terrorism." His early efforts to fight terrorism at home and abroad enjoyed congressional support from both parties: his aggressive military intervention against the Taliban-controlled government in Afghanistan in late 2001 proved extremely popular and helped cement his administration's image of toughness and resolve. Yet when the Bush administration expanded the war on terrorism to include military intervention in Iraq, justified on the basis of inaccurate reports that Iraq possessed weapons of mass destruction, these same policies became much more divisive. Though victorious in his 2004 reelection bid, George W. Bush's second term proved even more difficult than the first, with more Americans questioning the war in Iraq as U.S. casualties mounted. By the end of his second term, Bush's ratings had dropped to below 30 percent—in part the consequence of significant problems in the economy, exacerbated further by the Wall Street crisis of September 2008.

Barack Obama's presidency began—as most presidential terms do—buoyed by feelings of good will coming from both sides of the political aisle. A clear majority of the public hoped he would successfully tackle the economic crisis that befell the nation in 2008. They also hoped the young president was serious about his promises to bring "change" to Washington.

Obama's "honeymoon period" ended quickly, however, as the details of his administration's proposals for reform were laid bare for debate. President Obama benefitted from strong Democratic majorities in Congress; he muscled through his legislative agenda almost entirely on the strength of those majorities, and with little support from Republicans. The $787 billion fiscal stimulus bill (the American Recovery and Reinvestment Act of 2009) passed with the help of just three Republican Senators and no Republican House members; the landmark health care reform bill of 2010 was even more partisan, garnering not a single Republican vote from either branch of Congress. Obama thus learned an important political lesson: the rhetoric of bipartisanship does not easily translate into bipartisan votes. Regardless, Obama had just enough Democratic support to rack up some significant legislative successes during his first two years as president; few expected similar successes after the congressional elections of 2010.

Express Powers and Responsibilities of the President

Recognize the formal powers vested in the president under Article II of the Constitution

★ LO

Article II of the Constitution provides that the president of the United States holds executive power, but it is not very detailed about what constitutes executive power. In fact, the Constitution lists only four specific powers of the president: (1) commander in chief of the armed forces, (2) power to grant reprieves or pardons, (3) power to "make" treaties (subject to Senate approval), and (4) power to make certain appointments, including those of ambassadors and justices of the Supreme Court (again subject to Senate approval). Despite this limited number of constitutionally expressed powers, presidents today serve many important functions in the American political system. Noting these varied roles, political scientist Clinton Rossiter referred to the many different "hats" that the president must wear during the course of a week, or even during just one day.[7] Some of these are specified in the Constitution and laws of the United States, which conceive of a limited executive, but one who possesses the authority to react quickly and energetically to unexpected crises.

Head of State

The office of the presidency combines the political and symbolic functions that are often divided in other countries. As the nation's head of state, the president fulfills numerous formal duties and obligations on behalf of the country. Most visiting foreign heads of state meet directly with the president; sometimes those visits include an official "state dinner" at the White House hosted by the president and attended by key political leaders from throughout Washington. Article II of the Constitution also carves out a more formal role for the president in foreign affairs; the president's role in receiving ambassadors and other public ministers has often been interpreted as granting the president the discretion to give or deny official recognition to foreign governments. Although such a power may seem mostly honorary, it can have a real political impact in some circumstances. President Woodrow Wilson's refusal to recognize the new government of Mexico in 1913 caused considerable consternation among American supporters of the Mexican revolution, and led to growing tensions between the two neighbors. More recently, American presidents during the 1970s and 1980s refused to recognize the Palestine Liberation Organization as the legitimate representative of the Palestinian people, buttressing Israel's own hard-line stance against that organization.

President Obama at the 2009 G-8 Summit in L'Aquila, Italy, surrounded by (from left to right) Prime Minister Silvio Berlusconi of Italy, French President Nicolas Sarkozy, Russian President Dmitri Medvedev, U.N. Secretary General Ban ki Moon, and Libyan Leader Muammar Gaddafi.

OLI SCARFF/GETTY IMAGES

★ LO Explain how presidents use the veto, appointment and removal, and the pardon

Chief Executive and Head of Government

In his *Second Treatise of Government*, the political theorist John Locke argued that executive power was so fundamental that it predated civil society.[8] According to Locke, legislatures were ill-equipped to enforce their own laws because they need "perpetual execution," and legislatures sit only infrequently. Moreover, if the same entity both made and enforced the laws, it might be tempted to "suit the law to their own particular advantage," regardless of the law's language. Another political theorist, Baron de Montesquieu, also advocated the separation of legislative and executive powers—specifically, he decried the tendency of legislatures to exert too much influence over the executive, increasing the opportunity for abuse.[9]

Influenced in part by these arguments, the Framers of the Constitution vested all executive power in the president alone. Unfortunately, they failed to define that power with any specificity. At a minimum, the Constitution grants presidents alone the responsibility to execute laws of the United States, which encompasses the implementation and enforcement of measures passed by Congress; in other words, to see that Americans actually abide by those laws in practice. A president's failure to "take care that the laws be faithfully executed"—whether intentionally or due to negligent administration of his subordinates—can have obvious implications for the effectiveness of such laws. Actual levels of execution sometimes lie squarely within the discretion of the chief executive. Presidents Reagan and Clinton, for example, defined antitrust laws in markedly different ways simply by offering contrasting approaches to the execution of those laws. During the 1980s, Reagan's lack of enthusiasm for government intervention in the marketplace translated into the prosecution of far fewer antitrust actions than had been brought by previous administrations. By contrast, under President Clinton the Justice Department applied the antitrust laws enthusiastically, such as when it brought suit against the Microsoft Corporation in 1997 for monopolistic practices that stifled competition in the software industry. More recently, Republican President George W. Bush and the Democrats in Congress sparred not just over the written terms of the USA Patriot Act, but also over the Bush administration's aggressive enforcement of those provisions against some individuals, which gave the laws far more teeth than was originally anticipated.

The president's power to see that laws are faithfully executed also implies some power to hire and fire those charged with administrative authority to help execute federal laws. The **power of appointment** thus stands among the president's most important executive powers.[10] The Constitution specifically authorizes the president to appoint ambassadors and other public ministers, judges of the Supreme Court, and all other federal officers under his charge. Additionally, the president appoints all federal judges. Most of these appointments require the consent of the Senate. In recent years, senators have subjected the president's nominees to intense scrutiny, occasionally even rejecting the president's choices. President George W. Bush withdrew his second choice for the Supreme Court, White House Counsel Harriet Miers, before she had even received a formal Senate vote in October 2005.

Although Supreme Court nominees often receive the most intense investigation, the Senate may occasionally question other executive appointments. In 1989, the U.S. Senate rejected President George H. W. Bush's choice for defense secretary, John Tower, due to allegations that Tower had a drinking problem. Barack Obama's first choice as secretary of health and human services, the former Senate Majority Leader Tom Daschle, withdrew his name from consideration in February 2009 amid a growing controversy over his failure to accurately report and pay income taxes. Though Daschle might have garnered enough votes for confirmation from his former colleagues, he had nevertheless become a significant political liability for the new president.

The president's removal power has been a source of controversy as well. The Supreme Court's decision in *Myers v. United States* (1926) established that chief executives have the power to remove "purely executive officers" without congressional consent. Although federal judges and independent agency heads can be removed only by congressional action, Cabinet heads and military officials can be terminated by the president alone. In one famous instance during the Korean War, President Truman decided in 1951 to fire the extremely popular General Douglas MacArthur, commander of the UN forces in Korea. Of course political pressures may hamper the president's ability to fire executive branch officials. President Clinton was certainly frustrated by Attorney General Janet Reno's decision in late 1997 to authorize independent counsel Kenneth Starr's investigation into allegations of sexual harassment by Clinton. But removing Reno from office would have invited charges of evasion and cover-up, leading to even greater political problems for Clinton. Consequently, Reno survived as attorney general for the duration of Clinton's presidency.

Power of appointment
The president's constitutional power to hire and fire those charged with administrative authority to help execute federal laws, such as ambassadors, federal judges including those on the Supreme Court, and all other federal officers under the president's charge. Most of these appointments require the consent of the Senate.

Not only is the president responsible for the enforcement of all federal laws, he is also authorized by the Constitution to grant reprieves and pardons to individuals who violate those laws. The Founders vested this power in the chief executive because they believed that the prerogative of mercy, on which the pardon power is based, is most efficiently and equitably exercised by a single individual, as opposed to a body of legislators or judges. A **reprieve** reduces the severity of a punishment without removing the guilt; a full **pardon** relieves an individual of both the punishment and the guilt. A president's decision to exercise the pardon power can invite considerable negative comment and political backlash. Not surprisingly then, most presidents wait until the end of their presidential terms to grant pardons. Less than two months after being denied his bid for reelection in 1992, President George H. W. Bush pardoned six officials for their involvement in the Iran-Contra scandal from 1987, including former Defense Secretary Casper Weinberger. President Clinton issued 140 pardons on his last day in office in 2001, including one to Marc Rich, who had previously fled the country for tax evasion and whose wife was a major contributor to Clinton's political campaigns. No president received more criticism for granting a pardon than Gerald Ford, who as vice president succeeded to the presidency when Richard Nixon resigned in 1974. Ford's pardon of his former boss for involvement in the Watergate scandal helped undermine his prospects for election to the White House in his own right two years later.

Reprieve

The president's constitutional authority to reduce the severity of a punishment without removing the guilt for those who have violated the law.

Pardon

The president's constitutional authority to relieve an individual of both the punishment and the guilt of violating the law.

President Richard Nixon and Vice President Gerald Ford conferring on August 9, 1974, the day Nixon resigned from office.

HULTON ARCHIVE/STRINGER/GETTY IMAGES

Chief Diplomat

As chief diplomat of the United States, the president has the power to negotiate treaties and appoint diplomatic representatives to other countries, including ambassadors, ministers, and consuls. The president's power over treaties is limited to negotiation and execution—enactment of any treaties requires approval by two thirds of the Senate. Still, the power to negotiate and execute the terms of treaties affords the president immense authority in the field of foreign affairs. John F. Kennedy used this power to negotiate an end to the Cuban missile crisis in 1962;[11] Jimmy Carter personally presided over the negotiation of the Panama Canal Treaty of 1977–1978, which relinquished U.S. control over the canal by the year 2000. Every president during the latter stages of the Cold War conducted arms control negotiations with the Soviet Union, working to check the spread of nuclear weapons to other nations. Bill Clinton surprised many in his own party when he completed negotiations on the North American Free Trade Agreement, an economic treaty with Canada and Mexico that was favored primarily by Republican presidents who came before him.

Chief Legislator

Although Congress is the branch of government authorized to make laws, modern presidents are involved in nearly every stage of federal lawmaking.[12] The Constitution's express provision that the president recommend for the consideration of Congress "such measures as he shall judge necessary and expedient" barely hints at the president's real role in this context: major legislation is often the product of a give-and-take process between the president and congressional leaders. Indeed, the president plays a critically important role in helping to set the lawmaking agenda for Congress, especially when the president's party is also in control of the legislative branch of government. While campaigning for the White House, the future president will lay out a policy agenda; once elected, he will claim a legislative mandate to follow through on those campaign proposals. In the **State of the Union address**, an annual speech made to Congress laying out the status of the nation, the president typically proposes suggestions for legislation. The legislative programs of FDR's New Deal and Lyndon Johnson's Great Society were both influenced heavily by the executive branch. Similarly, Congress's reorganization of various executive branch agencies into a unified Department of Homeland Security in 2002 was based on a plan drafted by officials within the Bush administration. According to social scientist Paul Light, recent presidents have tended to offer fewer legislative proposals than presidents of the mid-twentieth century, consistent with the modern administrations' increased emphasis on reducing the size of the federal government.[13] Still, when a national crisis demands legislative solutions, Congress often looks to the president for leadership. House and Senate leaders made few significant modifications to their respective health care bills in 2009 without first huddling with President Obama and his top White House aides; and it was the president's willingness to meet frequently with moderate Democratic members of Congress that kept many in the fold for the final passage of health care reform in 2010.

The **White House Office of Legislative Affairs** serves as a liaison between the president and Congress and helps develop the strategy used to promote passage of the president's legislative agenda. Administration officials often testify before congressional subcommittees on behalf of legislation, and presidents meet with congressional leaders frequently throughout the lawmaking process to negotiate details and discuss strategy. Many bills have the president's imprint squarely upon them, even though the power of lawmaking rests formally with Congress. The president's legislative authority also includes the constitutional power to veto, or reject, legislation that he opposes. While Congress can technically override a veto by a two-thirds vote of both houses, barely 4 percent of presidential vetoes have been overridden in history.

During the twentieth century, vetoes became a routine form of political exercise for presidents, especially those confronting Congresses controlled by the opposite political party (See Table 7.1 on following page). For Richard Nixon, Gerald Ford, and George H. W. Bush, the only three presidents during this span who never enjoyed unified party rule, the veto became something of an art form. Nixon and Bush vetoed forty-three and forty-four bills, respectively. (Only eight of those vetoes were overridden.) Gerald Ford vetoed sixty-six bills in just two and a half years, but more than one in five were overridden, a clear sign of the limited power Ford held during his brief term as president. With Republicans controlling the House during George W. Bush's first six years in office, he did not need to veto any bill until July 19, 2006, when he vetoed the Stem Cell Research Enhancement Bill, legislation that would have eased restrictions on federal funding for embryonic stem cell research. However, after the Democrats' takeover of Congress in 2007, Bush vetoed eleven more bills sent to him by the Democratic Congress. During President Obama's first two years in office he vetoed two bills: (1) a continuing appropriations bill; and (2) legislation that would have made it easier for banks to foreclose on homes by allowing foreclosure documents to be accepted among multiple states.

Commander in Chief

One of the defining features of the American political system is its commitment to civil control of military, embodied in the president's status as head of the nation's armed forces. As commander in chief, the president is the nation's principal military leader, responsible for formulating and directing all military strategy and policy. Although the Constitution awards to Congress the formal power to "declare war," the balance of war-making power has shifted overwhelmingly from Congress to the

State of the Union address
An annual speech that the president delivers to Congress laying out the status of the nation and offering suggestions for new legislation.

White House Office of Legislative Affairs
A presidential office that serves as a liaison between the president and Congress. This office helps the president develop the strategy used to promote passage of the president's legislative agenda.

★ LO
Define the powers and limits of the president as commander in chief

TABLE 7.1 Vetoes Issued by Modern Presidents (through October 15, 2010)

President	Congresses	Regular Vetoes	Pocket Vetoes	Total Vetoes	Vetoes Overridden
Theodore Roosevelt	57th–60th	42	40	82	1
William Taft	61st–62nd	30	9	39	1
Woodrow Wilson	63rd–66th	33	11	44	6
Warren Harding	67th	5	1	6	0
Calvin Coolidge	68th–70th	20	30	50	4
Herbert Hoover	71st–72nd	21	16	37	3
Franklin D. Roosevelt	73rd–79th	372	263	635	9
Harry Truman	79th–82nd	180	70	250	12
Dwight Eisenhower	83rd–86th	73	108	181	2
John F. Kennedy	87th–88th	12	9	21	0
Lyndon B. Johnson	88th–90th	16	14	30	0
Richard M. Nixon	91st–93rd	26	17	43	7
Gerald Ford	93rd–94th	48	18	66	12
Jimmy Carter	95th–96th	13	18	31	2
Ronald Reagan	97th–100th	39	39	78	9
George H. W. Bush	101st–102nd	29	15	44	1
William Clinton	103rd–106th	37	1	38	2
George W. Bush	107th–110th	11	1	12	4
Barack Obama	111th	2	0	2	0

president during the past century, as modern executives have assumed the nearly unlimited power to send troops into combat.[14] Terming it a "police action," President Harry Truman sent troops to Korea in June 1950 without even asking Congress for a formal declaration of war. In 1973, over President Nixon's veto, Congress passed the War Power Resolution, which theoretically limits the power of the president to unilaterally commit troops to battle. Ignoring its provisions, Presidents Reagan, George H. W. Bush, and Clinton have deployed U.S. troops to invade Grenada (1983), Panama (1989), and Haiti (1994), respectively. Similarly, in February 2009 President Obama announced his plans to bolster the U.S. military presence in Afghanistan by over 17,000 new troops. Of course presidents are not entirely immune from public pressures in this context. In the two most recent Gulf War conflicts, the weight of popular opinion led both President Bushes to seek congressional authorization for the invasions of Iraq in 1991 and 2003.

★ LO Recognize the implied powers of the presidency not spelled out in the Constitution, including those exercised as the nation's crisis manager and political party leader

Implied Powers and Responsibilities of the President

Article II of the Constitution does not specifically spell out all the powers that a president may exercise; during the past two centuries presidents have assumed the right to exercise some "implied" or "inherent" powers not listed in the Constitution, and the Supreme Court has for the most part acceded in their right do so. These implied powers allow the president to act quickly in crisis situations, to serve as leader of his political party, and to issue executive orders and make executive agreements that do not require congressional approval.

Crisis Manager

More than any other official in government the president is in a unique position to respond quickly and effectively to unexpected crises. Consequently, Americans look immediately to the president under such circumstances to provide assurances, comfort, and where appropriate, a plan to address the difficulties. When a natural disaster strikes, the president will often visit the scene, meet with family members, and in many cases provide aid from the Federal Emergency Management Agency (FEMA). Domestic and international terrorism has posed special challenges for presidents in this regard. Even President Clinton's most bitter critics praised his efforts in 1995 when he led the nation in mourning the loss of 168 lives from a truck bombing at a federal building in Oklahoma City. In the days following the September 11 attacks, George W. Bush redefined his presidency as a fight against terrorism—his visits to "Ground Zero," the site of the attacks on the World Trade Center, and his address to a joint session of Congress created indelible images in the media and won him widespread public support. President Obama continually expressed his personal resolve to tackle the nation's economic crisis up to and after his inauguration as president in 2009: within weeks he pressed forward with a proactive economic stimulus plan in hopes that it might reassure the public that his administration was not taking a passive approach to the problem.

LUKE SHARRETT/THE NEW YORK TIMES/REDUX PICTURES

President Obama campaigning with New Jersey Governor (and fellow Democrat) John Corzine in 2009.

Party Leader

Once elected, the president of the United States assumes the position of de facto leader of his own political party. Not surprisingly, presidents are normally well attuned to how their political decisions will reflect on the party as a whole. A popular president is often expected to campaign for the party's congressional candidates, and if possible, help secure control of Congress for the party. Any assistance the president provides to congressional candidates seeking election may have an important side effect: the president may now have the leverage to demand support from those members of Congress for his own legislative programs. Similarly, the "coattail effect," by which congressional candidates and state and local officials benefit at the polls from the votes of the president's supporters, may strengthen the president's position with party members during the upcoming term.

Executive Orders and Agreements

On their own, presidents can issue **executive orders**, which are rules or regulations issued by the chief executive that have the force of law. Once thought to be an unconstitutional exercise of Congress's lawmaking power, executive orders have now become a routine feature of American government.[15] Since the beginning of the twentieth century, presidents have issued more than 13,000 executive orders

Executive orders
Rules or regulations issued by the chief executive that have the force of law and do not require the consent of Congress.

★ LO   Explain how
presidents exercise
power through executive
orders and agreements

regulating all manner of topics including affirmative action, civil service, federal holidays, the classification of government documents, public land designations, and federal disaster relief. Many executive orders deal with the nation's armed services: Clinton's "don't ask, don't tell" policy, which allowed homosexuals to serve in the military as long as they did not reveal their sexual orientation, was established by an executive order (albeit one that Clinton modified in response to congressional and public uproar). President George W. Bush issued more than 150 executive orders during his first term in office alone. On his first full day in office, Obama issued an executive order mandating that the interrogation of terrorism suspects not include torture.

Presidents may be reluctant to issue executive orders on especially controversial topics that may elicit a negative response from Congress, as any executive order can be partially or fully revoked by an act of Congress. FDR strategically issued executive orders to create agencies that Congress refused to establish; eventually, however, he was frustrated by the legislature's refusal to fund those agencies near the end of his presidency. Similarly, Richard Nixon's efforts to dismantle by executive order certain agencies created by his Democratic predecessors, such as the Office of Economic Opportunity, were often stymied, because the courts refused to allow the elimination of an agency established with the approval of Congress.

Executive agreement
A pact reached between the president and a foreign government that does not require the consent of Congress.

An **executive agreement** is a pact, written or oral, reached between the president and a foreign government. As with executive orders, these agreements do not require the consent of Congress, although Congress does have the power to revoke them. Executive agreements have become important tools by which presidents conduct foreign affairs. FDR agreed to trade U.S. destroyers for British military bases in 1940, more than a year before the United States formally declared war on Germany, thus implicitly supporting the British military cause against Germany. In recent years, the U.S. government's military alliances with Great Britain and other countries in response to Iraqi aggression have not been spelled out in any treaties that required the advice and consent of the Senate; rather, those alliances came in the form of executive agreements between President Bush and the British government.

Presidential Resources

★ LO   Describe the
other individuals and
offices in the executive
branch that contribute to
the modern presidency

Nearly a half century ago, Professor Richard Neustadt defined the central problem that all presidents face from the moment they are sworn into office: how do presidents mobilize the powers of the office to work for them? The federal bureaucracy has grown so vast that presidents cannot simply "command" the bureaucracy to do their will. So what exactly can presidents do to make their will felt within the executive branch, and to carry out their choices through that "maze of personalities and institutions called the government of the United States"?

In his landmark book, *Presidential Power: The Politics of Leadership*, Neustadt argued that the president's most fundamental power is the "power to persuade."[16] Presidents use this power most effectively by keeping themselves informed, employing a system of information that allows them to be at the center of the decision-making apparatus, and carefully cultivating the image of a powerful president. Modern presidents have tended to emphasize certain individuals and offices under their control that play critical roles in the success of their administrations.

The Vice President

After Vice President Martin Van Buren's successful election to the White House in 1836, few vice presidents rose to the presidency by running and winning on their own accord. In fact, after Van Buren no sitting vice president even emerged as a serious contender for the presidency until the Republicans nominated Richard Nixon in 1960. And the next sitting vice president after Van Buren to be elected president was George H. W. Bush in 1988.

Next in line for succession and thus "only a heartbeat away" from the presidency, vice presidents have often been relegated to the very fringes of presidential power.[17]

FDR barely communicated with John Nance Garner, who was vice president during FDR's first two terms in office. Of course, Garner did not have a very high opinion of the vice presidency either, referring to the position (in a sanitized version of his remarks) as not worth "a bucket of warm spit." When asked toward the end of his presidency what ideas Vice President Richard Nixon had offered within his own administration, President Dwight D. Eisenhower quipped: "If you give me a week, I might think of one." In fact, up through the 1950s, vice presidents maintained their principal

offices on Capitol Hill near the Senate Chamber, where they occasionally performed their one clearly defined constitutional responsibility: to preside over the Senate and to cast a vote in the event of a tie.

The vice presidency, however, has undergone a transformation in recent decades. Modern-day vice presidents have assumed roles as key advisers and executive branch officials working on behalf of the president. Walter Mondale developed U.S. policy on South Africa and was one of President Jimmy Carter's most trusted advisers. Al Gore headed the National Performance Review for the Clinton administration, leading to reforms to increase the federal government's efficiency and reduce its costs. Perhaps no federal official was more influential with President George W. Bush than Vice President Dick Cheney, the driving force behind Bush's controversial decision to invade Iraq in March 2003.[18] The current vice president, Joe Biden, has become famous for his salty language and verbal gaffes; but Biden is a trusted counselor to President Obama and the former Senator is credited with helping to press the administration's legislative agenda forward with his former colleagues.

Constitutionally, the vice president is first in line to succeed the president in the event of death or incapacitation. By statute, if the vice president is not available to serve, succession falls in turn to the Speaker of the House, the president pro tempore of the Senate, and then to Cabinet-level officials.

Vice President Joe Biden shakes hands with an Amtrak officer. Biden was a patron and supporter of Amtrak; when he was still a U.S. Senator he commuted 250 miles a day by train from his home in Wilmington, Delaware, when the Senate was in session.

The Cabinet

The Constitution specifically affords presidents the power to solicit the advice of the principal officers in each of the executive departments. Thus in addition to running their own executive departments within the large federal bureaucracy, principal officers also serve as key advisers. Together, they form the president's **Cabinet**. Today's Cabinet consists of fifteen heads of departments and six other important officials considered of "Cabinet rank." In reality, such a large body of individuals with different areas of expertise can serve only limited functions for a president, and recent chief executives have convened their full Cabinets to serve more as a sounding board and a communications device than as a significant instrument of policymaking. Nevertheless, in individual meetings Cabinet-level officials may still provide critical input to the president on issues related to their own departments.

The Executive Office of the President and the White House Staff

Created in 1939 to bring executive branch activities under tighter control, the Executive Office of the President (EOP) and its two thousand federal employees consists of numerous agencies that assist with the management and administration

Cabinet
The collection of the principal officers in each of the executive departments of the federal government who serve as key advisers to the president.

The White House Interns Program

College basketball star Joy Cheek found a pretty good job after graduating with a public policy degree from Duke University in 2010: she got to play professional basketball during the summer with the Indiana Fever of the WNBA. Joy maintains a back-up plan, however, in case her athletic dreams don't work out in the long run: she wants to work in politics. And in the summer of 2009 she got quite a head start toward that dream when she held a fourteen-week internship working in the office of the vice president on economic policy. While friends were working in fast-food restaurants or as lifeguards, Joy was attending weekly lectures with top White House officials, assisting at White House social events, and even hobnobbing with Vice President Biden.

The White House Internship program is one of the most prestigious of its kind, placing interns from across the country in one of twelve different White House offices, including the office of the Vice Presidency where Cheek landed. Competition for a spot in the program is normally quite stiff: Applicants go through a rigorous screening process that includes filling out a questionnaire, writing a pair of 300-word essays, and undergoing in-depth interviews. Yet the rewards of service are unarguable: Past White House interns of note include NBC news anchor Brian Williams, Fox news journalist Neil Cavuto, and the Academy Award–nominated screenwriter Nora Ephron.

If you are interested in getting first-hand experience working at the White House, you can apply online through the White House Web page (www.whitehouse.gov/about/internships/apply). But don't count on it being a particularly lucrative experience: summer White House interns are unpaid.

Former White House interns Brian Williams, nightly news anchor for NBC News (left), and Neil Cavuto of Fox News (right).

of executive branch departments. Some of these agencies, such as the Office of Management and Budget, the President's Council of Economic Advisors, the National Security Council, and the Office of the U.S. Trade Representatives, have near permanent status. Other EOP agencies come and go, depending on the policy priorities of the current administration. Thus during the height of the Cold War, the EOP included agencies that focused on preparedness and civil defense in the event of a nuclear attack.

The EOP also includes an expanded White House staff. Until 1939, this staff consisted mostly of assistant secretaries and clerks who helped the president with correspondence; the White House staff today consists of nearly six hundred employees and runs on an annual budget of almost $730 million. In charge of this bureaucracy is the **White House chief of staff**, who manages and organizes the staff to serve the president. Some modern presidents, including Ronald Reagan and George H. W. Bush, have adopted management styles that rely heavily on the chief of staff to control access to the president. Others, such as President Clinton, have utilized a "spokes-of-a-wheel" arrangement in which five or six different advisers have direct access to the president.[19] Regardless of the arrangement chosen, the White House chief of staff will have a significant hand in the success of the modern presidency. The principal duties of the White House staff include, but are not limited to, speech-writing, advance work for presidential appearances, scheduling, congressional relations, public relations, and communications.

White House chief of staff

The manager of the White House staff, which serves the president's organizational needs, including speechwriting, advance work for presidential appearances, scheduling, congressional relations, public relations, and communications.

The First Lady

All but one president (James Buchanan) have been married at some point in their lifetimes, and the spouses of sitting presidents, now referred to as first ladies, have come to assume an important role in the affairs of the nation. Until recently, presidents mainly relied on their spouses to help them perform social obligations, such as hosting state dinners. Woodrow Wilson's two wives broke somewhat with this mold: his first wife, Ellen, took public positions on bills being considered for Congress, and his second wife, Edith, served as an intermediary between the president and other government leaders while Wilson was recovering from a massive stroke in the fall of 1919. Eleanor Roosevelt, wife to Franklin Delano Roosevelt, charted a course for first ladies as aggressive public advocates. Mrs. Roosevelt launched one of the earliest civil rights organizations, the Southern Conference on Human Welfare; she actively supported the building of model communities; and she lobbied for refugees fleeing Nazi persecution. Occasionally, Mrs. Roosevelt even disagreed publicly with some of FDR's policies in foreign affairs.

SAUL LOEB/AFP/GETTY IMAGES

First Lady Michelle Obama speaking at an event related to her "Let's Move" campaign against childhood obesity.

Although none of the first ladies after Eleanor Roosevelt were willing to so boldly challenge their husbands' policies in the media, many did stake out policy areas where they could contribute, and some have become active members of their husband's administrations.[20] They have been assisted in this regard by a formal Office of the First Lady, now staffed by more than twenty aides. Rosalynn Carter lobbied Congress for mental health initiatives; Nancy Reagan became the public voice of the "Just Say No" to drugs campaign; and Barbara Bush (wife of George H. W. Bush) campaigned widely against the problem of illiteracy. A distinguished lawyer, Hillary Rodham Clinton led a task force in 1994 charged with reforming the nation's health care system; Mrs. Clinton's complex plan ultimately proved too ambitious, and it was rebuffed by Congress. In another series of unprecedented moves, Hillary Clinton ran for and won a seat in the U.S. Senate in 2000 and was reelected to the Senate in 2006; she was a front-running Democratic candidate for president (until she was defeated by Barack Obama in the Iowa primary), and became the secretary of state in 2009. Though an accomplished lawyer herself, Michelle Obama returned the office of the First Lady to its more common role as lobbyist for a cause, expounding the dangers of childhood obesity. Regardless of what roles first ladies may assume, modern presidents have increasingly come to rely on their spouses as advisers on a range of issues.

Although no woman has ever been nominated as a major party's candidate for the presidency, the day when that happens may be rapidly approaching. In 1984, Geraldine Ferraro, a member of Congress from New York, was the Democratic Party's candidate for vice president, a historic breakthrough to be sure. More recently, in 2008 the Republicans nominated Alaska governor Sarah Palin as the party's vice presidential candidate. Senator Hillary Clinton (D-NY) fell just short of capturing the Democratic presidential nomination, though she had been the early front-runner for the nomination from the time she first threw her hat into the race in early 2007. When a woman not only captures her party's nomination but goes on to win the presidency, a dilemma will be raised for the new chief executive in the event she is married: what role, if any, should be played by her spouse, who will be the first "first gentleman" in American history?

Important Presidential Relationships

★ LO   Recognize how the power of the presidency is enhanced by communications with the public, the Congress, and the media

The power of the president is influenced by the relations that a president develops and cultivates with three important constituencies: the public, Congress, and the news media.

The President and the Public

Catering to the needs and demands of the public mattered little to presidents prior to 1824, when presidential nominees were chosen by congressional leaders in secret caucuses. By contrast, the presidency today is a truly public institution that depends heavily on its public popularity for political effectiveness. Modern presidential nominations and elections are won on an arduous campaign trail in which aspiring chief executives must reach out, communicate with, and ultimately gain acceptance from large segments of the public. Once in office, presidents must remain constantly attentive to the sentiments of the public at large. FDR was the first president to rely on public opinion polls, and his administration utilized them to monitor support for his New Deal policies. Through his fireside chats, he reached into the living rooms of millions of Americans, winning their support for and confidence in his domestic and foreign policies.

Most modern presidents continuously engage the public to support administration policies, whether through the annual State of the Union address to Congress and other special televised messages, staged events, or interviews and press conferences with the media where they attempt to promote the benefits of their programs. Presidents Richard Nixon and Ronald Reagan preferred the "set piece" speech presented from the Oval Office during prime time; Presidents Jimmy Carter and Bill Clinton occasionally held "town meetings" to discuss issues in open forums with concerned citizens. In bypassing legislators and appealing directly to their constituents, modern presidents have perfected the art of what social scientist Samuel Kernell calls "going public."[21]

Some recent presidents have come under criticism for being too dependent on public opinion polls. President Clinton's critics charged that he too quickly withdrew support for some of his more controversial appointments when public opinion swung against them. But presidents may find themselves in even greater political trouble when they refuse to heed public opinion. President Johnson's escalation of troops in Vietnam during the late 1960s ignored growing public opposition against that war and undermined his hopes for reelection. Just as the Watergate scandal began to engulf Richard Nixon's presidency, his decision to hold press conferences less frequently only fed the impression that he was hiding from the public and fueled even more calls for his resignation. Whereas high levels of public support increase a president's chances to get legislation passed, precipitous drops in public support may stop a president's program in its tracks.

The President and Congress

The history of the American political system is marked by the ebb and flow of power between the president and Congress. For much of the nineteenth century, a form of "congressional government" prevailed, with most presidents acting as dutiful

Top: President Ronald Reagan giving a "set speech" from the Oval Office in 1986. Right: President Bill Clinton interacting with the public at a "town meeting" in 1993. Bottom: President Obama takes his campaign for health care to large, arena-sized audiences across America.

administrators of the laws passed by Congress. Buoyed by advances in communications technology that placed modern presidents at the center of American politics, presidents today play far more influential roles in the legislative process, at times even prodding Congress forward to meet their administrations' goals. Since the 1970s, the frequency of divided-party government, with the executive and the legislature controlled by opposing political parties, has placed the two branches in a near continuous battle over the nation's domestic policy agenda. Because credit for a program's success is rarely spread evenly among the two branches, tensions are inevitable and compromises often difficult to come by. President Reagan managed to get the Democrat-controlled House of Representatives to pass his program of tax decreases and spending cuts in 1981; when the economy rebounded a few years later, Reagan and the Republican Party benefited politically far more than did the Democrats. President Clinton's willingness to sign a welfare reform bill in 1996 aided him in that year's election, when he claimed to have lived up to his earlier promise to "end welfare as we know it." The Republican Congress that actually drafted and passed the welfare bill received far less credit for its accomplishments. In foreign policy, presidents continue to act nearly independent of Congress.

Presidents have many tools at their disposal to influence Congress. As party leader, the president can campaign for congressional candidates, and then leverage that assistance into support. Personal contacts by the president with members of Congress can be effective as well. The White House Office of Congressional Relations (OCR) serves as a liaison to Congress, rounding up support and monitoring events on Capitol Hill. Still, the most effective lobbying for a president's policies comes from members of Congress friendly to the administration, who persuade other members of Congress to vote in favor of the policies. The rewards for such service often come in the form of future appointments, pork-barrel projects for home districts or states, or financial support from the political party for future election bids. FDR rewarded Hugo Black, a key Senate supporter of the president's controversial 1937 plan to increase the size of the Supreme Court, with an appointment to the Court; Bill Clinton was prepared to reward Senate Majority Leader George Mitchell with the same prize in 1994, but held back because he needed Mitchell's support in Congress for a pending health care bill. (Despite Mitchell's efforts, Clinton's health care bill went down to defeat.)[22]

The President and the Media

The relationship between presidents and the media that cover their administrations is important. The media provide perhaps the most effective channel through which presidents can communicate information about their policies to the public. At the same time, the media's desire for interesting headlines to attract greater numbers of readers, listeners, viewers, and online observers leaves them to rely heavily on the executive branch for information. Effective media management has been a hallmark of the most successful modern presidents. Much of the responsibility rests with the **White House press secretary**, who plays an especially important role in briefing the press, organizing news conferences, and briefing the president on questions he may be forced to address.

The administration that ignores media management does so at its own peril. Social scientists Kathleen Hall Jamieson and Paul Waldman revealed how the mainstream media today does not so much report the news about presidents as create it, transforming "the raw stuff of experience into presumed fact" and "arranging facts into coherent stories" that can prove crucial to presidential success.[23] The media's focus on President George W. Bush talking with recovery workers at Ground Zero and issuing warnings to terrorists through a megaphone emphasized his toughness and compassion in dealing with the terrorist attacks of September 11, 2001. Yet nearly four years later that same press corps emphasized perceptions of President George W. Bush's aloofness aboard Air Force One after Hurricane Katrina killed thousands in and around New Orleans, Louisiana.

Today the president also relies on the White House director of communications to articulate a consistent and effective message to the public.[24] But even before that office came into being, chief executives felt the need to craft a message and hone their public images. Though known best for his fireside chats and effective public speeches, Franklin Roosevelt worked hard to cultivate good relations with the media, allowing his administration to set the news agenda and influence the content of the news. Many of his press conferences included off-the-record commentary that fed the media's appetite for information, yet allowed the president to change his position as circumstances changed. John F. Kennedy perfected the modern press conference in the East Room of the White House; his colorful banter with reporters played well as sound bites on the evening television news. Ronald Reagan's reputation as the "great communicator" was enhanced by positive media coverage. His administration perfected the use of "staged" or "pseudo" events, which presented the president in a positive light—perhaps visiting flag factories or reading Shakespeare to children at elementary schools—all packaged in time for the evening newscasts. Even when scandals rocked Reagan's second term in office, his mostly friendly relations with the press paid off when they painted him as the unwitting victim of his own administration's follies.

White House press secretary

The person on the White House staff who plays an especially important role in briefing the press, organizing news conferences, and even briefing the president on questions that may be asked.

NATIONAL ARCHIVES/GETTY IMAGES

President John Kennedy in June 1963, taking questions at one of his many press conferences.

Borrowing from Reagan's playbook, Presidents George W. Bush and Barack Obama have avoided live press conferences wherever possible, preferring controlled situations that could be molded to fit their respective messages. The Bush administration worked hard to cultivate the image of a president working hard for the American people—even while vacationing at his ranch in Crawford, Texas, the president was often pictured clearing brush and performing various chores, rather than simply relaxing. President Obama in particular relished hitting the road to drum up support for his policies at large pep rallies. Thus his aides urged him to travel widely while key legislation was being debated to capitalize on those particular strengths.

Although presidents and their staffs take great care to present a positive public image through the media, the glare of the spotlight can sometimes catch off-the-cuff commentary or statements from chief executives that would have best been left unsaid. Some of the more notable gaffes spoken by recent presidents include these remarks:

- "I am not worried about the deficit. It is big enough to take care of itself."

    —President Ronald Reagan

- "At breakfast, she was complaining that it is impossible to get a decent bagel in Washington."

    —President Bill Clinton, on wife Hillary's run for a U.S. Senate seat from New York

- "We see nothing but increasingly brighter clouds every month," referring to an improving economy.

    —President Gerald Ford, speaking to a group of businessmen

- "I don't see what's wrong with giving Bobby a little experience [as attorney general] before he starts to practice law."

    —President John Kennedy, reacting to critics who argued that his brother Robert was too young to be attorney general

- "When I need a little free advice about Saddam Hussein, I turn to country music."

    —President George H. W. Bush, at a country music awards ceremony

- "I would have made a good pope."

    —President Richard Nixon[25]

NOW & THEN

Making the Connection

When unexpected crises confront the nation—military, economic, or otherwise—leadership must come from the president of the United States. As the nation's chief legislator and executive, he can propose legislation to address the crisis and can implement that legislation in the best interests of the nation. As the nation's chief crisis manager, he must act boldly and decisively to reassure the nation that he has a plan to address whatever difficulties it may be facing. In the cases of FDR and Barack Obama, John Maynard Keynes's economic theories offered a basis for their administration's similar approaches to dealing with financial crises facing the nation. Other presidents have chosen markedly different approaches to leading the nation through economic difficulties. Both Presidents Ronald Reagan and George W. Bush, relied on the theory of supply-side economics to cure the nation's fiscal woes. Regardless of the approach adopted, modern presidents are expected to act decisively in times of crisis.

Unfortunately, the Constitution does not spell out all of the roles and responsibilities that have become central to the modern presidency. The office has evolved over the course of the nation's history, and much of that evolution has occurred in response to crisis situations, economic or otherwise. Unlike the Congress, the president is just one person and so can act quickly and decisively. Additionally, the president and the vice president are the only two officials elected by the entire nation—thus, the president alone can claim a mandate to act on behalf of the American people as a whole, rather than on behalf of a state, a district, or one political party. In times of crisis, citizens look to presidents for strength because they alone are in a position to provide it. For that reason more than any other, presidents only rarely have to demonstrate their continued relevance in the modern political system.

Immediately following his inauguration as president on January 20, 2009, President Obama could look forward to a "honeymoon period" with the press and the public during his first few months in office. The question was not whether that honeymoon would occur, but how, if at all, the newly elected president would take advantage of it. In the case of Obama, this period was marked by numerous legislative achievements: the $787 billion fiscal stimulus bill, a budget reconciliation bill, and massive intervention in the housing and credit markets.

Still, Obama's honeymoon period proved disappointing in at least one respect. Past U.S. presidents have found that during this initial period, even congressional opposition is likely to support some of the new president's more controversial initiatives. Ronald Reagan, for example, was able in 1981 to win support from the Democratic-controlled House of Representatives for some of the largest tax cuts in American history. FDR in 1933 was able to pass a record number of bills during his administration's first 100 days with help from many Republicans. Barack Obama's legislative victories, by contrast, were achieved almost entirely on the strength of Democratic congressional majorities.

Realistically, Barack Obama's honeymoon period began to wind down during May 2009, as his approval ratings plummeted into the 50 percent range on a regular basis. By then the nation was already growing frustrated with its continued economic woes, and many were willing to transfer at least some of the blame to the new administration (concerns about the growing deficit also hurt Obama's standing). Other presidential honeymoons have been cut short by pronounced presidential missteps. Gerald Ford enjoyed high approval ratings in 1974 when he took over the presidency following Richard Nixon's resignation; but when he pardoned the ex-president just a month into his own presidency, Ford suffered an immediate 30-point drop in his approval ratings. Bill Clinton rode a wave of high hopes into the White House in 1993. Yet when during his first week in office he announced his plans to allow gays in the military, support for his administration began to diminish.

Even the most careful presidents know that these honeymoons don't last forever. By the summer of a president's second year in office, the nation begins to turn its attention to the midterm elections; the following year, the president is usually gearing up to run for reelection. Best that the president simply takes advantage of his honeymoon while he can.

On www.cengage.com/dautrich/americangovernment/2e, find the Politics Inter-Active link for details on presidential agenda-setting and the short "honeymoon period" presidents work with during their first term in office. Consult as well the various links that relate to how different presidents began their administrations with ambitious policymaking agendas. Historical, popular, and global perspectives on the issue are also presented.

AP PHOTO

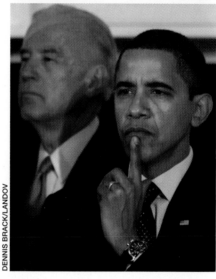

DENNIS BRACK/LANDOV

Top: President Gerald Ford announced on September 8, 1974, that he granted Nixon a "full, free and absolute pardon" for "all crimes committed against the United States" during Nixon's presidency.

Bottom: President Obama, flanked by Vice President Joseph Biden, listening intently during a meeting with the National Governors' Association early in his presidency. The new president faced immediate resistance to his proposals for economic recovery from Republican governors, among others.

Chapter 7 The Presidency

Chapter Summary

★ Where Do Presidents Come From? Presidential Comings and Goings

- Though theoretically any American who is at least thirty-five years old, a "natural born" citizen, and has lived in the United States for fourteen years is eligible to be president, the forty-three individuals who have held the office have been mostly older, well-educated, Caucasian Protestant men who have prior political experience.

- Only two presidents in history have ever been impeached by the House, and none were removed by the Senate. When a president does leave office, succession falls to the vice president.

★ The Evolution of the American Presidency

- The office of the president has evolved over the nation's history. Over time, it has accumulated more power. For the century after George Washington's term, Congress dominated the federal government, with only a few exceptions—namely during the presidencies of Andrew Jackson and Abraham Lincoln.

- The birth of the modern presidency occurred with the ascension of Theodore Roosevelt to office in 1901. His strong personality forced itself on the office. Taking strong pro-American positions in foreign policy and aggressive antimonopoly positions during the industrialization period, Roosevelt promoted power in the executive office.

- FDR's New Deal policies, in response to the failing economy of the 1930s, cemented a large role for the president in the American constitutional system. The growth of the federal bureaucracy under FDR significantly changed the role that the president would play and the power that office would yield.

- The emergence of the United States as a superpower after World War II cemented the role of the U.S. president as a dominant player in world and national politics. Contemporary presidents find themselves as the focal points of American politics, setting the political and legislative agenda and leading American foreign and domestic policy.

★ Express Powers and Responsibilities of the President

- The powers of the president, as expressly stated in the Constitution, are (1) to be commander in chief of the armed forces, (2) to grant reprieves or pardons, (3) to "make" treaties (subject to Senate approval), and (4) to make certain appointments, including those of ambassadors and justices of the Supreme Court (again subject to Senate approval).

★ Implied Powers and Responsibilities of the President

- Beyond the express powers granted to the president in the Constitution, presidents today also play a key role in setting the legislative agenda, managing national and international crises, and serving as leader of their political party.

- The singularity of leadership in the executive branch affords the president a unique position in the American political system, giving him the power to command the attention of the nation's people, Congress, and the media—thus enhancing the president's ability to persuade others what to do.

★ Presidential Resources

- The Cabinet, the Executive Office of the President, and the White House staff provide large organizational support for the president to administer federal programs and agencies and lead the national government.

★ Important Presidential Relationships

- The president enhances his power by continually communicating with the public, maintaining a strong working relationship with congressional leaders from both parties, and cultivating a good relationship with the media through strategic management of the White House's activities.

CourseMate

Key Terms

Cabinet (p. 215)

Executive agreement (p. 214)

Executive orders (p. 213)

Great Society (p. 205)

Impeachment (p. 197)

New Deal (p. 203)

Pardon (p. 210)

Power of appointment (p. 209)

Reprieve (p. 210)

State of the Union address (p. 211)

Twenty-second Amendment
    (p. 197)

White House chief of staff (p. 217)

White House Office of Legislative
    Affairs (p. 211)

White House press secretary
    (p. 220)

Resources

Important Books

Beschloss, Michael. *Presidential Courage: Brave Leaders and How They Changed America, 1789–2007.* New York: Simon & Schuster, 2007.

Dallek, Robert. *Hail to the Chief: The Making and Unmaking of American Presidents.* New York: Oxford University Press, 2001.

Greenstein, Fred. *The Hidden-Hand Presidency: Eisenhower as Leader.* New York: HarperCollins, 1982.

Greenstein, Fred. *The Presidential Difference: Leadership Style from Roosevelt to Clinton.* New York: Free Press, 2000.

Kernell, Samuel. *Going Public: New Strategies of Presidential Leadership.* Washington, DC: CQ Press, 1993.

Neustadt, Richard. *Presidential Power.* New York: John Wiley & Sons, 1980.

Peterson, Mark. *Legislating Together: The White House and Capitol Hill from Eisenhower to Reagan.* Cambridge, MA: Harvard University Press, 1993.

Internet Sources

http://www.whitehouse.gov/ (the home page of the White House including information on broader aspects of the presidency, a virtual library, and so on)

http://www.americanpresidents.org (C-SPAN-sponsored site on the presidency, including life portraits and a video archive of all American presidents)

http://www.archives.gov/presidential-libraries (the official National Archives site on presidential libraries, featuring links to all the individual libraries, a digital classroom, a research room with a searchable index, and so on)

NOW Ronald Reagan, the 41st President of the United States.

DAVID HUME KENNERLY/GETTY IMAGES

THEN Thomas Jefferson, the 3rd President of the United States

AP PHOTO

NOW &THEN

The Elusive Goal of Reducing the "Bloated" Bureaucracy

? *The new president took office armed with a mandate to reduce the size of the federal government. His successful campaign for the Oval Office featured an often-repeated pledge to reduce government excesses—the bureaucracy had grown rapidly in the years that preceded his leadership, and in his opinion the federal government needed to become more frugal and tighten its belt. Soon after winning election, the new chief executive set out to make good on his pledge. Commentators described this initiative by the new president as a "revolution" of sorts—one that would streamline government and reduce the burden of the federal bureaucracy on the American people. Hefty federal spending in previous years also encouraged him to make reducing the national debt a top priority. But the president soon realized that to accomplish other objectives he would need even greater resources and an even larger bureaucracy. Though he accomplished other policy objectives, he ultimately failed to make good on his pledge to reduce the size of government. Ironically, by the time he had left office, the federal government had grown bigger than it had been when he first arrived.*

CourseMate

NOW & THEN

DAVID HUME KENNERLY/GETTY IMAGES

NOW That certainly was the case during Ronald Reagan's presidency from 1981 through 1989. The "Reagan Revolution" aimed to reduce the burden of government. In his presidential campaign of 1980, Reagan criticized the federal government for growing beyond the means of the American people to support it. Getting rid of waste, reducing cumbersome red tape, eliminating expensive and inappropriate federal programs, and paying off the national debt were cornerstone themes of Reagan's campaign.[1] Accordingly, early in the Reagan administration a significant tax cut package was passed to reduce the size of the federal government. During his eight years in office, however, Reagan found that he often needed to increase the size of government to accomplish other objectives, such as defeating the Soviet Union in the Cold War, a feat that many historians now call the single greatest success of the Reagan administration. But such success came only after a substantial increase in the size of the federal bureaucracy and the budget to support that bureaucracy. Defense Department programs and budgets grew substantially during the Reagan years. Indeed, defense spending during this period amounted to the largest peacetime buildup in the nation's history. Ultimately, the Soviet Union proved no economic match for the United States, and Reagan's significant expansion of resources for the federal bureaucracy played a part in winning the Cold War. But in the process of winning it, Reagan reneged on his pledge to reduce the size of the federal government, thus leaving office in 1989 with a much larger bureaucracy than the one he inherited in 1981.

THEN Ronald Reagan was certainly not the first president to fall prey to this contradiction. Nearly two centuries earlier, Thomas Jefferson talked the talk of cutting the bureaucracy, but similarly failed to walk the walk of containing its growth. As with Reagan, political commentators of the time described Jefferson's triumph over John Adams as a "revolution" of sorts.[2] In his campaign, Jefferson stressed the need for "frugality" when it came to federal spending, and in his first inaugural address in 1801, he talked about the need to cut the waste. As president, Jefferson eliminated several federal agencies. In an effort to reduce the national debt, he closed down American embassies and cut the budgets of the Army and Navy.

Yet just like Reagan would do almost two centuries later, Jefferson pursued a policy agenda that ultimately required more government, more federal resources, and a larger bureaucracy. His agenda featured the expansion of the nation's borders, including the purchase of the Louisiana Territory from France, which more than doubled the geographic size of the United States. At a cost of $11,250,000 for the land and the assumption of $3,750,000 in French debts, the price tag was fairly steep for its time. Even more expensive, however, were the increases to the federal bureaucracy necessary to settle the region, fight the Indians who lived in the area, and fund a new agency called the General Land Office.[3] Many historians today view the Louisiana Purchase as President Jefferson's greatest accomplishment. To achieve it, however, Jefferson, like Reagan, had to forgo his commitment to reduce the size of the federal bureaucracy. When Jefferson left office in 1809, the federal bureaucracy was much larger than the one he had inherited in 1801.

AP PHOTO

Those aspiring to high office sometimes trumpet as one of their primary goals the downsizing of the bureaucracy. Reducing costs, rooting out inefficiencies in spending, improving program effectiveness, reducing unnecessary red tape, and eliminating waste are promises that strike a positive chord with many voters. Presidential candidates in particular often run campaigns focused heavily on just such a pledge. Once elected to office, however, they quickly learn that to accomplish their policy goals, the bureaucracy sometimes must grow rather than contract. By the end of their terms in office, they frequently discover that their work as chief executive has contributed more to increasing the size of government than to reducing it.

What Is Bureaucracy?

Bureaucracy is a term that usually conjures up negative images. It often refers to overgrown government, excessive rules and paperwork, or a burdensome process for getting something done. Political candidates extol the vices of "the unresponsive, fat bureaucracy" to strike a sympathetic chord with voters.[4]

Despite the negative connotations of the term, bureaucracy is necessary for any government. Laws must be enforced, programs must be administered, and regulations must be implemented. Without a federal bureaucracy, the government could not function. To be sure, there are many problems with bureaucracy. It is often hard to get things done in an efficient manner, or to fire workers who do not perform well, or to reward deserving workers. The buck often passes from one desk to another, and silly or irrelevant rules often dictate the actions of the bureaucrats. Despite its problems and the "bad rep" that the term often conjures up, bureaucracy is absolutely essential for any government to implement and carry out its laws and public policies.[5]

A **bureaucracy** is an organization set up in a logical and rational manner for the purpose of accomplishing specific functions. Sociologist Max Weber (pronounced VAY-ber), an early student of bureaucratic organizations, identified six characteristics of effective bureaucracies:[6]

1. **Bureaucracies are organized on the basis of specialization, expertise, and division of labor.** The organization is divided into subunits based on function, and subunits are staffed by employees who are qualified to administer those tasks.

2. **They are organized in a hierarchical manner with an identifiable "chain of command" from top to bottom.**

3. **A common set of rules for carrying out functions characterize the operation.** These rules are often referred to as standard operating procedures (SOPs). Employees are trained to know and use these SOPs so that functions are performed smoothly and consistently.

4. **Bureaucracies maintain good records, or a "paper trail," of actions taken and decisions made.** Good record maintenance enables periodic review, efficiency of operation, and proof of action.

5. **Bureaucracies are characterized by an air of professionalism on the part of employees.**

6. **The hiring and promotion process within effective bureaucracies is characterized by merit-based criteria and insulated from "politics."**

Bureaucracies are created within many types of organizations. Organizations typically exist to carry out a function, or set of functions. Bureaucracies are what actually carry out these functions. Large private companies typically have bureaucracies that divide labor functions into categories or departments such as sales, accounting, human resources, MIS (management information systems), and other divisions. Colleges and universities have bureaucracies that usually include an admissions department, a registrar's office, an academic counseling center, an athletics department, and so on. Even small organizations such as physicians' offices feature a bureaucracy that includes medical support staff (e.g., nurses), a front-office staff (receptionist and secretary), and business offices (accountant and medical insurance specialist).

Bureaucracy

An organization set up in a logical and rational manner for the purpose of accomplishing specific functions.

You, Your Parents, and the Dreaded FAFSA Form

You have probably seen it. Your parents or legal guardians have seen it. Most of your college friends have seen it too. It is the dreaded "FAFSA" (Free Application for Student Aid) form. The joy and satisfaction of getting accepted into college is often met with the red tape and complexity of applying for student financial aid. The FAFSA form must be filled out by all students applying for federal support to offset the increasingly high costs of college tuition. Most states and colleges also require the FAFSA to help make their own decisions about a student's financial need and thus the aid that may be required. The U.S. Department of Education begins accepting FAFSA applications on January 1 for eligibility during the school year that begins the following fall. FAFSA requires documentation for a myriad of financial information about college students and their legal guardians. If you have never seen the form, either because your parents have done the leg work for you or because you haven't applied for financial aid, take a look at it at on the Web at http://www.fafsa.ed.gov.

Financial planners and other consultants have built an industry out of aiding college students and their families in their efforts to navigate the cumbersome FAFSA form. The detailed financial information that FAFSA requires is not always handy—gathering that information can be an especially time-consuming and aggravating task. However, the goal of FAFSA remains a laudable one: to fairly and equitably distribute aid to college students based on documented financial need. Still, the challenge of filling out FAFSA and meeting all its requirements can offer a rude awakening indeed to prospective and returning students who have never before confronted the federal bureaucracy in all its glory.

For Critical Thinking and Discussion

1. What do you think about FAFSA? Is it too cumbersome or tedious?

2. Is the federal government transforming a simple process into one that is too complex to be effective? Or do you believe this form of red tape is necessary to ensure that colleges and universities can make fair decisions about financial aid for the nation's college students?

Most governments maintain bureaucracies to carry out specific governmental functions, and the federal government is no exception. As with political parties, there is no reference to the bureaucracy in the U.S. Constitution. But like parties, the federal bureaucracy is arguably one of the most important features of the American political system, because Americans have come to depend on it for many important things such as the defense of U.S. interests around the world, protection against terrorist attacks, cleaning up the destruction caused by natural disasters, a financial safety net for those who are unemployed or retired, the maintenance and expansion of the nation's roads and airways, and research for cures to such health problems as heart disease, cancer, and AIDS. In American government, the federal bureaucracy has traditionally come under the authority and jurisdiction of the president and the executive branch. As we will see, however, the modern federal bureaucracy is a complex set of agencies and organizations, parts of which are accountable to the legislative and judicial branches as well.

Citizens are more likely to come into direct contact with the bureaucracy than any other part of government, and so for many Americans the bureaucracy comes to symbolize what government is. A visit to an unemployment office to register for unemployment benefits, a check in the mail from the Social Security Administration, a trip to the Department of Motor Vehicles to renew a driver's license, or a visit to the Web site of the Consumer Protection Agency to inquire about the safety of a child's car seat—these are just a few of the many ways citizens interact with the bureaucracy.

The federal bureaucracy, in fact, is a huge set of organizations that is expected to serve many different functions. It includes hundreds of departments, offices, agencies, bureaus, councils, foundations, commissions, boards, services, and authorities. Each of these units, as Weber's analysis of bureaucracies suggests, specializes in an area of public policy, is hierarchically organized to carry out its particular duties, conducts its operation on the basis of a set of standard operating procedures, maintains records of its actions and decisions, is trained to carry out functions in a

FIGURE 8.1 The Organization of the Federal Bureaucracy

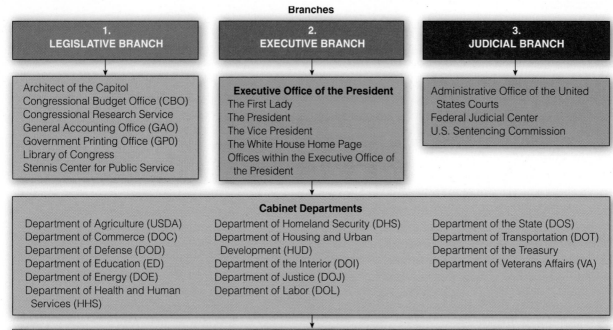

Branches

1. LEGISLATIVE BRANCH	2. EXECUTIVE BRANCH	3. JUDICIAL BRANCH
Architect of the Capitol Congressional Budget Office (CBO) Congressional Research Service General Accounting Office (GAO) Government Printing Office (GP0) Library of Congress Stennis Center for Public Service	**Executive Office of the President** The First Lady The President The Vice President The White House Home Page Offices within the Executive Office of the President	Administrative Office of the United States Courts Federal Judicial Center U.S. Sentencing Commission

Cabinet Departments

Department of Agriculture (USDA)
Department of Commerce (DOC)
Department of Defense (DOD)
Department of Education (ED)
Department of Energy (DOE)
Department of Health and Human Services (HHS)

Department of Homeland Security (DHS)
Department of Housing and Urban Development (HUD)
Department of the Interior (DOI)
Department of Justice (DOJ)
Department of Labor (DOL)

Department of the State (DOS)
Department of Transportation (DOT)
Department of the Treasury
Department of Veterans Affairs (VA)

Independent Agencies, Regulatory Agencies, and Government Corporations

Advisory Council on Historic Preservation
African Development Foundation
Central Intelligence Agency (CIA)
Commission on Civil Rights
Commodity Futures Trading Commission
Consumer Product Safety Commission (CPSC)
Corporation for National and Community Service
Defense Nuclear Facilities Safety Board
Election Assistance Commision
Environmental Protection Agency (EPA)
Equal Employment Opportunity Commission (EEOC)
Export-Import Bank of the United States
Farm Credit Administration
Federal Communications Commission (FCC)
Federal Deposit Insurance Corporation (FDIC)
Federal Election Commission (FEC)
Federal Housing Finance Board
Federal Labor Relations Authority
Federal Maritime Commission
Federal Mediation and Conciliation Service
Federal Mine Safety and Health Review Commission
Federal Reserve System
Federal Retirement Thrift Investment Board
Federal Trade Commission (FTC)
General Services Administration (GSA)
Institute of Museum and Library Services
Inter-American Foundation
International Broadcasting Bureau (IBB)
Merit Systems Protection Board
National Aeronautics and Space Administration (NASA)
National Archives and Records Administration (NARA)

National Capitol Planning Commission
National Council on Disability
National Credit Union Administration (NCUA)
National Endowment for the Arts
National Endowment for the Humanities
National Labor Relations Board (NLRB)
National Mediation Board
National Railroad Passenger Corporation (AMTRAK)
National Science Foundation (NSF)
National Transportation Safety Board
Nuclear Regulatory Commission (NRC)
Occupational Safety and Health Review Commission
Office of Compliance
Office of Government Ethics
Office of National Counterintelligence Executive
Office of Personnel Management
Office of Special Counsel
Overseas Private Investment Corporation
Panama Canal Commission
Peace Corps
Pension Benefit Guaranty Corporation
Postal Rate Commission
Railroad Retirement Board
Securities and Exchange Commission (SEC)
Selective Service System
Small Business Administration (SBA)
Social Security Administration (SSA)
Tennessee Valley Authority
Trade and Development Agency
United States Agency for International Development
United States International Trade Commission
United States Postal Service (USPS)

Source: From http://www.firstgov.gov.

Mixed Views on Bureaucracy

Public opinion surveys about the federal bureaucracy tend to provide mixed reviews. People generally support the idea of government addressing important problems, but many are of the opinion that when government does act it tends to waste money and act inefficiently. As the following figure shows, Americans exhibited mixed feeling about the expansion of the federal government in response to the economic problems during the recessionary period of 2007–2010. While a slim majority—53 percent—approved of government's expanded role to help improve the economy, they only supported that expansion for the short term. More than eight in ten Americans either disapproved of government's expanded role or wanted government's role to retract once the recession was over.

Americans were asked by the *USA Today/Gallup* Poll: "Thinking about the way the federal government has responded to the financial crisis in recent months, generally speaking, do you approve or disapprove of the expansion of the government's role in the economy?" Those who approved were then asked if they thought the role of government should be reduced once the crisis is over. Here is how they responded:

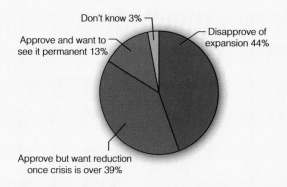

Source: USA Today/Gallup Poll, conducted March 27–29, 2009.

professional manner, and engages in hiring practices that are based on merit. The vast size and level of responsibility that these units have make the federal bureaucracy a complex and often confusing system to study.

What Does the Federal Bureaucracy Do?

Most of the federal bureaucracy is contained within the executive branch of government, and ultimately reports to the president of the United States.[7] Article II of the Constitution states that "the executive power shall be vested in a President of the United States of America." The executive power, or the power to carry out, administer, and enforce specific laws, then, falls mainly under the purview of presidential responsibility. The president uses the federal bureaucracy to exercise executive authority.

Policy Implementation

The full range of activities in which the federal bureaucracy engages is known as **policy implementation**. Policy implementation is the process of carrying out a law. Laws that are passed by Congress often include the development of new or modification of existing federal programs or services. In order to carry out the specific programs or services outlined in a law, the federal bureaucracy is assigned the task of implementation. For example, in 1935 Congress passed the Social Security Act to provide older Americans with a stable source of income during their retirement years and to offer support for the children of deceased workers. The Act created the Social Security Administration as the agency in the federal government that had the authority to carry out the provisions of the Act. Today, the Social Security Administration remains the unit in the federal bureaucracy responsible for maintaining records and authorizing benefits to those eligible for Social Security payments.

★ LO

Understand the critical role that the bureaucracy plays in the implementation of federal policy

Policy implementation
The process of carrying out laws, and the specific programs or services outlined in those laws.

Regulations
Rules or other directives issued by government agencies.

Implementation of a law requires translating the congressional legislation into action. Bureaucratic units begin the process of implementation by developing **regulations**, or a set of rules that guide employees of the agency in carrying out the program or service. These rules are supported by the force of law. The Social Security Administration, for example, has written a detailed set of regulations defining who is and who is not eligible for Social Security retirement benefits. The rules include a schedule for the amount of monthly payment benefit based on a person's age, the number of years he or she contributed to the Social Security system while working, and other criteria. Regulations are useful not only because they translate laws into actions, but, because they are written down and are usually very specific, they also provide a basis for employees in the bureaucracy to consistently apply them from one case to the next.

Once an agency drafts a set of regulations to implement a program, the regulations are published in the *Federal Register*. This federal government publication is widely accessible to elected leaders, interest groups, corporations, the media, and regular citizens. The agencies authoring the regulations have an open period where they accept comments on the proposed rules and decide whether to redraft based on the commentary they receive. If the agency refuses to redraft based on an objection, the objector can ask Congress to require the agency to modify the regulations; or the objector might take the matter to court on the basis that the agency was acting outside of Congress's intentions in the law.

Federal Register
The journal that publishes regulations that implement a federal program.

Bureaucratic Legislation

★ LO Explain "delegated authority" and describe the conditions under which such authority is granted

The types of laws passed by Congress are many and varied, and thus policy implementation encompasses many different bureaucratic activities. Some laws are very vague and offer agencies very little guidance about implementation. Other laws can be very specific in directing the agency how to implement it. When laws are vague, agencies are said to have **administrative discretion**, which gives them considerable freedom in deciding how to implement the law. Vague laws require an agency to spend more time and effort in developing regulations.

Administrative discretion
The freedom of agencies to decide how to implement a vague or ambiguous law passed by Congress.

Two policy areas where congressional legislation tends to be vague and where agencies have much latitude in making rules and regulations are environmental quality and workplace safety. Important pieces of legislation, such as the Clean Air Act and the Occupational Safety and Health Act, have given agencies such as the Environmental Protection Agency (EPA) and Occupational Safety and Health Administration (OSHA) much discretion in setting specific standards for car emissions, pollution, and workplace safety standards. This discretion usually is the product of at least one of two conditions. First, Congress often does not have the technical expertise to define how to achieve clean air or workplace safety, and so it gives agencies that have such technical capabilities the discretion to set standards. Second, Congress sometimes chooses not to deal with politically difficult issues such as how to clean up toxic-waste dumps, and so it shifts the responsibility to the bureaucracy, forcing an agency to resolve the problem. When an agency makes an unpopular decision as a result of Congress's "passing the buck," the agency's action contributes further to the negative image of bureaucracies.

Delegation of congressional power
Congress's transferring of its lawmaking authority to the executive branch of government.

When Congress writes vague legislation and thus transfers legislative authority to an agency, it gives that agency the effective power to make laws, a constitutional power that is supposed to rest with the Congress alone. When Congress does this, it is said to have **delegated congressional power**. Laws that relate to the authority of administrative agencies and the rules promulgated by those agencies are referred to as **administrative law**. Congress has delegated considerable legislative authority to the EPA and OSHA to craft both environmental and workplace safety laws. Similarly, Congress has delegated a substantial amount of authority to the Federal Reserve to manage the nation's economy. The "Fed" has the power to adjust the prime interest rate in response to economic conditions to encourage investments and ward off inflation.

Administrative law
A law that relates to the authority of administrative agencies and the rules promulgated by those agencies.

CHECK the List

Senator Proxmire's Top Ten Golden Fleece Awards

Stories of waste in bureaucratic spending always become fodder for calls to cut federal spending and eliminate unnecessary federal programs. Much of this "wasteful" spending is rooted in congressional pork-barrel spending, that is, spending on projects that benefit individual members' home districts. Perhaps no one took better aim at wasteful pork-barrel spending in the federal bureaucracy than U.S. Senator William Proxmire (D-WI). In 1975, Proxmire began what he called the "Golden Fleece Awards" to target bureaucratic agencies that spent money on wasteful programs. Proxmire announced 150 awards in all. Asked to identify the top ten most egregious spending wastes, Proxmire provided the following list:

✔ **Tequila fish.** The National Institute on Alcohol Abuse and Alcoholism for spending millions of dollars to find out if drunken fish are more aggressive than sober fish, if young rats are more likely than old rats to consume alcohol in order to reduce anxiety, and if rats can be turned into alcoholics.

✔ **The Great Wall of Bedford.** The U.S. Department of Commerce for spending $20,000 to build an 800-foot limestone replica of the Great Wall of China in Bedford, Indiana.

✔ **Buying Worcestershire sauce.** The Department of the Army for spending $6,000 to prepare a seventeen-page document that told the federal government how to buy a bottle of Worcestershire sauce.

✔ **The New Jersey Sewer Museum.** The Environmental Protection Agency for spending $1 million to preserve a Trenton, New Jersey, sewer as a historical monument.

✔ **Lessons in watching TV.** The Office of Education for spending $220,000 to develop a curriculum to teach college students how to watch television.

✔ **Tennis cheating.** The National Endowment for the Humanities for a $25,000 grant to study why people cheat and act rudely on tennis courts in Virginia.

✔ **Tailhook.** The Department of the Navy for using sixty-four planes to fly 1,334 officers to the Hilton Hotel in Las Vegas for a reunion of the Tailhook Association.

✔ **$2 million patrol car.** The Law Enforcement Assistance Administration for spending $2 million on a prototype police car that was never completed.

✔ **Basketball therapy.** The Health Care Financing Administration for Medicaid payments to psychiatrists for unscheduled meetings with patients who were attending basketball games, which cost the federal government between $40 million and $80 million.

✔ **Surfing subsidy.** The Department of Commerce for giving the Honolulu city government $28,000 to study how to spend $250,000 for a good surfing beach.

Source: Taxpayers for Common Sense Web site: http://www.taxpayer.net.

★ LO   Describe the
oversight function of Congress over the bureaucracy

Congressional oversight
Congress's exercise of its authority to monitor the activities of agencies and administrators.

Delegation of power from Congress to bureaucratic agencies is not, however, typically open-ended. Congress may cede law-making authority to the bureaucracy, but it does not relinquish all power. **Congressional oversight** is the term used to describe Congress's regular monitoring of bureaucratic agency performance for the purpose of achieving accountability. Although the vast bulk of bureaucratic agencies ultimately report to the president as chief executive, Congress through its oversight function commands a significant amount of accountability from executive agencies.[8]

If Congress is not satisfied with an agency's performance, it has a variety of means to coerce change: it can reduce or eliminate an agency's budget; it can refuse to confirm presidential appointments to that agency; it can eliminate the agency; it can conduct investigations into the activities and performance of the agency; or it can establish a new agency and shift resources and powers to it. This strong system of checks often renders the federal bureaucracy just as (if not more) responsive to Congress as to the president.

Specific congressional oversight functions may be carried out in a number of ways. Particular committees (or subcommittees) in Congress hold hearings, on either a regularly scheduled or an ad hoc basis, to review agency performance. For example, the House Armed Services Committee meets with the secretary of defense and Joint Chiefs of Staff to review Pentagon programs. The Senate Environment and Public Works Committee holds regular meetings with the administrator of EPA to review that agency's activities. The House Science and Technology Committee reviews the activities of NASA. In addition, the House Appropriations Committee is divided into a number of subcommittees, each of which regularly reviews pending authorizations for funding individual agencies. These subcommittees often scrutinize agency spending.

Two bureaucratic agencies under the direct control of Congress (rather than the president) that support the oversight function of congressional committees are the Congressional Budget Office (CBO) and the Government Accountability Office (GAO). These offices compile data on federal programs and are staffed with program review and accounting professionals who comply with members' and committees' requests for information on agency performance and cost. Congress uses the GAO to investigate the actions or inactions of an agency, and it uses the CBO to conduct research, such as program effectiveness studies.

Ben Bernanke, Chairman of the Federal Reserve Board, testifies before a Senate Budget Committee Hearing.

BLOOMBERG/GETTY IMAGES

★ LO   Understand
why Congress has provided some bureaucratic units with administrative judicatory authority

Bureaucratic adjudicating
Determining the rights and duties of particular parties within the scope of an agency's rules or regulations.

Bureaucratic Adjudication

Just as policy implementation sometimes includes the writing of legislation, it also may involve **bureaucratic adjudicating**, or determining the rights and duties of particular parties within the scope of an agency's rules or regulations. Such adjudication might include ruling on whether an individual is eligible to receive Social Security payments, or whether a company has violated an air pollution rule. Most adjudication takes place in the court system. However Congress, which has the authority to create federal adjudicating agencies, has placed judicial power in some bureaucratic agencies as well. For example, the Equal Employment Opportunity Commission

(EEOC) has the authority to adjudicate cases where an individual or group of individuals charges that a company has violated federal laws preventing discrimination in hiring or promotion practices in the workplace. The EEOC can try a case against a company, and if the finding is that the company violated federal law, the EEOC is authorized to prescribe a punishment or corrective action.

The EEOC and other agencies such as the EPA, the National Labor Relations Board, and the Federal Communications Commission (FCC) employ the personnel, procedures, and case law more typically seen in the judicial branch. Bureaucratic judicial personnel and powers include "administrative judges," appellate courts within the agency, and administrative hearings that resemble a trial. Ultimately, any administrative court decision may be appealed to the federal court system, because the power of adjudication ultimately rests in the hands of the judicial branch. In reality, however, federal courts routinely uphold cases appealed from administrative courts.

The Development of the Federal Bureaucracy

Describe how the federal bureaucracy has evolved over time, including substantial growth spurts as a result of the New Deal and Great Society programs and the Cold War ★ LO

The executive branch of government during the first four years of George Washington's presidency was extremely small. Congress created just three departments to aid the first president in executing the law: the Department of State to oversee foreign affairs, the Department of Treasury to oversee fiscal affairs, and the Department of War to oversee military affairs. Washington selected and the Senate confirmed Thomas Jefferson, Alexander Hamilton, and Henry Knox to lead these departments, respectively. Shortly after these departments were created, the president was authorized to hire an attorney general and a postmaster general. During the first year of the Washington administration, the federal bureaucracy employed only about fifty individuals.

As the role of government expanded, and as the United States added new territories, there was a need to expand the size of the federal bureaucracy. Military operations, such as those conducted during the War of 1812, required increased support services and agencies to support military operations. Westward expansion brought with it the need for federal services to settle the new areas. A centralized national bank required federal agencies to centralize the economic and monetary system. By the mid-1800s, Congress saw the need to create a new Cabinet department, the Department of the Interior, to manage federally owned lands and to aid in the westward expansion of the nation. The important role of farming in the nation's growth and development led to the establishment of the Department of Agriculture in 1862 to support and promote farming and farm product commercialization. The Department of Justice was established in 1870 to aid the attorney general in the post–Civil War era in prosecuting violators of federal law and representing the federal government in the courts.

In 1884, a Bureau of Labor was created to address the concerns of the labor force that arose with the growth of the industrial economy. Large-scale industrialization and economic development led to the development of a Commerce Agency in 1888 to help regulate interstate and foreign trade. These agencies were elevated to Cabinet status in the early 1900s to reflect the growing role they played in the federal government. The Great Depression set the stage for the election of Franklin Delano Roosevelt in 1932. The FDR administration advocated an activist role for the federal government in responding to the economic crisis. Consequently, FDR's New Deal created a myriad of new federal agencies to deal with the nation's fiscal woes, including the Social Security Administration, the Securities and Exchange Commission, the Civilian Conservation Corps, and a host of public works programs to provide jobs for the large number of unemployed. In 1936, Roosevelt established the Brownlow Committee (named for its chair Louis Brownlow) to investigate how to make the growing bureaucracy more efficient and more responsive to the president.[9]

© 2012 CENGAGE LEARNING

One Italian Writer Experiences American Bureaucracy

Americans tend to think that our bureaucracy is far too large, complex, and difficult for most average citizens to navigate. Of course the Italian bureaucracy can more than hold its own in a battle with the American version; it is renowned for its size, power, and grip on Italian government, as well as for its overall complexity for Italian citizens. In his book *Ciao, America!: An Italian Discovers the U.S.*, Italian journalist Beppe Severgnini offers a dose of perspective to Americans by chronicling the relatively pleasant experience he had with the bureaucracy in Washington, DC:

> For Italians coming to live in the United States, the greatest satisfaction . . . is grappling with American bureaucracy. Why is that? It's because, having trained on the Italian version, we feel like a matador faced with a milk cow. It's a pushover. . . . After sorting everything out, an Italian has a craving for a few more phone calls to make, some last-minute problem to unravel, or another clerk to convince. What now follows is the story of one short but exciting morning in action against the bureaucratic legions of Washington:

> The "battle station" was a phone booth at Sugar's, a Korean coffee shop on the corner of P and Thirty-fifth streets. Weapons and ammunition—five quarters, paper, pen, passport, map of the city, a good command of English, and a moderate degree of optimism. The first thing, in a country where everything is done over the phone, was to get a telephone. All this took was a call to C&P (the local—private and therefore efficient—equivalent of the Italian Telecom) to ask

> for a number. The clerk asked a few questions of the kind that any student on a beginner's English language course could answer—name, surname, age, address. At the end of the conversation, the same clerk told me, "Get your pen and write. This is your number. You'll be connected in twenty-four hours." Total time required for the transaction—ten minutes. Cost—twenty-five cents.

> At this point, it is necessary to connect your new phone to a long-distance carrier. Competition among AT&T, MCI, and Sprint is ruthless. Each provider offers special conditions, such as discounts on numbers you call frequently, on calls to a foreign country of your choice, at particular times of day or on certain days of the week. Time required to decide—fifteen minutes. Cost—nothing. Each company has its own free phone number (which in the USA begin with 1-800).

> But to apply for a Social Security number, which is the de facto equivalent in the United States of an identity card, the phone is not enough. You need to go to the appropriate office, where a clerk asks you questions and types your answers straight into a computer. Queue (sorry, line)—none. Forms—ditto. Interview time—five minutes.

> Then we made a visit to the police for a temporary parking permit. (Time—fifteen minutes. Cost—nothing.) After which to open a bank account, all you need to do is turn up with the money (essential), and proof of domicile. The address on a letter is okay. A photocopy of your rent contract is even better. A temporary checkbook is issued on the spot and you can choose the definitive version from a catalog. There's the classic model, the old-fashioned type, and one with Sylvester the cartoon cat on every check. My wife, of course, insisted on Sylvester. That was perhaps the most trying moment of the entire morning.

Source: Beppe Severgnini, *Ciao, America!: An Italian Discovers the U.S.* (New York: Broadway Press, reprint edition 2003), 13–14.

The committee unanimously agreed that the president's power should be enhanced to give the president greater authority as manager of the bureaucracy. The Brownlow Committee's recommendations led to the consolidation of presidential authority over the bureaucracy.

By 1940, the federal government accounted for 10 percent of the nation's gross domestic product (GDP), with $9.5 billion spent on federal programs, including the employment of about 700,000 Americans in the federal bureaucracy. The increased role of government led to greater demands for federal services, which in turn necessitated growth in the federal bureaucracy. Between 1940 and 1975, the federal bureaucracy experienced an unprecedented growth spurt. During this period, the number of federal employees more than tripled to 2.2 million; the federal budget increased to $332 billion; and the federal budget as a percentage of the gross domestic product reached 22 percent.[10]

Two factors accounted for this massive growth in the bureaucracy. First was President Lyndon B. Johnson's Great Society program of the 1960s. The Great Society encompassed numerous new laws aimed at social and economic improvements to American society through a highly activist role of the federal government. The post–World War II prosperity of the American economy allowed Johnson to convince a Democratic Congress that programs promoting social justice, a safety net for the impoverished, improvements to urban life, health care for the elderly, and greater access to educational opportunities should be guaranteed to all Americans and funded by the great wealth of the American economy. These programs had a large influence on growth of the bureaucracy through the 1970s.

A second factor contributing to the massive growth in the bureaucracy was the Cold War. World War II resulted in two superpowers, the United States and the Soviet Union, vying against each other for global influence. From 1945 to 1991, these superpowers developed expensive nuclear and other war technologies in search of military superiority. The federal budget for defense programs grew dramatically, as did the programs to support intelligence operations and aid to foreign nations for diplomatic purposes.

Getting Control of the Growing Bureaucracy

During the mid to late 1970s, the American economy began to slump. Whereas the prosperity of the 1960s facilitated the creation of a larger-size government to accomplish a number of policy goals, the sluggish economy of the late 1970s was unable to support the by now very large federal bureaucracy. Federal budget deficits began to accumulate, and the United States could no longer afford the huge federal bureaucracy that it had created. Ronald Reagan was elected president in 1980 with an agenda to scale back the federal bureaucracy. The Reagan administration targeted domestic programs to achieve the reduction in government. Since the 1980s, various administrations have attempted to reduce the size of the federal bureaucracy. The methods they have used include the following:

- Privatization. **Privatization** means replacing government-provided services with services provided by the private sector. The theory of privatization is that if private companies compete to provide services, the cost of those services will be less than if government provides those services directly. Additionally, some contend that private corporations can more flexibly adapt to changing circumstances because they are not weighed down by civil service restrictions and government red tape. Accordingly, a number of federal programs were privatized during the 1980s. For example, the U.S. Department of Labor frequently provided job training services to the unemployed during the 1960s and 1970s. Federal laws passed in the 1980s eliminated much of the federal management of job training and contracted out these services to private companies. More recently, the federal government has used a number of private contractors, including Halliburton (the company once run by former Vice President Dick Cheney) to help rebuild Iraq after the second Persian Gulf War, under the idea that the costs would be even greater if the federal government played a more direct role.

- Deregulation. The development of rules and regulations to achieve a policy goal requires units in the bureaucracy to ensure that such rules and regulations are followed. **Deregulation**, that is, eliminating government oversight and regulation of certain activities, results in less government to do the regulating. Prior to the mid-1970s, the trucking and railroad industries, long-distance telephone service, prices for air flights, and the activities of savings and loan institutions were regulated by the federal government. Deregulation of these and other activities resulted in the abolition of a number of federal agencies, including the Civil Aeronautics Board and eventually the Interstate Commerce Commission.

★ LO

Explain methods for attempting to control or reduce the size and scope of the federal bureaucracy through privatization, devolution, deregulation, and accountability

Privatization
The process of replacing government-provided services with services provided by the private sector.

Deregulation
The elimination of government oversight and government regulation of certain activities.

The United States contracted with a number of private firms to repair damage caused by the war in Iraq. Here, Iraqi men rebuild a house in Baghdad destroyed by a bomb.

■ Devolution. A central question in our federal system of government is which level of government—national or state—should have the authority to provide programs and services to citizens. The New Deal and Great Society programs gave the national government increased responsibility and authority for such services. In response to extensive growth of the national government, the 1980s witnessed a **devolution** of power and responsibility back to the states, mainly to shrink the size of the national government. For example, welfare reform in the mid-1990s shifted much responsibility for welfare from the federal to the state governments.

■ "Reinventing government." When Bill Clinton was elected president in 1992, he promised to "reinvent government." This promise translated into an eight-year effort to promote bureaucratic accountability. The Clinton administration instituted mechanisms such as customer satisfaction research with those who received federal services and freedom of information policies that gave the public and the news media access to government documents to help promote accountability. In addition, the Government Performance and Results Act, passed in 1997, required that agencies establish goals and set out a plan for achieving those goals. In the book *Reinventing Government*, David Osborne and Ted Gaebler describe how bureaucracy and other aspects of the public sector in the United States have undergone a transformation.[11] They contend that the "entrepreneurial spirit" brought to bear on government performance, which includes market-driven and business-oriented planning, has improved the effectiveness and efficiency of bureaucracy at all levels of government.

In addition to implementing these strategies for reducing the size of the federal bureaucracy, the Cold War, which concluded in 1991 with the collapse of the Soviet Union, put an end to escalating defense budgets to support the arms race with the Soviets.

The end of the Cold War and the implementation of strategies that contain, if not reduce, the size of the federal bureaucracy do appear to have reversed the decades-long trend toward increasing the size of government. Between 1990 and 2000, the number of civilian employees in the federal government declined by about 500,000,[12] and the percentage of the GDP accounted for by federal spending dropped from

Devolution

The transfer of power and responsibilities for certain regulatory programs from the federal government back to the states.

21.9 percent to 18.2 percent. Despite these efforts, however, federal spending on the bureaucracy continues to increase annually at a pace that exceeds inflation. In particular, defense spending to fight the war on terrorism and the war in Iraq in recent years have increased federal spending. Also, the Department of Homeland Security, created in response to the terrorist attacks of September 11, 2001, required increased federal dollars to protect the nation within its own borders.

More recently, the election of President Barack Obama and increased majorities of Democrats to Congress in 2008 during an economic recession ushered in a new growth spurt for the federal bureaucracy. A $787 billion federal spending plan to provide an economic stimulus along with a health care reform package and increased regulations of the financial services industry all significantly increased the scope and size of the bureaucracy. Most notably, the Obama administration championed the creation of a new Consumer Financial Protection Bureau designed to provide stricter regulations on the mortgage financing industry in particular.

The Organization of the Federal Bureaucracy

The federal bureaucracy is made up of a variety of different types of agencies that are empowered to carry out laws and federal programs. Some of these organizations have broad authority over a public policy area, whereas others have a narrow focus; some are empowered to implement laws and programs established by Congress, whereas others have the added responsibility of creating rules and policies, and adjudicating. Some report directly to the president, whereas others answer to both the president and Congress. Also, though most organizations in the federal bureaucracy are part of the executive branch, some are part of the legislative and judicial branches. Units of the federal bureaucracy include Cabinet departments, independent agencies, regulatory agencies, government corporations, and the Executive Office of the President.

★ LO

Define the different types of agencies in the federal bureaucracy including cabinet departments, independent agencies, regulatory agencies, government corporations, and the Executive Office of the President

Cabinet Departments

Amid the complex web of bureaucratic units is a select set of fifteen organizations called **Cabinet departments**, which are the major administrative organizations of the executive branch. These departments vary in terms of both size and importance. The Department of Defense, for example, employs nearly 1 million civilian workers and another 1.5 million military personnel. By contrast, the Department of Education has only about 5,000 employees.

At the head of each Cabinet department is a secretary (with the exception of the Justice Department, which is headed by the attorney general) who reports directly to the president. Along with a few other high-level presidential advisers and the vice president, these secretaries compose the president's Cabinet, a set of high-level administrators who report directly to the president. Cabinet heads and their deputies are nominated by the president and must be confirmed by the Senate. Typically, a secretary shares the same views as the president on policy matters and often is a loyal political supporter (if not close friend) of the chief executive. The "inner cabinet" is a term used to describe the secretaries of the most important departments in the cabinet—State, Defense, Treasury, and Justice. Whereas the Cabinet once served as the president's primary advisory panel, the growth in the Executive Office of the President, discussed later in this chapter, has shifted primary advisory responsibilities to that office.

Cabinet departments (sometimes referred to as executive departments) generally have a broad scope of authority over a particular policy area, such as the nation's military (the Department of Defense), federal law enforcement (the Department of Justice), the federal road and highway system (the Department of Transportation), and protecting the nation from terrorism and responding to emergency situations (Department of Homeland Security). The scope of activities in any one department tends to be so broad that most departments are best viewed as a collection of many different agencies and subagencies, each with a narrower policy focus.

Cabinet departments
Those federal agencies that qualify as the major administrative organizations of the executive branch.

TABLE 8.1 The Cabinet Departments

Department of State

The Department of State has been the leading U.S. foreign affairs agency since 1789, and the secretary of state is the president's principal foreign policy adviser. The State Department engages in the following activities: it leads in the coordination and development of U.S. foreign policy; it manages the foreign affairs budget and other foreign affairs resources; it represents the United States abroad, conveying U.S. foreign policy to foreign governments and international organizations through U.S. embassies and consulates in foreign countries and diplomatic missions to international organizations; and it negotiates agreements and treaties on issues ranging from trade to nuclear weapons.

Department of Treasury

The Treasury Department, also established in 1789, is entrusted with a broad range of duties and functions. It is responsible for paying all the bills of the federal government, collecting federal taxes, borrowing money for the federal government, printing money, and overseeing the operations of national banks. In addition to these monetary functions, the Department of the Treasury also oversees critical functions in enforcement and economic policy development. The Internal Revenue Service and the U.S. Mint are part of the Treasury Department.

Department of Defense

Called the Department of War when it was established in 1789, the Department of Defense currently employs nearly 1 million civilians, far more than any other agency in the federal bureaucracy. Most of these employees work at military bases around the United States. In 1947, the separate Departments of the Army, Navy, Air Force, Marines, and Coast Guard were reorganized into the new Department of Defense to achieve greater efficiency and coordination. In addition to its large civilian workforce, the Department is responsible for 1.5 million active-duty military personnel, and another 1.2 million in the Guard and Reserve.

Department of Justice

The Office of Attorney General was created in 1789 as an adviser to the president, and in 1870 was elevated to cabinet department status as the Department of Justice (DOJ). The role of DOJ is to prevent and control crime, to punish those who are guilty of unlawful behavior, to enforce the nation's immigration laws, and to administer the justice system. DOJ employs U.S. attorneys who prosecute offenders and represent the U.S. government in court. It also oversees the Federal Bureau of Investigation, the Drug Enforcement Administration, the Bureau of Prisons, and the United States Marshals Service, which protects the federal judiciary, apprehends fugitives, and detains people in federal custody.

Department of the Interior

The Department of the Interior (DOI), created in 1849, is responsible for maintaining and managing federally owned land, which includes about 20 percent of the nation's landmass. It maintains 900 dams and reservoirs that provide water to more than 30 million Americans. The department also handles federal relations with Native American tribes. Located within the department, the Bureau of Indian Affairs manages nearly 60 million acres of land held in trust by the United States. Finally, the DOI manages the national park system, which includes 388 parks and 540 wildlife refuges.

Department of Agriculture

The U.S. Department of Agriculture (USDA) was created in 1862 by Congress at the request of President Abraham Lincoln. At the time, nearly half of all U.S. workers were employed in farming. The USDA originally was created to provide farmers with seeds and information for improving farm production and services. Today, the USDA runs the school lunch, school breakfast, and food stamp programs; brings housing, telecommunications, and safe drinking water to rural farmland areas; is responsible for the safety of meat, poultry, and egg products; and provides research on farm technologies and safe food-handling practices.

Department of Commerce

The U.S. Department of Commerce and Labor was created in 1903 and was renamed the Department of Commerce (DOC) in 1913. Today, the DOC provides comprehensive statistical analysis of economic conditions in the United States, manages patent and trademark protection programs, and is responsible for conducting the U.S. Census. The department also provides grants to economically distressed areas for business and job development, promotes exports of U.S. manufactured goods, promotes the growth of minority-owned businesses, and runs the National Oceanic and Atmospheric Administration, which forecasts weather and environmental conditions.

TABLE 8.1 The Cabinet Departments *Cont'd*

Department of Labor

The Department of Labor was a bureau within the U.S. Department of Commerce and Labor and became a Cabinet-level department in 1913. Its mission is to promote the welfare of the job seekers, wage earners, and retirees of the United States by improving their working conditions, advancing their opportunities for profitable employment, protecting their retirement and health care benefits, helping employers find workers, strengthening free collective bargaining, and tracking changes in employment, prices, and other national economic measurements. The department administers a variety of federal labor laws including those that guarantee workers' rights to safe and healthful working conditions; a minimum hourly wage and overtime pay; freedom from employment discrimination; unemployment insurance; and other income support.

Department of Housing and Urban Development

The Department of Housing and Urban Development (HUD), created in 1965, is the federal department primarily responsible for dealing with the nation's housing needs. It administers programs that help cities and communities develop and rehabilitate. Many of HUD's activities focus on the nation's urban areas, providing housing assistance and public housing projects in many cities.

Department of Transportation

The Department of Transportation (DOT), established in 1966, sets federal transportation policy and works with state and local governments along with private-sector partners to promote a safe, secure, efficient, and interconnected national transportation system of roads, railways, pipelines, airways, and seaways. DOT is responsible for managing more than a dozen agencies, including the Federal Aviation Administration, the Federal Highway Administration, the National Highway Traffic Safety Administration, and the Federal Railroad Administration.

Department of Energy

The Department of Energy (DOE) was created in 1978 in response to an energy crisis spawned by a reduction in Middle East oil production. Today DOE helps protect national security by applying advanced science and nuclear technology to the nation's defense, manages programs to promote diverse energy sources, and is responsible for disposal of the nation's high-level radioactive waste.

Department of Education

The U.S. Department of Education, created in 1978, was originally one part of the Department of Health, Education, and Welfare. The department is responsible for administering a variety of federal programs supporting aid to local public schools and college tuition loan programs. The Office of Civil Rights within this department is responsible for administering Title IX of the Education Amendments of 1972 to the Civil Rights Act of 1964, which requires that educational institutions receiving federal funds maintain policies, practices, and programs that do not discriminate on the basis of sex. In accordance with Title IX, colleges must provide the same opportunities for sports team participation by women as they do for men.

Department of Health and Human Services

Created in 1978, the Department of Health and Human Services (HHS) administers more than 300 federal programs, covering a wide range of health and human services topics. These programs focus on medical and social science research, prevention of infectious disease outbreaks, immunization services, food and drug safety, financial assistance and services for low-income families, maternal and infant health, prevention of child abuse and domestic violence, substance abuse treatment and prevention, services for older Americans such as home-delivered meals, and comprehensive health services for Native Americans. HHS has the largest of the cabinet department budgets, over $500 billion for 2006.

Department of Veterans Affairs

This department, created in 1988, is charged with overseeing programs that promote the interest and general welfare of veterans of the U.S. military. The department operates the Veterans Health Administration and the Veterans Benefits Administration.

Department of Homeland Security

Created in 2002, the Department of Homeland Security (DHS) is the newest of the cabinet departments. It was created in response to the terrorist attacks of September 11, 2001. The department's main role is to protect the nation against further terrorist attacks within the nation's borders.

President Obama meets with his cabinet in the Cabinet Room at the White House.

CHIP SOMODEVILLA/
GETTY IMAGES

The U.S. Department of Labor, for example, is charged with promoting the American labor force and the interests of labor. It is organized into a large array of agencies and offices, each of which focuses on a particular aspect of labor issues. The Occupational Safety and Health Administration develops standards to promote safe workplace environments, and implements regulations to ensure that employers live up to these standards. The Bureau of Labor Statistics is responsible for compiling data on the labor force on a regular basis. The Office of Labor-Management Standards sets policies for the conduct of negotiations between employers and employees.

Likewise, the U.S. Department of Defense manages the armed forces, and is organized into a number of subunits, including the Army, Navy, Air Force, and National Guard. The hierarchical organization of departments facilitates the bureaucratic goals of area specialization, division of labor, and chain of command.

Although the head of a cabinet department advises and reports directly to the president, only Congress has the authority to create a new department or eliminate an existing one. The power to define the scope, authority, and indeed the very existence of a specific major department in the federal bureaucracy is an important "check" that Congress exercises over the president.

Special situations, and particularly crises, have led the U.S. government to create cabinet-level departments to deal with large-scale national problems. The creation of the Department of Defense in 1947, for example, was in response to large and costly inefficiencies in military operations during World War II. The Department of Energy was established in 1977 in response to the severe energy crisis and gasoline shortage that plagued the country during the 1970s. President Reagan successfully pressed for the creation of a Veterans Affairs Department in 1988 in order to promote his administration's appreciation of those who served in the U.S. military. The newest cabinet department is the Department of Homeland Security (DHS), established in 2002.

The Department of Homeland Security

The terrorist attacks of September 11, 2001, led to President George W. Bush's request to Congress to create the new department. At first, Bush resisted calls for another large unit in the federal bureaucracy. But given strong support in Congress and in the public for a unit to be in charge of the nation's security, he soon became an advocate of its creation. DHS represents a reorganization of twenty-two existing federal agencies into one Cabinet department. The reorganization was intended to improve the coordination and operations of these agencies in protecting the nation against threats to the homeland.

The primary areas of DHS are the following:

- Border and transportation security. This includes the U.S. Customs Service (previously part of the U.S. Department of Treasury) and the former Immigration and Naturalization Service (previously part of the U.S. Department of Justice).

- Emergency preparedness and response. This includes the Federal Emergency Management Agency, formerly an independent agency, and the National Domestic Preparedness Office (previously in the Federal Bureau of Investigation).

- Science and technology. This includes a variety of scientific research offices formerly part of the U.S. Departments of Energy, Defense, and Agriculture.

- Information analysis and infrastructure protection. This includes the Federal Incident Computer Response Center, which was previously part of the General Services Administration, and the National Incident Protection Center (formerly in the Federal Bureau of Investigation).

- The Secret Service, which was previously in the Treasury Department.

- The U.S. Coast Guard.

© 2012 CENGAGE LEARNING

In addition to maintaining the authority to carry out many of the nation's laws, the Cabinet also plays a symbolic role in the political system. Many interest groups provide input to the president through leaders in the Cabinet, and the voices of community and business leaders are often heard first by Cabinet department officials. As the highest-level units in the bureaucracy, Cabinet departments theoretically represent the most important policy areas. Increasingly, presidents have used their Cabinet secretary appointments to demonstrate diversity in government. For nearly two centuries, Cabinet secretaries were almost exclusively white men, but over the last twenty years presidents have used race and gender as factors influencing their appointments. President Clinton made history by naming women to the inner cabinet for the first time: Janet Reno as attorney general in 1993, and Madeleine Albright as secretary of state in 1997. President George W. Bush then made history by appointing the first African American to the inner cabinet: Colin Powell as secretary of state in 2001, and then an African American woman, Condoleezza Rice, as Powell's replacement in 2005; he also appointed the first Hispanic to the inner cabinet when he named Alberto Gonzales as the nation's attorney general during his second term in office. President Obama's cabinet is also diverse, featuring in prominent positions four women (Secretary of State Hillary Clinton, Secretary of Health and Human Services Kathleen Sebelius, Secretary of Homeland Security Janet Napolitano, and Secretary of Labor Hilda Solis) and two African Americans (Attorney General Eric Holder and U.S. Trade Representative Ron Kirk).

Formerly a governor of Arizona, Janet Napolitano was appointed Secretary of Homeland Security by President Obama in January 2008.

SCOTT J. FERRELL/CONGRESSIONAL QUARTERLY/GETTY IMAGES

Conflicts within the President's Cabinet

Presidents choose the leaders of their cabinets, and those chosen are most often high-level political supporters and friends of the president, as well as those who agree with the chief executive on key issues of public policy. Even though the president makes all these high-level appointments, conflicts between department heads are not uncommon. Discord among high-ranking officials may sometimes play out in the media and become a source of embarrassment to presidents. Most recently, a 2010 book by Bob Woodward entitled *Obama's Wars* depicts top White House officials in conflict over how to resolve the war in Afghanistan. Yet Cabinet leaders' differences of opinion on key policy matters may not always be a bad thing, because they give the president a variety of perspectives from which to make a choice.

From 1789 through 1793, President George Washington's Cabinet included Secretary of State Thomas Jefferson and Secretary of the Treasury Alexander Hamilton. Washington's desire for his Cabinet officers to work closely with each other and provide coordinated advice to him was soon dashed as severe conflicts broke out between these two men. Their primary disagreement was over Hamilton's proposal to create a central national bank. Hamilton believed that the federal government had the authority to establish such a bank, which he saw as necessary to solve the nation's economic problems. For Jefferson, the creation of a central bank exceeded the authority of the central government. The conflict between these top two Cabinet officials reflected a battle between Jefferson's "state's rights" beliefs and Hamilton's "strong central government" views. In the end, Washington sided with Hamilton, and a central bank was created.

From 1977 through 1979, President Jimmy Carter's foreign policy team included Secretary of State Cyrus Vance and National Security Advisor Zbigniew Brzezinski. Brzezinski was a close adviser to the president and over time came to take on more and more of the responsibilities normally under the purview of the secretary of state. For example, Carter in 1978 sent Brzezinski to Beijing to help normalize China–U.S. relations. As an emissary for Carter, Brzezinski assumed state functions beyond those of a policy adviser. The role Brzezinski played caused mounting friction between himself and Vance. This friction came to a head in 1979 over the U.S. response to the Iranian hostage crisis. Vance favored a policy of recognizing the Ayatollah Khomeini and negotiating with him, whereas Brzezinski favored U.S. military action to remove Khomeini. When Brzezinski convinced Carter to approve a plan to rescue the hostages by force (which failed), Secretary of State Vance resigned.

In 2003, George W. Bush found two of his inner-circle Cabinet secretaries locked in a profound battle over the question of whether or not the United States should militarily intervene in Iraq. Iraqi leader Saddam Hussein had continuously defied UN resolutions regarding inspections to locate sites used for the development of weapons of mass destruction. Secretary of State Colin Powell advocated a diplomatic solution, threatening the use of the U.S. military only if the UN would endorse such action. Secretary of Defense Donald Rumsfeld argued for U.S. military action even without UN approval (France, Germany, and Russia, and members of the UN Security Council had refused to support military intervention). In the end, President Bush sided with Rumsfeld, and the United States went to war with Iraq without the UN's full support. These conflicting positions between the president's top two foreign policy advisers reflect Rumsfeld's "hawkish" military perspective and Powell's more "realist" perspective. Powell resigned after President Bush's reelection in 2004; Rumsfeld remained defense secretary until December of 2006, resigning soon after the 2006 midterm elections.

Independent Agencies

A number of units in the federal bureaucracy do not have the high status of a Cabinet department but do report directly to the president. Whereas Cabinet departments tend to concentrate on broad areas, such as labor, energy, defense, or education, these **independent agencies**, which are not part of any executive Cabinet department, tend to focus on a narrower scope of issues. NASA, for example, focuses on the U.S. space program, whereas the Small Business Administration concentrates on low-cost

Independent agency
A department that focuses on a narrower set of issues than do higher-status Cabinet departments.

NASA is an independent agency with a highly trained technical and scientific staff. Pictured to the left is the NASA control room in Houston, Texas.

loans and support to encourage the development of small businesses. Independent agencies tend to be smaller than Cabinet departments. The heads of these agencies are appointed by and report to the president.

Regulatory Agencies

Regulatory agencies are responsible for implementing rules and regulations with respect to individual or corporate conduct related to some aspect of the economy. Such agencies are supposed to be staffed by nonpartisan individuals who are entrusted to make sound decisions that promote fairness and weed out corrupt practices on fiscal matters. To accomplish this, regulatory agencies (unlike Cabinet departments and independent agencies) are not under the control of the president. They are created by Congress and are run by independent boards or commissions that are not supposed to exert partisan influence.

The first regulatory agency was the Interstate Commerce Commission (ICC), created by Congress in 1887.[13] As with the creation of most regulatory agencies, the ICC was the federal government's response to widespread corruption. In the case of the ICC, the target was corruption in the railroad industry, which led to the high cost of railroad transportation. The ICC's scope of responsibility extended to regulation of commerce via not only railroad, but also pipeline, barge, automobile, and aircraft. The ICC established a complex set of rates for both passenger and freight transportation via the various modes of transport. ICC rules were intended to guarantee that transportation companies pay a fair fee on the value of property they used in carrying out their services. Congress abolished the ICC in 1995 because it determined that the agency was overregulating and thus stymieing growth in certain business sectors.

Today's federal bureaucracy includes a number of important regulatory agencies:

- The Federal Trade Commission (FTC). The FTC was established in 1914 and has the authority to develop and implement rules and regulations to encourage competition in industry. Over the years, the FTC has played an instrumental role in preventing "price fixing" policies of corporations.

- The Federal Communications Commission (FCC). The FCC was established in 1934 with the authority to regulate radio, television, and interstate telephone companies. Unlike newspapers, which are not regulated, radio and TV stations use public airwaves, making them subject to regulations developed and administered by the FCC.

Regulatory agency
A government body responsible for the control and supervision of a specified activity or area of public interest.

- The Securities and Exchange Commission (SEC). The SEC is responsible for rule making with respect to the stock market and corporate bookkeeping practices. It was created in 1934 in response to the stock market crash of 1929.
- The Equal Employment Opportunity Commission (EEOC). Created by Congress to help administer the Civil Rights Acts of 1964, the EEOC is charged with investigating violations of the act.
- The Environmental Protection Agency (EPA). The EPA was created in response to the environmental protection movement of the 1960s and 1970s. Concerns about air and water quality, as well as hazardous waste materials, led Congress to pass a number of important laws that addressed antipollution measures and empowered the EPA (in 1970) to implement environmental regulations. The EPA is the largest of the regulatory agencies.
- The Consumer Product Safety Commission (CPSC). Consumer advocacy was another movement that gained steam in the 1960s and 1970s. Efforts to make manufacturers produce products that were safer for consumers were an important feature of that movement. The CPSC was created in 1972 to protect the public against risks associated with consumer products.

The SEC, a regulatory agency, regulates the activities of traders on the busy floor of the New York Stock Exchange, pictured above.

Government corporations

Units in the federal bureaucracy set up to run like private companies that depend on revenue from citizens to provide their services.

Government Corporations

A small number of units in the federal bureaucracy are set up to run like private companies even though they serve an important public purpose. These are called **government corporations**. The idea behind a government corporation is that there is a market of customers who are willing to pay individually for the services provided by the corporation. The revenue on which the government corporation relies comes primarily from citizens paying for the service provided by the corporation. Unlike private corporations, government has a special interest in the solvency of government corporations because they serve an important public purpose. Consequently, when the revenue of a government corporation falls short of meeting expenses, government often will intervene to keep the unit in business.

The most widely known and used government corporation is the U.S. Postal Service (USPS), which employs nearly 1 million workers. The primary source of funds for the USPS comes from the sale of U.S. postage stamps. Similar to a private business, the USPS has a product to offer (mail delivery) and charges a fee (the cost of postage) for use of that service.

Another government corporation is the Tennessee Valley Authority (TVA), which serves the power needs of seven states in the Tennessee Valley and operates the system for navigation and flood control of the Tennessee River. Users of TVA's generated power pay for service, as do those who navigate on the Tennessee River. Another well-known government corporation is Amtrak, a railroad service operated by the National Railroad Passenger Corporation. Amtrak maintains more than 20,000 miles of track and operates 500 stations across the nation. Its revenue is largely derived from the sale of passenger tickets; however, in recent years low ridership has forced Congress to subsidize Amtrak from the general revenue fund.

The Executive Office of the President

The president of the United States has an office staff that reports directly to the president, provides advice and counsel, and helps the president manage the rest of the federal bureaucracy. **The Executive Office of the President** is managed by the White House Chief of Staff and includes a Communications Office, a press secretary, a Council of Economic Advisors (to provide advice and management of the bureaucratic agencies responsible to the economy), a National Security Council (to provide advice on foreign and military affairs), an Office of Management and Budget (to coordinate and provide data on the national budget), a White House Counsel (to provide legal advice to the president), an Office of Science and Technology, an Office of the U.S. Trade Representative, and an Office of National Drug Control Policy, among others.

CORBIS

Many of the federal bureaucracy's "alphabet soup" agencies were created as New Deal programs during the administration of President Franklin Delano Roosevelt. Pictured above are workers at one such agency, the Tennessee Valley Authority, seen here assembling a new power generator at the Cherokee Dam on the Holston River in east Tennessee.

Executive Office of the President
The staffers who help the president of the United States manage the rest of the federal bureaucracy.

The Federal Workforce

The federal bureaucracy encompasses an immense workforce. Currently it employs approximately 2 million civilian personnel, 85 percent of whom work outside of Washington, D.C.[14] In addition, there are about 1 million U.S. postal workers and another 1.7 million U.S. military personnel.

Political Appointees and Career Professionals

About 8,000 members of the federal workforce are presidential appointees, some of whom must be confirmed by the Senate. Those requiring Senate confirmation include Cabinet secretaries and the attorney general, heads of independent agencies, ambassadors, U.S. attorneys, and other high-level officers who have administrative responsibility. When a president's term of office expires, the new president generally fills these positions with new appointees. Presidential appointees are frequently referred to as "political" appointees because the job often represents a political reward for past service to the president or the president's political party.

Another 7,500 civilian federal employees are part of what is called the **Senior Executive Service (SES)**. These are senior officers in the federal bureaucracy who are career professionals. Those in the SES do not leave their positions when a new president takes office but work closely with presidential appointees and provide continuity

Senior Executive Service (SES)
Since the late 1970s, a defined group of approximately 7,500 career professionals in the federal bureaucracy who provide continuity in the operations of the bureaucracy from one presidential administration to the next.

in the operations of the federal bureaucracy from one presidential administration to the next. Congress established the SES in the late 1970s as a means of providing this continuity in leadership. Congress also spelled out a nonpartisan process for hiring SES officers based on educational background, work experience, and other qualifications.

Presidential appointees are largely selected to reflect the political orientation of the president, and senior executives are selected primarily to find highly qualified career professionals who will maintain stability in the operations of the bureaucracy. Together, these groups of employees provide leadership and senior management of the units in the federal bureaucracy.

The Civil Service

★ LO Appreciate the large scope of the federal workforce and the civil service rules governing federal employment

Civil service
The system whereby workers in the federal bureaucracy are supposed to be immune from partisan political maneuvering.

The vast majority of the federal bureaucracy workforce is known as the **civil service**. Similar to the SES, civil service workers in the federal bureaucracy are theoretically hired for their position based on their qualifications, and remain employees beyond the term of a particular president. Thus they are supposed to be immune from partisan political maneuvering. Civil service jobs were not always insulated from partisan politics, as they are today. To understand the rules and processes for employment in the federal bureaucracy, it is useful to examine how employment in the federal workforce has changed over the years.

During the early years of the American republic, continuous recruitment of well-educated, upper-middle-class men characterized the development of the federal bureaucracy. Presidents Washington, Adams, and Jefferson hired political, business, and social elites to carry out the activities of the federal bureaucracy. With the exception of top posts in government such as Cabinet secretaries, those in federal jobs usually remained from one presidential administration to the next. This tradition ensured an able and effective federal workforce, albeit a nondiverse one.

President Andrew Jackson, elected to office in 1828, undertook a massive restructuring of the federal workforce. Jackson ran for the presidency as a populist advocating for the interests of the "common man." Upon taking office, he chose to remove individuals in the bureaucracy who were not at all "common" and who found themselves politically at odds with the new president. Resistance among many in the bureaucracy to follow Jackson's orders, along with the president's own desire to see that the bureaucracy more closely reflected the demographics of American society, led Jackson to undertake a major overhaul of the bureaucratic workforce.

Spoils system
The postelection practice of rewarding loyal supporters of the winning candidates and party with appointive public offices.

Patronage
The act of appointing people to government positions in return for their partisan and/or political support.

Jackson replaced the long-term, upper-middle-class bureaucrats with political supporters and friends who came from many walks of life. This **spoils system** of hiring federal workers quickly became a steadfast American tradition. To the victors of presidential elections went the spoils of jobs in the federal government. Under this system of **patronage**, campaigning, political party activities, and governing became intertwined. Political parties enticed people to work on political campaigns by promising the payoff of a good federal job with an electoral victory. Often, those who were given a job were expected to return a percentage of their salary to the political party—a very clever fund-raising strategy. Strength of partisan support became the key criterion for landing and maintaining a good job.

Needless to say, this system of hiring workers produced a number of problems. Because qualifications to do the job were not important in the hiring decision, the bureaucracy became inefficient. Bureaucrats were more concerned about campaigning and supporting the political party than they were about doing their job. Further, the bureaucracy lacked any sort of continuity—for when the partisan control of the presidency changed hands, federal workers were fired en masse and replaced by a new set of underqualified political appointees.

By the time of the Civil War, the spoils system was entrenched and the bureaucracy was thoroughly corrupt. A civil service reform movement arose in the post–Civil War era, advocating an end to the spoils system and the development of a "professionalized" bureaucracy. Strong resistance from the political party bosses stalled the reform movement's agenda. But the 1881 assassination of President James Garfield by a disgruntled party worker who did not receive the federal job he thought he deserved gave strength to the movement. In 1883, Congress passed the **Pendleton Civil Service Reform Act**, which did the following:[15]

- It created a **merit system** for hiring many federal workers based on qualifications for the job, including educational background, related job experience, and performance on civil service tests.

- It prevented employees from losing their federal jobs when the presidency changed hands.

- It set up a Civil Service Commission to oversee federal hiring and firing practices.

Initially, the Pendleton Act applied only to a limited portion of the federal workforce, but it provided the basis for Progressive Era reformers of the early 1900s to develop a more professional bureaucracy through additional reform legislation. Today job qualifications in federal hiring and federal worker immunity from patronage are firmly rooted in the federal bureaucracy's employment practices. These principles now apply to more than 90 percent of federal workers.

The **Hatch Act of 1939** further insulated the civil service from partisan politics by (1) prohibiting the dismissal of an employee for partisan reasons (with the exception of certain high-level political appointments) and (2) prohibiting federal workers from running for office or actively campaigning for a political candidate. In the early 1990s, revisions to the Hatch Act relaxed some of the more stringent requirements of the law and allowed federal workers more flexibility in engaging in political activities. Those in the civil service can now participate in campaigns outside of their work hours, contribute money to a candidate or party, express partisan opinions, and wear campaign buttons, among other activities. However, under the current law, federal workers still cannot be candidates in a partisan election or use their official position to raise money or influence votes.

The **Civil Service Reform Act of 1978** replaced the Civil Service Commission with the Office of Personnel Management (OPM) and the Merit Systems Protection Board (MSPB). OPM and MSPB, bureaucratic agencies themselves, manage the civil service system today. Their functions include administering the system of federal hiring, protecting the rights of federal employees, conducting hearings and deciding cases where there are charges of wrongdoing in hiring and firing of employees, evaluating the effectiveness of federal hiring and retention practices, and regulating the ways in which federal workers can participate in politics.

Getting a Job in the Federal Government

Applying for a job in the federal government is much different from applying for a job at a company. For one thing, most federal jobs require that the applicant take and pass a civil service examination. And once you have a federal job, you may find that the job itself is much different than a job in the private sector. In his book *Insider's Guide to Finding a Job in Washington*, Bruce Maxwell lists four primary advantages of having a job in the federal bureaucracy:[16]

1. **The federal government is the nation's largest employer, and has lots of jobs.** In January 1999, in the Washington area the executive branch employed 293,584 people—and that's just civilians. Between January 1998 and January 1999, federal agencies and departments together hired an average of 3,272 new employees each month in the Washington area."

2. **Federal jobs provide excellent job security.** It's true that the federal government has been on a downsizing kick in recent years, but the vast majority of the job cuts have occurred through attrition and buyouts, not layoffs. The downsizing trend has now largely tapered off. In fact, between January 1998 and January 1999, the number of executive branch employees in the Washington area grew by 4,254."

Pendleton Civil Service Reform Act
The 1883 law that created a merit system for hiring many federal workers, protected them from being fired for partisan reasons, and set up a Civil Service Commission to oversee the hiring and firing process.

Merit system
A system of appointing and promoting civil service personnel based on merit rather than political affiliation or loyalty.

Hatch Act of 1939
The 1939 law that insulated the civil service from partisan politics by prohibiting employee dismissals for partisan reasons and by prohibiting federal workers from participating in political campaigns.

Civil Service Reform Act of 1978
The federal act that replaced the Civil Service Commission (the agency that oversaw federal hiring and firing practices) with the Office of Personnel Management (OPM) and the Merit Systems Protection Board (MSPB).

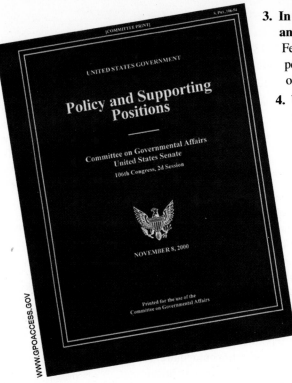

WWW.GPOACCESS.GOV

3. **In general, federal wages and benefits are good, and are comparable to those in the private sector.** Federal workers in the Washington area got a 3.68 percent pay hike in January 1999, raising the salary of the average white-collar employee to $59,307."

4. **Workers who retire from the federal government receive excellent pension benefits."** Job openings in the federal bureaucracy are advertised in what is known as a "vacancy announcement," which includes job title, pay grade level, application submission deadlines, where the job is located, a description of the job duties, a description of the requirements for the job, and procedures for applying for the position. The Office of Personnel Management (OPM) is the federal agency responsible for coordinating and distributing information on hiring and vacancy announcements in the federal government. OPM provides updated information on jobs at the following Web site: http://www.usajobs.opm.gov.

Pictured above is the "plum book," which provides a listing of all job openings in the federal bureaucracy.

Making the Connection

The federal bureaucracy has grown dramatically since the George Washington Administration. As new presidents seek to advance new policy goals, federal departments and agencies have been created and expanded. These agencies have aided presidents in accomplishing new feats and bringing the United States to world "superpower" status. Jefferson's expansion of the bureaucracy was necessary to accomplish the tremendous growth of the nation through the Louisiana Purchase. Reagan's expansion of the bureaucracy helped expand the defenses of the nation to the point that it helped win the Cold War. Many other presidents have found the bureaucracy necessary to help implement federal initiatives. These include Lincoln's efforts to withstand the secession of the southern states and preserve the Union; Theodore Roosevelt's drive to tame the corporate monopolies, Franklin Roosevelt's priming of the federal workforce to tackle the Great Depression, and Barack Obama's attempt to jumpstart the economy through a major stimulus spending plan.

Over the centuries, presidents, with the support of the American people, have used the bureaucracy to accomplish important policy goals. The bureaucracy has also served as the "whipping boy" in rhetorical campaigns for political office. In many instances the bureaucracy has earned its reputation as wasteful, inefficient, and bloated. But without the federal bureaucracy, the most important national initiatives could not have been realized. Even those presidents who campaigned on a platform to cut the bureaucracy ended up using it to advance important initiatives. The federal bureaucracy is an easy target of criticism, yet there is no denying the fact that it has contributed as much to the development of the American political system as any other part of the political system.

POLITICS InterActive!

Czars Aplenty in the U.S. Government

The official title of "czar" was once used by Russia to signify that nation's monarchial head. In previous centuries Russian czars, like other European monarchs such as kings and queens, were quite often dictators, reaching high office through undemocratic means while exercising broad legislative and executive authority. Today in the United States a number of positions in the executive branch of government are referred to unofficially as "czars." The title seems to have caught on for one of two reasons: either (1) the person selected for the job was expected to lead an effort to solve a particularly difficult problem (e.g., the "drug czar" coordinates the federal effort to mitigate the illegal drug trade in the United States), or (2) the person was selected by the president with the clear expectation that congressional approval was unnecessary. Often both reasons apply to the appointment of these special bureaucratic leaders. As coordinators of a very wide array of agencies, they usually enjoy close working relationships with the president. No wonder the modern czar is considered such a powerful force in American politics.

CHRIS USHER/CBS/LANDOV

Carol Browner, the White House "Energy Czar."

Presidents since Franklin D. Roosevelt have been making these special czarist appointments. During the administrations of FDR and most of his successors, the number of bureaucratic czars appointed per president was in the single digits. President Kennedy appointed none, Nixon just three, Reagan just one, and George H. W. Bush a mere two czars in all. A new trend began with George W. Bush, who created more than thirty of these positions, and continued with Barack Obama, who in his first fifteen months in office set a record number of czarist appointments at thirty-eight. While a handful of Obama's appointments have been confirmed by the Senate, the vast majority of them were never approved, making them the target of critics who believe the president has usurped congressional authority. The criticism may have reached its peak in August 2009 when Van Jones, President Obama's "Special Advisor" for "Green Jobs, Enterprise and Innovation," resigned when it was discovered that he supported a number of socialist policies. The Senate approval process might have turned up this concern much earlier.

Some of the high-profile Obama-appointed czars include the following:

- John Brennen, Assistant to the President for Homeland Security and Counterterrorism
- George Mitchell, Special Envoy to the Middle East
- Cameron Davis, Special Advisor to the EPA Administrator
- Paul Volcker, Chairman of the Economic Recovery Advisory Board
- Kenneth Feinberg, Special Master for TARP (Troubled Asset Relief Program) Executive Compensation
- Carol Browner, Assistant to the President for Energy and Climate Change
- Ed Montgomery, Director of Recovery for Auto Workers and Communities

Do you think that all high-level appointments made by the president should require congressional confirmation? Should czars be formally confirmed by the Senate just as all cabinet-level and many subcabinet-level appointments are? What accounts for the increased use of czars by Presidents George W. Bush and Barack Obama? Has the growth and increased complexity of the federal bureaucracy created an atmosphere wherein presidents need a special advisor to coordinate agencies in a specific problem area? Find the Politics InterActive link for details on czars in the federal government at www.cengage.com/dautrich/americangovernment/2e.

Chapter 8   The Federal Bureaucracy

Chapter Summary

★ What Is Bureaucracy?

- Though the term *bureaucracy* often conjures up negative images, the government could not function effectively without bureaucratic organizations.

- Most units in the vast federal bureaucracy are located within the executive branch of government, and most engage primarily in policy implementation. Such implementation begins with the development of regulations that guide employees of the agency in carrying out particular programs or services.

★ What Does the Federal Bureaucracy Do?

- Because Congress lacks technical expertise, it often gives agencies wide administrative discretion to decide how to implement laws. Sometimes Congress also delegates important programs to agencies because it wants to avoid thorny political issues.

- Congressional oversight of executive agencies may occur through legislative hearings or through the use of congressional agencies such as the CBO and GAO. Congress may threaten poorly performing agencies with reduced funding, a refusal to confirm appointments to the agency, or (in some extreme cases) the elimination of the agency altogether.

- Congress has placed judicial power in some bureaucratic agencies to help determine the rights and duties of parties within the scope of an agency's authority.

★ The Development of the Federal Bureaucracy

- The size of the federal bureaucracy exploded as the federal government played an increasingly active role in regulating the U.S. economy, overseeing new territories, and conducting overseas military operations. After FDR's New Deal was enacted during the 1930s, the federal government accounted for a sizeable portion of the nation's economy as a whole. The bureaucracy continued to expand in the 1960s and beyond to meet the needs of President Lyndon Johnson's Great Society program and to compete with the Soviet Union in the Cold War.

★ Getting Control of the Growing Bureaucracy

- Beginning in the 1980s, some administrations attempted to reduce the size of the federal bureaucracy through (1) the privatization of certain government-provided services, (2) the deregulation of some federal activities, (3) the devolution of various powers and responsibilities back to the states, and (4) efforts to promote greater bureaucratic accountability through initiatives such as the Government Performance and Results Act.

★ The Organization of the Federal Bureaucracy

- The federal bureaucracy is organized into fifteen Cabinet departments including the recently created Department of Homeland Security, numerous independent agencies that focus on a narrower scope of issues, regulatory agencies that implement rules and regulations of private conduct, government corporations, and the Executive Office of the President.

★ The Federal Workforce

- The federal workforce includes 8,000 presidential employees who received their positions through political patronage, a Senior Executive Service consisting of approximately 7,500 senior career professionals, and a vast number of civil service workers whose jobs are immune from partisan politics. Today most lower-level federal workers are hired through a merit system, rather than through the spoils systems that prevailed throughout much of the nineteenth and early twentieth centuries.

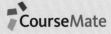

Key Terms

Administrative discretion (p. 234)
Administrative law (p. 234)
Bureaucracy (p. 230)
Bureaucratic adjudicating (p. 236)
Cabinet departments (p. 241)
Civil service (p. 250)
Civil Service Reform Act of 1978 (p. 251)
Congressional oversight (p. 236)
Delegation of congressional power (p. 234)

Deregulation (p. 239)
Devolution (p. 240)
Executive Office of the President (p. 249)
Federal Register (p. 234)
Government corporations (p. 248)
Hatch Act of 1939 (p. 251)
Independent agency (p. 246)
Merit system (p. 251)
Patronage (p. 250)

Pendleton Civil Service Reform Act (p. 251)
Policy implementation (p. 233)
Privatization (p. 239)
Regulations (p. 234)
Regulatory agency (p. 247)
Senior Executive Service (SES) (p. 249)
Spoils system (p. 250)

Resources

Important Books

Cook, Brian J. *Bureaucracy and Self-Government*. Baltimore: Johns Hopkins University Press, 1997.

Johnson, Ronald N., and Gary D. Libecap. *The Federal Civil Service System and the Problem of Bureaucracy*. Chicago: University of Chicago Press, 1994.

Neiman, Max. *Defending Government: Why Big Government Works*. Upper Saddle River, NJ: Prentice Hall, 2000.

Osborne, David, and Peter Plastrik. *Banishing Bureaucracy*. New York: Plume Books, 1997.

Stivers, Camilla, ed. *Democracy, Bureaucracy, and the Study of Administration*. Boulder, CO: Westview Press, 2001.

Wildavsky, Aaron. *The New Politics of the Budget Process*. 2nd ed. New York: HarperCollins, 1992.

Wilson, James Q. *Bureaucracy: What Government Agencies Do and Why They Do It*. New York: Basic Books, 1989.

Internet Sources

http://www.usa.gov/ (the U.S. government's official Web portal, this site provides links to all units and sub-units of the Executive Office of the President, the fifteen Cabinet departments, and most of the independent agencies, regulatory agencies, and corporations of the federal government)

NOW Judge Sonia Sotomayor, nominated to the U.S. Supreme Court, testifying at her Senate confirmation hearings in July 2009.

CHRISTY BOWE/CORBIS

THEN Solicitor General Thurgood Marshall, preparing to testify at his Supreme Court confirmation hearings in 1967.

AP PHOTO/JOHN ROUS

NOW & THEN

A Pathbreaking Appointment Offers a New Look—and Possibly a New Perspective—to High Court Deliberations

Demographically speaking, the U.S. Supreme Court has never been a truly representative judicial body. Eventually, presidents in the twentieth century made small inroads into promoting a more diverse Court, naming justices from different religions, for example. A racially and ethnically diverse Court, by contrast, took more time. Eventually a president recognized for his dedication to racial diversity in other facets of American politics took that cause to the high Court, nominating an individual who would become the first justice hailing from this significant racial minority. Though the president's opponents in the Senate would find other grounds for opposing the nominee, there would not be enough opposition to defeat the history-making appointment. And when the new justice was finally seated on the Court, the president would rightfully take credit for having moved the Court yet another step away from its more traditional all-white moorings.

LEARNING OBJECTIVES
★ WHAT YOU WILL LEARN ★

Types of Law

* ★ Compare different categories of law

The Structure of the U.S. Legal System

* ★ Recognize the role played by the fifty state judicial systems within the American system
* ★ Trace the development of the legal system

The Adversarial System of Justice

* ★ Contrast the inquisitorial system of justice with the adversarial system in the U.S.
* ★ Review the process by which a civil case proceeds from complaint to settlement or verdict
* ★ Understand the criminal justice system

Judicial Review and Its Implications

* ★ Define the power of judicial review

Limitations on Courts

* ★ Recognize the structural limitations on courts

Electing and Appointing Judges

* ★ Learn how state judges are selected
* ★ Learn how federal judges and Supreme Court justices are selected

How a Case Proceeds within the U.S. Supreme Court

* ★ Follow a Supreme Court case as it proceeds from writ of certiorari to final opinion

Why the Justices Vote the Way They Do

* ★ Examine the factors that influence judges

Current Debates over the Exercise of Judicial Power

* ★ Recognize some of the recurring debates about the proper role of courts

NOW & THEN

MARK WILSON/GETTY IMAGES NEWS/ GETTY IMAGES

NOW President Barack Obama's election as the nation's forty-fourth president broke perhaps the most visible racial barrier in American politics. Building on themes from his election campaign, Obama did not downplay the potential significance his own victory offered for race relations in America. And yet other racial barriers remained. Every session of the U.S. Supreme Court between 1967 and 2008 featured a bench made up of eight Caucasians and just one African American. While the Court included two Italian Americans (Antonin Scalia and Samuel Alito), Hispanics and Latinos, who together constitute the largest nonwhite ethnic group in the nation, remained unrepresented on the Court when Obama first took office.

President Obama dramatically altered that landscape when he nominated Judge Sonia Sotomayor, a woman of Puerto Rican descent, to the Supreme Court on May 26, 2009. Once confirmed, her appointment promised to diversify the high Court and gave Obama instant credibility with a large and powerful ethnic group. The road to Sotomayor's confirmation was rocky at times: Senate Republicans complained of comments she made about how the experiences of a "wise Latina woman" might help her reach better conclusions than a "white male who hasn't lived that life." But Sotomayor's strong academic pedigree, her extensive prosecutorial experience, and her seventeen years of judicial experience combined to secure the votes of every Senate Democrat and over twenty Senate Republicans, allowing her to coast to confirmation. Would Sotomayor's unique ethnic background give her a different perspective on the hardest cases? Debates over that question would be waged in the years to come.

THEN The thirty-sixth president of the United States, Lyndon Baines Johnson, was a product of the Texas hill country; as a young politician in the 1930s and 1940s, he cut his teeth on the rough-and-tumble, sometimes racist world of Texas politics. Few would have predicted that a politician hailing from that background would one day secure a legacy right next to Abraham Lincoln as the chief executive most responsible for advancing the cause of racial equality in America. Yet Johnson rightfully earned credit for shepherding civil rights and voting rights legislation through a Congress that had once seemed impregnable to such initiatives. With that legacy secure, President Johnson went a step further in 1967, appointing the African American solicitor general, Thurgood Marshall, to the all-white U.S. Supreme Court.

Marshall's credentials to become the first African American justice seemed impeccable: the former federal appeal judge made his name as a leading Supreme Court advocate on behalf of the NAACP, having successfully argued the landmark case of *Brown v. Board of Education*, among other cases. Eleven southern senators opposed Marshall's appointment by publicly emphasizing nonracial considerations: they claimed his addition to the Court would create a "built-in activist majority" that would favor criminal defendants at the expense of the public good. But Marshall's detractors were far outnumbered, and he coasted to confirmation by a 69–11 vote. Was Marshall's voting record as a Supreme Court justice for the next twenty-four years influenced by his race and background? On this one point, Marshall's enemies and supporters would both answer in the affirmative.

AP PHOTO

ecause justices serve for life, they are not normally accountable for judicial decisions rendered while on the bench. Their decisions are influenced by a number of factors: ideology, past experience as a jurist or in other government positions, and in all likelihood, the justice's personal characteristics and traits that help frame how he or she views a given set of facts or laws. Since the outset of the republic, presidents have pursued diversity for the high Court. During the nineteenth century the diversity they looked for was mostly geographical, as they sought representation for different regions; in the early part of the twentieth century, presidents sought to have different religions represented on the high Court. In recent decades presidents have occasionally emphasized ethnic and racial diversity as well. It may be impossible to prove that demographic traits and characteristics systematically affect the way a justice approaches a Supreme Court case, but presidents and senators clearly assume they will have some effect: otherwise, the emphasis on diversity would be for symbolic purposes only. No doubt Presidents Lyndon Johnson and Barack Obama thought their pathbreaking nominations of the first African American and Latina justices, respectively, would carry symbolic importance. But to cement their legacies in terms of actual judicial decision making, the two presidents and their supporters were no doubt hoping for more than just a symbolic effect.

Article III of the U.S. Constitution vests in the Supreme Court the power to decide legal cases or controversies that come before it. As one of the three primary branches of the federal government, the judiciary enjoys a special status in our constitutional system. Many scholars have suggested that courts enjoy heightened prestige over other actors in government as a result of their own conscious efforts to foster the perception that they somehow stand "above the political fray." The solemn formalities that pervade so many judicial proceedings conducted by "high priests of the law"—the black robes, the prohibition of cameras in the U.S. Supreme Court, and the general reluctance of judges to seek out publicity—contribute to a mythology about courts in general and to a "cult of the robe" that carries credence with many Americans.[1]

This chapter explores the nature of the federal judiciary and the specific role it plays in the U.S. political system by examining types of law and the manner in which the legal

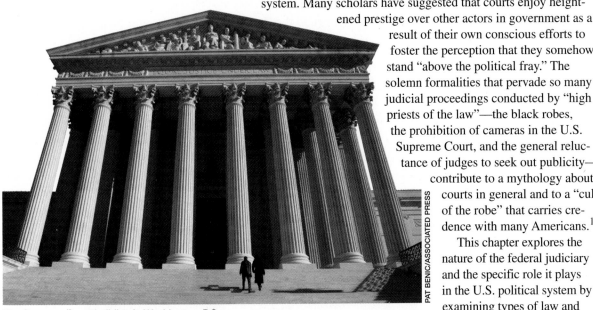

The Supreme Court building in Washington, DC.

PAT BENIC/ASSOCIATED PRESS

system in the United States is organized. It also explores the role state courts play in the political system and how individuals come to occupy all types of judgeships. The chapter then focuses on the U.S. Supreme Court more closely, with an eye toward learning how cases come to and are resolved by the nation's highest tribunal, and how that court is confronting some of the great issues of the day.

★ LO Compare different categories of law

Types of Law

The concept of law defies simple understanding. Although law is normally defined simply as "authoritative rules made by government," the philosopher John Locke argued that certain laws precede society and government. These natural laws are god-given, exist within human beings from the time they are born, and are intrinsic to the nature of individuals. Locke's notions of natural law (as distinguished from human-made or government-issued law) have influenced the legal systems of many nations, including the United States. Prior to the Civil War, opponents of slavery challenged its legitimacy with the claim that it ran counter to natural law. During the 1960s, civil rights advocates seeking to overhaul discriminatory practices presented similar arguments.

Still, even the foremost advocates of natural law concede that the rules imposed by sovereign governments enjoy some measure of legitimacy in most instances. Those rules and laws may be created and passed down in different ways. **Civil law** (also called "statutory law") refers to legislative codes, laws, or sets of rules that are enacted by authorized lawmaking bodies such as Congress, state and local legislatures, or any executive authority entrusted with the power to make laws.[2] **Common law** refers to judge-made law handed down through judicial opinions, which establish slowly evolving precedents over time. Many European legal systems, such as those in France, Germany, and Italy, are characterized as primarily "civil law systems" due to their extensive reliance on detailed legislative codes. The legal system in Britain, by contrast, is recognized as mainly a common law system. The modern U.S. legal system features a combination of these two approaches: although the common law held sway for most of the nation's history, legislatures in all fifty states and Congress during the past century have replaced many traditional common law rules with detailed legislative codes on a number of important topics, including commercial law, probate law, and various aspects of criminal law. Other categories of law include the following.

- Criminal law is the body of rules and regulations that declare what types of conduct constitute an "offense against society," and that prescribe the punishment to be imposed for those offenses. Criminal laws against murder, rape, and burglary can be found in almost any legal system. The body of noncriminal law—which includes the law of property, contracts, and other issues dealing with the private rights of citizens—is sometimes referred to as "civil law." (Be careful not to confuse references to "civil law" in this context with the "civil law" referenced earlier, which primarily concerns the enactment of statutes and codes.) Serious criminal offenses may lead to jail time; by contrast, those who violate noncriminal laws can be fined, but not imprisoned. Of course criminal law and civil law may touch on the same events—for example, a person alleged to have killed someone may be criminally prosecuted for murder and also separately sued in a "wrongful death action" for the same action. The two sets of proceedings are distinct and separate: The former football star and television personality O. J. Simpson was acquitted of criminal murder charges brought against him by the Los Angeles County district attorney, but subsequent civil suits were successfully brought against him by the victims' families.

- Constitutional law is the body of rules and judicial interpretations of rules found in the fundamental law of the nation or state, such as the Constitution of the United States. Normally constitutional law is considered "supreme" and overrides any statutes or executive decisions with which it comes into conflict.

- Administrative law is the body of rules, regulations, orders, and decisions issued by administrative agencies of a government, such as the Federal Trade Commission, the Environmental Protection Agency, or a state department of health.

- Public law, a term used more by academics than practitioners, refers to the laws and rules that govern disputes and issues involving the government directly acting in its official capacity. Constitutional, administrative, and criminal laws are all subcategories of the general rubric of public law.

- Private law refers to all parts of the law concerned with the definition, regulation, and enforcement of rights in cases where either (1) all the parties directly implicated are private individuals (such as a divorce settlement) or (2) the government is acting like any other private citizen when it sues or is being sued. For example, when a private person crashes his car into a government mail truck, the government's lawsuit against that person is usually a matter of private law rather than public law.

Significant overlap exists among all these categories of law. Knowing something about the different types of law is useful in helping to understand courts and the functions they serve in the American political system.

Civil law

This term has two meanings: (1) legislative codes, laws, or sets of rules enacted by duly authorized lawmaking bodies such as Congress, state and local legislatures, or any executive authority entrusted with the power to make laws; (2) the body of noncriminal laws of a nation or state that deal with the rights of private citizens.

Common law

Judge-made law handed down through judicial opinions, which over time establish precedents.

The Structure of the U.S. Legal System

Every court occupies a unique position within the larger hierarchy of state and federal courts. As a result, each court performs a variety of specific roles dictated by where it happens to be situated within the larger court structure.

★ LO   Recognize the role played by the fifty state judicial systems within the American system

State Legal Systems and State Courts

Most criminal and civil law matters in the United States first find their way into one of the fifty states' legal systems. Together, the state governments process nearly 35 million cases per year, more than 95 percent of the nation's litigation. About a third of the cases in state legal systems involve criminal matters. Each state system features its own unique characteristics and different nuances, an outgrowth of the states' different historical origins and significant population differences. Still, some common elements exist across all states.

Every state maintains trial courts, which do the bulk of work processing cases at the lower levels of the state legal system. These trial courts (often called "district courts" or "circuit courts" depending on the state or locality) may hear appeals from subordinate courts such as traffic courts; they also serve as sites for trials of more significant crimes. Thirty-nine of the fifty states have intermediate appellate courts, to which all appeals from trial courts must first be directed. All fifty states maintain at least one high Supreme Court. (Texas and Oklahoma have separate supreme courts for criminal and civil cases.) State supreme courts (or their equivalent of a different name) generally provide the final source of appeal for each state legal system.[3] To appeal beyond the state supreme court directly to the U.S. Supreme Court, a losing party must first exhaust all the remedies available at the state level, including losing his or her case at the state system's court of final appeal. He or she must also demonstrate there is a federal question at issue, whether based on the interpretation of a federal statute or of the U.S. Constitution.

In theory, state courts must comply with pronouncements from the U.S. Supreme Court over the meaning of the federal Constitution. The reality is much more complicated. During various periods of American history, rebellious state courts tried to evade certain Supreme Court pronouncements by distinguishing or limiting the Supreme Court ruling, and on occasion even by denying the Supreme Court's jurisdiction over the matter. The Virginia Supreme Court resisted various pronouncements of the U.S. Supreme Court in the early part of the nineteenth century; more than a

FIGURE 9.1
Common Features of a State Court System

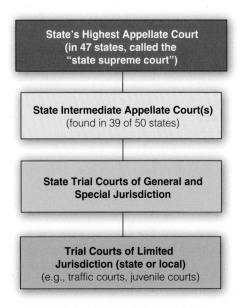

State's Highest Appellate Court (in 47 states, called the "state supreme court")

State Intermediate Appellate Court(s) (found in 39 of 50 states)

State Trial Courts of General and Special Jurisdiction

Trial Courts of Limited Jurisdiction (state or local) (e.g., traffic courts, juvenile courts)

century later, state courts sometimes ignored U.S. Supreme Court decisions protecting the accused. Although the Supreme Court can usually exert its will over defiant state courts, it must be willing to expend key institutional resources and prestige to do so.

Development of the Federal Court System

Trace the development of the legal system

Article III of the Constitution establishes a Supreme Court and any "inferior courts" that Congress may wish to create. Accordingly, Congress provided at the nation's outset for the creation of district and circuit courts, the latter of which bear little resemblance to modern circuit courts. Specifically, these early federal circuit courts were staffed by Supreme Court justices and district court judges, and they performed both trial and appellate functions. Thus in addition to their formal duties on the high court, Supreme Court justices in the early days of the Republic were also required to "ride circuit," traveling to their assigned circuits on a regular basis. (This practice formally ended when Congress reestablished the U.S. Courts of Appeals in 1891.)

During the nation's early history, the Supreme Court was seen as a weak third branch of government, with limited enforcement powers. With his ruling in *Marbury v. Madison* (1803),[4] Chief Justice John Marshall established the Court's power to review all acts of Congress for their constitutionality; even so, during Marshall's thirty-four-year reign as chief justice the Court struck down just one act of Congress as unconstitutional.

The Constitution makes no reference to the specific size of the Supreme Court. Thus Congress during the eighteenth and nineteenth centuries altered the size of the Court to consist of one chief justice and anywhere from five to nine associate justices serving on the Court at one time. Occasionally the issue of Court size comes up as a matter of strategic politics: In 1937 President Franklin Delano Roosevelt's ill-fated plan to expand the size of the Court (to up to fifteen members depending on the age of the sitting justices) was driven by the president's desire to appoint new justices who would support his New Deal program. Yet even some of President Roosevelt's own Democratic supporters opposed the plan. Since 1869 the Court's composition of nine members (one chief justice and eight associate justices) has remained essentially unchanged. Meanwhile, Congress has been active in creating, disbanding, and modifying the number of other judges that serve throughout the federal court system.

Cases today begin in the federal court system, rather than the state court system, only when they fit into one of three categories: (1) the lawsuit requires interpretation of the U.S. Constitution, a federal law, or a treaty of the United States; (2) the federal government is suing or prosecuting someone, or is itself being sued; or (3) the lawsuit is between two citizens of different states suing for an amount of more than $75,000. Many of the highest-profile legal cases in recent years became federal cases because they featured defendants accused of committing federal crimes. Included on this list are the trial of Oklahoma City bomber Timothy McVeigh and the prosecution of some of the terrorists involved (directly or indirectly) in the attacks of September 11, 2001. In recent decades Congress has become increasingly active in passing legislation to declare new federal crimes. Thus carjacking, the sale or possession of many types of illegal drugs, money laundering, and various other offenses are now considered federal crimes, and defendants who commit such offenses may face prosecution in federal courts.

The federal judicial system today also features a number of specialized courts, including tax courts, bankruptcy courts, and military courts. Most parties to a federal case start out in one of the ninety-four federal district courts located throughout the country. Federal district court judges have original jurisdiction (the power to rule in the first instance) over criminal and civil trials, and along with federal magistrates, they provide the initial sources of potential legal relief available in the federal judicial system.

FIGURE 9.2 The Federal Court System*

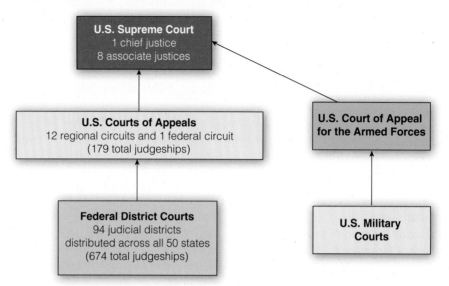

*Chart does not include specialized courts including courts of international trade, tax courts, claims courts, etc.

After the federal district court has rendered its judgment, appeal is available to one of thirteen federal appeals courts (also referred to as "circuit courts of appeals") across the country. With some exceptions, federal appeals are normally decided by a panel of three judges selected at random from the pool of ten or more judges authorized to serve on that court. In some cases, litigants can appeal from the three-judge panel to the full circuit court—this type of hearing is called "en banc." Because the San Francisco–based Ninth Circuit maintains a roster of forty-seven judges (spread out from Hawaii and California in the west, to Arizona, Nevada, Montana, and Idaho in the east), the phrase "en banc" on that court refers to eleven-judge panels that perform essentially the same function as en banc panels in other circuits.[5]

Litigants who receive an adverse judgment in the federal appeals court and wish to be heard in the U.S. Supreme Court may petition for a *writ of certiorari*, which is the pleading a losing party files with the Supreme Court asking it to review the decision of a lower court. Currently the Supreme Court enjoys near absolute discretion over its docket, and so it remains a long shot (less than 3 percent) that it will even grant the writ of certiorari in the first place.

Petitioning the U.S. Supreme Court for review is the final option available to state court litigants who suffer adverse decisions in the highest state court, and to federal court litigants who suffer adverse decisions after exhausting all forms of appeal in the federal court system. In a normal year, approximately half of the cases heard by the Supreme Court come from federal appellate courts and the other half from the fifty state court systems.

★ LO Contrast the inquisitorial system of justice with the adversarial system in the U.S.

The Adversarial System of Justice

Some European legal systems are based on an *inquisitorial system* of justice, in which judges, working on behalf of the government, are responsible for gathering information relevant to the disposition of a particular case. For example, in France—which adheres to the inquisitorial model—judges may initiate a criminal investigation against an individual, commission experts to investigate and report on special aspects of the crime, and even call witnesses and question them intensely.

By contrast, the American legal system is primarily an *adversarial system* of justice, in which opposing parties contend against each other for a result favorable to themselves. In jury trials judges act merely as independent referees overseeing the contest; in so-called bench trials where no jury is present, judges must still remain objective arbiters as they prepare to make final decisions on the merits.[6] In an adversarial system, the judge is entrusted only with ensuring that the litigants achieve procedural fairness and plays no active role in evidence gathering or in the advocacy of one side over the other. Supporters of this system contend that adversarial proceedings pitting zealous representatives of parties against one another offer the best prospect of allowing the judge or jury to determine the truth. Critics counter that inquisitorial systems tend to be free of the many strategic "maneuvers" parties so frequently practice in U.S. courtrooms, such as the withholding of crucial evidence or the presentation of evidence that bears only a minimal relationship to the actual facts at issue.

Elements of Civil Litigation

Countless disputes among individuals or entities are resolved quietly, long before the threat to litigate is even invoked. Still, whenever one private party contests another over the definition or enforcement of certain legal rights or the legal relationship that may exist between them, the disagreement may wind up in the form of a lawsuit brought before a judge in a court of law. Any such judicial contest, including all the events that lead up to a possible court event, is referred to as **litigation**. Although the procedural rules governing such private disputes vary widely from state to state and system to system, some elements of civil litigation are common among all systems. Normally the complaining party who chooses to initiate formal legal proceedings (usually called the **plaintiff**) does so by filing a **complaint**, which is a written document justifying why the court is empowered to hear the case and explaining why the plaintiff is entitled to some form of relief (usually an amount of money) under the current law. The target of the complaint, the **defendant**, normally must respond to the complaint with a formal written defense, in which he or she either admits to or denies what the plaintiff has said.

If the defendant convinces the judge either that the court has no power to hear the case (perhaps it was filed in the wrong court) or that there is no law that provides a remedy to the plaintiff, the case may be dismissed. If the defendant's argument is unsuccessful, the case then moves forward to the stage of pretrial litigation normally referred to as **discovery**. During discovery, each side has the right to find out what information the other side has about the case by requesting documents or materials, access to property, and/or examinations, or by offering answers to questions about the litigation either in written form or verbally at a deposition. Although the judge may play some role in supervising discovery at pretrial conferences, almost all such discovery occurs outside of the courtroom. Following the discovery stage of the proceedings, each side may file new written documents to the court contending that it now has overwhelming evidence in its favor or that the other side has discovered no evidence to prove its own contentions.

The vast majority of civil disputes never make it to trial. In some cases, one party may succeed in convincing the judge that no trial is necessary and that the judge should rule in that

A jury listens to an attorney present her case.

BOB DAEMMRICH/PHOTOEDIT

Litigation
Any judicial contest, including all the events that lead up to a possible court event.

Plaintiff
The party that chooses to initiate formal legal proceedings in a civil case.

Complaint
A document written by the plaintiff arguing why the court is empowered to hear the case and explaining why the plaintiff is entitled to some form of relief under the current law.

★ LO

Review the process by which a civil case proceeds from complaint to settlement or verdict

Defendant
The target of a plaintiff's complaint.

Discovery
A stage of pretrial litigation in which the plaintiff and defendant have the right to learn what information the other side has about the case by requesting documents or materials, access to property, and/or examinations, or by offering answers to questions about the litigation either in written form or verbally at a deposition.

party's favor immediately. Far more often, the sides agree to a legally binding "settlement" of claims made against each other, in which one side pays money to the other side, or agrees to cease and desist a certain practice in order to avoid the costs and uncertainties of trial. In civil litigation, judges often play an active role in encouraging the two parties to settle their differences out of court, saving resources for them and the judicial branch that would have been wasted in a long, drawn-out trial.

In some instances, the parties are not able to reach an out-of-court settlement, and a formal trial becomes necessary. In a "bench trial," the parties present evidence to a judge, rather than a jury of citizens. A jury trial usually takes far longer than a bench trial because of the many procedures required to prevent undue prejudice of the jury. Even if a jury trial is necessary, the judge still plays a role in the courtroom by ensuring that the jury is properly selected and that fair procedures are adhered to during the trial. One of the most crucial roles played by a judge in either type of trial is to rule on the admissibility of evidence that may be used to reach a decision. Only relevant evidence, which logically tends to prove or disprove a disputed fact, may be admitted into the trial proceedings. In civil cases, the complaining party is obligated to prove its allegations by a "preponderance of the evidence," which is generally thought to be anything greater than 50 percent. Although there is widespread disagreement on what this standard exactly means, it is clearly well below the high standard imposed on prosecutors in criminal cases to prove guilt "beyond a reasonable doubt."

Once the judge or jury has reached a final decision on the case, normally called the "verdict" in the case of a jury trial or the "judgment" in a bench trial, and the judge or jury has settled on a monetary amount to be awarded, the trial stage of the process comes to an end. Some posttrial motions may be available, and a dissatisfied party is also free to appeal the decision to a higher court.

The Criminal Justice System at Work

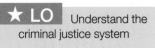

★ LO   Understand the criminal justice system

Although the rules of criminal procedure also vary widely, most criminal prosecutions begin with the arrest of a suspect by some law enforcement official at the federal, state, or local level. Once the suspect is formally accused, he or she is also referred to as the "defendant." Because some criminal charges may be later revealed as groundless or unsubstantiated, the government must quickly demonstrate in one of two ways that the charges against the defendant are valid. Some prosecutors elect to present initial evidence at a preliminary hearing held before a magistrate or trial judge, where they must demonstrate that there is probable cause to proceed to trial against the suspect. Far more often the prosecutor convenes a **grand jury**, whose duty it is to receive complaints, hear the evidence offered by the prosecutor, and determine whether a trial is justified. Grand juries comprise a greater number of jurors than an ordinary trial jury. Unlike regular juries, which hear only one case, grand juries may be asked to hear evidence on numerous cases over a period of several weeks or even months. Because the grand jury process is supervised entirely by the prosecutor, he or she maintains a distinct advantage—some say a prosecutor could get the grand jury to "indict a bologna sandwich." In the overwhelming majority of cases, the grand jury does indeed return a bill of **indictment** authorizing the government to proceed to trial against the defendant.

Whereas discovery is far-ranging and extensive in civil litigation, it is far more limited in criminal trials. Defense attorneys are usually under little or no obligation to provide any evidence at all to prosecutors; as a general matter, prosecutors are under an obligation to provide defense attorneys only with evidence that tends to "clear" the accused from alleged fault or guilt, although some states and localities provide additional discovery rights to the accused.

Most criminal prosecutions in the United States are resolved through a negotiated **plea bargain** between the defendant and the prosecutor.[7] Indeed, over 90 percent of convictions are the direct product of negotiated plea bargains. Many defendants seek to reduce their jail sentences by entering plea agreements that lead to lesser

Grand jury
A jury whose duty it is to hear the evidence offered by a prosecutor and determine whether a trial is justified.

Indictment
A decision by a grand jury authorizing the government to proceed to trial against the defendant.

Plea bargain
A pretrial negotiated resolution in a criminal case in which the defendants seek to reduce their jail sentences by pleading guilty and in return prosecutors are willing to trade down the severity of the punishment.

punishments. Much of the negotiation that occurs between prosecutors and defense attorneys is over the appropriate charges that will be formally filed, as most courts have adopted the equivalent of "going rates" for particular crimes.[8] Prosecutors willingly trade down penalties for crimes either because they are seeking that defendant's cooperation at another trial or because they wish to avoid the uncertainty and huge expenditure of resources that come with a trial.

In criminal cases that do go to trial, the burden rests squarely on the prosecutor to prove that the defendant committed the crime "beyond a reasonable doubt." Defendants, by contrast, do not have to prove their innocence. Unless a defendant waives the right to a jury trial, she or he must be tried by a jury of peers. State courts require anywhere between six and twelve jurors, whereas the federal court system require twelve jurors in all cases where a jury is present. Defendants, shielded by the Fifth Amendment privilege against self-incrimination, are under no obligation to testify. Numerous other constitutional safeguards are available to the defendant, including the right to a public and speedy trial and the right to directly confront witnesses. If the jury renders a "not guilty" verdict, the double jeopardy clause of the Fifth Amendment generally forbids the government from trying the defendant again for the same crime. A defendant who is convicted has a constitutional right to appeal the conviction or the resulting sentence to a higher court.

Although the burdens at trial appear to favor the accused, prosecutors generally have the benefit of experience in prosecuting many other defendants in the same court and can draw on a relatively large pool of resources (such as government investigators or medical examiners) to aid them in securing a conviction.

The Sixth Amendment has been interpreted to guarantee each indigent defendant the right to a government-provided lawyer in any instance where they face the possibility of jail time. Unfortunately, many public defenders' offices are overworked and underfunded, placing defendants at a relative disadvantage. By comparison, wealthy or well-connected defendants who do enjoy access to top legal talent and other resources at trial often fare much better. For example, in 1995 former pro football star O. J. Simpson was acquitted of charges of murdering his wife and a male friend of hers, thanks in no small part to the efforts of some of the nation's most well-known and highly regarded lawyers (nicknamed "the Dream Team" at that time by reporters). Clearly the American legal system does not always offer the same types of outcomes to those who are not similarly situated or well connected. For the vast majority of defendants, "justice" in the courtroom is meted out at lightning speed, with judges and prosecutors running through multiple criminal trials in a matter of hours with little opportunity to understand all the facts of a particular case. Public defenders only rarely have the chance to contest these trials with witnesses and evidence, lest they ignore all the other defendants under their charge. In sum, the picture of drama-filled trials seen so often on television or in the movies hardly depicts the reality of what goes on in this nation's criminal courtrooms.

Judicial Review and Its Implications

Define the power of judicial review

Courts in general, and judges in particular, serve in a variety of capacities: supervising the disposition of legal controversies between private parties, overseeing preliminary hearings or trials of criminal defendants, and ruling on important issues concerning the procedures to be followed or the evidence to be introduced at trial. Indeed, the role many judges play as "independent magistrates" is fundamental to the effective functioning of the American legal system. But courts and judges also play a significant and far-reaching role in overseeing the operations of the other branches of government, both by supervising conflicts between those branches and by protecting citizens against government action that may violate the Constitution.

This judicial authority has been magnified by the general recognition that American courts enjoy the added power of **judicial review**, by which they may declare acts of the other branches of the federal or state governments unconstitutional and

Judicial review
The power of a court to declare acts of the other branches of government or of a subordinate government to be unconstitutional and thus invalid.

Criminal Defense Attorneys as Heroes of the American Cinema

Few real-life criminal defense attorneys are likely to win popularity contests any time soon: after all, within the criminal justice system, they are the ones normally responsible for helping criminal defendants escape jail on technicalities. Yet when the public goes to the movies, the heroic image of the criminal defense attorney tends to predominate. In numerous Oscar-winning performances, the criminal defense attorney is the one who fights for a heroic cause (his or her factually innocent defendant) against the evil government prosecutors and lying witnesses who are seeking victory at all costs. The most famous of these cinematic attorneys was the character of Atticus Finch (played by Gregory Peck), who defended an innocent African American defendant in a racist Southern town in *To Kill a Mockingbird* (1962). Other defense attorneys followed in Atticus Finch's footsteps on the big screen, including Jake Brigance (played by Matthew McConaughey) in *A Time to Kill* (1996) and the irrepressible Vinny Gambini (played by Joe Pesci) in *My Cousin Vinny* (1992).

Actor Gregory Peck as Atticus Finch in *To Kill a Mockingbird*.

UNIVERSAL STUDIOS/GETTY IMAGES

Joe Pesci as Vinny Gambini in *My Cousin Vinny*.

BUREAU L.A. COLLECTION/CORBIS

For Critical Thinking and Discussion

1. Are criminal defense attorneys unfairly celebrated on the big screen?

2. Can you think of any examples in which a criminal defense attorney was not afforded heroic status in a full-length movie feature?

3. Why do you think popular culture tends to so often boil the criminal justice system down to a simple battle between good (defense attorneys) and evil? Are there any dangers to this pattern?

thus invalid. This dimension of judicial authority is not mentioned anywhere in the U.S. Constitution. Although Article VI of the Constitution declares the Constitution of the United States to be the "supreme law of the land . . . anything in the Constitution or laws of any state to the contrary notwithstanding," nowhere does the document explicitly vest any specific court (including the U.S. Supreme Court) with the authority to determine whether state laws are unconstitutional. Nor does the Constitution authorize the Supreme Court to serve as the authoritative interpreter of the document over the president, Congress, and other federal officials, all of whom are equally sworn to uphold the Constitution. In fact, scholars of the early constitutional period believe the drafters of the Constitution were unable to reach any consensus at all on this issue. How then did the power of judicial review arise?

The power of the Supreme Court to exercise judicial review was first established by the fourth chief justice of the United States, John Marshall, in the highly controversial case of *Marbury v. Madison* (1803).[9] With Thomas Jefferson's victory in the presidential election of 1800 and the Jeffersonian Republicans' rise to power in both houses of Congress the following year, nearly all of the nation's most powerful Federalists, including John Adams, Alexander Hamilton, and John Jay, were soon to be relegated to outsider status in the federal government. In his final hours as president, however, Adams appointed sixteen circuit court judges and forty-two new justices of the peace for the District of Columbia (all loyal Federalists); these positions were fully authorized by the Congress, and each of the individuals chosen for the posts was confirmed by the lame-duck Federalist Congress that remained loyal to Adams. President Adams also named John Marshall as chief justice of the United States. Although surrounded by partisan opposition in Washington, Marshall made the Supreme Court into the Federalist Party's beachhead, from which that party's judicial holdovers, enjoying the benefit of life tenure, could continue to espouse their vision of a powerful central government.

Immediately after Thomas Jefferson and his secretary of state James Madison formally took office in March 1801, they learned that several of the commissions for the new justices of the peace appointed by Adams had never been delivered—including one for William Marbury. When Jefferson ordered Madison to withhold the commissions, Marbury asked the Supreme Court to issue a *writ of mandamus*, a judicial order commanding an official (in this case, Madison) to perform a ministerial duty over which his discretion is limited (namely, the formal delivery of a duly signed and sealed commission). As authority for the Supreme Court's power to issue such a writ, Marbury cited the Judiciary Act of 1789, which appeared to give the U.S. Supreme Court exactly that authority.

Marbury was seeking to have the Supreme Court decide the case immediately, without first having to suffer a loss in a lower court. Because Chief Justice Marshall was an ardent Federalist, Marbury further assumed the Court would be sympathetic to his plight. In truth, it was Marshall who was really at fault in the case—as Adams's secretary of state, he had failed to properly mail the commission. Indeed, given his intimate knowledge of the facts, Marshall should have recused himself from the case, refusing to participate as a judge in the first place. Yet Marshall's Supreme Court rejected Marbury's request. Recognizing the tense political situation that surrounded the case—and all too aware that Jefferson might not abide by court order—Marshall lambasted the Jefferson administration for its refusal to perform their statutorily mandated duty, but denied that the Supreme Court possessed the power to issue the writ as requested.

Why the refusal to help his fellow Federalist? Marshall acknowledged that the 1789 law did in fact authorize the Court to issue such a writ in "original jurisdiction." But, Marshall ruled, that law was in explicit violation of Article III, Section 2, Clause 2, which did not specifically list "writs of mandamus" among the types of cases over which the Supreme Court had original jurisdiction. Nor could Congress extend the Court's original jurisdiction by mere statute. Thus, Marshall decided, the 1789 law was repugnant to the Constitution and was therefore null and void. With

Five of the Most Famous Twentieth-Century Trials

✔ **The Sacco-Vanzetti Trial (1921)**—The trial of two Italian anarchists for the murders of a local paymaster and his bodyguard sharply divided the public. Many thought two innocent men were being scapegoated in order to issue a more general warning against rising anarchist sentiment in the United States after World War I; others felt the trial of these two murderers had been fairly conducted in every respect. Both men were executed in 1927, six years after their convictions.

✔ **The Scopes "Monkey" Trial (1925)**—The prosecution of a high school biology teacher (John Scopes) for violating a state law that prohibited the teaching of evolution theory to students encapsulated a larger showdown being waged across the country between traditionalist forces grasping for the values of the past and modernists encouraging intellectual experimentation in education and elsewhere. The trial's carnival atmosphere (featuring lemonade stands outside the courtroom and chimpanzees performing in side shows) did not help Scopes—he was ultimately convicted and fined $100 by the court. Scopes's ordeal was eventually immortalized in the play *Inherit the Wind* (it also became a popular 1960 movie). The issue of whether public school teachers should teach evolution, creationism, or both continues to be a matter of debate in American politics today.

✔ **The "Lindbergh Baby" Trial (1935)**—The trial of German-born Bruno Hauptmann, accused of kidnapping the child of aviator Charles Lindbergh, seized the attention of the nation during the Great Depression. The trial raged on for a month as nearly 162 witnesses were called before a courtroom packed with such celebrity observers as writer Walter Winchell and entertainer Jack Benny. The jury returned a guilty verdict against Hauptmann after less than twelve hours of deliberation. A year after the verdict, Hauptmann was executed by electrocution.

✔ **The Rosenbergs Trial (1951)**—With the Cold War raging between the United States and the Soviet Union and the American public's fear of Communists on the rise, the trial of Julius and Ethel Rosenberg for conspiracy to commit espionage was certain to draw intense national attention. Although both defendants had been members of the Communist Party in the 1950s, evidence of espionage existed only against Julius; prosecutors charged his wife Ethel on much weaker evidentiary grounds in hopes of convincing her husband to talk. In fact, neither defendant ever confessed, and both were convicted and sentenced to death in the electric chair. The sentences were carried out in 1953.

✔ **The O. J. Simpson Murder Trial (1995)**—The investigation and trial of former football star O. J. Simpson for the murders of his wife, Nicole, and her friend Ronald Goldman provided the nation with an especially gripping drama that played out in the courtroom and on television over many months. What writer Dominick Dunne termed "the Super Bowl of all murder trials" pitted an all-star cast of defense attorneys (including F. Lee Bailey and Alan Dershowitz) against a Los Angeles District Attorney's office determined that Simpson not receive special treatment for his celebrity status. After a series of prosecution gaffes, including the infamous "glove incident" (paraded before the jury, Simpson was unable to fit on his hand the glove he allegedly wore the night of the murder), the celebrity defendant was ultimately acquitted on all charges. Months later, at a civil trial initiated by the families of the victims, Simpson was found "responsible" for the murders and was ordered to pay $33.5 million for his actions.

this decision, Marshall seized for the Court a power of judicial review over congressional laws that is unmentioned in the Constitution. The Supreme Court exercised this power only once more before the Civil War, although it has struck down well over 150 acts of Congress since then.

Two rulings more than a decade later further established the Supreme Court's authority in interpreting the Constitution. In *McCulloch v. Maryland* (1819),[10] the Court upheld the constitutionality of the Bank of the United States, thereby establishing the precedent that congressional power extends beyond those powers specifically listed in Article I of the Constitution. In *Martin v. Hunter's Lessee* (1816),[11] the Supreme Court ruled that the power of federal courts to review government actions for their constitutionality was not just applicable to other federal institutions; the supremacy clause ("The Constitution . . . shall be the Supreme Law of the Land") meant that the Supreme Court could also invalidate any actions of state governments that it believed to be in conflict with the U.S. Constitution. During his thirty-four years as chief justice, Marshall wrote 519 opinions, many of which remain influential commentary on constitutional power and authority. Under Marshall's leadership, the Court consistently rejected claims of state sovereignty that conflicted with federal interests. It was the special duty of the Supreme Court, Marshall believed, to make difficult judgments on the Constitution that either limited or affirmed the exercise of federal authority. In doing so, Marshall's court defined a strong role for the federal government, which was more clearly realized beginning in the twentieth century.

© 2012 CENGAGE LEARNING

In the two centuries since Marshall served as chief justice, the Supreme Court has invalidated more than 1,200 state laws. In 1958, it once again reaffirmed the principle of judicial supremacy in *Cooper v. Aaron*[12] in response to official defiance of a lower court's desegregation rulings: governors and state legislatures were bound to uphold decisions of the Supreme Court just as they were bound by oath to uphold the Constitution.

At times the exercise of judicial review has been extremely controversial. For example, the Supreme Court in *Dred Scott v. Sandford* (1857)[13] ruled that slaves were forever the property of their owners, even when they are brought temporarily into free states. The decision overturned a congressional law regulating the extension of slavery in the territories and may have helped to precipitate the Civil War four years later. During the Great Depression, the Supreme Court's rulings that many of FDR's New Deal proposals were unconstitutional instigated another constitutional crisis. Despite the uncertain beginnings that led to this practice and the tense moments in the nation's history that it has given rise to, judicial review of federal and state laws has become an unchallenged dimension of judicial power within the U.S. political system.

POOL/GETTY IMAGES

Former football star O. J. Simpson (left) confers with his "dream team" of high-priced legal talent at his murder trial in 1995.

Limitations on Courts

In Federalist No. 78, Alexander Hamilton deemed the judiciary "the least dangerous" branch because it had "no influence over either the sword or the purse . . . and can take no active resolution whatsoever." Despite Hamilton's opinion, courts have played a critically influential role in the American political system. When the Supreme Court aggressively interposes itself between aggrieved citizens and the government, as it did when it ordered desegregation of public schools in *Brown v. Board of Education* (1954),[14] or when it helps resolve some great political crisis, as it did when it ordered President Richard Nixon to hand over controversial tapes of White House conversations in *United States v. Nixon* (1974),[15] the judiciary appears more like an all-powerful branch than one that is weak and inconsequential.

The power of American courts is great, but the method by which courts participate in the political system is far more circumscribed than that of the other two branches. The limitations that courts must adhere to include the following:

1. **Courts cannot initiate or maintain lawsuits.** Unlike legislatures, which can propose and pass bills on their own initiative, judges in the United States cannot decide issues that are not currently before them in a legitimately filed lawsuit. If none of the actors in a controversy elect to involve the courts directly, the court has no role whatsoever in resolution of the conflict.

2. **Courts can hear only those lawsuits that constitute true "cases" or "controversies."** Article III imposes on the Supreme Court and all federal courts the same type of limitation that applies to nearly all other courts: judges may hear and resolve only those lawsuits that amount to legitimate "cases" or "controversies" and must ignore mere "hypothetical" or "theoretical" conflicts. Although most of these terms are fuzzy enough to give courts room to maneuver, in practice courts tend to refuse to decide lawsuits that are moot (that is, it is too late to provide any effective remedy), including lawsuits involving affirmative action programs and policies brought against educational institutions by applicants who have since enrolled in (and in many cases, graduated from) another institution. Courts are equally reluctant to decide cases that are not yet ripe (that is, the actual conflict is still sometime in the future). Accordingly, courts normally refuse to provide executives with what amounts to "legal advice" about future controversies that have not yet occurred. Courts similarly refuse to hear cases that were contrived by the parties in the form of collusion, or cases in which jurisdiction has not been properly invoked.

   The courts have also maintained a long-standing tradition of refusing to decide cases where the Constitution has explicitly entrusted the issue to be decided by one of the other branches of government; such issues are generally referred to as "political questions." Of course when attempting to justify its refusal to take on a political question, the court often engages in such extensive analysis of the underlying issues that it is hard to distinguish those opinions from analysis of the merits of the case itself. For example, in *Nixon v. United States* (2003),[16] the Supreme Court explained its refusal to reconsider the Senate's process of trying the impeachment of a federal judge, Walter Nixon, by issuing a lengthy opinion that reviewed in considerable detail the constitutional provisions entrusting the Senate with the "sole power" of trying impeachments. Related to the "case or controversy" rule is a requirement that courts impose on the parties themselves: courts will hear lawsuits only from parties that have proper **standing**, meaning that they are "uniquely" and "singularly affected" by the controversy. For example, courts usually reject lawsuits brought by individuals who are frustrated with the allotment of their tax dollars, because those individuals are not "singularly affected." Nor are individuals with a mere academic or political concern in a conflict allowed in court as parties to a case unless they have suffered some unique economic or physical burden related to the issue being decided. In the mid-twentieth century, Congress and many state legislatures have loosened these

Standing
The requirement that a party must be uniquely or singularly affected by a controversy in order to be eligible to file a lawsuit.

harsh standing requirements by authorizing lawsuits brought by large numbers of people with clearly defined common interests. Such **class action lawsuits** can proceed through the legal system even when not every member of the class has formally signed on. High-visibility class action lawsuits in recent years include those brought by tobacco users across the country and those by people who have suffered from the effects of asbestos.

3. **Courts must rely on other branches for enforcement.** Unlike the other branches of government, courts rely on other political institutions to put their opinions or orders into direct effect—police officers, marshals, and executive branch officers, among others, must carry out the courts' mandates. Whereas Congress can cut off funding to executive agencies that ignore its dictates, no similar tool is available to the judiciary. In the vast majority of instances, disobedience of the court is not in question. Yet when a court makes a controversial pronouncement, officials may be reluctant to adhere to the court's decision. In some rare cases, a court's decisions may be met with outright disobedience. Sometimes even courts may react negatively to another court's rulings: In July 2001, Chief Justice Roy Moore of the Alabama Supreme Court authorized the installation of a monument to the Ten Commandments in the Alabama state judicial building. Even after a federal district court ruled that the monument violated the separation of church and state, Moore refused to remove it; more than two years after installation of the monument, Moore was removed from office for defying the federal court's order.

In 1832, President Andrew Jackson declined to enforce the Supreme Court's decision in *Worcester v. Georgia*,[17] which ordered that a white Christian missionary be freed from a Georgia prison. Chief Justice Marshall had ruled that the Georgia law imprisoning the missionary for residing on Cherokee Indian property without permission violated a U.S.–Cherokee treaty; yet President Jackson declared—perhaps apocryphally—that "John Marshall has made his decision . . . now let him enforce it." (The missionary served his entire four-year mission in jail.) Sometimes even popular Supreme Court decisions face the threat of resistance. President Richard Nixon considered refusing to comply with the Supreme Court's 1974 decision in *United States v. Nixon* ordering him to hand over the secret tapes he made of conversations in the Oval Office.[18]

Controversial Supreme Court decisions in the 1950s and 1960s occasionally led to significant resistance on the part of ordinary citizens as well.[19] The landmark decisions in *Brown v. Board of Education*,[20] which first held that segregated public schools violated the equal protection clause and then commanded that public schools be desegregated "with all deliberate speed," met with violent reaction in the South. Ultimately President Dwight Eisenhower sent U.S. marshals to the South to enforce the desegregation decrees; otherwise, there might have been even greater resistance to the Court's controversial decisions. The Supreme Court's 1962 decision invalidating school-sponsored religious prayer in public schools (*Engel v. Vitale*[21]) goes ignored in many parts of this country even today—in one instance, a federal district court in Alabama was forced to prohibit prayer in public schools throughout the state in response to reports of widespread defiance.

In addition to these limitations, courts must also adhere to limitations that arise from the constitutional or statutory law. For example, Congress can by statute alter the Supreme Court's **appellate jurisdiction**, which is the power to review prior decisions handed down by state and lower federal courts. Thus Congress could in theory declare that federal courts as a whole are not empowered to hear abortion cases. In fact, foes of the Supreme Court's abortion decisions proposed just such a bill in the 1980s, but it was never passed. However, Congress cannot alter the Court's **original jurisdiction**, which is the power to hear a lawsuit at the outset. Article III authorizes the Court's original jurisdiction in cases involving ambassadors and cases in which states are the only parties.

© 2012 CENGAGE LEARNING

Class action lawsuit
A lawsuit filed by a large group of people with clearly defined common interests.

Appellate jurisdiction
The authority of a court to review decisions handed down by another court.

Original jurisdiction
The authority of a court to be the initial court in which a legal decision is rendered.

One final limitation on courts is harder to see, but is no less significant. Because judges and justices are normally appointed by politically accountable entities such as executives and legislatures, or in some states elected by the public itself, courts in general rarely stray too far from the reigning political majority. Social scientist Robert Dahl affirmed this hypothesis in his landmark 1957 article, "Decision-making in a Democracy."[22] Dahl's study of Supreme Court opinions revealed that although the Supreme Court often defies public opinion in the short run, its opinions usually fall in line with the dominant national majority coalition in the long run. The Court's eventual adaptability to shifts in the national mood, though much more subtle and slow-moving than the more political branches of government, has helped sustain it as a vital force in the American political system.

Electing and Appointing Judges

★ LO Learn how state judges are selected

The state and federal court systems differ dramatically in the way judges are selected. State court judges tend to be selected in one of five ways. Partisan elections are utilized in some states, with prospective and sitting justices required to campaign for their party's nomination and then to run in a general election. Nonpartisan elections, held in many other states, eliminate party designations from the election process. The "Missouri Plan" or merit plan selection process features a three-step process by which a judicial nominating commission initially screens candidates and then submits a list of three potential nominees to the governor, who then selects the judge from the list. Shortly thereafter, the new judge must then secure voter approval in a nonpartisan retention election.[23] Several other states authorize gubernatorial appointment of judges, in which the governor appoints judges, subject to approval of the state senate. Finally, a handful of states require that the state legislature appoint judges.

The selection of federal judges follows a more universal formula: all federal district court judges, federal appeals court judges, and Supreme Court justices are appointed by the president, subject to confirmation by a majority vote in the U.S. Senate. Whereas the Constitution dictates this formula for appointment of Supreme Court justices, Congress in its discretion authorized the appointment of lower federal court judges to require the Senate's advice and consent as well. Because all federal judges and Supreme Court justices hold their offices during "good behavior"—the functional equivalent of life tenure—they are thought of as more independent than those state judges who must run for reelection. In fact, the retention rate for state judges is often so high (due to low voter turnout and other factors) that even elected state judges tend to enjoy a large degree of independence in rendering decisions.

The Nomination Process

★ LO Learn how federal judges and Supreme Court justices are selected

During a single term in office a president can expect to make hundreds of federal judicial appointments. In practice, a tradition of deference to home-state senators (often called "senatorial courtesy") provides legislators in the upper chamber—especially those hailing from the president's party—with considerable influence over the selection of district court judges in their own states. (Senatorial courtesy also has a more limited impact on the selection of appeals court judges, as circuits cross individual state boundaries.) In recent decades, presidents have not only relied on senators' recommendations to generate nominees for judgeships; they also consider ideological factors and the personal characteristics of potential nominees.

Some modern presidents have sought to place their own ideological stamp on the lower courts (whether liberal or conservative) by utilizing a committee of White House and Justice Department attorneys to screen and suggest candidates.[24] The Reagan and George W. Bush administrations were especially active in seeking to use

CHIP SOMODEVILLA/GETTY IMAGES NEWS/GETTY IMAGES

the appointment of lower court judges as a means of moving the constitutional land-scape in a conservative ideological direction. When the presidency and the Senate are held by different parties, battles over judicial nominees may become especially fierce. In 2002 and 2007–2008, the Democrat-controlled Senate Judiciary Committee gave heightened scrutiny to President George W. Bush's more conservative nominees. Though in the minority, Senate Republicans sought to return the favor to President Obama, delaying many of his court nominees in 2009 and 2010.

President Barack Obama introduces his second nominee to the U.S. Supreme Court, Elena Kagan, in 2010.

Given its place atop the U.S. legal system, vacancies on the U.S. Supreme Court tend to draw far more political attention than do other judicial vacancies. Because the president, the U.S. Senate, and the media follow personnel changes on the Supreme Court more closely, the process by which justices are nominated and confirmed is a major news event. A president may have the opportunity to appoint several Supreme Court justices—Presidents George H. W. Bush and Bill Clinton appointed two justices each, whereas President Ronald Reagan appointed three associate justices and promoted one associate to chief justice (the justice responsible for administering the Court's affairs and heading the federal justice system as a whole) during his eight years in office. President George W. Bush appointed no justices during his first term, but filled two vacancies (including the chief justiceship) during the latter half of 2005. Bush's reelection helped him escape the fate suffered by President Carter, whose lone term in office witnessed no Supreme Court vacancies at all.

If a vacancy occurs in the position of chief justice, the president may choose to promote one of the eight associate Supreme Court justices to this prestigious position, as President Reagan did when he promoted William Rehnquist to the Court's center seat in 1986. More often, presidents reach outside the confines of the current Supreme Court for someone to take the position of chief justice. Chief Justice Earl Warren, for example, served as governor of California immediately prior to becoming chief justice in 1953. President George W. Bush also named an outsider, Judge John Roberts of the U.S. Court of Appeals for the D.C. Circuit, to succeed Rehnquist.

In choosing nominees to the high court, presidents in recent decades have considered several factors:

STEVE PETTEWAY, COLLECTION OF THE SUPREME COURT OF THE UNITED STATES

The U.S. Supreme Court Justices, as pictured at the start of the Court's Fall 2010 term. Standing, from left to right: Sonia Sotomayor, Stephen Breyer, Samuel Alito, and Elana Kagan. Seated, from left to right: Clarence Thomas, Antonin Scalia, John Roberts (Chief Justice), Anthony Kennedy, and Ruth Bader Ginsburg.

- The nominee's ideological and policy preferences. This factor has enjoyed a place of special importance in presidential calculations. A nominee's views on abortion, school prayer, and other hot-button issues may well tip the balance of the Court in favor of the president's stated views. Certainly there exists little evidence that presidents employ "litmus tests" on nominees, by which they might refuse to appoint individuals unless they explicitly state their views on such issues to the president in advance. President Dwight Eisenhower allegedly referred to his appointments of Chief Justice Earl Warren and Justice William Brennan as the "two biggest mistakes" of his presidency, because both men decided cases in a far more liberal direction than Eisenhower would have preferred. More recently, the elder George Bush may have been frustrated by the pro–abortion rights opinions of Justice David Souter, his first appointment to the Supreme Court. Still, most modern presidents have mobilized White House and Justice Department resources to conduct extensive research on each candidate's past writings and opinions in hopes of eliminating any surprises.

- Judicial competence. Most presidents have an interest in appointing especially qualified candidates for the high court, if only because it assists in speeding along the confirmation process. The American Bar Association (ABA), an interest group of lawyers, rates candidates for every federal judicial vacancy on a scale from "highly qualified" to "not qualified" on the basis of their legal background and accomplishments. Ethical considerations may also be considered, because the ABA may be reluctant to approve candidates who have previously been convicted of crimes, for example. Although a negative rating from the ABA does not always eliminate a candidacy, it may present significant obstacles in the Senate confirmation process. Early in his first term, President George W. Bush announced that he would no longer vet judicial candidates through the ABA prior to their formal nomination. Still, the ABA continued to rate those candidates after their nominations were submitted to the Senate. Two of President Bush's first three nominees for the high court, John Roberts and Samuel Alito, received the highest rating of "well qualified" just prior to their appearance before the Senate Judiciary Committee. (Bush's other nominee, Harriet Miers, withdrew her name from consideration before the ABA released its rating of her candidacy.)

- Political loyalty. Although loyalty has diminished somewhat as a priority in recent years, presidents still occasionally practice old-fashioned politics in the selection of Supreme Court nominees, choosing a justice based on a background of service to the president's party or to the president. During the twentieth century, well over 90 percent of all Supreme Court nominees were members of the president's political party. Of these, many emerged from the president's Cabinet, from the members of Congress loyal to the president's legislative program, or from other positions close to the chief executive or his subordinates at the time the appointment was made. Certainly the former president of the United States, William Howard Taft, was well positioned to tout his own appointment as chief justice of the United States; President Warren Harding placed Taft on the high court just seven years after Taft had left the White House.

TABLE 9.1 Current Membership of the U.S. Supreme Court

Member	Gender	Position	Date Born	Year Appointed (President)	Law School	Party	Religion
John Roberts	M	Chief Justice	1/27/55	2005 (Bush II)	Harvard	Republican	Roman Catholic
Antonin Scalia	M	Associate Justice	3/11/36	1986 (Reagan)	Harvard	Republican	Roman Catholic
Anthony Kennedy	M	Associate Justice	7/23/36	1988 (Reagan)	Harvard	Republican	Roman Catholic
Clarence Thomas	M	Associate Justice	6/23/48	1991 (Bush I)	Yale	Republican	Roman Catholic*
Ruth Bader Ginsburg	F	Associate Justice	3/15/33	1993 (Clinton)	Harvard/ Columbia	Democrat	Jewish
Stephen Breyer	M	Associate Justice	8/15/38	1994 (Clinton)	Harvard	Democrat	Jewish
Samuel Alito	M	Associate Justice	4/1/50	2006 (Bush II)	Yale	Republican	Roman Catholic
Sonia Sotomayor	F	Associate Justice	6/25/54	2009 (Obama)	Yale	Democrat	Roman Catholic
Elena Kagan	F	Associate Justice	4/28/60	2010 (Obama)	Harvard	Democrat	Jewish

* At the time of his 1991 appointment, Clarence Thomas regularly attended an Episcopal church but later returned to Roman Catholicism, the faith in which he had been raised.

- Demographic factors. A president may choose a candidate for the diversity the nominee adds to the demographics of the current Supreme Court.[25] As was noted at the outset, Lyndon Johnson appointed Thurgood Marshall as the first African American to the Court in 1967; Ronald Reagan appointed Sandra Day O'Connor as the first female justice in 1981; and President Obama appointed Sonia Sotomayor as the first Latina justice in 2009. Obama also appointed a second female, Elena Kagan, to the Court the following year, bringing the number of women on the Court up to three for the time being. The selection of nominees who can diversify the Court may pay political dividends for the White House as well: the president may be counting on such nominations to build support among certain groups.

- The current political environment. Supreme Court vacancies do not occur in a vacuum; presidents are well aware of the political conditions that surround a particular court vacancy, and more often than not they respond to it through their nomination choices. Such factors as low presidential approval ratings, a Senate controlled by the political opposition, or the need to achieve other legislative proposals may convince the president to select a more moderate or less controversial nominee. Thus President Bill Clinton—facing a challenging political environment during his first two years in office—chose two Supreme Court nominees during that period (Ruth Bader Ginsburg and Stephen Breyer) who were deemed acceptable by the ranking Republican member of the Senate Judiciary Committee, Sen. Orrin Hatch (R-UT). On the other hand, a president who enjoys a strong political position—as President Obama did in early 2009—may decide to name a more controversial Supreme Court nominee.

The Confirmation Process

Until the late 1960s, most confirmation processes tended to be little noticed events, drawing little public attention or press coverage. Beginning at that time, however, with the growth of federal regulatory schemes placing more and more cases in the federal courts, presidents began to routinely utilize judicial appointments as a means

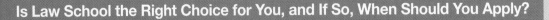

Is Law School the Right Choice for You, and If So, When Should You Apply?

Currently there are almost 200 American Bar Association–accredited law schools in the United States that award juris doctor degrees to students upon completion of three years or more of legal education. You are no doubt familiar with the names of many of these schools: Harvard, Yale, Columbia, the University of Chicago, and several others that enjoy sterling reputations and are well known around the world. Many graduates of these schools work in prestigious short-term clerkships for judges and then go on to enjoy their pick of legal jobs at extremely high starting salaries. Other law school graduates are not so fortunate, however. According to lawjobs.com, graduates of law schools ranked below the top twenty-five have a less than one in five chance of beginning their careers at a large law firm with relatively high starting salaries; and nearly 15 percent of all students at ABA-accredited schools either flunk out or are unemployed for at least nine months after graduation. Moreover, at forty-four ABA-accredited schools, fully 20 percent of students have flunked out or remain unemployed. Considering the high price of law school today (many students graduate with debts of $100,000 or more), these are daunting figures indeed.

Of course, for many college graduates who attend the right law school at the right moment in their young careers, legal education offers significant benefits, including the prospect of an exciting and lucrative career. Because the average age of entering law students across the nation is twenty-five years old (the average age is higher at top-ranked schools), most college graduates will consider other postgraduation opportunities before law school, both to prepare them for the rigors of law school and to enhance their chances of admission at top schools.

For Critical Thinking and Discussion

1. Are you considering law school immediately after graduation? If so, why?

2. Can you think of any benefits that accrue to law students who take time off after college?

3. Many college graduates apply to law school not so much because they dream of a legal career, but because they are unaware of any other promising options. Have you given thought to other types of graduate schools?

4. More college graduates apply to law school when economic times are especially difficult. Why do you think this is?

---

of shaping public policy. The confirmation process for those nominees was simultaneously opened up to unprecedented high levels of public scrutiny. All hearings for Supreme Court nominees have been televised live on C-SPAN since 1981. Interest groups have become increasingly active in confirmation proceedings, lobbying senators directly and testifying in favor of or against particular nominees. With the ideological stakes raised, presidents and their aides have become increasingly active in lobbying for their nominees.[26]

The Senate confirms the vast majority of Supreme Court nominees; between 1900 and 2010, fifty-nine of the sixty-three Supreme Court candidates who came up for a formal Senate vote on their respective nominations were confirmed. Nevertheless, controversial nominees in recent decades have experienced their share of public scrutiny—and in some cases, humiliation—when subjected to the glare of the confirmation process. One of Richard Nixon's nominees to the Supreme Court in 1970, Court of Appeals Judge G. Harrold Carswell of Florida, was rejected by the Senate in part because of his alleged links to white supremacist groups. Carswell was also dogged by charges that he was not competent to serve on the bench; to that came the deadly retort of one Senate supporter that "even the mediocre deserve some representation on the Supreme Court too." Despite all these obstacles, Carswell nearly survived Senate confirmation anyway—he was rejected by a six-vote margin. Frustrated by his defeat, Carswell resigned from the bench a few months later and ran unsuccessfully for the U.S. Senate in 1972.

Ronald Reagan's nomination of Judge Robert Bork to the Supreme Court in 1987 was defeated in the Senate amid a cloud of interest group cries that Bork would reverse liberal precedents on free speech and abortion.[27] Bork, a former Yale law professor, sported a record of opposition to many Supreme Court doctrines supported by political liberals, including the doctrine of constitutionally protected abortion rights that the Court articulated in *Roe v. Wade* (1973).[28] In his award-winning book, *The Selling of Supreme Court Nominees* (1994), University of Georgia Professor John Maltese notes that liberal interest groups that

PABLO MARTINEZ MONSIVAIS/ASSOCIATED PRESS

John Roberts, nominee for chief justice of the United States, testifying before the Senate Judiciary Committee in September 2005.

were determined to defeat Bork employed "a wide variety of tactics, including advertising, grass roots events, focus groups and polling" to increase public awareness of Bork's controversial positions.

The Reagan White House was caught off guard by the groundswell of opposition to Bork's nomination generated by the intense interest group–driven media campaign. By the time Senate confirmation hearings were held at the end of the summer, the campaign had taken its toll on Bork's candidacy: several senators, including Joseph Biden (D-DE), chairman of the Senate Judiciary Committee, had already been persuaded to oppose the appointment. The Senate eventually defeated Bork's nomination by a 58–42 vote. Presidents since then have come to understand the new politics of judicial confirmations, working closely with interest groups to mount their own campaigns in favor of judicial nominees. The Bork nomination gave rise to a new term in Washington's political lexicon—"to Bork," which defines the act of challenging a president's nominee through well-financed and organized interest group opposition.

The Bork confirmation fiasco also encouraged subsequent presidents to favor nominees who either possess no paper trail at all or who would be far more circumspect than Bork in their willingness to engage the Senate on constitutional issues. Accordingly, in 1990 the first Supreme Court vacancy of George H. W. Bush's presidency went to David Souter, a little known federal appeals judge who had logged most of his judicial career on the New Hampshire Supreme Court deciding technical issues of state law. Souter's position on issues such as abortion and the establishment clause were never really tested in the state court system, and senators on both ends of the political spectrum thus had little to work with when interrogating Souter. (He was confirmed easily by a 90–9 Senate vote.)

In recent years, the confirmation process for lower court nominees has been politicized as well, with battles being waged with extra ferocity over appointments to the U.S. courts of appeals. During the Clinton administration, Senate Republicans in control of that chamber often delayed nominees they felt were too liberal; Senate Democrats did the same to President George W. Bush's nominees in 2001. Before the Democrats regained control of Congress in the 2006 midterm elections, Senate Democrats opposed to some of George W. Bush's nominees on ideological grounds began to take advantage of Senate rules to stop votes on contested nominees. Specifically, they utilized the filibuster to block ten of President Bush's appellate court nominees during his first term in office. Bush renominated nine of those blocked nominees at the start of his second term, and a frustrated Republican Senate leadership began to consider rule changes to foreclose the use of filibusters against future nominees. Senate Democrats referred to any such rule change as the "nuclear option," because they were prepared to

When Supreme Court nominee Sonia Sotomayor went before the Senate Judiciary Committee during the summer of 2009, the symbolism of her nomination was obscured somewhat by the storm of political rhetoric flying in every direction. From the right came accusations that she would allow her gender and ethnicity to affect her decision making, and from the left came countercharges that critics were judging Sotomayor by a double standard as she was forced to appear bland and "mainstream" even while Latin Americans were celebrating the meaning of her path-breaking nomination.

Foreigners—especially those who hail from countries with a rich heritage of aristocracy and royalty—were perhaps less likely to ignore the symbolism of Sotomayor's "rags to riches" story. Just consider this commentary from BBC News Editor Justin Webb, who returned to the United Kingdom in 2009 after spending eight years as BBC's Washington-based editor.

Sonia Sotomayor, age 7

Justice Sonia Sotomayor

Out on route 17 in South Carolina, you can do very well or very badly. You can crash and burn, or you can fill up with cheap petrol and ride off into the sunset. If you do not like yourself in South Carolina, you can hire a self-drive hire truck and take it to Seattle. If you do not like your life and you have drive and luck, you can change it because—being American—you

believe you can change it. Sitting in a dingy apartment in New York watching Perry Mason on the TV, you can decide to make it big in law as eight-year-old Sonia Sotomayor once did. This summer, now in her fifties, she becomes a Supreme Court justice and the latest American story to send shivers down the spines of dreamers of the American dream.

But if Sonia Sotomayor is to make it big, there must be something creating the drive, and part of that something is the poverty of the alternative, the discomfort of the ordinary lives that most Americans endure and the freedom that Americans have to go to hell if that is the decision they take.

Source: Justin Webb, "Checking out of 'Hotel America,'" BBC Web site, August 1, 2009, accessed at http://news.bbc.co.uk/2/hi/programmes/from_our_own_correspondent/8176448.stm.

respond by shutting down Senate business through use of the filibuster rule in all other instances. On May 24, 2005, this growing crisis was averted, as a group of fourteen moderate senators (seven Republicans and seven Democrats) settled on a plan to allow several of Bush's most controversial nominees to be confirmed, in return for the promise that the filibuster would be reserved for use against judicial appointments when there are "extraordinary circumstances."

How a Case Proceeds within the U.S. Supreme Court

Writ of certiorari
The formal term for an order by which the Supreme Court acts in its discretion to review a case from a lower court.

The vast majority of cases that come before the U.S. Supreme Court arrive by a **writ of certiorari**, the formal term for an order by which the court acts in its discretion to hear a case on appeal. Losing parties in the highest state court, a federal circuit court, or (in extremely rare cases) a federal district court can properly file a "cert petition" with the Supreme Court, asking the Court to hear its case. Decisions to grant a writ of certiorari generally follow the *Rule of Four*—if four of the nine justices vote to hear the case, it is placed on the Court's official docket of cases that it will hear during the coming year. Of the many thousands of cert petitions that arrive at the Court during a given year, barely more than 1 percent (fewer than ninety overall) are normally granted.

In theory, the justices decide to hear only those cases that are considered so important that they justify intervention at such a high level. Two other factors may also increase the likelihood that the Supreme Court will grant a writ of certiorari: (1) when the federal government intervenes in the case; or (2) when there is a split among two or more of the U.S. circuit courts of appeals on a similar issue. Additionally, some justices as a matter of strategy may vote to deny the petition for cert, even when they think the lower court case was wrongly decided, because they do not want their colleagues to transform the lower court precedent into a Supreme Court edict applicable throughout the land. Regardless of the justices' many motives, denial of a cert petition theoretically casts no aspersions whatsoever on whether a case has been wrongly or rightly decided, although it does allow the lower court decision to stand as the controlling legal decision for the parties in that case. For example, the Supreme Court's 1997 denial of a cert petition in a case concerning affirmative action at the University of Texas did not necessarily imply high Court dissatisfaction with

FIGURE 9.3 From Cert Petition to Final Judgment in the U.S. Supreme Court

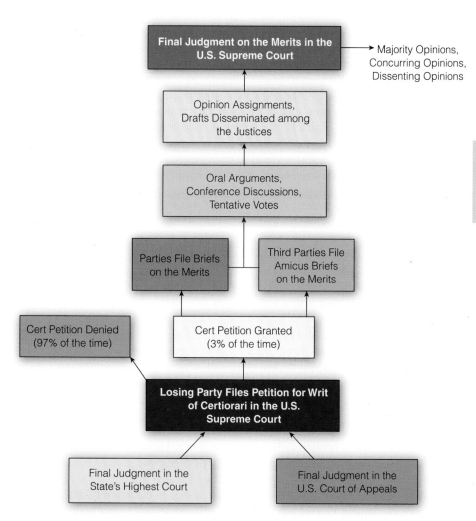

★ LO

Follow a Supreme Court case as it proceeds from writ of certiorari to final opinion

In some exceptionally rare cases, a final judgment from a federal district court may receive expedited review from the U.S. Supreme Court and thus bypass the U.S. Court of Appeals.

affirmative action; rather, it simply left intact a U.S. Court of Appeals decision that applied only to the three states in that circuit: Texas, Mississippi, and Louisiana. The U.S. Supreme Court waited until six years later to articulate new rules for affirmative action that would become applicable in all fifty states.

If the Court elects to issue a writ of certiorari and hear a case, both the losing and winning parties in the lower court file written documents called **briefs** arguing why constitutional or federal statutory law weighs in favor of their respective positions. Outside parties with an interest in the litigation may also elect to file briefs, known formally as **amicus curiae briefs** (*amicus curiae* is Latin for "friend of the court"), expressing their own views on how the Court should decide a particular case. Interest groups frequently file amicus briefs in Supreme Court cases that affect their members; in doing so, they offer a version of "expert testimony" on the law, albeit with their own strategic bent on the issue in question. The American Medical Association, for example, routinely files amicus briefs in abortion cases; the American Trial Lawyers Association may express its opinion in cases interpreting rules of trial procedure through amicus briefs as well. In some of the more high-profile cases, literally hundreds of such briefs may be filed, offering the court an admittedly informal tally of the state of public opinion on the issue.

The **solicitor general** argues on behalf of the U.S. government in most cases where the federal government is a party. That office also stands among the most influential "friends of the court," filing amicus briefs on behalf of the federal government in approximately a quarter of all cases heard by the Supreme Court each year. Acting through the solicitor general, the U.S. government has enjoyed a disproportionate share of success in affecting Supreme Court case discretionary grants of review and case outcomes.[29]

After all party and amicus briefs have been filed, the Supreme Court justices normally hear oral arguments from opposing counsel in the Supreme Court's chamber. Attorneys licensed to practice before the Supreme Court present their client's view of the law and facts within an allotted period of time (normally thirty minutes); most of that time is actually spent answering questions and inquiries from the justices. If a justice is truly undecided, he or she may be affected in the margins by the positions of advocates at oral arguments; the give-and-take with the lawyers may also suggest ways to more effectively draft the final opinion. Still, there remains little evidence that the oral arguments actually shift the votes of most justices. Regardless, the hearings in the Supreme Court chamber can still offer moments of high drama, such as when Richard Nixon's attorneys argued for an especially broad interpretation of executive privilege in the 1974 Watergate tapes case. Their argument was ultimately rejected, and Nixon resigned just days after the Court's decision was handed down.

Shortly after the oral arguments are completed and the case has been formally submitted, the justices meet in conference to discuss the case, offer initial votes, and assign opinions. The chief justice presides over all conferences, which culminate in the assignment of opinions to be researched and written by individual justices in accordance with the conference discussions. Each justice employs four clerks—selected from a pool of the top law school graduates from across the country—who work behind the scenes researching the law and creating initial drafts of written opinions according to the justice's specific wishes. In some cases clerks enjoy even more influence over the justices they work for, assisting them as they sort through competing legal arguments.

A **majority opinion** requires agreement of at least five of the Court's nine members; only a majority opinion carries the force of law. The chief justice has just one vote like his colleagues, but if he is in the majority, the chief justice also has the crucial power to choose who will write the Court's main opinion. (If the chief justice is not in the majority, the senior-most associate justice in the majority retains that power of assignment.) Individual justices may choose to write other opinions either on their own or on behalf of a minority of justices. A **concurring opinion** agrees

Briefs

Written documents filed by parties in an appealed case arguing why constitutional or statutory law weighs in favor of their respective positions.

Amicus curiae briefs

Written documents filed by outside parties in the case with an interest in the outcome of the litigation expressing their own views on how the Court should decide a particular case.

Solicitor general

The lawyer representing the U.S. government before the U.S. Supreme Court.

Majority opinion

The opinion of a majority of members of the U.S. Supreme Court, which carries the force of law.

Concurring opinion

The opinion of one or more justices that agrees with the end result reached by the majority but disagrees with the reasons offered for the decision.

with the end result reached by the majority but disagrees with the reasons offered for the decision. A **dissenting opinion**, on the other hand, disagrees with the result reached by the majority. Justices write concurring and dissenting opinions both to register their differences with the majority and to lay the groundwork for the future, when those alternate grounds may one day secure the support of a Court majority.

Dissenting opinion
The opinion of one or more justices who disagree with the result reached by the majority.

The dissents written by Oliver Wendell Holmes Jr., who served on the U.S. Supreme Court from 1902 to 1932, established him as one of the most important legal thinkers in American history. When President Theodore Roosevelt appointed Holmes to the U.S. Supreme Court in 1902, the Court majority at the time appeared to be favorably disposed to protect the rights of big business. Armed with his own "realist" view of law that emphasized the "necessities of the time," Holmes dissented vigorously from the Court's majority opinions invalidating industrial reform laws and other progressive legislation. With speech restrictions on the rise in America during and immediately after World War I, Holmes eventually adjusted his own philosophy to promote a broader conception of free speech under the Constitution. Along with fellow justice Louis Brandeis, Holmes dissented from the majority's opinions allowing the government to punish minority views. (Holmes also made famous the metaphor of a "marketplace of ideas" and cautioned that even liberal protections of free speech would not protect a man from "falsely shouting 'fire!' in a crowded theater.") For Holmes, "the life of law" was never logic; rather, it was "experience." Justices after Holmes came to embrace his practical, real-world approach to the law. For instance, in *New York Times v. Sullivan* (1964),[30] the Supreme Court built on Holmes's theories about the First Amendment to apply a more protective approach to libel law, making it harder for public officials to sue newspapers that criticized their actions.

MPI/GETTY IMAGES

The Great Dissenter, Justice Oliver Wendell Holmes Jr., was appointed to the Supreme Court by President Theodore Roosevelt in 1902. Holmes's dissenting opinions on behalf of the freedom of expression would garner the support of Supreme Court majorities several decades later.

Once drafts of the justices' opinions in a case have been circulated and finalized, the decision can be announced. Occasionally the justices can shift their votes near the end of the process. For example, in 1986 Justice Lewis Powell seemingly resolved his own inner struggles over the scope of privacy rights when he chose to join Justice Byron White's four-person opinion in *Bowers v. Hardwick*.[31] Powell's vote gave White the slim majority and determined that the right to homosexual sodomy would not receive constitutional protection until 2003, when the Court overturned *Bowers* in *Lawrence v. Texas*.[32] Powell later publicly recanted his support of *Bowers*, proving that his inner struggle had actually continued. Normally the justices issue written opinions only, but on special occasions, the justices may even decide to read from key passages of the opinion they authored.

Why the Justices Vote the Way They Do

Examine the factors that influence judges

★ LO

Although it is difficult to determine what causes Supreme Court justices to vote as they do on certain issues, social scientists and legal scholars have identified a number of factors that may play a role in a judge's decision making:

■ Legal rules and precedents. The law itself—including constitutional law, statutes, rules and regulations, and past court decisions interpreting those sources—may be unambiguous enough to counsel one particular application to the case at hand. Previous court decisions are especially hard to avoid—when judges follow the decisions of past judges ruling in similar cases, they are adhering to the long-standing doctrine of "stare decisis," which is Latin for "stand by the decision" that has already been settled. For example, though Justice Byron White dissented from the original decision in *Miranda v. Arizona* (1966)[33] providing unprecedented rights

AMERICAN GOVERNMENT In Historical Perspective

Cases That Kept a Nation on Edge

Decisions of the U.S. Supreme Court are often highly watched and frequently have a profound impact on the political system. Sometimes, a decision of the Court is characterized by both high visibility and huge consequences. Following are three points in the nation's history when all eyes were on the Supreme Court's decision.

In 1819, the nation was suffering from a financial panic brought on by intense inflation, overextended investments in manufacturing, the collapse of foreign markets, and the contraction of credit nationwide. Exacerbating these ills was the mismanagement of the Second Bank of the United States, which had been chartered by Congress in part to provide stability during just such a crisis. In fact, the national bank had also increased the hardship on state banks by offering competition for scarce resources. When several states passed laws that either taxed the national bank or restricted its operations, the very constitutionality of a national bank came under question in a case (*McCulloch v. Maryland*) that weaved its way up to the U.S. Supreme Court. The economic solvency of various state banks rested on the Court's decision, and many eagerly awaited the Court's verdict. The suspense ended in 1819, when John Marshall, speaking for a unanimous Court, upheld the national bank of the United States as constitutional and rendered it immune from inferior entities.

In 1951, Americans were gripped by a "red scare," brought on by rising tensions in the Cold War with the Soviet Union. Back at home, Senator Joseph McCarthy (R-WI) was charging that Communists had infiltrated the State Department and the U.S. Army. Two years earlier, eleven top leaders of the U.S. Communist Party had been convicted in a high-profile trial for violating the Smith Act of 1940, which made it a crime to "knowingly and willfully advocate" the necessity or propriety of overthrowing the government. All eleven appealed their convictions to the U.S. Supreme Court, claiming that the Smith Act violated the First Amendment guarantee of freedom of speech; McCarthy's forces triumphed: the Court ruled on June 4, 1951, that the First Amendment did not bar the government from making the advocacy of violent overthrow of the government a criminal act. McCarthy's personal comeuppance would have to wait three and a half more years until December 1954, when the Senate voted to censure McCarthy for his abusive conduct by a 67–22 vote.

In 2000, more than a month after Election Day, Florida's twenty-five electoral votes remained up for grabs between presidential contenders George W. Bush and Al Gore. Although an electronic recount of the state's ballots indicated that Bush held a slim lead, Gore claimed that voter confusion had led the machine recount to inaccurately record the "intent of the voter," and his lawyers demanded a manual recount of the ballots in four counties. The Florida Supreme Court agreed with Gore's position, but the U.S. Supreme Court stopped the recount and agreed to hear the case on expedited review. With a nation of citizens left wondering if the outcome of the election would be resolved in time for the January inauguration, a narrowly divided Supreme Court issued its 5–4 decision on the evening of December 12, 2000. The Court's five more conservative justices ruled that a manual recount of the ballots in the disputed counties would violate the Constitution's equal protection clause and was thus invalid. With no time left to conduct a complete manual recount of the ballots in the entire state under a more uniform standard, Gore conceded the election the following evening to Bush. Five weeks later, Bush was sworn in as the forty-third president of the United States.

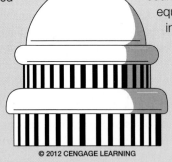

© 2012 CENGAGE LEARNING

to the accused, in later decisions he actively applied the *Miranda* holding to other cases, deferring to a high Court precedent that he personally opposed. Although the language of Supreme Court opinions suggests that stare decisis is always at work, often more than one reasonable interpretation of a law or legal opinion exists. In recent years, some judges have turned to international law and judicial opinions handed down in foreign courts as well. Most notably, Justice Anthony Kennedy in *Lawrence v. Texas* (2003) cited the European Court of Human Rights in support of the Court's protection of homosexual privacy rights. Defenders of this practice claim that because Americans share some values with the wider civilization, judges should be able to cite any and all sources of law in rendering their decisions; critics respond that there is no basis for U.S. judges to impose foreign "moods or fads" on Americans.

- Changes in circumstances. Sometimes changes in real-life conditions and circumstances may influence how laws are interpreted. In the school desegregation cases of the 1950s, the Supreme Court openly considered the newly discovered harmful effects of segregation on African American children. Similarly, in 1973, the Supreme Court took into account changes in modern medicine when it formulated the definition of constitutionally protected abortion rights in *Roe v. Wade*. Some jurists and scholars believe such changes in circumstances are irrelevant—rather, they view the Constitution as fixed in time and thus limited in scope to what the Framers envisioned. The search for the Framers' original intent about the Constitution is often referred to as "originalism." By contrast, other judges and scholars advocate the more flexible view of the Constitution as a "living, breathing document," which must adapt to changing circumstances and conditions.

- Ideological "attitudes." Many political scientists argue that Supreme Court justices' personal attitudes (liberal or conservative on law enforcement issues, free speech, and so forth) influence their judicial decision making. This model of understanding how justices decide cases has been labeled "the attitudinal model." Defenders of the model cite numerous statistics that support their understanding of the way judges decide cases. For example, William O. Douglas was a New Deal liberal who voted in the liberal direction in criminal procedure cases nearly 90 percent of the time and in civil rights cases 93 percent of the time.[34]

- Personal traits and characteristics. Males and females may approach political events differently; accordingly, the gender of a Supreme Court justice affects his or her reaction to legal issues and cases to some degree. Just as some demographic groups tend to be more conservative, justices who fit into those groups may be expected to vote accordingly. A justice's personal experiences may also play a role in how he or she judges. Biographers of Justice Oliver Wendell Holmes, for example, contend that Holmes's near-death experiences as a soldier in the Civil War colored his approach to judging.[35]

- Intracourt politics. A justice's interest in maintaining good relations with fellow justices may push him or her to vote in a certain way; behind-the-scenes bargaining and negotiating have also been features of Supreme Court politics throughout its history. In the late 1950s and early 1960s, Chief Justice Earl Warren and Justice William Brennan were famed for their ability to sway undecided justices in their favor; by contrast, Justice Felix Frankfurter's condescending attitude toward his fellow justices persuaded few and alienated many.

- External political pressures. Although Supreme Court justices enjoy life tenure and are thus theoretically immune to outside political pressures, the reality is much more complicated. Aware that the Court's prestige often rests on its ability to persuade the other branches, as well as the public, to comply with the Court's decisions, justices often react to the political environment that surrounds the Court when issuing legal opinions. *Roe v. Wade* survived its widely predicted demise in 1992 because at least two conservative justices feared its reversal would deal a blow to the Supreme Court's prestige. Public opinion may also play a role in determining the language of opinions and even the outcome of some cases.

Current Debates over the Exercise of Judicial Power

American courts often find themselves the subject of controversy. Many of the recurring debates over the proper role of courts include the following:

■ Judicial restraint versus judicial activism. The Supreme Court struck down several New Deal statutes in the 1930s; a few decades later, it invalidated state laws banning the use of contraceptive devices (in 1965) and state laws restricting the right to abortion (in 1973). Critics of those decisions protested the exercise of judicial activism by the high Court. Specifically, they charged that rather than deferring to the elected branches of government as a general matter, the justices responsible for those controversial decisions had effectively turned the Court into a "super legislature" that makes social policy. More recent cases like *Lawrence v. Texas* (2003), in which the Court struck down a state law banning homosexual sodomy, have revived those charges once again. Critics of judicial activism argue in favor of a philosophy of judicial restraint by which judges act more slowly and incrementally, affording the democratically elected branches considerable discretion to enact whatever laws they choose, so long as there is no clear and unambiguous prohibition against those laws in the Constitution itself. (Given the "elegant vagueness" of the Constitution's language, advocates of judicial restraint believe those instances are rare indeed.)

Supreme Court Justice Antonin Scalia, speaking at a Federalist Society Gala in 2007.

■ Electing judges versus appointing judges. Federal judges are appointed by the president with the advice and consent of the Senate and then serve for life. Many state judges are appointed as well, for either fixed or indefinite terms; others must run for election and then must seek reelection to stay on the bench. These varying methods of judicial selection may have significant implications on judicial decision making. Appointed judges no longer accountable to the public or to any political processes enjoy increased independence in their decision making. Although many judicial elections pose little or no challenge to the incumbents, these election contests have become dramatically more contested in recent decades. For instance, in 1986 conservative groups disgruntled with liberal decisions rendered by the highest state court in California campaigned successfully to defeat three of its more liberal justices in recall elections, including Chief Justice Rose Bird. What elected judges may lack in independence they make up for in accountability; unlike judges appointed for life, elected judges should be more responsive to the public as a whole. The debate over judicial selection mechanisms often boils down to a question of how to strike the proper balance between the competing interests of judicial independence and accountability to the public.

■ Law versus politics. Do judges sit on a court of law, or is their institution simply another political body exercising its political will? Certainly the judicial process is fashioned to trumpet the court's role as a legal body that transcends ordinary politics. The judicial robes, magisterial courtrooms, and reliance on formality give rise to this "cult of the robe" as the "apolitical" branch. Canons of judicial ethics require that judges avoid even the appearance of impropriety by not participating in political debates and lobbying other branches on various matters. At the same time, the U.S. Supreme Court in particular often finds itself at the storm center of American politics. In some instances the other branches actually come to the court in search of legal answers to what are essentially political problems. The Court's 5–4 decision in *Bush v. Gore* (2000),[36] which ended the manual recounts for the 2000 presidential election in Florida and made George W. Bush the president-elect, illustrates just one way that law and politics can become intertwined. In extremely rare cases, the elected branches essentially abdicate their responsibility to act altogether, forcing the courts to step in by enforcing judicial decrees. For example, federal courts have on rare occasions supervised the construction of prisons and the implementation of busing programs. The highly political manner in which judges are chosen and the ambiguous nature of so many legal provisions mean that the tension between law and politics is perhaps inevitable in the U.S. political system.

■ Cameras in the courtroom. The Constitution guarantees to every criminal defendant a public trial; courts can satisfy that requirement by allowing the media and some members of the public access to the trial. Many states go a step further, allowing television cameras in state courtrooms, but the federal judicial system has so far resisted any such development. Do lawyers play up to the television cameras, undermining the interests of justice? It's hard to say. When O. J. Simpson was tried for murder in a California courtroom in 1995, the trial received gavel-to-gavel television coverage. Afterward, several of the lawyers in his case became full-fledged media stars, appearing on their own talk shows.

In April 2005, Senator Charles Grassley (R-IA) introduced in Congress the so-called Sunshine in the Courtroom Act, which would allow cameras into federal courtrooms. Specifically, the bill would give the presiding federal judge in every case the authority to determine whether cameras would be permitted, and if so, for how long. Even if such legislation one day passes, it is unlikely that cameras will appear any time soon in the U.S. Supreme Court, where Chief Justice John Roberts continues to defer to a handful of older justices who remain adamantly opposed to television coverage. Justices Stephen Breyer and Antonin Scalia have both spoken publicly against the move. Indeed, Scalia noted his objection in especially stark terms during a 2005 interview: "I think there's something sick about making entertainment out of other people's legal problems … I don't like it in the lower courts, and I don't particularly like it in the Supreme Court."[37] Until the makeup of the current courts changes significantly, Supreme Court observers unable to observe oral arguments in person will have to settle for audiotapes of the oral arguments made available a short time later.

© 2012 CENGAGE LEARNING

Making the Connection

In the modern era, some presidents have placed added emphasis on the need to diversify the Court, moving it beyond the all-white tribunal that presided up through the 1960s. President Lyndon Johnson named the first African American (Thurgood Marshall); President Barack Obama named the first Latina (Sonia Sotomayor). Both nominations generated some controversy, but both were eventually confirmed by comfortable margins. As a result, the Court would look different and—in the eyes of many—the Court's decision making would be influenced by the addition of new and unique perspectives. Does the racial and ethnic identity of a Supreme Court justice affect his or her judicial decision making, or does the law mean the same thing to those of every race, ethnicity, gender, etc.? Such a connection may be difficult to prove, though many of those who supported the two nominations were no doubt hoping for exactly that result.

Since 1973, the Supreme Court's controversial decision in *Roe v. Wade* has galvanized the nation like few other Supreme Court decisions in history. By a 7–2 vote, the Court in *Roe* struck down abortion laws in forty-six states and the District of Columbia. Opposition to *Roe* exploded from the outset, with a pro-life camp forming in heated resistance to the decision. Self-labeled "right to life" groups gained even more legitimacy when President Ronald Reagan made opposition to *Roe v. Wade* part of his litmus test for all judicial appointments. In response to *Roe v. Wade*, several states passed laws limiting abortion in various ways, such as requiring parental consent for minors to obtain abortions, twenty-four-hour waiting periods, and spousal notification, among others. Some, but not all, of these laws were upheld in *Planned Parenthood v. Casey* (1992), which upheld the basic holding of *Roe v. Wade* while also modifying it in significant ways. Meanwhile, pro-choice groups have increased their own lobbying activities to defend the *Roe v. Wade* decision from attack.

Pro-life protesters in Washington, DC, march in opposition to the Supreme Court's decision in *Roe v. Wade*.

Since the early 1980s, no Democratic presidential nominee has been able to escape the requirement of professed support for the decision.

President George W. Bush's appointment of Samuel Alito to replace the more moderate Sandra Day O'Connor on the U.S. Supreme Court fed the growing expectation that *Roe v. Wade* might be overturned by the increasingly conservative Supreme Court in the not-so-distant future.

What effect would the overturning of *Roe v. Wade* have on the American political landscape? On www.cengage.com/dautrich/americangovernment/2e, find the Politics InterActive link for details on what life might look like if *Roe v. Wade* were overturned, including links that provide information about the issues surrounding court decisions on abortion in historical, popular, and global perspectives.

Chapter Summary

★ Types of Law

- Law encompasses the authoritative rules made by government. The term *civil law* refers to statutes enacted most often by legislative bodies; common law consists of the rulings handed down by judges that establish precedents. Other types of law include criminal, civil, constitutional, and administrative law.

★ The Structure of the American Legal System

- Each of the fifty states maintains its own court system, which includes trial courts and appellate courts.
- Article III of the U.S. Constitution established the judicial branch, including the U.S. Supreme Court.
- Federal district courts are the trial courts. Their decisions may be appealed to the U.S. courts of appeals, whose decisions may be reviewed by the U.S. Supreme Court. The decision of a state supreme court that raises federal issues may also be brought directly to the U.S. Supreme Court.

★ The United States' Adversarial System of Justice

- The American legal system is an adversarial system of justice, in which opposing parties contend against each other for a result favorable to themselves, and judges act merely as independent referees.
- In the U.S., disputes between parties may be settled through civil litigation. Those accused of crimes are prosecuted through a criminal law system. The vast majority of criminal prosecutions are settled by plea-bargaining.

★ Judicial Review and Its Implications

- Chief Justice John Marshall's opinion in *Marbury v. Madison* (1803) established the Supreme Court's authority to review the constitutionality of any act passed by Congress.

★ Limitations on Courts

- Courts in the United States cannot initiate lawsuits; they can only hear true controversies; their decision affects only those parties that are part of a case; and they have no ability to enforce their decisions.

★ Electing and Appointing Judges

- State judges are selected in various ways depending upon the jurisdiction: some are appointed by governors or legislatures; others must run in an election; still others are chosen by a merit plan system.
- All federal court judges are nominated by the president and must be confirmed by the U.S. Senate.

★ How a Case Proceeds within the U.S. Supreme Court

- In order to grant a writ of certiorari to review a case, four of the nine justices must approve.
- After briefs are filed and oral arguments are heard, the justices vote on the merits and issue their majority opinion accordingly. Concurring and dissenting opinions may also be issued.

★ Why the Justices Vote the Way They Do

- Various factors influence a judge's decision making, including legal precedents, new circumstances, ideological attitudes, personal traits, intracourt politics, and external pressures.

★ Current Debates over the Exercise of Judicial Power

- Justices who frequently overturn state and federal laws may be accused of judicial activism; critics of such activism advocate judicial restraint, deferring to democratically elected legislatures.
- State judges who must run for election occasionally face some opposition, which forces them to be more responsive to the public. Appointed judges, by contrast, enjoy more independence.
- A majority of justices continues to oppose allowing television cameras to cover oral arguments.

CourseMate

Key Terms

Amicus curiae briefs (p. 282)

Appellate jurisdiction (p. 273)

Briefs (p. 282)

Civil law (p. 261)

Class action lawsuit (p. 273)

Common law (p. 261)

Complaint (p. 265)

Concurring opinion (p. 282)

Defendant (p. 265)

Discovery (p. 265)

Dissenting opinion (p. 283)

Grand jury (p. 266)

Indictment (p. 266)

Judicial review (p. 267)

Litigation (p. 265)

Majority opinion (p. 282)

Original jurisdiction (p. 273)

Plaintiff (p. 265)

Plea bargain (p. 266)

Solicitor general (p. 282)

Standing (p. 272)

Writ of certiorari (p. 280)

Resources

Important Books and Articles

Abraham, Henry J. *Justices, Presidents, and Senators: A History of the U.S. Supreme Court Appointments from Washington to Clinton*. Lanham, MD: Rowman & Littlefield, 2007.

Baum, Lawrence. *American Courts: Process and Policy*. Boston: Houghton Mifflin, 2007.

Baum, Lawrence. *The Supreme Court*. Washington, DC: CQ Press, 2006.

Dahl, Robert. "Decision-making in a Democracy: The Supreme Court as a National Policy-Maker." *Journal of Public Law*, vol. 6 (1957): 279–295.

Epstein, Lee, and Jack Knight. *The Choices Justices Make*. Washington, DC: CQ Press, 1998.

Maltese, John A. *The Selling of Supreme Court Nominees*. Baltimore: Johns Hopkins University Press, 1995.

McCloskey, Robert G. *The American Supreme Court*. 4th ed. Chicago: University of Chicago Press, 2004.

Rosenberg, Gerald. *Hollow Hope: Can Courts Bring About Social Change?* Chicago: University of Chicago Press, 1993.

Segal, Jeffrey A., and Harold J. Spaeth. *The Supreme Court and the Attitudinal Model Revisited*. New York: Cambridge University Press, 2002.

Toobin, Jeffrey. *The Nine: The Secret World of the Supreme Court*. New York: Doubleday, 2007.

Yalof, David A. *Pursuit of Justices: Presidential Politics and the Selection of Supreme Court Nominees*. Chicago: University of Chicago Press, 1999.

Internet Sources

http://www.uscourts.gov (the home page of the U.S. federal judiciary, which includes information about the U.S. Supreme Court, the U.S. courts of appeals, U.S. district courts, and U.S. bankruptcy courts)

http://www.findlaw.com (the most comprehensive source of no-cost legal research available on the Internet; includes a legal search engine and links to organizations, law schools, and so on)

http://www.supremecourtus.gov (the U.S. Supreme Court's own Web site, which features recent decisions, briefs, and other important information about the nation's highest court)

http://www.oyez.org (this Web site features a searchable database of select Supreme Court opinions and audio excerpts of oral arguments from the Supreme Court; also includes a virtual tour of the U.S. Supreme Court building)

10 Public Opinion

NOW President George W. Bush greets troops at Fort Benning, Georgia, in January 2007 as they prepare for deployment to Iraq.

AP PHOTO/GERALD HERBERT

THEN President Lyndon B. Johnson greets the troops at Fort Campbell, Kentucky, in July 1966.

CORBIS

NOW & THEN

The Highs and Lows of Presidential Popularity

The nation was in crisis due to the tragic events of that day. In the wake of the tragedy, a stunned nation was willing to put its partisan differences aside. The record-breaking high approval ratings registered by the president in the days that followed the national tragedy confirmed that the nation was rallying behind its leader, giving him the benefit of the doubt and hoping that he would lead the nation through the crisis. As a result, the president and his administration would benefit from an influx of political capital during his initial year in office, allowing the president to embark on an unusually ambitious agenda for change. Over the course of time, however, the president's honeymoon period with the public was destined to come to an end; he would see his popularity slowly erode following the White House's decision to fight a war that played out over many years and eventually cost many American lives. Just as his young presidency had benefitted from record-high approval ratings in the wake of a national tragedy, his time in office would end with exceedingly low approval ratings as a result of a long and unpopular war.

LEARNING OBJECTIVES
★ WHAT YOU WILL LEARN ★

Public Opinion in American Politics
★ Understand both the theoretically important role that public opinion plays in American democracy and the tactical function public opinion plays in the policymaking process

How Is Public Opinion Expressed?
★ Learn the different ways in which public opinion may be expressed, including public opinion polls, rallies and protests, blogging, voting, and contributing time and money to campaigns

The Levels of Public Opinion
★ Distinguish between the different levels of public opinion, from broad values and beliefs, to partisan and ideological orientations, to attitudes and opinions on specific items

How Informed Is Public Opinion?
★ Assess the mass public's level of knowledge about American politics and the capacity of the public to contribute to the political process

How Does Public Opinion Form?
★ Recognize that political socialization is a life-long process and know a number of important factors (such as the family, schools, friends, religion) that contribute to the development of political opinions

How Is Public Opinion Measured?
★ Explain the differences between a scientific poll and an unscientific poll
★ Identify criteria for asking unbiased poll questions

Interpreting Public Opinion Data
★ Assess the findings from a poll along the dimensions of direction, intensity, and continuity of public opinion

CourseMate

NOW & THEN

George W. Bush's Job Approval Ratings Trend

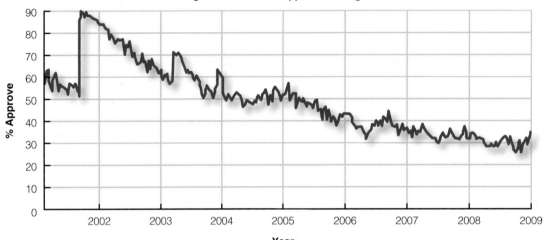

Source: The Gallup Organization. © 2009 The Gallup Organization.

NOW   The young presidency of George W. Bush was stunned on September 11, 2001, by the terrorist attacks on the World Trade Center in New York City and on the Pentagon in Washington, DC. The nation's citizens were shocked as well. In this time of extreme national crisis, Americans of all ideological persuasions dropped their partisan leanings and threw their support behind Bush, hoping that the tough-talking Texan was the right man to lead the nation through the tragedy. A Gallup poll conducted after the attacks showed that Bush did, in fact, register the highest approval ratings—90 percent—ever recorded by the polling organization. Americans gave President Bush every benefit of the doubt as he responded to the events of that day. Benefiting from this rally-around-the-flag sentiment, Bush was dealt a hand of enormous political capital and presidential power, and in 2003 he used that capital to launch a war that deposed Iraqi dictator Saddam Hussein and removed his government from power, basing his decision to attack on intelligence that Saddam Hussein had been developing weapons of mass destruction. Bush quickly claimed victory, but the declaration turned out to be premature: the U.S. army and its allies found no weapons of mass destruction, and the invasion touched off a civil war between hostile Iraqi factions that would fester throughout the Bush presidency, costing thousands of American lives and hundreds of billions of dollars. By the time Bush was settling into his final year in office in 2008 a full five years after the invasion of Iraq, his approval ratings had reached a Gallup Poll record low of 25 percent.

THEN On the evening of November 22, 1963, just hours after President John Kennedy was assassinated in Dallas, Texas, Vice President Lyndon Baines Johnson took the presidential oath of office aboard Air Force One. The new president and his nation were still in shock at the events that had unfolded earlier that day. Glued to the television, the nation wondered who was responsible and whether the nation's security was at risk. They looked to the new president for hope and leadership, and Democrats as well as Republicans quickly rallied to support him. In a Gallup poll conducted shortly after Johnson took the oath, a near record 79 percent approved of his performance, affording him considerable presidential power. Johnson would use his lofty position in the following year and a half to push for civil rights legislation, secure a landslide election victory, and initiate comprehensive "Great Society" legislation aimed at improving education and defeating poverty. He also used his position to escalate a war against the communist threat in Vietnam, Laos, and Cambodia. President Johnson first deployed 3,500 U.S. combat units to the ground war in 1965. Initially, the public overwhelmingly supported the deployment. Over the next five years, however, the Johnson administration sent more and more combat troops to Vietnam to fight against the communist-backed North Vietnamese army and the guerrilla-type tactics they employed. The war continued to rage on with no end in sight as the number of American casualties grew and the costs of the war mounted. All of this took a serious toll on President Johnson's standing in the polls, as his popularity gradually declined to a low of 35 percent during his final year in office. Like George W. Bush, Lyndon Johnson saw the highest of highs and the lowest of lows in the court of public opinion.

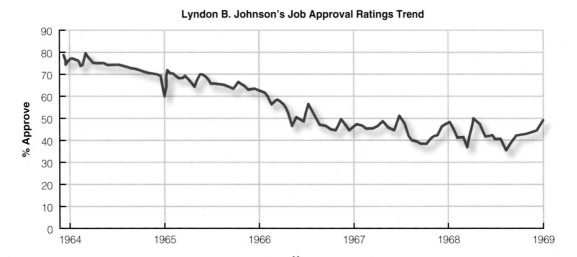

Lyndon B. Johnson's Job Approval Ratings Trend

% Approve

Year

Source: The Gallup Organization. © 1970 The Gallup Organization.

For political leaders and citizens alike, the appetite for information on what the public thinks has always been hearty. Today, this appetite is fed through the large number of opinion polls whose results are disseminated through newspapers, magazines, television, radio, and the Internet. The methods of gauging public opinion have advanced quite dramatically over the nation's history, and this advancement has been driven in no small part by the obsession to know "what Americans think." The nation's democratic roots, featuring a commitment to majoritarian rule and the notion of "consent of the governed," raise public opinion to a lofty status in the workings of American politics. Indeed, the willingness of officials to heed the people's voice has become firmly entrenched in the American political culture. A president's authority to govern is, in part, influenced by his standing in the polls. When public support is high, a president enjoys a great deal of persuasive power, as Presidents Johnson and Bush did in 1963 and 2001, respectively. When public support dropped for both presidents, each man was reduced to a weak lame duck with little or no power to influence American politics. Knowing this, modern presidential candidates invest heavily in conducting significant numbers of public opinion polls throughout their election campaigns. Even when they are victorious, presidents continue to invest in conducting polls while in office.

Scientific measurement of public opinion is a relatively recent phenomenon in American politics. But the significant role that public opinion plays in the formulation of policy is as old as American democracy itself. Understanding what public opinion is, how it is expressed, how it forms, and how it is measured in contemporary politics is critical to understanding how American government works.

Public Opinion in American Politics

★ LO Understand both the theoretically important role that public opinion plays in American democracy and the tactical function public opinion plays in the policymaking process

The concept of public opinion is central to the American system of government. But the way in which public opinion is gauged and its relevance and uses in the American political system have changed over the nation's history. The U.S. Constitution begins with the words "We the People," highlighting the important role of the *public* in the creation of the government. Nonetheless, there is no mention of the term *public opinion* in the Constitution. The word *democracy* literally translated (from its Greek roots *demos kratos*) means "rule by the people," and thus the opinions of the public take on a particularly important role in governing. The American system of government was founded on a set of democratic principles, first articulated by Plato and Aristotle and later popularized by political philosophers of the eighteenth-century Enlightenment, such as Montesquieu.[1] These principles herald the role of the public in governing and in consenting to what government does.

From the time of the Founders up through the present day, the virtues of public opinion and its role in American democracy have been continually extolled. James Madison argued that the "public voice" and its formal role in voting provided primary justification for adopting the proposed Constitution. Borrowing from the political theories of John Locke, Madison acknowledged that government must serve the "will of the people." Andrew Jackson's presidency encouraged and empowered the rise of the "common man" to express his opinion for the purpose of influencing government.

Political leaders recognize that public opinion plays not only a theoretically important role in our democratic form of government, but an important tactical role as well. Political scientist E. E. Schattschneider, in an influential book titled *The Semisovereign People*, argued that "public opinion can emerge as a key factor in any political context," and that public opinion often is responsible for determining the outcome of important political battles. Long before Schattschneider, President Abraham Lincoln expressed this idea based on his own experiences, saying: "Public sentiment is everything. With public sentiment, nothing can fail; without it, nothing can succeed."[2]

Though most scholars, elected leaders, and everyday citizens would agree that **public opinion** is and should be very important in our system of government, the concept remains hard to define and measure. Many scholars regard public opinion

Public opinion
The summation of individual opinions on any particular issue or topic.

MANUEL BALCE CENETA/ASSOCIATED PRESS

as simply the summation of individual opinions on any particular issue or topic. Political scientist V. O. Key Jr., however, defined public opinion more specifically as "those opinions held by private persons which government finds it prudent to heed." As an input in the American political system, public opinion must not only exist, Key argued, but it must also be "heeded" or at least heard by those making policy decisions.[3]

Public opinion is a vague, though important, concept. It is regularly used by presidents to justify their policies, by political candidates to mount campaigns, by interest groups to promote their causes, by journalists to describe public preferences, and by scholars to understand the American government. Today public opinion polls—for better or worse—have become the yardstick through which public opinion is understood and evaluated. The barrage of polls released daily by major media organizations provides a plethora of data defining the American psyche. There are, however, numerous practices in addition to polling through which public opinion in America may be expressed.

Protesters at an April 2006 rally in Washington, DC, calling for American intervention to stop genocide in Darfur. Protests are an important expression of public opinion in the United States.

How Is Public Opinion Expressed?

The formal constitutional mechanism by which public opinion influences the federal government is the free, open, and regular election of House members. Since ratification of the Seventeenth Amendment in 1913, the direct election of U.S. senators has served as yet another constitutional means for the expression of public opinion. Chapter 14 covers this form of expressing public opinion in detail. Voting is one important expression of public opinion and provides guarantees that officials are responsive to voters. In many state and local elections, voters are asked to respond to referendum questions, which empower the public to directly resolve policy issues. But there are a number of additional ways beyond voting in which public opinion has an influence on government. The First Amendment's guarantees that the people have the right to free speech, to peaceably assemble, and to petition their

★ LO

Learn the different ways in which public opinion may be expressed, including public opinion polls, rallies and protests, blogging, voting, and contributing time and money to campaigns

Shaping Public Opinion, One Blog at a Time

Though many politically aware Americans still express their opinions on politics in traditional ways such as by writing letters to their local newspaper or by participating in live protests, millions of others have taken advantage of home computers with modems to post comments on the Internet through the use of political web logs, or "blogs." Blogs vary widely in form, but most feature some form of personal commentary, references to data, and links to other sources on the Internet related to the topic of discussion (often these links are to other political blogs).

Do blogs provide "objective journalism"? Most bloggers don't even aspire to that goal. Rather, they simply aim to provide up-to-date, personal perspectives on current political topics. Nor do readers hold most bloggers accountable for their lack of objectivity either—liberals tend to flock to more liberal blogs such as *The Daily Kos* and *Talking Points Memo*, while conservatives frequent conservative bloggers' sites, such as *Powerline* or the blog of conservative author Michelle Makin. Indeed, many bloggers proudly state their political biases up front. Regardless, the danger remains that like-minded audiences will simply accept bloggers' opinions as the truth without any further research or reflection. Consider that Brigham Young University political scientist Richard Davis recently discovered that most people

CAROL T. POWERS/THE NEW YORK TIMES/REDUX

Pictured above is Ana Marie Cox, founder of the popular "Wonkette," a blog about life in Washington.

who closely follow both political blogs and traditional news media tend to believe the content on blogs is more accurate.

For Critical Thinking and Discussion

1. Do you go to blogs to shape your own political opinions? Why or why not?
2. Do you tend to visit blogs that reinforce your own biases and attitudes, or do you look for blogs that challenge your opinions?
3. What can bloggers add to coverage of an ongoing political event, such as a major party political convention, that traditional journalists may have difficulty capturing?

---

government pave the way for political rallies and protest rallies, which are important manifestations of public opinion.

Supporting a candidate and engaging in attempts to elect an individual or political party to office through a monetary contribution or a contribution of time and effort is another way that public opinion is expressed. Likewise, contributing time or money to an interest group or political action committee enables individuals to express their opinion indirectly and may have a significant impact on what government does.

Public opinion is also expressed through the news media. Journalists often provide commentary on politics and public issues through talk radio shows, Web sites, editorial pages, and television news talk shows that provide perspectives on public opinion. Individual citizens may also use the media to express their opinion, by writing letters to the editor or by posting on a political blog. In addition, members of the public often choose to express their opinion directly to elected officials by contacting them, via either a letter or e-mail, a phone call, or the Internet, for their views on a particular issue.

Yet perhaps the most visible and widely used expression of public opinion in contemporary politics is the public opinion poll. Most major and many smaller media organizations today regularly conduct polls on politics and policy issues, and publish

the results of those polls in the form of news stories. The *USA Today*/Gallup poll, the CBS/*New York Times* poll, the Fox News/ Opinion Dynamics poll, and the NBC/*Wall Street Journal* poll are only a few examples of media-based polls that, on a regular basis, provide data on American public opinion.

The Levels of Public Opinion

Public opinion exists at three basic levels— the broad level of values and beliefs, an intermediate level of political orientations, and the specific level of preferences about particular topics.

Values and Beliefs

At the highest, most abstract level are the **values and beliefs** of the American people. Values are the broad principles underlying the American political culture that most citizens support and adhere to; they represent that which people find most important in life. Beliefs are the facts derived from values that people take for granted about the world. Although there are a number of values that Americans hold dear, political scientist Samuel Huntington[4] has identified four politically relevant values that are widely accepted in the American political culture and serve as the basis for defining political beliefs on which there is great consensus in America: liberty, equality, individualism, and the rule of law.

The vast majority of Americans support the idea of basic freedoms and liberties, such as freedom of religion and freedom of speech. These liberties are embedded in our political culture and serve as the basis for many government policies. Because Americans value liberty, for example, they believe that people should have the right to choose a religion or not to choose a religion, the right to publicly disagree with the president or the party in power, and the right to publish articles or news stories without government retribution.

Likewise, a majority of Americans firmly value the concept stated in the Declaration of Independence that "all men are created equal." Regardless of economic status, race, or gender, the American public on the whole subscribes to the belief that all people should be treated equally under the law and that all people should have equal opportunities for economic success.

Americans also show a strong propensity to support the value of individualism. Over the years, Americans have consistently shown a preference for rewarding individual hard work and for limiting the role of government.[5] Jefferson's maxim that "that government is best which governs the least" presumes that society will advance by encouraging individuals to succeed and leads to a faith in capitalism and free enterprise as the optimal economic system. Also, the Puritan work ethic that served as an important value in early American society continues to be reflected in Americans' affinity for the value of individualism.

MARK WILSON/GETTY IMAGES

Kindergarten students in a Maryland classroom learn to appreciate the values associated with the American flag.

★ LO

Distinguish between the different levels of public opinion, from broad values and beliefs, to partisan and ideological orientations, to attitudes and opinions on specific items

Values and beliefs
The broad principles underlying the American political culture that citizens support and adhere to.

Finally, the value of the "rule of law" encourages a strong belief in the legitimacy of the U.S. Constitution, in the importance of elections as a way to configure government, and in the beliefs that the opinion of the majority should prevail, that those in the minority should have the right to challenge the majority, and that those accused of a crime should be entitled to fair procedures.

Unlike other levels of public opinion, values and beliefs are unique in that they generally receive a high level of support and consensus. Whether individuals are Democrats or Republicans, from the far right or the far left, elites or more representative of the masses—the vast majority generally subscribe to these broad values. Accordingly, values are the level of public opinion that define our political culture; widespread agreement and support for them is thus critical to the maintenance of the American political system.

Political Orientations

Political orientations

The translation of values and beliefs into a systematic way of assessing the political environment.

Values and beliefs are very broad and abstract notions held by Americans that provide general guidance to people in thinking about politics. **Political orientations** are the translation of these values and beliefs into a systematic way of assessing the political environment. Although there may be broad consensus about values and beliefs among Americans, the translation of these values into an organized way of thinking about politics and issues is considerably more varied.

The two primary ways in which Americans orient themselves toward political topics and issues are partisanship (see Figure 10.1) and political ideology. Partisanship, which is discussed in a later chapter, features a psychological attachment to one of the main political parties, generally either the Democrats or the Republicans.[6] A partisan identification provides an orientational mechanism for understanding how to apply one's values and beliefs to the political world. Consider, for example, the political debate over affirmative action policies. A Democratic orientation largely applies the value of equality and the belief that people of all races and creeds should enjoy equal opportunities, therefore suggesting support for affirmative action programs, which attempt to level the playing field and make corrections for policies that have historically benefited white males. A Republican orientation, on the other hand, generally places a higher priority on the value of individualism and the belief that government should not interfere with individual initiatives to succeed, thus suggesting opposition to affirmative action programs. Partisan orientation often helps people translate values into specific opinions.

Political ideology

A philosophical guide that people use to help translate their values and beliefs into political preferences.

Liberal ideology

A political orientation that favors a more assertive role in the redistribution of economic resources, but emphasizes individual freedom on a range of social issues.

Conservative ideology

A political orientation that generally favors government activism in defense of more traditional values on social issues, but favors government restraint in economic redistribution.

Likewise, political ideology provides an orientation for translating values into specific opinions. **Political ideology** is a philosophical guide that people use to help translate their values and beliefs into specific political preferences. The dominant ideologies in America are liberalism and conservatism. The contemporary **liberal ideology**, which is more closely associated with the modern Democratic Party, prefers that government take a more assertive role in the redistribution of economic resources, but that government advocate positions that emphasize individual freedom on a range of social issues. Today's **conservative ideology**, which is more closely identified with the Republican Party, favors government activism in defense of more traditional values on social issues, but prefers government restraint in economic redistribution.

The liberal and conservative camps largely agree on the basic values and beliefs of the American political culture—in the rule of law and majority rule and minority rights and in the idea that the free enterprise system will generally guarantee the most robust economy. But liberals and conservatives often differ when seeking to translate these values and beliefs into actual policies.

Partisanship and political ideology are two very important topics in the study of American public opinion. They provide a framework for individuals to translate broad values and beliefs into preferences for issue positions and political candidates. These orientations help people to efficiently form opinions and express those opinions. Partisanship and political ideology also enable both political leaders and

FIGURE 10.1 Partisanship in America

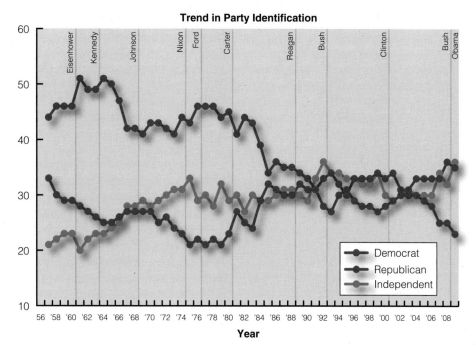

Trend in Party Identification

Source: www.people-press.org/party-identification-trend/.

An important and well-studied political orientation of the American public is political partisanship, which provides a framework through which many Americans make sense of the often complex and confusing political world. Partisanship is quite influential in helping individuals form opinions on policy preferences as well as perceptions of political leaders and candidates for office. As the graph indicates, the distribution of partisanship among the American public has remained relatively stable over the past fifty years.

scholars to better understand why Americans think what they think about particular issues and vote the way they vote in elections.

The political orientations of Americans tend to be quite stable and lasting[7]—more so than the specific preferences that people have toward policies and political actors. The stability in American political orientations provides an order and consistency to American public opinion, which ultimately promotes stability in the political system as a whole.

Political Preferences

The most discussed level of public opinion is the particular **political preferences** that Americans have on policy issues, their attitudes regarding the performance of political leaders and institutions, and their candidate preferences in elections. Support for the minimum wage, gun control proposals, the use of U.S. troops in fighting terrorism, abortion policy, campaign finance reform proposals, tax increases, or tax cuts are all specific policy issues on which the American public expresses opinions. In addition to policies, Americans also hold specific opinions about the performance of their elected leaders such as the president, as well as their confidence in institutions such as Congress, the U.S. Supreme Court, and the military.

What Americans think about the minimum wage, the performance of the president, or the candidates in a political campaign is highly influenced by their political orientations. For example, an individual who identifies as a Republican and considers herself ideologically conservative is much less likely to say she approves of President Obama's performance than would a Democrat who considers himself to be liberal.

Political preferences
The attitudes people maintain regarding the performance of political leaders and institutions, their candidate preferences in elections, and specific policy issues.

How Informed Is Public Opinion?

As discussed earlier in this chapter, American democracy relies on public opinion to choose leaders and inform public policy. This reliance is based on an important assumption about democracy—that citizens have the necessary information and skills to be able to understand political issues and provide informed input. Since the time of Plato and Aristotle, political philosophers have dealt with questions about this important assumption: is the public capable of democracy?

In the *Federalist Papers*, Alexander Hamilton and James Madison expressed concerns about the fickleness of public opinion and the potential "tyranny of the masses," which could lead to instability in governance.[8] Hamilton's solution for this problem was a republican form of government, in which the public chooses leaders who run the government, rather than a direct democracy in which the public rules directly.

FIGURE 10.2 American Political Preferences and Opinions on Selected Issues

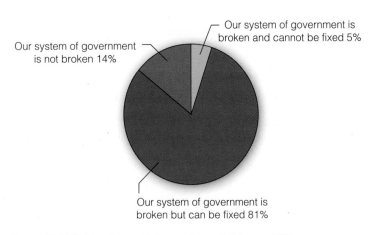

Which of the following comes closest to your view?

Our system of government is broken and cannot be fixed 5%

Our system of government is not broken 14%

Our system of government is broken but can be fixed 81%

Source: CNN/Opinion Research Corporation poll, February 2010.

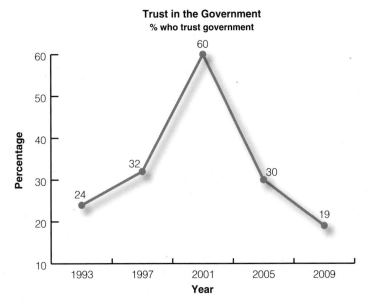

Trust in the Government
% who trust government

Source: CNN/Opinion Research Corporation poll, February 2010.

Suspicions about the capacity of the public for meaningful contributions to governance were also articulated quite well by Walter Lippman in the early twentieth century.[9] Lippman, a well-known public opinion scholar, delivered withering attacks on ordinary citizens' lack of knowledge regarding politics. He argued that citizens invest very little energy and effort in acquiring information about politics, and as a consequence, the public lacks the necessary knowledge for their opinions to provide value. Subsequent research in the 1960s and 1970s, most notably by Philip Converse and his colleagues in *The American Voter*, used scientific surveys to support the argument that ordinary citizens tend to be ill-informed about political issues, ill-equipped to understand politics, and quite fickle in how they stand on issues.[10]

More contemporary studies indicate that the American public today is uninformed about politics. For example, a May 2008 national survey[11] of Americans found:

- 73 percent did not know that the Bill of Rights prohibits the official establishment of religion in the United States.

- 79 percent could not identify the Gettysburg Address as the source of "Government of the people, for the people and by the people."

- 50 percent could not name the three branches of the federal government.

- 25 percent could not name any power of the federal government.

- 35 percent could not name one country that was an enemy of the United States during World War II.

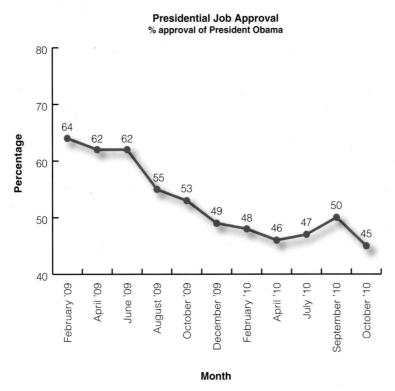

Presidential Job Approval
% approval of President Obama

The approval rating that Americans give to the performance of the president is also subject to wide shifts. This figure shows the approval rating for first two years of the Barack Obama presidency.

Source: CNN/Opinion Research Corporation poll.

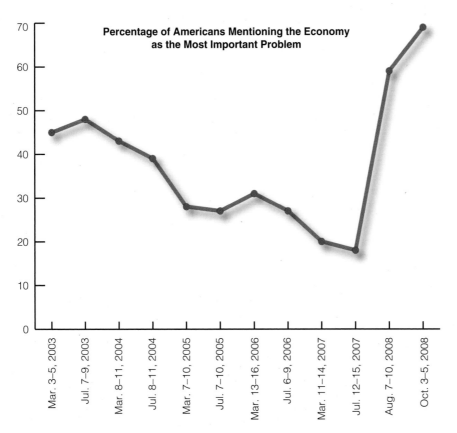

Percentage of Americans Mentioning the Economy as the Most Important Problem

The Gallup Organization regularly asks the American people what they think is the most important issue facing the country. A common answer is the economy, which jumped in late 2008 as the economy tumbled.

Source: The Gallup Organization. ©2003–2008 The Gallup Organization.

MIKE BLAKE/REUTERS/LANDOV

Voters in Glendale, California, waiting to cast their ballot in the November 2006 elections.

In addition, many surveys show that the public's level of expressed interest in politics is quite low. During the 2007 presidential primary campaign, for example, the Pew Center found that only one in five voters said that they were "very interested" in following the races—and this represented an increase of seven percentage points over interest in the race in 2003. With such little knowledge of and lack of interest in politics, should public opinion even be considered an important factor in making public policy? How much confidence should we have in the outcome of elections where the voters know little about the candidates and the issues?

Some political scientists have come to the defense of the American public in this regard. V. O. Key Jr., in his work *The Responsible Electorate*,[12] stated that although "many voters act in odd ways indeed," if one studies the electorate more carefully one would find that "voters are not fools." Key observed that "'in the large, the electorate behaves about as rationally and responsibly as we should expect, given the clarity of the alternatives presented to it and the character of the information available to it." If political leaders don't rationally discuss issues and provide a framework for voters to use to understand politics, it is not the voters who should be blamed, but rather the leaders. Considering this caveat, Key extolled the capacity of the public to form stable, responsible opinions and to contribute to the governing process.

Benjamin Page and Robert Shapiro extended Key's ideas in their book *The Rational Public*.[13] They used decades of public opinion poll data to show that over the long haul, public opinion on many issues does remain fairly stable, and when it does change, it moves in logical directions. The aggregate responses of the public in polls, Page and Shapiro found, make sense and demonstrate rationality. They also found that the public makes distinctions between important policy areas and that public opinion tends to form meaningful patterns, consistent with a set of underlying beliefs and values.

The link between public opinion on an issue and public policy is a difficult one to establish. Page and Shapiro report that over the long haul, there does seem to be a relationship between public attitudes on policy issues and the public policies that emerge from government. These researchers also argue that when public opinion shifts, a corresponding shift in public policy is likely to follow.

Political scientist Samuel Kernell has noted a more indirect link between public opinion and public policy:[14] political actors (most notably the president) who have high levels of public support are generally better able to get legislation passed. President Bush, for example, in 2003 was able to get Congress to pass a new tax cut package in part because of the high job performance ratings Americans gave him at that time. High levels of public support may be translated into an officeholder's greater political power to influence the legislative process.

How Does Public Opinion Form?

Through voting, opinion polls, protest rallies, communications with leaders, and newspaper editorials, public opinion is expressed and provides an important input for public policymaking. But how do individuals develop their particular political orientations, and how do they come to hold their specific political preferences? How do the more deep-seated values and beliefs form? What influences the values that people hold, their partisan and ideological orientations, and their opinions on specific issues?

Political socialization is the process by which an individual acquires values, beliefs, and opinions about politics. Political socialization is a lifelong process, beginning in early childhood and continuing throughout an individual's life. The learning process that leads to the acquisition of values and opinions not only applies to politics—it also applies to other orientations of people, including their beliefs about religion and culture.

Just as there are a number of factors and influences that lead individuals to consider themselves Democrats or Republicans or supporters of gun control or gun rights, there are also numerous factors and influences that lead people to choose a particular religion, such as Protestant or Catholic, or to choose no religion at all. Socialization is important not only in the development of political learning for individuals, but also in the transmission of fundamental beliefs and values of the American political culture from one generation to the next.

Though political socialization is a lifelong process, there are certain times in life when political learning is greater. For example, the political socialization that occurs early in life has a more profound impact on political orientations than learning that occurs in adulthood. The impressions and information that are acquired while the individual is younger tend to be most influential and the longest lasting. Psychologists refer to this as the **primacy tendency**.

Though early political learning tends to be most profound, socialization to politics remains at work through a number of influences over the course of a person's life. A number of factors and institutions, known as **agents of political socialization**,[15] have been identified as having a particularly relevant impact on one's socialization to politics.

Certainly demographic factors such as race, ethnicity, gender, age, and economic status go a long way toward defining individuals' identities, and can influence their political values. But a list of the most important agents of political socialization also includes such influences as family, friends and peer groups, schools, the media, and religion. Collectively, these agents promote the acquisition of the political values, beliefs, and opinions that an individual comes to hold.

Family

Because much of the early years in a person's life are dominated by experiences with the family, the primacy tendency leads many to develop values and beliefs consistent with parents' values and beliefs. Parents begin to teach their children about the political world early in the child's life. They transfer feelings about such concepts as authority, freedom, democracy, and racial prejudice to their children in both

Recognize that political socialization is a lifelong process and know a number of important factors (such as the family, schools, friends, religion) that contribute to the development of political opinions

★ LO

Political socialization
The process by which an individual acquires values, beliefs, and opinions about politics.

Primacy tendency
The theory that impressions acquired while an individual is younger are likely to be more influential and longer lasting.

Agents of political socialization
Factors that have a significant impact on an individual's socialization to politics.

ERIC FOWKE/PHOTOEDIT

Parents provide an important influence in socializing their children to appreciate American political values. Above, a father teaches his son to appreciate the values associated with Independence Day.

AMERICAN GOVERNMENT In Global Perspective

What the World Thinks about the United States

The Pew Global Attitudes project asks other nations what they think about Americans. One journalist, Andisheh Nouraee, had this take on a recent Pew survey about Americans:

The Pew Global Attitudes Project is an ongoing series of worldwide public opinion surveys designed to help Americans understand what the rest of the world is thinking about important issues. The [2006] survey asked 16,000 people in 15 countries what they think about several important political issues. Most important to us, the poll asked what people think about us. . . . Sit back and enjoy the bad news: The world doesn't like us . . . only four [countries] had majorities who say they have a favorable opinion of the United States.

The United States' worst favorability ratings come from the Muslim countries in the survey. Only 30 percent of Indonesians and Egyptians view the U.S. favorably. In Pakistan, it's 27 percent; in Jordan, 15 percent; and in Turkey, only 12 percent of the people polled said they have a favorable opinion of the United States. Those numbers are especially disturbing when you consider that those countries are all considered friends of the U.S. And Turkey is not only a democracy, it's a member of NATO. If that's what our Muslim friends think of us, imagine what our Muslim enemies must think.

The only country with a large Muslim population whose citizens view the U.S. favorably is Nigeria. Don't cheer up just yet, though. When Pew divided the Nigerian respondents into Muslims and Christians, they found that just 32 percent of Nigerian Muslims like us. Nigeria's overall pro-America numbers were so high, it turns out, because an astonishing 89 percent of Nigerian Christians like us. According to Pew, more Nigerian Christians view the U.S. favorably than the Americans do.

The other stunner from the "How they like us now?" survey is the sharp decline of the United States' favorability rating in Spain. Only 23 percent of Spaniards view the U.S. favorably this year, down from 41 percent last year. Remember, they're not only an ally, but they actually sent troops to Iraq when we asked. Of the 14 countries surveyed, only two of the countries have majorities who say they have some or a lot of confidence in Bush's international leadership. Those two countries: Nigeria and India.

In Great Britain, our greatest ally that isn't actually touching us, 30 percent of those surveyed say that they at least have some confidence in Bush's international leadership. In France, that number dips to 15 percent; in Spain, 7 percent; and in Turkey, just 3 percent of those surveyed said they have at least some confidence in Bush's international leadership. Three percent! That's one out of every 33 people. It makes me wonder if the people who said they have confidence in Bush even heard the question correctly. . . .

Source: Andisheh Nouraee, "What do foreigners think of America these days?" http://atlanta.creativeloafing.com/gyrobase/Content?oid=oid%3A93423.

formal and informal ways. By standing at attention during the playing of the national anthem or attending a Memorial Day service, parents are informally communicating important values about politics. Telling children that skin color should not affect how to think about a particular person or explaining why it is important to vote in an election are formal ways political information is communicated.

These early formal and informal cues from parents have a long-term and lasting impact on a child's political socialization. Over the years, researchers have found that children whose parents are more involved in politics tend to be more involved in politics themselves. The transference of party identification from parent to child is also significant. Children who grew up in homes where parents regard politics as important also tend to regard politics as important throughout their lives. Because children generally want to be like their parents, the many cues, both formal and informal, that they receive from their parents are a strong influence on the formation of political orientation.

Friends and Peer Groups

As children grow older, they begin to interact with people outside of their immediate family. They seek friendships with others and show a desire to get along with social groups. Children acquire a great deal of new political learning through their friends and associates, as well as from the social groups that they seek to join. Often, the values, beliefs, and opinions of social peers are the same as or similar to those of the family, so friends and peers reinforce what was learned from parents. For example, wealthy people tend to live together in particular neighborhoods, and so as children from wealthy families find friends and peers, they are likely to find people who have been socialized by their parents in ways similar to themselves.

By the fifth or sixth grade, children become cognitively equipped to better understand the world of politics. Whereas previous learning tends to be based on unquestioned acceptance of what is being communicated, young adults have the ability to critically analyze new information. This cognitive skill development comes at a time in life (young adolescence) when friends and peer groups are particularly influential. Thus the desire to get along and to form social relationships has an important influence on political learning at this point in life.

The Schools

Part of the curriculum in many school systems across the United States focuses on the development of political values, such as respect for authority, legitimacy of our political institutions, patriotism, and capitalism. Classes in civic education and American government, the daily morning pledge of allegiance to the flag, and pictures of American presidents are just some of the mechanisms by which schools act as an agent of socialization.

BOB DAEMMRICH/PHOTOEDIT

High schools, such as this one in Austin, Texas, help to teach the values of the democratic process by providing mock trials in which students learn how our legal system works.

Actress and comedian Tina Fey made several appearances on the comedy show *Saturday Night Live* impersonating Republican vice presidential nominee Sarah Palin and helping to influence what voters thought about the candidate.

Stephen Colbert, of TV's popular *Colbert Report*, uses the medium of cable television to provide political humor.

Schools serve as an important mechanism for the positive development of attitudes about basic American democratic values, thus promoting general positive attitudes about the legitimacy of the democratic system. Research conducted by David Easton and his colleagues in the 1950s and 1960s demonstrated that schools promoted a positive affective attachment to the concept of "democracy" by the third grade.[16] During the early grades, children acquire beliefs regarding a citizen's role in politics—obeying laws, voting, and paying attention to political events.

Political socialization from the school is not limited to elementary and high school. The college experience also has an important socializing effect on citizens' political development. College graduates tend to be more likely to vote and participate in politics, they are more likely to follow news and political campaigns, and they are better able to understand the political world in which they live. The effects of formal education, even beyond the specific civics education curriculum of the earlier grades, make an important positive contribution to an individual's political socialization.

The Media

Americans spend a great deal of time accessing news information and being entertained by the mass media. It is not surprising, then, that the media act as an important agent of political socialization as well. Information that citizens glean from media news coverage about political events and political campaigns has an impact on their values, beliefs, and opinions. Research has shown that heavy users of the news media are more politically informed than lighter users;[17] they are also more supportive of basic American values, such as individualism, equality, and free speech rights.

The media's impact as a socialization agent extends beyond the provision of news information. Entertainment television, the movies, talk radio, and other media forms also inspire various types of political learning. Studies have shown, for example, that entertainment television tends to promote negative stereotypes of women and minorities, which may reinforce negative attitudes about race or affirmative action. Use of Internet Web sites and blogs may also help shape a person's political outlook.

Religion

Throughout American history, religious organizations have played an important role in the political socialization process. The values of individualism and hard work were important influences in establishing a capitalist economy and continue to underpin economic policy in the United States. These values, based on the Protestant work ethic, continue to influence the socialization process. More recently, the Christian-based fundamentalist movement has utilized religious teaching to influence opinions about political issues. The Catholic Church's opposition to abortion affects many Catholics' position on that issue.

How Is Public Opinion Measured?

When Americans think about the term *public opinion* in contemporary politics, they often focus on the results of public opinion polls. A **public opinion poll** is a method of measuring the opinions of a large group of people by selecting a subset of the larger group, asking them a set of questions, and generalizing the findings to the larger group.

Public opinion poll
A method of measuring the opinions of a large group of people by asking questions of a subset of the larger group and then generalizing the findings to the larger group.

Public opinion polls are not the only way that public opinion in America is either expressed or understood, but polls have become the most obvious and important instrument for gauging public opinion. Polls provide information that elected leaders use in making public policy, thus providing an important way for public sentiment to influence public policy. Polls have also become a centerpiece of elections, used both by the candidates to shape a winning strategy and by journalists to provide news coverage of campaigns.

Polling has become a huge industry in the United States. To the public, the most visible polls are those that are regularly conducted by media organizations, asking Americans what they think about a variety of topics, such as who they plan to vote for in an upcoming election, how they rate the job the president is doing, how they feel about the condition of the economy, and many other topics. Media polls are conducted with the purpose of broadcasting results as news stories. However, the polling industry extends far beyond media polls. Candidates at all levels conduct polls to identify strategies for waging a successful election campaign. Federal, state, and local government agencies conduct polls to evaluate the successes and failures of public programs. Interest groups conduct polls to promote their agendas.

Even though polls have come to play an important and visible role in American politics, the manner in which they are conducted is often misunderstood, and questions about their accuracy are often raised. What makes a poll "scientific"? How is it possible to interview 1,000 Americans and conclude how more than 200 million Americans think? How can two polls be conducted on the same topic and produce different findings? An understanding of polling techniques can help answer these questions.

The History of Political Polling

The immediate predecessor to modern scientific polling in the United States dates back to the 1824 presidential campaign. Newspapers such as the *Boston Globe*, *New York Herald*, and *Harrisburg Pennsylvanian* attempted to gauge voter attitudes about the presidential candidates and predict the election outcome that year by conducting what has come to be known as the **straw poll**. A straw poll gathers the opinions of people who are conveniently available in a particular gathering place. (Today, many refer to these polls as "convenience" polls.) Back in 1824, the newspapers sent "counters" to public places (such as taverns and public meetings) to ask patrons and attendees who they planned to vote for in the upcoming election. Newspaper publishers quickly found a hearty appetite among readers for stories that attempted to predict the outcome of political races—an appetite modern media executives continue to find quite strong today.

Straw poll
An unscientific poll that gathers the opinions of people who are conveniently available in a gathering place.

Polling Problems in Presidential Elections

"Dewey Defeats Truman"? "Gore defeats Bush"? Not so, as it turned out. Still, that didn't stop public opinion pollsters from convincing many in the media that Thomas Dewey would be elected president in 1948, and that Al Gore would be the winner in 2000. More than fifty years apart, the polls played an important role in two predictions that caused considerable confusion. Then, in 2008, the pollsters struck again. . . .

In 1948, polls leading up to Election Day predicted that New York Governor Thomas Dewey would soundly defeat President Harry S. Truman. The Gallup Poll, the Roper Poll, and other opinion polling organizations consistently found Dewey ahead throughout much of the fall campaign. The scientific sampling methods they employed had been used by these same organizations in successfully calling the winner of every presidential race since 1936. The problem? All the major pollsters stopped their preelection polling at least two weeks before Election Day. In fact, Dewey did maintain a large lead throughout the campaign, a lead that had not changed up through mid-October.

The polls projected Thomas Dewey to defeat President Harry Truman in 1948. The polls were wrong, but they led many newspapers across the country to prematurely project Truman's defeat as they went to press.

So the pollsters just stopped polling. Then, in the final weeks of the campaign, Truman's furious and aggressive campaign schedule began to make a difference, and voter opinions began to shift in favor of the incumbent president. Yet the pollsters didn't pick

Early straw polls assumed that the accuracy of polls was based on the total number of respondents who were included in each poll. The larger the number of respondents, the more accurate the results, so it was thought. Straw polls remained the basic methodology for conducting polls for more than a century.[18]

By the early 1930s, the most famous national straw poll was the *Literary Digest* poll. In addition to conducting straw polls on policy issues, this poll correctly predicted the winner of the 1920, 1924, 1928, and 1932 presidential elections. The *Literary Digest* conducted its polls by mailing ballots to millions of people. Mailing addresses were obtained from the *Digest*'s own readership lists as well as telephone directories and automobile registration lists. The *Digest* assumed its accuracy in predicting election outcomes was based on the large number of ballots that it counted from voters across the country.

In the 1936 election between Franklin Roosevelt and Alfred Landon, the *Literary Digest* collected ballots from more than 2 million people and confidently predicted that Landon would receive 55 percent of the vote, Roosevelt would get 41 percent, and the remaining 4 percent would go to Union Party candidate William Lemke. The actual election results stunned the *Literary Digest* and its many readers. Roosevelt won the election with a whopping 61 percent of the popular vote. Landon garnered 36.5 percent, whereas Lemke won less than 2 percent. The missed projection put the *Literary Digest* out of business.

This widely publicized missed call by the *Literary Digest* is explained by the faulty assumption of the straw poll methodology—the assumption that the greater

W. EUGENE SMITH/TIME & LIFE PICTURES/GETTY IMAGES

up these changes. Thus their confident prediction that Dewey would win proved wrong, and the *Chicago Daily Tribune* became famous for running the presses with its premature headline: "Dewey Defeats Truman."

In 2000, the presidential election between Republican George W. Bush and Democrat Al Gore proved once again the pollsters could be fallible. In the last few weeks of the campaign, many respected polling organizations showed a tight race between the two candidates. The Voter News Service (VNS), a company that conducted polls of voters almost immediately after they exited voting booths (aptly termed "exit polls"), was supported in 2000 by ABC, CBS, NBC, CNN, Fox, and the Associated Press. On Election Day that year, VNS conducted exit polls in each of the fifty states as a way of predicting the winner in each state, thus facilitating an accurate prediction of the Electoral College outcome. For each of the fifty states in the previous seven presidential elections, network exit polling correctly predicted the presidential winners. When the polls in Florida closed at 8 PM, VNS began tabulating its results, including its results in Florida, and sent the results to the media organizations that supported VNS. Based on the Florida exit poll data, the networks declared Gore the winner in Florida, which gave him enough Electoral College votes to win the election. Unfortunately, Florida was so close, and balloting was so complicated in that state, that the exit poll call was problematic. The flawed exit poll prediction complicated an already confusing election night for the television networks. It would take more than five weeks after Election Day, and a U.S. Supreme Court decision, to declare George W. Bush the winner in Florida, and thus the winner of the presidential election.

In 2008, preelection pollsters struggled to accurately project the outcome of several Democratic Party primaries. Most notable were the polls associated with the New Hampshire primary. *USA Today*/Gallup, CBS, Fox, and a number of other organizations conducting polls in New Hampshire all concluded that Barack Obama would win the Democratic primary. Some of the polls indicated that Obama would defeat Hillary Clinton by more than 10 points. The nation and particularly the pollsters were surprised to find on election night that Clinton had defeated Obama. Clinton's surprise win in the nation's first primary came days after Obama's defeat of Clinton in the first caucus in Iowa and helped fuel a long and bitter battle for the Democratic presidential nomination.

---

the number of respondents, the more accurate the poll. The number of interviews in a poll is only one of a number of factors that affect poll accuracy. In 1936, the United States was still fighting the effects of the Great Depression, when many Americans had difficulty making ends meet. Those Americans with telephones, automobiles, and subscriptions to the *Literary Digest* (the sources of the mailing addresses for the ballots) tended to be wealthier, less affected by the Depression, and disproportionately less likely to support the liberal economic policies of FDR's New Deal.

At the time, the *Literary Digest* debacle was aptly explained by several researchers who had already begun to conduct polls with more accurate methodologies. Chief among these was Dr. George Gallup, who was applying probability sampling methods to the polls he conducted. During the 1936 campaign, Gallup argued that the *Literary Digest* methodology was producing faulty results. His cries fell on many deaf ears until after the election, when his advice sowed the seeds for a healthy polling industry based on more scientific methods.

Scientific Sampling

The polling procedures popularized by Gallup in the aftermath of the 1936 election relied on the principles of probability theory, and focused on the sampling of the population under study.[19] A *sample* is a subgroup of people from a population who are studied for the purpose of learning something about the

BILLY E. BARNES/PHOTOEDIT

An NBC News exit pollster interviews a voter shortly after she casts her ballot. Exit polls allow the networks to project winners and losers before the polls close.

College Students Making Their Voices Heard

The economic recession of 2007–2010 slammed virtually all sectors of the American economy, including public higher education. Losses in state revenue and drops on college endowments forced many institutions to raise the cost of college tuition. As college boards of trustees began to approve sometimes large tuition hikes in 2009 and early 2010, a grassroots movement, spurred by the social networking site Facebook, various blogs, Twitter, and other types of social media, formed to speak out against these tuition increases. The Internet chatter culminated in a "March 4, 2010, Day of Action to Defend Public Education." Numerous rallies and marches to protest the cost hikes occurred on college campuses across the country that same day, including (1) more than 300 students blocking a major highway near the University of California at Davis; (2) fifteen students storming the chancellor's office at the University of Wisconsin–Milwaukee; and (3) more than 200 professors at the University of Illinois protesting pay cuts.

Protesters at the University of California express concern over college tuition increases on March 4, 2010 (picture from the March 5, 2010, *USA Today*).

For Critical Thinking and Discussion

1. Have you participated in a protest rally or march on campus? If not, why not?

2. Marches and protests as an expression of public opinion are more common on college and university campuses than they are other in other venues. Why do you think colleges and universities tend to foster this form of expression in particular?

---

whole population. Based on the laws of probability, it is possible to draw a sample from a population, administer a set of questions to those in the sample, and understand something about the entire population, within a known level of error.

A **scientific sample** is one that uses probability theory as a guide to selecting people from the population who will compose the sample. Random selection of respondents in the sample is key to achieving a scientific, or representative, sample. *Random sampling* is achieved by giving each possible respondent in the population a known chance of being selected in the sample. There are a number of ways of achieving a random sample.

Scientific sample
A randomly selected subgroup drawn from a population using probability theory.

★ LO Explain the differences between a scientific poll and an unscientific poll

Unscientific Polls

In a scientific poll, the results of the poll are generalizable to a population that is represented by the sample of people who are interviewed. **Unscientific polls** differ from scientific ones in that the sample of people who are interviewed is not representative of any group beyond those who register their opinion. There are many examples of unscientific polls in politics. What makes a poll unscientific is the way respondents are selected for the sample. If the vast majority of people in a population are given a chance of being sampled, then the poll is scientific. If not, then the sample represents nothing beyond itself. In an unscientific sample, some individuals in the population have no chance of being included. Many unscientific polls are conducted even today. A good example is the television call-in poll. Often television news shows that deal with political topics will offer viewers an opportunity to call an 800 or 900 number

Unscientific poll
A poll in which the sample of people interviewed is not representative of any group beyond those who register their opinion.

to answer a poll question. These polls are unscientific because only those people who are viewing the show have an opportunity to respond. E-mail surveys conducted by CNN.com and ESPN.com are similarly unscientific surveys. The sample of people who call in is not representative of any group beyond the callers themselves. Other examples of unscientific polls include the following:

- **Log-in polls.** A poll question pops up as you enter your computer's Web browser with the question: Do you think Sarah Palin would make a good president? Click here for "yes" or click here for "no." Many services, such as Yahoo!, Netscape, and MSN, include questions such as these on their home page, and then present a tally of the results. This type of poll is an unscientific one, because only those people who click on the browser and decided to take the time to answer the question have their opinion registered. Those who don't have a computer (for example, poorer and older people), those who don't have Internet access, and those who are less interested in politics have no chance or far fewer chances of being selected for such a poll. The results of those polls represent nothing more than the people who answer the question.

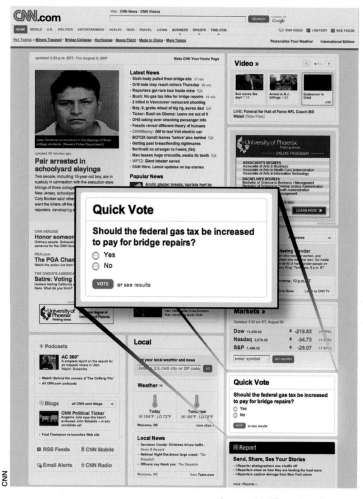

An unscientific poll as it appears to those who visit CNN's Web site.

- **SLOPs, or self-selected listener opinion polls.** Television and radio news/talk shows sometimes conduct polls during the course of a broadcast by offering an 800 or 900 phone number for registered listeners to call and express their opinion on some topic. SLOPs are also known as "call-in" polls. These polls are unscientific because only those people who happen to be tuned in to the broadcast have any opportunity to be included in the sample.

- **CRAPs, or computerized response audience polling.** This kind of poll is often used by local news organizations. Telecommunications equipment places a call, and automated voice systems ask the poll questions. Respondents are asked to use the keypad of their telephone to register their answers to the questions. The extremely high rate of refusal (for example, most people hang up when they hear the automated voice) renders them highly unscientific.

- **Intercept polls.** Have you ever been in a shopping mall when someone with a clipboard comes up to you and asks if you would answer some questions? If so, you've been solicited to participate in an intercept poll (that is, an interviewer "intercepted" you). Respondents in such polls are conveniently selected into the sample because they are spotted by the interviewer. Because people who are at shopping malls or other public places are not representative of all people, this is regarded as an unscientific type of poll.

The *Literary Digest* mishap highlights the problem with unscientific samples—those people who have no chance of being included in the sample may be very different from those who are included. Voters who had no car or published telephone number had no chance of being selected in the *Literary Digest* sample. Even though the total number of people in the sample was quite high (more than 2 million), it was not representative of the population of voters because less-well-off people had little to no chance of being included in the sample. Today's reliance on telephone surveys to gauge public opinion has come under attack on the basis that cell phone numbers are not sampled and thus systematically exclude younger Americans from the sampling (because younger people are more likely to rely on cell phones).

Pseudo-Polls

Recently, some unscrupulous political campaigns and political action committees (PACs) have been disguising themselves as pollsters for the purpose of planting messages with voters, rather than measuring public opinion. Some of these campaigns or PACs present themselves as pollsters for the purpose of fund raising as well. These phone calls have come to be known as **pseudo-polls**. As the term implies, there is no polling going on with a pseudo-poll. Pretending to be pollsters, callers often contact tens of thousands of voters and ask hypothetical (that is, untrue) questions about their political opponents—such as "Did you happen to know that John Smith is reported to have beaten his wife in the past—does this make you any less likely to support him in his race for senator?" Respondents to the call believe they are being interviewed by a legitimate polling firm and take away from the conversation a contrived and false message about a political candidate. This type of pseudo-poll is called a "push poll," because the intention of the call is to "push," or influence, people to vote a particular way.

Another type of pseudo-poll is referred to as "FRUGing," or fund raising under the guise of polling. This is an unethical practice that tricks people into thinking they are being polled by a legitimate organization, when they are really being set up for a fund-raising attempt. "SUGing," or selling under the guise of polling, is a pseudo-poll that engages in telemarketing. The individual—who will ultimately receive a sales pitch at the end of the call—believes that she or he is answering a legitimate poll.

Sample Size

A fundamental characteristic of a scientific public opinion poll is the nature of the procedures used to draw a sample from the population. The size of the sample is also a factor in poll quality. **Sampling error** is the term used to indicate the amount of error in the poll that results from interviewing a sample of people rather than the whole population under study. Sampling error is largely a function of sample size: the larger the sample size, the less sampling error with the poll. However, there is a law of diminishing returns associated with increasing the size of the sample.

For example, a national scientifically drawn sample of 200 Americans has a sampling error of about +/–7 percent at the 95 percent level of confidence. This means that with a sample of 200, chances are ninety-five in a hundred that the sample will produce results within seven points above or below the survey result. By increasing the sample size by 400 respondents, from 200 to 600, the sampling error is reduced to +/–4 percent. An additional 600 respondents in the sample, bringing the sample size to 1,200, reduces the sampling error to +/–3 percent.

Media organizations that report poll findings often attempt to convey information about the poll to help the reader/audience understand the sampling error associated with the results. Typically, a news report on a poll will include a statement like this: "The survey was conducted by telephone with a random sample of 1,200 American adults. Sampling error for the survey is +/–3 percent at the 95 percent level of confidence."

What does this statement mean? Suppose the poll found that 60 percent of the respondents approved of the job that Barack Obama was doing as president. The statement indicates that there was a "random sample" of American adults. This means that the poll was a scientific poll, and the results can be generalized to the full American adult public.

With any scientific poll, there is sampling error, and probability theory allows us to calculate what the sampling error might be. This calculation is thus expressed as a "confidence interval," or range, which is reported to be +/–3 percent of the poll

Pseudo-poll

Phone calls from members of political campaigns or PACs who present themselves as pollsters for the purpose of planting messages with voters rather than measuring public opinion.

Sampling error

The amount of error in a poll that results from interviewing a sample of people rather than the whole population under study; the larger the sample, the less the sampling error.

BLUE JEAN IMAGES/GETTY IMAGES

A telephone interviewer for a public opinion polling firm asks a randomly selected voter whom she will vote for in an upcoming election.

result (or a six-point range). The level of confidence typically reported is at the "95 percent level of confidence" (meaning that ninety-five out of one hundred similarly conducted polls would produce results in this range). Thus what the statement says, then, is that we can be 95 percent confident that the approval rating for President Obama is somewhere between 57 and 63 percent.

In addition to random selection and sample size, the quality of the sample is affected by "nonresponse" error. Once a sample is selected, it is necessary to contact and conduct interviews with those in the sample. Rarely is it possible to obtain an interview with 100 percent of those sampled. Some people refuse to be interviewed, some are not home when contacts are made, and others screen their phone calls through an answering machine or caller ID system. Nonresponse is problematic when those who do not respond tend to answer the questions differently than those who do respond. The goal is to achieve as high a response to the poll as possible in order to limit possible nonresponse error.

Modern-day scientific polls of Americans and voters typically use a probability technique known as **random-digit dialing (RDD)** to obtain scientific telephone samples. RDD uses known information about telephone area codes and exchanges and randomly assigns the last four digits to these. Because about 90 percent of the households in the United States have active telephone lines, almost everyone living in a house with a telephone has some chance of being selected in the sample.

Asking Questions on Polls

Accurate and reliable polls require not only scientific sampling procedures, but also significant attention to the way in which polling questions are asked. The way in which a question is worded can have a large impact on the type of answers that are given by survey respondents. Consider the following example of a question asked on a national survey conducted by the Roper Organization in 1993: "Does it seem possible or does it seem impossible to you that the Nazi extermination of the Jews never happened?" More than one in five respondents to the poll indicated that they thought it was possible that the Holocaust never happened. The results from this question led to a series of news stories expressing concern that nearly one-quarter of the American public questioned the reality of the Holocaust. However, researchers noted an important problem with the wording of the question; namely, it included a double negative. It is difficult for respondents, particularly in a telephone interview (where they are not

Random-digit dialing (RDD)

A probability technique for scientific telephone polling that randomly assigns the last four digits to known information about telephone area codes and exchanges.

Identify criteria ★ LO
for asking unbiased poll questions

looking at the words of the question), to interpret what it means to "seem impossible" that something "never happened." The confusing question led to the exaggerated survey result. To test the notion that the question was confusing, the Gallup organization instead asked this question in a 1994 survey: "In your opinion, did the Holocaust definitely happen, probably happen, probably not happen, or definitely not happen?" In this form of the question, only 2 percent said that the Holocaust probably did not happen, and 0 percent said that it definitely did not happen.

Another example of how wording can influence the responses to a question involves two questions, on separate surveys, intended to measure attitudes about the legality of flag burning. A CBS/*New York Times* poll asked, "Should burning or destroying the American flag as a form of political protest be legal or should it be against the law?" Fourteen percent said it should be legal, and 83 percent said it should be against the law. A Gallup poll asked the question this way: "The Supreme Court ruled that burning the American flag, though highly offensive, is protected under the free speech guarantee of the First Amendment to the Constitution. Do you agree or disagree?" Thirty-eight percent agreed that flag burning should be legal based on this question—fully twenty-four percentage points higher than what was

CHECK the List

Items That Should be Disclosed about Any Publicly Released Poll

Many polls conducted in the United States are intended to provide information for public consumption. These polls are referred to as "public polls." The *USA Today*/CNN/Gallup Poll, the *New York Times*/CBS Poll, and the Harris Interactive Poll are just a few of the organizations that regularly conduct polling intended for public consumption.

There are so many polling organizations, people often have a hard time ascertaining the quality of a poll. The National Council on Public Polls (NCPP) is an association of organizations that regularly conduct public polls. Members of NCPP have articulated the following list of items that should be disclosed about any poll that is released publicly, as a way to help the poll consumer evaluate the quality of the poll:

✔ The name of the organization that sponsored or paid for the poll

✔ The dates of interviewing

✔ The method for obtaining the interviews (for example, telephone, e-mail, in-person)

✔ A definition of the population that was sampled

✔ The size of the sample (that is, the number of interviews conducted)

✔ The size and description of subsamples, if the poll relies primarily on less than the total sample

✔ The complete wording of questions on which the poll results are based

✔ The percentages from the poll on which conclusions are based

Source: A list articulated by members of the National Council on Public Polls.

found with the CBS/*New York Times* question. In this case, the context in which Gallup framed the question—that the Supreme Court said flag burning was legal based on the First Amendment—produced the different result.

The polling community of practitioners and scholars has, over the years, conducted a number of experiments to test how question wording can influence the results of polls. Listed here are of some of the key recommendations for guidelines in constructing good poll questions:[20]

1. **Avoid double-negatives in questions (as in the Holocaust question example cited above).**

2. **Keep the question as simple as possible, using words that people with a limited vocabulary might understand.**

3. **Don't include more than one question within a question—such an error is called a double-barreled question.** An example of a double-barreled question is, "Do you approve or disapprove of the job that President Obama is doing in handling the economic and domestic affairs of the nation?" Respondents might have different answers to the president's performance in economic versus other domestic affairs.

4. **The questions should not lead the respondent to a particular answer.** The following is an example of a leading question: "Do you approve of the job that Barack Obama is doing as president?" Because only the "approve" option is stated in the question, some respondents might likely answer "yes, they approve," when they might have answered that they "disapprove" had that option been provided as well.

5. **Don't expect honest answers to socially unacceptable response questions.** For example, using illegal drugs is not only illegal but regarded as socially unacceptable. So one should not necessarily expect all drug users to answer honestly a question about their own use of drugs.

Interpreting Public Opinion Data

Assess the findings from a poll along the dimensions of direction, intensity, and continuity of public opinion ★ LO

Understanding public opinion requires attention not only to the scientific aspects of sampling and the wording of questions, but also to the analysis and interpretation of the results of a poll. In assessing results, analysts are concerned with three important characteristics of public opinion data: direction, intensity, and continuity.[21]

To understand the **direction** of public opinion, the analyst seeks to find which position or preference a majority of people hold as their opinion. On most topics, there are two possible directions in which public opinion might lean—a positive direction or a negative direction. For example, with respect to presidential approval, respondents might either approve or disapprove of the job the president is doing. Similarly, the public might either trust or distrust their political leaders; or they might support or oppose a proposal for a policy that makes it more difficult to buy a handgun. On any given opinion question, direction is a basic characteristic that the analyst seeks to gauge.

Intensity is also an important characteristic of public opinion. Often, the analyst seeks not only to find the direction of opinion but also to determine how strongly or how committed the public feels about the opinion that it holds. Consider the responses to the following question asked to a national sample of Americans in 2000: "Do you agree or disagree with this statement—companies should be allowed to advertise tobacco products on television?" Those polled were asked a follow-up question: "Do you strongly or mildly (agree/disagree) with this?" The results were as follows:

Strongly agree	24 percent
Mildly agree	27 percent
Mildly disagree	10 percent
Strongly disagree	37 percent

Direction (of public opinion)
A tendency toward a particular preference, usually (though not always) characterized as either positive or negative.

Intensity (of public opinion)
The degree of strength or commitment the public feels about the opinion it holds.

The direction of opinion in this case only marginally swings in agreement that companies should be able to advertise tobacco on TV. Fifty-one percent, a bare majority, agreed with this statement, and 47 percent disagreed. The direction of opinion only modestly endorses the statement. However, the follow-up question sheds additional light on the intensity of opinion. Among those who agree, they are about evenly divided, 24 percent to 27 percent, between strongly and mildly agreeing. Those who disagree are much more intense in their feelings, with 37 percent strongly and only 10 percent mildly disagreeing.

Continuity is a third important characteristic of public opinion. Political preferences may remain very stable over time, they may gradually change, or they may fluctuate wildly over short periods of time. Continuity (or "changeability," its opposite) is often an important dimension of public opinion. The presidential approval rating is often analyzed from the context of the continuity/change dimension. When major political events occur, we often see change.

Continuity (in public opinion)
A tendency for political preferences to remain generally stable over time.

Making the Connection

Public opinion plays an important role in any system of government. Even authoritarian regimes such as the French government under King Louis XVI in the late eighteenth century, Czarist Russia in the early twentieth century, and the Soviet Union in the late twentieth century were susceptible to being overthrown by the forces of the popular will. But in a democratic society, public opinion is freely expressed and willingly heeded by those running the government. In contemporary American politics, there are a variety of ways in which public opinion may be expressed. As Presidents Lyndon Johnson and George W. Bush quickly learned, public opinion can change drastically over a president's term, keeping chief executives and other public officials continuously accountable to the popular will.

Modern technology and the advancement of social science research have enabled political scientists, journalists, political candidates, and elected leaders to measure accurately and understand better not only what public opinion is, but also how and why it changes. Modern presidents have the resources of scientific public opinion polls at their disposal and use them quite extensively. But although the scientific opinion poll is a modern phenomenon, the importance of public opinion has always been central to the life of American politics.

POLITICS InterActive!

Tracking the Latest Public Opinion Polls

From March 22 to March 26, 2010, four separate organizations conducted national polls measuring approval of President Barack Obama's job performance. Gallup placed Obama's approval rating at 51 percent; the Rasmussen Poll found that 48 percent approved of Obama's performance; the Quinnipiac Poll said 45 percent approved; and the *Washington Post* found that it was 53 percent. What might account for the differences between these four polls' findings? Is it sampling error? The wording of the question used to measure presidential job approval? The way the different pollsters went about selecting a sample? The way the questions were administered to respondents?

Use the links below to find out how these organizations conduct their polls and how they measure presidential approval. What are the differences in the methodology of these various pollsters, and how might those differences contribute to different findings?

- http://www.gallup.com
- http://www.rasmussenreports.com
- http://www.quinnipiac.edu
- http://www.washingtonpost.com

On www.cengage.com/dautrich/americangovernment/2e, find the Politics InterActive link for details about the presidential approval rating and how other major polling organizations measure it and what they have found.

The Gallup Poll, which has conducted preelection polls for CNN and *USA Today*, tracks voters' intentions throughout the fall campaigns. This graph shows Gallup's tracking from early September through the end of October in the 2008 presidential race.

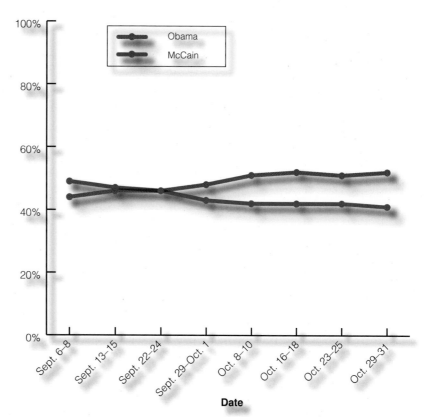

Source: The Gallup Organization. © 2008 The Gallup Organization.

Chapter Summary

★ Public Opinion in American Politics

- Public opinion plays an important role in ensuring that citizens' beliefs are embraced in a democracy; public opinion also plays a tactical role for political officials, influencing the outcome of many important political battles.

★ How Is Public Opinion Expressed?

- Public opinion may be expressed through a variety of means including public opinion polls, voting, free speech and assembly, political blogging, the support of particular candidates for political office, and the contribution of time and efforts to interest groups.

- The news media also serve as an outlet for public opinion, whether by publishing articles about important individuals' opinions or by sponsoring their own public opinion polls on politics and policy issues. Still, many members of the public prefer to express their opinions directly to elected officials through letters, phone calls, or e-mails. Blogs have become an increasingly popular way for individuals to express their views on issues.

★ The Levels of Public Opinion

- Public opinion exists at its most abstract level in the form of values and beliefs; it exists in a more specific form through political orientations, which translate values and beliefs into a systematic way of assessing political realities, and in an even more specific way in the form of particular political preferences.

★ How Informed Is Public Opinion?

- Many noted scholars in the early and mid-twentieth century argued that the public lacks the necessary knowledge for their opinions to provide value. Contemporary surveys continue to confirm that the public maintains a low interest in politics generally, and that most Americans are uninformed about basic political facts.

- By contrast, a number of other scholars, beginning with V. O. Key Jr. in the 1960s, have argued that regardless of its specific knowledge of politics, the public as a whole behaves quite rationally over the long haul, expressing stable opinions that move (if at all) in logical and meaningful directions based on their values and beliefs.

★ How Does Public Opinion Form?

- Individuals' opinions are shaped in part by political socialization; impressions formed during youth often last well into adulthood. Opinions are also shaped by demographics (race, ethnicity, gender, age, and so on), family members, friends and peer groups, schools, the media, and religious organizations.

★ How Is Public Opinion Measured?

- Public opinion polls measure the opinions of a large group of people by selecting a subset of the larger group and then generalizing the findings from the small group back to the large group. To ensure that the poll is scientific, the sample must be chosen randomly using probability theory through techniques such as random-digit dialing. Unscientific polls can produce misleading results.

- The way in which questions on a poll are worded is also an important factor in assessing the quality of a poll. Misleading questions, whether intentional or unintentional, may produce faulty results.

★ Interpreting Public Opinion Data

- The proper interpretation of public opinion data requires attention to the direction, intensity, and continuity of the public's expressions. With regard to the third characteristic, political preferences may fluctuate wildly over short periods of time.

CourseMate

Key Terms

Agents of political socialization (p. 305)

Conservative ideology (p. 300)

Continuity (in public opinion) (p. 318)

Direction (of public opinion) (p. 317)

Intensity (of public opinion) (p. 317)

Liberal ideology (p. 300)

Political ideology (p. 300)

Political orientations (p. 300)

Political preferences (p. 301)

Political socialization (p. 305)

Primacy tendency (p. 305)

Pseudo-poll (p. 314)

Public opinion (p. 296)

Public opinion poll (p. 309)

Random-digit dialing (RDD) (p. 315)

Sampling error (p. 314)

Scientific sample (p. 312)

Straw poll (p. 309)

Unscientific poll (p. 312)

Values and beliefs (p. 299)

Resources

Important Books and Journals

Delli Carpini, Michael X., and Scott Keeter. *What Americans Know About Politics and Why It Matters.* New Haven, CT: Yale University Press, 1996.

Fowler, Floyd. *Survey Research Methods.* Newbury Park, CA: Sage Publications, 1995.

Hibbing, John R., and Elizabeth Theiss-Morse. *Congress as Public Enemy: Public Attitudes Toward American Political Institutions.* Cambridge: Cambridge University Press, 1995.

Igo, Sarah. *The Averaged American: Surveys, Citizens, and the Making of a Mass Public.* Cambridge, MA: Harvard University Press, 2007.

International Journal of Public Opinion (quarterly journal that serves as a source of public opinion analysis for academics and polling professionals).

Key, V. O., Jr. *The Responsible Electorate.* New York: Knopf, 1960.

Key, V. O., Jr. *Public Opinion and American Democracy.* New York: Knopf, 1967.

Page, Benjamin I., and Robert Y. Shapiro. *The Rational Public: Fifty Years of Trends in Americans' Policy Preferences.* Chicago: University of Chicago Press, 1992.

Public Opinion Quarterly (quarterly journal that features important theoretical contributions to opinion and communication research, analyses of current public opinion, and investigations of methodological issues involved in survey validity).

Schattschneider, E. E. *The Semisovereign People: A Realist's View of Democracy in America.* New York: Holt, Rinehart and Winston, 1960.

Stonecash, Jeffrey M. *Political Polling: Strategic Information in Campaigns.* New York: Rowman and Littlefield, 2003.

Traugott, Michael W., and Paul J. Lavraskas. *The Voter's Guide to Election Polls.* New York: Chatham House, 2000.

Zaller, John. *The Nature and Origin of Mass Opinion.* Cambridge: Cambridge University Press, 1992.

Internet Resources

http://www.gallup.com (the Web site for Gallup poll data)

http://www.aapor.org (the home page for the American Association for Public Opinion Research, the association for pollsters and people who study polls)

http://www.ropercenter.uconn.edu (Web site for the Roper Center for Public Opinion Research, which includes the largest collection of public opinion data in the world)

11 Interest Groups

NOW Former lobbyist Jack Abramoff.

AP PHOTO/GERALD HERBERT

THEN Rep. Oakes Ames (R-MA) served in Congress from 1863-1873.

LIBRARY OF CONGRESS PRINTS AND PHOTOGRAPHS
DIVISION WASHINGTON, D.C.

NOW & THEN

Lobbying Scandals with a Ring of Familiarity

? *The relationship between government and private interests has always been difficult to navigate. Lobbying legislators to favor or oppose certain legislation may be a time-honored practice, and yet so-called legislative favors granted in return for some financial interests can quickly cross the line and betray the public trust. Interest groups that advocate their position in the halls of Congress sometimes cross that line. In one instance, private financial interests hoped to capitalize on the greed of certain members of Congress, who were willing to accept rewards from these organizations in return for providing a piece of the expanding government largesse. The group's original cause may well have been noble, but once the public trust was violated, public faith in the entire operation was compromised. And because corruption knows no bounds, even the original cause of the interest groups was eventually undermined by those who tried to circumvent the rules of the political process.*

LEARNING OBJECTIVES
★ WHAT YOU WILL LEARN ★

Pluralism and the Interest Group System

★ Appreciate the function of interest groups as a mechanism by which groups of people attempt to influence government to advance shared goals

★ Define pluralism as the theory that public policy is largely the product of a variety of different interest groups competing with one another to promote laws that benefit members of their respective groups

★ Assess both the benefits and criticisms of the interest group system in the United States

★ Compare the role of interest groups to that of political parties

Interest Groups in Action

★ Understand the reasons for the growth of interest groups in the United States during the twentieth century

★ Evaluate the critical role interest groups play in influencing policymaking through structures such as iron triangles and issue networks

★ Assess solidary benefits as one of the reasons people join interest groups

★ Assess the factors that contribute to each interest group's level of influence on policy

Types of Interest Groups

★ Distinguish between economic interest groups and noneconomic interest groups according to their primary purpose and cite examples of each type of group

★ Explain the "free rider" problem that many interest groups face

How Interest Groups Achieve Their Goals

★ Identify the activities interest groups engage in to achieve their goals and influence public policy

NOW & THEN

AP PHOTO/GERALD HERBERT

NOW During the past two decades, many Native American tribes—buoyed by passage of the 1988 Indian Gaming Regulatory Act—have undergone a rags-to-riches story. Millions of Americans have visited tribe-run casinos located on reservations where gaming is now permitted. Many Native American tribes benefited from that federal legislation, and in the 1990s tribal leaders wanted to press their advantage further. Thus several tribes, including the Mississippi Choctaw, hired lobbyist Jack Abramoff to represent them before Congress. Abramoff proved especially effective in this role, helping defeat federal legislation that would have assessed the unrelated business income tax (UBIT) on Native American casinos. House Majority leader Tom DeLay (R-TX) was one of many House members who played a role in this and other victories. According to some media reports, Abramoff may have done more than just "argue forcefully" on the tribes' behalf: he allegedly spent millions of dollars to influence politicians. In addition to offering many members of Congress free meals at his restaurant, Abramoff maintained four skyboxes at major sports arenas for political entertaining at a cost of over $1 million a year. Joining Abramoff on one vacation in 2000 was DeLay, whose airfare to London and Scotland was allegedly charged to an American Express card issued to Abramoff.

Abramoff also defrauded the very Native American tribes he had been hired to serve. By overbilling Indian gambling interests and orchestrating lobbying activities against his own clients, Abramoff attempted to play both sides of the fence. Abramoff pleaded guilty to numerous charges in 2006. The Abramoff lobbying scandal led to the downfall of House Majority leader DeLay and to charges brought against many other members of Congress and their aides.

THEN Immediately after the Civil War, railroads were the dominant economic interest in Washington, DC. Seeking legislative support, the Union Pacific Railroad in particular exerted pressure on well-known Congressmen of the time such as Representative James Brooks (D-ME), and Senators James Harlan (R-IA) and James Willis Patterson (R-NH). Ironically, the key individual responsible for that pressure was a fellow Congressman, Oakes Ames (R-MA). As an influential member of the House, Ames obtained contracts for his family firm for the construction of the Union Pacific; he even installed his brother Oliver Ames as president of the railroad in 1866. In 1872 the railroad established a front company, known as Crédit Mobilier, as part of a financial scam to funnel money back to the railroads through their own construction contracts. Ames then allowed members of Congress to purchase railroad shares at face rather than market value; in return, the members agreed to ignore illegal corporate transactions and to help produce dividends for the railroads they now owned. Ames's scheme eventually ensnared the sitting vice president of the United States, Schuyler Colfax, as well as his successor as vice president, Henry Wilson. Ames was censured after a House investigation; Colfax was nearly impeached. In addition, Ames's actions nearly ruined the Union Pacific railroad, which went bankrupt in the 1870s. But at a time when corruption laws were still in their infancy, many politicians escaped with nothing more than "the embarrassment of public exposure."

LIBRARY OF CONGRESS PRINTS AND PHOTOGRAPHS
DIVISION WASHINGTON, D.C.

During these two critical periods in American history, private groups and economic interests exerted their will on the public institutions of government to such a great extent that all distinctions between public and private seemed to break down. No one could question the importance of the railways during the post–Civil War period; meanwhile Native Americans—downtrodden for so long in American society—had finally risen to a position of economic prominence in the 1990s, and their success was welcomed in many corners. Unfortunately, the aggressive lobbying on behalf of these two groups went too far.

Interest groups today play a central role in formulating public policy, directing the regulation of certain industries, and even influencing important court decisions. Indeed, there is little doubt about the size and magnitude of their influence throughout the American political system. Of course the vast majority of interest groups are law-abiding, positive forces in government. A key issue remains, however: how far do we allow such groups to press their interests in government, before they become a negative force in democracy?

This chapter assesses the workings and performance of American politics from the perspective of interest group activity. What are interest groups? How do they work? Who belongs to them? Which ones are more and less powerful? How do they exert influence on what government does?

Pluralism and the Interest Group System

★ LO Appreciate the function of interest groups as a mechanism by which groups of people attempt to influence government to advance shared goals

The U.S. political system provides numerous opportunities for people to influence public policy. Voting in elections to choose leaders offers one such opportunity. The guarantees of freedom of speech to speak one's mind about political issues and freedom of the press to critically assess issues and leaders' performance are others. Public opinion polls are yet another mechanism that solicits input from the masses.

But perhaps the most natural—and arguably the most influential—form of public input into government arrives by way of the activities of interest groups. James Madison, in Federalist No. 10, admonished that "the latent causes of faction are thus sown in the nature of man."[1] By faction, Madison was referring to what we now term interest groups. Madison was concerned about the potential influence of factions on the government. But at the same time, he understood that people were by nature drawn toward the organization of collective interests and the use of that organization to influence government action. Madison expected that if enough interest groups vied to influence policy, they would cancel each other out.

What Is an Interest Group?

★ LO Define pluralism as the theory that public policy is largely the product of a variety of different interest groups competing with one another to promote laws that benefit members of their respective groups

An **interest group** (also referred to as a "pressure group" or "organized interest") is an organization of people with shared goals that tries to influence public policy through a variety of activities. Every individual has interests, and interest groups are a mechanism for people with shared goals to protect or advance their own interests. People can try to influence government on their own—such as by calling or writing their elected representatives to voice their opinion, or by voting in an election. Another way that people can influence government is by joining a group that is organized to accomplish an objective.

Senior citizens, for example, have a shared interest in securing cost-of-living adjustments (COLAs) in the Social Security system that disburses checks to them each month. Each year, the president and Congress determine the percentage rate increase in the COLA. The larger the increase, the higher will be an individual's monthly Social Security check. Each individual senior citizen might call his or her representatives in Congress to try to influence the vote for a larger COLA increase. Another way senior citizens may try to influence government is by joining and supporting AARP (formerly the American Association for Retired People), an interest group that, among other activities, tries to influence government to approve large increases in the annual COLA for Social Security. AARP is large, with many resources and lobbyists to influence legislators. Though an individual citizen's call to a representative may carry some weight, it is no match for the vast resources and activities of the AARP.

Interest group

An organization of people with shared goals that tries to influence public policy through a variety of activities.

Interest groups link people with government policies. The linkage created by interest groups is constitutionally protected by the First Amendment, which guarantees the people's right "to peaceably assemble and petition the government for redress of grievances." People assembling in groups that carry out activities to foster group members' goals is a common activity in Washington, in the fifty state capitals, and in thousands of local governments.

Alexis de Tocqueville, a Frenchman who toured the United States in the early 1830s and observed the early workings of the U.S. political system, was struck by the extent to which group association and activity dominated the American system. In his now-classic 1835 book titled *Democracy in America*,[2] de Tocqueville praised the extent to which group activity underpins American democracy. More than his fellow French citizens and other Europeans that he observed, de Tocqueville found that Americans were particularly prone to organize in groups and use their associations to influence the political process.

Pluralism refers to the theory that public policy largely results from a variety of interest groups competing with one another to promote laws that benefit members of their respective groups. By contrast, **majoritarianism** refers to the theory that public policy is a product of what majorities of citizens prefer. Whereas the majoritarian perspective focuses on public opinion, voting results, and mass representation to describe how democracy in America actually works, the pluralist perspective suggests that in fact "the majority rarely rules."

Political scientist Robert Dahl, an architect of pluralist ideas, suggested in *A Preface to Democratic Theory*[3] that the American people are represented in government primarily through interest group activity. The products of public policy are largely a function of support for and membership in interest groups that compete for influence through activities such as lobbying. The U.S. political system, according to Dahl, offers a number of "access points" for any given group to provide input. These access points include Congress, executive branch offices, the courts, elections, and the news media. David B. Truman, another political scientist, has advanced the notion that group activity and mobilization are natural consequences of shared concerns.[4] The free and open competition among groups advances the democratic system, just as a free and open marketplace of ideas promotes the adoption of the best ideas in society.

The Pros and Cons of Interest Groups

The political power that emanates from groups of people organizing for the purpose of influencing government outputs can be quite strong. "Are interest groups good or bad for American democracy?" is a question akin to the old cliché "Is the glass half full or half empty?" The answer, of course, depends on one's perspective. Madison himself recognized that interest groups were powerful and that they could be dangerous. But he also acknowledged that factions could not be eliminated. Channeling them into productive devices for promoting public input was a primary challenge his generation faced in framing the government.

Interest groups in America invite criticism from some circles and praise from others. Listed below are the primary arguments regarding the advantages and disadvantages of interest group activity:

The Pros. Many observers today sing the praises of an interest group system that advances the interests of the people. Their arguments in support of interest groups include the following:

- Interest groups provide all groups in society with an opportunity to win support for their ideas and positions. The vast number of interest groups represents a wide array of political opinions, economic perspectives, and social class differences.

- By their very nature, humans seek out others who have ideas similar to their own. Joining groups and working for the interests of the group is a natural inclination of citizens and should be encouraged as a method of representation in our democracy.

Pluralism
The theory that public policy largely results from a variety of interest groups competing with one another to promote laws that benefit members of their respective groups.

Majoritarianism
The theory that public policy is a product of what majorities of citizens prefer.

Assess both the ★ LO
benefits and criticisms of the interest group system in the United States

In the Words of French Political Philosopher Alexis de Tocqueville

Alexis de Tocqueville, a French observer of the American political system, praised the role that interest groups played in American politics. After touring the United States in the early 1830s, de Tocqueville wrote *Democracy in America*, published in 1835, in which he made the following observations about interest groups, or "associations" as he referred to them, in the United States:

> The [citizen] of the United States learns from birth that he must rely on himself to combat the ills and trials of life. . . . If some obstacle blocks the public road halting . . . traffic, neighbors at once form a deliberative body; this improvised assembly produces an authority which remedies the trouble before anyone has thought of the possibility beyond that of those concerned . . . associations are formed to combat moral troubles; intemperance is fought in common. Public security, trade and industry, and morals and religion all provide the aims for associations in the United States. There is no end to which

> the human will despair of attaining by the free action of the collective power of individuals.

> When a political association is allowed to form centers of action at certain important places in the country, its activity becomes greater and its influence more widespread. There men meet, active measures are planned, and opinions are expressed with that strength and warmth which the written word can never attain.

> Freedom of association has become a necessary guarantee against the tyranny of the majority. In the United States once a party has become predominant all public power passes into its hands. . . . The most distinguished men of the opposite party . . . must be able to establish themselves outside of it. . . . The omnipotence of the majority seems to me such a danger to the American republics that the dangerous expedient used to curb it is actually something good. Here I would repeat something which I have put in other words when speaking of municipal freedom: no countries need associations more—to prevent either the despotism of parties or the arbitrary rule of a prince—than those with a democratic social state.

- The right of association is a basic right protected implicitly by the First Amendment to the U.S. Constitution, which affords individuals the right "peaceably to assemble."

- A wide array of diverse groups in society—rich and poor, urban and non-urban, male and female, Northern and Southern, liberal and conservative—potentially may organize and attempt to influence government. The system is fair in that it gives all groups an equitable opportunity to compete.

The Cons. Many other observers of the U.S. political system are quite critical of the power exerted by interest groups. In *The Power Elite*, C. Wright Mills[5] characterizes interest groups as a tool of the political elite rather than a system that enables broad participation in influencing public policy. Along this line, many criticize the ability of wealthy corporations and individuals to exert disproportionate influence on government through well-financed interest group activities. John Heinz and his colleagues argue further that the influence of interest groups is contingent on a number of factors and that their influence may be quite limited.[6] Other criticisms of interest groups include the following:

- Use of interest groups to make public policy is unfair because groups supported by the wealthy have far greater resources to promote their interests in the political system.

- Large corporations exist to maximize profits. They dominate the interest group system and tend to be ruthless in achieving their policy goals. The interest group system thus promotes the advancement of interests that do not always strive for the common good.

- The amount of interest group activity is so great that it has made it difficult to get things done in government. Too many groups are operating, slowing down the policymaking process to a state of gridlock in many arenas.

- Interest group leaders are not elected, distinguishing them from many of the policymaking institutions that have been constitutionally ordained—such as Congress and the executive branch. Thus interest group dominance of the political system is an affront to democracy.

- Interest groups work to concentrate benefits for the few while distributing costs to the many.

Interest Groups versus Political Parties

Compare the role of interest groups to that of political parties ★ LO

Political parties also link people to government policies. However, parties differ from interest groups in two important ways. First, parties today mainly focus on elections by endorsing candidates and working for their election to office. Most interest groups do not run candidates for office as parties do (although interest groups often endorse candidates). Interest groups commonly find other access points of government to accomplish their goals—access points such as the courts, the committee system in Congress, and executive agencies.[7]

A second important difference between interest groups and political parties is that groups tend to focus narrowly on special issues or sets of issues (hence the term *special interests*), whereas major parties are generally all-encompassing and are guided by broader ideological approaches to governing, rather than by a specific policy position. In short, the major parties are generalist whereas groups are focused. Consequently, there are few political parties, but many, many interest groups. Groups do not try to appeal to as many individuals as possible; rather, they appeal to those whose special interests are advocated by the group. For example, the National Rifle

LEWIS W. HINE/TIME LIFE PICTURES/GETTY IMAGES

Women and children in 1890 labor at a food processing plant.

Association (NRA) does not try to recruit gun control advocates because they are less likely to help promote the group's interests. Conversely, parties try to appeal to as many people as possible to optimize their electoral success.

Interest Groups and Social Movements

Social movement
A large informal grouping of individuals and/or organizations focused on specific political or social issues.

A number of **social movements** have been identified in American history, such as the civil rights, consumer safety, women's rights, and environmental movements of the 1960s and 1970s. These large informal groupings of individuals were often spawned directly from particular interest groups. The consumer protection movement, for example, was driven by the activities of the group Public Citizen, formed by consumer activist Ralph Nader. The American drive toward equality has produced a number of important social movements that utilized organized interests.

Movements have been political (for example, women's suffrage in the early 1900s), economic (for example, labor rights in the late 1800s and early 1900s), and social (for example, the civil rights movements of the 1960s). These movements have all been propelled by the activities of interest groups.

Interest Groups in Action

Interest groups have always played an important role in American politics. Even in the colonial period, groups such as the Sons of Liberty gathered members, collected donations, and organized protests to achieve the goal of American freedom from British taxation. The Sons of Liberty were successful in their aims because they tied their actions to the economic interests of their members. As Madison acknowledged, economic interests tend to be the type of concerns that are most salient to people and thus move them to collective action.

In 1886, the American Federation of Labor (AFL) was formed as the first broad-based national labor union. The AFL was originally established to advocate the rights of craft unions and ensure the terms of union contracts. Organized and led by Samuel Gompers for forty years, it attracted many members and raised funds to promote laws benefiting organized labor. The AFL was the principal advocate for establishing a cabinet department, the U.S. Department of Labor, to administer labor programs. This department continues to serve as one of the largest executive departments in the nation. In the 1950s, the AFL merged with the Congress of Industrial Organizations (CIO) to create the AFL-CIO, an interest group still very active in promoting the labor agenda.

The National Association of Manufacturers (NAM) was organized in 1885 for the purpose of advancing the interests of the manufacturing businesses. Though setting protective tariffs was its core objective, the NAM also became a primary opponent of the AFL and other labor interest groups. The goals of organized labor (such as higher wages for workers, better working conditions, increased benefits, and job security) and the goals of business owners (maximizing profits) often came into conflict.

Tensions between labor and business interests intensified with the tremendous growth of the American economy beginning in the late 1800s and continued to mount as the economy expanded. Large companies, focusing on maximizing profits (which in turn appealed to shareholders), opposed laborers' demands for increased wages, better working conditions, and worker benefits. Today, labor and business interest groups continue to be among the largest and most powerful interest groups in the nation.

The Growth of Interest Groups

★ LO Understand the reasons for the growth of interest groups in the United States during the twentieth century

Perhaps the most significant factor leading to an increase in the number of interest groups has been the overall growth in government. Interest groups attempt to advance their agenda by influencing various aspects of government. As the number of government programs and agencies has expanded, along with their reach,

AARP: The Behemoth of Interest Group Politics

AARP boasts over 40 million members, making it one of the largest interest groups in America. A principal reason for AARP's popularity is that its eligibility for membership is straightforward: one must be fifty years of age or older. Formerly known as the American Association of Retired Persons, AARP adopted its acronym as its official name in 1999, as its activities broadened beyond those directly related to advocating for the interests of retirees. In 2009, AARP reported spending about $30 million in lobbying government activities at the state and federal levels.

AARP now not only advocates for its membership, but it also provides a wide variety of services, including Medicare Supplemental insurance, discounts on rental cars, cruise and vacation packages, long-term care insurance, and legal services.

The size of AARP, along with the broad scope of its activities, have invited criticisms and led to some controversies. For example, 60,000 members quit the organization in 2009 over its endorsement of President Obama's health care reform proposals. The AARP also came under fire in 2003 for lobbying in

favor of the Medicare Prescription, Drug, Improvement and Modernization Act. An Annenberg Public Policy Report concluded that AARP had a conflict of interest in advocating for this legislation because it earns income from the sale of health and life insurance policies, which benefit from the Act's provisions. Indeed, AARP concedes that it was paid over $650 million in royalties from insurance companies which sold products to AARP members through an AARP reference in 2008 alone. Meanwhile, those same member services and advocacy tactics—controversial as they may be—make AARP one of the largest and most successful interest groups in the American political system.

WILLIAM THOMAS CAIN/GETTY IMAGES

Members of the well-organized and very powerful AARP at a political rally.

opportunities for influencing what government does through interest group activities have expanded as well.

The New Deal programs of the 1930s and the Great Society programs of the 1960s led to tremendous growth in the federal government and huge increases in the federal budget. Government began to assume a more active role not only in promoting its economic policies but in promoting social policies as well. In response, a vast number of interest groups formed. Both proponents and opponents of a more active government organized interest groups to advocate their views. As the number of interest groups advocating economic issues expanded, so too did the number of groups promoting ideological perspectives, positions on single issues, and political reforms.

Although interest groups have been part of the American system since its beginning, the number of groups has increased dramatically over the past half-century. Between 1960 and 2000, the number of official associations increased by 400 percent (from

5,843 to 23,298); the total amount of lobbying spending in Washington increased from $1.43 billion in 1998 to $3.47 billion in 2009; and from 1998 through 2009 the total number of registered lobbyists in Washington, DC, increased from 10,403 to 13,739.[8] Major political developments, such as the antiwar movement, the civil rights movement, and the Watergate scandal of the Nixon administration, mobilized a better-educated mass public to become increasingly concerned about political issues. This heightened concern about social and political issues fostered a significant amount of new interest group activity. The sophisticated use of mass-media technologies such as television, the computer, and the Internet has facilitated the ability of groups to emerge and flourish.

Another factor contributing to the increase in interest group activity has been the escalating cost of financing political campaigns. As costs have increased, interest groups have come to play a greater role in supporting political parties and the election of candidates. The Federal Election Campaign Act of 1971 placed limits on individual and corporate contributions to political campaigns. As a means of financing campaigns through alternative methods, interest groups have formed **political action committees (PACs)**. Currently PACs can contribute up to $5,000 directly to campaigns, so long as each PAC contributes to at least five different candidates in an election year. As we will see in Chapter 15. PACs are a source of much controversy because many political candidates have become dependent on PAC money to wage successful campaigns.

Iron Triangles, Issue Networks, and the Influence of Groups

The influence of interest groups is buoyed by the process in which public policy is created and modified. In any policy area, three key sets of actors interact to produce public policy: (1) congressional committees and subcommittees assigned to a specific policy area, (2) executive agencies of government that have the authority to administer policies in a particular area, and (3) private interest groups that have an interest in influencing that policy area. Members of congressional committees, managers of agencies, and leaders of interest groups all have vested interests in the specific policy area. As political scientist Theodore Lowi has noted, although these parties may not always agree on particular positions, they all seek to promote policies favorable to their interests, and they come to depend on one another for support and influence. Together, this network of actors dominates the development of public policies. This durable and seemingly impenetrable three-sided network has come to be known as the **iron triangle** of policymaking.[9]

The development of U.S. defense policy illustrates how iron triangles work. The armed services and defense committees and subcommittees in Congress are responsible for appropriating funds for defense contracts (such as for the building of new military aircraft). Members of Congress on these committees are committed to maintaining a strong national defense, and they control the purse strings for developing new defense systems. Leaders in the U.S. Department of Defense are responsible for implementing defense systems under the orders of the president and rely on congressional committees to fund strong systems. Private contractors such as Pratt & Whitney (an airplane engine manufacturer) employ the engineers and researchers to design superior systems and provide valuable information to the congressional committees and the defense department.

The committees and the Department of Defense depend on Pratt & Whitney for advanced engine technologies, advice on aircraft design, and the capacity to produce cutting-edge aircraft engines. Pratt & Whitney benefits from winning federal contracts to produce defense systems. The congressional committees, Defense Department managers, and corporate leaders and lobbyists from Pratt & Whitney are familiar with one another, depend on one another, and use one another in the development of defense systems. The iron triangle approach to public policymaking has institutionalized the role of interest groups in the exercise of American democracy.

Political action committee (PAC)

The political arm of an interest group that promotes candidates in election campaigns primarily through financial contributions.

★ LO   Evaluate the critical role interest groups play in influencing policymaking through structures such as iron triangles and issue networks

Iron triangle

A three-sided network of policymaking that includes congressional committees (and subcommittees) in a specific policy area, executive agencies with authority over that area, and private interest groups focused on influencing that area.

RÜSTEM GÜRLER/ISTOCKPHOTO.COM

ALEX WONG/GETTY IMAGES

Musician Moby (left) with Congressman Edward Markey (D-MA) talk to the press at a news conference on Internet freedom in 2006. Moby and Markey both support limiting the influence of giant companies on the Internet.

Though an iron triangle refers to the interdependent relationship between legislators, bureaucrats, and lobbyists in a particular policy area, it is also possible to identify a broader set of actors who all have a vested interest in an area of public policy and try to collectively influence their policy area. Political scientists have used the term **issue networks** to describe this broader array of actors beyond legislators, bureaucrats, and lobbyists who try to influence a particular policy area. These include congressional staff people, journalists or other members of the media who often report on the policy area, and researchers who have done work on and are experts in the policy area.[10]

Membership in Groups

Many Americans belong to interest groups, and many businesses, nonprofit organizations, and public entities belong to interest groups as well. It is estimated that about four in five citizens belong to at least one interest group. Many of the more common groups Americans belong to include labor unions (such as the AFL-CIO, which boasts a total of about 11 million members), professional associations (such as the 240,000 physicians and medical students who belong to the American Medical Association), and organizations such as the AARP to which many of the nation's senior citizens belong. As many as 3 million businesses across the United States belong to the U.S. Chamber of Commerce.[11]

Although the number of Americans who belong to interest groups is high, certain types of people are more likely than others to engage in interest group activity. Americans with higher incomes and greater resources, and those who are better educated and employed in professional occupations, are much more likely to belong to groups. Those with more financial resources tend to better appreciate the utility of group membership and interest groups' impact on the political process; wealthier individuals are also more likely to have the resources to support interest group activities. Thus many critics of interest group politics charge that the pluralist model of democracy favors the upper middle class and upper class of society. Because those with more resources can and do support interest groups, they are more likely to influence public policy to their financial advantage.

Issue network
The broad array of actors (beyond just the iron triangle) that try to collectively influence a policy area in which they maintain a vested interest.

★ LO
Assess solidary benefits as one of the reasons people join interest groups

NEWSCOM

Pictured above are railroad workers on strike in southeastern Pennsylvania in November 2009. The strike shut down bus, train, and trolley service in Philadelphia.

Material benefits (of group membership)
The specific, tangible benefits individuals receive from interest group membership, such as economic concessions, discounts on products, etc.

Purposive benefits (of group membership)
Rewards that do not directly benefit the individual member, but benefit society as a whole.

Solidary benefits (of group membership)
Satisfaction that individuals receive from interacting with like-minded individuals for a cause.

Various reasons have been proposed to explain why people or organizations might join and support certain interest groups. One is that they receive specific, tangible benefits from membership. These are referred to as **material benefits**[12] of group membership. For instance, local units of the National Education Association (NEA) work for its teacher members to win salary increases, and so the benefits of membership often produce a favorable material benefit to teachers in the form of higher wages. Many interest groups provide their members with other material benefits such as health and auto insurance discounts, magazine subscriptions, and free products.

Another reason why interest groups are appealing are the **purposive benefits** (or expressive benefits) of membership.[13] Purposive rewards are those that do not directly benefit the individual member, but benefit society more generally. Some interest groups, for example, are committed to the goal of improving the environment and promoting policies that better protect the natural environment. The Sierra Club is one such organization that endorses these goals, and members of the Sierra Club receive purposive benefits from membership and support of the group's activities.

A third type of incentive for interest group membership is the **solidary benefits**[14] of membership, or the satisfaction that individuals receive from interacting with like-minded individuals for a cause. Solidary rewards derive less from the interest group's goals and more from the process of interacting with others to achieve a goal. For example, a union worker who attends a labor rally to support increases in a new contract may receive satisfaction from simply being with colleagues in support of a cause.

What Makes Some Groups More Powerful Than Others?

Although there are thousands of interest groups operating in the United States, some groups are more successful than others in promoting their cause and affecting public policy to their liking. There are three general characteristics of an interest group, which may have significant bearing on how powerful that group's influence will be in Washington:

1. **The size of the membership.** There is, undoubtedly, power in numbers. The larger the number of members of an interest group, the more powerful that group will be in affecting public policy. Large membership alone makes elected leaders responsive to a group's concerns. An interest group with a large number of members can increase its power and influence by convincing its members to vote for a candidate or candidates. The Christian Coalition of America (CCA) is a Christian political advocacy group that includes fundamentalists, evangelicals, Pentecostals, and many members of mainline Protestant churches as well. Officials of the CCA often communicate with the organization's huge membership regarding the endorsement of candidates. Not surprisingly, the CCA attracts the attention of candidates as well as officeholders who plan on running for another term. Groups with large numbers of members also have an advantage in raising funds to support their activities. With many members, the potential for fund raising is great. And funding goes a long way in advancing the effectiveness of interest group activities. A good example of a group that exhibits strength through numbers is the American Farm Bureau Federation (AFBF), which boasts 4.7 million members and has proven especially effective at promoting policies that provide large subsidies and other benefits to American farmers. A bilateral trade agreement between the United States and Russia in late 2006 was a testament to AFBF influence, as it substantially expanded the export market for U.S. farmers.

Governor Mike Huckabee (R-AR), a contender for the Republican Party's presidential nomination in 2008, speaks at the annual Conservative Political Action Conference in Washington, DC, in March 2007.

MARK WILSON/GETTY IMAGES

The Top Ten Most Influential Interest Groups

Each year, *Fortune* magazine lists the ten most influential interest groups in the nation based on a survey of Washington, DC, political players. The following groups made a recent top ten list.

✔ 1. **AARP.** AARP provides services for senior citizens, including consumer and policy advocacy, health care information, and tax counseling.

✔ 2. **The National Rifle Association (NRA).** The NRA is dedicated to preserving the rights of law-abiding citizens to purchase, own, and use their own firearms. The Institute for Legal Action is the lobbying arm of the NRA.

✔ 3. **The National Federation of Independent Businesses (NFIB).** This is the largest advocacy group in the nation that represents small businesses. Among other things, NFIB supports a simpler tax system and lower taxes on businesses, and it opposes minimum wage increases and the expansion of the Family Medical Leave Act.

✔ 4. **American Israel Public Affairs Committee (AIPAC).** AIPAC is a strong advocate of a pro-Israel foreign policy for the U.S. government.

✔ 5. **The American Federation of Labor–Congress of Industrial Organizations (AFL-CIO).** The goal of the AFL-CIO is to empower working people by giving them a strong voice in the workplace and in government policymaking.

✔ 6. **The Association of Trial Lawyers of America (ATLA).** ATLA, the world's largest trial lawyers association, promotes policies that enhance fairness for injured persons in the judicial process and aid lawyer effectiveness in pursuing such claims.

✔ 7. **The U.S. Chamber of Commerce.** This is the world's largest federation of businesses. Among other things, it lobbies to reduce government's regulation of businesses and improve trade opportunities for U.S. firms doing business abroad.

✔ 8. **National Right to Life Committee (NRLC).** NRLC was formed in response to the *Roe v. Wade* decision in which the Supreme Court protected abortion under certain circumstances from government regulation. The NRLC has lobbied to make abortion laws more stringent.

✔ 9. **The National Education Association (NEA).** NEA focuses on advancing public education in the United States. It lobbies for improved teacher preparation, better working conditions for teachers, and increased resources for the nation's schools.

✔ 10. **The National Restaurant Association.** This is the leading business association for the restaurant industry.

2. **The wealth of the members.** The number of members is an important indicator of the potential amount of money that interest groups might be able to raise. But just as important is the wealth of the membership. Certain interest groups enjoy a huge advantage when it comes to the average wealth of its members. For example, the American Trial Lawyers Association (ATLA) is made up of trial

lawyers who, by virtue of their occupation, are quite wealthy when compared to average Americans. Thus, whereas the number of members of the ATLA is only about 60,000, the wealth of its membership and the consequent level of financial contributions from members provide sufficient resources to make it an especially powerful interest group in Washington.

3. **The dedication of members to the goals of the group.** In addition to the number of members and wealth of members, groups that have a loyal following based on member commitment to the cause of the group can be a powerful resource.[15] The National Right to Life Committee (NRLC) is a good example. The NRLC organized and began to solicit members and contributions in 1973, after the *Roe v. Wade* decision legalized abortion. NRLC's members tend to be dedicated to right-to-life positions and willing to contribute much time, effort, and resources to advance its pro-life agenda.

Types of Interest Groups

Although interest groups represent a wide array of interests in American society, there are two basic types of interest groups—economic groups and noneconomic groups. Many groups engage in both economic and noneconomic pursuits, but most can be classified as either primarily economic or noneconomic in nature.

Economic Groups

Although the specific goals of different interest groups vary greatly, the vast majority of groups in America have goals that are economic in nature. Two out of every three interest groups in America are **economic interest groups**, or groups that exist to promote favorable economic conditions and economic opportunities for their members. Economic groups also tend to be the largest and most powerful groups because members of such groups maintain a vested personal financial stake in having the group achieve its goals.

As well as being the most numerous, economic groups also tend to be the best organized and most influential interest groups. Because economic interests are those that generally inspire more concern from businesses and citizens alike, they tend to feature greater individual involvement, commitment, resources, and organization.

There are thousands of interest groups that focus primarily on advancing the economic goals of its members. These groups include private businesses, labor unions, business and industry associations, and professional associations.

Business Groups.
The largest companies in the nation and the world typically maintain internal units that function as an interest group for the company. Very large companies, such as General Motors (GM) and IBM, for example, have their own interest groups. Such companies typically have wide and varied interests. GM, for example, is affected by environmental laws (tougher air pollution laws often require GM to spend more on technologies to reduce emissions in their cars), labor laws (increases in the minimum wage require higher pay for some workers), and product safety laws (increased safety standards might increase the cost of assembling a car). GM needs a well-staffed interest group to try to influence these and many other types of legislation.

Most businesses belong to associations, and often these associations engage in interest group activities to advocate for the interests of their members. Some associations are very broad in scope, such as the U.S. Chamber of Commerce, with its 3 million members. These businesses range from small neighborhood auto mechanics to large billion-dollar financial institutions. The Chamber seeks to broadly advance the interests of business owners.

Another type of business association is a **trade association**. A trade association typically focuses on one particular industry, and members of the association are

★ LO

Distinguish between economic interest groups and noneconomic interest groups according to their primary purpose and cite examples of each type of group

Economic interest group
An organized group that exists to promote favorable economic conditions and economic opportunities for its members.

Trade association
A business association that focuses on one particular industry, with membership drawn exclusively from that industry.

drawn exclusively from that industry. Businesses in a particular trade often face similar types of concerns, and the trade association looks out for the specific interests of a classification of businesses. For example, the American Society of Travel Agents (ASTA) is a trade association whose 24,000 member institutions include travel agencies, hotels, airlines, car rental agencies, and the like. ASTA promotes legislation and regulations favoring the travel industry.

Businesses, business associations, and trade associations have an advantage over associations and other organizations whose members are individual citizens or consumers. Businesses quickly see the advantage of joining an association, which collectively advocates for the interests of like businesses. Individuals, however, are less likely to join and contribute to an association that advocates for such things as consumer protection. Because there are so many consumers, an individual consumer is less likely to see a benefit in his or her own contribution. But because there are fewer businesses that belong to any given trade association, businesses are more likely to perceive a benefit from participating in the organization. As Mancur Olson, a well-known scholar on interest groups, put it, smaller groups are more likely to organize and associate because members can more readily see the benefits and "logic of collective action."[16] That is, people with common interests working together in groups are more effective than the same number of people working independently.

Certainly members of smaller groups are more likely to perceive direct benefits from their membership; smaller groups are also less likely to suffer from the free rider problem. **Free riders** are those individuals who do not join or contribute to an interest group that is representing their interests. Thus, they enjoy the benefits of membership without paying for the costs. The free rider problem is more

★ LO   Explain the "free rider" problem that many interest groups face

Free rider
An individual who does not join or contribute to an interest group that is representing his or her interests.

A meeting of the Airline Pilots Association in Atlanta, Georgia, where union organizers discuss concerns of the pilots.

BARRY WILLIAMS/GETTY IMAGES

common in larger groups, which may have trouble convincing individuals to contribute due to each individual's perception that others will work to achieve the group's goal.

Labor Unions.

Whereas business groups promote the interests of companies and corporations, labor unions promote the interests of American workers. Initially, labor unions emerged from the expansion of the U.S. economy in the late 1800s and early 1900s. The new technologies that resulted from the Industrial Revolution led to the rapid growth of large-scale farming and manufacturing and created many new jobs. Many business owners exploited their laborers, providing low pay, few benefits, and often poor and unsafe working conditions. Workers then organized into unions, using the threat of a strike to improve their conditions.

In the early 1940s, as many as 35 percent of workers in America were union members. Over the years, however, the percentage of union workers has declined. Today only about 13 percent of workers belong to a union. An important reason for this decline relates to changes in the type of jobs that Americans hold. Skilled and unskilled laborers are most likely to be unionized, but these types of jobs represent an increasingly smaller proportion of the workforce. Professional and service jobs, which are less likely to be unionized, now dominate the American workforce, and so union membership has declined. Rather than unionizing, professionals tend to organize and join professional associations. Some professionals, however, have unionized. The largest union in the United States today is a teachers' union, the National Education Association.

Unions differ from professional associations in that the laws provide certain bargaining rights to unions. Union membership may be required for all employees as well. State laws vary on this issue. Some states are **open shop**, which means that employees in that state maintain the option of whether or not to join a certified union. Of course in open shop states, workers who do not join the union may benefit from union activities without "paying the price"—another form of the "free rider" problem. Since 1947, the federal Taft-Hartley Act has technically banned the **closed shop**, which requires union membership as a condition of employment in a unionized workplace. Still, unions have successfully convinced some state legislatures that because all workers enjoy the benefits of union advocacy (for example, promoting pay increases and so on), all workers should at least be required to pay dues to the union. Thus many states allow so-called **union shops**, which require that employees in unionized workplaces either join the union or pay the equivalent of union dues to it after a set period of time.

Professional Associations.

Higher levels of education and advances in technology have transformed the American workforce over the past half-century. One of the major changes has been an increase in professional, technical, and service jobs, and a decrease in the number of skilled and unskilled labor jobs. Professionals have organized to promote and protect their economic interests through membership in professional organizations, which lobby on their behalf.

Two large and growing classes of professionals are lawyers and medical doctors, both of which have high-profile and powerful interest groups—the American Bar Association (ABA) for lawyers and the American Medical Association (AMA) for doctors. The medical and legal professions are regulated by state governments, and the AMA and ABA have been quite successful in influencing the regulatory process—for example, by establishing licensing requirements for doctors and lawyers.

Another large and influential professional association is the National Association of Realtors (NAR), with a total membership of over 700,000, an annual budget of over $60,000,000, and an organizational staff of more than 400 people. The size, budget, and organization of NAR provide it with ample resources to advocate the interests of the nation's real estate agents.

Open shop
The law that allows employees the option of joining or not joining the certified union at a unionized workplace.

Closed shop
The law that requires employees to become members of the union as a condition of employment in unionized workplaces.

Union shop
The law that requires that employees in unionized workplaces either join the union or pay the equivalent of union dues to it after a set period of time.

TABLE 11.1 Who Spends the Most on Lobbying?

In 2009, interest groups spent more than $3 billion on lobbying activities in Washington, D.C. This table shows the biggest spenders from 1998 through 2009.

Organization	Total
U.S. Chamber of Commerce	$606,758,180
American Medical Association	$220,832,500
General Electric	$196,410,000
AARP	$175,702,064
American Hospital Association	$174,890,431
Pharmaceutical Research and Manufacturers of America	$173,403,920
AT&T Inc.	$150,471,757
Northrup Grumman	$143,005,253
Exxon Mobil	$138,886,942
National Association of Realtors	$138,417,380
Blue Cross/Blue Shield	$136,317,077
Business Roundtable	$134,030,000
Edison Electric Institute	$133,955,999
Verizon Communications	$132,534,841
Lockheed Martin	$122,430,423
Boeing	$121,528,310
General Motors	$106,914,000
Southern Co.	$104,620,694
Freddie Mac	$96,194,048

Source: Center for Responsive Politics, http://www.opensecrets.org.

Noneconomic Groups

Economic groups exist primarily to advance the commercial and financial interests of its members. Whereas economic interests dominate pluralist activities, many other interest groups advocate for primarily noneconomic concerns. Three general categories of **noneconomic interest groups** are public interest groups, issue or ideological groups, and government groups.

Noneconomic interest group

An organized group that advocates for reasons other than their membership's commercial and financial interests.

Public interest group

An organized group that promotes the broad, collective good of citizens and consumers.

Public Interest Groups. **Public interest groups** promote the broad, collective good of citizens and consumers. Many public interest groups seek to promote political reforms that enhance the role of the public in the political process. The League of Women Voters is one such group. Initially formed as an interest group that promoted women's suffrage, the League has become a leading advocate for improving turnout among all citizens in elections. The League of Women Voters has also taken the lead in promoting candidate engagement on issues of importance to the voters by sponsoring campaign debates.

Another highly active public interest group is Common Cause. This group's literature describes itself in the following way: "Common Cause is a nonprofit, nonpartisan citizen's lobbying organization promoting open, honest and accountable government. Supported by the dues and contributions of over 200,000 members in every state across the nation, Common Cause represents the unified voice of the people against corruption in government and big money special interests."[17]

Common Cause promotes reforming the political system in ways that enhance the role of the average citizen. Thus it supports laws limiting elected officials from taking gifts from special interests, banning large speaking honoraria for members of Congress, and reforming the presidential campaign finance system. Ironically, Common Cause also tries to limit the role interest groups play in the electoral process.

Ralph Nader and the various citizens' advocacy groups he helped to start (including Public Citizen and the Center for Auto Safety) are among the nation's leading public interest groups. Nader's best-selling book *Unsafe at Any Speed: The Designed-in Dangers of the American Automobile* forced the president of General Motors to publicly admit to the U.S. Senate that the company ignored automobile safety problems. Nader's Raiders, the name later given to the hundreds of young activists who arrived in Washington, DC, to help Nader investigate government corruption, were highly influential in pushing automobile safety legislation in the late 1960s, which dramatically raised safety standards for cars and trucks. Their efforts effectively launched a widespread consumer movement, which remains strong. Today these groups advocate campaign finance reform, monitor the health care industry, and promote consumer safety and consumer rights, among other public interest activities.

Fred Wertheimer, formerly the president of Common Cause.

Issue and Ideological Groups. Interest groups that focus on specific issues and ideological perspectives are known as **issue and ideological groups**. Abortion, women's rights, and the environment are just a few of the policy issues that have produced interest groups such as the National Right to Life Committee (pro-life), Americans for Free Choice (pro-choice), the National Organization for Women (NOW; women's rights), and the Sierra Club and the Nature Conservancy (both environmental groups). Each of these groups maintains effective lobbies on behalf of its positions.

Some groups have a broader focus than a particular issue or set of policy issues. These are known as ideological groups, and they promote a more general ideological approach on how government should deal with a host of issues. Both liberal and conservative ideological groups operate in the American pluralist system. The Americans for Democratic Action (ADA), for example, is an interest group that promotes government policies with a liberal orientation. Since 1947, the voting records of members of Congress on certain issues have served as the standard measure of political liberalism. The ADA supports candidates for office whose votes on key issues score a high "liberal quotient."

The American Civil Liberties Union (ACLU) is an interest group that advocates for the civil rights and liberties of American citizens. Specifically, the ACLU adamantly supports the rights of the accused, free speech rights, free press rights, religious liberty rights, and many other liberties guaranteed by the Bill of Rights. The ACLU has also become a strong advocate for students' rights, the rights of workers, lesbian/gay rights, and immigrants' rights.

The Christian Coalition of America (CCA) is another ideological group that has become a lobbying powerhouse in recent decades; it offers a vehicle to become involved in influencing public policy. The CCA's agenda advocates pro-life positions, promotes the role of religion as a part of what government does, favors reducing tax burdens on families, and supports victims' rights.

Issue and ideological group
An organized group that focuses on specific issues and ideological perspectives.

DIANA WALKER/TIME & LIFE PICTURES/GETTY IMAGES

"Before the Lecture Begins, Students from PIRG Have an Announcement...."

If you have spent significant time on a college campus, you have probably heard about PIRG (Public Interest Research Group). PIRG is a federation of state-based public interest groups that, in the words of its Web site, "stand up to powerful special interests on behalf of the American public" (see http://www.uspirg.org/about-us). State PIRGs are particularly active in recruiting students on college campuses. At the start of the semester, student members of PIRG ask professors for a few minutes of class time to pitch PIRG-related activities to the class. For many students, this is their first exposure to an interest group. Those who join will quickly get involved in PIRG's public interest causes and sometimes even become interns and get course credit for the experience.

For Critical Thinking and Discussion

1. Does PIRG operate on your campus?
2. What other interest groups are active at your college?
3. Have you ever been asked to get involved in PIRG or another interest group's activities?
4. What kinds of interest groups are you most willing to support?

JEFF GREENBERG/ALAMY

A college student in Florida solicits signatures on a petition for Florida PIRG.

Government Interest Groups. Most interest group activity organizes private concerns (of either individuals or businesses) for the purpose of influencing public policy. But private interests are not the only ones represented in the pluralist system. Groups representing the interests of governments also operate in this complex system.

Cities and states across the nation have organized to exert influence on the federal government. Most states and large cities employ their own lobbyists in Washington, DC. But states, cities, and other governments also organize collectively through a variety of interest groups, which are generally referred to as **intergovernmental lobbies**. The National League of Cities, for example, is an interest group that advocates for the broad interests of local governments. Another intergovernmental lobby advancing the cause of the nation's cities is the U.S. Conference of Mayors. The Council of State Governments and the National Governors Association lobby on behalf of the states' interests.

Not only do state and local governments lobby in Washington, DC, but foreign governments also organize and lobby. Many nations have embassies in the Washington, DC, area, and many of these embassies engage in interest group activities of their own.

Intergovernmental lobby

Any interest group that represents the collective interests of states, cities, and other governments.

How Interest Groups Achieve Their Goals

Identify the activities interest groups engage in to achieve their goals and influence public policy

★ LO

Interest groups engage in a number of activities to advance the goals of the group and influence public policy. These activities usually involve lobbying, supporting candidates and parties in election campaigns, mounting persuasion campaigns, and litigating.

Lobbying

Interest groups attempt to influence elected and other public leaders to make decisions that are favorable toward the group's goals. **Lobbying** is the term used to describe how interest groups go about influencing government officials. Lobbyists are the professionals who do the lobbying.

Lobbying
The means by which interest groups attempt to influence government officials to make decisions favorable to their goals.

Lobbyists provide information to public officials, with the hope that the information will convince the official to vote or act in a manner favorable to the group's interest. Lobbyists perform a valuable function to public officials by providing not only information and perspectives on issues, but expertise as well. In the iron triangle system, lobbyists seek access to members of Congress and to managers in executive agencies in a particular policy area. Public officials come to depend on the lobbyists for information and knowledge. For example, managers in the Department of Defense and members of Congress on the Armed Services Committee rely on lobbyists from Pratt & Whitney for information on emerging jet engine technologies, engine performance data, and other information, which allows the military to plan and improve the nation's defenses.

Similarly, the congressional committees responsible for workplace safety standards and the Occupational Safety and Health Administration (OSHA), the executive agency responsible for administering those standards, depend on the lobbyists representing labor unions and product safety groups for data and information on workplace hazards, and recommendations for remediation. Of course, these same public officials are likely to be lobbied by business interests concerned about the increased costs associated with remediation of hazards.

Lobbyists communicate with public officials in many different ways, including formal presentations, written memos and policy papers, informal e-mails or notes, face-to-face meetings, or informal discussions over a meal or a drink. The most effective lobbyists are those who provide valuable, truthful information on policy issues and who make persuasive arguments. Having a good working relationship with public officials and a quality reputation provides the lobbyist with access to officials, which is crucial to the lobbyist's success.

A common depiction of lobbying is that of an individual offering money, gifts, trips, or other goods in return for a favorable action, such as a congressperson's vote on a particular bill. Though such activities do take place, in modern times they have become the exception rather than the rule. The activities of lobbyists today are strictly regulated by federal and state governments. Lobbyist gift-giving and bribery of public officials is illegal in most states and can be prosecuted. States require lobbyists to provide financial statements, report expenses, and maintain official registration for interest groups and individuals who provide lobbying services.

Lobbyists are regularly seen in the halls of the Capitol building and the House and Senate office buildings. They are also common fixtures in the halls and offices of the state capitol buildings. Many lobbyists own their own lobbying firms and contract with interest groups to provide services, similar to the way that an organization might hire a law firm to conduct legal work. More commonly, however, lobbyists are employed by businesses, associations, or other organizations to lobby for that employer alone. Large organizations and businesses have the resources to hire full-time lobbyists; contract lobbyists often work for smaller organizations that do not have the resources to hire their own full-time lobbying staff.

High-Powered Lobbyists in American History

Today lobbyists are as important in policymaking as members of Congress themselves. But this is nothing new in American politics. Lobbying has been part of the American political system since the colonial era. Some of the nation's most successful lobbyists over time include the following:

Benjamin Franklin. Most students of American history recognize Benjamin Franklin as a founding father, political philosopher, and inventor/scientist. But Franklin was also a lobbyist and quite a successful one. The colonies of Pennsylvania, Georgia, and Massachusetts hired him to lobby on their behalf before the British Parliament from 1757 to 1770. Franklin's greatest lobbying success was securing the repeal of the Stamp Act in 1766.

Tommy Corcoran. "The Cork," as he was known in Washington circles, set the mold for today's most successful lobbyists. He was a trusted friend and adviser to President Franklin Delano Roosevelt during the New Deal era, when Corcoran successfully lobbied Congress on behalf of the White House for many new government programs, including the Securities and Exchange Commission, the Tennessee Valley Authority, and the Federal Housing Administration. He also placed hundreds of attorneys in jobs to run these New Deal agencies. A well-connected insider, The Cork established a private lobbying practice in 1942, where his many connections in government proved valuable for his private-sector clients. From the 1940s until the 1960s, he was the most powerful and influential lobbyist in Washington.

John Podesta. After serving as President Bill Clinton's fourth and final chief of staff from 1998 through 2001, John Podesta parlayed his top spot in the West Wing into a high-profile, influential, and lucrative lobbying career. He founded and is the current president of the Center for American Progress, a liberal think tank highly influential with Democrats in Congress. Podesta's understanding of White House operations earned him the position of director of the Obama–Biden transition team, where he played a key role in the selection of individuals to fill the highest level executive appointments. Today, he remains highly influential among Obama administration insiders, many of whom owe their appointment to him.

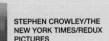
STEPHEN CROWLEY/THE NEW YORK TIMES/REDUX PICTURES

John Podesta, former chief of staff and current president and founder of the Center for American Progress.

Grassroots lobbying
Communications by interest groups with government officials through the mobilization of public opinion to exert influence on government action.

A form of lobbying that has been used more frequently in recent years is known as **grassroots lobbying**. The idea behind grassroots lobbying is that interest groups communicate with government officials by mobilizing public opinion to exert influence on government action. Because elected leaders are often quite sensitive to the opinions of voters, if a group can demonstrate that public opinion supports a particular position or that the public is willing to contact officials to express their view, officeholders will respond favorably because they want to enhance their chances of being reelected to office. Interest groups with a large number of members are particularly effective at grassroots lobbying, mainly because they can produce large numbers of potential votes in a given election. AARP, with more than 40 million members, has successfully used grassroots methods of lobbying to put pressure on Congress to protect the Social Security and Medicare systems—two primary goals of AARP.

TABLE 11.2 Big Givers to Campaigns

These ten organizations were the biggest contributors to American political campaigns between 1989 and 2010. AT&T and the National Association of Realtors gave about equally to Democrats and Republicans, while the remaining top ten givers heavily tilted toward giving to Democratic Party candidates.

Organization	Contributions
AT&T, Inc.	$44,228,128
American Federation of State, County and Municipal Employees	$41,945,511
National Association of Realtors	$35,643,323
International Brotherhood of Electrical Workers	$31,544,407
Goldman Sachs	$31,544,275
American Association for Justice	$31,465,429
National Education Association	$30,162,867
Laborers Union	$28,993,900
Teamsters	$27,992,624
Service Employees International Union	$27,933,732

Source: Center for Responsive Politics, March 2010.

Supporting Candidates and Parties in Elections

Interest groups are also quite active in electoral politics, providing resources for candidates and parties that support the interest groups' goals. PACs, described earlier in this chapter, are an important instrument through which interest groups provide financial support to candidates and political parties.

In addition to providing financing to support candidates, groups can play an important role in campaigns in other ways as well. For example, a labor union might endorse a candidate and communicate that endorsement to its members, urging members to vote for the candidate. A group might also use its resources to hire a phone bank to make "get out the vote" phone calls on behalf of a candidate or slate of candidates. Groups have also provided support by drafting speeches for candidates on policy matters or hosting rallies for office seekers.

Business groups tend to support Republican candidates, largely because Republicans are more likely to agree with their goals. Similarly, labor unions tend to support Democratic candidates because Democrats are likely to support labor's positions on many issues, such as increases in the minimum wage and family leave laws. On social issues, Republican candidates tend to receive the support of conservative groups, such as pro-life groups and groups advocating stiffer crime control measures. Groups that advocate a more liberal social agenda (such as the ACLU and Sierra Club) tend to support Democratic candidates, whose issue agenda is more consistent with the group goals.

Litigation

Interest groups have also become quite adept at using the court system as a means of achieving their goals. Groups regularly initiate lawsuits, request injunctions, defend members, and file briefs. Consumer product safety groups, for example, regularly file for injunctions in courts seeking to order companies to cease the sale of products that are unsafe.

Senators and Representatives Who Became Lobbyists

Some of the most sought-after lobbyists by corporations and organizations are former elected officials, especially former senators and representatives, who are well acquainted with how government works and retain personal relationships with many of their former colleagues who remain in Congress. In 1999, the Center for Responsive Politics reported that 129 former members of Congress were registered as lobbyists in Washington. Federal law requires that a member wait one year after leaving office before lobbying. Former members of Congress who are now highly paid lobbyists include former Congresswoman Pat Schroeder, former Senator Robert Packwood, and former Senator Tom Daschle.

Pat Schroeder, a Democrat from Colorado, was first elected to the House of Representatives in 1972 and served there until 1997. Her quarter-century in the House included time as chair of the Congressional Caucus on Women's Issues, as a member of the Armed Services Committee, and as chair of a House select committee on children, youth, and families. She was the primary author of the Family and Medical Leave Act of 1993. Schroeder also chaired a subcommittee on intellectual property rights and became the House's foremost expert on copyright issues. Schroeder is now a successful Washington lobbyist. Putting her experience in copyrights and intellectual property rights to good use, she recently became president and chief executive officer of the Association of American Publishers, which is the main trade association for the publishing industry.

Former Representative Pat Schroeder (right, seen here with Vice President Dick Cheney's wife, Lynne) as president of the Association of American Publishers in 2005.

Robert Packwood, a Republican from Oregon, served nearly three decades in the Senate. He was regarded as a shrewd, legislatively accomplished liberal on many social issues, such as abortion rights and family planning. Immediately after he won reelection to a fifth term in the Senate, a story appeared in the *Washington Post* accusing him of sexual harassment. Packwood's strong record of support for feminist issues made the charges of harassment, and his denial of them, especially controversial. Packwood resigned from the Senate in 1995 after an ethics committee recommended his expulsion for sexual misconduct. The cloud of controversy surrounding his departure from the Senate, however, did not diminish his potential

Former Senator Bob Packwood.

for a career as a lobbyist. One year to the day after his resignation, he became a lobbyist with the Sunrise Research Group. Packwood's clients include Northwest Airlines, Verizon Communications, and the National Association of Real Estate Investment Trusts.

Tom Daschle, a Democrat from South Dakota, served as Senate majority leader from June 2001 through January 2003. Daschle was first elected to the Senate in 1986 and became the Senate Minority leader just eight years later—in the history of the U.S. Senate, only Lyndon Johnson served fewer years before being elected to lead his party. When Daschle lost his reelection bid in 2004, he immediately took a job with the lobbying arm of the law firm Alston & Byrd. Consequently, health care clients including CVS, Abbott Laboratories, and HealthSouth soon flocked to the firm: eventually 60 percent of the firm's lobbying receipts came from that one industry alone. Few were surprised when President-elect Barack Obama sought Daschle to head up his administration's health care initiative in 2009. Unfortunately for Obama, Daschle had been a sloppy accountant: he had failed to pay all the taxes (and interest) he owed on his earnings as a health care consultant and was forced to withdraw his name from consideration.

Former Senator Tom Daschle

Some interest groups focus primarily on the courts to achieve their goals. For example, the ACLU regularly initiates lawsuits in circumstances in which it believes the government is compromising individual civil liberties. The ACLU is very active in litigating gender discrimination cases. One of the advantages of interest group litigation is its capitalization of interest groups' financial resources; average citizens do not have sufficient resources to initiate so many lawsuits. Also, because interest groups often specialize in particular kinds of lawsuits, they are able to litigate more skillfully.

Another way interest groups use the court system to exert influence is by the filing of amicus curiae ("friend of the court") briefs, which are companion briefs supporting an argument or set of arguments in an existing Supreme Court case.[18] Although the interest group is not a direct litigant in a matter, it can use an amicus brief to further or better articulate a position and thus aid litigants in their respective case.

Interest groups have also influenced the court system by engaging in lobbying activities to influence the appointment of judges. Pro-life and pro-choice groups are very active in supporting or opposing particular judicial nominees, based on the nominees' position and past decisions on abortion cases. The American Bar Association uses a rating system to rank individuals nominated for federal judgeships that has become extremely influential in the appointment process.

©BETTMANN/CORBIS

ACLU attorney Ruth Bader Ginsburg in 1977. Sixteen years later Ginsburg became an associate justice on the U.S. Supreme Court.

Persuasion Campaigns

Many interest groups run media campaigns to persuade the public to support their position on issues. Some of this persuasion occurs during election campaigns when groups create and place ads intended to help a political candidate or political party achieve victory. But increasingly, groups have run such campaigns outside of election campaigns to persuade or educate others to the group's way of thinking.

Groups have developed sophisticated public relations operations to communicate their positions. They use tactics such as "targeted mass mailings," in which they mail a pamphlet or other document to a large list of individuals that the group is attempting to influence. For example, the Americans for Democratic Action maintains a list of voters who are not registered with any particular political party. The ADA often sends mailings to those on the list to try to persuade them to support the ADA's position on a particular issue. In addition to mass mailings, groups regularly use television, radio, newspapers, magazines, or even billboards to communicate positions and try to persuade. They also use the Internet to send messages to the wider public.

© 2012 CENGAGE LEARNING

Making the Connection

Interest groups have become firmly entrenched within the American political land-scape. Their influence is both certain and controversial. More than two centuries ago, James Madison expressed concerns about the influence of "factions." Today, many observers of American politics continue to express concerns about the influence of groups and the value of pluralism as a mode of governance. Nevertheless, interest groups offer an important and unique linkage between American citizens' varied interests and public policy. This does not diminish the importance of other linkages, such as free and open elections. But the linkage offered by interest groups is unique in that it allows citizens to exert influence by interacting with one another and collectively attempting to influence what government does.

Few would argue with the premise that interest groups have been responsible for leading the charge in promoting political and social policies that have significantly improved the lot of millions of Americans. At the same time, the relationship between interest groups and government actors can become uncomfortably close, if not downright corrupt. Nearly a century and a half apart, both the railways and the Native American tribes were interest groups that exerted a strong influence on government policymaking. Both sets of interests were well-respected for their contribution to the American landscape. Yet when Oakes Ames and Jack Abramoff, respectively, attempted to influence public policies and agreements using greed as an enticement, the democratic system suffered. Like everyone else in a democracy, interest groups must be free to press their own agenda, but not so free that they may trample the agendas of so many others.

Named after a section of the United States tax code, "527s" are a relatively new tool used by interest groups to try to influence the outcome of elections in America. A 527 group is a politically oriented organization that enjoys tax-exempt status under current law, and thus is subject to no limits on the amount of soft money it can raise and spend. The group then uses the money it raised to develop and air "issue" advertisements. Although 527 groups cannot produce ads that directly tell voters which candidate or party to vote for in a particular election, they generally target positions on particular issues and craft advertisements that attempt to convince voters how they should think about those issues. Thus many 527 ads have amounted

to negative attacks on the personality or character of particular candidates. In short, 527s have found a way to make an end run around the campaign finance system.

Spending by the 527s is significant. In 2008, 527 groups spent nearly $500 million on national, state, and local election contests. In the 2004 presidential election year, the 527s spent over $600 million. In the 2006 midterm election year, they spent $430 million.

In 2004, a 527 known as the Swift Boat Veterans for Truth was responsible for producing and airing the "swift boat" ads that attacked John Kerry's character by questioning his

SCOTT OLSON/GETTY IMAGES

John McCain speaks at the annual meeting of the National Rifle Association, which endorsed him for president.

military record. In 2008, 527s were behind many of the negative attacks on Barack Obama that decried his association with controversial figures such as William Ayers and Rev. Jeremiah Wright.

Go to www.opensecrets.org/527s to find out which individuals and organizations provide the bulk of financial support to the 527s. Which industries have been most active in forming these groups? What kinds of ads have they produced? Who do you think benefits more—Democratic or Republican candidates—from 527 activities? Some 527 groups cite the First Amendment to defend their activities. Do these groups legitimately contribute to the "marketplace of ideas," or is this an example of "free speech run amuck"?

On www.cengage.com/dautrich/americangovernment/2e, find the Politics Inter-Active link for details on 527s. Consult as well the various links that relate to 527 advertisements. Historical, popular, and global perspectives on the 527s are also offered.

★ Pluralism and the Interest Group System

- Interest groups are a popular mechanism by which groups of people attempt to influence government to advance their shared goals.

- Pluralism is the theory that public policy largely results from a variety of interest groups competing with one another to promote laws that benefit members of their respective groups.

- Many praise the interest group system in the United States because it provides all groups in society with access and a fair opportunity to compete for influence over public policy.

- The interest group system is also criticized for allowing wealthy corporations and individuals a disproportionate influence on public policy, encouraging many groups to promote their own causes even if they run counter to the public interest, and significantly slowing down the policymaking process.

- Unlike political parties, interest groups usually do not run their own candidates for public office, and they tend to focus more narrowly on special issues or sets of issues.

★ Interest Groups in Action

- The growth of interest groups in the United States during the twentieth century was a product of the tremendous growth of government in general over that same period and the increased concerns about political issues that are expressed by a better-educated mass public.

- Interest group influence over public policy is theoretically informal; in reality, interest group participation has become ingrained in the process through structures such as iron triangles and issue networks.

- Individuals tend to join or support interest groups in order to receive material benefits, purposive benefits (those that benefit society more generally), and solidary benefits based on individuals' satisfaction from interacting with like-minded people in pursuit of a goal.

- Large interest groups must always concern themselves with the problem of "free riders," those who benefit from interest group activities on their behalf without ever joining or contributing to that interest group.

- The most successful interest groups tend to maintain a large membership of individuals, at least some of whom are wealthy, as well as a loyal following based on members' commitment to the cause.

★ Types of Interest Groups

- Economic interest groups that pursue favorable monetary benefits for their members include business groups such as industry trade associations, labor unions, and professional associations. Non-economic interest groups that pursue goals other than the commercial interests of their members include public interest groups, issue or ideological groups, and government interest groups.

★ How Interest Groups Achieve Their Goals

- Interest groups achieve their goals through lobbying activities, supporting candidates in election contests, litigating, and mounting persuasion campaigns.

CourseMate

Key Terms

Closed shop (p. 339)

Economic interest group (p. 337)

Free rider (p. 338)

Grassroots lobbying (p. 344)

Interest group (p. 326)

Intergovernmental lobby (p. 342)

Iron triangle (p. 332)

Issue and ideological group (p. 341)

Issue network (p. 333)

Lobbying (p. 343)

Majoritarianism (p. 327)

Material benefits (of group membership) (p. 334)

Noneconomic interest group (p. 340)

Open shop (p. 339)

Pluralism (p. 327)

Political action committee (PAC) (p. 332)

Public interest group (p. 340)

Purposive benefits (of group membership) (p. 334)

Social movement (p. 330)

Solidary benefits (of group membership) (p. 334)

Trade association (p. 337)

Union shop (p.339)

Resources

Important Books

Berry, Jeffrey M. *The Interest Group Society.* New York: Longman, 1997.

Cigler, Alan, and Burdett Loomis, eds. *Interest Group Politics*, 7th ed. Washington, DC: CQ Press, 2006.

Goldstein, Kenneth M. *Interest Groups, Lobbying and Participation in America.* New York: Cambridge University Press, 1999.

Lowery, David, and Holly Brasher. *Organized Interests and American Government.* New York: McGraw-Hill, 2004.

Olson, Mancur. *The Logic of Collective Action: Public Goods and the Theory of Groups.* Cambridge, MA: Harvard University Press, 1965.

Rozell, Mark J., Clyde Wilcox, and David Madland. *Interest Groups in American Campaigns: The New Face of Electioneering.* Washington, DC: CQ Press, 2005.

Salisbury, Robert H. *Interests and Institutions: Substance and Structure in American Politics.* Pittsburgh, PA: University of Pittsburgh Press, 1992.

Tocqueville, Alexis de. *Democracy in America.* Edited by J. P. Mayer. Garden City, NY: Harper Perennial, 1988.

Internet Sources

http://www.opensecrets.org (Web site of the Center for Responsive Politics; includes facts and figures relating to lobbying activities, associations giving to political candidates, PACs, and sources of support for interests groups)

http://www.aflcio.org (AFL-CIO)

http://www.nlc.org (National League of Cities)

http://www.uschamber.org (U.S. Chamber of Commerce)

http://www.citizen.org (Public Citizen, Ralph Nader's watchdog organization)

12 The Media and Politics

COURTESY OF WHITEHOUSE.GOV

NOW The Obama White House web page promoting the health care reform bill in 2009.

THEN A still shot from a TV news broadcast in 1963 showing Birmingham, Alabama, firemen hosing down protesters.

CHARLES MOORE/BLACK STAR/ALAMY

NOW & THEN

A New Medium Assists in the Cause of Landmark Legislation

The battle being waged was the culmi-nation of decades of debate that had thus far resulted in little legislation of any consequence. Now the president and his congres-sional allies were emboldened, and they sought to pass landmark legislation—but would they be able to overcome all the legislative hurdles that stood in their path? Their initiative this time would find an unexpected ally in the form of a powerful new medium. Those who tried to misrepresent the legislation would be held accountable; misleading arguments by the opposition could be verified thanks to a medium that offered unprecedented and convenient access to information. Public opinion was still bitterly divided on the reform, but this new medium would help the president win the highly contentious legislative battle. Indeed, without the help of this new medium, the president's persistent leadership might not have proved adequate to the challenge.

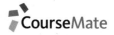

CourseMate

NOW & THEN

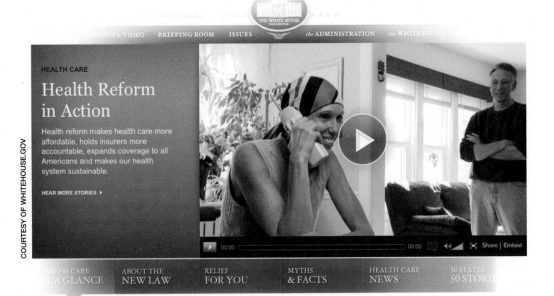

COURTESY OF WHITEHOUSE.GOV

HEALTH CARE

Health Reform in Action

Health reform makes health care more affordable, holds insurers more accountable, expands coverage to all Americans and makes our health system sustainable.

HEAR MORE STORIES ▶

NOW Early in his presidency, Barack Obama was determined to achieve legislative success on a subject that had proved elusive to so many of his predecessors: comprehensive health care reform. Franklin Roosevelt was forced to remove compulsory health care provisions from the social security legislation in 1935; Harry Truman had seen his proposal for national health care defeated as well. More recently, President Bill Clinton had made health care reform the centerpiece of his first term as president, only to see his plan soundly defeated in 1994 by a well-organized opposition. In these earlier battles, the American Medical Association and other opponents capitalized upon public fears that the legislation might separate individuals from their own doctors; many citizens had been overwhelmed by media campaigns that monopolized the airways with negative aspects of the legislation. The Obama administration's efforts to pass health care would not be so hindered, thanks in part to the Internet, which delivers virtually unlimited amounts of information to the vast majority of American homes. The Internet effectively brought the full debate over health care out into the open, exposing backroom deals and revealing the exaggerations inherent in arguments made both for and against the various bills under consideration. Ultimately the Obama administration took advantage of the Internet to sell its plan to the far left as well as the far right. The legislation eventually overcame all obstacles in its path, including a Republican party-line filibuster, which it cleared by just one vote. President Obama was thus able to seize the upper hand by a narrow margin. Had the public not been privy to the immense amounts of information pouring forth from the Internet, the arguments against the administration's plan might once again have proven too difficult to overcome.

THEN Health care reform was not the only proposed change to benefit from a new medium that reached millions. President John F. Kennedy's assassination in 1963 did not end his administration's hopes that it might see civil rights legislation pass before the 1964 presidential election. In fact, Kennedy's successor, Lyndon Johnson, pressed for civil rights legislation beginning in early 1964. Past presidents had tried and failed to pass civil rights laws: In 1947 President Truman was rebuffed in his hopes for legislation that addressed segregation. President Eisenhower pursued a centrist agenda on civil rights, but the best he could achieve was to establish a bipartisan civil rights commission and a civil rights division in the Justice Department; the 1957 Civil Rights Act had such a narrow impact that it proved a disappointment to civil rights leaders. Kennedy's ambitious civil rights agenda might have met a similar fate had the plight of African Americans in the South not been seen by the rest of the nation through extensive and unprecedented television coverage. Footage from television cameras allowed viewers at home to witness police officials directing full-pressure water hoses on African American school children, police dogs set loose on civil rights demonstrators, and numerous brutal beatings. Donations to the civil rights movement increased dramatically once the public outside the South became an eyewitness to these dramatic events, and legislative leaders from both parties soon felt public pressure to overcome the objections of opponents. After waiting out a fifty-four-day filibuster, the Senate eventually joined the House in approving major civil rights legislation. On July 2, 1964, President Lyndon Johnson signed the Civil Rights Act into law. Clearly the "small screen" had played a large role in the process.

A still shot from a television report showing a Birmingham fireman hosing down protesters in 1963.

BETTMANN/CORBIS

Chapter 12 The Media and Politics

355

Consider the following facts about media consumption in the United States: the average American spends more time watching television than working or going to school; all forms of media considered, the average person is engaged in media consumption for 3,500 hours each year—that's almost 40 percent of the 8,760 hours that exist in a year. There are even more TV sets per household than there are toilets. The media clearly have a pervasive presence in the everyday life of most Americans. From listening to radio "shock jocks" like Howard Stern, to watching popular television shows such as *American Idol*, to catching up on the latest news from around the world on CNN or a newspaper Web page, Americans make ample use of media sources available to them.

The news media serve a number of important political functions in the United States and operate through a large and growing number of outlets. Political leaders constantly monitor and attempt to influence news stories printed in newspapers and broadcast on television. Voters' primary source of information about political candidates and political issues is the news media. The technologies of television and the Internet allow citizens to observe events on the battlefield, look into the eyes of presidential candidates, and watch tragedies unfold such as the devastation unleashed on New Orleans and other parts of the Gulf Coast by Hurricane Katrina in 2005—many of these events unfold live from around the world in front of viewers in their own homes. Not only do the media serve as an important information source, but they also help set the political agenda, provide perspective and commentary on issues and political candidates, and help keep government accountable to the people.

The Media in American Politics

Most news media organizations in the United States are owned by private companies, which, like most other private companies, seek to make a profit. Unlike other industries, however, the media enjoy a special constitutionally granted protection. The First Amendment to the U.S. Constitution specifically provides that "Congress shall make no law . . . abridging the freedom . . . of the press." When the First Amendment was adopted in 1791, the press was mostly a small collection of newspapers and magazines. Over the years, the press, now more commonly referred to as the media, has expanded to include radio, television, book publishers, music producers, the Internet, and motion pictures.

One early event that helped shape America's perspective on freedom of the press was the trial in 1735 of newspaper printer Peter Zenger, who in the *New-York Weekly Journal* published a series of articles highly critical of the British-appointed governor of New York. Zenger was arrested on charges of criminal libel. He was defended by Philadelphia lawyer Andrew Hamilton, who won the case with his argument that Zenger had printed the truth and the truth cannot be considered libelous. Hamilton's argument thus established the principle of truth as a defense against libel.

The argument for a free press in United States today largely rests upon the concept of the "free marketplace of ideas," a phrase coined by Supreme Court Justice Oliver Wendell Holmes in his dissenting opinion in *Abrams v. United States* (1919), which suggests that allowing people to freely communicate their ideas will provide a larger variety of ideas to consider. Encouraging the publication and dissemination of a wide variety of political ideas offers citizens a diversity of opinions and perspectives and facilitates the free flow of information about local, national, and global events. Of course, for ideas to flow freely, government must be prevented from using its power to stifle perspectives with which it disagrees.

Government Regulation of the Media

Congress created the Federal Communications Commission (FCC) in 1934 to regulate the electronic media (primarily radio and eventually television) through the licensing of broadcasters and creating rules for broadcasters to follow. The FCC does not have authority to regulate the print media, such as newspapers. In fact, regulation

DAILY NEWS

EXTRA! EXTRA!

© 2012 CENGAGE LEARNING

★ LO Understand the purpose and evolution of the Federal Communications Commission of print media is rare, and courts have consistently treated the right of print media to publish free of government regulation. Some electronic media require broadcast frequencies that are scarce and thus need to be regulated to ensure the orderly transmission of programs.

Among the tools that the FCC may employ to regulate the activities of broadcasters is the threat of revoking a license or fining a station for violating its rules. The FCC has used these tools to limit the language and type of sexual material that broadcasters might use. For example, the FCC imposed fines on the owners of radio stations that broadcast "shock jock" Howard Stern. Stern's program often includes graphic descriptions of sexual acts and sex games, as well as language that the FCC deems unacceptable. Some of those stations fined then dropped the Stern show from their program schedule. To avoid further legal battles with the FCC, in 2005 Stern moved his show to a satellite radio station, which is not subject to FCC regulations because satellite radio is purchased by users and does not rely on the publicly controlled airwaves.

One of the most celebrated instances of the FCC clamping down on material in broadcast transmission involved comedian George Carlin's "Seven Dirty Words" skit, which satirized attitudes toward vulgar language. In the skit, Carlin continually repeated the seven words that you can't say on TV or radio. The piece was played on a radio station licensed to the Pacifica Foundation. Prior to playing the piece, the announcer warned the audience about its content. Nevertheless, a listener complained to the FCC, and the FCC in turn warned the radio station not to replay the piece. The station challenged the FCC's authority to regulate programming content, and the case made its way to the U.S. Supreme Court in *FCC v. Pacifica Foundation* (1978).[1] In that case the Supreme Court upheld the FCC's power to regulate the broadcast media on the criteria of indecent material.

The FCC's **equal time rule** mandates that radio and TV stations must offer equal amounts of airtime to all political candidates who want to broadcast advertisements. This rule also now includes a provision requiring that if a station broadcasts the president's State of the Union message, then that station must also provide free airtime for the opposing political party to broadcast a response.

From 1950 through the late 1980s, the FCC also enforced the so-called fairness doctrine, requiring broadcasters to set aside time for public affairs programming. The proliferation of news sources and technologies for transmitting electronic messages during the 1980s effectively ended the FCC's fairness doctrine requirements. These changes in technologies also resulted in the passage of the 1996 Telecommunications Act, which shifted the emphasis of government policy from regulating to facilitating competition. This law deregulated cable television providers, eliminated monopolies held by local phone companies, and allowed local phone companies to provide long-distance phone services. The Telecommunications Act transformed the FCC from a regulator of the telecommunications industry into an aggressive supporter of competition within that industry.

> **Equal time rule**
> The FCC mandate that radio and TV stations offer equal amounts of airtime to all political candidates who want to broadcast advertisements.

Functions of the Media in American Politics

> Describe the various functions that the media serve in the American political system
> ★ LO

Throughout the history of the United States, the media have come to serve a number of functions in the political system, all of which promote the free flow of information to the public. Principal functions of the media include (1) providing objective coverage of events, (2) facilitating public debate, and (3) serving as government watchdog.

Providing Objective Coverage of Events.

The media's most basic role involves monitoring events around the nation and the world and communicating those events to the public. Through modern communications technologies, the media have become proficient at reporting major events as they happen. Live coverage of presidential addresses, campaign debates, war operations, prominent trials, natural disasters, and other important world events have made their way almost instantaneously onto front-page headlines and into television's round-the-clock news coverage.

CHECK the List

Six Lapses in Journalistic Ethics

Journalists, editors, news directors, and publishers are constantly faced with ethical dilemmas in carrying out their jobs. Deciding what kinds of stories to cover, whether a particular story is appropriate to publish, and whether a news source is reliable are just some of their responsibilities. Accuracy (making sure that what is published or aired is truthful), fairness (presenting all sides of a story), and confidentiality of sources (protecting the identity of news sources) are generally regarded as important guidelines to ethical behavior in journal-

ism. The Society of Professional Journalists adopted a code of ethics in 1973 (and modified it in 1996) that provides fairly specific guidelines to help those in journalism make ethical decisions.*

Ethical codes, however, are merely guidelines. They are not enforceable laws. There have been a number of highlighted cases in recent years in which a serious breach of ethics led to a fair amount of criticism of organizations and specific individuals involved. The following are six recent examples.

✔ ***Newsweek* magazine and the treatment of Iraqi detainees.** Relying on a confidential source, *Newsweek* ran a story in May 2005 that accused American military personnel of using unethical techniques to get Iraqi prisoners at Guantanamo Bay to talk. One such technique the magazine reported was flushing pages of the Koran down the toilet in front of the prisoners. Some observers charged that the *Newsweek* article inspired severe anti-American rioting in parts of the Muslim world, with seventeen deaths attributed to the incident. About a week after publication of the article, *Newsweek* retracted the story, indicating that its source had provided inaccurate and misleading information. Later, however, other prisoners corroborated the story.

✔ ***The New York Times* and John McCain's alleged affair.** On February 21, 2008, the *New York Times* published a 3,000-word front-page article alleging that Senator John McCain, the GOP's presumptive nominee for president, had an extramarital affair with Vicki Iseman, a telecommunications industry lobbyist, eight years earlier during his 2000 run for the presidency. The story offered no direct evidence of an affair, but reported that a top McCain campaign advisor had to take special precautions to keep the two apart during the 2000 campaign. The story generated massive attention and criticism. McCain and Iseman immediately denied the story. In fact, Iseman later said that she had never even been alone with McCain and that she had supplied the *New York Times* with ample information refuting the story that the newspaper never published. The aide that the *Times* had relied on for the story, it turned out, had left McCain's campaign in 2007 on bad terms after losing an internal power struggle.

✔ **Jayson Blair, *New York Times*.** When the *New York Times* discovered in 2003 that Blair, a reporter for the newspaper, had not only made up facts and quotes but had also plagiarized in thirty-six of seventy-three articles published under his byline, he was fired. Blair's ethical missteps also led the *New York Times* to fire executive editor Howell Raines for allowing the situation to happen.

✔ **Jack Kelley, *USA Today*.** In early 2004, this *USA Today* foreign correspondent resigned amid allegations that he made up stories, plagiarized, and took money from his newspaper for translation services that never happened. Kelley's ethical lapses included lifting hundreds of passages from other publications, contriving at least twenty stories, and falsely attributing information he published to "U.S. intelligence sources."

✔ ***Dateline NBC*.** In 1992, the NBC television program *Dateline* produced a segment showing how pickup trucks manufactured by General Motors had a proclivity to explode when they collided with other vehicles—but the producers of the show failed to disclose that they rigged the crash and faked the explosion. NBC was highly criticized for both faking the explosion and then not disclosing that fact to the public.

✔ **Mike Barnicle, *Boston Globe*.** In 2003, Barnicle wrote a series of articles published in the *Boston Globe* that used clever quotes and lines picked up from comedian George Carlin's book, *Brain Droppings*. Barnicle did not attribute the lines to Carlin, and the *Boston Globe* fired him for this breach of journalistic ethics.

*The Society of Professional Journalists' Code of Ethics can be found at http://www.spj.org/ethicscode.asp.

Providing information about news and events is perhaps the most basic and most important function of the media. Factual news information is an essential component of evaluating events and forming political opinions. Operating free of government control, the U.S. media can provide objective coverage of events to the American public. **Objectivity** refers to the media reporting events factually, accurately, fairly, and equitably—an important goal for many journalists. In addition to providing factual information about events, objective journalism requires signaling when important events occur and providing perspectives on all sides of an issue or policy debate. The goal of objectivity, however, is itself the subject of some debate. Objectivity is hard to define and measure, and journalists sometimes take a shortcut by trying to give equal weight to all sides without making any judgments of their own. This approach permitted Senator Joseph McCarthy to falsely but very publicly accuse people of being Communists in the 1950s; it let cigarette companies get away with denying that smoking causes cancer; and it prolonged the current national debate on global warming. Journalism professor Philip Meyer has advocated for a science-based definition of objectivity by getting journalists to seek more independent verification of facts.[2]

Numerous media formats strive to provide objective coverage of news information. Most of the content of newspapers (with the notable exception of the editorial pages) is aimed at objectively covering news events and politics at the global, national, and local levels. The twenty-four-hour cable news channels, such as CNN, Fox News, and MSNBC, provide news of events on a continuous basis. Many other formats are aimed at providing an objective look at news information to readers and viewers.

Moreover, the proliferation of cable television has broadened the role of the media as provider of information. Channels like the Biography Channel, the History Channel, local government access channels, and C-SPAN now offer programming that gives historical context to local, national, and international events.

Facilitating Public Debate.
In addition to monitoring and reporting events, the media also facilitate public dialogue and debate on important political issues. By helping frame issues, offering perspectives on how a problem might be solved, and providing context and commentary on political campaigns, the media serve a vital role in a democratic system that depends heavily on voters to make informed choices in elections.

The media facilitate public debate through a variety of forms, both print and electronic. Newspaper editorials provide perspectives on policy debates and political candidates. Syndicated columnists such as David Broder, Anna Quindlen, and George Will publish columns in numerous newspapers around the nation on a regular basis, presenting their own perspectives on issues. Most newspapers dedicate space on their editorial pages for citizens to write opinion pieces ("op-eds") and letters to the editor offering their point of view. Many news magazines adhere to a liberal or conservative approach to discussing issues or evaluating candidates for office. *The Nation*, for example, has a liberal perspective, whereas *The National Review* presents a conservative perspective. Even magazines devoted to one perspective or another, however, usually offer a forum for readers to assess issues. Radio talk shows that offer perspectives on politics, such as those of conservative radio talk show host Rush Limbaugh or liberal political commentator Ed Schultz, also facilitate public debate, as do television programs like MSNBC's *Countdown with Keith Olbermann* and Fox News' *Hannity's America*, which often feature debates between the anchors and their ideological opponents.

These media formats go beyond objectively reporting news to analyzing events and presenting arguments from varying ideological perspectives that readers and viewers can evaluate and use in forming their own opinions about public policies and political candidates.

Objectivity
The journalistic standard that news reporting of events must be factual, accurate, fair, and equitable.

Government Watchdog. Since the founding of the nation, American political culture has been characterized by a healthy skepticism about government. To govern is to have power, and power (in the minds of many) corrupts. The federal system that divides power between the federal government and state and local governments, the system of shared power among the legislative, executive, and judicial branches of government, and the system of checks and balances among these three branches are mechanisms that help guard against the potential abuse of government power. The news media also help prevent the abuse of government power through their role as government watchdog. In this role, the media are sometimes referred to as the fourth branch of government, or the "fourth estate," checking the power of the other branches. Rooting out corruption and abuses of power through investigative journalism is a core function of the American media, no less important today than it was two centuries ago.

More than a century ago, a group of journalists, who came to be known as "muckrakers"[3] (they were given this name by President Theodore Roosevelt), investigated and exposed corporate and political corruption in American life, including the corrupting effect of corporate contributions on presidential candidates who won office. In the late 1800s, corporate wealth was concentrated in a handful of companies in the railroad and banking industries, and those companies bought favors and influence with various presidential administrations. The muckrakers exposed the rash of influence peddling and by doing so helped spawn new laws curbing corporate contributions to federal campaigns.

Pulitzer Prize-winning investigative reporters Carl Bernstein and Bob Woodward in 1973. Woodward and Bernstein investigated the Watergate scandal of the Nixon administration in 1973 and 1974 for the *Washington Post*.

Perhaps the most well-known case of the media uncovering and exposing government corruption was the investigative reporting of *Washington Post* reporters Bob Woodward and Carl Bernstein in the early 1970s concerning the Watergate corruption scandal of President Richard M. Nixon's administration. Their work led in part to the resignation of President Nixon in 1974 for his role in covering up the details of the Republican-led break-in of Democratic National Headquarters in the Watergate Hotel during the 1972 presidential campaign.[4] Woodward and Bernstein largely depended on an anonymous administration source, who came to be known as "Deep Throat," for information that ultimately exposed the White House cover-up of a number of criminal activities in Nixon's 1972 campaign for reelection. It was not until thirty years later, in 2005, that Mark Felt, who at the time of the Watergate break-in was deputy director of the FBI, publicly announced that he was in fact "Deep Throat."

The media also exercise their watchdog function through television programs such as *60 Minutes*, *Dateline*, and *Meet the Press* and through Internet Web sites set up by groups like Common Cause, which provides data on the negative influence of corporate donations on political campaigns. The media also carry out their watchdog function through books. For example, the 2008 book *What Happened* by Scott McClellan, former press secretary to President George W. Bush, severely criticized the president and top Bush administration officials for waging a propaganda campaign to convince the American public that war with Iraq was necessary.

Historical Development of the Media

Before the American Revolution, the news media consisted of a handful of newspapers that were published by printers.[6] The main job of the printer was not to publish a newspaper, but rather to prepare official documents (such as marriage licenses, deeds to land, and government documents), political pamphlets, and religious books. Newspapers of the time mostly featured notices of public events and advertisements for local merchants. These early newspapers carried little information about politics or news events.

The political events that led up to the American Revolution and the events of the Revolution itself changed the nature and functions of the colonial newspapers. Many colonists were intensely interested in the disputes with Great Britain and eager for news about the battles of the Revolution. Newspapers responded to these interests with news stories about the events. Stories about the economic turmoil of the post-Revolution period, particularly the bitter partisan fight between the Federalists and Anti-Federalists over ratification of the Constitution, also appeared in the nation's early newspapers.

The Era of the Partisan Press

The Federalist/Anti-Federalist battle ushered in the **partisan press era**, a period characterized by newspapers supporting a particular political party. This period lasted from the late 1700s through the mid-1850s. Newspapers advocating the Federalist position that favored a stronger central government included John Fenno's *Gazette of the United States* and Noah Webster's *American Minerva*. The Anti-Federalists and later the Jeffersonian-Republicans, who supported states' rights, had their own partisan newspapers, such as the *National Gazette* and the *National Intelligencer*.

Partisan newspapers appealed mostly to readers who already agreed with the political positions advocated by those publications. Partisan-oriented news eventually became big business, and government printing contracts to partisan publications became a regular part of the spoils system.

During the early nineteenth century, a number of technological developments had a significant impact on the newspaper business. The invention of the rotary press in 1815 enabled the mass production of newspapers. The invention of the telegraph and the development of the telegraph system across the United States in the 1840s provided for the widespread electronic dissemination of news information. The expansion of the railroad system across the nation facilitated the mass distribution of newspapers across the continent. These developments allowed newspapers to print news events more quickly and distribute their publications to a larger number of people in a shorter period of time. These technologies also helped reduce production costs, making newspapers affordable for most Americans. The term *penny press* aptly described the low cost of newspapers during the early to mid-nineteenth century.

By the 1850s, newspapers found that they could increase their circulation by distancing themselves from particular partisan positions. Eyeing ever-larger markets, newspapers began to appeal to all Americans. Journalists began to tout the goals of objective reporting of the facts, rather than providing a biased or partisan perspective on events. By the end of the nineteenth century, the technological innovations and the desire of newspaper publishers to reach larger numbers of readers and maximize profits through the selling of advertisements had transformed the newspaper industry from a mostly partisan press to one focused on objective reporting of the news.

The Emergence of Electronic Media

The development of the radio in the early twentieth century provided a new means for Americans to get information about politics. Most notably, communication from the media source to the audience was instantaneous. In addition, the technology

★ LO
Appreciate the evolution from a partisan press to a media focused on objectivity

Partisan press era
The period from the late 1700s to the mid-1800s when newspapers typically supported a particular political party.

★ LO
Explain how changes in technology have transformed the nature of the media

Can the Media Be Trusted to Tell the Truth?

A frequent question raised by critics of the news media is whether or not Americans can trust the truthfulness of news stories. Periodically during the course of American history, journalists have sensationalized stories as a way to "shock" audiences and increase sales of their own publications. Sometime these journalists play loose with the facts, and even fabricate stories outright. Those tactics may work to increase profits in the short run, but the cost to the reputation of American journalism has been significant indeed. Consider the following two cases:

In 1898, William Randolph Hearst was a wealthy newspaper magnate on a mission to incite a war against Spain. During the late 1800s, many American journalists had engaged in what has come to be known as "yellow journalism" to attract more readers and bolster the profits of newspaper owners. The yellow journalism of the late

©CORBIS

William Randolph Hearst

nineteenth century was marked by sensational photos, hoaxes, and even some fake interviews. Hearst, a leading practitioner of the art, became the owner and publisher of nearly thirty newspapers including the *San Francisco Examiner*, the *New York Journal*, and the *Chicago American*. In 1898, his newspapers' coverage of the explosion of the battleship *Maine* in Havana Harbor suggested that Spain was responsible for the blast, even though no hard evidence existed. Many historians believe that Hearst's accounts played a role in leading the United States to war with Spain in the Spanish-American War. He used the techniques of yellow journalism to build a media empire, but at the same time his methods eroded public confidence in news reporting in general, and in his own publications in particular.

In 1998, Matt Drudge was another culprit in the increasing public dismay with the media. Drudge and his *Drudge Report* certainly personify many of the problems that plague the reputation of the news media in the

allowed political leaders to directly communicate with the American people. The first radio station was KDKA in Pittsburgh, established in 1923. The first network of radio stations, which was established in 1926 as the National Broadcasting Company (NBC), provided common programming and newscasts that were made available to the first truly mass audiences.

President Franklin Delano Roosevelt, delivering one of his famous "fireside chats" in 1933.

AP PHOTO

Franklin Delano Roosevelt, elected president in 1932, used the radio to deliver comforting and inspiring messages to the nation, then suffering in the midst of the Great Depression. FDR's weekly radio addresses, which the president called "fireside chats," represented the first significant use of this medium by a political leader to communicate to the nation's people. In addition to FDR's fireside chats, radio commentators such as Father Charles Coughlin (Detroit's

Internet age. Touted as a top Internet "news" source, the *Drudge Report* first became famous in 1998 for its coverage of the President Bill Clinton/White House intern Monica Lewinsky sex scandal. As the first to report over the Internet the lurid sexual details of White House encounters between Clinton and twenty-one-year-old Lewinsky, the *Drudge Report* "scooped" the story. Scandal surrounding the sexual encounters between Clinton and Lewinsky provided the material that attracted Drudge's readers to his Web site. Yet as fast as Drudge has been to report stories, he has sometimes proven to be quite unreliable. Rumors, rather than substantiated facts, serve as the basis for many of his stories. Early in 2004, Drudge "revealed" unsubstantiated stories about alleged marital affairs of Democratic presidential candidate John Kerry. None of the stories proved to have any basis in fact. Critics charge that when Drudge's stories fail to materialize, he doesn't hesitate to exaggerate the facts to increase his readership. Recent polls show that confidence in the news and newsmakers has dropped since the increase in sensationalized news that dates back at least to the 1980s.[†]

Matt Drudge

AP PHOTO/MICHAEL CAULFIELD

*The *Drudge Report* can be found at http://www.drudgereport.com.
[†]See the 2006 General Social Survey, conducted by the National Opinion Research Center at the University of Chicago.

anti-Semitic "fighting priest") and Louisiana Senator Huey Long popularized radio as a medium that could provide a great deal of political commentary and debate. During World War II, Americans eager for news about the progress of the war turned to the radio for information. Edward R. Murrow's live radio reports from London during the Nazi bombings of that city and from other battle sites captivated the nation.

In the 1950s, Joe Pyne of radio station KABC hosted the first political talk radio show. Pyne challenged the status quo political views of the times, invited call-in questions from listeners, and promoted confrontation and debate. Pyne's style and format laid the foundation for many of today's popular political talk radio shows.

A number of technological advancements have had a large impact on the scope and importance of the news media through American history, but none has had a more profound influence than the invention of television. In the post–World War II boom of the American economy, the nation quickly adopted TV as its primary medium for getting news about politics and the world. NBC and CBS developed the standard TV news show format in the early 1950s with a fifteen-minute daily news program. The program featured a news anchor reading the news, supported by film footage and reporters. (This format—now modified into a half-hour program produced each evening—continues to be widely used today by all the major networks.) In the 1950s, TV networks broadcast the Army–McCarthy hearings of the U.S. Senate that exposed Senator Joseph McCarthy as a crude bully and resulted in

Left: Chet Huntley and David Brinkley deliver the evening news for NBC in 1965. Right: CBS news anchor Walter Cronkite, pictured here in 1969, was a very popular and trusted newsman for CBS news.

his censure for ethical misconduct. Live television coverage of the Republican and Democratic national conventions set the standard for live broadcasts of major political events. The networks also sold advertising time to the major party candidates in the presidential election of 1952, revolutionizing the way in which candidates would wage their bids for elective office.

Presidential Debates and the Power of Television.

A defining moment in revealing the political power of electronic media was the live television broadcast of the debates between Republican Richard Nixon and Democrat John Kennedy, candidates in the presidential election of 1960. For the first time, all Americans were able to watch a live debate between the candidates. Many observers credit Kennedy's favorable TV performance as an important factor contributing to his razor-thin victory over Nixon in the November election. During the first of three televised debates, Kennedy won over the audience with his relaxed and self-assured manner before the camera; by contrast, Nixon seemed nervous and uncomfortable. Nixon prepared for the debate by studying briefing documents, but spent little time practicing debate style. Kennedy, on the other hand, spent a great deal of time practicing answers to questions out loud. For the two days prior to the first debate, Kennedy and his inner circle of advisers didn't leave the practice session in their hotel room. On the night of the debate, a tanned Kennedy looked strong and healthy. He wore a navy blue suit that contrasted sharply with the light walls of the TV studio. Nixon, on the other hand, looked ill and underweight. Just before the debate he had been hospitalized with an infection, exhausted from a hard week of campaigning. He wore makeup to cover up his five o'clock shadow and dressed in a light gray suit that blended into the background.

The candidates debated the important issues and both did well in articulating their positions. But TV analysts reported that Kennedy won the debate. His stage presence, practice addressing the camera, tanned complexion, hand gestures, and commanding appearance compared favorably to the somber, pale Nixon. It was a lesson that no future presidential candidate would forget.

Interestingly, research on this debate[7] reveals that those who listened to the debate on the radio thought Nixon won, whereas those who watched the debate on TV tended to think that Kennedy won, proving that the medium through which events are communicated can indeed influence the way in which people evaluate those events. That the medium itself may have an important effect on the way in which people receive and perceive news was suggested by communications researcher Marshall McCluhan, who summarized this idea with his memorable phrase "the medium is the message."[8]

JOHN P. FILO/CBS/LANDOV

AP PHOTO/REED SAXON

Left: Katie Couric of *CBS Evening News* became the first female solo anchor on a major network's evening news. Right: Brian Williams, NBC's evening news anchor.

Live televised debates between the candidates for president did not occur again until 1976, when Republican President Gerald Ford and Democratic challenger Jimmy Carter met. This time both candidates were well prepared to convey the image they wanted to the American viewing audience. Dressed to coordinate with the set background, prepped with numerous practice sessions, and made up to ensure a favorable skin color tone, both Carter and Ford sought to communicate a positive image. Live broadcasts of presidential campaign debates have been a part of every presidential election contest since 1976.[9]

Television has transformed virtually every aspect of political campaigns and government policymaking. Prior to TV, the vast majority of voters never saw more than a still picture of the candidates, and most learned about them from reading newspaper accounts of their statements, speeches, and activities. Television, however, has allowed viewers to observe candidates live and in action, and to see how they deliver a speech and respond to questions. Television has also given candidates the opportunity to develop an "image" through carefully planned media appearances and strategically designed political advertisements.

JIM BOURG-POOL/GETTY IMAGES

The first of the three debates between 2008 presidential candidates John McCain (left) and Barack Obama (right) took place at the University of Mississippi in Oxford on September 26, 2008.

Presidential Press Conferences.

The power of televised images has also altered the governing process. Whereas President Woodrow Wilson was the first to hold regular and formal presidential news conferences, President Dwight D. Eisenhower was the first to hold regular news conferences as we know them today, as a means of explaining his administration's policies and appealing directly to the public for support. Before Eisenhower, the news media's access to the president was primarily through appointments that the chief executive would give to favored reporters. Eisenhower opened up the press conference to reporters from all types of news organizations. The questions were not prescreened, and Eisenhower addressed whatever topics were on reporters' agendas. This format for addressing the nation, coupled with the capability of television to show Americans the event, opened up the presidency to the public.

Eisenhower's successor, President John F. Kennedy, quickly mastered the art of the presidential press conference. He made events seem even more dramatic and intriguing by allowing TV to broadcast them live. Kennedy's preparedness on issues, strong intellect, charismatic personality, and sense of humor made his press conferences interesting and successful events. President Lyndon B. Johnson continued the press conference tradition set by his predecessors, but such events became more difficult for Johnson as America's involvement in the Vietnam War escalated, with press questions increasingly focused on war casualties and military ineffectiveness.

Eisenhower, Kennedy, and Johnson averaged about two press conferences every month, but Presidents Nixon, Ford, Carter, and Reagan held fewer—less than one per month. Nixon, Ford, and Carter each dealt with crisis situations (Vietnam, Watergate, a severe energy crisis, and the Iranian hostage crisis), which led to uncomfortable open questioning from journalists, and so each president cut back on the number of conferences. Reagan, despite his acting background and ease in front of a camera, had a difficult time dealing with reporters' questions in a press conference setting, and so he began a weekly radio address as a regular means of communicating with the American public. All presidents since Reagan have used this form of weekly address to speak to the nation.

President Bill Clinton increased the number of presidential press conferences to an average of two per month, based on his ability to use this format quite effectively. However, the number of Clinton

Christina Aguilera lends her familiar face to a Rock the Vote poster. MTV, a popular media outlet for young people, airs this campaign prior to major elections.

press conferences was reduced sharply during the period when he faced his biggest crisis in office, over his relationship with White House intern Monica Lewinsky. President George W. Bush, who like Reagan was often ill at ease at responding to questions in a press conference situation, averaged only one press conference per year. Staged events, one-on-one interviews with reporters, televised speeches, and the weekly radio address were Bush's preferred means of communicating to the public through the media. Like his predecessor, President Obama has also held few press conferences, preferring public appearances, staged events, and use of his White House Web page to communicate with the public.

With each successive presidential administration, White House staffs have become better equipped at using television to influence the public through direct communication. Press conferences, presidential addresses, and carefully staged presidential appearances (such as President Bush's visit to an aircraft carrier upon his declaration of victory in 2003 in the war against Iraq) are typical of the means by which the White House uses the media to muster support for the president's agenda.

The Mass Media Today

★ LO
Understand the large variety of media that cover news and provide opinion about government and politics, including both traditional media and "new" media

Today's mass media include a variety of channels of communication through which news content is disseminated to audiences. Channels of communication may be either print or electronic. Print media largely include newspapers, magazines, and books. Electronic media include television, radio, the Internet, and movies. In addition, forms of content on any medium may be classified as either news or entertainment. In newspapers, for example, the first section of most publications is entirely devoted to news stories and editorials. Subsequent sections might include other news such as sports news or business news. Typically there is an entertainment section that includes movie reviews, comics, crossword puzzles, recipes, and so forth. Television stations also provide news programming in the forms of news broadcasts, investigative reporting shows, and political talk shows, and entertainment programming in the form of sitcoms, soap operas, reality TV programs, and drama shows.

Even media sources that are intended primarily to provide entertainment programming sometimes include content that may fall within the realm of politics. One very popular show that combines news with comedy is *The Daily Show*, hosted by political comedian Jon Stewart. During recent presidential elections the cable television station MTV broadcast programming that attempted to increase voter turnout among young people.

The Print Media

The modern print media mostly include newspapers, magazines, and books. Use of these print media has declined in recent decades. *Time* and *Newsweek* are popular weekly magazines devoted to providing in-depth coverage of current events, though their readership too has declined as consumers of news increasingly turn to electronic sources of information. These and other news magazines often rely on photojournalism to support their longer stories to engage readers.

Books also enjoy an important place in American journalism. *Plan of Attack*, a 2004 book by Bob Woodward, documented the role of the Bush administration in preparing for the second Iraq War. Woodward, through interviews with top White House sources including the president and the secretary of state, concluded that the Bush administration had actively begun preparations for war long before the U.S. invasion and well before notifying Congress of its intentions. Woodward's work became an important topic during the 2004 presidential campaign. Thirty years earlier in a book called *All the President's Men*, co-written with Carl Bernstein, Woodward documented the Nixon administration's role in the Watergate affair.

A century ago there were about 2,200 newspapers published daily; today there are only about 1,500 daily newspapers—a 30 percent decline—purchased by about 76 million readers. Once the prime source of news for Americans, newspapers now take a backseat to television as the nation's main news source (see Figure 12.1, p. 368). Just as the number of newspaper readers has declined steadily since the 1950s, today the Internet seems to be becoming a more popular source of news and as a result, the number of newspaper readers is falling at an even greater rate than before.

FIGURE 12.1 The News Sources That Americans Use

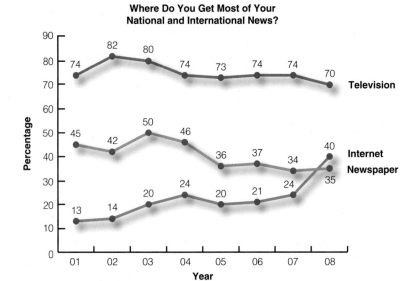

Where Do You Get Most of Your National and International News?

Source: http://pewresearch.org/pubs/1066/internet-overtakes-newspapers-as-news-source.

The vast majority of newspapers are regional metropolitan and suburban publications. They range from those that cover large metropolitan areas, such as the *Chicago Tribune*, the *Miami Herald*, the *Dallas Morning News*, and the *San Francisco Chronicle*, to those covering much smaller towns. A handful of newspapers such as the *New York Times*, the *Wall Street Journal*, and *USA Today* are considered national dailies and are designed to appeal to a national readership. The *New York Times* trumpets its supposed status as the "paper of record" of events from around the world; the *Wall Street Journal* has the niche of being the nation's leading newspaper on financial markets and commerce; *USA Today*'s format of brief stories along with colorful graphics and pictures has helped it attract a nationwide following.

Wire services provide a clearinghouse for news as it is occurring. The largest wire service by far is the Associated Press (AP). The AP employs a large number of reporters throughout the nation and around the world to write stories on news events. Newspapers and television and radio stations that are members of the AP share the news services it produces. Using the AP as their news source allows smaller regional newspapers and local TV and radio stations to cover events from around the world in an efficient, informative, and cost-effective manner.

The Electronic Media

The major electronic media are television, radio, and the Internet. Television and radio have played an important role in American politics for many decades, and the Internet has been responsible for more recent changes in the news and the way in which Americans use the news. The Internet, along with other relatively new media technologies such as DVDs, fax machines, cell phones, satellites, and cable TV, have come to be known as the **new media** (or "digital media"), which have revolutionized the news business at every level.

Television. With its mass adoption by households in the early 1950s, television became and has remained the primary source of news for most Americans. More than 98 percent of households in the United States report having at least one television set. News programming on TV is provided mostly by broadcast television networks and their local affiliates. The broadcast networks include ABC, CBS, and NBC. Cable television stations, such as CNN, Fox News, and MSNBC, provide twenty-four-hour

★ **LO** Assess changes in audience and readership patterns, and the impact of those changes on news coverage

New media
Media outlets that rely on relatively newer technologies for communicating, such as the Internet, DVDs, fax machines, cell phones, satellites, cable TV, and broadband.

news programming as well. Other cable stations, such as C-SPAN and local public access stations, provide specialized coverage—for example, the live broadcast of congressional debates and committee meetings.

The defining characteristic of television is its visual nature.[10] The implied "reality" of seeing video of events, or live broadcasts of events, can be quite powerful, as civil rights demonstrators learned in the mid-1960s. Compared to the written word, the spoken word, or even still pictures, video communicates events "as they are," and so is regarded by viewers as more trustworthy and "real." Many argue that film footage of reporters covering the Vietnam War contributed to the erosion of public support for America's involvement there. The daily barrage of video showing dead soldiers brought new meaning to Americans' understanding of war and helped influence President Lyndon Johnson's decision not to seek reelection in 1968. In 2004, video of Americans captured and mutilated by Iraqi insurgents as a protest against the U.S. military occupation of Iraq captured a great deal of attention and reduced support for the Bush administration's policy. Likewise, vivid pictures of American mistreatment of Iraqi detainees at Abu Ghraib prison did not help the Bush administration's effort to defeat the Iraqi insurgents.

New satellite technologies further facilitate the live and instantaneous coverage of events not only around every corner of the globe, but also from the moon, Mars, and Jupiter. The new high-tech satellites provide an opportunity for people to view events as they occur even from the outer reaches of the universe, such as the live pictures sent back from satellites on the 2004 U.S. spaceship mission to Mars.

AP IMAGES/PAUL DRINKWATER

Keith Olbermann hosts the liberal-oriented news commentary program *Countdown with Keith Olbermann* on cable television station MSNBC.

Radio. Contemporary radio largely programs commercial music, with several minutes of each hour allotted for news, sports, traffic reports, and weather forecasts. These short news reports are an important source of information (particularly for commuters who use their cars to get to and from work or school) about news events and politics. A number of radio stations carry a specialized form of radio programming referred to as **talk radio**, in which one or more hosts provide commentary and often invite listeners to call in to the show and offer their own opinions. Talk radio steadily gained popularity in the late 1980s and early 1990s, marked by a growing interest in political talk shows, as increasing numbers of commuters with cell phones began to take time while sitting in traffic to listen to these shows and call in to offer their own views.

Some of the more popular call-in shows focus on politics. The hosts often provide an ideological perspective on policies, issues, and political candidates and campaigns. Listeners of a particular ideological persuasion enjoy hearing what the host and others have to say, and a small number call in to offer their own views. Many local radio stations provide political talk radio programs, ranging from very modestly ideological debates to extremely partisan ones. Several nationally syndicated shows have also attracted an especially large listening audience, such as conservative commentator Rush Limbaugh's show.

A trend in ownership of radio is the purchase of smaller, local radio stations by large media organizations. Critics of this trend contend that the large corporate owners typically impose standardized programming through satellite feeds, thus depriving them of their local character.

Talk radio

A specialized form of radio programming on which one or more hosts provide commentary and often invite listeners to call in to the show and offer their own opinions.

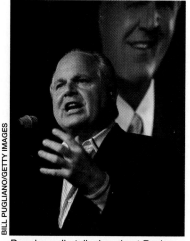

BILL PUGLIANO/GETTY IMAGES

Popular radio talk show host Rush Limbaugh, a favorite of conservatives across America.

The Internet. In 1993, a group of students at the University of Illinois developed MOSAIC, the first graphical Internet browser. MOSAIC allowed users to view pictures and color images on the World Wide Web. MOSAIC soon went commercial and became Netscape, and by the mid-1990s it was attracting tens of millions of users. Coupled with huge worldwide increases in sales of personal computers through the 1990s, the ease and user-friendliness of accessing the Internet made the medium an attractive source of news and information for people around the world.

The Internet's rise as a mass medium has many implications for news, information, and the American political system. One such effect is the way in which people use the Internet compared to other news sources. From the viewers' perspective, television watching is a passive activity. Once they've tuned into a particular channel, viewers have no other choice but to get whatever news is being presented. They cannot ask questions or seek specific answers to questions they might have. Likewise, listening to a radio broadcast is a fairly passive activity for listeners unless, of course, they choose to call in to the show. While reading a newspaper, people can pick and choose the articles they prefer to read. However, newspapers are also limited in the amount of content they can provide, and readers cannot query a newspaper to get answers on specific questions they might have.

The Internet, however, allows users to pursue exactly the kind of news and information they are interested in. Search engines such as Google and Yahoo allow Internet users to find whatever they are looking for. Furthermore, most news Web sites include a "search" feature that allows users to search the Web site and/or newspaper database for information relevant to a particular query.

Unlike other media, the Internet also enables individual users to be their own mass publisher. Most word processing packages include the option of "save as Web page." A simple set of keystrokes enables users to place information, data, and graphics on their own Web page. Web design software enables users to put a Web page on a server and thus make that page available to millions of other Internet users to access. In this way, Internet users can publish material that is accessible to a mass audience.

Most newspapers and television stations maintain Web sites that include the organization's news content, and links to other sources, such as the Associated Press. Many of these sites also include a searchable database of archived news stories. Some of the most used news Web sites are CNN (http://www.cnn.com) and the *New York Times* (http://www.nytimes.com). With searchable indices to past stories, links to other sites, online forums, and audio and video files, these sites offer a broad array of content that users can easily access.

The Internet has transformed the flow of news and information about politics in other ways as well. It has become a common source of information about political campaigns, because candidates for office often create a Web page and post it on a server for voters to access. A wide variety of "chat rooms" and online forums serve as venues for users to post their opinions, ask questions, and engage in dialogue on political issues. **Blogs** (derived from the term *weblogs*) are also becoming popular among many Internet users. In 2008, for example, the significant amount of fund-raising and voter communication by Obama supporters substantially buoyed that campaign's success. Blogs provide a combination editorial page, personal Web page, and online diary offering personal observations in real time about news events and issues. Some of the more popular blogs are published by journalists and political commentators.

About 65 percent of Americans report that they use personal computers on a regular basis, and most of these PCs are connected to the Internet. Those who use the Internet are more likely to be younger, middle- and upper-class, better educated, and nonminority—a disparity that has been referred to as the **digital divide**. Greater access to the Internet facilitates access to news and information, and those who have access clearly enjoy an advantage. However, as computers and Internet access costs decline, and as younger generations with computer skills replace older generations,

Blogs

Internet sites that include a combination of editorial page, personal Web page, and online diary of personal observations in real time about news events and issues.

Digital divide

The large differences in usage of the Internet between older and younger people, lower- and middle/upper-class people, lesser and better educated people, and minority groups and nonminority groups.

You and Your Blog Can Make a Difference

Political blogs have significantly changed the way that people across the country participate in American politics. They offer anyone with a computer and access to the Internet the opportunity to publish their political opinions in the mass media, to share ideas and perspectives with others, and to debate and challenge the positions of those with whom they disagree. Of the literally millions of political blogs to be found on the Internet, most are associated with a particular partisan or ideological perspective.

While political bloggers may be found all around the world, Americans between the ages of eighteen and thirty-five have been especially active in contributing their ideas in this particular marketplace, sometimes termed the "blogocracy." Some of their efforts have had a significant impact on political events. For example, during the 2006 Virginia Senate campaign, a supporter of Democratic candidate Jim Webb was following Webb's opponent, incumbent Senate George Allen, with a video camera. Annoyed at being followed, Allen referred to the Webb supporter as a "Macaca," which is a term that refers to a species of monkey and is considered an ethnic slur. The videotaper, S. R. Sidarth, was also a blogger, and immediately posted the video of Allen's slur on YouTube. Many other blogs and national news organizations began to cover the clip of Allen's slur. The posting is credited both with clinching Webb's narrow victory in the race, and in stifling Allen's presidential ambitions for 2008.

Another way some bloggers have influenced politics is through the "moneybomb," a blog-driven grassroots fundraising campaign that is usually generated over a short period of time: supporters use the blogs to create a frenzied atmosphere to quickly raise money. Bloggers who supported Massachusetts GOP senate candidate Scott Brown initiated a moneybomb for him in his 2010 special election once Brown came within striking distance of winning Ted Kennedy's reliably Democratic seat. The effort raised $10 million.

College students, like the one pictured, can publish blogs from anywhere on campus.

For Critical Thinking and Discussion

1. Have you ever posted comments on a blog, whether your own, a friend's, or simply as a reply to another blogger's comments?

2. Find a blog that aligns with your own political interests or attitudes and read at least a week's worth of posting and comments. What do you notice? Do opinions tend to get debated or echoed within that blog?

3. What are the advantages and disadvantages of engaging in this form of political participation?

the digital divide is likely to become less and less pronounced. Public libraries have provided another remedy to the digital divide. In 1996, 28 percent of all libraries had public access to the Internet. Today, 95 percent of libraries offer Internet access to patrons. Eager to gain access, the number of visitors to public libraries has increased by nearly 20 percent over the past six years.

Ownership of the Media

The Framers of the Constitution were clearly committed to the freedom of the press. Government ownership of the press was then and is today regarded as a threat to the basic freedoms that Americans enjoy. If government controls the news and the flow

★ LO

Learn that the ownership of media organizations is concentrated in large corporations

of information to citizens, it holds too much power. Private ownership of the media allows for the free and open exchange of ideas. Ironically, some today argue that the concentration of ownership of the news media by large nonmedia corporations, such as General Electric and the Disney Corporation, has stifled diversity in news content and blurred the line between what is news and what is entertainment. One large corporation that owns multiple media outlets has become the norm, whereas in the past most media outlets were independently owned. It is also argued that ownership of media organizations by a conglomerate such as GE might compromise the objectivity of the news. When NBC, which is owned by GE, reports on a story about GE, might that story be biased?

The big three television networks—ABC, CBS, and NBC—have dominated television viewership since the early 1950s. By 1956, more than nine in ten stations were affiliated with one of these networks. Over the past several decades, the growing popularity of cable and satellite TV challenged the predominant position of the three networks. With hundreds of channels now available, the three networks' share of the viewing market continues to shrink. This competition led the networks to focus on greater efficiencies in the day-to-day operation of their businesses. By the mid-1980s, all three networks had experienced a change in corporate ownership, and all three now are part of "vertically integrated" corporations that are involved in video production as well as national and local distribution. In the late 1980s, competition between the networks further increased with the addition of the Fox Network.

NBC is currently owned by the megacorporation General Electric (GE); the CBS network, formerly owned by Viacom, is now its own corporation; the Disney Corporation owns and operates the ABC network; and Fox, the newest of the major networks, is owned by the News Corporation. Table 12.1 suggests the extent to which these four corporate owners control the nation's media.

Not all television and radio stations in the United States are privately owned. The Public Broadcasting Act of 1967 created the Corporation for Public Broadcasting

TABLE 12.1 Corporate Ownership of the Four Major Television News Outlets

TV Network	NBC	CBS	ABC	Fox
Corporate Owner	General Electric (GE)	CBS Corporation	Disney Corporation	News Corporation
Network TV Affiliates Owned	10	16	10	25
Cable TV Channels Owned	MSNBC, CNBC, Bravo, the Weather Channel, Oxygen, Telemundo	Showtime, CBS College Sports Network	Disney Channel, ESPN, ABC Family	Fox Sports, Fox Family, Fox Kids, FX, Fox News, Fox Movie Channel, Fox Business Network, Fox Classics, Fox College Sports, FX Networks, Speed Channel, FUEL TV, National Geographic Channel
Other Holdings	Manufactures electrical appliances, electrical power equipment	Simon & Schuster (book publisher)	ESPN magazine, Disneyland, Disneyworld	HarperCollins (book publisher), newspapers

(CPB), which is responsible for distributing federal funds to support public, non-commercial radio and television stations. These stations have had a difficult time surviving economically in a marketplace dominated by commercial interests. CPB funds the Public Broadcasting Service (PBS), which was formed in 1969 to distribute programming to the nation's public television stations. CPB-funded radio programs are distributed by National Public Radio (NPR), American Public Media, and Public Radio International to member stations.

The 1967 law provided much-needed support for noncommercial TV and radio and has established a rather impressive network of stations that provide some very popular programming. *Morning Edition* and *All Things Considered* are highly regarded radio news shows with a very loyal following; the same goes for the PBS-supported *News Hour with Jim Lehrer*. *Frontline* is a popular, award-winning investigative reporting program supported by PBS. Documentary series on the Civil War, produced by Ken Burns, and other such topics have been well-received by large audiences. PBS has also supported a significant amount of children's educational programming, including *Sesame Street*.

PBS and NPR member stations do not generally engage in commercial advertising. They rely instead on funds from the CPB and on donations from businesses and individuals to support their broadcasting operation. For example, in 1999 General Motors provided a major ten-year commitment of support to PBS to finance productions by Burns, including documentaries on major league baseball and jazz music. Individual pledges of support are typically solicited through on-air membership drives and corporate underwriting of programming. There are nearly 400 PBS television stations, many of which are aligned with communications departments in colleges and universities across the nation.

An important assumption underlying federal support for public broadcasting is that government is obligated to ensure that offerings are diverse and that an ample number of educational programs are developed. Federal support for public TV and radio, however, is often a political hot potato. Conservatives claim that public television has a liberal bias, and many have attempted, unsuccessfully, to curb federal funding for CPB.

The Effects of the Media

There is no doubt that Americans rely on the media for news and information about politics. What is less clear is the influence that media exposure has on citizens' opinions (Does watching a news story on the increase in crime rates make the viewer more fearful of crime?) and behavior (Does reading an article about Barack Obama's community organizing experiences lead a reader to vote for or against him on Election Day?).

Researchers can quite easily gauge the exposure and use of the media. It is much more difficult, however, to identify the impact of media exposure on opinions and behavior. Citizens are constantly bombarded by news stories from a variety of different media. Isolating how one news story, or even several stories in one medium, influences opinions or behaviors is very hard to determine.

Despite the difficulty of proving media effects, political leaders and candidates for election certainly act as though the effects are powerful. Leaders constantly try to influence campaign stories and news stories to favor their own positions. Presidents use press conferences to send messages and attempt to win public support. Candidates buy advertising time to try to influence voters. Political parties orchestrate events at party conventions to send favorable partisan messages to voters.

Early research studies of media effects examined how citizen exposure to media content during a campaign influenced how they voted. In classic books on the subject (such as *The Voter Decides* and *The American Voter*), the media were credited with having little or no effect on voters' decisions. These studies, which led to a

★ LO

Describe the different theories that have been developed to explain the effect that exposure to news has on viewers/readers

theory known as **minimal effects theory**, found that deep-seated, long-term political attitudes had a much greater influence on the vote decision.[11] Such enduring and pre-existing attitudes lead to selective perception and retention of news content. People evaluate news material from their own partisan perspective (selective perception) and tend to process and remember the material more consistent with their preexisting attitudes (selection retention).[12]

Moreover, preexisting attitudes often influence what kinds of news people choose to pay attention to in the first place (selective exposure). Psychologists suggest that people's desire to achieve cognitive consistency and avoid cognitive dissonance explains why they process new information in such a way as to assimilate with existing attitudes. These early studies that found "minimal effects" were largely focused on partisan elections and attempted to evaluate the effects of media exposure on the vote decision.

Subsequent research, though not refuting the findings of the media's minimal effects on partisan behavior, examined other areas where media exposure might have an impact. **Social learning theory**, for example, argued that viewers imitate what they view on television through observational learning.[13] Television's focus on sex and violence has led to a large number of studies that try to assess whether exposure to such material leads viewers to become more violent with reduced moral standards. Some of this research suggests that viewers do learn negative, antisocial behavior from TV.

Social learning theory
The theory that viewers imitate what they view on television through observational learning.

Some communications researchers have advanced the notion of *priming*,[14] which suggests that the activation of one thought also activates other thoughts, and exposure to media provides cues to people on this thought activation process. For example, watching the Road Runner beat up on Wile E. Coyote in the old Warner Brothers cartoon may make one child act violently against another child after watching the cartoon. The rash of injuries related to the show *Jackass* is another example of the priming theory in action.

Critics of media often use social learning and priming theories to advocate for government controls of the media. The Telecommunications Act of 1996, for example, required television set manufacturers to include a V-chip in new units to allow parents to block programs they did not wish their children or families to view. Another law passed in 1997 required the television industry to develop a rating system for television shows based on the show's level of sex, violence, and profanity. Studies that demonstrated a connection between TV exposure and negative behavior were important pieces of evidence used to promote support for the V-chip requirement and the TV ratings system.

Cultivation theory
The theory of media effects that suggests that heavy television exposure helps develop an individual's overall view of the world.

The **cultivation theory** of media effects suggests that heavy television exposure helps develop an individual's overall view of the world.[15] According to this theory, the emphasis on violence and crime in both news and entertainment programming would lead the heavy viewer to overestimate and be disproportionately concerned about the extent of crime and violence.

Agenda setting theory
The theory that holds that although the effects of television exposure may be minimal or difficult to gauge, the media are quite influential in telling the public what to think about.

A final theory of media effects is best known as **agenda setting**. This theory suggests that although the effects of exposure may be minimal or difficult to gauge, the media are quite influential in telling the public what to think about. For example, Monica Lewinsky's affair with President Bill Clinton was a lead story in the news throughout 1998, and the prominent placement of that story in numerous media outlets helped to keep it a popular topic of conversation. Daily news coverage of the number of soldiers and civilians killed in Iraq focuses public attention on the U.S. military engagement there.

The media set the public agenda for the issues and activities that many Americans choose to think about and talk about. Prominently placed and frequently repeated headlines in newspapers, lead stories on television news shows and on talk radio, and highlighted stories on well-trafficked Web sites set the stage for public discourse. Citizens pick up a newspaper or flip on an all-news TV station to become informed

The Commercial Success of Fox News

The Fox News Channel, created by Australian media mogul Rupert Murdoch in 1996, is today the nation's most watched cable news network. Because its opinion shows are hosted by well-known conservative commentators such as Bill O'Reilly, Glenn Beck, and Sean Hannity, many believe that Fox's news format, too, is designed to promote conservative political programming. However, Fox News maintains that its news programming, which runs from 9 AM to 4 PM and 6 PM to 8 PM daily, remains fair and unbiased.

Along with O'Reilly, Beck, and Hannity, Fox News airs shows hosted by former Arkansas Governor (and Republican presidential candidate) Mike Huckabee, Shepard Smith, Greta Van Susteren, and Neil Cavuto. All of these shows typically rank in Neilson's top ten cable news shows. Fox's primary competition within the cable news industry comes from CNN and MSNBC. For the past few years, however, Fox News has decisively won the battle for viewers; in fact, the size of the Fox audience is larger than that of CNN and MSNBC combined. By the end of 2009, Fox News ranked second in the Neilson ratings for all cable networks (behind only the USA Network), while CNN and MSNBC ranked fifteenth and twenty-sixth, respectively.

Often a target of Fox News commentators, the Obama administration has been especially critical of this popular news outlet. In October 2009, the Obama administration's then director of communications, Anita Dunn, declared that her bosses were going to

Fox News conservative talk show host Bill O'Reilly draws a very high audience for his nightly cable TV show, *The O'Reilly Factor.*

take on Fox: "We are going to treat them the way we would treat an opponent. . . . We don't need to pretend that this is the way legitimate news organizations behave." Despite these and other criticisms, Fox News has continued to increase its domination of cable news programming.

For Critical Thinking and Discussion

1. What do you think accounts for the success of Fox News? Why has it been so much more successful than CNBC or CNN in attracting large audiences?

2. Do you think that Fox's coverage of the news is truly "objective," or does it reflect a conservative perspective? Likewise, does MSNBC's news programming reflect a liberal perspective?

about what is happening in their community, the nation, and the world. In this sense, the news media have a powerful impact on public debate.[16] As news media scholar Doris Graber has noted, "When media make events seem important, average people as well as politicians discuss them and form opinions. This enhances the perceived importance of these events and ensures even more public attention and, possibly, political action."[17]

Criticisms of the News Media

Though Americans rely on the media for information about what is going on in the nation and around the world, the news media are also the subject for a number of criticisms. For example, despite the vast array of news sources available, most

★ LO

Identify common criticisms of media coverage of politics, including bias, sensationalism, and the concentration of corporate ownership

Foreign Press: All Obama, All the Time

President Obama's political opponents often like to complain that he is more popular abroad than he is at home. There may be good reason for this frustration, dating back to Obama's exceedingly positive treatment by the foreign press during his 2008 run for the presidency. *Politico*'s Michael Calderone took special note during that campaign of how the German press seemed to be rooting for Obama to win:

> *Christoph von Marschall, the Washington bureau chief of the Berlin-based newspaper* Der Tagesspiegel, *wrote in Sunday's* Washington Post *about the "dirty little secret" of the Obama campaign: snubbing the foreign press. But lack of access hasn't stopped the ink from flowing. Barack Obama's face adorns newspaper and magazine covers worldwide, as reporters flock to foreign capitals for the presumptive Democratic presidential nominee's five-country tour following stops in Afghanistan and Iraq.*
>
> *Marschall, for one, said that he's written several Obama-related pieces already this past week, and will continue over the next few days,* focusing on the trip's impact on the U.S. election. Back in Berlin, he estimated that 10 to 15 reporters will cover Obama's upcoming speech from various angles, filling up column inches in the newspaper's national, local and cultural pages. . . . Toby Harnden, U.S. editor of the Daily Telegraph, *told* Politico *that it's almost as if the overwhelmingly popular Obama had been "designed by a committee of Europeans" with the goal of creating their ideal American presidential candidate.*
>
> *. . . . In an effort to satisfy voracious reader appetites for all things Obama,* Der Spiegel *published a 6,300-word story, with the candidate adorning the cover. The font was nabbed from Germany's version of "American Idol." "Europeans have fallen in love with the Democrat, mostly because he's not Bush," Cordula Meyer and several* Der Speigel *colleagues wrote. . . . "The German press, looking from Berlin, behaves as if the election of Obama is a foregone conclusion," said Josef Joffe, publisher-editor of* Die Zeit, *a weekly German newspaper. "He's being celebrated like a victorious Roman general who comes back from the conquest of Gaul or something."*

Source: Michael Calderone, "Foreign Press: All Obama, All of the Time," www.politico.com/news/stories/0708/11972.html, *Politico,* June 22, 2008.

CARSTEN KOALL/GETTY IMAGES NEWS/GETTY IMAGES

Barack Obama addresses a crowd of enthusiastic Germans in June 2008.

news programming follows a standard format that makes it appear the same to the public. Many newspapers are owned by a handful of publishers (such as the Tribune Company and Gannett) and follow a standard format for news. Similarly, just a few companies own many of the nation's radio stations and TV stations and employ a similar format in their programming. Critics charge that this concentration in ownership could result in a handful of companies promoting their own political objectives.

Another criticism of the private ownership of the media stems from the premise that the media, like most other privately owned companies, are in business primarily to make money. For the media, increasing profits requires attracting larger audiences and more readers, and as many media companies have found, providing higher-quality news programming on politically important topics does not always guarantee increased audience ratings or numbers of readers. Rather, news that provides more entertainment tends to get larger audience shares.

Often, the result is news that is characterized by "sensationalized" content. Stories that highlight or exploit crime, violence, disasters, personal conflicts, competition, and scandals tend to increase the sale of newspapers and improve the ratings of TV news programs. Thus the profit motive of private ownership drives companies in the news business to disproportionately cover events that include sensationalized content. Stories like the death of Michael Jackson, the foibles of *Jon and Kate Plus Eight,* and the extramarital affairs of John Edwards, Tiger Woods, New York Governor Elliot Spitzer, and South Carolina Governor Mark Sanford all received a tremendous amount of coverage at the expense of other, more important stories.

Sensationalism extends to coverage of elections as well. Studies of election coverage have found that most news dwells more on stories about the candidates' personal background than on their positions on the issues. Political scientists note that this emphasis on covering "character" issues rather than policy positions characterizes modern presidential election campaign news. In 2000, for example, much of the coverage of candidate George W. Bush in the final week before the election focused on a drunk-driving charge that occurred while he was young. In 2004, significant coverage targeted the military service of the candidates, including Bush's "questionable" military record in the Alabama Air National Guard and John Kerry's record as a Vietnam War soldier and protester. More recently in 2008, a significant amount of coverage focused on Barack Obama's association both with his outspoken pastor Jeremiah Wright and with William Ayers, a cofounder of the Weather Underground, a radical leftist organization. Critics of election coverage also charge that there is too much focus on preelection polls and the competitiveness of the "horse race," which crowds out the more substantive coverage of the issues and the candidates' positions on them.

Another common criticism of the news media is that they are politically biased. Some critics, for example, charge that corporate owners of media organizations are more likely to hold a conservative ideology, which is reflected in their news products. Others cite studies indicating that journalists and reporters tend to hold a more liberal philosophy, and that this orientation seeps into their stories. Certainly there is evidence to support the assertions that owners and managers are more conservative than the citizenry as a whole, and that journalists are more liberal. But the issue of whether personal ideology or partisanship is reflected in news stories is less clear. In some elections, research has demonstrated that newspaper and TV news programs have shown a pro-Republican bias, whereas in others it has found a pro-Democratic bias.[18]

NOW & THEN

Making the Connection

The media serve a number of important functions in the American political system. In addition to providing information, signaling events, and "watchdogging" what government does, the media also provide an infrastructure that leaders use to communicate with citizens. In the examples used at the outset of this chapter, we saw how Presidents Johnson and Obama took advantage of relatively new media (television and the Internet, respectively) to successfully win long-term political struggles to pass civil rights and health care reform legislation.

Technological innovations have served to change the forms and nature of the media throughout the course of American history. These changes have opened up new opportunities for presidents and other leaders to help shape a political agenda and successfully bring an important policy idea to fruition. These changes have also had the effect of bringing news and information to audiences with more and more speed and efficiency.

The America media remain as important a political institution as any in our system of government. Americans' demand for information, the appetite of journalists to keep tabs on government performance, and political leaders' reliance on the media to communicate with citizens all serve to make the media stronger today that they have ever been.

The media may have both a negative and positive influence on the way students treat and perceive each other in class and on campus.

ROBERT W. GINN/PHOTOEDIT

Comedy Television: A New Rite of Passage for Presidents and Candidates

The night of March 3, 2008, presented a crucial moment in Senator Hillary Clinton's bid for the Democratic presidential nomination. She trailed Senator Barack Obama in the delegate count, and with a dwindling number of contests remaining on the calendar, the following day's primaries in Texas and Ohio could make or break her campaign. How did she choose to spend her time, her most precious commodity, on this critical evening? Hanging out via satellite with Jon Stewart on Comedy Central's *The Daily Show*, a daily half-hour political satire, usually targeted at politicians such as Clinton. "It is pretty pathetic," Clinton joked from Austin, Texas, with Stewart. "I only wish you were out on the campaign trail with us . . . you could make fun of us in person rather than by remote."

Two years later, on March 10, 2010, President Barack Obama found himself in the midst of a crucial national tour to sell his health care reform legislation to the American people. The president took precious time during this campaign to make a rare stop at *The David Letterman Show*, reaching an audience that might not watch the nightly news programs or cable news networks. Facing some criticism that his health care proposals had racist overtones, the President quipped to Letterman: "I think it's important to realize that I was actually black before the election." Letterman responded: "How long have you been a black man?"

AP PHOTO/GERALD HERBERT

President Obama appears on the *Tonight Show with Jay Leno* in an effort to promote his administration's legislative agenda in March 2009.

Americans, and particularly younger Americans, increasingly rely on comedy shows for their political news. Comedic commentary on politicians and political events has become a prime source of news for many Americans, and presidents and candidates know that all too well. Stops on *The Daily Show*, Comedy Central's *The Colbert Report*, *The Tonight Show with Jay Leno*, and *The David Letterman Show* can do wonders for book sales, presidential aspirants, and presidents who are trying to advance a policy goal. So long as television comedians strike a chord with these prized audiences, presidential candidates and presidents will continue to seek out appearances on these shows at every opportunity.

On www.cengage.com/dautrich/americangovernment/2e, find the Politics Interactive link for a discussion of comedy news shows. Note how *The Daily Show*'s coverage of elections in particular can affect an election campaign. Consult as well the various links that explore how the structure of the American news media has changed, and where these comedy news shows fit in the new pecking order.

Chapter 12   The Media and Politics

Chapter Summary

★ The Media in American Politics

- The media serve a number of important functions in the political system, all of which promote the free flow of information to the public. These functions include providing objective coverage of events, facilitating public debate, and serving as government watchdog.

- Congress created the Federal Communications Commission (FCC) in 1934 to regulate the electronic media through licensing of broadcasters and creating rules for broadcasters to follow. The FCC does not have authority to regulate the print media, because the courts have consistently treated the right of print media to publish free from government regulation.

★ Historical Development of the Media

- From the nation's founding through the 1850s, news in America was largely provided by a partisan press, made up of newspapers supported by a particular political party.

- Over the past 150 years, the standards for news reporting have become less focused on serving political party interests and more focused on "objectivity."

- Technological change has greatly altered the news media. The invention of the rotary press in 1815 facilitated the mass printing of papers; the railroad system provided for speedy distribution of papers; the invention of the radio provided instantaneous coverage of events as they unfolded; and television brought taped and live footage of news events into people's homes.

★ The Mass Media Today

- Politics and political events, such as presidential campaigns, debates, and news conferences, are widely covered by media organizations.

- Today's mass media comprise large and varied types of news outlets, including radio, television, books, newspapers, and magazines. They also include the so-called new media facilitated by the Internet, satellites, cell phones, broadband, and other newer technologies.

- Corporate ownership of news media outlets today is characterized by large nonmedia corporations, such as General Electric and the Disney Corporation. Some argue that this concentration of large corporate ownership has stifled diversity in news content and blurred the line between what is news and what is entertainment.

- Although the big three television networks—ABC, CBS, and NBC—have dominated television viewership since the early 1950s, the growing popularity of the Fox network, as well as cable and satellite TV, have begun to offer stiff competition.

- The Public Broadcasting Act of 1967 created the Corporation for Public Broadcasting (CPB), which is responsible for distributing federal funds to support public, noncommercial radio (NPR) and television (PBS) stations.

★ The Effects of the Media

- The effects of exposure to news on readers/viewers are the subject of much debate. A number of theories—including social learning, minimal effects, cultivation, and agenda setting—seek to explain how the news media influence what people think about politics.

★ Criticisms of the News Media

- Media performance is often the subject of criticism. Some of the major sources of discontent with media performance include the concentration of corporate ownership of media outlets, sensationalized coverage of relatively unimportant events, and ideological bias in news reporting.

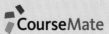
CourseMate

Key Terms

Agenda setting theory (p. 374)

Blogs (p. 370)

Cultivation theory (p. 374)

Digital divide (p. 370)

Equal time rule (p. 357)

Minimal effects theory (p. 374)

New media (p. 368)

Objectivity (p. 359)

Partisan press era (p. 361)

Social learning theory (p. 374)

Talk radio (p. 369)

Resources

Important Books

Anderson, David M., and Michael Cornfield, eds. *The Civic Web: Online Politics and Democratic Values.* New York: Rowman and Littlefield, 2003.

Dautrich, Kenneth, and Thomas Hartley. *How the News Media Fail American Voters.* New York: Cambridge University Press, 1999.

Epstein, Edward. *News from Nowhere.* New York: Random House, 1973.

Graber, Doris A. *Mass Media and American Politics.* Washington, DC: CQ Press, 2004.

Iyengar, Shanto, and Jennifer A. McGrady. *Media Politics: A Citizen's Guide.* New York: W. W. Norton, 2006.

Jamieson, Kathleen Hall, and Paul Waldman. *The Press Effect: Politicians, Journalists and the Stories That Shape the Political World.* New York: Oxford University Press, 2003.

Meyer, Philip. *Precision Journalism: A Reporter's Introduction to Social Science Methods.* New York: Rowman and Littlefield, 2002.

Murray, David, Joel Schwartz, and S. Robert Lichter. *It Ain't Necessarily So: How the Media Remake Our Picture of Reality.* New York: Penguin Books, 2002.

Patterson, Thomas E. *The Mass Media Election: How Americans Choose Their President.* New York: Praeger, 1980.

Schroeder, Alan. *Presidential Debates: Forty Years of High-Risk TV.* New York: Columbia University Press, 2000.

Thurber, James A., Candice J. Nelson, and David A. Dulio, eds. *Crowded Airwaves: Campaign Advertising in Elections.* Washington, DC: Brookings Institution Press, 2002.

Internet Resources

http://www.people-press.org (the site for the Pew Research Center for the People & the Press, which provides polling and other data on the news media)

http://www.mediaresearch.org (a media watchdog Web site containing a variety of reviews and research on media issues)

http://www.freedomforum.org (the site for the Freedom Forum Foundation, with information and analysis on news media issues and First Amendment debates)

http://www.knightfdn.org (the site for the Knight Foundation, an organization that provides programs and research on journalism topics)

13 Political Parties

NOW Tea Party activists wearing themed costumes march in a tax-revolt rally in 2009.

PHIL MCCARTEN/REUTERS/LANDOV

THEN A rally of the Populists' movement in Willowdale Township, Kansas, during the early 1890s.

FOTOSEARCH/GETTY IMAGES

NOW &THEN

An Upstart Political Movement Takes on the Two-Party System

? *The two major political parties waged a ferocious battle in the midterm election campaign. The majority party, which controlled the White House and both houses of Congress, believed its recent electoral successes had given it a mandate to act. Accordingly, it used its strong majorities to muscle through landmark legislation. The opposition party was energized by "smaller government" enthusiasts who celebrated their status within the party of "No!" They denounced the majority as reckless "tax and spend," big government fanatics. In this era of deep skepticism about government, a new political movement was also taking shape. Frustrated with both major parties, this group of crusaders used an anti-elitist appeal to lash out at the establishment. The opposition party clearly benefitted from this new movement, as it was more closely aligned to the new group's ideology. This association led to strong gains for the opposition party on Election Day. And yet having benefitted from their links to this new anti-government movement, the party that now seized control of Congress soon faced a dilemma of its own: Should it embrace the upstarts' more radical, anti-government agenda—and in the process risk painting their entire party as out of touch with the political mainstream?*

History of Political Parties in the United States

* Explain how a party system developed in the United States despite the Founders' attempt to create a political system without parties
* Trace the historical development of the modern Democrat and Republican Parties
* Define "critical elections" and party realignment and dealignment in the United States and cite examples of their occurrence

The Functions of Political Parties

* Identify and explain the three broad functions of political parties

Why a Two-Party System?

* Understand the historical and legal factors that contributed to the development of the two-party system in the United States
* Explain the role that third parties have played in U.S. elections

Party Organizations

* Learn how party organizations operate at the national, state, and local levels, including how they define party platforms and help their candidates win elections

Are Parties in Decline?

* Learn the factors that have contributed to a decline in political parties over the past few decades and assess the future prospects for the parties

NOW & THEN

AP PHOTO/ALAN DIAZ

marcorubio

Marco Rubio, a successful Republican Tea Party candidate from Florida, tells supporters after his 2010 election victory: "Our nation is heading in the wrong direction and we have both parties to blame."

NOW In 2009 and 2010, President Barack Obama and the Democrats muscled through an economic stimulus bill and landmark legislation addressing health care and financial reforms. The Republican minority held firm in its opposition to unprecedented spending, happily embracing their status as the party of "No." As deficits ballooned, the Republicans viewed the 2010 elections as an opportunity to reverse their electoral misfortunes in 2006 and 2008. At the same time, a political movement known as the "Tea Party" arrived on the political scene. Espousing principles of "fiscal responsibility," "adherence to the Constitution," and limited government, the Tea Party opposed what it regarded as excessive government spending by both major parties. The Tea Party movement had aided the cause of the more extreme conservative GOP contestants in primary contests, as its energetic band of followers occasionally frustrated Republican moderates. Still, the vast majority of Tea Party movement supporters were Republicans, and in the 2010 midterm elections the GOP recaptured the House and reduced the Democratic margin in the Senate. Tea Party candidates such as Rand Paul of Kentucky and Marc Rubio of Florida celebrated their Senate election victories with warnings that the Republican Party could not take their support for granted. For Republican congressional leaders in the new 112th Congress, a significant challenge lay ahead. Just how determined would Tea Party Republicans be in advancing their more extreme agenda? Would such an agenda threaten Republican gains in the years to come?

THEN After winning the White House and securing majorities in both houses of Congress in the 1888 elections, Republicans looked to the upcoming elections of 1890 and 1892 with considerable trepidation. Republican President Benjamin Harrison and his administration had significantly expanded the federal government's powers: the Republicans raised import duties to protect American businesses against global competition, expanded the money supply through the issuance of certificates backed by silver, increased pensions for military veterans, and passed the Sherman Anti-Trust Act to regulate the power and growth of monopolies. Democrats now became the party of "No!" With the 1890 elections approaching, they berated the "billion dollar" Congress for raiding the treasury, and voters quickly took to the Democrats' anti-silver, small government message to give them back control of Congress. The subsequent arrival of the "People's Party," known also as "Populists," soon complicated matters for Democrats eager to oust Harrison from office in the 1892 election. The Populists were radicals who crusaded against banks, railroads and elites in general; their natural allies were the Democrats, and after running some candidates of their own, the Populists eventually supported William Jennings Bryan, the Democratic nominee for president in 1896. Democrats benefitted in the short term from the Populists' energetic following, but in 1894 and beyond the Populists occasionally allied with like-thinking Republicans, forcing Democrats to rethink the benefits of allying themselves too closely with a radical political movement.

A cartoon from 1896 depicts William Jennings Bryan at the head of an army of fellow Populists, preparing to attack Washington, DC.

IN BATTLE ARRAY. — AND THERE 'S NOT MUCH DOUBT ABOUT THE RESULT.

THE GRANGER COLLECTION, NYC — ALL RIGHTS RESERVED.

Political movements organized around an anti-government, anti-establishment message are not uncommon in American politics. The "Know Nothing" movement was a nativist American political group that opposed major party positions on immigration and naturalization in the 1840s and 1850s; Father Charles Coughlin and Huey Long offered a form of anti-business populism in the 1930s. The Populist movement of the 1890s and the Tea Party movement of more recent times fall in line with that tradition, exciting an enthusiastic and passionate base of followers. Though such movements rarely break through with successful presidential candidates of their own, they do affect congressional and presidential elections significantly in the short run: the party in power may find itself on the short end of this sudden burst of enthusiasm, and the outparty can benefit greatly from the movement's skepticism over government. But then the political party that benefits electorally from the populist movement must accommodate its new partner, and in the process it may be forced to stray far from more mainstream policy positions. So goes the challenge of major political parties, which may gain in the short term from such political movements, but then must learn to live with them without losing their mass appeal.

Political parties are the lifeblood of American politics. New laws are enacted through the debate and negotiation of party leaders in government; individuals are recruited and promoted as political candidates through the apparatus of the political party structure; voters evaluate campaigns and candidates largely through a partisan looking glass. At the national, state, and local levels, the two major political parties set the tone, control the agenda, and run the government. Parties have been the dominant organizational framework through which our government has worked for over 200 years, even though the U.S. Constitution makes no mention of parties.

More than 60 years ago, the American Political Science Association (APSA) focused the scholarly community's attention on what it referred to as responsible party government.[1] The "responsible party government" model depicts the proper role of parties as organizations that offer clear programs and policy positions to voters. Voters make choices on the basis of those programs, and when victorious in elections, the party works toward achieving those programs and policies. At the time of the next election cycle, voters hold the party accountable for what it has accomplished.

The extent to which parties actually resemble the responsible party model has been the subject of much debate over the past half century. Moreover, despite the large role parties play in the American political system, many observers argue that parties are organizationally weak, particularly when compared to parties in other democracies around the world. Whereas most European parties have clearly defined constituencies based on social class, regional, ethnic, or religious division, American political parties are often ideologically vague, aligning with broader constituencies and gravitating toward more centrist positions on issues. And despite their prevalence in politics, there are indications that the influence of parties is on the decline.

The Founders who drafted the Constitution designed a federal system without political parties. They envisioned a system that would be run by independent-minded people who served out of a sense of civic virtue. James Madison's famous Federalist No. 10 deplores "factions," as he calls them. Madison and his colleagues largely looked upon parties (the equivalent of extremely large factions) as tools of the politically ambitious that would tend to promote corruption and bias in the political system.

Parties are also important in other democracies around the globe. Left: British Prime Minister David Cameron of the Conservative Party. Right: Israeli Prime Minister Benjamin Netanyahu of the Likud Party.

Senators Who Leave Their Party Loyalties Behind

Only twenty individuals in U.S. Senate history have been willing to leave their political party while serving as an incumbent senator (six of those switched from the Republican Party to the short-lived "Silver Republican party" during the 1890s). Senators may switch parties for any of several reasons, including (1) because their views are no longer aligned with their current party; (2) because they hope to increase power by moving from the minority party to the majority party; and (3) because the party base within their constituency is threatening to defeat renomination, while the opposing party offers greater prospects for nomination. This final rationale was offered by Senator Arlen Specter of Pennsylvania, who switched from the Republicans to the Democrats in April of 2009 to avoid impending defeat in the 2010 Senate Republican primary. (The switch failed to save him, as Specter lost the Democratic primary instead). Regardless of his motives, the move had key implications for the Obama Administration's legislative agenda, as it laid the groundwork for a filibuster-proof Democratic majority.

While Specter's defection was clearly significant, it did not actually shift control over the Senate from one party to another. By contrast, consider the following two cases in which a party switch brought a change in partisan control of the Senate:

Senator Arlen Specter of Pennsylvania, campaigning in the 2010 Democratic primaries.

In 1953, Senator Wayne Morse of Oregon formally abandoned the Republican Party, to which he had been affiliated as a U.S. senator for eight years. Though reelected to office as a Republican in 1950, Morse formally became an independent at the beginning of the 1953 legislative session. Following the defection what had been an even split between the ninety-six senators was suddenly transformed into a

Senator Wayne Morse of Oregon.

48-47 advantage for the Democrats. Morse's control over the levers of power proved short-lived, however, as the death of nine senators and the resignation of another led to many reversals of party control during the course of the 83rd Congress, which convened between 1953 and 1955. In 1955 Morse formally switched allegiances to the Democratic Party and remained a Democrat until his death in 1974. As a senator, Morse was well known for his proclivity to defy his party's leadership . . . no matter which party that happened to be at a given time.

In 2001, only five months into the first session of the 107th Congress, Senator Jim Jeffords (R-VT) left the Republican Party to become an independent caucusing with the Democrats. Before his defection, the Senate had been exactly split (50–50) between the Republicans and the Democrats; Vice President Dick Cheney had thus cast the deciding vote in favor of his fellow Republicans' control. Jeffords' switch—spurred by the Senate Republicans' refusal to fully fund the Individuals with Disabilities Education Act—gave the Democrats a 50–49 advantage and thus a majority in the Senate.

Despite some of the Founders' disdain for political parties, they have become central to the American political system. E. E. Schattschneider, a well-regarded student of American politics, observed in 1942 that "democracy is unthinkable, save in terms of the parties."[2] The Democratic and Republican parties not only have become important political institutions in their own right, but they play a central role in running government at all levels, and they organize and provide context to voters.

Political parties are organizations that seek to win elections for the purpose of influencing the outputs of government. They are typically guided by a political philosophy, rooted in particular values and an ideological approach to governing. The philosophy, values, and ideological approach generally lead to specific issue positions espoused by leaders of a party and the candidates who run for office under a party's label. Some minor parties focus less on the unrealistic assumption that they might win elections and more on articulating an ideological approach to governing and supporting particular issue positions. As in any organization, parties include leaders as well as citizens. In American politics, parties provide an important link between citizens and their leaders, playing a key role in recruiting citizens and relying on them for support at election time.

Political party
An organization that seeks to win elections for the purpose of influencing the outputs of government.

History of Political Parties in the United States

★ **LO** Explain how a party system developed in the United States despite the Founders' attempt to create a political system without parties

Even though the Founders frowned on political parties and made no provision for them in the federal government they designed, not long after the first government under the new U.S. Constitution took office in 1791, a number of the architects of the Constitution became strong advocates of particular parties.[3] Perhaps more than anything else, this contradiction serves to highlight not only the importance of political parties to the practice of democracy, but also the necessity of parties. In the United States, competition between the political parties has kept any one group or "faction" from becoming too powerful for too long. The Constitution provides various safeguards against the accumulation of power in the form of checks and balances. Paradoxically, though parties are not mentioned at all in the Constitution, competition between political parties has proven to be a significant check against tyranny.

The First Parties in America

The history of political parties in the United States traces back to colonial America, when supporters of the English crown aligned with the British Tory Party, and advocates of a new independent American nation aligned themselves with the British Whig Party. Benjamin Franklin and other founders still considered themselves Tories up through the early 1770s, and during the American Revolution colonists who supported Britain were called Tories or Loyalists. The period following the war ushered in new challenges as leaders of the new American nation debated the relationship that should exist between the national government and the state governments. Ultimately this debate created two new parties (or "factions" as many still called them in the eighteenth century). The U.S. Constitution that replaced the Articles of Confederation significantly enhanced the structure, power, and importance of the national government. The debate over ratification of the new Constitution pitted the Federalists, who supported a stronger federal government, against the Anti-Federalists, who opposed a strong federal government and supported state sovereignty.[4]

More formal, identifiable political parties emerged and began to assume the critical function of supporting candidates for elective office during the first administration of George Washington. Once again, the issue that spurred the emergence of parties as vehicles for nominating candidates was the distribution of power between the federal and state governments under the Constitution. The Federalists continued to support a stronger federal government and the policies of the Washington administration, which promoted the power of the national government. Most Federalists also favored maintaining close ties with Great Britain. President Washington did not consider himself a member of the Federalist Party; he despised parties and refused to endorse their presence in the politics of the new country. Yet many of Washington's supporters, led by Alexander Hamilton, organized the Federalist Party and used the organization to recruit candidates for office.

The Federalist Party was soon challenged by the Democratic-Republican Party, which asserted that the Washington administration was assuming greater powers than those the Constitution granted to the federal government. It also criticized the federal government's favorable relations with Britain, preferring France as a closer European ally. As early as 1792, the Democratic-Republicans were organized and led by Thomas Jefferson and James Madison—the same Madison who ten years earlier had authored in Federalist No. 10 perhaps the most eloquent argument *against* factions that has ever been written. In the congressional elections of 1792, Democratic-Republican candidates won a majority of seats in the House of Representatives. George Washington was unopposed for president, but the Democratic-Republicans backed George Clinton against Federalist John Adams for the vice presidency. Adams, however, won reelection to the vice presidency by an electoral vote margin of 77 to 50.

Every presidential and congressional election since 1796 has featured some form of party competition. In this early period of American political parties, the Federalists drew most of their support from the northern states, whereas the Democratic-Republicans had greater support in the southern and mid-Atlantic states. Sectional differences in partisan support have characterized American politics for much of the nation's history. In the first competitive presidential election of 1796, the Federalists endorsed John Adams and the Democratic-Republicans endorsed Thomas Jefferson. Adams won seventy-one electoral votes and Jefferson won sixty-eight votes, making Adams president and Jefferson vice president. Not anticipating political parties, the Constitution allowed for the election of a president and vice president who stood very far apart on critical issues of the day.

By the time of the election of 1800, the parties were highly organized. Each of the two political parties endorsed a slate of candidates for president and vice president to avoid the problem of having two separate parties occupy those offices. The party organization selected presidential electors, who dutifully cast their constitutionally granted two votes to their party's candidates. The Federalists nominated both John Adams and Charles Pinckney, whereas the Democratic-Republicans endorsed Thomas Jefferson and Aaron Burr. Jefferson and Burr each received seventy-three electoral votes, thus producing an Electoral College tie for the presidency. By the provisions of the Constitution, the election was then to be decided by the House of Representatives. After a fair amount of debate and politicking, the House eventually selected Jefferson on the thirty-sixth ballot. Clearly the system of selecting the president needed to be modified from one that did not recognize the importance of political parties in the electoral process to one that did.

The Twelfth Amendment deferred to the reality of parties in presidential elections. Ratified prior to the election of 1804, this amendment formally separated the Electoral College vote for president and vice president. Rather than having electors cast

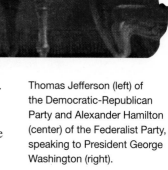

MPI/GETTY IMAGES

Thomas Jefferson (left) of the Democratic-Republican Party and Alexander Hamilton (center) of the Federalist Party, speaking to President George Washington (right).

two ballots for president, electors were now to cast separate votes for president and vice president. This modification in the electoral process helped avoid the problem that had occurred in 1796 of having a president and vice president locked in partisan struggle, as well as the problem in the 1800 election that resulted in two candidates from the same party tied for the presidency.

The election of 1800 marked the beginning of the end for the Federalist Party. The Federalists would never again win a presidential election, and their strength in Congress diminished steadily over the next two decades. The Democratic-Republicans enjoyed party dominance to such an extent that the Federalists were virtually extinct after the election of 1820. Interestingly, this lack of competition from the Federalists during the first two decades of the nineteenth century had the effect of fragmenting the Democratic-Republicans. In 1824, the Democratic-Republican Party put forth several sectional candidates, but no candidate received a majority of electoral votes. (Andrew Jackson won ninety-nine votes, John Quincy Adams took eighty-four, and another seventy-four votes were scattered among other candidates.) Eventually, the House of Representatives decided in favor of Adams. The result was a Democratic-Republican Party in disarray.

A Second Party System Emerges

★ LO Trace the historical development of the modern Democrat and Republican Parties

Disillusioned by the outcome of the 1824 election, Andrew Jackson eventually formed a new political party, the Democratic Party, which remains one of the two major parties still competing in American politics today. Jackson's support in 1824 derived from many of the new states that had been added to the union as a result of westward expansion. Many such states, including Jackson's home state of Tennessee, allowed voters to choose presidential electors directly, rather than following the traditional practice of authorizing the state's congressional delegation (known as the "congressional caucus") to choose electors. Because he received more popular votes than John Quincy Adams in 1824, Jackson felt the presidency was rightfully his that year. However, Henry Clay, the fourth-place candidate, allied himself with Adams, thereby giving Adams enough votes for victory. When Adams became president he appointed Clay as secretary of state. Jackson and his supporters accused Clay of making a "corrupt bargain" by trading his votes to Adams in exchange for his appointment as secretary of state. Those who remained loyal to John Quincy Adams began calling themselves the National Republicans. The next presidential election would be a contest essentially between two splinter groups (Democrats and National Republicans) of the now defunct Democratic-Republicans.[5]

Jackson took his case directly to the people and ran for president again in 1828, this time as a Democrat. He ran a populist campaign, arguing that the people should have a greater say in selecting the president, and developed

Jackson Forever!
The Hero of Two Wars and of Or'eans!
The Man of the People!
HE WHO COULD NOT BARTER NOR BARGAIN FOR THE
PRESIDENCY!
Who, although "*A Military Chieftain,*" valued the purity of Elections and of the Electors, **MORE** than the Office of **PRESIDENT** itself! Although the greatest in the gift of his countrymen, and the highest in point of dignity of any in the world,
BECAUSE
It should be derived from the
PEOPLE!
No Gag Laws! No Black Cockades! No Reign of Terror! No Standing Army or Navy Officers, when under the pay of Government, to browbeat, or
KNOCK DOWN
Old Revolutionary Characters, or our Representatives while in the discharge of their duty. To the Polls then, and vote for those who will support
OLD HICKORY
AND THE ELECTORAL LAW.

Election poster in 1828 for Andrew Jackson's presidential campaign. Jackson is the founder of today's Democratic party.

BETTMANN/CORBIS

The Importance of Having Honest Two-Party Elections

The 2009 Pew Global Attitudes Survey queried people from around the world about a variety of democratic ideals that characterize American political culture. One of those ideals is the value of "honest two-party elections." This graph shows the percentages of both middle-class and lower-income citizens from countries around the world who say that honest two-party elections are "very important."

A Chilean voter casts a ballot in Santiago during a recent national election. Since democracy was restored to Chile in 1990, voters in that nation tend to place high value on honest two-party elections, as shown on the right.

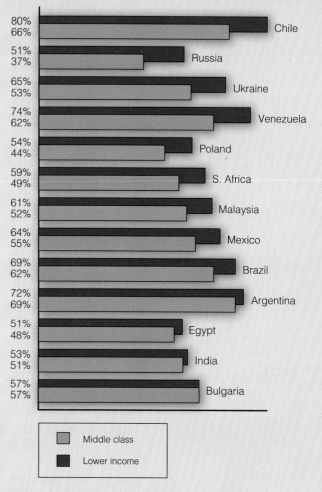

Country	Middle class	Lower income
Chile	80%	66%
Russia	51%	37%
Ukraine	65%	53%
Venezuela	74%	62%
Poland	54%	44%
S. Africa	59%	49%
Malaysia	61%	52%
Mexico	64%	55%
Brazil	69%	62%
Argentina	72%	69%
Egypt	51%	48%
India	53%	51%
Bulgaria	57%	57%

Source: Pew Global Attitudes Project, http://pewglobal.org/2009/02/12/the-global-middle-class.

his campaign theme around the Adams–Clay "corrupt bargain." Jackson's theme caught fire with the voters, and the nation's continuing westward expansion, along with voting reforms and increased suffrage in eastern states, suddenly expanded the role of voters in selecting presidential electors. Thus, in a campaign that was essentially decided by the people, puritanical John Quincy Adams proved no match for the flamboyant Jackson, still revered as the general who led American forces to victory in the Battle of New Orleans, the final military engagement of the War of 1812. And Jackson's newly established Democratic Party emerged as a national force to be reckoned with.

The election of 1828 also permanently changed the nature of campaigns, and with them, the nature of parties. The precedent for a presidential election influenced by the masses was now set, and the era of congressional delegations selecting presidential electors was over. Parties quickly recognized the need to organize in states and localities to accommodate the new process of selecting presidential electors. Party organizations became larger and more powerful as they developed into critical instruments in campaigns. This era also established the tradition of holding **national party conventions**. These conventions drew together party delegates from across the states for several purposes. First, the delegates were responsible for choosing the party's presidential candidate and vice presidential candidate. Second, the delegates

National party convention

A large meeting that draws together party delegates from across the nation to choose (or formally affirm the selection of) the party's presidential and vice presidential candidates.

Chapter 13 Political Parties

Party platform

A document outlining the party's position on important policy issues.

articulated their **party platform**, a document outlining the party's position on important policy issues. Third, the conventions coordinated the activities of parties across the states. National party conventions remain a central event both in the presidential selection process and in the organization of modern political parties in general.

The Democratic Party held its first national party convention in 1832, once again nominating Andrew Jackson for president. The National Republicans again nominated Henry Clay, who lost to Jackson in the November election. Several years later a new political party, the Whigs, which was made up of a coalition of National Republicans and other groups, emerged as a principal competitor to the Democrats. By the 1840s, the Democrats and Whigs dominated not only election contests, but also leadership and committee assignments in Congress. Soon those two parties became the primary vehicles through which legislation was sponsored and then shepherded through the Congress.

From 1836 through 1856, the Whigs and the Democrats shared the presidency and the vast majority of seats in Congress. Both parties were truly national parties, with organizations in each of the states. The issue of slavery, however, soon became the principal issue on the American political agenda. The Civil War would transform American politics forever, and a product of this transformation was the demise of the Whig Party. Within the Whigs, there were strong differences of opinion over the slavery issue, which led to the decline of the Whigs as a national force by the late 1850s. New, smaller parties emerged, such as the Free Soil and Know-Nothing parties, but none of those parties was able to attract large numbers of voters over an extended period of time. By the late 1850s, a new Republican Party had emerged to absorb these smaller parties and replace the Whigs as the major opposition party to the Democrats.

The Modern Party System in America: Democrats versus Republicans

The year 1856 marked the first presidential election when the precursors to the modern Democratic and Republican parties faced off for office. Democratic nominee James Buchanan defeated Republican candidate John Fremont by 174 to 114 electoral votes. Since 1856, every presidential election but one has featured the Democrats and Republicans as the only two major political parties in serious contention for the White House. (The lone exception occurred in 1912, when former Republican President Theodore Roosevelt, the nominee of the newly formed Progressive or "Bull Moose" Party, ran second to Woodrow Wilson, the Democrat. Incumbent President William Howard Taft, the Republican nominee, finished a distant third.) In 1860, Democratic Party support for states' rights and Republican Party support for national power and preservation of the Union divided the parties over the issue of slavery. Republican Abraham Lincoln's successful campaign that year helped his party capture the presidency and a majority in both houses of Congress. It also precipitated the Civil War. With the eventual secession of eleven Southern and Democrat-heavy states, the Republican Party came to dominate politics for the next decade.

Critical election

An election that produces sharp changes in patterns of party loyalty among voters.

Like the election of 1828, the election of 1860 is considered by many scholars to be a **critical election** in the modern era of American parties. The theory of critical elections, developed by political scientist V. O. Key Jr., posits that certain elections can be characterized as producing sharp changes in patterns of party loyalty among voters.[6] This occurred in 1860 when voter support for parties realigned along the issue of slavery, based primarily on a North versus South division. Until 1860, the Democratic Party had enjoyed support from urban and industrial areas in both the North and the South and the demographic and social groups associated with those regions. The Civil War shifted these alignments to a North–South division, thus rendering the 1860 contest a critical election. The theory of critical elections suggests that every such election is accompanied by some type of electoral realignment,[7] a lasting reconfiguration of how certain groups of voters align with the parties.

JOE RAEDLE/NEWSMAKERS/GETTY IMAGES

Washington State Democrats
Presidential Caucus
Saturday, Feb. 7, 2004, 10:00 am

Precinct _____

Location _____

RON WURZER/GETTY IMAGES

©LYNNE FERNANDES/THE IMAGE WORKS

The elephant is the symbol of the Republican Party. The donkey is the symbol for the Democratic Party.

The first president elected under the Democratic Party banner was Andrew Jackson. The seventh U.S. President was labeled a "jack ass" by his opponents during the election of 1828 for his populist campaign slogan, "Let the People Rule." Jackson used the critique to his advantage, invoking the donkey symbol often during his eight years in the White house.

In the 1870s, political cartoonist Thomas Nast continued to popularize the donkey symbol. A staunch Republican, Nast was also responsible for choosing the elephant as a symbol of his own party. In an 1874 cartoon that ran in *Harper's Weekly*, Nast drew a donkey wearing lion's clothes, which scared away all the other zoo animals, including the elephant which was labeled "the Republican vote."

Since then, both the donkey and elephant have symbolized the two major parties in the United States.

When the last of the former Confederate states was readmitted to the union in 1870, the Democratic Party once again began to assert itself in national politics. The Civil War had cemented a "solid South" stronghold for the Democratic Party that would continue for a century. Republicans remained the favored party in the northern and midwestern states, although some major cities in the North (including New York City) tended toward the Democratic Party. Republicans dominated the presidency for the remainder of the century, winning six of the next eight presidential contests.

A third realigning election in the modern party era occurred in 1896. That election did not result in a clear shifting of voter preferences from one party to another; rather, it marked the rise of the Republican Party to a near total consolidation of power and voter support in the northern and western states, as well as the continued Democratic Party dominance in southern states. Republican candidate William McKinley won the 1896 election, and with it a realignment of new allegiances to the Republican Party. Indeed, the only Democrat to capture the presidency between 1896 and 1932 was Woodrow Wilson, and Wilson's initial success was more a consequence of Theodore Roosevelt's split with the Republican Party than it was a result of an expanded Democratic base. Roosevelt, a Republican president from 1901 to 1909, formed the Progressive "Bull Moose" Party and ran as its presidential candidate in 1912. He in effect split the Republican vote, handing Democrat Woodrow Wilson an Electoral College victory.

In 1912, the Republican Party's progressive and conservative wings split, giving the Democrats the White House and a majority in both houses of Congress. Within six years, however, Republicans regained control of Congress and were well positioned to retake the White House in 1920. During the sixty-two-year period from 1870 to 1932, the two major parties developed their party

Five Critical Elections in U.S. History

Scholar V. O. Key Jr.'s theory of critical elections argues that certain presidential elections have produced realignments of voter groups to specific political parties. These elections tend to be ones in which voters are highly engaged and intensely involved. They are also marked by disruptions of normal voting patterns, and the new voting patterns that emerge are often lasting. Many political scientists agree that there have been at least five such critical elections in the nation's history:

✔ **1. The election of 1828.** No candidate received a majority of electoral votes in the election of 1824. The House of Representatives awarded the election to John Quincy Adams, even though Andrew Jackson won more Electoral College votes than Adams. Jackson mounted a populist campaign in 1828 to avenge his loss in 1824, arguing for broader popular participation in the election of the president. His message caught fire, catapulting him into office and establishing a new alignment of voters, which represented in Jackson's words the "common man," for the Democratic Party.

✔ **2. The election of 1860.** Slavery was the defining issue in the election of 1860, which saw the emergence of the Republican Party as the second major party (the Democrats being the other one) in American politics. Republican Abraham Lincoln won the support of the northern establishment, including bankers, industrialists, merchants, and laborers. Southern whites supported the Democrats, an allegiance that continued for the long haul. The Republican Party won seven of the next nine presidential races.

✔ **3. The election of 1896.** By 1896 new problems plagued the nation, pitting the interests of the older agrarian economy against the industrialists. The realignment of voters over these problems did not result in a realignment to a Democratic majority; rather, it reinforced Republican dominance as new groups of voters were becoming aligned with the Republican Party. Farming and mining interests in the West, along with industrial worker interests in the Northeast, supported Republican initiatives to reduce corporate industrialism. Republican William McKinley won on a platform advocating a high protective tariff, a single gold standard, and an aggressive foreign policy. The Republicans would remain the dominant party up until the Great Depression of the 1930s.

✔ **4. The election of 1932.** Economic depression was foremost on people's minds during the election of 1932. Fourteen million people lost their jobs during the time between the stock market crash in 1929 and this election. Hundreds of financial institutions failed, wiping out the life savings of millions. The gross national product fell by one third. All this occurred during the administration of Republican President Herbert Hoover. Hoover's limited attempts to deal with the economic depression were inconsequential, paving the way for a realignment of working-class voters, immigrants, and union members to the Democratic Party under the leadership of Franklin Delano Roosevelt. FDR advocated a strong activist role for government to solve the nation's economic woes.

✔ **5. The election of 1968.** The election of Richard M. Nixon in 1968 marked the end of Democratic domination of the presidency. The Democratic Party candidate would win only three of the ten presidential races between 1968 and 2004. In this time period, Republicans also captured majorities of both houses of Congress. The election of 1968 ushered in what many refer to as a period of "dealignment," when neither party has a lock on the electorate.

President Franklin Delano Roosevelt, a Democrat, campaigning for reelection in Hartford, Connecticut, in 1936.

organizations and shored up their voting coalitions. They institutionalized their power in Congress by creating the party caucuses and electing party leaders. Also, during this period the Democrats and Republicans developed party organizations so strong that the two-party Democrat–Republican system would become permanently institutionalized in American politics.

A fourth realigning election in the modern party era resulted from shifting party allegiances in the midst of the Great Depression. Republican President Herbert Hoover was elected in 1928, less than a year before the stock market crash of 1929 sent the economy into a tailspin. Hoover and the Republicans adopted some limited measures to deal with the economic disaster, but they maintained their party's traditional conservative faith in the dynamics of the market to solve economic problems. Franklin Delano Roosevelt, the Democratic candidate opposing Hoover in 1932, advocated a substantially larger and more activist role for government in dealing with the Depression. Roosevelt's pledge of a "New Deal" and an activist government won the support of the urban working class, people of lower socioeconomic status, new immigrants, and many Catholics and Jews. The shift in allegiances from the Republican Party to the Democratic Party in 1932 (FDR carried forty-two states and 60 percent of the vote) had a lasting impact on voters. Adding the "New Deal coalition" to the "solid Democratic South" resulted in Democratic Party domination of American politics for at least the next thirty-six years. The policies of Democratic Presidents Roosevelt, Harry Truman, John F. Kennedy, and Lyndon Johnson during this era, supported by large Democratic majorities in Congress, were the product of the powerful New Deal coalition established in 1932.

Since 1968, however, both the New Deal coalition and the Democrats' solid grip on the South have declined.[8] At the same time, the century-long southern hostility toward the Republican Party of Abraham Lincoln has diminished, as many conservatives in the South have become attracted to the Republican Party and its socially conservative agenda. Between 1969 and 2010, the Democrats controlled the White House for just fourteen years, whereas the Republicans held the White House for twenty-eight years. During that same period, the Democrats controlled both chambers of Congress for twenty-four years and the Republicans for ten years, with eight years of split majorities in the House and Senate. No clear

©SCHERL/SV-BILDERDIENST/THE IMAGE WORKS

critical elections appear to have occurred over this time frame, and few patterns in voter realignment are obvious. Indeed, some political scientists have argued that the term **dealignment**[9] best describes the behavior of voters since the 1960s. Dealignment refers to the decline in both voter attachment to parties and clarity of party coalitions.

The 2010 election results provided new evidence of voters' lack of attachment to either of the two major political parties. After successive election cycles in which the Democratic Party took significant strides toward reestablishing itself as a lasting majority, many independents and disaffected Republicans who had voted for Democrats in 2006 and 2008 returned to the Republican fold in 2010. As a result, the Republicans retook control of the House and reduced the Democrats' margin of control in the Senate to just six seats. More telling, many voters cast their lots with so-called Tea Party candidates who had criticized both major parties for their extravagant spending during the previous decade. As the Democrats and Republicans struggle with their long-term political identities, movements like the Tea Party will continue to hold their feet to the fire, threatening the long-term party attachments that had been so prevalent in the past.

★ LO   Identify and explain the three broad functions of political parties

The Functions of Parties

Political parties serve a number of critical functions in the American political system at the national, state, and local levels of government. They give organizational coherence to both the operations of popular elections and the management of government. The functions that political parties serve have become inseparable from the principles that define how Americans choose leaders and how elected leaders formulate and administer public policies.

Contesting Elections

Free and open elections are the hallmark of the American republican form of government. With winning elections as their principal goal, political parties promote the prominence, competitiveness, and significance of elections in America. By winning elections and occupying seats in the government, members of the party can influence public policy. The larger the number of elective seats that a party controls, the greater the party's potential influence on policy outcomes. Thus contesting elections lies at the core of a political party's functions.

To contest elections most effectively, the two major parties in the United States have developed a large set of party organizations. These organizations, which operate at the national, state, and local levels, are engaged in a number of activities directed toward winning elections. These activities include fund-raising, organizing events and meetings, providing funding to candidates who are running for office, recruiting and organizing volunteers who want to work for the election of candidates, and purchasing services (for example, polling services, political advertisements, campaign materials such as bumper stickers, direct mail to homes, and so forth) to promote the election of candidates. Many election contests feature a candidate from the party currently in office (the incumbent candidate) defending his or her record against an alternative candidate from the party out of power. The fact that political parties are organized to contest elections and offer alternative proposals for making public policy promotes the responsiveness of elected officials to the voters: by offering voters alternative candidates more in line with public opinion, parties provide an effective mechanism for voters to remove leaders from office through elections. The alternative candidates offered by the Democratic and Republican parties also serve to organize the process of competitive elections in the United States, because the vast majority of elections feature a Democratic candidate and a Republican candidate running against each other. Some elections include independent or third-party candidates, and in some

The Republicans versus the Democrats . . . at a College Campus Near You

The College Republican National Committee and the College Democrats of America are two extremely active organizations, maintaining chapters on college campuses in all fifty states. These chapters serve as both an active recruiting tool for party membership and to support partisan activities in elections. Campus chapters for these groups provide a forum for students to discuss issues, participate in social events, hear speakers in their party, organize letter writing campaigns and phone banks, and conduct voter registration drives.

The College Republicans were founded in 1892. They have fifty state federations, more than 1,800 college chapters, and over 250,000 members. The College Republicans have served as a launching pad for many GOPers who have gone on to prominent political careers, including Grover Norquist, president of Americans for Tax Reform; U.S. Senators Rick Santorum and Roger Wicker; Rick Davis, campaign manager for John McCain's 2008 presidential bid; and Karl Rove, Fox News contributor and former political advisor to George W. Bush, to name just a few. The College Democrats, founded in 1932, can also boast of its history of launching great Democratic political careers, including that of Democratic National Committee chair and former Virginia Governor Tim Kaine, former Vermont Governor Howard Dean, and House Speaker Nancy Pelosi. Interestingly, former Democratic Senator and later Secretary of State Hilary Clinton was the president of the Wellesley College chapter of the

AP PHOTO/LINGBING HANG

A meeting of the College Republicans on the campus of West Virginia University.

College Republicans. If you are an aspiring Democrat or Republican looking for a place to launch a political career, your college's chapter of Democrats or Republicans may be the place to start. Or, if you feel strongly about one of the parties, your college chapter is a place where you can make a difference.

For Critical Thinking and Discussion

1. Does your college maintain chapters for the College Democrats and College Republicans? If so, which one is more popular on your campus? Does their relative popularity reflect the relative popularity of the two parties in the local region or the state?

2. If you are already a member, what kind of activities does your chapter engage in that help promote the national party's cause?

elections a Democratic candidate or a Republican candidate runs unchallenged. But most election contests feature some form of competition between candidates from the two major parties.

Recruiting and Nominating Candidates

Political parties are the main vehicles through which candidates for office are recruited and screened. The fact that parties exist to win elections gives them the incentive to recruit candidates to run for office under the party label. Parties want to find candidates who will represent the party well, and thus they provide a "weeding out" process resulting in higher-quality candidates.

Most recruiting and promoting of candidates begins at the local party level. Individuals interested in politics often donate their time and efforts to working for political parties by, among other things, attending and participating in party meetings, distributing campaign literature, and driving candidates to campaign events. Local organizations tend to reward this service work with nominations for local offices, such as a seat on a local school board or a planning and zoning board. Successful candidates for these local offices often move up through the ranks of the local party organization to earn the endorsement and nomination of their party for higher office.

Providing a Framework for Voters to Make Vote Choices

Political parties also provide a useful framework for voters who must choose among candidates for elective office. Without even knowing the names of particular candidates for office, voters may be cued in to those candidates' political, ideological, and policy perspectives on the basis of a candidate's party. Most voters associate the political parties with at least broad approaches to governing, if not positions on specific policy issues. For example, on the role that government should play in fixing economic problems, most voters perceive the Democratic Party to be more likely to support an active role for government, whereas Republicans are perceived as having a more "hands off" approach, preferring economic problems to correct themselves through the free market.

The organizational framework for voters to assess candidates is the political party. This framework helps voters more easily process and evaluate campaign information. Party labels thus offer voters an efficient shortcut mechanism for choosing among candidates. For instance, the Democratic Party and candidates running under that label are often regarded by voters as being more liberal or left of center in their position on issues, whereas candidates under the Republican Party label are viewed as being more conservative or right of center. Party identification is the psychological connection that voters have with a political party that influences other attitudes (such as one's position on gun control) as well as voting behavior. **Party identification**, an individual's feeling of attachment to a particular political party, is a political attitude that begins to form early in a person's life and generally remains quite stable throughout his or her lifetime. The authors of *The American Voter*,[10] a classic book on American voting behavior, described party identification as "generally a psychological identification which can persist without legal recognition or evidence of formal membership." Party identification serves an important role in forming attitudes on particular issues and making vote decisions.

Scientific surveys usually measure party identification by asking questions such as: "Generally speaking, do you think of yourself as a Republican, a Democrat, an independent, or what?" Scholars began measuring party identification in the 1950s, and research on the concept has revealed several important findings. First, although

CAROLYN KASTER/AP PHOTO

Senators Hillary Clinton (D-NY) and Barack Obama (D-IL) waged a long battle for the 2008 Democratic presidential nomination.

Party identification
The psychological attachment that an individual has to a particular party.

Partisan Differences on Social Issues

Americans who consider themselves Democrats tend to have different perspectives on social issues than those who consider themselves Republicans. The following data from a May 2010 Gallup Poll indicate how partisan groups differ on what is considered to be morally acceptable.

Percentage Viewing Matters as "Morally Acceptable," by Party ID
Ranked by party difference (Democrat vs. Republican)

	Democrat %	Independent %	Republican %	Difference pct. pts.
Gay or lesbian relations	61	61	35	26
Abortion	51	39	26	25
The death penalty	52	66	76	24
Embryonic stem cell research	68	62	47	21
Having a baby outside of marriage	61	59	41	20
Premarital sex	67	64	47	20
Buying/Wearing clothing made of animal fur	54	61	67	13
Divorce	73	74	61	12
Doctor-assisted suicide	52	46	40	12
Cloning animals	34	32	27	7
Suicide	18	16	11	7
Gambling	64	60	59	5
Extramarital affairs	7	7	3	4
Medical testing on animals	58	57	62	4
Cloning humans	11	7	8	3
Polygamy	6	12	5	1

Source: Gallup Poll, May 2010. © 2010 The Gallup Organization.

the number of independents has grown slightly over the years, there are many more party identifiers than there are independents. Indeed, the majority of Americans today identify with a political party. Second, whereas the Democratic Party had more identifiers than the Republican Party from the mid-1940s to the 1980s, the number of Democrats and Republicans is nearly equal today. As a consequence, the two major parties enjoy pretty much equal amounts of support from the American public. Third, despite these shifts, party identification in the electorate is quite resistant to change. Thus, from one election to another, voting patterns remain remarkably stable and rarely deviate from either a Democratic or Republican victory. Fourth, party identification plays a very important role in helping voters make voting decisions: as shown in Figure 13.1 (p. 400), the vast majority of Republican identifiers vote for Republican candidates and the vast majority of Democratic identifiers vote for Democratic candidates.[11]

FIGURE 13.1 Party Identifiers Who Say They Will Support the Party Line

In the 2008 presidential election, candidates that Democratic voters supported:

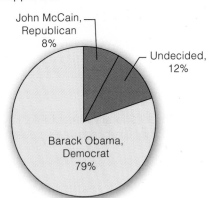

John McCain, Republican 8%

Undecided, 12%

Barack Obama, Democrat 79%

In the 2008 presidential election, candidates that Republican voters supported:

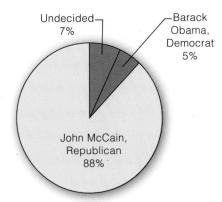

Undecided 7%

Barack Obama, Democrat 5%

John McCain, Republican 88%

Source: Fox News/Opinion Dynamics Poll, September 2008.

Normal vote

The percentage of voters that can be expected with reasonable certainty to cast a ballot for each of the two major political parties.

Party identification is also an important concept for candidates and party leaders in plotting campaign strategies and contesting elections. As political scientist Phillip Converse has noted, a **normal vote**[12] can be expected for any given election contest. That is, a certain percentage of voters can be expected to cast a ballot for the Democrats, whereas another predictable percentage can be expected to vote for the Republicans. The strategy designed to win an election, and the chances that the strategy will result in a victory, largely depend on the normal vote distribution. The larger the margin of one party's normal vote, the less competitive the race. The competitiveness of the race can also be influenced by the number of the nonpartisan voters.

Though party identification is defined as a psychological attachment that an individual has to a particular political party and is regarded by political scientists as an attitude, formal membership in a political party is generally associated with the process of voter registration. In addition to making a citizen eligible to vote, the voter registration process in many states includes registering as a member of a political party. In some states, membership in a political party is a necessary precondition for voting in that political party's primary elections to select the candidates who will represent the party in a general election. States with open primaries do not limit the nomination process to voters of one party. State laws govern how a citizen becomes a member of a political party and thus eligible to vote in the party's primary election contests. In most states, it is possible to register to vote without being a member of any particular party. The rules for becoming a member of a party vary widely from state to state.

Providing Organization for the Operations of Government

The majority party organizes its respective institution to accomplish the task of governing.[13] The leadership organization in the House and Senate is based primarily on majority-party leadership. The top leadership position in the House of Representatives is the Speaker of the House, who is always chosen by the majority-party caucus of the House. The chief leadership position in the Senate is the majority leader, who is selected by the majority-party caucus in the Senate. Members of the majority party chair committees in both houses of Congress. Leaders in Congress then try to implement the campaign pledges and platforms advocated by their party during the previous election campaigns. The executive branch, headed by the president, includes various departments and agencies that conduct the work of the federal government. Partisanship and loyalty to the president's political party are important factors that influence whom the president appoints to lead these agencies and departments.

The policy agenda and important policy decisions are largely the result of the political party organization and partisan leadership of these key branches of government. The greater a party's control over the key governing institution, the more power that party has in influencing public policy. When the Democratic Party has a majority in both the House and the Senate and occupies the presidency, the Democratic Party has virtual control over what laws get passed. For example, the 1932 elections brought FDR, a Democrat, into the White House and resulted in increased Democratic majorities in both houses of Congress. The result of this dominance was passage of numerous laws promoting active government involvement in dealing with the Great Depression.

Divided government,[14] on the other hand, refers to split party control of Congress and the presidency. Because both houses of Congress are required for passing new laws, when the majority party in at least one house of Congress differs from the party occupying the presidency, a form of divided government exists. For example, beginning in January 2007 the Democrats controlled both houses of Congress while Republican President George W. Bush was still in the White House. The presence of divided government often makes it difficult for either party to advance its policy goals and objectives.

Whereas the first 150 years of the republic was mostly characterized by one party controlling both branches of government, the last half century has been dominated by divided government. For example, during the eight years that Republican Ronald Reagan was president, the Democrats held a majority of seats in the House of Representatives, and they continued to do so through Republican George H. W. Bush's administration that followed. During the administration of Democratic President Bill Clinton, the Republicans maintained a majority of seats in both houses for the last six of Clinton's eight years in office. For the first six months of George W. Bush's presidency, the Republicans held control of the House, while the Senate was split 50–50 among Democrats and Republicans, with the tie-breaking vote going to Vice President Dick Cheney. The defection of Vermont Senator James Jeffords from the Republican Party in mid-2001 gave the Democrats a majority in the Senate, resulting in a divided government. After the 2002 elections, Republicans reasserted control over the Senate, and united government under Republican control was established for the next four years. Yet with a Democratic sweep of the House and Senate in November 2006, President Bush was forced to navigate through the perils of divided government for the remainder of his time in office.

The Democratic Party ended divided government for a two-year period with Barack Obama's 2008 presidential election victory over Republican challenger John McCain. In addition, the Democratic Party caucuses increased their margins in both the House of Representatives and the Senate for the 111th Congress. Those large margins of control proved short-lived, however, as the Republicans in 2010 gained over 60 House seats to retake the majority in that chamber and reduced Democratic margins in the Senate as well. Divided party government thus returned to Washington once again in 2011.

FIGURE 13.2 Partisan Voting in Congress

Every year, *Congressional Quarterly* measures the percentage of partisan votes taken in the House and Senate. A roll call vote is considered partisan if a majority of one party votes against a majority of the other. The percentage of partisan voting has hovered around a relatively high 50 percent in the House for the past two decades and stayed there during 2009, at 51 percent. But in the Senate, it was a whopping 72 percent—the highest percentage of partisan votes ever tallied in that chamber.

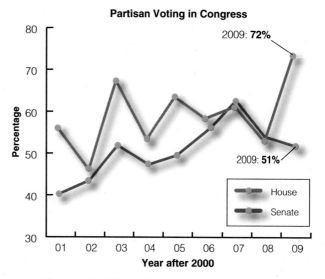

Source: Congressional Quarterly.

Divided government
Split party control of Congress and the presidency.

Many observers of American politics question the rationality of an American electorate that so often sends one party to the presidency, yet keeps the opposite party in control of Congress. The stalemate or gridlock that may result from divided government is problematic to some. Still, many Americans believe that divided government has its benefits; certainly divided control tends to intensify the checks and balances on power envisioned by the framers of the Constitution.

Why a Two-Party System?

Political parties are an integral part of many of the world's democracies. Contemporary party systems are largely a product of the unique characteristics, history, issues, and social class structure of any given nation.

Though party systems in a democracy vary in numerous ways, they may generally be classified into one of two general types: (1) **two-party systems** and (2) **multiparty systems**. The United States features a two-party system, dominated by the Democratic and Republican parties.[15] The vast size and organizational structure of the two major parties, coupled with the fact that these two parties win the great majority of elections, appropriately classifies the United States as a two-party system. Other democracies feature as many as ten parties of relatively equal stature. The nations with multiparty systems typically include parties organized on the basis of political ideologies (such as the socialist party or conservative party), particular economic interests (such as the agricultural party or the industrial party), religion, geography, or positions on a single issue or set of issues.

In the United States, there is a wide range of ideological views, economic interests, religious orientations, ethnic groups, and geographic disparities. Other nations with such a wide diversity of interests typically rely on multiple parties to represent these different components of the population. However, in the United States a two-party model has persisted now for more than two centuries.

Two-party system

A party system dominated by two major parties that win the vast majority of elections.

Multiparty system

A political system in which many different parties are organized on the basis of political ideologies, economic interests, religion, geography, or positions on a single issue or set of issues.

Former Massachusetts Governor Mitt Romney, campaigning for the GOP presidential nomination in 2008. Romney lost the nomination contest to Senator John McCain.

MIKE SEGAR/REUTERS /LANDOV

Reasons for the Two-Party System in the United States

What are the factors that contribute to the American two-party model? A key factor is the Electoral College system for selecting the president of the United States. In order to win the presidency, a candidate must obtain a majority, not simply a plurality, of votes in the Electoral College. Naturally, this requirement encourages groups of voters to align with one of the major political parties, lest their votes be wasted. Minority groups, such as blue-collar union members, which have no chance of achieving a majority of votes as a single unified party, have found it in their best interest to support one of the two major parties in a presidential election. Being part of a winning coalition yields more influence than being in a smaller unified group with no chance of winning.

A second important factor that promotes the two-party system is the winner-take-all process that prevails in selecting members of Congress. In U.S. congressional elections, only the candidate with the most votes in a single district wins the seat. For example, in a race for a Senate seat, if the Democratic candidate receives 40 percent of the vote, the Republican 35 percent, the Reform Party candidate 15 percent, and the Green Party 10 percent, the Democratic candidate with the 40 percent plurality is elected to Congress. By contrast, in other democracies, such as Israel, France, and Germany, forms of **proportional representation** are used. Under this system, the percentage of the vote that a party receives is reflected in the number of seats that that party occupies in the national legislature. In Israel, for example, a party that receives as little as 1.5 percent of the vote nationally is entitled to at least one seat in the 120-seat Knesset (the Israeli legislature). Whereas a proportional representation system gives minor parties representation in the legislature, the winner-take-all system does not. A third party must win the most votes in any given election contest to win a seat. The winner-take-all system promotes the two-party system and prevents smaller parties from achieving even minimal representation in the national legislature.

A third factor promoting the two-party system is the ideological nature of public opinion in America. Most Americans are ideologically centrist, or moderate, with few considering themselves strong ideologues. The lack of strong ideological differences helps explain why only two parties dominate American politics. Neither the Democratic nor the Republican Party can afford to be too strongly ideological because to be so would risk building a winning coalition in elections.

A fourth factor promoting the two-party system are the laws and regulations that govern campaigns in United States, which tend to benefit the major parties at the expense of third parties. For example, in order to qualify for matching federal funds for presidential campaigns and many state gubernatorial campaigns, candidates must demonstrate a minimum level of support in prior elections and/or primary elections. Most minor parties, however, are eligible to receive such funds only after the election is over. They receive public funding in federal elections, for example, if (1) they receive 5 percent of the popular vote and (2) they appear on the ballot in at least ten states.

★ LO

Understand the historical and legal factors that contributed to the development of the two-party system in the United States

Proportional representation

A system of electing a national legislature in which the percentage of the vote that a party receives is reflected in the number of seats that the party occupies.

NICHOLAS KAMM/AFP/GETTY IMAGES

Robert Barr, the Libertarian Party candidate for president in 2008.

Because money to finance a campaign is necessary during, rather than after, the campaign, third parties are at a serious disadvantage. The lack of a history and lack of public interest in third-party primary elections precludes most from receiving federal or state funding in these elections. For a third party's candidate to appear on election ballots in the states, the party must meet a number of criteria, including petitions supporting the candidate and often significant fees.

★ LO   Explain the role that third parties have played in U.S. elections

Minor and Third Parties

Despite the dominance of the Republican and Democratic parties over the past century and a half, a number of third parties have contested elections in the United States. The most recent third party of note was the Green Party, from which Ralph Nader launched his presidential campaign during the 2000 election.* Most third-party candidates fail to register even one percentage point of the popular vote in presidential elections, and few third-party candidates are found in the U.S. Congress, in state legislatures or governorships, or in local government. For the past 150 years, not one president has been elected who did not run as either a Democrat or Republican.

Even the few-and-far-between third-party candidacies that have attracted a sizeable percentage of popular votes in presidential elections have experienced only short-lived success (see Table 13.1). The Progressive or "Bull Moose" Party of Theodore Roosevelt, for example, garnered 27 percent of the vote in 1912, but failed to establish itself as a permanent threat to the two major parties. Its success was largely based on Roosevelt's stature and popularity, and by 1916 Roosevelt had returned to

TABLE 13.1 Important Third-Party Candidacies in Presidential Races

Third parties are by no means a new phenomenon in American politics. Despite their tendency to be short-lived and their relative lack of success in capturing elective office, third-party movements endure, often affecting which major-party candidate wins office. The following is a select list of third parties, their respective candidates, and their vote totals in presidential elections.

Year	Party	Candidate	% of Popular Vote
1832	Anti-Masonic	William Wirt	8
1856	Know-Nothing	Millard Fillmore	22
1892	Populist	James Weaver	9
1912	Bull Moose	Theodore Roosevelt	27
1912	Socialist	Eugene V. Debs	6
1924	Progressive	Robert La Follette	17
1948	States' Rights	Strom Thurmond	2
1948	Progressive	Henry Wallace	2
1968	American Independent	George Wallace	14
1980	National Unity	John Anderson	7
1992	United We Stand America	Ross Perot	19
1996	Reform	Ross Perot	9
2000	Green	Ralph Nader	3
2004	Independent	Ralph Nader	1

* Nader was technically the Green Party candidate for president in 1996 as well, but he was only on 22 state ballots that year, and his candidacy labored under a self-imposed spending limit of $5,000. In the 2004 presidential election the Green Party candidate was Texas attorney David Cobb; Nader ran as an independent in 2004.

the Republican fold. Likewise, Ross Perot, running as an independent in the 1992 presidential race, captured nearly 20 percent of the popular vote. But his attempt to match his 1992 success met with disappointment in his 1996 bid, when he took only 9 percent of the popular vote. By 2000, Perot's Reform Party showed up as barely a blip in the vote totals.[16]

Third parties face a number of obstacles in their attempt to become viable. First, their mostly negligible chance of winning at the outset leads many voters to sense that a vote for a third party would be wasted. The strong historical and cultural institutionalization of the American two-party system is another obstacle third parties face. The sizeable number of voters who identify themselves as either a Democrat or Republican inclines most voters to support major-party candidates in elections. In addition to the legal barriers already discussed, media coverage of campaigns also plays a role; the media tend to focus most coverage on the two major parties, with little attention given to third-party candidacies.

Still, third parties persist. Despite their limited success in winning important government positions, they often have substantial influence on the outcome of elections. Third-party candidates in hotly contested presidential races have on occasion siphoned off enough votes from one of the major-party candidates to provide an Electoral College victory to the other major party. Twice since 1832 a third party has won more than 20 percent of the popular vote in a presidential race, and five times during this period a third party has won at least 10 percent of the popular vote.

Political scientist James Q. Wilson, a student of third parties, has identified four basic types of third parties. **Economic protest parties** tend to emerge in times of economic recession. In the 1892 election, for example, the Populist Party advocated the free coinage of silver, as an alternative to the gold standard. (The Populists won 9 percent of the popular vote.) Similarly, Ross Perot's campaign in 1992 expressed strong discontent with the economic policies of the George H. W. Bush administration, including the budget deficit and trade policies. Perot won 19 percent of the popular vote.

A second type of third party is the **ideological party**, which promotes broad ideas about the purpose and role of government. In the United States, the Libertarian Party advocates an extremely minimalist role for government, whereas the Socialist Party stands at the opposite end of the spectrum, advocating a much broader and significant role for government. Third is the **issue party**, which tends to form on the basis of a single issue. After a short period of time, issue parties generally fade away. An example is the Liberty Party, which advocated abolition of slavery. It appeared in several elections prior to 1848, when it merged with the Free Soil Party. (The Free Soil Party was a precursor to the Republican Party, which ran a candidate for president beginning in 1856.)

Finally, there are **factional parties**—pieces from one or both of the major parties that have split off to form a separate party. Theodore Roosevelt formed the Progressive Party and ran in the 1912 election after he lost the Republican Party nomination to President William Howard Taft. Roosevelt won 28

AP PHOTO/J. SCOTT APPLEWHITE

Economic protest party
A party that emerges in times of economic recession to express discontent with the ruling party.

Ideological party
A party that promotes broad ideas about the purpose and role of government.

Issue party
A party that tends to form on the basis of a single issue.

Factional party
A party that has split off from one of the major parties.

Green Party candidate Ralph Nader in 2000.

TABLE 13.2 Third Parties Today

Despite the lack of electoral success by third parties, many continue to operate in the United States today. Listed here are a few of them, along with a description of their reason for being.

Party	Description
1. Natural Law Party	This party advocates "all-party" government, which it defines as "bringing together the best ideas, programs, and leaders from all political parties and the private sector to solve and prevent problems." The party argues that bringing the individual lives of people and national policies into harmony with the "natural law" will best solve the nation's problems.
2. Constitution Party	This party bases the foundation of its political activities on religious principles of Christianity. It argues that the U.S. Constitution established a "republic under God, rather than a democracy."
3. Reform Party	Ross Perot ran as a candidate in the 1992 presidential election under the organization "United We Stand America." He ran to protest the leadership of both the Republican and Democratic parties and won 19 percent of the popular vote. In 1996, Perot reorganized under the Reform Party name and won 9 percent of the popular vote. Former Republican Pat Buchanan was a Reform Party candidate for president in 2000, receiving 0.5 percent of the popular vote.
4. Libertarian Party	This party endorses the notion that government should be small and limited, interfering as little as possible with the lives of citizens. The Libertarian Party argues that "individuals have the right to exercise sole dominion over their own lives [and] they have the right to live in whatever manner they choose so long as they do not interfere with the rights of others." Libertarians place a premium on individual liberties and personal responsibility.
5. Socialist Party	Whereas the Libertarians support a very limited role for government, the Socialist Party supports active government involvement in providing equitable distributions of resources in society. Socialists endorse a strong government role in providing health care, jobs, housing, and education, among other public programs. Although Bernie Sanders won election in 2006 as a U.S. senator from Vermont running as a self-described "Democratic Socialist," he does not belong to the Socialist Party.
6. Green Party	The foundation of the Green Party rests on pro-environmentalist positions like "Green" parties in other democracies, such as Germany and France. In the United States, the Green Party is also identified with a number of social justice causes, including feminism, promotion of diversity, and global responsibility. Green Party candidate Ralph Nader took 2.7 percent of the popular vote in the 2000 election, finishing in third place.

percent of the popular vote to Taft's 23 percent, helping Democrat Woodrow Wilson to win the presidency. Similarly, in 1924 Senator Robert La Follette of Wisconsin left the Republican Party to form a newer version of the Progressive Party and took 17 percent of the popular vote. In 1980, Republican Congressman John Anderson of Illinois, after failing to achieve the Republican Party's nomination for president, formed the National Unity Party; in the election Anderson received 7 percent of the popular vote.

★ LO Learn how party organizations operate at the national, state, and local levels, including how they define party platforms and help their candidates win elections

The Party Organizations

Political parties exist through party organizations at the national, state, and local levels. Though most elected government officials are members of the Democratic or Republican parties, political parties also exist as organizations outside of the government. These party organizations, which often count millions of volunteers among their members, articulate positions on issues; enlist members from the public at large; recruit candidates who will run under the party label for elective office; raise money from individuals, corporations, and interest groups; and provide organizational and campaign services to candidates who are running for office.

Andrew Jackson is regarded as the father of the **national party organization**. Up until the election of 1828, a party's candidates for president and vice president were nominated by the party congressional caucus. Jackson changed this process by establishing a national party convention to be held several months before a presidential election. The convention brings together state and local party leaders to nominate the party's candidates for president and vice president. In addition to party leaders, the national conventions today include delegates from the states elected by members of the party in presidential primary elections.

Since the middle of the nineteenth century, both the Democratic and Republican national party organizations have been run by a **national committee**, which oversees the conduct of the presidential campaign and develops strategy for each party's congressional elections as well. The national committees, consisting of state and local party representatives, are run by a **national committee chair** chosen soon after the presidential election has concluded.

At the national level, the committees, chairs, and party organization largely provide a supportive role during the presidential campaign. Once providing a core advisory role to a presidential candidate, the national organizations today are more involved in helping their candidate raise money and campaign for office. Strategy, planning, and advising are now handled mostly by the candidate's own campaign staff, which typically includes a media consultant, a pollster, a campaign manager, and various other campaign consultants. The modern-day national party organization is also less influential in determining who the nominee will be and more responsive to the victorious candidate's personal campaign staff. They do maintain greater influence in assisting state and local party efforts to win elections by providing polling and media consulting services, campaign management services, and financial resources.

In the modern era, state and local party organizations tend to be more influential in the nomination of candidates, in developing and organizing campaigns, and in providing a cue to voters about their vote selections. Voters pay less attention to campaigns in state and local elections and therefore depend more on partisan cues in their choice of candidates. State legislative and local election campaigns generally have limited resources to mount significant image-building campaigns for candidates. Candidates are thus more dependent on the resources of the state and local party organizations for financing. Local party organizations provide "get out the vote" services by funding phone banks to contact voters directly. State and local organizations also fund and make available polling services and media consulting services to candidates in less visible races. Benefiting from these services, candidates for local and state offices may feel the need to be more responsive to the party organizations.

Local party organizations also provide the grassroots manpower for soliciting mass participation in political activities. These activities include implementing voter registration drives, organizing political fund-raisers and rallies, and staffing phone banks to make direct contact with voters urging them to vote for their party's candidates. Local organizations also provide the mechanism for identifying and recruiting talented citizens to become candidates for elective office. They provide the "farm team" for potential candidates for higher offices, such as governor, member of Congress, and senator.

Are Parties in Decline?

Many political scientists contend that the political party is in a state of decline in America. Bolstering this claim is the dealignment thesis described earlier in this chapter, which holds that voters today are less attached to parties and tend to be more independent-minded than they were up through the 1960s. Political scientist Martin Wattenberg[17] argues that increased negativity toward the parties has

National party organization
The institution through which political parties exist at the national, state, and local levels, primarily focused on articulating policy positions, raising money, organizing volunteers, and providing services to candidates.

National committee
The committee that oversees the conduct of a party's presidential campaign and develops strategy for congressional elections.

National committee chair
The head of the national committee for one of the two major parties.

★ LO
Learn the factors that have contributed to a decline in political parties over the past few decades and assess the future prospects for the parties

Barack Obama accepts the presidential nomination of the Democratic Party at that party's national convention in 2008.

PAUL J. RICHARDS/AFP/
GETTY IMAGES

contributed to party decline. Wattenberg suggests further that the mass media have contributed to this decline by neglecting to cover parties. Prior to the 1960s, voters depended mainly on parties to provide information about political issues and candidates; now voters turn to the media as the prime information source. Furthermore, the medium of television allows candidates today to bypass parties and appeal directly to the public for support. Many candidates now run campaigns that de-emphasize parties and focus primarily on the candidate's image.

Scholars have also noted a decline in the organizational linkages between officeholders and the political parties. Patronage, the practice by which victorious parties offer loyal party members jobs in government, declined substantially during the past century. Under the patronage system, parties were able to retain the strong support of many of their members by offering the prospect of a good government job if the party was victorious. The civil service and other reforms seriously limited a political party's ability to offer jobs or other favors in return for supporting the party. Although these reforms have eroded the power of parties, they have also improved the quality of government officials and reduced corruption in government affairs.

Changes in the way candidates are nominated by a party have also reduced the power of party organizations. Until recently, parties exerted powerful control over the process by which an individual becomes a candidate wearing the party label in a general election. Without endorsement of the party organization, candidates for president, Congress, and state and local office once were virtually precluded from running under the party label. However, reforms in the 1960s and 1970s reduced the party organization's role in the nomination process. The **direct primary election**, which provides for the nomination of a candidate based on an open election among all party members, has empowered rank-and-file party members rather than party leaders to choose the party's nominees. Direct primaries make it easier for candidates who are not necessarily approved by the party organization to wear the party label in a general election.

Some scholars, however, are not so convinced that parties are on the decline. They argue that although certain aspects of parties are declining, in other ways parties are showing a resurgence in relevance.[18] For example, parties have adapted quite well to candidate-centered campaigns by servicing candidate organizations. In 2006, the Democratic Party supported some candidates who actually de-emphasized their party identification, and thus helped forge victories for Democrats in congressional districts that were considered moderate-to-conservative. Additionally, party-line voting in the House and the Senate has been highly disciplined in recent years. In the 110th Congress (2007–2008), for example, senators voted with their party's position on legislation an average of 83 percent of the time. Not much changed during the 111th Congress: when health care reform came up for a series of final votes in the Senate in late 2009 and early 2010, all 100 senators voted down the line with their party leadership's position on the issue.

Whether they are declining or not, at the moment parties remain alive and quite active in American politics. Even though voter partisanship may have waned, party identification still remains a strong determinant of vote choice. Although the parties may be less visible to voters, they continue to exert considerable influence over voting decisions. The Democratic and Republican Party organizations are well funded and include millions of party workers. Party organizations provide money and expertise to candidates to help them achieve electoral success. The president remains the recognized leader of the party label he wears, and the party with a majority of seats in each house of Congress maintains clear control of the legislative agenda. Although the power of the party may have declined, it is clear that "the party" is far from over in American politics.

Direct primary election
An open election, rather than an election by party leaders, to choose candidates for the general election.

Making the Connection

The Founders never intended for a two-party system to take hold in the republic they so carefully designed; and yet two-party systems have dominated U.S. politics for over two centuries, beginning with the rivalry between Federalists and the Democratic-Republicans in the 1790s, and extending all the way up to the present, when the Democrats and modern-day Republicans take turns controlling our government. Sometimes both major parties—despite all their built-in political advantages—lose touch with passionate strains of popular opinion. This is most likely to occur when the public grows increasingly skeptical about government as a whole.

In such instances, an upstart political movement may suddenly arrive on the scene, connecting with the interests of a segment of the electorate that seeks a brand new means of influencing government. In the 1890s it was the "People's Party" (also known as the Populists) that made its voice heard; in 2010 the Tea Party movement lent its support to numerous anti-government candidates and helped to shift party control of Congress in the process. If history is a guide, those movements tend to be short-lived, exerting significant influence in a series of election cycles before one or both of the major parties bring the movement's energetic set of followers into their own party's fold. Will the major political party that is most successful in this regard be willing to incorporate the upstart movement's ideas into their policy agenda as well? That was the dilemma that faced the Democratic Party in the 1890s, and which faces the Republican Party in 2011 and beyond.

Tea
4
Two

© 2012 CENGAGE LEARNING

POLITICS InterActive!

A Democrat Even a Republican Nominee Could Love

E ver since he was elected to the U.S. Senate for the first time in 1988, Senator Joseph Lieberman of Connecticut has been something of a political enigma. In 1998, he was the first prominent Democrat to publicly challenge Bill Clinton for the poor judgment the president exercised in his affair with Monica Lewinsky. However, Lieberman then voted against removing Clinton from office by impeachment the following year. While voting as a classic liberal on social issues, Lieberman has cultivated his reputation as an extreme conservative on military and war issues. Indeed, he was one of the Senate's strongest advocates for continued prosecution of the controversial war in Iraq. And though Lieberman was tapped as the Democratic Party's

nominee for vice president in 2000, the Connecticut senator's status as a Democrat became tenuous after the party's voters in Connecticut rejected him as their nominee for the Senate in 2006. Lieberman ran for reelection that fall as an independent and coasted to victory.

Lieberman continued to caucus with the Democrats after his 2006 election victory, helping secure that party's majority control in the Senate. Still, the Democratic leadership in the 110th and 111th Congresses could no longer take his support for granted. One significant indication of Lieberman's break with his Democratic past occurred during the 2008 presidential campaign, when Lieberman declared his support

JOE RAEDLE/GETTY IMAGES

Senator Joseph Lieberman (I-CT), right, with 2008 Republican presidential candidate John McCain at the Republican National Convention.

for Republican Senator John McCain's candidacy over all the Democratic contenders for the White House, including his own home state colleague, Senator Christopher Dodd (D-CT). A serious contender to be McCain's choice for vice president (McCain chose Alaska Governor Sarah Palin instead), Lieberman even received a prominent speaking position at the 2008 Republican National Convention. By contrast, the long-time Democrat was nowhere to be found at the Democratic National Convention in Denver, Colorado, held the previous week. More recently, Lieberman refused to support health care reform legislation until President Obama and the Democratic majority agreed to drop the "public option" provision of that legislation.

On www.cengage.com/dautrich/americangovernment/2e, find the Politics Interactive link for a discussion of the narrow working margin in the Senate, and a list of the moderate Democrats and Republicans who are most influential when no one party enjoys a large margin of control over the Senate. Consult as well the various links that relate to other famous mavericks that have confounded their own party leadership time and time again.

Chapter 13 Political Parties

Chapter Summary

★ History of Political Parties in the United States

- Because many of the founders frowned on parties and other factions, the Constitution nowhere mentions or contemplates parties. Nevertheless, the debate over ratification of the Constitution gave rise to two parties: the Federalists and the Anti-Federalists. The United States has had a two-party system ever since.

- Every presidential and congressional election since 1796 has featured some form of party competition. National party conventions and national party organization originated during Andrew Jackson's presidency. The Democratic and Republican parties have dominated since 1856.

- Certain elections, such as those of 1860, 1896, and 1932, are considered "critical elections" because they produced sharp and lasting changes in patterns of party loyalty among voters.

- Some political scientists have termed the era since 1968 as a period of dealignment, characterized by a decline in voter attachment to parties and in clarity of party coalitions.

★ The Functions of Political Parties

- The two major parties have developed large organizations that exist at the national, state, and local levels. They assist in fund-raising for candidates, recruiting and organizing volunteers to work for candidates, and purchasing political services to promote the election of candidates.

- Party identification develops early in a person's political life, psychologically connecting the individual to a political party, which in turn influences other attitudes and voting behavior.

- Majority-party leadership in Congress organizes that branch to accomplish the task of governing. Partisanship also influences a president's policy positions and appointments.

- When divided party government exists, it becomes difficult for either party to advance its policy goals and objectives.

★ Why a Two-Party System?

- The U.S. party system has been dominated by Democrats and Republicans since the election of 1856. This two-party system is perpetuated by several factors, including the need for a majority of Electoral College votes (not just a plurality) to win the presidency outright, and a winner-take-all system that makes it especially hard for third parties to succeed to any degree.

- Third-party candidates rarely attract a significant percentage of popular votes in presidential elections because voters perceive that votes for such a candidate would be wasted and because various legal barriers make it hard for third-party candidates to receive government funding.

★ Party Organizations

- The two major political parties have organizations at the national level, at the state level in all fifty states, and at the local level in most cities and towns across the nation. These organizations are active in developing party platforms, recruiting candidates to run for office, and providing financial support and other resources to aid the candidates electorally.

★ Are Parties in Decline?

- The decline of patronage and the prevalence of the direct primary election have contributed to the belief that parties are now in decline. Regardless, party identification remains an especially strong determinant of vote choice in America today.

CourseMate

Key Terms

Critical election (p. 392)
Dealignment (p. 396)
Direct primary election (p. 409)
Divided government (p. 401)
Economic protest party (p. 405)
Factional party (p. 405)
Ideological party (p. 405)

Issue party (p. 405)
Multiparty system (p. 402)
National committee (p. 407)
National committee chair (p. 407)
National party convention (p. 391)
National party organization
  (p. 407)

Normal vote (p. 400)
Party identification (p. 398)
Party platform (p. 392)
Political party (p. 388)
Proportional representation
  (p. 403)
Two-party system (p. 402)

Resources

Important Books

Aldrich, John H. *Why Parties? The Origin and Transformation of Party Politics in America.* Chicago: University of Chicago Press, 1995.

Beck, Paul Allen. *Party Politics in America,* 5th ed. New York: Longman, 1997.

Bibby, John F. *Politics, Parties and Elections in America.* Belmont, CA: Wadsworth, 2002.

Blevins, David. *American Political Parties in the 21st Century.* New York: McFarland & Co., 2006.

Conley, Richard S. *The Presidency, Congress and Divided Government.* College Station: Texas A&M University Press, 2002.

Green, John C., and Daniel Shay, eds. *The State of the Parties: The Changing Role of Contemporary American Parties.* New York: Rowman and Littlefield, 1996.

Keith, Bruce E., David E. Magleby, Candice J. Nelson, Elizabeth Orr, Mark C. Westlye, and Raymond E. Wolfinger. *The Myth of the Independent Voter.* Berkeley: University of California Press, 1992.

Milkis, Sydney M. *The President and the Parties: The Transformation of the American Party System Since the New Deal.* London: Oxford University Press, 1993.

Rosenstone, Steven J., Roy L. Behr, and Edward H. Lazarus. *Third Parties in America.* Princeton, NJ: Princeton University Press, 1984.

Wattenberg, Martin P. *The Decline of American Political Parties, 1952–1996.* Cambridge, MA: Harvard University Press, 1998.

Internet Sources

Web sites of various political parties:

http://www.natural-law.org (Natural Law Party)

http://www.constitutionparty.com (Constitution Party)

http://www.gp.org (Green Party)

http://www.rnc.org (Republican Party)

http://www.democrats.org/ (Democratic Party)

Another useful Web site:

http://www.electionstudies.org/ (information on partisanship and party identification from the National Election Study can be found at this Web site)

14 Voting and Participation

NOW Barack Obama, campaigning for the presidency in 2008.

CHRIS CARLSON/AP PHOTO

THEN John F. Kennedy, campaigning for the presidency in 1960.

PAUL SCHUTZER/TIME LIFE PICTURES/GETTY IMAGES

NOW &THEN

A Young, Charismatic Campaigner Energizes Voters and Overcomes the Weight of History

One of the youngest candidates ever to run for the presidency, this Democrat burst on the national political scene sporting a remarkable talent for energizing the base of a party that had been shut out of the White House for the past eight years. Young people newly drawn to electoral politics were attending his political rallies in droves. Yet a significant obstacle stood in his way: Americans had never before elected to the White House someone from his demographic group. He incurred other attacks as well, first from his formidable Democratic Party rival from the U.S. Senate, and later from his Republican opponent, each of whom attempted to convince voters that this new brand of politician was in fact an intellectual elitist out of touch with mainstream America. All these attacks proved unsuccessful. A majority of Americans responded to his message of change by electing him president of the United States. In connecting with voters and winning the presidential race, this new president overcame the weight of history by becoming the first person in his demographic group to occupy the Oval Office.

LEARNING OBJECTIVES
★ WHAT YOU WILL LEARN ★

The Legal Structure for Voting in the United States

★ Assess the role of state governments in managing elections

★ Evaluate the effect of various constitutional amendments on the expansion of voting rights in the United States

★ Appreciate the wide diversity of voter registration systems implemented in the fifty states

Exercising the Franchise

★ Assess the influence of different factors in influencing voter turnout, including interest in politics, sense of civic duty, the perception that one's vote can make a difference, education, income, age, and social group pressures

★ Explore the influence of political campaigns on turnout and in affecting "high stimulus" elections

★ Analyze the trends in U.S. voter turnout over the past six or seven decades

★ Compare and contrast voter turnout in the United States with voter turnout in other democracies

Making a Vote Choice

★ Understand the various factors that explain vote choices

Political Participation beyond the Voting Booth

★ Appreciate the many forms of political participation beyond voting, including communicating concerns to officials, civil disobedience, and protest activities

NOW & THEN

CHRIS CARLSON/AP PHOTO

NOW   A mere state senator from Illinois, Barack Obama burst on the political scene with a fiery, impassioned keynote speech at the 2004 Democratic National Convention. Not only was he young, charismatic, and a gifted orator, but he was also African American. Though the Democrats were defeated in the 2004 presidential contest, Obama was elected to the U.S. Senate. Soon thereafter he capitalized on the popularity and fame of his keynote speech to launch his own run for the presidency in 2008. His youth and vigor attracted record numbers of new voters to the Democratic Party, raised voting turnout in Democratic primaries to record numbers, and helped him defeat well-known U.S. Senator and former First Lady Hillary Clinton for the Democratic presidential nomination. Campaigning on an agenda for "change," Obama's youth and energy contrasted sharply with the more somber personality of his eventual Republican opponent, Senator John McCain. After eight years of Republican rule from George W. Bush in the Oval Office, voters were looking for something new and altogether different—and they found it in the charismatic and inspirational Obama. Ultimately voter turnout reached new highs in 2008, helped in no small part by Obama's electric candidacy. Voters from recent Republican strongholds including Colorado and Virginia—states that went for Republican George W. Bush in 2000 and 2004—helped the young Democrat make political history as the first African American to win the White House.

THEN   Nearly a half century before Obama's historical run, Senator John F. Kennedy of Massachusetts exploded on the nation's political map with his own run at the vice presidency during the Democratic National Convention of 1956. He eventually lost the nod to fellow Senator Estes Kefauver of Tennessee, who became the choice of presidential nominee Adlai Stevenson. Still, the youthful and charismatic Kennedy had caught the eye of his party faithful (as well as the nation at large) with his convention appearance and narration of the keynote film. Four years later he capitalized on that stardom to mount his own successful campaign for the Democratic presidential nomination. Kennedy was young, charismatic, and a gifted and inspirational speaker, yet he had his own glass ceiling to overcome—Kennedy was Catholic, and no Catholic had ever made it all the way to the White House. Kennedy's youthful energy proved an asset throughout the campaign, first in helping him overcome a formidable primary challenge from Senate Majority Leader Lyndon Johnson and later in his hard-fought general election contest against his Republican opponent, Vice President Richard Nixon. Kennedy generated considerable voter interest by drawing large crowds at political rallies and high turnout in primary contests. His general election campaign called for a "New Frontier" of change for America, mobilizing many new voters in the process. Kennedy's charisma contrasted sharply with the rather dull personality of his Republican opponent, Richard Nixon. After eight years under Republican Dwight D. Eisenhower, voters from such Republican strongholds as Michigan and Pennsylvania—both states that twice went overwhelmingly for Eisenhower—helped Kennedy make history as the first (and so far, only) Catholic to occupy the White House.

PAUL SCHUTZER/TIME LIFE PICTURES/GETTY IMAGES

Chapter 14 Voting and Participation

MORRY GASH/AP PHOTO

Democratic presidential hopeful Senator Barack Obama (D-IL) and his wife Michelle at a rally in St. Paul, Minnesota, in June 2008.

P olitical participation takes many forms in American politics.[1] At the core of participation is the act of voting. Open and free elections held on a regular basis are the hallmark characteristic of a democratic government. Voting provides the critical linkage between citizens' preferences and governmental authority. The United States is not a direct democracy in which every citizen is invited to deliberate the issues and vote on public policy. Rather, the U.S. system is a **representative democracy**, sometimes referred to as an indirect democracy or republican form of government, in which citizens choose the individuals who are then responsible for making and enforcing public policy. The people do not directly rule, but they have the opportunity to exercise power vicariously by choosing as their leaders those whom they prefer.

The core principle underlying representative democracy is **majoritarianism**, or majority rule, which means that among the choices presented to voters, the choice that is supported by the most voters (that is, receives the most votes) is the choice that prevails. When a majority makes its choice, the consent of the governed is satisfied. Given the diversity of opinions and interests among people in our society, it is unrealistic to assume that all, or even most, voters will agree on one choice. But the will of the people is accomplished when the majority decides.

Voting is the mechanism that ensures that the majority will rule. Times change, and so do people's opinions and preferences. Therefore, representative democracy not only requires an election in the selection of leadership, but also requires that elections occur on a regular basis so that the government's authority reflects changing majority views. Regular and periodic elections allow the majority of voters to continue to exercise ultimate control over the direction of public policy.

In this chapter, we explore historical and legal factors related to who has the right to vote, how Americans exercise their right to vote, and the factors that influence the making of a vote choice. Voting, of course, is not the only way citizens participate in the political process. They also contribute time and money to parties and candidates, write letters and contact public officials, express thoughts on policy issues and political candidates in blogs, attend town meeting and rallies, and engage in protests such as sit-ins, boycotts, and marches (see Figure 14.1). We examine these forms of political participation as well.

Representative democracy

System of government in which citizens elect the individuals who are responsible for making and enforcing public policy.

Majoritarianism

The principle that the choice that is supported by the most voters is the choice that prevails.

Voting

The political mechanism that ensures that the majority will rule.

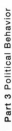

FIGURE 14.1 The Ways in Which Americans Participate in Politics

Americans participate in politics in a number of different ways. The following chart lists some of the more common methods of political participation, along with the percentage of Americans who have engaged in each type of activity.

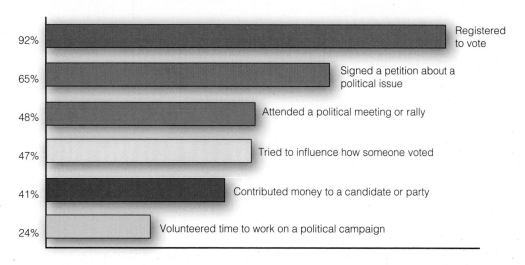

- 92% — Registered to vote
- 65% — Signed a petition about a political issue
- 48% — Attended a political meeting or rally
- 47% — Tried to influence how someone voted
- 41% — Contributed money to a candidate or party
- 24% — Volunteered time to work on a political campaign

Source: 2008 national survey of 2,500 American adults, conducted by Intercollegiate Studies Institute (ISI).

The Legal Structure for Voting in the United States

★ LO
Assess the role of state governments in managing elections

The **franchise**, or suffrage, is the right to vote. When speaking about majority rule, it is important to ask, "majority of whom?" Article I, Section 4 of the U.S. Constitution assigns the system of voting, including the definition of who is granted suffrage, to the states. Voting registration, voter eligibility, methods of casting ballots, and the tallying of official results are all functions reserved for states. The original Constitution prescribes eligibility requirements for federal officeholders (representatives, senators, and the president) and lays out the system for selection of the president and vice president, but it says nothing about who can vote in the elections for these officials. Constitutional amendments have been ratified and federal laws have been passed that prevent states from discriminating in granting suffrage rights; but technically, there exists no absolute constitutional right to vote in the first place.

Franchise (or suffrage)
The right to vote.

Toward Universal Suffrage

★ LO
Evaluate the effect of various constitutional amendments on the expansion of voting rights in the United States

The states have exercised significant authority in defining who is eligible to vote. For many years states regularly denied minorities, women, young adults, Native Americans, and the poor the right to vote for officeholders at the local, state, and national levels of government. In addition, a number of states prescribed property ownership requirements that prevented many people from being eligible to vote. Some states at various points in the nation's early history sought to broaden the right of suffrage. New Jersey, for example, allowed women the right to vote in the early 1800s, and some northern states provided for black suffrage prior to the Civil War.[2] But the goal of **universal suffrage**—or the right of all citizens to vote—has been an elusive one throughout American history. Restrictions on voting rights have systematically denied the right of particular groups of people to participate in choosing their leaders.

Two centuries of government under the Constitution, however, have been marked by steady progress toward the goal of extending the franchise to all Americans. In the first federal elections in 1788, voting rights were limited to white men who owned property; whereas in the most recent federal elections of 2008, all citizens

Universal suffrage
The idea that all citizens in a nation have the right to vote.

When One Vote Made the Difference

Does your vote matter? Few elections are decided by one vote. However, there have been very important elections throughout American history that prove the exception rather than the rule. In some instances, a single vote made a huge difference. According to PBS's "The Democracy Project," these important elections were decided by a handful of votes:

1846 One vote decided on war with Mexico. In 1846, the Mexican army invaded Texas and President Polk asked for a Declaration of War. The Senate did not want to go to war, and the declaration passed by only one vote. The United States won the war against Mexico and with that victory added five states—Arizona, New Mexico, Nevada, Utah and California.

1867 One vote gave the United States the state of Alaska. The Alaska Purchase of 1867 was ratified by just one vote—paving the way for the territory to be America's largest state when it became part of the United States in 1958.

1876 One vote gave Rutherford B. Hayes the presidency of the United States. In the 1876 presidential election, Samuel Tilden received a half million more popular votes than Hayes. The Electoral College was not in agreement about who should be America's next leader. A special commission was formed to make the final decision. The commission decided, although Hayes had lost the actual vote by the citizens of the United States, he had won the electoral vote by just one ballot: 185 to 184.

1916 One vote in each of the voting districts of California reelected President Wilson. If Wilson's opponent, Charles E. Hughes, had received an additional vote in each one of California's voting precincts, he would have defeated Wilson.

1948 One vote per voting precinct gave Harry Truman the presidency. If Truman's opponent, Thomas E. Dewey, had received one vote more per precinct in Ohio and California, there would have been a tie and the House of Representatives would have decided the election. And because Dewey had more support in the House than Truman, Dewey would have won.

Source: http://pbskids.org/democracy/vote/onevote2004.html

of the United States aged eighteen or older (who were not otherwise prohibited from voting due to a felony conviction or some similar offense) enjoyed the legal right to vote. Enfranchisement was not achieved quickly, nor did it happen as the result of one or two events. Rather, the process of extending the right to vote to all American adults occurred over centuries of time, and with much opposition.

The Civil War presented the first major challenge to the disenfranchisement of a particular class of people, namely, African Americans. Prior to the Civil War, African American slaves not only did not have the right to vote, they had no rights at all. In the infamous U.S. Supreme Court decision *Dred Scott v. Sanford* (1857), the Court ruled that slaves were property, that they had no rights under the law, and that they were not and could never become legal citizens of the United States. Immediately after the surrender of Confederate forces in 1865, President Abraham Lincoln gave an address suggesting that freed slaves be given the franchise. The idea met with some resistance, even among the northern states. However, the so-called Civil War

amendments to the Constitution not only ended the institution of slavery (the Thirteenth Amendment) and granted citizenship to former slaves (the Fourteenth Amendment), but the **Fifteenth Amendment**, passed in 1870, guaranteed that "the right of citizens of the United States to vote shall not be abridged by the United States or any state on account of race, color, or any previous condition of servitude." The Fifteenth Amendment was the first formal action granting the federal government the power to enforce voting rights over the states.

The Fifteenth Amendment, however, did not deter some officials from the former Confederate states from finding ways to deny African Americans their newly won voting rights after Reconstruction ended in 1877. Threats, beatings, destruction of property, and other intimidation tactics, often ignored by local police, effectively kept blacks from coming to the polls on Election Day.[3] In addition, some states sought legal means to prevent blacks from voting. They passed laws instituting a **poll tax** that required individuals to pay a fee before being allowed to vote; they required potential voters to pass a **literacy test** to prove that they could read and write. Because most blacks were poor, they were often unable to pay the poll tax (usually about $30). Blacks also tended to have less education (in some states it had been illegal to teach slaves to read and write), so they frequently could not pass the literacy tests, which were often deliberately difficult and unfairly applied to minorities to prevent them from voting. From the late 1800s through the first half of the twentieth century, these methods posed a substantial barrier to black turnout in federal elections, which typically was about 10 percent. These laws also depressed turnout of poor people in general.

The civil rights movement of the 1960s addressed the problems associated with the disenfranchisement of blacks. Two important products of this movement were the Twenty-fourth Amendment and the Voting Rights Act of 1965. The **Twenty-fourth Amendment**, passed in 1964, outlawed poll taxes by making unconstitutional any law that made payment of a tax a voting eligibility requirement in federal elections.[4] The Voting Rights Act of 1965 denied states the right to use literacy tests as a requirement for voting; it also provided African Americans with protection from intimidating tactics that had been used to keep them away from the polls.

The past century also witnessed the enfranchisement of women. Though passage of the Fifteenth Amendment in 1870 granted African American men the legal right to vote, women would not receive the same constitutional guarantee until 1920 with the passage of the **Nineteenth Amendment**. In 1848, some 200 delegates—women and men—met in Seneca Falls, New York, to issue a call for women's rights, including the right to vote. The Civil War years diverted the nation's attention from women's rights to other pressing problems.[5] Attempts to include a women's right to vote in the Fifteenth Amendment proved unsuccessful, although women began voting in some states well before passage of the Fifteenth Amendment. By the late nineteenth century, some of the new western states, such as Utah, Wyoming, Colorado, Idaho, Washington, and California, enacted women's suffrage laws. Despite continued opposition from leaders, including President Woodrow Wilson and many states in the Northeast, popular sentiment and a well-organized lobbying effort eventually led to the passage of the Nineteenth Amendment.

Three other groups have successfully won the right to vote through federal legislation and constitutional amendment. Until the early twentieth century, Native Americans had neither citizenship nor voting rights; but federal laws passed in 1924 made it illegal for states to deny Native Americans the franchise. In 1961, the **Twenty-third Amendment** to the Constitution gave residents of the District of Columbia the right to vote in presidential elections. Because the District is not a state, its residents had not been allowed to participate in presidential elections. The Twenty-third Amendment allocates electoral votes to the District using the same formula by which electoral votes are allocated to a state: the total number of representatives it would have in the House, if it were a state, plus two. Today, the District of Columbia has a total of three electoral votes. In 1971, in the midst of the Vietnam War when many young Americans were dying in battle, Congress passed and the states ratified the **Twenty-sixth Amendment**, which lowered the voting age to eighteen in all local, state, and federal elections.

Fifteenth Amendment
The amendment to the Constitution that guaranteed the franchise regardless of race, color, or any previous condition of servitude.

Poll tax
The requirement that individuals pay a fee before being allowed to vote.

Literacy test
The requirement that individuals prove that they can read and write before being allowed to vote.

Twenty-fourth Amendment
The constitutional amendment that outlaws poll taxes.

Nineteenth Amendment
The constitutional amendment that guarantees women equal voting rights.

Twenty-third Amendment
The constitutional amendment providing electoral votes to the District of Columbia, thus giving District residents the right to vote in presidential elections.

Twenty-sixth Amendment
The constitutional amendment that lowered the voting age to eighteen in all local, state, and federal elections.

Although the administration of election and voting rules is largely controlled by the states, a significant number of federal laws and constitutional amendments have extended voting rights in the United States. Collectively, these laws prevent states from discriminating against particular groups of citizens with respect to their right to vote. Unfortunately, racism and other forms of discrimination continue to exist and thus continue to affect voting rights in America. Subtle forms of discrimination, including intimidation tactics by groups such as the Ku Klux Klan, may scare individuals into not voting. But more overt discriminatory tactics, supported by some state and local laws, have largely been erased. As a society the United States, over many years, has progressed toward the democratic ideal of universal suffrage. Today in the United States, the only adults legally disenfranchised are convicted felons in prison (forty-seven states), on probation (twenty-nine states), and on parole (thirty-two states).

Voter Registration Laws

Just as the extension of the franchise has evolved over the years, so has the system of voter registration. Most states today have voter registration systems in which individuals must qualify in order to become eligible to vote. The responsibility for qualifying lies with the individual. States do not compile and maintain a list of individuals who are eligible to vote. Rather, individuals must take it upon themselves to demonstrate their qualifications and file the appropriate paperwork to become eligible.

Massachusetts, in 1800, was the first state to require individuals to register to vote.[6] A handful of states followed Massachusetts's lead, but not until after the Civil War did most states adopt voter registration systems. Many of the voter registrations systems that were adopted between the 1870s and the early 1900s made it harder for immigrants, the less educated, and those less familiar with the political system to vote. A leading force behind the institution of voter registration systems was the populist movement of the late nineteenth century, which largely included white, middle-class, native-born Americans. In the northern states, registration laws were intended to make it more difficult for new European immigrants to vote; in the West, the intention was to make voting by new Chinese and Japanese immigrants more difficult; in the South, registration was aimed at limiting the black vote; and the source of concern in the Southwest was Mexican immigrants. Most states today still rely on some form of self-initiated voter registration, which continues to present an obstacle to voting for some people. A person must first find out how to register, remember to register in advance of Election Day, and then spend time registering. Many states require proof of age and citizenship, and many also impose a length-of-residence qualification, requiring a potential voter to prove that he or she has resided in the state for a specified period of time.[7]

A number of organizations and public interest groups have lobbied state legislatures and Congress to simplify and ease voter registration requirements in order to allow more people to vote on Election Day, including those who fail to register in advance of the election. North Dakota is the only state that does not currently require registration, and three states—Maine, Minnesota, and Wisconsin—permit voters to register on Election Day. The National Voter Registration Act of 1993, often called the **Motor Voter law**, mandates that when an individual applies for or renews a state driver's license, the state must also provide that individual with voter registration materials. The idea behind the law is that combining the process of registering to vote with the more routine task of obtaining a driver's license makes voter registration easier. Research suggests that although this law has increased voter registration, it has not increased actual turnout.[8]

Exercising the Franchise

A number of factors explain why people decide to cast a ballot on Election Day. An individual's interest in politics is one important factor. People who are more interested in politics tend to follow news about campaigns to a much greater degree than those who are less interested, and those who are more interested are more likely to vote.

★ LO Appreciate the wide diversity of voter registration systems implemented in the fifty states

Motor Voter law
The federal law that mandates that when an individual applies for or renews a state driver's license, the state must also provide that individual with voter registration materials.

★ LO Assess the influence of different factors in influencing voter turnout, including interest in politics, sense of civic duty, the perception that one's vote can make a difference, education, income, age, and social group pressures

AMERICAN GOVERNMENT In Global Perspective

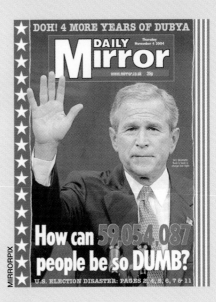

One British Newspaper Asks: "How Can 59 Million People Be So DUMB?"

The outcome of the 2004 presidential election—with George W. Bush winning reelection—was a source of frustration for many around the world. Many in other countries had questioned the U.S. use of military force in 2003 in Iraq without UN support. When it became clear that there were no weapons of mass destruction hidden in Iraq (a primary Bush justification for the war), President Bush became even more unpopular world-wide. The headline in the November 4, 2004, issue of the *Daily Mirror* placed emphasis on world skepticism of Bush's leadership and questioned the 59 million American voters who reelected Bush to another term as president.

Interest in politics, however, is only one factor that leads people to vote. Another is a person's sense of "civic duty," or the belief that being a good citizen requires one to vote. Many people who are not very interested in politics show up to vote nonetheless because they have a sense of civic duty.[9] From a young age, most Americans are socialized to believe that participating in elections is characteristic of the good democratic citizen, and so they feel an obligation to cast a vote even though they may not be particularly interested in elections and campaigns.

Another factor that influences some people to vote is the perception that their vote can have an impact on the outcome of an election. Individuals who feel strongly about a particular issue, set of issues, or a candidate may want to vote on the theory that if the election is close, their vote might actually make a difference in the outcome. Indeed, the sense that one's vote can make a difference contributes to higher turnout in elections that are perceived to be close.

Finally, for some people social group pressure can be a motivating factor in deciding to vote. Voting is often regarded as the "right" thing to do, and some people feel that casting a ballot is expected of them by others. This sense of social pressure to do what is acceptable by society's standards can increase the likelihood that a person will vote.

Who Turns Out to Vote?

An individual's interest in politics and attentiveness to news about politics and campaigns, sense of civic duty, and sense of political efficacy (that is, the belief that one's vote can make a difference) all lead to higher rates of **voter turnout**, which is the percentage of eligible voters who show up to vote on Election Day. In addition to these "political" factors that help to distinguish between citizens who are more or less likely to vote, there are a number of demographic characteristics that also help to explain turnout. A person's gender, age, and level of education are all related to the decision to vote (see Figure 14.2, p. 424).

In many elections, younger people tend to pass up the opportunity to vote at greater rates than middle-aged and older people do. Youth nonvoting is often attributed to the more transient nature of younger people's lives.[10] At about age eighteen, many

Voter turnout
The number of people who turn out to vote as a percentage of all those eligible to vote.

FIGURE 14.2 Differences in Voter Turnout among Demographic Groups in 2008 Presidential Election

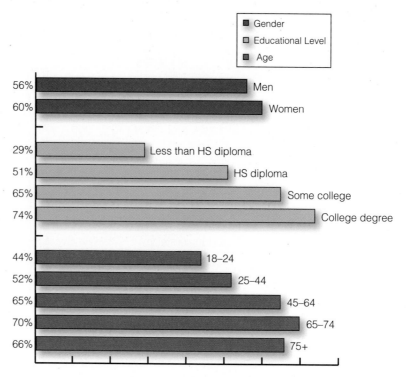

Source: Current Population Survey, U.S. Bureau of the Census 2008.

young people leave their parents' home to go to college or to take a job or to start their careers. Younger Americans are less rooted in a community, have had less time to register to vote, and are experiencing major changes in their social and personal situation. Voting tends to be less of a priority under these changing circumstances. As people age, buy a home, have a family, and reside in a particular community for a period of time, they become more socially attached and are more likely to vote.

Two other demographic groups are substantially more likely to vote—better-educated Americans[11] and wealthier Americans.[12] These two factors are related, because higher levels of education also lead to higher relative affluence and social status. The process of being educated sharpens a person's mind, improves the individual's ability to understand problems in society, and equips him or her to deal with complex information, such as the issues discussed in political campaigns. Education also enhances a person's appreciation for democracy and sense of civic duty. A better understanding of the issues and appreciation for the democratic process encourage higher levels of voter participation.

How Do They Vote? Methods of Casting a Ballot

Once a person decides to vote, there are several different ways in which a ballot can be cast. In the United States, five different methods of voting are generally used: (1) hand-counted paper ballots, (2) mechanical lever machines, (3) computer punch cards, (4) optical scan cards, and (5) electronic voting systems. Each of the fifty states has the authority to administer elections, and most states delegate most of the work to counties or other localities. In all, more than 10,000 jurisdictions at the county level or below are responsible for carrying out the important task of collecting and tabulating votes.

Paper ballots were the only method of voting used in the United States during the first 100 years of the nation's history. Originally the paper ballots used were produced by a political party and listed only the candidates belonging to the party

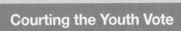

Courting the Youth Vote

Candidates and political parties often try to increase turnout as a means of enhancing their candidates' prospects in an election. However, nonpartisan organizations may engage in special efforts to encourage the so-called youth vote in particular. These organizations may target young voters primarily for two reasons: (1) young voters represent the future of American democracy, and (2) youth turnout has tended to be lower than turnout among older Americans. Even in 2008—when youth vote increased substantially as compared to past presidential elections—barely more than half of eligible voters aged eighteen to twenty-nine voted, leaving that group well behind turnout rates of the electorate as whole (more than 60 percent or more of eligible Americans voted in 2008).

Among the many organizations that run programs to encourage young voters to exercise their voting rights are the following:

- Rock the Vote, which claims to have registered more than 2 million new voters in 2008 alone;

- 18 in '08, which provides programs on college campuses and produces documentaries that encourage youth voting and other political participation;

- CIRCLE (Center for Information and Research on Civic Learning and Engagement), which conducts research on the dynamics of young people's voting behavior (see www.civicyouth.org);

- YouthVote.org, a Web site that provides a plethora of information for young people to learn how to register to vote and why it is important to do so.

For Critical Thinking and Discussion

1. Have you ever been approached by a group or organization asking you either to register to vote or to turn out to vote in a particular election?

2. Did they make a special appeal to you on the basis of your age? How important was that appeal in your decision to vote (or not vote)?

3. Why do you think college-age students turn out in relatively lower numbers?

---

that produced the ballot. On Election Day, the party would make the ballot available to the voter, who would then place it in the ballot box. In 1856, many jurisdictions began using a form of the paper ballot known as the "Australian secret ballot," which lists all the candidates for each office being contested, and voters then choose which candidate they prefer. (The other four methods of voting also employ the characteristics of the Australian ballot: all possible choices are displayed for all offices, the voter marks choices through some mechanism, and those choices are secret.) Paper ballots are still currently used in about 3 percent of precincts, mostly in rural areas.

The first real technological advance in voting technologies came with the introduction of the *lever voting machine* in 1892. A voter enters a voting booth and chooses candidates listed on a posted ballot by pulling a lever. The votes are recorded by advances in a counting mechanism that are made when the voter leaves the booth. The lever machine does not require a paper ballot and does not require (or allow) manual counting of ballots. When the polls close, poll workers simply read the numbers recorded by the counters. About 22 percent of precincts currently use lever machines.

Punch cards, which debuted in 1964, were the first computerized method of vote counting. Voters record choices by punching holes in appropriate locations on a card. These cards are computer readable. The piece of card that is punched out is called the *chad*. Unlike lever machines, the punch cards may be saved as a record of the vote, and manual recounts of the actual votes are possible. The punch card system is the most widely used in the United States, with about 37 percent of precincts using this method. Much of the controversy regarding the Florida vote for president in 2000 dealt with the issue of whether a "hanging" chad (a chad that had been punched but was still clinging to the punch card by a fiber) should be counted as a legal vote.

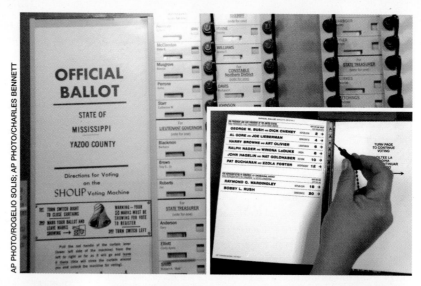

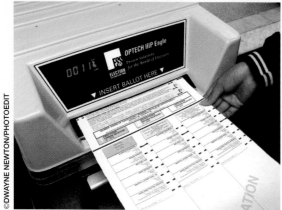

Clockwise from top left: the traditional paper ballot method of casting a vote, a mechanical voting lever machine, the computer punch card method of voting, the touch-screen computer ballot, and optical scanning card technology.

Optical scan ballots are a method of voting based on the same technology as that used to grade standardized tests such as the SAT. Given a paper card and a pencil, voters mark their selections by filling in boxes or ovals on the card. The ballots are then scanned by a computer for vote tabulation. As with punch cards and paper ballots, a permanent record of the vote is kept and is available for manual counting. About 25 percent of precincts use optical scan voting systems.

Electronic voting is similar to lever machine voting in that it involves no paper record of the individual votes; however, the technology is much more sophisticated. Voters select candidates from a ballot, which may be posted on the voting machine or displayed on a computer screen. Typically, voters make their choices by pushing a button or touching the computer screen, then submit their selections by pushing a specific button. The votes are stored in the computer. Write-in votes are entered via a keypad. About 7 percent of precincts use electronic voting systems.

In addition to these five main voting methods, several other methods are currently under development. One is Internet voting, which would allow voters to cast their ballots online using their personal computer (as long as the computer had online access) to vote. At present, the biggest obstacle to implementing Internet voting systems is ensuring authenticity and anonymity in the voting process.

Why Don't People Vote?

Despite the numerous factors that motivate people to vote, many in fact do not vote. Voter turnout is a measure of how engaged Americans are in voting in any given election contest. High turnout is considered a healthy sign for a democratic system. It implies that people are engaged in political issues, spend the time to contribute to the system, and take responsibility for selecting leaders. Lower turnout is often viewed as a by-product of alienation, mistrust, and lack of confidence in the political system.

Economist Anthony Downs originally offered an explanation for nonvoting based on a theory known as *rational choice*.[13] He argued that voters might decide not to vote because they reason that the costs of obtaining and understanding information about candidates and campaigns outweigh the benefits of making a vote choice. It is a rational choice, therefore, to decide not to vote, or to vote on the basis of certain "shortcuts" such as a candidate's political party.

Elections are plentiful in the United States and are held for many different offices at many different levels of government. Turnout varies from one type of election to another. Some elections draw much more media attention and thus engender more interest than others. Some feature much more political advertising and so provide more cues to voters. Some elections are inherently viewed as more important and so inspire a greater sense of civic duty among voters.

In 1966, political scientist Angus Campbell and his colleagues identified five factors that distinguish between "high stimulus" elections (in which turnout tends to be higher), and "low stimulus" elections (in which turnout is generally lower).[14] The factors that characterize a high stimulus election are (1) greater levels of media coverage, (2) higher significance of the office, (3) campaigns in which voters assign high importance to an issue, (4) more attractive candidates, and (5) perceptions of a close race. Campbell and his colleagues argue that events external to voters may stimulate interest in elections and thus increase the likelihood that individuals will turn out to vote on Election Day. For example, when big issues such as war and peace are at stake, people are more likely to take an interest in the election and vote.

Presidential elections tend to produce the highest levels of turnout because (1) they are heavily covered by the media; (2) there is more spending on political advertisements, particularly on television, thus making the campaign more visible to voters; and (3) the presidency is the most significant office in the U.S. political system. In presidential races where an issue important to many voters is at stake, such as problems with the economy in 1992 or the Vietnam War in 1968 or the war with Iraq and terrorism in 2004, turnout tends to be especially high. Races for higher office typically deal with bigger issues and feature candidates who are more attractive to voters. For these reasons, turnout in presidential races, and to a lesser extent in contests for U.S. senators and state governors, tends to be higher than turnout in elections for lower state offices and local races.

A well-documented trend from 1960 through 2000 was the declining rate of voter turnout in U.S. elections. Prior to 2004, turnout hovered around 50 percent for eight presidential elections. In fact, the election of 1996 marked the first time since 1908 that turnout actually dipped below the 50 percent mark, with only 49.1 percent of Americans of voting age going to the polls. For the past two presidential elections, however, voter turnout has trended upward (60 percent in 2004 and 58 percent in 2008). Voter turnout is lower in midterm congressional elections (that is, the congressional elections that occur midway through a president's term). Forty-one percent of American adults cast a ballot in the 2006 elections.

Figure 14.3 (p. 428) depicts the trend in voter turnout for presidential elections covering the past half century. It shows that the downward trend in turnout from 1960 through 2000 has been reversed, with turnout in 2004 reaching the 60 percent level.

★ LO

Analyze the trends in U.S. voter turnout over the past six or seven decades

Voting in the United States Compared with Other Democracies

Many observers of elections note that voter turnout rates are lower in the United States than they are in other democracies. From 1992 through 2000, the average turnout rate in the United States for presidential elections was 52 percent. Over the same period, the average turnout rate in all federal elections (including midterm congressional races) was 45 percent. During roughly the same period of time, turnout in other nations, as shown in Figure 14.4 (p. 429), was much higher.[15]

★ LO

Compare and contrast voter turnout in the United States with voter turnout in other democracies

FIGURE 14.3 Voter Turnout in U.S. Congressional and Presidential Elections

The following shows trends in voter turnout from 1960 through 2008 for presidential year elections and midterm congressional elections.

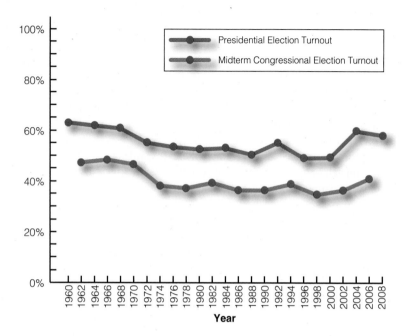

Several explanations have been offered to account for both the lower turnout rates in the United States compared to other democracies as well as the trend toward declining rates of turnout in the United States over the past half century:

1. **There are a large number of elections in America, making the opportunity to participate less of a novelty.** U.S. turnout rates may be lower than those in other democracies of the world simply because there are so many elections held in the United States.[16] The U.S. system of federalism produces several layers of government—national, state, and local. At the federal level, elections are held for president, the Senate, and the House of Representatives. At the state level, there are gubernatorial races as well as elections for other statewide offices, including attorney general, state treasurer, and other state agency heads. At the local level, there may be elections for mayor, city council, sheriff, local judges, and so on. Furthermore, for many of these offices there are two elections: a primary election to elect the party candidate and a general election to determine the office winner. Also, in many states and localities there are often special elections on referendum questions and bond issues. Opportunities for participation in elections in the United States are so plentiful that they have become commonplace events. The vast number of elections may help explain lower rates of voting in any one contest. Switzerland, which also has a large number of elections, also has relatively low turnout compared to other democracies.

2. **Tuesdays are workdays.** Traditionally, most elections in the United States have been held on Tuesdays. Most working people work on Tuesday, and so it may be inconvenient or difficult for many voters to find the time to vote on this day. People report having less and less free time in our society, which can account in part for declining turnout. In many other countries, elections are held on weekends or over a period of a number of days, making it easier for people to find the time to cast a vote.

3. **Voting in the United States usually requires advance registration.** As described earlier in this chapter, voters in most U.S. states are required to register to vote prior to Election Day. In other countries, voter registration is often

automatic; that is, citizens of legal age are automatically registered to vote. Thus voters simply need to show up at the voting place on Election Day. In countries where registration is automatic, 100 percent of eligible voters are thus registered; in the United States, where registration is usually a separate process, typically about 70 percent of eligible individuals have registered to vote.

4. **Over the past fifty years, perceptions both that participation can make a difference in what government does (that is, voters' sense of "internal efficacy") and that government is responsive to the people ("external efficacy") have declined.** Many researchers have concluded that the decline in political efficacy,[17] which is accompanied by declines in political trust and in confidence in political institutions, has produced lower rates of voter turnout. As people come to feel that they are less able to influence the system and that the system is less responsive to them, they may become less likely to vote.

5. **Extensions of the franchise lead to short-term declines in turnout.** Ironically, events that have expanded the franchise have been followed by lower rates of voter turnout. Following passage of the Fifteenth Amendment in 1870, which enfranchised former male slaves, the turnout rate dropped in 1872; passage of the Nineteenth Amendment in 1920, granting women the right to vote, led to an overall drop in turnout; and passage of the Twenty-sixth Amendment in 1971 that lowered the voting age to eighteen led to lower turnout rates. One explanation for this phenomenon is that many newly eligible voters are not yet registered to vote and may require some time and socialization to get into the habit of voting.

6. **Voting in the United States is not compulsory.** Some democracies, including the United States, regard the franchise as a right.

FIGURE 14.4 Voter Turnout around the World

Voter turnout varies a great deal from one country to another. This figure depicts average voter turnout from 1991 through 2000 in a number of the world's democracies. The turnout rates are expressed as the percentage of the voting age population that actually voted in national elections. For the United States, the percentage includes both presidential and midterm congressional elections.

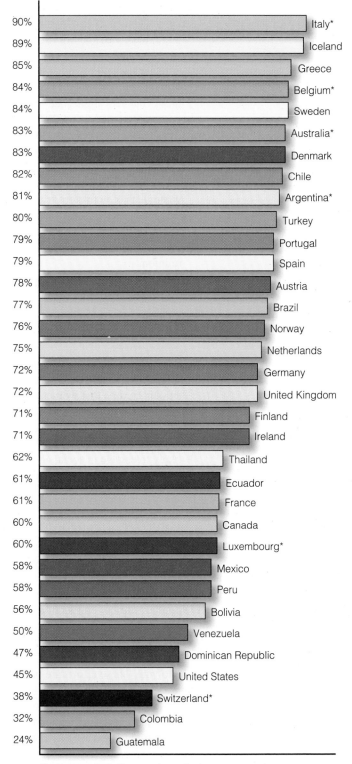

90%	Italy*
89%	Iceland
85%	Greece
84%	Belgium*
84%	Sweden
83%	Australia*
83%	Denmark
82%	Chile
81%	Argentina*
80%	Turkey
79%	Portugal
79%	Spain
78%	Austria
77%	Brazil
76%	Norway
75%	Netherlands
72%	Germany
72%	United Kingdom
71%	Finland
71%	Ireland
62%	Thailand
61%	Ecuador
61%	France
60%	Canada
60%	Luxembourg*
58%	Mexico
58%	Peru
56%	Bolivia
50%	Venezuela
47%	Dominican Republic
45%	United States
38%	Switzerland*
32%	Colombia
24%	Guatemala

*Denotes a country that has compulsory voting laws.

Source: International Institute for Democracy and Electoral Assistance.

Accordingly, citizens have the opportunity to exercise their right to vote or they may choose not to vote. By contrast, some democracies have compulsory voting laws requiring citizens to vote. These nations assert that voting is a citizen's responsibility. Belgium, in 1892, was the first country to adopt compulsory voting. According to the International Institute for Democracy and Electoral Assistance, thirty-two countries have compulsory voting laws on the books. Twenty-four countries enforce these laws to some degree, and of them, nine—Australia, Belgium, Cyprus, Fiji, Luxembourg, Nauru, Singapore, Switzerland, and Uruguay—have strict enforcement policies.

Punishments for not voting in countries with compulsory voting laws include large fines, possible imprisonment (although imprisonment is generally the punishment for not paying a fine), and disenfranchisement. In Belgium, individuals who do not vote in four elections over a fifteen-year period are stripped of their voting rights. In Bolivia, voters are given vouchers after they vote, and these vouchers are needed to receive a salary from a bank during a three-month period after an election. In Greece, it is very difficult to get a passport or driver's license without showing proof of having voted.

Many arguments can be made in favor of or against compulsory voting laws, but one thing is certain: countries with compulsory voting laws have much higher turnout rates than countries without such laws. In Italy, for example, where lists of nonvoters are publicized, turnout has been around 90 percent. Though compulsory voting laws certainly increase turnout, many critics argue that the right to vote implicitly includes the right not to vote, just as the right to practice the religion of one's choice also includes the right not to practice a religion.

7. **There has been a decline in "social capital."** Political scientist Robert Putnam has noted a general decline in **social capital**, which is the extent to which individuals are socially integrated into their community.[18] Over the past half century, Americans have become less socially connected because they are not as likely to be members of organizations such as political parties, labor unions, civic groups, or even bowling leagues. As reasons for this decline, Putnam cites the increase of women in the workforce and corresponding reduction in the amount of time that women have available to spend on social and community activities. Other factors for the decline include the increase in residential mobility, and technological innovations like radio, television, and the Internet. People today are more likely to stay home and watch TV or surf the Internet and less likely to engage in social activities with other people. Voting is, in part, a social activity. The decline in social capital may be responsible, at least in part, for the general decline in voting.

Is Nonvoting a Problem?

Although turnout has declined, the American political culture encourages people to vote. Over the years, voting has evolved from a privilege offered to a relatively few number of people to a right enjoyed by all. The League of Women Voters, Common Cause, and other groups regularly engage in campaigns to increase voter registration and stimulate turnout on Election Day. Candidates often stress the importance of voting, and the nation's educational system promotes the values of exercising the franchise, even to those not yet of age to vote. Even the television station MTV invested time and money into the popular "Rock the Vote" campaign to encourage young people to vote. These efforts are predicated on the assumption that voting is important and that, conversely, nonvoting is problematic.

So to what extent is low voter turnout a problem in our democracy? Two main arguments support the contention that nonvoting is problematic. The first holds that low voter turnout rates are a symptom of a weak democracy. The essence of what makes a democracy is the link between what a majority of citizens prefer and those who are given the authority to govern. Voting is the mechanism that creates this link.

Social capital

The "social connectedness" of a community, or the extent to which individuals are socially integrated into their community.

© 2012 CENGAGE LEARNING

With low turnout, majorities of all citizens do not rule. When barely 50 percent of eligible voters cast ballots, successful candidates can hardly claim to have captured majority support. George W. Bush won the 2000 presidential election, for example, but less than 25 percent of all American adults voted for him.

The second argument contends that low turnout awards distinct advantages to the affluent, higher-socioeconomic groups in our society. As we have seen, turnout rates are lower among less educated and lower-income groups. Thus, nonvoting affords better-educated and wealthier groups of people more power in determining the winner of a political race.

There are also reasons, however, why nonvoting may not be a cause for concern. Perhaps nonvoting produces an electorate that is more informed, more aware of the important issues, and better able to make vote choices for the candidates who most deserve election to office. Former Senator Sam Ervin once said, "I don't think it's a problem that apathetic, lazy people don't vote." Voting simply for the sake of voting may not produce good choices. Though ideally all citizens should become informed and cast a vote based on their information, many people lack the capacity or interest to cast a truly meaningful vote.

Another reason why nonvoting may not be a problem rests on the premise that voting is a voluntary right, just as the rights of free speech, religious choice, and peaceful assembly are voluntary. Our society does not compel citizens to speak out on issues, to declare a religious affiliation, or to contribute time or money to any particular cause or political party. So why should it expect people to exercise their right to vote? Furthermore, for many people nonvoting may be their expression of satisfaction with the status quo.

Making a Vote Choice

Understand the various factors that explain vote choices ★ LO

After an individual registers to vote and makes a decision to vote, the final phase of the voting decision is to make a choice among the candidates who are running for office. In covering American politics, the news media spend a tremendous amount of time and resources analyzing how voters will vote in a contest, particularly in presidential elections. For this reason, preelection polling has become a centerpiece of American political campaign strategy as well as news coverage (see Figure 14.5, p. 432). Years before a presidential election takes place, media polls query American voters on the potential candidates and assess the level of support voters offer these candidates. Months before the election, daily tracking polls monitor how voters are thinking and changing from day to day.

Likewise, political scientists' primary focus of research on American political behavior is on how voters make up their minds about who they will vote for. Research has identified a number of different factors that act as cues to individual voters in helping them make a vote decision. Collectively, these factors are referred to as "determinants of vote choice."

Candidate Familiarity

The most basic voting cue is simple name recognition and familiarity with a candidate. Many voters pay little attention to politics and political campaigns. Recognizing the name of a candidate on a ballot, then, offers an important voting cue. If voters recognize one candidate's name and no others, they are much more likely to vote for the name they recognize. Likewise, the more familiar voters are with a candidate, the more likely they are to vote for that candidate. In lower-visibility elections, such as primaries and local elections, name recognition plays a large role in the voting decision. However, even in statewide and presidential races (particularly presidential primaries), familiarity with a candidate can be an important cue to voters. High name recognition and voter familiarity propelled George W. Bush to the top of the pack in the Republican presidential primaries during the 2000 campaign. High name recognition of former first lady Hillary Clinton allowed her to gain

FIGURE 14.5

Accuracy of the Gallup Poll in Predicting Voter Behavior

Preelection polls offer candidates, journalists, and voters detailed information on the dynamics of an election contest. How well the polls actually predict vote choices is a frequently voiced concern. One of the best-known opinion polls in the United States is the Gallup Poll, which has been conducting preelection polls since the 1936 presidential election. This figure shows Gallup's prediction for the percentage of the vote that the winner would receive in each presidential election from 1936 to the present, along with the actual percentage of the vote that the winner got on Election Day. Only once did Gallup make an incorrect prediction—in 1948, it predicted that Dewey would defeat Truman.

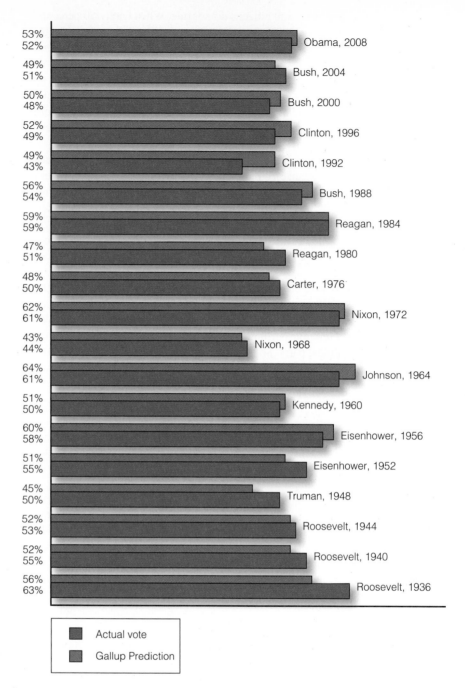

	Actual vote
	Gallup Prediction

Source: The Gallup Organization. ©1936–2008 The Gallup Organization.

frontrunner status early on in the race for the 2008 Democratic presidential nomination. In many congressional House races, incumbents tend to win reelection at rates in excess of 90 percent in large part because voters recognize their names and are less familiar with the challengers.

Party Identification

Political parties play many important roles in the American political system. Often voters form a psychological attachment to a party that helps them organize their political information and offers an important cue to vote choice. As discussed in Chapter 13, party identification is the term for this psychological attachment to a political party. Party identification tends to be a long-term predisposition—once it is

Television Presidents Paving the Way for Voter Open-Mindedness

When Barack Obama became the first African American to take the oath of office as U.S. president in 2009, he overcame racial barriers thought to be impenetrable just two decades earlier, when many voters dismissed Jesse Jackson's run for the presidency as a sideshow. Still, those among the tens of millions who watched Obama's inauguration as the forty-fourth president should be forgiven if the whole thing seemed a bit . . . *familiar*. Consider that on October 29, 2002, almost six years before Obama's election victory, viewers of the popular Fox series *24* were greeted by a television breakthrough of sorts, when African American character actor Dennis Haysbert was introduced in his new role as U.S. President David Palmer. More than four years later, on January 14, 2007, *24* fans were introduced to the sight of yet another African American president: this time it was David Palmer's brother Wayne (played by D. B. Woodside).

Other historical breakthroughs in television's depiction of the American presidency are notable as well. On May 14, 2007, the fictional Latin American Congressman Matthew Santos (played by Jimmy Smits) was sworn is as the new U.S. president in the final episode of the critically acclaimed drama series *The West Wing*. Women presidents have also appeared in prime time, both in the short-lived 2005 drama series *Commander in Chief* (Academy Award–winning actress Geena Davis played President Mackenzie Allen), as well as in the seventh season of *24*, when Allison Taylor (played by Cherry Jones) became the latest fictional chief executive.

For his part, Dennis Haysbert has argued that his role as an African American president may have actually benefited Barack Obama: "If anything, my portrayal of David Palmer, I think, may have helped open the eyes of the American people." This may be a case of reality not so much mimicking popular culture as being influenced by its more open-minded mores.

For Critical Thinking and Discussion

1. What role does race or gender play in voters' assessments of candidates?

2. Can a fictional television series influence the way voters think about real-life candidates and their political viability? If so, how?

3. Do historical electoral breakthroughs (such as the election of the first African American or woman as president) require that voters first undergo a fundamental change in attitudes?

Pictured above are Dennis Haysbert as President David Palmer on *24*, Geena Davis as President MacKenzie Allen on *Commander-in-Chief* and Jimmy Smits as President Matthew Santos on *The West Wing*.

Source: Simon Reynolds, "Haysbert: '24' President Helped Obama," Digitalspy.com, July 2, 2008.

formed, it usually remains with an individual over the course of his or her life. Party identification, then, is an important determinant of vote choice.[19]

Party identification is particularly powerful in influencing a vote decision in lower-profile political races: those in which no particularly serious issues are at stake, the candidates are not well-known, and the news media pay little attention to covering the race. In such contests, those who identify with a political party are most likely to turn out to vote, and those who turn out usually vote for the candidate associated with their political party.[20]

For example, elections for the House of Representatives tend to be lower profile than presidential or Senate races. Among the 435 congressional districts across the country, more than 350 are considered to be "safe seats" for one of the two major parties. Safe seats are districts where the party affiliation of the voters is so one-sided that the candidate who wears that party's label is virtually assured of victory.

It should be noted, however, that overall party identification and its impact on vote choice have been in a state of decline.[21] Over the past fifty years, voters have become less likely to identify as either a Democrat or a Republican, and more likely to say that they are independent. Decline in confidence in the political parties, campaigns that are more focused on the candidates than on the candidate's party, and increased television news coverage of campaigns are cited as primary reasons for the drop in party identification.

Still, two thirds of voters continue to identify with one of the major parties, and thus party identification remains the single best predictor of how an individual might vote in an election. Identifying with a partisan perspective provides a shortcut for voters in making candidate choices. More broadly, party identification enables people to more readily make sense of their political world.

Issue Voting

For voters who identify themselves as Democrats, the Democratic Party's candidate is likely to hold an issue position that they favor; the same is true for voters who identify as Republicans. For voters who identify themselves as independents, however, a candidate's party does not serve as a determinant of vote choice. For these voters, a candidate's position on a particular issue or set of issues is a voting cue.

Voting on the basis of issues is more likely to occur in certain types of elections.[22] First, when a particular issue captures the attention of many people in the electorate, voters are more likely to use a candidate's position on that issue to form a vote decision. For example, in the 1968 presidential race, American involvement in the Vietnam War was a central concern for many voters, and many voted on the basis of the two candidates' positions on the war.[23]

Second, issue voting occurs more often when an issue is of particular personal concern to a voter. In 2008, for example, American voters were concerned about a poorly performing economy and the crisis on Wall Street, and thus many cast a vote on the basis of the candidates' proposals for addressing the economic crisis. Third, issue voting is much more likely to occur when the candidates hold clearly distinct positions on issues.

Anthony Downs's rational choice approach to understanding voting turnout also applies to making a vote choice. Downs suggested that in making a choice, voters examine the issue positions of the candidates and assess how close they are to the voters' own positions. The candidate whose positions on the issues are closer to the voter's earns the vote.

Issue voting is often regarded as the most sophisticated type of voting behavior. Notions of the "ideal democratic citizen" describe such a person as someone who is informed about issues, has developed a position on those issues, and then compares that position to the positions of the candidates. Voting on the basis of such a calculation requires political knowledge and attentiveness to campaigns. Though issues remain important to many voters and take on higher levels of importance under certain circumstances, most research indicates that other shortcut factors, such as party identification, are more commonly used to make choices.

The Top Ten and Bottom Ten Popular Vote Winners in Presidential Elections

The ten presidential election winners who received the highest percentage of the popular votes:

✔	1.	Lyndon Johnson	Democrat	1964	61.3%
✔	2.	Franklin Roosevelt	Democrat	1936	60.8%
✔	3.	Richard M. Nixon	Republican	1972	60.6%
✔	4.	Warren G. Harding	Republican	1920	60.4%
✔	5.	Ronald Reagan	Republican	1984	59.0%
✔	6.	Herbert Hoover	Republican	1928	58.2%
✔	7.	Franklin Roosevelt	Democrat	1932	57.4%
✔	8.	Theodore Roosevelt	Republican	1904	57.4%
✔	9.	Andrew Jackson	Democrat	1828	56.0%
✔	10.	Ulysses S. Grant	Republican	1872	55.6%

The ten presidential election winners who received the lowest percentage of the popular vote:

✔	1.	John Quincy Adams	National Republican	1824	30.5%
✔	2.	Abraham Lincoln	Republican	1860	39.8%
✔	3.	Woodrow Wilson	Democrat	1912	41.9%
✔	4.	Bill Clinton	Democrat	1992	43.2%
✔	5.	Richard Nixon	Republican	1968	43.4%
✔	6.	James Buchanan	Democrat	1856	45.3%
✔	7.	Grover Cleveland	Democrat	1892	46.1%
✔	8.	Zachary Taylor	Whig	1848	47.4%
✔	9.	Benjamin Harrison	Republican	1888	47.9%
✔	10.	Rutherford B. Hayes	Republican	1876	48.0%

Retrospective Voting

In issue voting, a voter assesses the candidates' issue positions and casts a vote based on which candidate the voter thinks will do a better job in dealing with that issue in the future. However, a voter's past experience with a candidate or a political party also can be an important determinant of vote choice. **Retrospective voting**, a concept developed by political scientist Morris Fiorina, posits that evaluations of incumbents' past performance in office provide important cues for voters in deciding whether to vote for that incumbent.[24] Voters who believe that an incumbent has done a good job are likely to vote for the officeholder, whereas if they judge that an incumbent's job performance has been poor, they are likely to vote against the officeholder. Voter assessments of the economy and the performance of the president in handling economic conditions are especially important in a voter's retrospective evaluation of an incumbent. Bill Clinton's victory over incumbent George H.

Retrospective voting

An explanation of vote choice that asserts that voters' evaluations of a candidate's past performance in office provides an important cue for vote decisions.

W. Bush in the 1992 presidential election was largely the result of voters' negative evaluations of Bush's handling of the nation's economy. Likewise, Ronald Reagan's defeat of incumbent President Jimmy Carter in 1980 was based on voters' perception that Carter performed poorly in dealing with economic problems and the Iranian hostage crisis.

In retrospective voting, the evaluation of the incumbent provides the determination of vote choice. In other words, a voter's assessment of the incumbent's job performance provides a shortcut decision rule on voting for or against the incumbent. Pollsters often measure this assessment through a "job approval rating" question. The percentage of voters who approve of the incumbent's job performance often reflects the percentage of the vote that the incumbent receives in a reelection bid.

Candidates for office often try to encourage voters to think retrospectively, if it is in their strategic interest to do so. In the 1980 presidential campaign, while the nation was experiencing economic problems and an extended international crisis with hostages being held in Iran, challenger Ronald Reagan defeated incumbent Jimmy Carter in part by asking the voters, "Are you better off today than you were four years ago [before Carter took office]?" Similarly, in 1992, challenger Bill Clinton questioned the integrity of President George H. W. Bush by repeating a TV clip of the president saying "Read my lips, no new taxes"—a pledge Bush had made in 1988 but did not keep.

Candidate Image Voting

The image, personal traits, and other characteristics of the particular candidates in a campaign can also influence the way people vote. Especially in higher-stimulus elections, where candidates make ample use of television advertisements to build an image, voter perceptions of candidates' qualities are important. Perceptions of candidate image include such characteristics as honesty, trustworthiness, leadership ability, concern for voters, integrity, intelligence, and sense of humor.

Candidates for office who have more favorable images than their opponents among voters tend to fare much better in election contests. In eleven of the thirteen presidential elections between 1952 and 2000, the candidate who had the higher "image score" from questions asked on the American National Election Survey won the election. The two exceptions were 1960, when John Kennedy and Richard Nixon shared an identical score in a very close election that Kennedy won, and in 1984 when Walter Mondale and Ronald Reagan shared an identical score (Reagan went on to a decisive victory).

In today's media age, candidates have found that image development is an efficient means of persuading swing voters how to vote. Thus, candidates often use television advertising to build their own favorable image or, conversely, to depict their opponents as having negative image characteristics. Visual images on television are useful in conveying symbolic, image-oriented messages. Bill Clinton in 1996 built a successful campaign around a theme that he would continue to improve the nation's economic future (his theme was captured in the slogan "building a bridge to the twenty-first century"). Ronald Reagan in 1984 cemented his strong leadership image in his campaign for reelection (with the TV ad slogan "It's morning again in America").

★ LO   Appreciate the many forms of political participation beyond voting, including communicating concerns to officials, civil disobedience, and protest activities

Political Participation Beyond the Voting Booth

Though voting tends to be the most popular form of political participation in the United States, it is by no means the only way Americans participate. In a 2000 survey conducted by the National Election Study, about 1 percent of people questioned said they had themselves run for political office, about 2 percent said they had participated in a political protest, and the same percentage said they had attended a political meeting. About one in twenty Americans report having contributed money to a political candidate or party and only slightly more have displayed campaign materials on themselves (for example, worn a campaign button) or their property (for instance, put a bumper sticker on their car). More common forms of nonvoting participating include writing a letter to or contacting a public official and belonging to a political organization, with about 30 percent of Americans claiming to do each.

Though all of these forms of political participation enrich American political culture, activities that protest something often gain the most visibility. One recent protest movement that gained a national following is the so-called Tea Party movement. Beginning in early 2009, a series of anti-tax protests emerged in response to the federal government's increase in spending to combat the economic recession. The Tea Party protests challenged the Barack Obama-Democratic Party policies of deficit spending and proposals to reform the nation's health care insurance system. The term *Tea Party* was chosen strategically to reference the Boston Tea Party, whose goal was to protest Britain's taxation policies toward the colonies during the American Revolutionary period. "TEA" is also used as an acronym for "taxed enough already." In addition to organizing protest rallies across the nation (annually on April 15, or "tax day," for example), Tea Party organizers were particularly active during the summer and fall of 2009 in voicing their concerns at congressional Democrats' constituent meetings promoting health care reform proposals.

The Tea Party also influenced a number of congressional races in the 2010 midterm elections. The movement helped conservative Republicans such as Rand Paul (R-KY) and Marco Rubio (R-FL) coast to general election victories in the Senate. At the same time, some Tea Party-supported candidates who won their GOP primary election against more moderate Republican candidates (such as Christine O'Donnell, who defeated the more moderate governor, Mike Castle, in the primary) were defeated in the general election.

Protests can take one of three forms: legal protests in which citizens play by the "rules of the game" to speak out against a government policy, acts of nonviolent civil disobedience, and illegal protest activities that often include violence.

Marches, sit-ins, and rallies are forms of legal protests; such activities are designed to call attention to an issue that the protesters feel is not receiving adequate attention in the standard political process. Protesters are exercising their First Amendment right "peaceably to assemble and to petition the government for a redress of grievances." Many legal peaceful protests have raised awareness of an issue to a level that forces the normal legislative process to address it. A number of protest movements paved the way for substantial changes in public policy. Protests against the Vietnam War, for example, during the late 1960s and early 1970s led, in part, to American withdrawal from the Vietnam War. After World War I, protests among women's groups demanding the right of women to vote led to the adoption in 1920 of the Nineteenth Amendment granting women suffrage. Successful

AP PHOTO/ED REINKE

Republican U.S. Senate candidate Rand Paul addresses supporters at his primary election victory celebration in Bowling Green, KY, on May 18, 2010. Paul, who was backed by the Tea Party movement, went on to win in the general election and now represents Kentucky in the Senate.

JUSTIN SULLIVAN/GETTY IMAGES

Members of the Tea Party movement protest outside a hotel in San Francisco before President Obama arrives for a fundraiser on May 25, 2010.

© 2012 CENGAGE LEARNING

protests are often begun by small groups of individuals who feel strongly about an issue and are willing to spend the time and effort to make their case.

Protests make for good television because they generally feature conflict, a grievance, and individuals who are outspoken about the particular cause. Well-organized groups who engage in protests on hot-button issues, such as environmental groups, pro-life or pro-choice groups, and anti–death penalty groups, have become adept at informing the news media about the protests ahead of time and engaging articulate speakers to make their case. The media attention often provides protesters an opportunity to ensure that their causes reach the policy agenda of governing institutions.

The second type of protest behavior, *civil disobedience*, involves protesters engaged in illegal but nonviolent activity. The goal of the protesters is to break laws that they feel are unjust, and the protesters willingly accept the consequences for breaking the law. Blacks protesting segregation laws in the southern states during the 1950s and 1960s would intentionally break those laws as a way of drawing attention to the problem of segregation.

Finally, a third type of protest behavior involves violent protests. In 1992, a number of rioters in south central Los Angeles took to the streets after a jury acquitted several white police officers in a case where the officers had been caught on videotape brutally beating a black man they had stopped for a traffic violation. The rioters were protesting accusations of racial bias in the Los Angeles criminal justice system. The protesters looted businesses, stopped traffic, pulled a white truck driver out of his vehicle and severely beat him, and caused much damage to property.

Making the Connection

Barack Obama, like John F. Kennedy, inspired historic numbers of Americans to participate in the political process by casting their ballots. In both 2008 and 1960, these young energetic candidates mobilized millions of new and first-time voters. Their emergence on the political scene altered the political landscape by tipping the balance of the turnout among certain demographic groups (Obama's candidacy increased turnout among African Americans, while Catholics rushed to the polls to vote for Kennedy) and thus shifted the White House from one party to another. While voter turnout does not often exceed the 60 percent mark as it did in 1960 and 2008, majorities of adult Americans do regularly participate in presidential elections every four years, and in doing so they help influence decisions about the future of the country.

Americans participate not only by voting in elections. As in the historic elections of 1960 and 2008, millions of Americans regularly participate in rallies for political candidates, contribute money to interest groups and political campaigns, and donate time to political causes that are of concern to them. Outside of elections, many Americans regularly write letters to the editor, post entries on political blogs, sign petitions, and speak to their elected officials. Participation is part and parcel of the American political culture.

POLITICS InterActive!

Genetics and Political Participation

For decades political scientists have used empirical methods to unwrap the mysteries of why some people participate in politics and others do not. "Rational choice" theorists have used a cost-benefit analysis to explain such participation, based on the premise that if the perceived costs outweigh the perceived benefits, an individual will "sit out" an election. Others have used social-psychological explanations such as the perceived benefits of group membership, the strength of a person's attachment to a political party or candidate, and the level of interest in the campaign or the candidates. Still others have focused on such additional factors as sense of civic duty, proximity to the polling place, and barriers to registration. Some of the research has identified patterns of participation, but no clear and convincing factors have been identified that consistently explain participation with any large degree of confidence.

Some recent research, however, may hold the key to unlock the mystery of political participation. A study released by a group of political scientists in 2008 found a strong relationship between an individual's genetic makeup and his or her propensity to participate in politics. The research found that individual genetic differences account for a significant amount of variation in political participation, even after controlling for the effects of many of the more common factors researchers have associated with participation, such as education, age, income, socialization factors, and attitudes. The researchers—James H. Fowler, Laura A. Baker, and Christopher T. Dawes—discussed the findings of their study in an article entitled "Genetic Variation in Political Participation," published in the May 2008 issue of the *American Political Science Review*. In conducting their study, the researchers examined a national panel of over 800 twins, along with nearly 400 twins in southern California. They discovered that a wide variety of types of political activity, including running for office, attending political rallies, and contributing money to candidates and parties, could be partially explained by genetic factors.

On www.cengage.com/dautrich/americangovernment/2e, find the Politics InterActive link for details on the role of genetics and political participation. Consult as well the various links that relate to biological factors and politics. Historical, popular, and global perspectives on the issue are also presented.

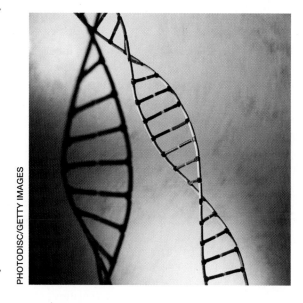

PHOTODISC/GETTY IMAGES

Chapter Summary

★ The Legal Structure for Voting in the United States

- Traditionally, the states and not the federal government have had authority in running elections. However, state attempts to disenfranchise certain groups have been thwarted by constitutional amendments and federal laws. Although the goal of universal suffrage may not be fully realized today, over the centuries the United States has moved closer to this goal.

- The constitutional amendments that have limited states' ability to disenfranchise voters include the Fifteenth Amendment (guaranteeing African American men the franchise), Nineteenth Amendment (women's suffrage), Twenty-fourth Amendment (outlawing poll taxes), and Twenty-sixth Amendment (guaranteeing the vote to those eighteen years of age).

- States are responsible for maintaining a system of voter registration, and the systems vary widely from state to state. Only one state (North Dakota) does not require voters to register to vote as a prequalification to voting. Through the Motor Voter law, the federal government has tried to encourage higher levels of voter registration.

★ Exercising the Franchise

- Among the factors that have been identified as relating to a citizen's propensity to vote are interest in politics, sense of civic duty, the perception that one's vote can make a difference, level of education, level of income, age, and social group pressure.

- The nature of the times and type of political campaign can also influence turnout. High stimulus elections, in which the issues are very important or the races are more visible, tend to produce higher voter turnout. Presidential elections generally promote the highest levels of turnout, and the less visible local races inspire the lowest levels of turnout.

- Although there has been a general declining trend in voter turnout in the United States over the past six or seven decades, recent presidential and midterm congressional elections have seen a modest increase in voting. This may be the result of voter concerns about U.S. military involvement in Iraq.

- Voter turnout in the United States tends to be lower than turnout in other democracies. Reasons that account for the lower U.S. turnout are the fact that there is no compulsory voting in the United States, the wide variation in states' voter registration requirements, the vast number of U.S. elections, and the tradition of holding elections on one weekday.

★ Making a Vote Choice

- A number of factors serve to explain the vote choices that voters make. These "determinants of the vote" include name recognition and candidate familiarity, party identification, the convergence between candidate issue positions and voter issue preferences, retrospective evaluations of the candidates' past performance, and voter assessment of the personal characteristics of the candidates.

★ Political Participation beyond the Voting Booth

- Though voting provides the critical link between people and government output in a representative democracy, there are many other ways that citizens participate beyond voting, ranging from writing or contacting an official about a concern, to civil disobedience and protest activities.

CourseMate

Key Terms

Fifteenth Amendment (p. 421)
Franchise (or suffrage) (p. 419)
Literacy test (p. 421)
Majoritarianism (p. 418)
Motor Voter law (p. 422)
Nineteenth Amendment (p. 421)
Poll tax (p. 421)

Representative democracy (p. 418)
Retrospective voting (p. 435)
Social capital (p. 430)
Twenty-fourth Amendment (p. 421)

Twenty-sixth Amendment (p. 421)
Twenty-third Amendment (p. 421)
Universal suffrage (p. 419)
Voter turnout (p. 423)
Voting (p. 418)

Resources

Important Books

Alvarez, R. Michael, and Thad Hall. *Electronic Elections: The Perils and Promises of Digital Democracy*. Princeton, NJ: Princeton University Press, 2008.

Conway, M. Margaret. *Political Participation in the United States*. Washington, DC: CQ Press, 2000.

Flanigan, William H., and Nancy H. Zingale. *Political Behavior in the American Electorate*, 12th ed. Washington, DC: CQ Press, 2009.

Niemi, Richard, Herbert F. Weisberg, and David Kimball. Controversies in Voting Behavior, 5th ed., Washington DC: CQ Press, 2010.

Patterson, Thomas E. *The Vanishing Voter: Public Involvement in an Age of Uncertainty*. New York: Alfred A. Knopf, 2002.

Rosenstone, Steven J., and John Mark Hansen. *Mobilization, Participation and Democracy in America*. New York: Macmillan, 1993.

Teixeira, Ruy A. *The Disappearing American Voter*. Washington, DC: Brookings Institution Press, 1992.

Internet Sources

http://www.electionstudies.org/ (home to the American National Election Study, which includes survey data on voter opinion and behavior for national elections since 1952)

http://www.fairvote.org (Web site of the Center for Voting and Democracy; includes a host of articles, data, and information on voting rights and voting turnout)

http://www.cawp.rutgers.edu/ (Web site for the Center for American Women and Politics at Rutgers University; contains data, program information, and fact sheets on the role of women in elections and voting)

http://www.generationvote.com (Web site containing information on voting and participation geared toward younger voters)

15 Campaigns and Elections

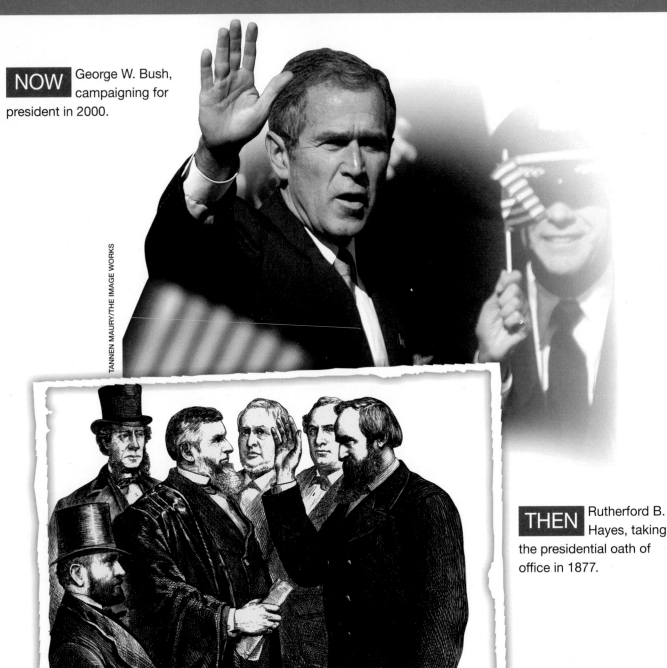

TANNEN MAURY/THE IMAGE WORKS

NOW George W. Bush, campaigning for president in 2000.

THEN Rutherford B. Hayes, taking the presidential oath of office in 1877.

CORBIS

NOW &THEN

The Stolen Election?

All the experts were predicting a close election. The sitting president was not running for reelection, and so he would not play any visible role in the campaign. Politics, including the campaign itself, had been particularly divisive, due in part to heightened partisan tensions on Capitol Hill. Electorally, the partisan differences broke down by geography, as North and South lined up behind different candidates. But the hard-fought campaign finally ended, and Election Day drew to a close. All that remained was to count the votes and determine which candidate would be the next president. But Election Day came and went, and weeks passed following that first Tuesday in November without a declared winner. The Democratic Party's candidate had won the popular vote, but in presidential elections the Electoral College vote determines the winner. The vote margins in several states were very close, particularly in Florida. Voting irregularities in that state were the subject of considerable concern. The Electoral College outcome depended on the resolution of these voting disputes and the recount of the vote in certain districts, including some key districts in Florida. Ultimately, it was the U.S. Supreme Court, and that body's Republican appointees, that decided the election: by the Court's ruling, the new president would be the Republican Party candidate—and not the Democratic Party candidate who had received more popular votes. Millions of Americans were left frustrated with a process that seemed to only marginally reflect the public's will.

LEARNING OBJECTIVES
★ WHAT YOU WILL LEARN ★

American Presidential Elections
in Historical Perspective

★ Understand the current system for choosing U.S. presidents

★ Trace the historical evolution of the presidential selection process

The Prenomination Campaign

★ Assess the role of the prenomination campaign and the "invisible primary" in winnowing the field of candidates

The Nomination Campaign

★ Identify the function of primaries and caucuses, and explain how the timing of those contests plays a role in the outcome of the nomination process

★ Describe the role of national party conventions

The General Election Campaign

★ Compare and contrast incumbent races and open elections

★ Assess the various factors that contribute to the selection of vice presidential running mates

★ Analyze strategic campaign objectives that focus on securing a winning coalition of states

★ Evaluate the role of televised presidential debates and television advertising

★ Explain the Electoral College system

Campaign Funding

★ Understand the impact money has on presidential campaigns, and recognize the laws governing campaign finance

Congressional Campaigns and Elections

★ Assess the power of incumbency in congressional elections

★ Explain why turnout levels vary in presidential elections and midterm elections

★ Identify and define the "coattail effect" of presidential elections

CourseMate

NOW & THEN

A judge evaluates a questionable ballot due to a "hanging chad" after the 2000 presidential election in Florida.

RHONA WISE/AFP/GETTY IMAGES

NOW   George W. Bush, the Republican Party candidate for president, was not declared the winner of the November 7, 2000, presidential election until more than a month had passed. Democrat Al Gore won the popular vote by about 500,000 votes. But on the evening of the election, with a number of states showing very close presidential races, the outcome of the electoral vote remained in question.

The campaign had been an especially hard-fought contest. The sitting president, Bill Clinton, played only a minimal role in the campaign, as the Gore campaign feared the scandals that rocked Clinton's second term might hurt Gore as well. Politically, the nation was largely divided along partisan lines, with Democrats providing the basis for Gore's coalition in the Northeastern states and Republicans contributing the strongest block for Bush in the South. The vote margins were close in a number of states—New Mexico, New Hampshire, Oregon, and Pennsylvania, to name a few. But the closest race, and the one that eventually became mired in controversy regarding voting irregularities, was in Florida with its twenty-five electoral votes.

In the weeks following Election Day, as votes in that state were recounted, lawyers for both the Bush and the Gore campaigns filed suits over how to count partially punched out paper ballots that still contained confetti-like bits of paper (the so-called hanging chads). Florida's Republican Secretary of State, Katherine Harris, reported directly to Governor Jeb Bush, the brother of George W. Bush; she also had been George W. Bush's Florida campaign co-chair the year before. Not surprisingly, Harris formally certified the results of the Florida vote in favor of George W. Bush before the recounts were concluded. Eventually, it was the court system, and in particular the U.S. Supreme Court, that decided the controversial election. By a 5–4 decision (the five justices in the majority were all conservatives appointed by Republican presidents), the Court ruled that the vote recounts must cease and that Harris's vote certification would stand.

THEN Some 124 years earlier, the election of 1876 was similarly mired in controversy, with many observers later referring to it as the "stolen election."[1] Like the 2000 campaign, the 1876 contest was expected to be close. The sitting president, Ulysses S. Grant, whose administration was plagued by political scandals, stayed clear of the campaign. Partisan differences that lingered after the Civil War remained a source of tensions in the reconstructed United States. Northern states provided the foundation of an electoral coalition for the Republicans whereas southern states amassed a voting bloc for the Democrats. The popular vote count across the nation gave Democratic candidate Samuel Tilden a 250,000-vote margin over Republican candidate Rutherford B. Hayes. Disputes over the vote counts in several states, including South Carolina, Louisiana, and especially Florida, left the winner of the contest in doubt for more than two months after Election Day.

Each candidate claimed that he had won the popular vote in Florida; the Democratic electors sent one set of Electoral College vote counts to the U.S. Senate, and the Republican electors sent their own vote count. The Republican-controlled Senate appointed a commission, with an equal number of Democrats and Republicans, plus one "neutral" Supreme Court Justice (who happened to be a Republican). The commission, by one vote, awarded all of the disputed electoral votes to Hayes, the Republican, who was declared the winner.

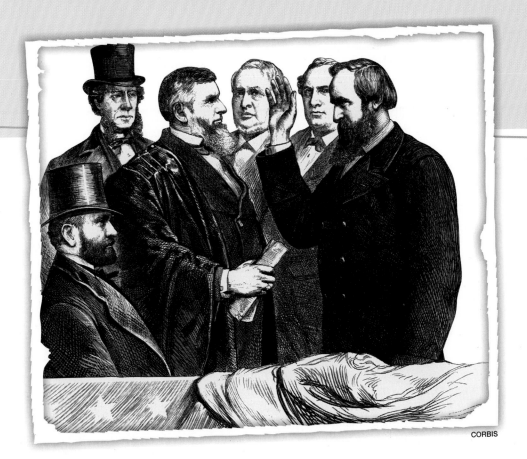

CORBIS

T he U.S. Constitution calls for a presidential election every four years and congressional elections every two years. Without skipping a beat, the United States has met this constitutional requirement for more than two centuries. Through a Civil War, two world wars, and several major economic depressions, elections—the hallmark of American democracy—have taken place like clockwork.

In designing this representative democracy, the Founders intended a system that demanded accountability from elected officials. Elections for president and Congress provide this accountability. Regular and free elections are the linchpin underlying democracy in America. Every year Americans are invited to cast ballots in elections for many local, county, and statewide races, but no election receives more attention than the race for the presidency.

★ LO   Trace the historical evolution of the presidential selection process

American Presidential Elections in Historical Perspective

The U.S. Constitution says nothing about political parties or the process by which individuals become candidates for the presidency. The Founders assumed that electors, chosen by the states (and heavily influenced by the House of Representatives), would identify and evaluate potential candidates, and then the Electoral College would select the chief executive.[2] Parties, or "factions" were frowned on; the selection of president was intended to be the product of a select group of rational, wise men making choices at a lofty level above partisan politics.

Although their intentions for presidential selection were noble, the Founders' expectations about how a president would actually be chosen proved to be quite naïve. Political parties, though weaker today than in the past, have provided the framework for presidential elections since 1796. Each of the two major parties holds nomination contests in the fifty states to select the party's candidate in the general election; the nominees compete in the general election.

The presidential selection process that has evolved over the past two centuries of U.S. nationhood is long and complex. The manner in which the 2008 selection process occurred was not based on some elaborate constitutional design. Rather, this complicated and quirky process is the result of more than 200 years of modification and evolution. Over the years, two distinct phases of the presidential selection process have developed: the nomination phase and the general election phase.

The Nomination Phase

★ LO   Understand the current system for choosing U.S. presidents

In the nomination phase of the presidential election process, the political parties select specific people to run as the presidential and vice presidential candidates in the general election. This duo is referred to as the "party ticket." The Constitution did not account for a nomination phase because the Founders did not anticipate that a two-party system would emerge. The first two presidential elections did not even include political parties. Rather, the electors from the states all agreed that George Washington should be president in 1789 and again in 1792. Nevertheless, divisions within the federal government erupted and political alliances began to form during Washington's administration. These alliances resulted in the first two major political parties, the Federalists and their opponents, who eventually became known as the Democratic-Republicans. In 1796, when Washington decided not to seek a third term, each of these parties sought to win the presidency by recruiting and supporting candidates.[3]

The Federalists in Congress supported John Adams and the Democratic-Republicans threw their support to Thomas Jefferson. Electors, who were largely chosen by state legislatures, followed the cues of their partisan leadership in casting their electoral votes, and Adams, the Federalist-supported candidate, won the general election with seventy-one electoral votes, whereas Jefferson received sixty-eight electoral votes. The nomination process in 1796 reflected a significant level of party discipline in the casting of ballots among electors. In the elections of 1800, 1804, and 1808, both the Federalists and the Democratic-Republicans used informal meetings and discussions

AMERICAN GOVERNMENT In Global Perspective

A U.S. Presidential Candidate Captures the Imagination of Foreigners

Egyptian political scientist and former parliamentarian Mona Makram Ebeid attended the 2008 Democratic National Convention in Denver, Colorado. Upon his return to Egypt, he wrote a piece in the *Egypt Daily News* (on October 7, 2008) calling Barack Obama a charismatic leader in a nation that represents the world's "emotional centrality."

. . . Obama has thrived in his career by turning campaign stops into emotional experiences. He has thrived also because of big crowds and small donors. At his convention speech, he looked like a star of a rock concert and the crowd responded accordingly. Attendees chanted, danced and shook miniature American flags in unison. His speech hit the kind of emotional high notes that have thrilled his followers. I believe that this success was due to his cleverly setting himself as a breakthrough candidate who was uniquely well placed to "turn the page of history" at a moment when so many voters are frustrated with the Bush administration's record of failures and alarmed at the prospect of American decline . . .

The rapt faces of attendees at the 2008 Democratic National Convention in Denver reflect the historical moment as Barack Obama becomes the first African American to win the nomination for president from one of the nation's two major political parties.

The U.S. presidential elections are watched with passion around the world not because of America's power but because of its emotional centrality. . . . The rest of the world would certainly embrace a less fearful and more open post-9/11 America. Choosing Barack Obama, a symbol of hope, would do more to restore the image of the United States in the world than anything else. A rejection of the promise he represents would be a symptom of that nation's historical decline. . . .

to choose a party nominee. Democratic-Republicans dominated electoral politics from 1812 through 1828, as the Federalist Party eventually disappeared.

In 1824, however, a significant split occurred within the Democratic-Republican Party. Andrew Jackson, who had the support of many common people, challenged party favorite John Quincy Adams. Jackson won both the popular vote and a plurality of the electoral vote, but no candidate received a majority of electoral votes. By constitutional provision, the election was sent to the House of Representatives, which voted Adams the victor. Jackson then founded a new party, the Democratic Party,[4] which is, of course, one of the two major parties still in existence today. Jackson and his followers believed in the enfranchisement of all white men, rather than just the propertied class—during what became known as the Jacksonian era, white male suffrage was dramatically expanded throughout the country. Specifically, more and more state political parties adopted open caucuses, in which party members formally met to provide input as to who their party should nominate for elective office.

Electoral reforms during the Progressive era of the early 1900s opened participation in the nomination process to a greater number of Americans. The direct primary gave voters an opportunity to cast a ballot for delegates, who would in turn be sent to a national convention for the purpose of choosing a presidential nominee. The state of Florida was the first to hold a direct primary in a presidential election, in 1900. Although direct primaries did allow greater numbers of people the opportunity help select delegates, until the 1960s it was still the political elite of a party (governors, mayors, party chairs, and other officials) that selected most of the delegates and thus had the most input in choosing the party's presidential nominee.

The political unrest of the 1960s, spurred by anti–Vietnam War activism, led to further changes that gave voters in primaries even more weight in selecting party nominees. Benefiting from the increased percentage of convention delegates chosen through open primaries, Jimmy Carter, the little-known governor of Georgia, won the Democratic Party's nomination in 1976. A political outsider, Carter was able to appeal directly to average voters. Carter not only won the nomination, but he also went on the win the presidency that year. His victory demonstrated to candidates in both the Democratic and Republican parties that securing sufficient numbers of delegates to win the nomination requires direct appeals to voters, whether through party caucuses or, more likely, through party primary contests.

The General Election Phase

The unanticipated emergence of political parties not only established a nomination process, but it also forced a change in the Founders' design for selecting presidents. The Founders intended the state legislatures to pick well-qualified "electors," who would meet on a specified day in their state to decide who was the best choice to become president. At the end of the day, these electors would then cast votes for president. The states then sent their vote totals to the president of the U.S. Senate (the sitting vice president), who counted the votes before Congress. The candidate with a majority of votes became president, and the second-place finisher became vice president. If no one candidate received a majority of the votes, the election was to be decided by the House of Representatives with each state delegation having one vote to select the new president. The Senate was to select the vice president.

In the 1800 presidential race, nearly all of the Federalists voted for John Adams and Charles Pinckney (sixty-five and sixty-four votes, respectively) and all of the Democratic-Republicans voted for Jefferson and Aaron Burr, each of whom received seventy-three votes. Although it was generally agreed that Jefferson was the leader of the Democratic-Republican ticket, Burr challenged Jefferson in the House (because the election was a tie, the House state delegations had to choose the new president). Ultimately the House decided in favor of Jefferson, who became president, with Burr then becoming vice president. It was clear that the presidential election system needed fixing.[5]

The Twelfth Amendment to the Constitution, passed in 1804, provided for separate balloting for president and vice president by requiring that electors designate one of their two votes for president and the second of their two votes for vice president. This amendment greatly reduced the possibility that future elections would end in a tie.

Several other amendments to the Constitution have altered the presidential selection process. The Twenty-second Amendment, ratified in 1951, limits presidents to two four-year terms in office (or ten years if a vice president serves out the term of a president). The Twenty-third Amendment, ratified in 1961, provides the District of Columbia with three electoral votes. Because the District is not a state, it has no senators or voting members in the House.

The modern presidential selection system, then, is an amalgamation of the Founders' design, modified by constitutional amendments and changes that occurred over time. This all makes for a complex system of picking a president. Although there are many caveats and exceptions to the rules, the contemporary presidential selection process generally consists of five stages:

1. **The prenomination campaign.** After a new president is selected, potential candidates for the next presidential election (four years hence) begin to explore the possibility of running. The ability to raise money, garner support from key leaders in the party, and attract the attention of the news media all contribute to each candidate's decision of whether to enter the race.

2. **The nomination campaign.** From January through June of the presidential election year, parties in each state hold either a primary or caucus in which the party delegates from the state commit to candidates. Each party has different criteria for allocating the number of delegates that a state will get. The candidate who receives a majority of delegates wins the party nomination.

AMERICAN GOVERNMENT In Historical Perspective

The Comeback Kids of Presidential Elections

Losing a presidential election can be an enormous letdown, but it hasn't stopped a number of high-profile losers from making a comeback. Six men who lost a general election contest have come back to be elected president.

In 1796, Thomas Jefferson lost a bitter campaign to John Adams by only three electoral votes. But Jefferson came back to defeat Adams in 1800 and win reelection in 1804.

In 1808, James Monroe lost his bid for the White House in the nomination process, but then went on to win the 1816 election and ran unopposed in 1820 (the only other presidential candidate to run unopposed was George Washington).

In 1824, Andrew Jackson lost his initial bid for the presidency to John Quincy Adams in a contest that was decided by the House of Representatives (because no candidate received a majority of electoral votes). But in 1828, Jackson came back to defeat Quincy Adams and then won reelection in 1832.

In 1836, William Henry Harrison unsuccessfully ran for the presidency (he was defeated by Martin Van Buren). But like Jackson and Jefferson before him, Harrison avenged his loss with another run at the man who defeated him and won the election of 1840. Harrison never had the opportunity to run for reelection because he died a month after taking office.

In 1884, Grover Cleveland won the election, but was defeated by Benjamin Harrison (William Henry Harrison's grandson) in 1888. Cleveland and Benjamin Harrison ran again in 1892, and this time Cleveland defeated Harrison, thus becoming the first and only chief executive to serve two nonconsecutive terms.

In 1968, the "comeback kid" was Richard Nixon, who had served eight years as vice president under President Dwight Eisenhower. In 1960, Nixon ran against John F. Kennedy and lost. Nixon then ran for governor of California, but lost that race as well. Despite Nixon's quip to the press after his gubernatorial loss that "you won't have Nixon to kick around anymore," he won the Republican nomination in 1968 and defeated Hubert Humphrey in a very close contest. Nixon won reelection in 1972 by a landslide, but midway through his term was forced to resign as a result of the Watergate scandal.

3. **The national conventions.** Each political party holds a national convention during the summer to showcase their candidate. Prior to the convention, the candidates select their vice presidential running mates. Although the conventions used to play an important role in defining the party platform and selecting the party's nominee, today the conventions are largely publicity events for the ticket and other stars in the party, as well as an opportunity to critique the opposing party.

4. **The general election campaign.** Because national party conventions today generally affirm rather than choose party nominees, presidential candidates usually begin waging their general election campaigns before the conventions, as soon as it becomes clear who will be the two major-party nominees. (These decisions generally occur some time in spring of the election year.) Most recent campaigns have included a series of televised debates between the presidential and the vice presidential candidates and a significant amount of advertising and campaigning in key states.

5. **The Electoral College decision.** The winner of the presidential election is decided on the basis of the vote count in the Electoral College. The number of electoral votes for each state is equivalent to the state's allotment of House members plus two (for the state's two U.S. senators). In all but two states, the candidate who wins the popular vote automatically receives all of the electoral votes from that state. (Currently in Maine and Nebraska, the votes for president are counted for each congressional district; candidates get one elector for each district they win, and the candidate who wins the state overall gets an additional two electors.) Nationwide, the candidate who receives an outright majority of electoral votes wins the election.

President-elect Barack Obama and his wife Michelle, with their daughters Malia and Sasha, at the November 2008 election night rally in Chicago's Grant Park. Thousands of supporters gathered in the park to celebrate Obama's victory.

Prenomination campaign

The political season in which candidates for president begin to explore the possibility of running by attempting to raise money and garner support.

The Prenomination Campaign

Although the presidential campaign officially begins with the first state contest for delegates in January of the election year, the real campaign for president actually begins much earlier, soon after the previous presidential election has concluded. As part of the **prenomination campaign**, behind-the-scenes candidates who are thinking about making a run often begin to "test the waters" by talking to party insiders, shoring up early commitments of support, lining up a campaign staff, beginning a fund-raising operation, traveling around the country making speeches and appearances, setting up "exploratory committees" to assess the feasibility of making a formal declaration of official candidacy, and then making the official announcement. Shortly after the 2004 election, Senators John McCain, Barack Obama, and Hillary Clinton established exploratory committees and began raising money for their 2008 campaigns.

The prenomination campaign also marks the beginning of the "weeding out" process. Early on, many would-be candidates find insufficient support from party insiders. Others cannot raise sufficient funds to be competitive. Some tire too quickly of the arduous and time-consuming schedule necessary for launching a run for the presidency. These and other obstacles begin the process of narrowing the field of candidates.

In 2008, with no incumbent president or vice president in contention, more than ten candidates from each of the two major parties seriously explored their presidential prospects during late 2006 and early 2007.

The **invisible primary** is the competition between candidates seeking the party nomination for front-runner status. A candidate gains front-runner status by winning broad support from important people within the party, raising more money than others, and achieving top position in the public polls conducted by leading news organizations. Front-runners tend to receive more coverage in the news, thus promoting their name recognition and popularity as candidates.

Invisible primary

The competition among candidates seeking the party nomination for front-runner status prior to the primaries and caucuses.

CHIP SOMODEVILLA/GETTY IMAGES

Within the Democratic Party, the invisible primary leading up to the 2008 primaries and caucuses began as a battle primarily among former First Lady and U.S. Senator from New York Hillary Rodham Clinton, former North Carolina Senator and 2004 vice presidential candidate John Edwards, Illinois Senator Barack Obama, Delaware Senator Joseph Biden, Connecticut Senator Christopher Dodd, Governor Bill Richardson of New Mexico, and Ohio Congressman Dennis Kucinich. On the Republican side, the contest for the 2008 nomination shaped up chiefly as a battle among Arizona Senator John McCain, former Tennessee Senator Fred Thompson (who was also an actor on the popular television show *Law and Order*), former Massachusetts Governor Mitt Romney, and former New York City Mayor Rudolph Giuliani.

The fortunes of individual candidates can change in a hurry once the invisible primary has concluded. By the end of the invisible primary in 2007, it became clear that based on their fundraising and showing in the national polls, the three major contenders for the Democratic nomination would be Senators Clinton, Obama, and Edwards. On the Republican side, the invisible primary concluded with Romney and Giuliani at the top of the pack.

Left to right, former North Carolina Senator John Edwards, Illinois Senator Barack Obama, New Mexico Governor Bill Richardson, and New York Senator Hillary Rodham Clinton spar with each other during a debate among Democratic nominees early in 2008. While Edwards and Richardson struggled to win delegates, and thus bowed out of the nomination contest before it had formally concluded, Obama and Clinton continued to battle over the Democratic nomination all the way until June.

The Nomination Campaign

The invisible primary may go a long way toward winnowing the field down to a handful of realistic contenders for major-party nominations; still, as Mitt Romney and Rudy Giuliani learned in 2008, money and attention can go only so far—contenders for the presidency must ultimately deliver victories in state primaries and caucuses or risk seeing their financial and volunteer

AP PHOTO/CHARLIE NEIBERGALL

Fred Thompson, former senator from Tennessee and an actor on TV's *Law & Order*, campaigning for the Republican Party's presidential nomination in Iowa in October 2007.

Arizona Senator John McCain and former Massachusetts Governor Mitt Romney, here seen engaging in a testy dialogue during a debate among Republican presidential hopefuls in late 2007. McCain eventually defeated Romney and several other rivals to secure the 2008 Republican nomination. Once McCain's nomination was secure, Romney transformed from being McCain's foremost critic into one of his steadfast supporters and even garnered serious consideration from McCain for the vice presidential nomination later that summer.

AP PHOTO/MARK TERRILL

★ LO Identify the function of primaries and caucuses, and explain how the timing of those contests plays a role in the outcome of the nomination process

Presidential primary
A statewide election to select delegates who will represent a state at the party's national convention.

Open primary
An election that allows voters to choose on the day of the primary election the party in which they want to vote.

Closed primary
An election that requires voters to declare their party affiliation ahead of time.

Caucus
A method of choosing party nominees in which party members attend local meetings at which they choose delegates committed to a particular candidate.

support dry up in a hurry. Given the reduced importance of party conventions in influencing nomination decisions in the modern era, success in the earliest primaries and caucuses may be crucial.

Primaries and Caucuses

The nomination of a candidate by a political party is the product of state-to-state contests in which delegates are committed to those candidates seeking the party's nomination. There are two basic methods by which states allocate delegates: presidential primary elections and caucuses.[6] A **presidential primary** is a statewide election to select delegates who will represent a state at the party's national convention.[7] In this election, voters choose among delegates who are committed to a particular candidate. The delegates who win go to the national convention and cast their vote for a party nominee to run in the general election. In 2008, more than forty-five states used the presidential primary method of delegate selection. There are two types of primaries held by states. The less common approach is the **open primary**[8] in which voters can show up at the voting booth on the primary Election Day and declare whether they want to vote in the Democratic Party primary or the Republican Party primary; they then cast their vote in the primary they have chosen. A **closed primary**[9] election, by contrast, requires voters to declare a party affiliation ahead of time. When the voters show up to vote on primary Election Day, they are eligible to vote only in the party in which they are registered. Many states that use the closed primary have modified their requirements by allowing voters who have previously declared no party affiliation to show up at the polls on Election Day and declare a party, and thus vote in that party's primary.

A handful of states including Iowa, Nevada, and Maine do not hold presidential primary elections; instead they use the caucus method to select delegates for the national party convention. In the **caucus** method, party members are invited to attend local meetings at which they choose delegates who make a commitment to a candidate for the party nomination. These delegates in turn attend more regionalized meetings and select delegates from that group. Depending on the size of the state and the number of regions, this process continues until a slate of delegates attends a statewide convention, or caucus. At this statewide caucus, attendees again vote for a slate of delegates, who are committed to a candidate, to send to the party's national convention.

The first state contest for delegates, normally the Iowa caucus, launches the process by which delegates from the states commit to candidates for the party nomination. About one week after the Iowa caucus comes the New Hampshire primary,[10] which has traditionally been the first state primary election in which delegates commit to candidates.[11] Each of the fifty states (along with the District of Columbia, the U.S. Virgin Islands, American Samoa, and Guam) holds either a caucus or primary election, and in each of these contests delegates commit to candidates. The calendar of state caucuses and primaries, beginning in January and extending into June, is referred to as the nomination campaign. Through the **nomination campaign**, a candidate attempts to win a majority of delegates in the caucus and primary contests to lay claim to be the winner of the party's nomination.

The Traditional Importance of the Iowa and New Hampshire Contests

Iowa and New Hampshire are small states with relatively few delegates. The Iowa Democratic caucus in 2012 will have 52 delegates at stake, and the 2012 New Hampshire Democratic primary will have a total of thirty-one delegates at stake. To win the Democratic nomination campaign, a Democratic candidate needs to amass support from more than 2,200 delegates. In pure delegate count, larger states such as California with 448 delegates, Florida with 220, and New York with 276, are much more important. Why, then, do Iowa and New Hampshire enjoy such disproportionately great influence in the nomination process? The answer is timing. Iowa and New Hampshire have so much influence over the nomination campaign because they have traditionally been the first two contests held. The news media focus a tremendous amount of attention on these initial competitions. Winners of the Iowa and New Hampshire contests receive a great amount of attention in the news, whereas losers tend to get written off as "unelectable."

The importance of the early contests has led to a phenomenon known as **frontloading**,[12] a trend that has occurred over the past five or six presidential elections in which states have moved their primary or caucus contests earlier in the year to attract greater attention from the candidates and the media. A state that holds its contest early makes itself more important in the nominee selection process. In 1988, the time between the Iowa caucus and the date by which most states had chosen their convention delegates was more than twenty weeks.

In 2008, the majority of delegates were selected within a four-week period, from January 3 to February 5. The rush to move the contests earlier caused considerable confusion in the Democratic nomination race in 2008. In an attempt to ensure that New Hampshire would remain the first contest, the Democratic National Committee passed a rule that any state that moved its primary earlier than February 5 (Super Tuesday) would forfeit its delegates.

Nomination campaign
The political season in which the two major parties hold primaries and caucuses in all the states to choose party delegates committed to specific candidates.

Frontloading
The recent trend of states moving their primaries and caucuses earlier in the year to attract greater attention from the candidates and the media.

HULTON-DEUTSCH COLLECTION/CORBIS

Harold Stassen holds the record for most attempts to win a party nomination—ten. Stassen, a Republican governor of Minnesota, first attempted to win the Republican nomination in 1948. His tenth and final attempt was in 1992. In only two elections (1956 and 1972) between his first and last attempts was Stassen not a contender for the Republican nomination. Pictured here are Stassen supporters at the 1948 Republican convention.

TABLE 15.1 Tentative Schedule of Primaries and Caucuses for the 2012 Presidential Election (determined at the time this book went to print)

Primaries and Caucuses 2012	State
Monday, January 16	*Iowa caucuses*
Tuesday, January 24	New Hampshire
Saturday, January 28	*Nevada caucuses,* South Carolina
Tuesday, January 31	Florida
Tuesday, February 7 (Super Tuesday)	Alabama, California, Connecticut, Delaware, Georgia, Missouri, New Jersey, New York, Oklahoma, Tennessee, Utah
Saturday, February 11	Louisiana
Tuesday, February 14	Maryland, Virginia
Tuesday, February 21	Wisconsin, *Hawaii GOP caucuses*
Tuesday, February 28	Arizona, Michigan
Tuesday, March 6	*Minnesota caucuses,* Massachusetts, Ohio, Rhode Island, Texas, Vermont
Tuesday, March 13	Mississippi
Tuesday, March 20	*Colorado caucuses,* Illinois
Tuesday, April 24	Pennsylvania
Tuesday, May 8	Indiana, North Carolina, West Virginia
Tuesday, May 15	Nebraska, Oregon
Tuesday, May 22	Arkansas, Idaho, Kentucky
Tuesday, June 5	Montana GOP, New Mexico, South Dakota

Nevertheless, the states of Michigan and Florida both moved their primaries to January, disqualifying both states' primary outcomes, which had favored frontrunner Hillary Clinton. Ironically, the closeness of the ensuing race between Barack Obama and Clinton throughout the spring of 2008 meant that considerable attention would be paid to later contests held in Pennsylvania, North Carolina, and Indiana.[13]

For 2012, both major political parties have agreed to somewhat reverse the front-loading process. Specifically, no primary or caucus will occur prior to the Iowa caucuses on January 16. Also, only Iowa, New Hampshire, South Carolina, Nevada, and Florida will be allowed to hold contests before February. States that allocate their delegates proportionate to the vote outcome will be permitted to hold contests as early as the first Tuesday in March, as a way to encourage greater voter turnout. States that allocate all delegates to the contest winner (the "winner-take-all" states) may hold contests beginning on the first Tuesday in April. This plan is intended to spread out the primaries and caucuses, giving candidates more time to campaign in more states, and at the same time preserve the unique role that Iowa and New Hampshire have played in the nomination process. The tentative slate of contests can be seen in Table 15.1 (all contests are primaries unless otherwise noted).

★ **LO** Describe the role of national party conventions

The Nominating Conventions

The national conventions for the Democratic and Republican parties were once used to discuss the party platform and, most important, to choose the candidate who would represent the party in the general election. The images of the smoke-filled back rooms where deals were cut and delegates were lobbied to throw their support behind a particular candidate were very real. For most of our nation's history, the major parties selected candidates for the presidency in this way. Much of the brokering and deal making took place by skilled political operators at the national conventions.

The 1968 Democratic National Convention, held in Chicago, was characterized by a great deal of divisiveness and discord, much of which was captured on national network television. Vietnam War protesters outside of the convention hall were beaten by Chicago police under the direction of Chicago mayor and "political boss" Richard J. Daley.

AP PHOTO/MICHAEL BOYER

Chicago has been a frequent host to national party conventions. Twenty-five national conventions have been held in the Windy City, eleven Democratic and fourteen Republican. The second most frequent hosting city is Baltimore, which has seen ten conventions. The 1968 Democratic convention in Chicago was characterized by violent protests over the Vietnam War.

Tension reigned inside the convention center as well, with antiwar supporters of Eugene McCarthy and George McGovern clashing with the party regulars supporting Hubert Humphrey. Television brought the negative images of the divided Democratic Party into American homes, seriously damaging the Democratic ticket. Four years later, television coverage again captured a disunited Democratic Party at the national convention in Miami, where delegates fought into the wee hours of the morning to nominate a party nominee (George McGovern finally won the nomination. The Democrats were not the only party to suffer discord and division. In 1976, grassroots support for Ronald Reagan spoiled any momentum incumbent President Gerald Ford hoped to generate at the Republican National Convention.

By the mid-1980s, both major political parties, recognizing the influential role that television was playing in election politics, had begun to adjust their agenda for the national conventions. With the frontloading process allowing candidates to capture a majority of delegates prior to the national convention, the parties began to choreograph their conventions and use them as advertisements for the party ticket. Today's conventions tend to avoid airing any intraparty differences. Instead, they are "anointing" ceremonies for the party ticket. They feature popular members of the party endorsing the nominees and include prerecorded videos highlighting the nominees' record of public service and family values.[14]

At the 2008 Democratic national convention, for example, a video of Barack Obama's life highlighted his experience as a community organizer in Chicago and his commitment to his family. His wife and brother-in-law spoke on his behalf. Former President Bill Clinton and Senator Hillary Clinton added words of praise for the ticket, and vice presidential candidate Joe Biden delivered his own "prime time" speech promoting Obama. Likewise, speakers at the Republican National Convention touted John McCain's military service. His wife, Cindy McCain, offered a brief testimonial on his behalf as well, and McCain's vice presidential running mate, Sarah Palin, gave a stirring speech that was widely regarded as the highlight of the convention.

The 2012 GOP and Democratic nominating conventions remain important political events. Rather than playing a crucial role in selecting the party nominee and debating the policy positions of the party, however, these conventions provide a week-long forum for the parties and their nominees to introduce themselves to voters and to formally kick off the general election campaign.

The General Election Campaign

A number of factors provide context for understanding general election campaigns in the American political system. These include whether or not an incumbent is running, the candidate's pick for the number two spot on the ticket, the strategy for achieving a winning coalition of states, the presidential debates, political advertisements, and finally the vote in the Electoral College.

Incumbent Race versus Open Election

★ LO Compare and contrast incumbent races and open elections

General election campaigns for president are highly visible, very well funded, and among the most noteworthy of events in the American political system. Sometimes the contest is an **incumbent race**, or one between a sitting president and a challenger, such as the 2004 contest between President George W. Bush and challenger John Kerry. In an incumbent race, the focus of the campaign tends to revolve around the performance of the incumbent over the past four years. In this sense, incumbent races are often viewed as a referendum on the performance of the current occupant of the White House.

Incumbent race
General election race pitting a person currently holding the office against a challenger.

In all, there have been eleven incumbents who lost their bids for another term. Five of these incumbent losses occurred over the past 100 years: in 1912 Woodrow Wilson defeated President William Howard Taft; in 1932 Franklin Delano Roosevelt defeated President Herbert Hoover; in 1976 Jimmy Carter defeated President Gerald R. Ford; in 1980 Ronald Reagan beat President Carter; and in 1992 Bill Clinton defeated President George H. W. Bush.

In 2004, incumbent President George W. Bush touted his accomplishments and tried to convince voters that he was best able to lead in the war on terrorism, based on his response to 9/11 and military actions in Afghanistan and Iraq. Bush also claimed that the tax cuts he signed earlier in his term set the stage for a rebound to the national economy. In his campaign, Kerry harshly criticized Bush's "rush to war" in Iraq without building international support and without establishing a connection between Al Qaeda and Saddam Hussein. Kerry also blamed the policies of the Bush administration as the reason why the economy was still performing poorly. In incumbent races, the outcome often is determined on the basis of public evaluations of the incumbent. In the end, Bush's defeat of Kerry in 2004 was based on the president's ability to convince voters that he deserved another term in office.

In 1996, Bill Clinton ran for reelection against Republican nominee Senator Bob Dole. The huge economic boom of the middle 1990s along with a period of relative worldwide peace all but doomed the Dole campaign, as voters tended to reward the incumbent Clinton for the period of peace and prosperity that the nation was enjoying. Four years earlier, in 1992, President George H. W. Bush was not as fortunate, nor was President Jimmy Carter when he lost his bid for reelection in 1980. In both 1980 and 1992, consumer confidence was low and voters largely blamed the incumbents for the woes of the economy. In both of those contests, the incumbents were ousted.

The 2012 presidential contest is likely to pit the Democratic incumbent President Barack Obama against a Republican challenger, with Obama's record as president serving as the main focus of the campaign. At the time this book went to press, the list of possible Republican presidential contenders in 2012 was a long one, headed by former Governor Mitt Romney of Massachusetts, Governor Haley Barbour of Mississippi, former Governor Mike Huckabee of Arkansas, former House Speaker Newt Gingrich, former Pennsylvania Senator Rick Santorum, and former 2008 vice presidential candidate Sarah Palin.

Open election
General election race in which neither candidate is the incumbent. (Open elections for Congress are normally called "open seat elections.")

In **open elections**, neither candidate is an incumbent. Open seat elections tend to be far less focused on the past. In 2000, for example, Democrat Al Gore was the sitting vice president, running for president. Rather than trying to take credit for being part of the Clinton team, Gore chose to distance himself from Clinton to demonstrate that he was his "own man"—and to avoid being associated with the negative baggage of Clinton's presidency (namely the Monica Lewinsky scandal and Clinton's impeachment trial). Gore was eventually able to dissociate himself from Clinton, but in the end he was defeated by the Republican candidate George W. Bush.

YOUR PERSPECTIVE on American Government

Getting Involved in Political Campaigns

Politics is very much on the minds of college-age Americans today. In 2008, a record 35.6 percent of college freshmen said that they had frequently discussed politics in the past year. (The previous high was 33.6 percent in 1968, at the height of the Vietnam War.) In the most recent presidential campaign, college students were more interested and more active than ever before. Students who work on election campaigns may find themselves performing such simple tasks as stuffing envelopes or walking door-to-door to distribute leaflets. Those who are technologically savvy may assist campaigns in other ways—for example, by helping to create Facebook profiles or fan pages on the Internet. In 2008 College Republicans nationwide socially networked through a Web site called Student Tools for Online Republican Mobilization, or STORM. Have you ever volunteered time to work on a political campaign? About 11 percent of college freshmen in 2008 said they did. (This figure was up by about three percentage points from 2004.) More college freshmen also report that they are likely to engage in a political protest (6.1 percent in 2008, as compared to 4.9 percent in 1966).

For Critical Thinking and Discussion

1. Why do you think your peers were so energized about the 2008 presidential election?

2. Do you think college students' participation made a difference in 2008?

3. Do you think the trend toward increased college student participation will continue in the 2012 presidential race?

Note: Data presented are from "Presidential Race Raised Student Political Involvement" by Mary Beth Marklein in *USA Today*, January 22, 2009.

Even less common are presidential election contests when neither the incumbent president of the United States nor the incumbent vice president is actively seeking to win the White House. Because President George W. Bush was constitutionally prohibited from seeking a third term, and Vice President Dick Cheney declined to make a bid for the White House in his own right, the 2008 presidential election became the first in eighty years to feature a truly open-ended contest for the presidency. (Although neither President Harry Truman nor Vice President Alben Barkley was a major-party nominee in 1952, both pursued the Democratic nomination for a short period of time before dropping out of the race.) The last open-ended election before 2008 occurred in 1928, when neither President Calvin Coolidge nor Vice President Charles Dawes were ever serious candidates for their party's nomination.[15]

The Choice of a Vice Presidential Candidate

Another important aspect of campaign strategy is the selection of the vice presidential running mate. Significant amounts of thought and fanfare go into the selection. Vice presidential candidates are quite visible on the campaign trail and can provide a boost to the ticket. The choice of running mate often attempts to balance the ticket geographically; John Edwards, for example, was from the southern state of North Carolina, a factor deemed important by the 2004 Democratic nominee, John Kerry,

★ LO

Assess the various factors that contribute to the selection of vice presidential running mates

457

The vice presidential candidates in 2008 were Democrat Delaware Senator Joe Biden (top) and Republican Alaska Governor Sarah Palin (above).

AP PHOTO/CHARLIE NEIBERGAL

AP PHOTO/STEPHAN SAVOIA

who was from Massachusetts, a New England state. Vice presidential candidates are often chosen on the basis of their ideological leanings. Ronald Reagan selected George H. W. Bush as his running mate in part because Reagan was viewed as far to the political right and needed a running mate who was more moderate. By contrast, the more moderate Bob Dole chose the ideologically conservative Jack Kemp as his choice for vice president in 1996 to mobilize conservative Republican voters.

A fair amount of scrutiny goes into the process of selecting a vice presidential running mate, because some have turned out to be liabilities for the ticket. In 1972, when it was revealed that Senator Thomas Eagleton had been hospitalized for nervous exhaustion and had received electroshock therapy, an embarrassed George McGovern quickly replaced him on the ticket with the former U.S. Ambassador to France, Sargent Shriver. Similarly, it became clear in 1988 that George H. W. Bush's selection of Dan Quayle as his running mate was problematic after disclosure of Quayle's attempts to avoid the military draft during the Vietnam War. Bush kept Quayle on the ticket, however, and went on to win the 1988 election. Many observers questioned George W. Bush's decision to keep Vice President Dick Cheney on the ticket in 2004, given the perception that Cheney was the driving influence behind the decision for early and swift American military action in Iraq, where weapons of mass destruction were never found.

In 2008, John McCain's selection of the relatively unknown Alaska governor, forty-four-year-old Sarah Palin, earned him plaudits from social conservatives. But the choice also led to excessive scrutiny of McCain's selection process for the vice presidential slot after Palin stumbled in several interviews with the mainstream media. Palin was also regarded by some as being too inexperienced to sit just "a heartbeat away" from the presidency. By comparison, Barack Obama's selection of Senator Joseph Biden of Delaware received relatively little scrutiny.

Gathering a Winning Coalition of States

★ LO Analyze strategic campaign objectives that focus on securing a winning coalition of states

Battleground states
States identified as offering either major-party candidate a reasonable chance for victory in the Electoral College.

A central feature of any general election campaign is each candidate's plan to put together a coalition of states sufficient to win a majority of electoral votes. At the outset of the campaign, states may be divided into three categories: strong Republican states, strong Democratic states, and the so-called **battleground** (or "swing") **states**, those which either candidate has a reasonable chance of winning. The map in the "Check the List" feature depicts this categorization of states for the 2008 presidential campaign. The blue states were considered safely Democratic and the red were considered safely Republican; the gold states were the ones up for grabs.

In 2008 both the Republican nominee, John McCain, and the Democratic nominee, Barack Obama, set their sights on twelve battleground states in particular. (See the "Check the List" box). John Kerry's narrow Electoral College loss to President George W. Bush in 2004 (Kerry fell short of the winning total by just eighteen Electoral College votes) pointed Obama's way to victory: If he could hold all of Kerry's winning states, while picking up just one or two of the battleground states won by

Top Twelve Battleground States in 2008

In the presidential campaign of 2008, the vast majority of states saw relatively little activity in terms of candidate appearances and television advertising. Instead, the candidates for both major parties targeted a few select states for concentrated activity. They spent most of their resources of time and money on these battleground states because, as each candidate knew well ahead of time, these were where the election outcome would be decided.

Certainly there were some surprises in 2008. Georgia—considered a secure McCain state—did end up in the Republicans' column, but by only a five-point margin. Meanwhile the battleground state of New Mexico ended up in the Obama victory column by a comfortable fifteen-point margin. But overall the twelve battleground states of 2008 held true to their status.

Popular Vote Outcomes in the 2008 Presidential Election

	State	Obama (D)	McCain (R)
✔	North Carolina	49.9%	49.5%
✔	Missouri	49.3%	49.5%
✔	Indiana	49.9%	49.0%
✔	Florida	50.8%	48.4%
✔	Ohio	51.2%	47.2%
✔	Montana	46.7%	50.1%
✔	Virginia	51.8%	47.3%
✔	Colorado	52.6%	45.8%
✔	New Hampshire	54.6%	44.6%
✔	Pennsylvania	54.6%	44.3%
✔	Nevada	55.1%	42.7%
✔	New Mexico	56.9%	41.8%

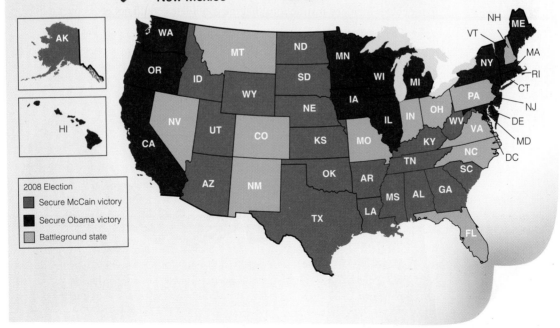

2008 Election
- Secure McCain victory
- Secure Obama victory
- Battleground state

Bush, he could secure victory. Accordingly, Obama invested considerable resources in the battleground states of Ohio and Florida, either of which would provide him with the necessary margin for success. Obama's campaign also focused its attention on the three battleground states that Bush had won comfortably: North Carolina, Virginia, and Colorado. Meanwhile the McCain camp was on the defensive, fighting to hold onto all these states, while looking for a breakthrough in Pennsylvania, where Kerry had won in 2004. On Election Day 2008, Obama's strategy reaped rewards for the Democratic ticket: Obama won a clear majority of the twelve battleground states and thus coasted to victory in the Electoral College.

The Presidential Debates

★ LO Evaluate the role of televised presidential debates and television advertising

The media and the public have come to expect that a presidential campaign will feature debates between the presidential candidates, and sometimes between the vice presidential candidates as well. Candidates may not believe it is in their strategic interest to debate their opponents (for example, a candidate who is ahead in the polls might prefer to play it safe and not run the risk of losing a debate and perhaps the lead in the campaign). Still, both major-party candidates usually agree to debate so that they aren't portrayed as being "afraid" to do so. The expectation of a set of debates, however, is a relatively recent phenomenon in presidential elections. The first debates that generated a high level of interest and scrutiny were those between John F. Kennedy and Richard M. Nixon in the 1960 election campaign. Some political scientists today credit Kennedy's victory as partly the result of his strong performance in the debates.[16]

The next set of debates occurred in 1976, between Gerald Ford and Jimmy Carter. Each presidential campaign since then has included debates between the presidential candidates and sometimes also between the vice presidential candidates. The 2004 campaign, for example, featured three debates between the presidential candidates and one between the vice presidential candidates. The debates between presidential candidates George W. Bush and John Kerry included one debate on the economy and one debate on foreign affairs with questions asked by a journalist, and a "town meeting" debate in which the candidates were asked questions by a randomly selected group of American voters; in the vice presidential debate, a journalist asked questions of the candidates. (The presidential debates are discussed in further detail in Chapter 12.)

The schedule of debates and the rules governing their conduct are the product of intense negotiation between the campaigns. In 2008, the detailed set of rules for the four debates included instructions that the candidates could not cross over a line on

Democratic presidential nominee Barack Obama and Republican presidential nominee John McCain shake hands before their second presidential debate.

PAUL J. RICHARDS/AFP/GETTY IMAGES

the stage separating them, time limits on answering questions and offering rebuttals, and a restriction for the final two debates that the candidates could not ask questions of each other.

Despite the large amount of attention both the campaigns and the media pay to the debates, the impact that debates have on the election outcome is unclear. Many researchers have documented that those who tend to watch the debates already have moderate to strong convictions regarding who they want to win, and these convictions often shape how an individual voter evaluates the candidate's performance in the debates. Though polls sometimes show that the voters tend to identify a debate "winner," there is far less evidence to show that this has any impact on voter intentions. The first of the debates often gets the most attention, and yet many of the media-dubbed "winners" of first debates, whether Walter Mondale in 1984, Michael Dukakis in 1988, Ross Perot in 1992, or John Kerry in 2004, have ended up on the short side of the electoral vote count on Election Day. In 2008 Barack Obama performed well in all three of his debates against John McCain, and while those performances did not secure his final victory, polls indicated that they helped reassure many undecided voters that the junior senator from Illinois was indeed ready to be president. Some observers of elections indicate that although debates may not have a direct impact on vote intentions, they can change the dynamics of a campaign, which in turn may influence the outcome.[17]

The Advertising

Television advertisements have become a staple of presidential campaign strategies.[18] They are used to heighten name recognition, communicate core messages to voters, and offer reasons why one should vote for (or against) a particular candidate. Television advertising uses a variety of different techniques to accomplish these goals. The most controversial of these techniques is the attack or "negative" ads that candidates often use to portray their opponents in a bad light.[19] Television ads can be very effective at convincing voters to support a candidate—particularly voters who are undecided on any particular candidate or who are politically independent rather than identifying themselves as a Democrat or a Republican. Whereas other forms of campaign communication (such as televised debates, political news columns, political talk shows on radio and TV, and news broadcasts) are provided in formats that appeal to voters who are interested in the campaign and have already made up their mind about who they will vote for, televised advertisements may be placed during certain shows or at certain times when independents and undecided voters are tuning in. The unsuspecting audience is captive to the short advertisement, which provides a unique opportunity for a campaign to attract votes.

The Electoral College Vote

Unlike elections for most public offices in the United States, the outcome of the popular vote does not necessarily determine who wins the presidential election. The winner of the presidential election is the candidate who receives a majority of the 538 votes in the **Electoral College**. As the opening to this chapter demonstrated, in the highly controversial 1876 and 2000 presidential elections the popular vote winner lost the presidential race. Similarly, John Quincy Adams won the 1824 election despite losing the popular vote, as did Benjamin Harrison in 1888.

How does the Electoral College work? The Constitution allocates each state a certain number of electoral votes, based on the sum of the number of senators (two) plus representatives (currently anywhere from one to fifty-three) that a state has in the U.S. Congress. The Twenty-third Amendment to the Constitution allocated three electoral votes to the District of Columbia. The number of seats a state has in the House of Representatives may change as a result of the official census conducted every ten years. Thus the number of electoral votes that a state has may change as well. The total number of electoral votes remains fixed at 538, and a candidate must receive a majority—270—to win the presidency (see Figure 15.1, p. 462).

Explain the
Electoral College system

★ LO

Electoral College
The constitutional mechanism by which presidents are chosen. Each state is allocated Electoral College votes based on the sum of that state's U.S. senators and House members.

FIGURE 15.1 The Electoral College Map

This map of the states depicts the number of electoral votes each state has as a result of the 2000 U.S. census. The states shaded in red are those states whose electoral votes were cast for Republican John McCain in 2008. The blue states' electoral votes went to Democrat Barack Obama.

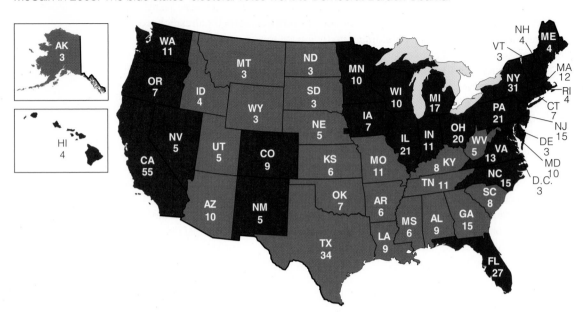

The minimum number of electoral votes possible for any one state is three because the Constitution guarantees to each state two senators and one House member. A number of states have three electoral votes: Vermont, Wyoming, North Dakota, South Dakota, Alaska, Montana, and Delaware. California currently has the largest number of electoral votes with fifty-five (fifty-three members of the House and two senators).

Even small states with as few as three electoral votes can influence the outcome of an election. In 2000, George Bush received 271 electoral votes, only one vote more than the 270 majority he needed to win. Had just one of the small states that gave Bush its three electoral votes voted for Gore, Bush would not have won the election.

Over the past sixty years, the U.S. population has shifted with the southern and western states gaining population and the northeastern and Midwestern states losing. Consequently, the numbers of electoral votes in states such as Florida, California, Texas, and Arizona have grown, and the number of votes allocated to states like New York, Pennsylvania, Ohio, and Illinois has declined. Early projections from the 2010 census indicate that this trend will continue, which should add even more electoral strength to some regions, while subtracting from others. Based on figures from the Bureau of the Census, it is likely that the 2012 electoral vote count in Texas will swell from thirty-four to thirty-eight. The following states are likely to gain at least one additional electoral vote as well: Arizona, Florida, Georgia, Nevada, South Carolina, Utah, and Washington. By contrast, Ohio's total will decline from twenty to eighteen, and each of the following states are likely to lose at least one electoral vote: Illinois, Iowa, Louisiana, Massachusetts, Michigan, Minnesota, New Jersey, New York, and Pennsylvania.

Article II of the Constitution gives the state legislature of each state the authority to appoint **electors**, one for each electoral vote that a state has been allocated. During the first few presidential elections, most states used the state legislature to select the individuals who would be the state's electors.[20] By 1860, however, states gradually shifted to using the popular vote outcome in the state to allocate electors, or the so-called **unit rule**. The unit rule (or "winner take all" system) means that the candidate who receives the most votes among the popular votes cast for president in a state will receive all the electoral votes from that state. At present only two states, Maine and

Electors

Individuals appointed to represent a state's presidential vote in the Electoral College; in practice, voters in presidential elections vote for a slate of electors committed to a particular candidate, rather than voting directly for the candidate.

Unit rule

The system in forty-eight states by which the candidate who wins the most votes among popular votes cast for president in a state receives all the electoral votes from that state; also known as the "winner take all" system.

Nebraska, do not use the unit rule. Rather, in those states the popular vote winner in each congressional district receives the electoral vote from that district, and the two votes that derive from the state's Senate seats are awarded to the statewide popular vote winner. In 2004, voters in Colorado defeated a referendum to allot electoral votes as Maine and Nebraska currently do.

In practice, the voters in a presidential election vote not for the actual candidate but for the slate of electors who commit to the candidate for whom the voters cast their ballots. Interestingly, the electors who pledge themselves to a candidate are under no constitutional obligation to actually cast their electoral vote for that candidate. In fact, electors do sometimes break their pledge. In seven of the last fifteen presidential elections, at least one individual elector has not voted for the candidate that won the popular vote in their state. The most recent deviation occurred in 2004, when a Minnesota elector pledged to vote for John Kerry cast his presidential vote for "John Ewards" [sic] instead. That misvote may have been an accident. By contrast, in 2000, Washington, DC, elector Barbara Lett-Simmons, while pledged to vote for Democrats Al Gore and Joe Lieberman, intentionally cast no electoral votes as a protest against the District of Columbia's lack of statehood. To date, however, these rare broken promises (or mistakes) have not had an impact on an election outcome—and only nine of the 21,829 electoral votes cast since 1796 deviated from the vote that was expected of an elector.[21]

The significance of the unit rule is illustrated by the outcome of the 2000 presidential election. In Florida, which had twenty-five electoral votes, the popular vote distribution between Bush and Gore was very close. For nearly one month after the election, controversies surrounding the vote count and the ballot in Florida left uncertain which candidate won the most popular votes in the state. What loomed in the balance was all of Florida's twenty-five electoral votes—and the election victory. Without Florida, Gore had 267 electoral votes—just three votes shy of victory, whereas Bush had 246. Because the unit rule applied to Florida's twenty-five votes, all twenty-five would be allocated on the basis of which candidate received the most popular votes.

The Founders' original intent in creating the Electoral College was to keep the presidential selection process out of the direct hands of the people. They felt that the people were best represented by the House of Representatives, whose members were elected directly by voters. But the Founders questioned the ability of the general public to select the chief executive. Rather, they believed that the more knowledgeable, wise, and politically thoughtful members of each state's legislature should be empowered with the authority to appoint electors who would choose from the best of the best.

But as the meaning of democracy changed and as American politics opened up to greater political participation, states began to use the popular vote as a means of allocating their electoral votes. Why, then, do we continue to use this rather complicated, indirect system for voters to choose their president? Why not simply use the sum total of the popular vote to choose a winner? The most basic answer is explained by politics, not necessarily logic. The Electoral College system benefits smaller states. For example, Wyoming's population of approximately 494,000 represents 0.17 percent of the potential popular vote. But its three electoral votes constitute 0.56 percent of the electoral vote total. Because every state starts off with two electoral votes (for its two U.S. senators), smaller states end up with disproportionately more voting power in the Electoral College than in the popular vote. In recent years, the states that benefit from the Electoral College system have tended to be dominated by Republican legislatures. Because changing the Electoral College system requires a constitutional amendment, and because amendment procedures require approval by three fourths of the state legislatures, any attempt to change the system is unlikely to win the support of a sufficient number of state legislatures, enough of which are small enough to benefit from the Electoral College. Despite the many proposals that have been offered to reform or eliminate the Electoral College, it seems likely, at least for the foreseeable future, that the Electoral College is here to stay.

Appealing to Voters the Old Fashioned Way . . . by Writing a Book

Stump speeches, TV ads, press conferences, and visits to the county fair are staples in a modern presidential candidate's campaign playbook. More recently, a new item has been added to this list: authoring a book. Putting one's name on a book provides the candidate with an unfiltered opportunity to comprehensively make the case for his or her candidacy and gain credibility with voters. Back in 1999, the year before his first run for the presidency, John McCain wrote *Faith of My Fathers: A Family Memoir*, in which he described his grandfather's, father's, and his own commitment to the U.S. Navy. In 2008, just as he was embarking on his successful quest to become the Republican presidential nominee, he followed up with *Why Courage Matters: The Way to a Braver Life*. Barack Obama, the 2008 Democratic nominee, has written several books. In *Change We Can Believe In* (2008) and *The Audacity of Hope* (2008), he described his views of how to bring about change to American politics. In *Dreams from My Father*, written four years earlier, he described his earlier life as a son of a black father and white mother. Other candidates also put their pen to work on their own behalf: Republican candidate Ron Paul wrote *The Revolution: A Manifesto* (2008), in which he expounded his vision of a libertarian approach to governing. Democratic hopeful Hillary Clinton wrote *Living History* (2003) to promote the role she played as First Lady during the Clinton administration and perhaps to pave her road to the presidency five years later.

Critics charge that these books are filled with vague platitudes that offer only a limited glimpse into the candidates' real positions. Moreover, in many cases ghostwriters (perhaps one of the candidate's own campaign speechwriters) are largely responsible for the language used. Still, no one expects these campaign "tomes" to go away soon, if only because they provide an excuse for candidates to embark on a book-signing tour that can serve to kick off a future presidential campaign. Possible candidates for the 2012 Republican nomination have wasted no time putting pen to paper in preparation for their own potential campaigns. Sarah Palin wrote *Going Rogue: An American Life* (2010), in which she chronicled growing up in Alaska and her life as a vice presidential candidate. That same year, Mitt Romney wrote *No Apology: The Case for American Greatness*, which touted the impressive contributions of America to the world. You should have little problem finding these and other campaign books at a bookstore near you.

For Critical Thinking and Discussion

1. Have you read any books written by a presidential candidate? If so, did the book change the way you viewed the candidate? Did you become more or less supportive of the candidate?

2. How much influence do you think candidate-authored books have? How would you compare the influence of a book to the influence of television ads or a candidate's web page?

★ LO Understand the impact money has on presidential campaigns, and recognize the laws governing campaign finance

Campaign Funding

Waging a political campaign, particularly a presidential campaign, is becoming increasingly expensive.[22] In 2008, all the candidates together raised more than $1.7 billion, nearly double the amount raised in 2004, and more than four times the amount raised in 2000. Barack Obama's campaign alone raised $745 million. Campaign financing, then, is one of the most important functions of a political campaign. Hiring a professional staff to develop and implement a successful campaign, producing and airing TV commercials and radio spots, renting campaign headquarters office space, conducting polls to monitor the course of the campaign, and producing buttons, bumper stickers, and signs all cost money. Good candidates have demonstrated a high capacity for raising money to wage a campaign.

Sources of Funding

Where do campaigns find financial support? They find money from individual citizens, from interest groups and political action committees, and from political parties.

Companies, groups, and individuals all have vested interests in the political system, and each may provide support (including monetary contributions) to promote candidates who advocate their own positions on issues. Our system of politics encourages people and groups to participate in the political process, and this participation includes financial contributions to campaigns. Indeed, giving money to candidates may be seen as a healthy sign that people are engaged in the political process and want to participate in making a difference.

Beginning in the 1970s, parties and candidates turned to political action committees (PACs) to address the new realities of political campaigns, particularly regarding fund-raising and limits on individual contributions. PACs are the arms of interest groups that raise and give money to political candidates. Any group that wishes to participate in financing campaigns must create a PAC and register it with the Federal Election Commission (FEC). There are more than 4,000 PACs currently registered with the federal government (see Figure 15.2). Of the $1 billion raised by House and Senate campaigns in 2004, about 30 percent came from the fund-raising efforts of PACs.

In addition to individual and PAC contributions, the political parties play an important role in financing political campaigns. Both major parties have national and statewide committees, which raise money and give money to candidates to fund campaigns. In 2000, the national party committees each collected and spent about $200 million to help fund their candidates. Typically, the parties support House and Senate candidates, particularly those who have a competitive chance of winning.

Another important source of campaign funding comes from the individual candidates' House and Senate campaigns. Members of Congress who hold safe seats are very effective at raising money for their own campaigns. These campaigns, because they are for safe seats, tend not to need a great deal of funding. So the incumbents use their campaign war chests to help fund the campaigns of their colleagues in more competitive races. Often they do so through the formation of a PAC.

Though not the norm, some federal candidates for office use their own personal wealth to fund their campaigns. In 1992 and 1996, independent presidential candidate Ross Perot spent millions of dollars of his own personal fortune (Perot's personal

FIGURE 15.2 The Growth of Political Action Committees

The federal campaign finance legislation of the 1970s was the first vigorous attempt to monitor and regulate the money that was raised and spent on political campaigns. These laws applied to the regulation of hard money, which was money raised directly by and spent by the political candidates. They influenced the creation of political action committees (PACs), which raise and spend soft money—funds for political campaigning independent of the political candidates. In 1974, there were only 608 PACs registered with the federal government; by 2002, 4,027 PACs were registered. This figure shows the total amount of receipts and expenditures of all PACs registered with the federal government from the 1975–1976 election cycle to the 2007–2008 election cycle.

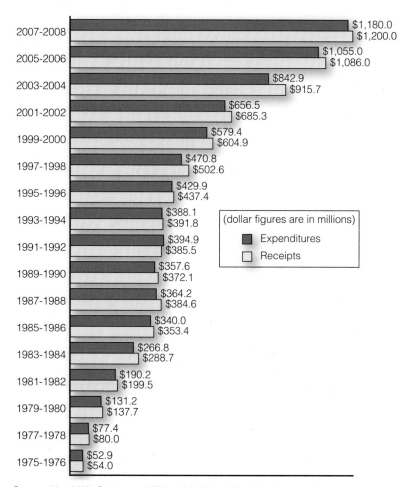

Source: Harold W. Stanley and Richard G. Niemi, *Vital Statistics on American Politics 2004–2005*, 103 (Washington, DC: CQ Press, 2006). Copyright ©2006 CQ Press, a division of Sage Publications. Data for 2005-2008 are from www.fec.gov/press/press2009/20090415pac/20090424pac.shtml.

wealth is in the billions of dollars). Similarly, Democratic Senator Jon Corzine from New Jersey spent more than $50 million of his own money to win a Senate seat in 2000 (his Republican competitor spent over $30 million of his own money).

The federal government and a handful of state governments (including Arizona, Connecticut, North Carolina, and Maine) maintain some form of public campaign financing as well. Although candidates cannot be forced to participate in public financing schemes, which restrict their expenditures, the government may entice their participation by offering them significant public funds in return for their agreement to abide by personal campaign spending limits. The federal government's presidential election financing system allows major-party candidates to draw on funds received when taxpayers check a box on their tax returns agreeing to donate to the fund. In 2004, presidential candidates were eligible to receive approximately $70 million each if they agreed to limit their campaign expenditures. Yet neither of the two major-party candidates in 2004, George W. Bush and John Kerry, elected to participate in the federal financing scheme. By rejecting the use of such public financing, they were able to freely spend throughout the primaries and general election campaign without regard to any federally imposed limits. In 2008, John McCain accepted the $85 million he qualified for in public financing to fund his general election campaign. Barack Obama, however, declined public financing and continued to privately raise funds through the general election—a decision based on his widespread success in raising campaign money during the primaries.

In recent presidential election cycles, candidates have been able to take advantage of the Internet as yet another means of fund-raising. In 2000, Bill Bradley raised more than $2 million via the Internet for his campaign for the Democratic presidential nomination. (He ended up losing his bid for the nomination to Al Gore.) Then, in the 2004 race for the Democratic presidential nomination, a little-known former governor from the small state of Vermont, Howard Dean, waged an impressive campaign by tapping into the vast potential of the Internet and online fund-raising. His followers, who came to be known as "Deaniacs," tended to be younger Americans, a group much more inclined to use the Internet, to IM (instant message), and to blog. The Dean campaign translated this orientation of his followers into the most successful Internet fund-raising campaign that American politics had ever seen. As Wired.com reported during the nomination campaign in early 2004:

> The biggest news of the political season has been the tale of this small-state governor who, with the help of Meetup.com and hundreds of bloggers, has elbowed his way into serious contention for his party's presidential nomination . . . Dean has used the Net to raise more money than any other Democratic candidate. He's also used it to organize thousands of volunteers who go door-to-door, write personal letters to likely voters, host meetings, and distribute flyers.

Dean raised an unprecedented $40 million in his campaign for the nomination. This amount exceeded that of all his competitors for the nomination, and the vast bulk of his campaign war chest was derived from small, individual donations solicited through the Internet. Although Dean's campaign collapsed after the candidate suffered unexpected losses in Iowa and New Hampshire and though most of his $40 million war chest was depleted by the first primary contest, Dean's success at Internet fund-raising was nonetheless quite impressive. Then in 2008 Barack Obama's campaign substantially raised the stakes in fundraising through the Internet by raising over $200 million through that medium. His appeal to voters through the Internet represents a significant achievement in the use of this new technology in campaign politics. As Americans increasingly come to rely on the Internet, it is likely that political candidates will follow Dean's and Obama's examples and harness this technology for fundraising and other campaigning.

Regulating Campaign Financing

Congress and the states have passed many and varied laws to regulate the conduct of campaign contributions. These laws are not intended to prevent individuals or groups from giving money. Rather, they attempt to prevent a "quid pro quo," or a donation in return for an elected official voting or acting in a certain way in direct response to accepting the campaign gift.

The first significant piece of federal legislation aimed at regulating campaign financing was the **Federal Election Campaign Act (FECA)**, passed in 1971 and amended in 1974. The law required that all federal candidates accurately disclose campaign contributions and document all campaign expenditures. Subsequent amendments to FECA imposed legal limits on campaign contributions by individuals ($1,000 to each candidate per election cycle; $5,000 to PACs per year; and $20,000 to national party committees per year). Additionally, FECA imposed an outright ban on certain campaign contributions by corporations, unions, national banks, and foreign nationals, among others.

All these provisions targeted so-called **hard money** contributions that go directly to candidates and their campaign committees. FECA did little to stem the influx of **soft money** funds to political parties and political advocacy groups that are not contributed directly to candidate campaigns and that do not expressly advocate the election of a particular candidate. In the two decades following FECA, the two major political parties have strategically spent soft money on administrative and party building activities, as well as on issue ads that do not specifically promote an individual candidate, but that nevertheless attempt to affect the election outcome.

The **Federal Election Commission (FEC)** was established in 1974 to enforce all campaign financing rules and regulations, including limits on campaign contributions. Today, the FEC is the federal agency in charge of enforcing election laws. Provisions for public funding of presidential campaigns were subsequently passed in 1976 and 1979.

Critics have voiced a number of complaints about the system of campaign finance regulations. For one thing, the original limits on individual contributions—fixed by legislation in the 1970s—were never indexed to inflation. This oversight was addressed in legislation in 2002 which mandated that limits be indexed for inflation every two years. For example, in 2005–2006 individuals were able to give up to $2,100 to candidates and up to $26,700 to national party committees.

Another complaint concerns the failure of the system to adapt to modern campaign dynamics. As a result of frontloading, presidential primary elections are now bunched up earlier and earlier in the general election campaign; yet the strict limits on expenditures imposed on those who accept public financing do not really account for these new campaign realities, which compel candidates to spend a considerable amount of their money during a relatively short period of time.

In recent years, advocates of campaign finance reform have focused their greatest criticism on soft money in the form of **independent campaign expenditures**. These are monies that PACs or individuals spend to support political campaigns but that do not directly contribute to them. FECA banned the unlimited use of independent expenditures to directly support the election of one candidate or the defeat of another candidate, but those funds could still be used to build the party as a whole. For example, a PAC can produce and support a political advertisement that endorses a particular party's position on an issue and pay for the airtime to broadcast that ad on television. The money for the ad is not donated to a campaign per se, but instead is spent on services that support the campaign; thus, the money spent is considered an "independent" expenditure. The U.S. Supreme Court in **Buckley v. Valeo (1976)**[23] ruled that Congress could limit campaign contributions consistent with the First Amendment, but that it could not limit independent campaign expenditures or personal money spent by candidates on behalf of their own campaigns. Twenty years later in *McConnell v. F.E.C.* (2003),[24] the Court extended that ruling to apply to spending by political parties as well. Thus political parties themselves often sponsor television ads that talk more generally about issues facing the country without mentioning any individual candidate or race; of course most political experts acknowledge that these ads may have a significant impact on individual campaigns.

The most recent reform attempts have focused on soft money and independent campaign expenditures. Senators John McCain (R-AZ) and Russell Feingold (D-WI) were particularly critical of the loopholes in campaign financing that have allowed

Federal Election Campaign Act (FECA)
The federal legislation passed in 1971 that established disclosure requirements and restricted individual campaign contributions.

Hard money
Donations made directly to political candidates and their campaigns that must be declared with the name of the donor (which then becomes public knowledge).

Soft money
Money not donated directly to a candidate's campaign, but rather to a political advocacy group or a political party for "party building" activities.

Federal Election Commission (FEC)
The agency created in 1974 to enforce federal election laws.

Independent campaign expenditure
Political donations that PACs or individuals spend to support campaigns, but do not directly contribute to the campaigns.

Buckley v. Valeo (1976)
The 1976 Supreme Court opinion that held that spending money to influence elections is protected First Amendment speech, and that prohibited limitations on independent expenditures or personal money spent by candidates on their own campaigns.

Bipartisan Campaign Reform Act (BCRA) of 2002

Also called the McCain-Feingold Act, the federal legislation that (1) restricted soft money spent by political parties, (2) regulated expenditures on ads that refer to specific candidates immediately before an election, and (3) increased limits on hard money donated directly to candidates and their campaigns.

★ **LO** Assess the power of incumbency in congressional elections

★ **LO** Explain why turnout levels vary in presidential elections and midterm elections

★ **LO** Identify and define the "coattail effect" of presidential elections

Midterm congressional elections

Congressional elections held midway between successive presidential elections.

Coattail effect

The potential benefit that successful presidential candidates offer to congressional candidates of the same political party during presidential election years.

soft money to go unregulated by the Federal Election Commission. They cosponsored legislation designed to better regulate the way campaigns are financed and how the money is spent. In 2002, Congress passed the **Bipartisan Campaign Reform Act (BCRA)**, popularly known as the McCain-Feingold Act, which prohibited national parties and candidates for federal office from accepting soft money (i.e., that which is not subject to regulation by the FEC). The BCRA also raised limits on contributions to a particular candidate for federal office from $1,000 to $2,000. The U.S. Supreme Court, in 2010, struck down as unconstitutional several other provisions of the BCRA, including certain limits on corporate and union funding of broadcast ads right before an election.

Congressional Campaigns and Elections

Although presidential elections typically receive the most attention from the media and the public, many other elections also occur regularly, including those that send members to the two houses of Congress. In each presidential election year, all 435 seats in the House of Representatives are contested, as are one third of the seats in the Senate. Midway between successive presidential elections are the **midterm congressional elections**, in which all 435 House seats are contested again and another one third of the Senate seats are voted on (senators serve six-year terms, and the 100 Senate elections are staggered so that about one third of the seats are contested every two years).

Midterm elections for Congress differ from presidential-year elections in important ways.[25] First, voter turnout tends to be lower in the midterm contests. Without the large-scale attention the presidential race receives, voter interest and engagement in the midterm elections are lower, and thus turnout tends to suffer. Even in the highly charged midterm elections of 2006, voter turnout was just 41 percent, almost fifteen percentage points below voter turnout figures for the preceding presidential election.

Second, midterm elections fail to offer congressional candidates what has come to be known as the **coattail effect**. In a presidential election year, the names of candidates for Congress typically are listed below the name of their party's candidate for president on the ballot. Thus, voters' selection of congressional candidates may be influenced by their choice for president. The congressional candidates, in effect, ride the coattails of the presidential candidate.[26] For the coattail effect to be apparent, the outcome of the presidential race typically needs to be a landslide victory for the winner, such as in 1984 when President Ronald Reagan soundly defeated Democrat Walter Mondale. For the first time in decades, the 1984 elections ushered in a Republican majority to the U.S. Senate. By contrast, George W. Bush's narrow victory in 2004 did not appear to produce a coattail effect.

Third, in midterm elections there has been a discernible trend—though often not very strong—that favors congressional candidates in the party opposite the president's party in midterm contests. When a president wins, especially by a large margin, the coattail effect distorts what would normally occur in any given congressional race. Yet in midterm elections, without the president's name at the top of the ballot, the absence of the coattail gives the advantage to the opposing party. In the modern era, the party in opposition to the president has managed to regain control of Congress only in the midterm elections when the president's popularity is waning. Thus in 1946 and then in 1994, the Republicans wrestled both houses of Congress back from the Democrats at midterm elections during the presidencies of Democrats Harry Truman and Bill Clinton, respectively. More recently in 2006, voters upset about the state of the war in Iraq dealt a devastating blow to the Republicans' control of Congress: though many Republican incumbents in the House and Senate were ousted from office that year, not one Democratic House member or Senator lost a seat in the 2006 midterm elections. The Democrats successfully rode the public's antiwar sentiment to regain control of both houses of Congress midway through the second term of Republican President George W. Bush.

True to form, the 2010 midterm elections once again offered a rebuke to the political party holding the White House. Running on a platform that opposed

Democratic spending initiatives and promised to rein in the size of government, Republican House candidates transformed a 178-seat minority into a 240-seat majority. By taking more than 60 seats away from the Democrats, Republicans enjoyed a level of midterm election success not seen by either party in decades. Republicans were also successful in the Senate, shrinking the Democrats' 18-seat margin of control down to just 6 seats.

More important than presidential coattails or any other factor in congressional elections, however, is the **power of incumbency**. Incumbent members of Congress, particularly those in the House, are returned to office by voters at amazingly high rates. In a normal year of House races, an incumbent who is running for

A dejected Senator Russ Feingold (D-WI) concedes defeat on November 2, 2010. Feingold served three terms in the U.S. Senate, but could not hold on for a fourth term against the electoral tide that swept many Republicans into office in 2010.

TABLE 15.2 Safe Seats in Congress

The vast majority of the 435 seats in the House of Representatives, each of which are contested every two years, and the 100 U.S. Senate seats, each of which is contested every six years, are safe seats for incumbents who are running for reelection. Even if there is not an incumbent running for reelection, most of these seats tend to be safe for one of the two major political parties. The 2010 midterm elections proved to be a bit of an anomaly, as 51 Democratic House incumbents in all lost their general reelection bids.

The table below shows the number of incumbents defeated and the number of seats that switched from one party to another in each congressional election since 1980*. Keep in mind that in each election year, 435 House races and thirty-three or thirty-four Senate races are usually contested.

Year	Incumbents Defeated	Open Seats Where Party Changed	Total Changes	Incumbents Defeated	Open Seats Where Party Changed	Total Changes*
	House of Representatives			**Senate**		
1980	30	11	41	9	3	12
1982	23	8	31	2	2	4
1984	16	6	22	3	1	4
1986	6	15	21	7	3	10
1988	6	3	9	4	3	7
1990	15	6	21	1	0	1
1992	24	19	43	4	0	4
1994	35	26	61	2	6	8
1996	21	14	35	1	3	4
1998	6	11	17	3	3	6
2000	6	12	18	6	2	8
2002	4	8	12	3	1	4
2004	5	5	10	1	7	8
2006	22	9	31	6	0	6
2008	17	13	30	5	3	8
2010**	53	10	63	2	4	6

* Figures include only shifts from one major party to the other party.

** Results from 2010 midterm elections include only those races decided as of November 5, 2010.

Source: Harold W. Stanley and Richard G. Niemi, *Vital Statistics on American Politics 2005-2006* (Washington, DC: CQ Press, 2006), 48-49. Copyright ©2006 CQ Press, a division of Sage Publications; updated by authors

Power of incumbency
The phenomenon by which incumbent members of Congress running for reelection are returned to office at an extremely high rate.

Safe seat
A congressional seat from a district that includes a high percentage of voters from one of the major parties.

Marginal seat
A seat in a congressional district that has relatively similar numbers of Democratic and Republican voters.

Franking privilege
The traditional right of members of Congress to mail materials to their constituents without paying postage.

reelection stands a better than 90 percent chance of being returned to office.[27] What accounts for such a high return rate? First, name recognition of the candidate is a significant factor in lower-profile congressional races, and incumbents, because they have been in office, tend to have higher name recognition than do challengers. Second, the vast majority of congressional districts and thus the vast majority of seats in Congress are dominated by either the Republican Party or the Democratic Party. Congressional seats from districts that include either a high percentage of Democratic voters or a high percentage of Republican voters are dominated by their respective majority party and are referred to as **safe seats**. A far smaller number of districts tend to have similar numbers of Democratic and Republican voters and are known as **marginal seats**. In the redistricting of congressional districts that periodically takes place, the political parties try to configure districts to their own partisan advantage. This maneuvering tends to create a large number of safe seats and often very few marginal seats (see Table 15.2, p. 469).

Finally, incumbent members of Congress enjoy financial advantages, such as the **franking privilege**, which allows members to mail materials to their constituents without paying postage.

Making the Connection

Elections and campaigns are central features of the republican form of government in the United States. The number of elections is many, the cost of campaigns is high, and the process for selecting the nation's chief officeholder, the president of the United States, is long and complex. Several times in the nation's history the complicated procedure for selecting a president has resulted in considerable controversy, as in the elections of 1876 and 2000. Yet through these controversies and many others, the U.S. political system has maintained free, open, and regular elections since George Washington was unanimously chosen as the nation's first president in 1789. U.S. presidential elections evoke a great deal of passion, engage the interest of millions of voters, persuade vast numbers of citizens and groups to contribute large amounts of money, and focus attention on the great issues of the day. Thus campaigns and elections duly serve their purpose in providing an important connection between Americans and their government.

POLITICS InterActive!

Campaign Donations: Just a Click Away

One significant development in the financing of the 2008 presidential primaries and caucuses was the success Democratic candidate Barack Obama enjoyed in raising many small donations using the Internet. According to the nonpartisan Campaign Finance Institute, Obama raised $101 million in small individual contributions of $200 or less through March 31, 2008. The vast majority of these small donations were made through the Internet. As compared to larger donations solicited directly from individuals, these Internet donations offered Obama numerous advantages: (1) they provided his campaign with broad-based funding at very little cost, as compared to more expensive methods such as events, telemarketing, and direct mail; (2) they required little time or effort on the part of the candidate himself; and (3) they filled the campaign's coffers without the risk of influence buying that accompanies larger contributions from a smaller number of individuals. Howard Dean, a candidate for the Democratic nomination in 2004, became the first presidential candidate to tap funds so successfully in this way—his campaign raised $50 million in the third quarter of 2003 with an average donation size of $80. In 2008, Obama refined and built on Dean's model, helping Obama secure his party's presidential nomination.

On www.cengage.com/dautrich/americangovernment/2e, find the Politics Inter-Active link for information about the Internet campaign financing phenomenon, including analysis of which candidates have benefited the most from Internet donations in recent election cycles. Historical, popular, and global perspectives on the issue are also presented.

ANDREW HARRER/BLOOMBERG/GETTY IMAGES

Chapter Summary

★ American Presidential Elections in Historical Perspective

- The system for choosing U.S. presidents includes two distinct phases: a nomination phase (during which major-party nominees are chosen) and a general election phase (in which a new president is selected).

- From 1796 up through the 1830s, the nomination process was dominated by officials of the two major parties who chose party nominees based on informal discussions.

- Andrew Jackson and the Democratic Party he founded gave the "common man" increased influence in choosing nominees; by the twentieth century, electoral reforms such as the direct primary gave voters in many states a formal opportunity to cast a ballot for delegates, who would in turn choose their party's nominees at a national convention.

★ The Prenomination Campaign

- Modern presidential elections begin with a prenomination campaign waged by potential candidates to raise money and gain the support of key party leaders. A candidate's failure to raise sufficient funds in this "invisible primary" may cause him or her to drop out of the race before any formal primaries or caucuses have been held.

★ The Nomination Campaign

- Nomination campaigns focus on attaining victories in presidential primaries and caucuses. The Iowa caucus and the New Hampshire primary have traditionally come at the beginning of the nomination calendar, and so they tend to disproportionately influence the final outcomes. In recent elections, many states have attempted to move their primaries and caucuses up on the calendar in a process known as frontloading.

- National party conventions used to play an important role in helping choose party nominees; today they are mostly made-for-television affairs, anointing the party ticket with speeches offering testimonials to the nominees.

★ The General Election Campaign

- General election races may be either incumbent races (pitting a sitting president against a challenger) or open elections (with no incumbent in the race). In the former, the election often amounts to a referendum on the performance of the president over the previous four years.

- Presidential candidates choose their running mates (the vice presidential candidates) strategically to address specific weaknesses of the presidential candidate or to boost the ticket's prospects in certain geographical areas.

- To win the presidency, a candidate must put together a coalition of states sufficient to win a majority of the 538 Electoral College votes, which are allocated to each state based on the sum of the number of senators and the number of representatives. The candidate who does well in battleground states will normally win the 270 or more votes necessary to secure a majority.

- Televised presidential debates between major presidential candidates occurred for the first time in 1960 and have been held in every presidential election since 1976. These debates tend to receive a large amount of attention from the press and the public, but their impact on the final election outcome remains unclear.

★ Campaign Funding

- Campaign funding is critical to the success of individual candidates. Election laws since 1974 have limited the amount individuals or organizations can give to candidates (hard money). The Bipartisan Campaign Reform Act (BCRA) of 2002 went a step further, restricting expenditures to political parties or advocacy groups that are theoretically independent of specific candidates or campaigns (soft money). The Federal Election Commission enforces all such limitations that have been upheld as constitutional by the U.S. Supreme Court.

★ Congressional Campaigns and Elections

- In congressional elections, the power of incumbency is more important than any other factor. Unlike midterm elections, congressional elections that coincide with presidential elections tend to garner greater voter turnout, and members of the successful presidential candidate's party sometimes benefit from the coattail effect.

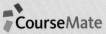

Key Terms

Battleground states (p. 458)

Bipartisan Campaign Reform Act (BCRA) of 2002 (p. 468)

Buckley v. Valeo (1976) (p. 467)

Caucus (p. 452)

Closed primary (p. 452)

Coattail effect (p. 468)

Electoral College (p. 461)

Electors (p. 462)

Federal Election Campaign Act (FECA) (p. 467)

Federal Election Commission (FEC) (p. 467)

Franking privilege (p. 470)

Frontloading (p. 453)

Hard money (p. 467)

Incumbent race (p. 456)

Independent campaign expenditure (p. 467)

Invisible primary (p. 450)

Marginal seat (p. 470)

Midterm congressional elections (p. 468)

Nomination campaign (p. 453)

Open election (p. 456)

Open primary (p. 452)

Power of incumbency (p. 470)

Prenomination campaign (p. 450)

Presidential primary (p. 452)

Safe seat (p. 470)

Soft money (p. 467)

Unit rule (p. 462)

Resources

Important Books

Abramson, Paul R., John H. Aldrich, and David W. Rohde. *Change and Continuity in the 2008 Elections.* Washington, DC: CQ Press, 2010.

Edwards, George. *Why the Electoral College Is Bad for America.* New Haven, CT: Yale University Press, 2004.

Magleby, David B., ed. *Financing the 2000 Election.* Washington, DC: Brookings Institution Press, 2002.

Mayer, William G., and Andrew Busch. *The Frontloading Problem in Presidential Nominations.* Washington, DC: Brookings Institution Press, 2003.

Wayne, Stephen J. *The Road to the White House 2008*, 8th ed. Boston: Wadsworth Press, 2008.

Internet Resources

http://www.electoral-vote.com (a Web site that uses polling data from each state to estimate and map the Electoral College vote outcome; provides historical data on Electoral College outcomes and statewide polls)

http://www.livingroomcandidate.org/ (the Museum of the Moving Image produces this valuable site, which contains televised campaign advertisements of candidates since the 1952 election)

http://www.opensecrets.org (this site, maintained by the Center for Responsive Politics, contains a wealth of information about PACs, campaign finance, and links to the Federal Election Commission's data)

Appendix

Declaration of Independence

In Congress, July 4, 1776.
A DECLARATION
By the Representatives of the United States of America,
In General Congress Assembled.

When in the Course of human Events, it becomes necessary for one People to dissolve the Political Bands which have connected them with another, and to assume among the Powers of the Earth, the separate and equal Station to which the Laws of Nature and of Nature's God entitle them, a decent Respect to the Opinions of Mankind requires that they should declare the causes which impel them to the Separation.

We hold these Truths to be self-evident, that all Men are created equal, that they are endowed by their Creator with certain unalienable Rights, that among these are Life, Liberty, and the Pursuit of Happiness—That to secure these Rights, Governments are instituted among Men, deriving their just Powers from the Consent of the Governed, that whenever any Form of Government becomes destructive of these Ends, it is the Right of the People to alter or abolish it, and to institute new Government, laying its Foundation on such Principles, and organizing its Powers in such Form, as to them shall seem most likely to effect their Safety and Happiness. Prudence, indeed, will dictate that Governments long established should not be changed for light and transient Causes; and accordingly all Experience hath shewn, that Mankind are more disposed to suffer, while Evils are sufferable, than to right themselves by abolishing the Forms to which they are accustomed. But when a long Train of Abuses and Usurpations, pursuing invariably the same Object, evinces a Design to reduce them under absolute Despotism, it is their Right, it is their Duty, to throw off such Government, and to provide new Guards for their future Security. Such has been the patient Sufferance of these Colonies; and such is now the Necessity which constrains them to alter their former Systems of Government. The History of the present kind of Great Britain is a History of repeated Injuries and Usurpations, all having in direct Object the Establishment of an absolute Tyranny over these States. To prove this, let Facts be submitted to a candid World.

He has refused his Assent to Laws, the most wholesome and necessary for public good.

He has forbidden his Governors to pass Laws of immediate and pressing importance, unless suspended in their Operation till his Assent should be obtained; and when so suspended, he has utterly neglected to attend to them.

He has refused to pass other Laws for the Accommodation of large Districts of People, unless those People would relinquish the Right of Representation in the Legislature, a Right inestimable to them, and formidable to Tyrants only.

He has called together Legislative Bodies at Places unusual, uncomfortable, and distant from the Depository of their public records, for the sole Purpose of fatiguing them into Compliance with his Measures.

He has dissolved Representative Houses repeatedly, for opposing with many Firmness his Invasions on the Rights of the People.

He has refused for a long Time, after such Dissolutions, to cause others to be elected; whereby the Legislative Powers, incapable of Annihilation, have returned to the People at large for their exercise; the State remaining in the mean time exposed to all the Dangers of Invasion from without, and Convulsions within.

He has endeavoured to prevent the Population of these States; for that Purpose obstructing the Laws for Naturalization of Foreigners; refusing to pass others to encourage their Migrations hither, and raising the Conditions of new Appropriations of Lands.

He has obstructed the Administration of Justice, by refusing his Assent to Laws for establishing Judiciary Powers.

He has made Judges dependent on his Will alone, for the Tenure of their Offices, and the Amount and Payment of their Salaries.

He has erected a Multitude of new Offices, and sent hither Swarms of Officers to harass our People, and eat out their Substance.

He has kept among us, in Times of Peaces, Standing Armies, without the consent of our Legislatures.

He has affected to render the Military independent of and superior to the Civil Power.

He has combined with others to subject us to a Jurisdiction foreign to our Constitution, and unacknowledged by our Laws; giving his Assent to their Acts of pretended Legislation:

For quartering large Bodies of Armed Troops among us:

For protecting them, by a mock Trial, from Punishment for any Murders which they should commit on the Inhabitants of these States:

For cutting off our Trade with all Parts of the World:

For imposing Taxes on us without our Consent: For depriving us, in many Cases, of the Benefits of Trial by Jury:

For transporting us beyond Seas to be tried for pretended Offences:

For abolishing the free System of English Laws in a neighbouring Province, establishing therein an arbitrary Government, and enlarging its Boundaries, so as to render it at once an Example and fit Instrument for introducing the same absolute Rule into these Colonies:

For taking away our Charters, abolishing our most valuable Laws, and altering fundamentally the Forms of our Governments:

For suspending our own Legislatures, and declaring themselves invested with Power to legislate for us in all Cases whatsoever.

He has abdicated Government here, by declaring us out of his Protection and waging War against us.

He has plundered our Seas, ravaged our Coasts, burnt our Towns, and destroyed the Lives of our People.

He is, at this Time, transporting large Armies of foreign Mercenaries to compleat the Works of Death, Desolation, and Tyranny, already begun with circumstances of Cruelty and Perfidy, scarcely paralleled in the most barbarous Ages, and totally unworthy the Head of a civilized Nation.

He has constrained our fellow Citizens taken Captive on the high Seas to bear Arms against their Country, to become the Executioners of their Friends and Brethren, or to fall themselves by their Hands.

He has excited domestic Insurrections amongst us, and has endeavoured to bring on the Inhabitants of our Frontiers, the merciless Indian Savages, whose known Rule of Warfare, is an undistinguished Destruction, of all Ages, Sexes and Conditions.

In every stage of these Oppressions we have Petitioned for Redress in the must humble Terms: Our repeated Petitions have been answered only by repeated Injury. A Prince, whose Character is thus marked by every act which may define a Tyrant, is unfit to be the Ruler of a free People.

Nor have we been wanting in Attentions to our British Brethren. We have warned them from Time to Time of Attempts by their Legislature to extend an unwarrantable Jurisdiction over us. We have reminded them of the Circumstances of our Emigration and Settlement here. We have appealed to their native Justice and Magnanimity, and we have conjured them by the Ties of our common Kindred to disavow these Usurpations, which, would inevitably interrupt our Connections and Correspondence. They too have been deaf to the Voice of Justice and of Consanguinity. We must, therefore, acquiesce in the Necessity, which denounces our Separation, and hold them, as we hold the rest of Mankind, Enemies in War, in Peace, Friends.

We, therefore, the Representatives of the UNITED STATES OF AMERICA, in GENERAL CONGRESS, Assembled, appealing to the Supreme Judge of the World for the Rectitude of our Intentions, do, in the Name, and by Authority of the good People of these Colonies, solemnly Publish and Declare, That these United Colonies are, and of Right ought to be, FREE AND INDEPENDENT STATES; that they are absolved from all Allegiance to the British Crown, and that all political Connection between them and the State of Great-Britain, is and ought to be totally dissolved; and that as FREE AND INDEPENDENT STATES, they have full Power to levy War, conclude Peace, contract Alliances, establish Commerce, and to do all other Acts and Things which INDEPENDENT STATES may of right do. And for the support of this Declaration, with a firm Reliance on the Protection of divine Providence, we mutually pledge to each other our Lives, our Fortunes, and our sacred Honor.

John Hancock

Georgia:
Button Gwinnett
Lyman Hall
George Walton

North Carolina:
William Hooper
Joseph Hewes
John Penn

South Carolina:
Edward Rutledge
Thomas Heyward, Jr.
Thomas Lynch, Jr.
Arthur Middleton

Maryland:
Samuel Chase
William Paca
Thomas Stone
Charles Carroll of Carrollton

Virginia:
George Wythe
Richard Henry Lee
Thomas Jefferson
Benjamin Harrison
Thomas Nelson, Jr.
Francis Lightfoot Lee
Carter Braxton

Pennsylvania:
Robert Morris
Benjamin Rush
Benjamin Franklin
John Morton
George Clymer
James Smith
George Taylor
James Wilson
George Ross

Delaware:
Caesar Rodney
George Read
Thomas McKean

New York:
William Floyd
Philip Livingston
Francis Lewis
Lewis Morris

New Jersey:
Richard Stockton
John Witherspoon
Francis Hopkinson
John Hart
Abraham Clark

New Hampshire:
Josiah Bartlett
William Whipple

Massachusetts:
Samuel Adams
John Adams
Robert Treat Paine
Elbridge Gerry

Rhode Island:
Stephen Hopkins
William Ellery

Connecticut:
Roger Sherman
Samuel Huntington
Oliver Wolcott

New Hampshire:
Matthew Thornton

November 23, 1787

TO THE PEOPLE OF THE STATE OF NEW YORK

Among the numerous advantages promised by a well-constructed Union, none deserves to be more accurately developed than its tendency to break and control the violence of faction. The friend of popular governments never finds himself so much alarmed for their character and fate, as when he contemplates their propensity to this dangerous vice. He will not fail, therefore, to set a due value on any plan which, without violating the principles to which he is attached, provides a proper cure for it. The instability, injustice, and confusion introduced into the public councils, have, in truth, been the mortal diseases under which popular governments have everywhere perished; as they continue to be the favorite and fruitful topics from which the adversaries to liberty derive their most specious declamations. The valuable improvements made by the American constitutions on the popular models, both ancient and modern, cannot certainly be too much admired; but it would be an unwarrantable partiality, to contend that they have as effectually obviated the danger on this side, as was wished and expected. Complaints are everywhere heard from our most considerate and virtuous citizens, equally the friends of public and private faith, and of public and personal liberty, that our governments are too unstable, that the public good is disregarded in the conflicts of rival parties, and that measures are too often decided, not according to the rules of justice and the rights of the minor party, but by the superior force on an interested and overbearing majority. However anxiously we may wish that these complaints had no foundation, the evidence of known facts will not permit us to deny that they are in some degree true. It will be found, indeed, on a candid review of our situation, that some of the distresses under which we labor have been erroneously charged on the operation of our governments; but it will be found, at the same time, that other causes will not alone account for many of our heaviest misfortunes; and, particularly, for that prevailing and increasing distrust of public engagements, and alarm for private rights, which are echoed from one end of the continent to the other. These must be chiefly, if not wholly, effects of the unsteadiness and injustice with which a factious spirit has tainted our public administrations.

By a faction, I understand a number of citizens, whether amounting to a majority or a minority of the whole, who are united and actuated by some common impulse of passion, or of interest, adversed to the rights of other citizens, or to the permanent and aggregate interests of the community.

There are two methods of curing the mischeifs of faction: the one, by removing its causes; the other, by controlling its effects.

There are again two methods of removing the causes of faction: the one, by destroying the liberty which is essential to its existence; the other, by giving to every citizen the same opinions, the same passions, and the same interests.

It could never be more truly said than of the first remedy, that it was worse than the disease. Liberty is to faction what air is to fire, an aliment without which it instantly expires. But it could not be less folly to abolish liberty, which is essential to political life, because it nourishes faction, than it would be to wish the annihilation of air, which is essential to animal life, because it imparts to fire its destructive tendency.

The second expedient is as impracticable as the first would be unwise. As long as the reason of man continues fallible, and he is at liberty to exercise it, different opinions will be formed. As long as the connection subsists between his reason and his self-love, his opinions and his passions will have a reciprocal influence on each other; and the former will be objects to which the latter will attach themselves. The diversity in the faculties of men, from which the rights of property originate, is not less an insuperable obstacle to a uniformity of interests. The protection of these faculties is the first object of government. From the protection of different and unequal faculties of acquiring property, the possession of different degrees and kinds of property immediately results; and from the influence of these on the sentiments and views of the respective proprietors, ensues a division of the society into different interests and parties.

The latent causes of faction are thus sown in the nature of man; and we see them everywhere brought into different degrees of activity, according to the different circumstances of civil society.

A zeal for different opinions concerning religion, concerning government, and many other points, as well of speculation as of practice; an attachment to different leaders ambitiously contending for pre-eminence and power; or to persons of other descriptions whose fortunes have been interesting to the human passions, have, in turn, divided mankind into parties, inflamed them with mutual animosity, and rendered them much more disposed to vex and oppress each other than to co-operate for their common good. So string is this propensity of mankind to fall into mutual animosities, that where no substantial occasion presents itself, the most frivolous and fanciful distinctions have been sufficient to kindle their unfriendly passions and excite their most violent conflicts. But the most common and durable source of factions has been the various and unequal distribution of property. Those who hold and those who are without property have ever formed distinct interests in society. Those who are creditors, and those who are debtors, fall under a like discrimination. A landed interest, a manufacturing interest, a mercantile interest, a moneyed interest, with many lesser interests, grow up of necessity in civilized nations, and divide them into different classes, actuated by different sentiments and views. The regulation of these various and interfering interests forms the principal task of modern legislation, and involves the spirit of party and faction in the necessary and ordinary operations of the government.

No man is allowed to be a judge in his own case, because his interest would certainly bias his judgment, and, not improbably, corrupt his integrity. With equal, nay with greater reason, a body of men are unfit to be both judges and parties at the same time; yet what are many of the most important acts of legislation, but so many judicial determinations, not indeed concerning the rights of single persons, but concerning the rights of large bodies of citizens? And what are the different classes of legislators but advocates and parties to the causes which they determine? Is a law proposed concerning private debts? It is a question to which the creditors are parties on one side and the debtors on the other. Justice ought to hold the balance between them. Yet the parties are, and must be, themselves the judges; and the most numerous party, or, in other words, the most powerful action must be expected to prevail. Shall domestic manufactures be encouraged, and in what degree, by restrictions on foreign manufactures? are questions which would be differently decided by the landed and the manufacturing classes, and probably by neither with a sole regard to justice and the public good. The apportionment of taxes on the various descriptions of property is an act which seems to require the most exact impartiality; yet there is, perhaps, no legislative act in which greater opportunity and temptation are given to a predominant party to trample on the rules of justice. Every shilling with which they overburden the inferior number, is a shilling saved to their own pockets.

It is in vain to say that enlightened statesmen will be able to adjust these clashing interests, and render them all subservient to the public good. Enlightened statesmen will not always be at the helm. Nor, in many cases, can such an adjustment be made at all without taking into view indirect and remote considerations, which will rarely prevail over the immediate interest which one party may find in disregarding the rights of another or the good of the whole.

The inference to which we are brought is, that the *causes* of faction cannot be removed, and that relief is only to be sought in the means of controlling its *effects*.

If a faction consists of less than a majority, relief is supplied by the republican principle, which enables the majority to defeat its sinister views by regular vote. It may clog the administration, it may convulse the society; but it will be unable to execute and mask its violence under the forms of the Constitution. When a majority is included in a faction, the form of popular government, on the other hand, enables it to sacrifice to its ruling passion or interest both the public good and the rights of other citizens. to secure the public good and private rights against the danger of such a faction, and at the same time to preserve the spirit and form of popular government, is then the great object to which our inquiries are directed. Let me add that it is the great desideratum by which this form of government can be rescued from the opprobrium under which it has so long labored, and be recommended to the esteem and adoption of mankind.

By what means is this object attainable? Evidently by one of two only. Either the existence of the same passion or interest in a majority at the same time must be prevented, or the majority, having such coexistent passion or interest, must be rendered, by their number and local situation, unable to concert and carry into effect schemes of oppression. If the impulse and the opportunity be suffered to coincide, we well know that neither moral nor religious motives can be relied on as an adequate control. They are not found to be such on the injustice and violence of individuals, and lose their efficacy in proportion to the number combined together, that is, in proportion as their efficacy becomes needful.

From this view of the subject it may be concluded that a pure democracy, by which I mean a society consisting of a small number of citizens, who assemble and administer the government in person, can admit of no cure for the mischiefs of faction. A common passion or interest will, in almost every case, be felt by a majority of the whole; a communication and concert result from the form of government itself; and there is nothing to check the inducements to sacrifice the weaker party or an obnoxious individual. Hence it is that such democracies have ever been spectacles of turbulence and contention; have ever been found incompatible with personal security or the rights of property; and have in general been as short in their lives as they have been violent in their deaths. Theoretic politicians, who have patronized this species of government, have erroneously supposed that by reducing mankind to a perfect equality in their political rights, they would, at the same time, be perfectly equalized and assimilated in their possessions, their opinions, and their passions.

A republic, by which I mean a government in which the scheme of representation takes place, opens a different prospect, and promises the cure for which we are seeking. Let us examine the points in which it varies from pure democracy, and we shall comprehend both the nature of the cure and the efficacy which it must derive from the Union.

The two great points of difference between a democracy and a republic are: first, the delegation of the government, in the latter, to a small number of citizens elected by the rest; secondly, the greater number of citizens, and greater sphere of country, over which the latter may be extended.

The effect of the first difference is, on the one hand, to refine and enlarge the public views, by passing them through the medium of a chosen body of citizens, whose wisdom may best discern the true interest of their country, and whose patriotism and love of justice will be least likely to sacrifice it to temporary or partial considerations. Under such a regulation, it may well happen that the public voice, pronounced by the representatives of the people, will be more consonant to the public good than it pronounced by the people themselves, convened for the purpose. On the other hand, the effect may be inverted. Men of factious tempers, of local prejudices, or of sinister designs, may, by intrigue, by corruption, or by other means, first obtain the suffrages, and then betray the interests, of the people. The question resulting is, whether small or extensive republics are more favorable to the election of proper guardians of the public weal; and it is clearly decided in favor of the latter by two obvious considerations:

In the first place, it is to be remarked that, however small the republic may be, the representatives must be raised to a certain number, in order to guard against the cabals of a few; and that, however large it may be, they must be limited to a certain number, in order to guard against the confusion of a multitude. Hence, the number of representatives in the two cases not being in proportion to that of the two constituents, and being proportionally greater in the small republic, it follows that, if the proportion of fit characters be not less in the large than in the small republic, the former will present a greater option, and consequently a greater probability of a fit choice.

In the next place, as each representative will be chosen by a greater number of citizens in the large than in the small republic, it will be more difficult for unworthy candidates to practice with success the vicious arts by which elections are too often carried; and the suffrages of the people being more free, will be more likely to centre in men who possess the most attractive merit and the most diffusive and established characters.

It must be confessed that in this, as in most other cases, there is a mean, on both sides of which inconveniences will be found to lie. By enlarging too much the number of electors, you render the representatives too little acquainted with all their local circumstances and lesser interests; as by reducing it too much, you render him unduly attached to these, and too little fit to comprehend and pursue great and national objects. The federal Constitution forms a happy combination in this respect; the great and aggregate interests being referred to the national, the local and particular to the State legislatures.

The other point of difference is, the greater number of citizens and extent of territory which may be brought within the compass of republican than of democratic government; and it is this circumstance principally which renders factious combinations less to be dreaded in the former than in the latter. The smaller the society, the fewer probably will be the distinct parties and interests composing it; the fewer the distinct parties and interests, the more frequently will a majority be found of the same party; and the smaller the number of individuals composing a majority, and the smaller the compass within which they are placed, the more easily will they concert and execute their plans of oppression. Extend the sphere, and you take in a greater variety of parties and interests; you make it less probable that a majority of the whole will have a common motive to invade the rights of other citizens; or if such a common motive exists, it will be more difficult for all who feel it to discover their own strength, and to act in unison with each other. Besides other impediments, it may be remarked that, where there is a consciousness of unjust or dishonorable purposes, communication is always checked by distrust in proportion to the number whose concurrence is necessary.

Hence, it clearly appears, that the same advantage which a republic has over a democracy, in controlling the effects of faction, is enjoyed by a large over a small republic,—-and is enjoyed by the Union over the States composing it. Does the advantage consist in the substitution of representatives whose enlightened views and virtuous sentiments render them superior to local prejudices and schemes of injustice? It will not be denied that the representation of the Union will be most likely to possess these requisite endowments. Does it consist in the greater security afforded by a greater variety of parties, against the event of any one party being able to outnumber and oppress the rest? In an equal degree does the increased variety of parties comprised within the Union, increase this security. Does it, in fine, consist in the greater obstacles opposed to the concert and accomplishment of the secret wishes of an unjust and interested majority? Here, again, the extent of the Union gives it the most palpable advantage.

The influence of factious leaders may kindle a flame within their particular States, but will be unable to spread a general conflagration through the other States. A religious sect may degenerate into a political faction in a part of the Confederacy; but the variety of sects dispersed over the entire face of it must secure the national councils against any danger from that source. A rage for paper money, for an abolition of debts, for an equal division of property, or for any other improper or wicked project, will be less apt to pervade the whole body of the Union than a particular member of it; in the same proportion as such a malady is more likely to taint a particular county or district, than an entire State.

In the extent and proper structure of the Union, therefore, we behold a republican remedy for the diseases most incident to republican government. And according to the degree of pleasure and pride we feel in being republicans, ought to be our zeal in cherishing the spirit and supporting the character of Federalists.

PUBLIUS

February 8, 1788

TO THE PEOPLE OF THE STATE OF NEW YORK

To what expedient, then, shall we finally resort, for maintaining in practice the necessary partition of power among the several departments, as laid down in the Constitution? The only answer that can be given is, that as all these exterior provisions are found to be inadequate, the defect must be supplied, by so contriving the interior structure of the government as that its several constituent parts may, by their mutual relations, be the means of keeping each other in their proper places. Without presuming to undertake a full development of the important idea, I will hazard a few general observations, which may perhaps place it in a clearer light, and enable us to form a more correct judgment of the principles and structure of the government planned by the convention.

In order to lay a due foundation for that separate and distinct exercise of the different powers of government, which to a certain extent is admitted on all hands to be essential to the preservation of liberty, it is evident that each department should have a will of its own; and consequently should be so constituted that the members of each should have as little agency as possible in the appointment of the members of the others. Were this principle rigorously adhered to, it would require that all the appointments for the supreme executive, legislative, and judiciary magistracies should be drawn from the same fountain of authority, the people, through channels having no communication whatever with one another. Perhaps such a plan of constructing the several departments would be less difficult in practice than it may in contemplation appear. Some difficulties, however, and some additional expense would attend the execution of it. Some deviations, therefore, from the principle must be admitted. In the constitution of the judiciary department in particular, it might be inexpedient to insist rigorously on the principle: first, because peculiar qualifications being essential in the members, the primary consideration ought to be to select that mode of choice which best secures these qualifications; secondly, because the permanent tenure by which the appointments are held in that department, must soon destroy all sense of dependence on the authority conferring them.

It is equally evident, that the members of each department should be as little dependent as possible on those of the others, for the emoluments annexed to their offices. Were the executive magistrate, or the judges, not independent of the legislature in this particular, their independence in every other would be merely nominal.

But the great security against a gradual concentration of the several powers in the same department, consists in giving to those who administer each department the necessary constitutional means and personal motives to resist encroachments of the others. The provision for defense must in this, as in all other cases, be made commensurate to the danger of attack. Ambition must be made to counteract ambition. The interest of the man must be connected with the constitutional rights of the place. It may be a reflection on human nature, that such devices should be necessary to control the abuses of government. But what is government itself, but the greatest of all reflections on human nature? If men were angels, no government would be necessary. If angels were to govern men, neither external nor internal controls on government would be necessary. In framing a government which is to be administered by men over men, the great difficulty lies in this: you must first enable the government to control the governed; and in the next place oblige it to control itself. A dependence on the people is, no doubt, the primary control on the government; but experience has taught mankind the necessity of auxiliary precautions.

This policy of supplying, by opposite and rival interests, the defect of better motives, might be traced through the whole system of human affairs, private as well as public. We see it particularly displayed in all the subordinate distributions of power, where the constant aim is to divide and arrange the several offices in such a manner as that each may be a check on the other—-that the private interest of every individual may be a sentinel over the public rights. These inventions of prudence cannot be less requisite in the distribution of the supreme powers of the State.

But it is not possible to give to each department an equal power of self-defense. In republican government, the legislative authority necessarily predominates. The remedy for this inconveniency is to divide the legislature into different branches; and to render them, by different modes of election and different principles of action, as little connected with each other as the nature of their common functions and their common dependence on the society will admit. It may even be necessary to guard against dangerous encroachments by still further precautions. As the weight of the legislative authority requires that it should be thus divided, the weakness of the executive may require, on the other hand, that it should be fortified. An absolute negative on the legislature appears, at first view, to be the natural defense with which the executive magistrate should be armed. But perhaps it would be neither altogether safe nor alone sufficient. On ordinary occasions it might not be exerted with the requisite firmness, and on extraordinary occasions it might be perfidiously abused. May not this defect of an absolute negative be supplied by some qualified connection between this weaker department and the weaker branch of the stronger department, by which the latter may be led to support the constitutional rights of the former, without being too much detached from the rights of its own department?

If the principles on which these observations are founded be just, as I persuade myself they are, and they be applied as a criterion to the several State constitutions, and to the federal Constitution it will be found that if the latter does not perfectly correspond with them, the former are infinitely less able to bear such a test.

There are, moreover, two considerations particularly applicable to the federal system of America, which place that system in a very interesting point of view.

First. In a single republic, all the power surrendered by the people is submitted to the administration of a single government; and the usurpations are guarded against by a division of the government into distinct and separate departments. In the compound republic of America, the power surrendered by the people is first divided between two distinct governments, and then the portion allotted to each subdivided among distinct and separate departments. Hence a double security arises to the rights of the people. The different governments will control each other, at the same time that each will be controlled by itself.

Second. It is of great importance in a republic not only to guard the society against the oppression of its rulers, but to guard one part of the society against the injustice of the other part. Different interests necessarily exist in different classes of citizens. If a majority be united by a common interest, the rights of the minority will be insecure. There are but two methods of providing against this evil: the one by creating a will in the community independent of the majority that is, of the society itself; the other, by comprehending in the society so many separate descriptions of citizens as will render an unjust combination of a majority of the whole very improbable, if not impracticable. The first method prevails in all governments possessing an hereditary or self-appointed authority. This, at best, is but a precarious security; because a power independent of society may as well espouse the unjust views of the major as the rightful interests of the minor party, and may possibly be turned against both parties. The second method will be exemplified in the federal republic of the United States. Whilst all authority in it will be derived from and dependent on the society, the society itself will be broken into so many parts, interests, and classes of citizens, that the rights of individuals, or of the minority, will be in little danger from interested combinations of the majority. In a free government the security for civil rights must be the same as that for religious rights. It consists in the one case in the multiplicity of interests, and in the other in the multiplicity of sects. The degree of security in both cases will depend on the number of interests and sects; and this may be presumed to depend on the extent of country and number of people comprehended under the same government. This view of the subject must particularly recommend a proper federal system to all the sincere and considerate friends of republican government, since it shows that in exact proportion as the territory of the Union may be formed into more circumscribed Confederacies, or States oppressive combinations of a majority will be facilitated: the best security, under republican forms, for the rights of every class of citizens, will be diminished; and consequently the stability and independence of some member of the government, the only other security, must be proportionately increased. Justice is the end of government. It is the end of civil society. It ever has been and ever will be pursued until it be obtained, or until liberty be lost in the pursuit. In a society under the forms of which the stronger faction can readily unite and oppress the weaker, anarchy may as truly be said to reign as in a state of nature, where the weaker individual is not secured against the violence of the stronger; and as, in the latter state, even the stronger individuals are prompted, by the uncertainty of their condition, to submit to a government which may protect the wear as well as the more powerful. It can be little doubted that if the State of Rhode Island was separated from the Confederacy and left to itself, the insecurity of rights under the popular form of government within such narrow limits would be displayed by such reiterated oppressions of factious majorities that some power altogether independent of the people would soon be called for by the voice of the very factions whose misrule had proved the necessity of it. In the extended republic of the United States, and among the great variety of interests, parties, and sects which it embraces, a coalition of a majority of the whole society could seldom take place on any other principles than those of justice and the general good; whilst there being thus less danger to a minor from the will of a major party, there must be less pretext, also, to provide for the security of the former, by introducing into the government a will not dependent on the latter, or, in other words, a will independent of the society itself. It is no less certain than it is important, notwithstanding the contrary opinions which have been entertained, that the larger the society, provided it lie within a practical sphere, the more duly capable it will be of self-government. And happily for the *republican cause*, the practicable sphere may be carried to a very great extent, by a judicious modification of mixture of the *federal principle*.

PUBLIUS

Presidents of the United States

Name of President	Dates of Service	Political Party Affiliation	Vice President(s)	Major Party Candidate(s) Defeated in General Election
George Washington	1789–97		Adams	
John Adams	1797–1801	Federalist	Jefferson	Jefferson
Thomas Jefferson	1801–09	Democratic-Republican	Burr/Clinton	Adams, Pinckney
James Madison	1809–17	Democratic-Republican	Clinton/Gerry	Pinckney, D. Clinton
James Monroe	1817–25	Democratic-Republican	Tompkins	King
John Quincy Adams	1825–29	Democratic-Republican/Democratic	Calhoun	Jackson
Andrew Jackson	1829–37	Democratic	Van Buren	J. Q.Adams, Clay
Martin Van Buren	1837–41	Democratic	Johnson	Harrison
William Harrison	1841	Whig	Tyler	Van Buren
John Tyler	1841–45	Whig	vacant	
James Polk	1845–49	Democratic	Dallas	Clay
Zachary Taylor	1849–50	Whig	Fillmore	Cass
Millard Fillmore	1850–53	Whig	vacant	
Franklin Pierce	1853–57	Democratic	King/vacant	Scott
James Buchanan	1857–61	Democratic	Breckinridge	Fremont
Abraham Lincoln	1861–65	Republican	Hamlin/Johnson	Breckinridge, Douglas, McClellan
Andrew Johnson	1865–69	Democratic	vacant	
Ulysses S. Grant	1869–77	Republican	Colfax/Wilson/vacant	Seymour, Greeley
Rutherford B. Hayes	1877–81	Republican	Wheeler	Tilden
James Garfield	1881	Republican	Arthur	Hancock
Chester Arthur	1881–85	Republican	vacant	
Grover Cleveland	1885–89	Democratic	Hendricks/vacant	Blaine

Name of President	Dates of Service	Political Party Affiliation	Vice President(s)	Major Party Candidate(s) Defeated in General Election
Benjamin Harrison	1889–93	Republican	Morton	Cleveland
Grover Cleveland	1893–97	Democratic	Stevenson	Harrison
William McKinley	1897–1901	Republican	Hobart	Bryan
Theodore Roosevelt	1901–09	Republican	vacant/Fairbanks	Parker
William Taft	1909–13	Republican	Sherman/vacant	Bryan
Woodrow Wilson	1913–21	Democratic	Marshall	T. Roosevelt, Taft, Hughes
Warren G. Harding	1921–23	Republican	Coolidge	Cox
Calvin Coolidge	1923–29	Republican	vacant/Dawes	Davis
Herbert Hoover	1929–33	Republican	Curtis	Smith
Franklin D. Roosevelt	1933–45	Democratic	Garner/Wallace/ Truman	Hoover, Landon, Wilkie, Dewey
Harry Truman	1945–53	Democratic	vacant/Barkley	Dewey
Dwight Eisenhower	1953–61	Republican	Nixon	Stevenson
John F. Kennedy	1961–63	Democratic	Johnson	Nixon
Lyndon Johnson	1963–69	Democratic	vacant/Humphrey	Goldwater
Richard Nixon	1969–74	Republican	Agnew/vacant/Ford	Humphrey, McGovern
Gerald Ford	1974–77	Republican	vacant/Rockefeller	
Jimmy Carter	1977–81	Democratic	Mondale	Ford
Ronald Reagan	1981–89	Republican	G. H.W. Bush	Carter, Mondale
George H. W. Bush	1989–93	Republican	Quayle	Dukakis
William Clinton	1993–2001	Democratic	Gore	G. H. W. Bush, Dole
George W. Bush	2001–2009	Republican	Cheney	Gore, Kerry
Barack Obama	2009–present	Democratic	Biden	McCain

A

Administrative discretion The freedom of agencies to decide how to implement a vague or ambiguous law passed by Congress.

Administrative law A law that relates to the authority of administrative agencies and the rules promulgated by those agencies.

Affirmative action Programs, laws, or practices designed to remedy past discriminatory hiring practices, government contracting, and school admissions.

Agenda setting theory The theory that holds that although the effects of television exposure may be minimal or difficult to gauge, the media are quite influential in telling the public what to think about.

Agents of political socialization Factors that have a significant impact on an individual's socialization to politics.

Amendments Modifications or additions to the U.S. Constitution passed in accordance with the amendment procedures laid out in Article V.

Amicus curiae briefs Written documents filed by outside parties in the case with an interest in the outcome of the litigation expressing their own views on how the Court should decide a particular case.

Anarchy A state of lawlessness and discord in the political system caused by lack of government.

Anti-Federalists Those who opposed ratification of the proposed Constitution of the United States.

Appellate jurisdiction The authority of a court to review decisions handed down by another court.

Articles of Confederation The document creating a "league of friendship" governing the thirteen states during and immediately after the war for independence; hampered by the limited power they vested in the legislature to collect revenue or regulate commerce, the Articles eventually proved unworkable for the new nation.

Authoritarianism A form of government in which one political party, group, or person maintains such complete control over the nation that it may refuse to recognize and may even suppress all other political parties and interests.

Authority The ability of public institutions and the officials within them to make laws, independent of the power to execute them.

B

Bail An amount of money determined by a judge that the accused must pay to a court as security against his or her freedom before trial.

Battleground states States identified as offering either major-party candidate a reasonable chance for victory in the Electoral College.

Bicameral legislature A legislature composed of two separate chambers.

Bill A proposed law presented for consideration to a legislative body.

Bill of attainder An act of a legislature declaring a person (or group) guilty of some crime, and then carrying out punishment without a trial. The Constitution denies Congress the ability to issue a bill of attainder.

Bill of Rights The first ten amendments to the U.S. Constitution, which protect various rights of the people against the new federal government.

Bipartisan Campaign Reform Act (BCRA) of 2002 Also called the McCain-Feingold Act, the federal legislation that (1) restricted soft money spent by political parties, (2) regulated expenditures on ads that refer to specific candidates immediately before an election, and (3) increased limits on hard money donated directly to candidates and their campaigns.

Block grants Grants from the federal government to the states that may be used at the discretion of states to pursue more generalized aims.

Blogs Internet sites that include a combination of editorial page, personal Web page, and online diary of personal observations in real time about news events and issues.

Briefs Written documents filed by parties in an appealed case arguing why constitutional or statutory law weighs in favor of their respective positions.

***Brown v. Board of Education* (1954)** The 1954 U.S. Supreme Court decision that declared school segregation to be unconstitutional.

***Buckley v. Valeo* (1976)** The 1976 Supreme Court opinion that held that spending money to influence elections is protected First Amendment speech, and that prohibited limitations on independent expenditures or personal money spent by candidates on their own campaigns.

Bureaucracy An organization set up in a logical and rational manner for the purpose of accomplishing specific functions.

Bureaucratic adjudicating Determining the rights and duties of particular parties within the scope of an agency's rules or regulations.

C

Cabinet The collection of the principal officers in each of the executive departments of the federal government who serve as key advisers to the president.

Cabinet departments Those federal agencies that qualify as the major administrative organizations of the executive branch.

Casework The direct assistance that a member of Congress provides to a constituent, community group, or a local or state official.

Caucus A method of choosing party nominees in which party members attend local meetings at which they choose delegates committed to a particular candidate.

Checks and balances A system of limits imposed by the Constitution that gives each branch of government the limited right to change or cancel the acts of other branches.

Civil law This term has two meanings: (1) legislative codes, laws, or sets of rules enacted by duly authorized lawmaking bodies such as Congress, state and local legislatures, or any executive authority entrusted with the power to make laws; (2) the body of noncriminal laws of a nation or state that deal with the rights of private citizens.

Civil liberties Those specific individual rights that are guaranteed by the Constitution and cannot be denied to citizens by government. Most of these rights are in the first ten amendments to the Constitution, known as the Bill of Rights.

Civil rights Those positive rights, whether political, social, or economic, conferred by the government on individuals or groups.

Civil Rights Act of 1964 The federal law that banned racial discrimination in all public accommodations, including those that were privately owned; prohibited discrimination by employers and created the Equal Employment Opportunity Commission to investigate complaints of discrimination; and denied public funds to schools that continued to discriminate on the basis of race.

Civil Rights Act of 1968 The federal law that banned race discrimination in housing and made interference with a citizen's civil rights a federal crime.

Civil service The system whereby workers in the federal bureaucracy are supposed to be immune from partisan political maneuvering.

Civil Service Reform Act of 1978 The federal act that replaced the Civil Service Commission (the agency that oversaw federal hiring and firing practices) with the Office of Personnel Management (OPM) and the Merit Systems Protection Board (MSPB).

Civil War Amendments The Thirteenth Amendment (ratified in 1865) banished slavery from all states and U.S. territories. The Fourteenth Amendment (ratified in 1868) granted full U.S. and state citizenship to all people born or naturalized in the United States and guaranteed to each person "the equal protection of the laws." The Fifteenth Amendment (1870) forbade the denial or abridgement of the right to vote by any government on account of race.

Class action lawsuit A lawsuit filed by a large group of people with clearly defined common interests.

Closed primary An election that requires voters to declare their party affiliation ahead of time.

Closed rule A rule of procedure adopted by the House Rules Committee that severely limits the ability of members of Congress to amend a bill.

Closed shop The law that requires employees to become members of the union as a condition of employment in unionized workplaces.

Cloture A Senate debate procedure that permits that body to end debate and force a vote on a bill by a vote of sixty senators.

Coattail effect The potential benefit that successful presidential candidates offer to congressional candidates of the same political party during presidential election years.

Common law Judge-made law handed down through judicial opinions, which over time establish precedents.

Complaint A document written by the plaintiff arguing why the court is empowered to hear the case and explaining why the plaintiff is entitled to some form of relief under the current law.

Concurrent powers Those powers shared by the federal and state governments under the Constitution.

Concurring opinion The opinion of one or more justices that agrees with the end result reached by the majority but disagrees with the reasons offered for the decision.

Confederation A system of government (or "league") in which two or more independent states unite to achieve certain specified common aims.

Conference committee A joint committee of Congress appointed by the House of Representatives and the Senate to resolve differences on a particular bill.

Congressional agencies Government bodies formed by and relied on by Congress to support members of Congress in performing their functions.

Congressional district A geographic region (either a state itself or a region located entirely within one state) whose residents select one member to represent it in the House of Representatives.

Congressional oversight Congress's exercise of its authority to monitor the activities of agencies and administrators.

Congressional personal staff A group of workers who assist an individual member of Congress in performing his or her responsibilities.

Conservative ideology A political orientation that generally favors government activism in defense of more traditional values on social issues, but favors government restraint in economic redistribution.

Constitutional Convention Meeting of delegates from twelve states in Philadelphia during the summer of 1787, at which was drafted an entirely new system to govern the United States.

Continuity (in public opinion) A tendency for political preferences to remain generally stable over time.

Cooperative federalism The doctrine of federalism that affords Congress nearly unlimited authority to exercise its powers through means that often coerce states into administering and/or enforcing federal policies.

Critical election An election that produces sharp changes in patterns of party loyalty among voters.

Cultivation theory The theory of media effects that suggests that heavy television exposure helps develop an individual's overall view of the world.

D

Dealignment A decline in voter attachment to parties and in clarity of party coalitions.

Declaration of Independence Formal document listing colonists' grievances and articulating the colonists' intention to seek independence; formally adopted by the Second Continental Congress on July 4, 1776.

Defendant The target of a plaintiff's complaint.

Delegation of congressional power Congress's transferring of its lawmaking authority to the executive branch of government.

Democracy Form of government in which the people, either directly or through elected representatives, hold power and authority. The word *democracy* is derived from the Greek *demos kratos*, meaning "rule by the people."

Deregulation The elimination of government oversight and government regulation of certain activities.

Devolution The transfer of power and responsibilities for certain regulatory programs from the federal government back to the states.

Digital divide The large differences in usage of the Internet between older and younger people, lower- and middle/upper-class people, lesser and better educated people, and minority groups and nonminority groups.

Direct democracy A system of government in which all citizens participate in making policy, rules, and governing decisions.

Direction (of public opinion) A tendency toward a particular preference, usually (though not always) characterized as either positive or negative.

Direct primary election An open election, rather than an election by party leaders, to choose candidates for the general election.

Discovery A stage of pretrial litigation in which the plaintiff and defendant have the right to learn what information the other side has about the case by requesting documents or materials, access to property, and/or examinations, or by offering answers to questions about the litigation either in written form or verbally at a deposition.

Dissenting opinion The opinion of one or more justices who disagree with the result reached by the majority.

Divided government Split party control of Congress and the presidency.

Double jeopardy clause The constitutional protection that those accused of a crime cannot be tried twice for the same crime.

Dual federalism The doctrine of federalism that holds that state authority acts as a limit on congressional power under the Constitution.

E

Economic equality May be defined as providing all groups the equality of opportunity for economic success, or as the equality of results. In the United States, the latter has been the more common understanding of economic opportunity.

Economic interest group An organized group that exists to promote favorable economic conditions and economic opportunities for its members.

Economic protest party A party that emerges in times of economic recession to express discontent with the ruling party.

Electoral College The constitutional mechanism by which presidents are chosen. Each state is allocated Electoral College votes based on the sum of that state's U.S. senators and House members.

Electors Individuals appointed to represent a state's presidential vote in the Electoral College; in practice, voters in presidential elections vote for a slate of electors committed to a particular candidate, rather than voting directly for the candidate.

Enumerated powers Express powers explicitly granted by the Constitution such as the taxing power specifically granted to Congress.

Equal time rule The FCC mandate that radio and TV stations offer equal amounts of airtime to all political candidates who want to broadcast advertisements.

Establishment clause The clause in the First Amendment that prohibits government from enacting any law "respecting an establishment of religion." Separationist interpretations of this clause affirm that government should not support any religious activity. Accommodationists say that support for a religion is legal provided that all religions are equally supported.

Exclusionary rule The legal rule requiring that all evidence illegally obtained by police in violation of the Bill of Rights must be "excluded" from admission in a court of law, where it might have assisted in convicting those accused of committing crimes.

Executive agreement A pact reached between the president and a foreign government that does not require the consent of Congress.

Executive Office of the President The staffers who help the president of the United States manage the rest of the federal bureaucracy.

Executive orders Rules or regulations issued by the chief executive that have the force of law and do not require the consent of Congress.

Ex post facto laws A law that punishes someone for doing something in the past, at a time when the act was not illegal. The Constitution denies government the ability to write laws ex post facto.

F

Factional party A party that has split off from one of the major parties.

Federal Election Campaign Act (FECA) The federal legislation passed in 1971 that established disclosure requirements and restricted individual campaign contributions.

Federal Election Commission (FEC) The agency created in 1974 to enforce federal election laws.

Federalism The doctrine underlying a system of government in which power is divided between a central government and constituent political subunits.

Federalist Papers A series of articles authored by Alexander Hamilton, James Madison, and John Jay, which argued in favor of ratifying the proposed Constitution of the United States; the *Federalist Papers* outlined the philosophy and motivation of the document.

Federalists Those who supported ratification of the proposed Constitution of the United States between 1787 and 1789.

Federal Register The journal that publishes regulations that implement a federal program.

Fifteenth Amendment The amendment to the Constitution that guaranteed the franchise regardless of race, color, or any previous condition of servitude.

Filibuster The action by a single senator or a minority of senators to block a bill from passage by refusing to end discussion.

Franchise (or suffrage) The right to vote.

Franking privilege The traditional right of members of Congress to mail materials to their constituents without paying postage.

Free exercise clause The religious freedom clause in the First Amendment that denies government the ability to prohibit the free exercise of religion. Debate over the clause has largely focused on whether government laws can force adherents of a certain religion to engage in activities that are prohibited by their religious beliefs or prevent them from performing acts that are compelled by their religious beliefs.

Free rider An individual who does not join or contribute to an interest group that is representing his or her interests.

Frontloading The recent trend of states moving their primaries and caucuses earlier in the year to attract greater attention from the candidates and the media.

Full faith and credit clause The provision in Article IV, Section 1 of the Constitution that forces states to abide by the official acts and proceedings of all other states.

G

Gerrymandering The drawing of House district boundaries to the benefit of one political party over another. The term is named for Elbridge Gerry, a Massachusetts delegate to the Constitutional Convention, who (as governor) redrew districts in this fashion to favor the Democratic-Republicans.

Gibbons v. Ogden (1824) The Supreme Court case that held that under the Constitution, a federal license to operate steamboats overrides a state-granted monopoly of New York water rights.

Good faith exception An exception to the exclusionary rule that states if a search warrant is invalid through no fault of the police, evidence obtained under that warrant may still be admitted into court.

Government The collection of public institutions in a nation that establish and enforce the rules by which the members of that nation must live.

Government corporations Units in the federal bureaucracy set up to run like private companies that depend on revenue from citizens to provide their services.

Grand jury A jury whose duty it is to hear the evidence offered by a prosecutor and determine whether a trial is justified.

Grants-in-aid Grants from the federal government to states that allow state governments to pursue specific federal policies, such as highway construction.

Grassroots lobbying Communications by interest groups with government officials through the mobilization of public opinion to exert influence on government action.

Great Compromise A proposal also known as the "Connecticut Compromise" that provided for a bicameral legislature featuring an upper house based on equal representation among the states and a lower house whose membership was based on each state's population; approved by a 5–4 vote of the state delegations.

Great Society A set of aggressive federal domestic policies proposed by President Lyndon Johnson and passed by Congress in the 1960s that further enhanced the role of the presidency.

H

Hard money Donations made directly to political candidates and their campaigns that must be declared with the name of the donor (which then becomes public knowledge).

Hatch Act of 1939 The 1939 law that insulated the civil service from partisan politics by prohibiting employee dismissals for partisan reasons and by prohibiting federal workers from participating in political campaigns.

I

Ideological party A party that promotes broad ideas about the purpose and role of government.

Impeachment The first step in a two-step process outlined in Article II, Section 4 of the U.S. Constitution to remove a president or other high official from office. The House of Representatives, by majority vote, may impeach if the official has committed "treason, bribery, or other high crimes or misdemeanors." The second step requires a conviction in the Senate by a two-thirds vote.

Incorporation The process by which the U.S. Supreme Court used the due process clause of the Fourteenth Amendment to make most of the individual rights guaranteed by the Bill of Rights also applicable to the states. Incorporation provided that state and local governments, as well as the federal government, could not deny these rights to citizens.

Incumbent race General election race pitting a person currently holding the office against a challenger.

Independent agency A department that focuses on a narrower set of issues than do higher-status Cabinet departments.

Independent campaign expenditure Political donations that PACs or individuals spend to support campaigns, but do not directly contribute to the campaigns.

Indictment A decision by a grand jury authorizing the government to proceed to trial against the defendant.

Individualism The value that individuals are primarily responsible for their own lot in life and that promotes and rewards individual initiative and responsibility. This value underlies America's reliance on a capitalist economy and free-market system.

Intensity (of public opinion) The degree of strength or commitment the public feels about the opinion it holds.

Interest group An organization of people with shared goals that tries to influence public policy through a variety of activities.

Intergovernmental lobby Any interest group that represents the collective interests of states, cities, and other governments.

Invisible primary The competition among candidates seeking the party nomination for front-runner status prior to the primaries and caucuses.

Iron triangle A three-sided network of policymaking that includes congressional committees (and subcommittees) in a specific policy area, executive agencies with authority over that area, and private interest groups focused on influencing that area.

Issue and ideological group An organized group that focuses on specific issues and ideological perspectives.

Issue network The broad array of actors (beyond just the iron triangle) that try to collectively influence a policy area in which they maintain a vested interest.

Issue party A party that tends to form on the basis of a single issue.

J

Jim Crow laws Laws used by some southern states that required segregation of blacks and whites in public schools, railroads, buses, restaurants, hotels, theaters, and other public facilities. The laws excluded blacks from militias and denied them certain education and welfare services.

Joint committee A committee composed of members of both the House and the Senate that is investigative in nature.

Judicial review The power of a court to declare acts of the other branches of government or of a subordinate government to be unconstitutional and thus invalid.

K

Katz test The legal standard that requires the government to attain a warrant demonstrating "prob-

able cause" for any "search" that violates a person's actual and reasonable expectation of privacy.

L

Layer cake federalism Description of federalism as maintaining that the authority of state and federal governments exists in distinct and separate spheres.

Legitimacy The extent to which the people afford the government the authority and right to exercise power.

Lemon test The legal test that determines if a government statute aiding public or private schools is an unconstitutional violation of the establishment clause. The statute is unconstitutional if the statute has no secular purpose, if its principal or primary effect advances or inhibits religion, or if it fosters "an excessive government entanglement with religion."

Libel Printing or disseminating false statements that harm someone.

Liberal ideology A political orientation that favors a more assertive role in the redistribution of economic resources, but emphasizes individual freedom on a range of social issues.

Limited government The value that promotes the idea that government power should be as restricted as possible.

Literacy test The requirement that individuals prove that they can read and write before being allowed to vote.

Litigation Any judicial contest, including all the events that lead up to a possible court event.

Lobbying The means by which interest groups attempt to influence government officials to make decisions favorable to their goals.

Logrolling The trading of influence or votes among legislators to achieve passage of projects that are of interest to one another.

Loose construction Constitutional interpretation that gives constitutional provisions broad and open-ended meanings.

M

Majoritarianism (1) The principle that the choice that is supported by the most voters is the choice that prevails; (2) the theory that public policy is a product of what majorities of citizens prefer.

Majority caucus The members of the party that has the majority of seats in a particular chamber.

Majority leader In the Senate, the controlling party's main spokesperson who leads his or her party in proposing new laws and crafting the party's platform. The Senate majority leader also enjoys the power to make committee assignments. In the House, the majority leader is the controlling party's second in command, who helps the Speaker to oversee the development of the party platform.

Majority opinion The opinion of a majority of members of the U.S. Supreme Court, which carries the force of law.

Majority rule The notion that the will of the majority should guide decisions made by American government.

Marble cake federalism Description of federalism as intertwining state and federal authority in an inseparable mixture.

Marginal seat A seat in a congressional district that has relatively similar numbers of Democratic and Republican voters.

***Martin v. Hunter's Lessee* (1819)** The Supreme Court case that established that state governments and state courts must abide by the U.S. Supreme Court's interpretation of the federal Constitution.

Material benefits (of group membership) The specific, tangible benefits individuals receive from interest group membership, such as economic concessions, discounts on products, etc.

***McCulloch v. Maryland* (1819)** The Supreme Court case that established that Congress enjoys broad and extensive authority to make all laws that are "necessary and proper" to carry out its constitutionally delegated powers.

Merit system A system of appointing and promoting civil service personnel based on merit rather than political affiliation or loyalty.

Midterm congressional elections Congressional elections held midway between successive presidential elections.

Minimal effects theory The theory that deep-seated, long-term political attitudes have much greater influence on an individual's vote decisions than does news media coverage.

Minority caucus The members of the party that has a minority of seats in a particular chamber.

Minority leader The leader of the minority party in each chamber.

***Miranda* warning** The U.S. Supreme Court's requirement that an individual who is arrested must be read a statement that explains the person's right to remain silent and the right to an attorney.

Monarchy A form of government in which one person, usually a member of a royal family or a royal designate, exercises supreme authority.

Motor Voter law The federal law that mandates that when an individual applies for or renews a state driver's license, the state must also provide that individual with voter registration materials.

Multiparty system A political system in which many different parties are organized on the basis of political ideologies, economic interests, religion, geography, or positions on a single issue or set of issues.

N

National committee The committee that oversees the conduct of a party's presidential campaign and develops strategy for congressional elections.

National committee chair The head of the national committee for one of the two major parties.

National party convention A large meeting that draws together party delegates from across the nation to choose (or formally affirm the selection of) the party's presidential and vice presidential candidates.

National party organization The institution through which political parties exist at the national, state, and local levels, primarily focused on articulating policy positions, raising money, organizing volunteers, and providing services to candidates.

National supremacy doctrine Chief Justice John Marshall's interpretation of federalism as holding that states have extremely limited sovereign authority, whereas Congress is supreme within its own sphere of constitutional authority.

Natural law According to John Locke, the most fundamental type of law, which supersedes any law that is made by government. Citizens are born with certain natural rights (including life, liberty, and property) that derive from this law and that government cannot take away.

Necessary and proper clause The clause in Article I, Section 8 of the Constitution that affords Congress the power to make laws that serve as a means to achieving its expressly delegated powers.

New Deal An set of aggressive federal domestic policies proposed by President Franklin Roosevelt in the 1930s and passed by Congress as a response to the Great Depression; it ultimately transformed the presidency into an institution marked by permanent bureaucracies and well-established repositories of power.

New Jersey Plan A proposal known also as the "small states plan" that would have retained the Articles of Confederation principle of a legislature where states enjoyed equal representation.

New media Media outlets that rely on relatively newer technologies for communicating, such as the Internet, DVDs, fax machines, cell phones, satellites, cable TV, and broadband.

Nineteenth Amendment The constitutional amendment that guarantees women equal voting rights.

Nomination campaign The political season in which the two major parties hold primaries and caucuses in all the states to choose party delegates committed to specific candidates.

Noneconomic interest group An organized group that advocates for reasons other than their membership's commercial and financial interests.

Normal vote The percentage of voters that can be expected with reasonable certainty to cast a ballot for each of the two major political parties.

O

Objectivity The journalistic standard that news reporting of events must be factual, accurate, fair, and equitable.

Oligarchy A form of government in which a small exclusive class, which may or may not attempt to rule on behalf of the people as a whole, holds supreme power.

Open election General election race in which neither candidate is the incumbent. (Open elections for Congress are normally called "open seat elections.")

Open primary An election that allows voters to choose on the day of the primary election the party in which they want to vote.

Open rule A rule of procedure adopted by the House Rules Committee that permits amendments to a bill.

Open shop The law that allows employees the option of joining or not joining the certified union at a unionized workplace.

Original jurisdiction The authority of a court to be the initial court in which a legal decision is rendered.

Overriding a veto The power of the Congress to enact legislation despite a president's veto of that legislation; requires a two-thirds vote of both houses of Congress.

P

Pardon The president's constitutional authority to relieve an individual of both the punishment and the guilt of violating the law.

Partisan press era The period from the late 1700s to the mid-1800s when newspapers typically supported a particular political party.

Party identification The psychological attachment that an individual has to a particular party.

Party platform A document outlining the party's position on important policy issues.

Patronage The act of appointing people to government positions in return for their partisan and/or political support.

Pendleton Civil Service Reform Act The 1883 law that created a merit system for hiring many federal workers, protected them from being fired for partisan reasons, and set up a Civil Service Commission to oversee the hiring and firing process.

Plaintiff The party that chooses to initiate formal legal proceedings in a civil case.

Plea bargain A pretrial negotiated resolution in a criminal case in which the defendants seek to reduce their jail sentences by pleading guilty and in return prosecutors are willing to trade down the severity of the punishment.

***Plessy v. Ferguson* (1896)** The Supreme Court case that upheld a Louisiana segregation law on the theory that as long as the accommodations between the racially segregated facilities were equal, the equal protection clause was not violated. The Court's ruling effectively established the constitutionality of racial segregation and the notion of "separate but equal."

Pluralism The theory that public policy largely results from a variety of interest groups competing with one another to promote laws that benefit members of their respective groups.

Pocket veto The indirect veto of a bill received by the president within ten days of the adjournment of Congress, effected by the president's retaining the bill unsigned until Congress adjourns.

Policy implementation The process of carrying out laws, and the specific programs or services outlined in those laws.

Political action committee (PAC) The political arm of an interest group that promotes candidates in election campaigns primarily through financial contributions.

Political culture The values and beliefs about government, its purpose, and its operations and institutions that are widely held among citizens in a society; it defines the essence of how a society thinks politically and is transmitted from one generation to the next.

Political equality A condition in which members of different groups possess substantially the same rights to participate actively in the political system. In the United States, these rights include voting, running for office, petitioning the government for redress of grievances, free speech, free press, and the access to an education.

Political ideology A philosophical guide that people use to help translate their values and beliefs into political preferences.

Political orientations The translation of values and beliefs into a systematic way of assessing the political environment.

Political party An organization that seeks to win elections for the purpose of influencing the outputs of government.

Political preferences The attitudes people maintain regarding the performance of political leaders and institutions, their candidate preferences in elections, and specific policy issues.

Political socialization The process by which an individual acquires values, beliefs, and opinions about politics.

Politics The way in which the institutions of government are organized to make laws, rules, and policies, and how those institutions are influenced.

Poll tax The requirement that individuals pay a fee before being allowed to vote.

Popular sovereignty The idea that the ultimate source of power in the nation is held by the people.

Pork-barrel legislation A government project or appropriation that yields jobs or other benefits to a specific locale and patronage opportunities to its political representative.

Power The ability to get individuals to do something that they may not otherwise do, such as pay taxes, stop for red lights, or submit to a search before boarding an airplane.

Power of appointment The president's constitutional power to hire and fire those charged with administrative authority to help execute federal laws, such as ambassadors, federal judges including those on the Supreme Court, and all other federal officers under the president's charge. Most of these appointments require the consent of the Senate.

Power of incumbency The phenomenon by which incumbent members of Congress running for reelection are returned to office at an extremely high rate.

Preemption The constitutional doctrine that holds that when Congress acts affirmatively in the exercise of its own granted power, federal laws supersede all state laws on the matter.

Prenomination campaign The political season in which candidates for president begin to explore the possibility of running by attempting to raise money and garner support.

Presidential primary A statewide election to select delegates who will represent a state at the party's national convention.

President pro tempore In the absence of the vice president, the senator who presides over the Senate session. By tradition, this is usually the senator from the majority caucus who has served the longest number of consecutive years in the Senate.

Primacy tendency The theory that impressions acquired while an individual is younger are likely to be more influential and longer lasting.

Prior restraint The government's requirement that material be approved by government before it can be published.

Privatization The process of replacing government-provided services with services provided by the private sector.

Proportional representation A system of electing a national legislature in which the percentage of the vote that a party receives is reflected in the number of seats that the party occupies.

Pseudo-poll Phone calls from members of political campaigns or PACs who present themselves as pollsters for the purpose of planting messages with voters rather than measuring public opinion.

Public interest group An organized group that promotes the broad, collective good of citizens and consumers.

Public opinion The summation of individual opinions on any particular issue or topic.

Public opinion poll A method of measuring the opinions of a large group of people by asking questions of a subset of the larger group and then generalizing the findings to the larger group.

Purposive benefits (of group membership) Rewards that do not directly benefit the individual member, but benefit society as a whole.

R

Racial profiling The law enforcement practice of taking race into account when identifying possible suspects of crimes.

Random-digit dialing (RDD) A probability technique for scientific telephone polling that randomly assigns the last four digits to known information about telephone area codes and exchanges.

Reapportionment The allocation of a fixed number of House seats to the states.

Redistricting The act of redrawing congressional boundaries to achieve equal representation in each of the congressional districts.

Regulations Rules or other directives issued by government agencies.

Regulatory agency A government body responsible for the control and supervision of a specified activity or area of public interest.

Reporting legislation The exclusive power of standing committees to forward legislation to the full House or Senate. Neither chamber can vote on a bill unless the committee votes to approve it first.

Representative democracy A form of government designed by the U.S. Constitution whereby free, open, and regular elections are held to allow citizens to elect individuals who govern on their behalf and who are responsible for making and enforcing public policy; also referred to as *indirect democracy* or a *republican* form of government.

Reprieve The president's constitutional authority to reduce the severity of a punishment without removing the guilt for those who have violated the law.

Reserved powers Those powers expressly retained by the state governments under the Constitution.

Retrospective voting An explanation of vote choice that asserts that voters' evaluations of a candidate's past performance in office provides an important cue for vote decisions.

Rules Committee A committee in the House of Representatives that determines the rules by which bills will come to the floor, be debated, and so on.

Safe seat A congressional seat from a district that includes a high percentage of voters from one of the major parties.

Sampling error The amount of error in a poll that results from interviewing a sample of people rather than the whole population under study; the larger the sample, the less the sampling error.

Scientific sample A randomly selected subgroup drawn from a population using probability theory.

Select committee A committee established by a resolution in either the House or the Senate for a specific purpose and, usually, for a limited time.

Senior Executive Service (SES) Since the late 1970s, a defined group of approximately 7,500 career professionals in the federal bureaucracy who provide continuity in the operations of the bureaucracy from one presidential administration to the next.

Separation of powers The principle that each branch of government enjoys separate and independent powers and areas of responsibility.

Shays's Rebellion Armed uprising by debt-ridden Massachusetts farmers frustrated with the state government.

SLAPS test A standard that courts established to determine if material is obscene based in part on whether the material has serious literary, artistic, political, or scientific value. If it does, then the material is not obscene.

Social capital The "social connectedness" of a community, or the extent to which individuals are socially integrated into their community.

Social contract From the philosophy of Jean-Jacques Rousseau, an agreement people make with one another to form a government and abide by its rules and laws, and in return, the government promises to protect the people's rights and welfare and promote their best interests.

Social equality Equality and fair treatment of all groups within the various institutions in society, both public and private, that serve the public at large, including in stores, theaters, restaurants, hotels, and public transportation facilities among many other operations open to the public.

Social learning theory The theory that viewers imitate what they view on television through observational learning.

Social movement A large informal grouping of individuals and/or organizations focused on specific political or social issues.

Soft money Money not donated directly to a candidate's campaign, but rather to a political advocacy group or a political party for "party building" activities.

Solicitor general The lawyer representing the U.S. government before the U.S. Supreme Court.

Solidary benefits (of group membership) Satisfaction that individuals receive from interacting with like-minded individuals for a cause.

Sovereignty The supreme political power of a government to regulate its affairs without outside interference.

Speaker of the House The leader of the House of Representatives, responsible for assigning new bills to committees, recognizing members to speak in the House chamber, and assigning chairs of committees.

Spoils system The postelection practice of rewarding loyal supporters of the winning candidates and party with appointive public offices.

Standing The requirement that a party must be uniquely or singularly affected by a controversy in order to be eligible to file a lawsuit.

Standing committee A permanent committee that exists in both the House and Senate; most standing committees focus on a particular substantive area of public policy, such as transportation, labor, foreign affairs, and the federal budget.

State of the Union address An annual speech that the president delivers to Congress laying out the status of the nation and offering suggestions for new legislation.

Straw poll An unscientific poll that gathers the opinions of people who are conveniently available in a gathering place.

Strict construction Constitutional interpretation that limits the government to only those powers explicitly stated in the Constitution.

Strict scrutiny A legal standard set in *Brown v. Board of Education* for cases related to racial discrimination that tends to invalidate almost all state laws that segregate racial groups.

Supremacy clause The provision in Article VI, Clause 2 of the Constitution that provides that the Constitution and federal laws override any conflicting provisions in state constitutions or state laws.

Symbolic speech Nonspoken forms of speech that might be protected by the First Amendment, such as flag burning, wearing armbands at school to protest a war, or camping out in public parks to protest the plight of the homeless.

Talk radio A specialized form of radio programming on which one or more hosts provide commentary and often invite listeners to call in to the show and offer their own opinions.

Theocracy A form of government in which a particular religion or faith plays a dominant role in the government.

Three-Fifths Compromise A compromise proposal in which five slaves would be counted as the equivalent of three free people for purposes of taxes and representation.

Title IX The section of the Federal Educational Amendments Law of 1972 that prohibits the exclusion of women from an educational program or activity receiving financial assistance from the federal government. Courts have interpreted those provisions to force colleges and universities to provide as many athletic teams for women as they do for men.

Trade association A business association that focuses on one particular industry, with membership drawn exclusively from that industry.

Twenty-fourth Amendment The constitutional amendment that banned poll taxes in federal elections.

Twenty-second Amendment Passed in 1951, this constitutional amendment restricts any one person from being elected to the presidency "more than twice," or from acting as president for longer than two and a half terms.

Twenty-sixth Amendment The constitutional amendment that lowered the voting age to eighteen in all local, state, and federal elections.

Twenty-third Amendment The constitutional amendment providing electoral votes to the District of Columbia, thus giving District residents the right to vote in presidential elections.

Two-party system A party system dominated by two major parties that win the vast majority of elections.

U

Unfunded mandate A directive from the federal government to the states requiring that they perform certain functions, with no accompanying funds to support those functions.

Union shop The law that requires that employees in unionized workplaces either join the union or pay the equivalent of union dues to it after a set period of time.

Unitary system of government A system of government in which the constituent states are strictly subordinated to the goals of the central government as a whole.

Unit rule The system in forty-eight states by which the candidate who wins the most votes among popular votes cast for president in a state receives all the electoral votes from that state; also known as the "winner take all" system.

Universal suffrage The idea that all citizens in a nation have the right to vote.

Unscientific poll A poll in which the sample of people interviewed is not representative of any group beyond those who register their opinion.

V

Values and beliefs The broad principles underlying the American political culture that citizens support and adhere to.

Veto The constitutional procedure by which the president refuses to approve a bill or joint resolution and thus prevents its enactment into law.

Virginia Plan A proposal known also as the "large states plan" that empowered three separate branches of government, including a legislature with membership proportional to population.

Voter turnout The number of people who turn out to vote as a percentage of all those eligible to vote.

Voting The political mechanism that ensures that the majority will rule.

Voting Rights Act of 1965 The federal law that invalidated literacy tests and property requirements and required select states and cities to apply for permission to the Justice Department to change their voting laws. As a consequence, millions of African Americans were effectively reenfranchised in the South.

W

Warrant A document issued by a judge or magistrate that allows law enforcement to search or seize items at a home, business, or anywhere else that might be specified.

Whip (majority and minority) Member of Congress elected by his or her party to count potential votes and promote party unity in voting.

White House chief of staff The manager of the White House staff, which serves the president's organizational needs, including speechwriting, advance work for presidential appearances, scheduling, congressional relations, public relations, and communications.

White House Office of Legislative Affairs A presidential office that serves as a liaison between the president and Congress. This office helps the president develop the strategy used to promote passage of the president's legislative agenda.

White House press secretary The person on the White House staff who plays an especially important role in briefing the press, organizing news conferences, and even briefing the president on questions that may be asked.

Writ of certiorari The formal term for an order by which the Supreme Court acts in its discretion to review a case from a lower court.

Chapter 1

1. See Thomas Hobbes, *Leviathan* (London: A. Crooke, 1651).
2. For a collection of Rousseau's work, see Jean-Jacques Rousseau, *The Social Contract and Discourses,* translation and commentary by G. D. H. Cole (London: Guernsey Press, 1983).
3. Harold Lasswell, *Politics: Who Gets What, When and How* (New York: McGraw-Hill, 1936).
4. John Locke, *Two Treatises of Government,* ed. Peter Laslett (Cambridge: Cambridge University Press, 1960).
5. Alexis de Tocqueville, *Democracy in America, 1835,* ed. Richard Hefner (New York: Penguin Books, 1956).
6. Robert Goidel, Donald A. Gross, and Todd G. Shields, *Money Matters* (Lanham, MD: Rowman & Littlefield, 1999), 17.
7. Morris Fiorina, *Culture War? The Myth of a Polarizing America* (New York: Pearson Longman, 2005).

Chapter 2

1. Fred Anderson, *The War That Made America: A Short History of the French-Indian War* (New York: Viking, 2005).
2. Robert Middlekauff, *The Glorious Cause* (New York: Oxford University Press, 1982).
3. Events of these years are nicely recounted in Pauline Maier, *From Resistance to Revolution: Colonial Radicals and the Development of American Opposition to Britain, 1765–1776* (New York: W. W. Norton, 1992).
4. *The Political Writings of Thomas Paine, Vol. 1* (Boston: J. P. Mendum Investigator Office, 1870).
5. David McCullough, *John Adams* (New York: Simon & Schuster, 2001), 119; Joseph Ellis, *Founding Brothers* (New York: Knopf, 2000), 212–213.
6. Pauline Maier, *American Scripture: Making the Declaration of Independence* (New York: Vintage, 1998).

7. Merrill Jensen, *The Articles of Confederation: An Interpretation of the Social-Constitutional History of the American Revolution, 1774–1781* (Madison: University of Wisconsin Press, 1959).
8. For an account of Massachusetts public policy during this period, see Van Beck Hall, *Politics without Parties: Massachusetts 1780–1791* (Pittsburgh: University of Pittsburgh Press, 1972).
9. Robert Gross, ed., *In Debt to Shays* (Charlottesville: University of Virginia Press, 1993).
10. Christopher Collier, *Decision in Philadelphia: The Constitutional Convention of 1787* (New York: Ballantine Books, 2007).
11. For a discussion of the Founders' silence on slavery, see Joseph Ellis, *Founding Brothers* (New York: Knopf, 2000), 81–119.
12. Jacob E. Cooke, ed., *The Federalist* (Middletown, CT: Wesleyan University Press, 1961).
13. Saul Cornell, *The Other Founders: Anti-Federalism and the Dissenting Tradition in America 1788–1828* (Chapel Hill: University of North Carolina Press, 1999).
14. Henry Mayer, *A Son of Thunder: Patrick Henry and the American Republic* (Charlottesville: University of Virginia Press, 1992).
15. Paul Murphy, *The Historic Background of the Bill of Rights* (New York: Taylor & Francis, 1990).
16. See Jefferson–Madison correspondence republished in Philip Kurland, ed., *The Founders' Constitution* (Indianapolis: Liberty Fund, 2000).
17. Indeed, there may be numerous legal problems implicated by the holding of such a convention, as noted in Russell Caplan, *Constitutional Brinksmanship: Amending the Constitution by National Convention* (New York: Oxford University Press, 1988).
18. One of the better recent works on Marshall's tenure at the Court is R. Kent Newmyer, *John Marshall*

and the Heroic Age of the Supreme Court (Baton Rouge: Louisiana State University Press, 2002).
19. 17 U.S. 316 (1819).
20. See Robert Bork, *The Tempting of America* (New York: Simon & Schuster, 1990).
21. Lawrence Tribe, *Constitutional Choices* (Cambridge, MA: Harvard University Press, 2004).
22. John Hart Ely, *Democracy and Distrust* (Cambridge, MA: Harvard University Press, 1980).
23. 5 U.S. 137 (1803).

Chapter 3

1. Stanley R. Sloan, *NATO, The European Union and the Atlantic Community: The Transatlantic Bargain Reconsidered* (New York: Rowman & Littlefield, 2002).
2. See *McCulloch v. Maryland*, 17 U.S. 316 (1819).
3. 14 U.S. 304 (1816).
4. *Goodrich v. Department of Public Health*, 798 N.E. 2d 941 (Mass 2003).
5. In California, same-sex marriages were performed under the authority of a state supreme court ruling between June 16, 2008, and November 4, 2008, before a voter initiative reinstated that state's previous ban on the practice.
6. For example, in *Supreme Court of New Hampshire v. Piper*, 470 U.S. 274 (1985), the Supreme Court interpreted the privileges and immunities clause of Article IV to forbid states from excluding nonresidents from admission to the practice of law.
7. See *New Jersey v. New York*, 523 U.S. 767 (1998).
8. Stanley Elkins and Eric McKitrick, *The Age of Federalism: The Early American Republic 1788–1800* (New York: Oxford University Press, 1995).
9. 17 U.S. 316 (1819).
10. 22 U.S. 1 (1824).
11. H. W. Brands, *Andrew Jackson: His Life and Times* (New York: Doubleday, 2005).

12. 53 U.S. 299 (1852).

13. *Railroad Retirement Board v. Alton Railroad Co.*, 295 U.S. 330 (1935); Carter v. Carter Coal Co., 298 U.S. 238 (1936).

14. William E. Leuchtenburg, *The Supreme Court Reborn: The Constitutional Revolution in the Age of Roosevelt* (New York: Oxford University Press, 1995).

15. *Heart of Atlanta Motel v. United States*, 379 U.S. 241 (1964); *Katzenbach v. McClung*, 379 U.S. 294 (1964).

16. For an application of the term to welfare policy, see Pamela Wilson, *Welfare Policymaking in the States: The Devil in Devolution* (Washington, DC: Georgetown University Press, 2002).

17. David Savage, *Turning Right: The Making of the Rehnquist Supreme Court* (New York: Wiley, 1993).

18. 505 U.S. 144 (1992).

19. 521 U.S. 898 (1997).

20. 514 U.S. 549 (1995).

21. 529 U.S. 598 (2000).

22. 527 U.S. 706 (1999).

23. John T. Noonan Jr., *Narrowing the Nation's Power: The Supreme Court Sides with the States* (Berkeley: University of California Press, 2003).

24. William Watkins, *Reclaiming the American Revolution: The Kentucky and Virginia Resolutions and Their Legacy* (New York: Palgrave Macmillan, 2004).

25. *New State Ice Co. v. Liebmann*, 285 U.S. 262, 311 (1932).

26. See BEA News Release No. 08–11, "State Personal Income Tax 2007" (released March 26, 2008).

27. Timothy Conlan, *New Federalism: Intergovernmental Reform from Nixon to Reagan* (Washington, DC: Brookings Institution Press, 1988).

Chapter 4

1. David McCullough, *John Adams* (New York: Simon & Schuster, 2001), 504.

2. Antonin Scalia, "Law and the Winds of Change." Remarks made at the 24th Australian Legal Convention, Perth, West Australia, September 21, 1987.

3. Alexander Hamilton, James Madison, and John Jay, *The Federalist Papers,* ed. Clinton Rossiter (New York: New American Library, 1971).

4. Jefferson–Madison correspondence in Philip Kurland, ed., *The Founders' Constitution* (Indianapolis, IN: Liberty Fund, 2000).

5. 32 U.S. 243 (1833).

6. Thomas Jefferson first coined that phrase in a letter he wrote as president to the Baptists of Danbury, Connecticut, in 1802. George Seldes, ed., *The Great Quotations* (Secaucus, NJ: Citadel Press, 1983), 369.

7. 319 U.S. 624 (1943).

8. 374 U.S. 398 (1963).

9. 406 U.S. 205 (1972).

10. 98 U.S. 145 (1878).

11. 494 U.S. 872 (1990).

12. Carolyn N. Long, *Religious Freedom and Indian Rights: The Case of* Oregon v. Smith (Lawrence: University Press of Kansas, 2000).

13. Noah Feldman, *Divided by God* (New York: Farrar, Straus and Giroux, 2005).

14. 370 U.S. 421 (1962).

15. 374 U.S. 203 (1963).

16. 472 U.S. 38 (1985).

17. 536 U.S. 639 (2002).

18. 403 U.S. 602 (1971).

19. 505 U.S. 577 (1992).

20. 530 U.S. 290 (2000).

21. 249 U.S. 247 (1919).

22. 341 U.S. 494 (1951).

23. 304 U.S. 144 (1938).

24. 395 U.S. 444 (1969).

25. Harry Kalven, *A Worthy Tradition: Freedom of Speech in America* (New York: Harper & Row, 1988).

26. 376 U.S. 254 (1964).

27. Anthony Lewis, *Make No Law: The Sullivan Case and the First Amendment* (New York: Vintage Books, 1992).

28. 403 U.S. 713 (1971).

29. 413 U.S. 15 (1973).

30. 521 U.S. 844 (1997).

31. John W. Johnson, *The Struggle for Students' Rights:* Tinker v. Des Moines *and the 1960s* (Lawrence: University Press of Kansas, 1997).

32. *Tinker v. Des Moines* (393 U.S. 503 (1969)).

33. 391 U.S. 367 (1968).

34. 491 U.S. 397 (1989).

35. Robert Justin Goldstein, *Flag Burning and Free Speech: The Case of* Texas v. Johnson (Lawrence: University Press of Kansas, 2000).

36. Philippa Strum, *When the Nazis Came to Skokie: Freedom for Speech We Hate* (Lawrence: University Press of Kansas, 1999).

37. 528 U.S. 343 (2003).

38. Milton Heumann and Thomas W. Church, eds., *Hate Speech on Campus* (Boston: Northeastern University Press, 1997).

39. 554 U.S. _____ (2008).

40. 561 U.S. _____ (2010)

41. Lucas A. Powe Jr., *The Warren Court and American Politics* (Cambridge, MA: Belknap Press of Harvard University, 2002).

42. 389 U.S. 347 (1967).

43. 367 U.S. 643 (1961).

44. *Kyllo v. United States*, 533 U.S. 27 (2001).

45. It should be noted, however, that a majority of states have chosen to use grand juries, even without being compelled to do so by the U.S. Constitution.

46. 384 U.S. 436 (1966).

47. Gary Stuart, *Miranda: The Story of America's Right to Remain Silent* (Tucson: University of Arizona Press, 2004).

48. 372 U.S. 335 (1963).

49. 536 U.S. 304 (2002).

50. Austin Sarat, *When the State Kills* (Princeton, NJ: Princeton University Press, 2002).

51. 381 U.S. 479 (1965).

52. John W. Johnson, Griswold v. Connecticut: *Birth Control and the Constitutional Right of Privacy* (Lawrence: University Press of Kansas, 2005).

53. 410 U.S. 113 (1973).

54. N. E. H. Hull and Peter Charles Hoffer, Roe v. Wade: *The Abortion Rights Controversy in American History* (Lawrence: University Press of Kansas, 2001).

55. 505 U.S. 833 (1992).

56. 550 U.S. 124 (2007).

57. 539 U.S. 558 (2003).

Chapter 5

1. Juan Williams, *Eyes on the Prize: America's Civil Rights Years, 1954–1965* (New York: Penguin, 1988).

2. Louis R. Harlan, *Booker T. Washington: The Making of a Black Leader* (New York: Oxford University Press, 1975).

3. David Levering Lewis, *W. E. B. DuBois, 1868–1919: Biography of a Race* (New York: Owl Books, 1994).

4. 347 U.S. 483 (1954).

5. 60 U.S. 393 (1856).

6. Eric Foner, *Reconstruction: America's Unfinished Revolution* (New York: Harper, 2000).

7. 83 U.S. 36 (1872).

8. 109 U.S. 3 (1883).

9. 163 U.S. 537 (1896).

10. For a comprehensive account of the NAACP's strategy, see Richard Kluger, *Simple Justice* (New York: Vintage Books, 1975).

11. 358 U.S. 1 (1957).

12. Jennifer Hochschild, *The New American Dilemma: Liberal Democracy and School Desegregation* (New Haven, CT: Yale University Press, 1984).

13. See Taylor Branch, *Pillar of Fire: America in the King Years, 1963–65* (New York: Simon & Schuster, 1999).

14. Charles Whalen and Barbara Whalen, *Longest Debate: A Legislative History of the Civil Rights Act* (Santa Ana, CA: Seven Locks Press, 1984).

15. 438 U.S. 265 (1978).

16. Howard Ball, *The Bakke Case: Race, Education and Affirmative Action* (Lawrence: University Press of Kansas, 2000).

17. 515 U.S. 200 (1995).

18. 539 U.S. 306 (2003).

19. 539 U.S. 244 (2003).

20. Edward N. Wolff, "Racial Wealth Disparities: Is the Gap Closing?" Public Policy Brief No. 66 (Annandale-on-Hudson, NY: Levi Economics Institute of Bard College, 2001).

21. "Vital Signs: Statistics That Measure the State of Racial Inequality," *Journal of Blacks in Higher Education*, no. 44 (Summer 2004).

22. Michael Jones and Eileen Poe-Yamagata, *And Justice for Some* (Washington, DC: Building Blocks for Youth Press, 2000).

23. 208 U.S. 412 (1908).

24. 335 U.S. 464 (1948).

25. 368 U.S. 57, 61 (1961).

26. 404 U.S. 71 (1971).

27. 411 U.S. 677 (1973).

28. 429 U.S. 190 (1976).

29. U.S. Merit Systems Protection Board, "Sexual Harassment in the Federal Workplace: Trends, Progress, Continuing Challenges" (Office of Policy Evaluation, U.S. Merit Systems Protection Board Document).

30. 517 U.S. 620 (1996).

Chapter 6

1. Woodrow Wilson, *Congressional Government* (Baltimore: Johns Hopkins University Press, 1981; originally published in 1885).

2. For a good discussion of the Constitutional Convention and issues related to Congress, see Charles Stewart III, "Congress and the Constitutional System," in *Institutions of American Democracy: The Legislative Branch,* ed. Paul J. Quirk and Sarah A. Binder (New York: Oxford University Press, 2005).

3. Alexander Hamilton, James Madison, and John Jay, *The Federalist Papers* (Chicago: The New American Library of World Literature; reprinted in 1961).

4. Thomas Mann, *Unsafe at Any Margin: Interpreting Congressional Elections* (Washington, DC: Brookings Institution Press, 1978).

5. Paul Finkelman and Peter Wallenstein, *The Encyclopedia of American Political History* (Washington, DC: CQ Press, 2001), 55–56.

6. See, for example, *Baker v. Carr,* 369 U.S. 186 (1962); *Reynolds v. Sims,* 377 U.S. 533 (1964); *Wesberry v. Sanders,* 376 U.S. 1 (1964).

7. See James Madison, Federalist No. 63.

8. For a discussion of leadership in Congress, see Burdett A. Loomis, *The Contemporary Congress,* 3rd ed. (Boston: Bedford St. Martin's, 2000), chap. 6.

9. See Eric Schickler, "Institutional Development of Congress," in *Institutions of American Democracy: The Legislative Branch,* ed. Quirck and Binder (New York: Oxford University Press, 2005), chap. 2.

10. A classic work on congressional committees is Richard F. Fenno Jr., *Congressmen in Committees* (Boston: Little, Brown, 1973).

11. See Stephen S. Smith and Christopher Deering, *Committees in Congress,* 2nd ed. (Washington, DC: CQ Press, 1990).

12. See Roger Davidson and Walter Oleszek, *Congress and Its Members,* 4th ed. (Washington, DC: CQ Press, 1994).

13. A classic piece on the topic is John Manley, "Wilbur Mills: A Study of Congressional Influence," *American Political Science Review* 63 (1969): 442–464.

14. Eric Redman, *The Dance of Legislation* (Seattle: University of Washington Press, 1974).

15. For a discussion of the motivations for senators to filibuster, see Sarah A. Binder and Stephen S. Smith, *Politics or Principles? Filibustering in the United States Senate* (Washington, DC: Brookings Institution Press, 1997).

16. Morris P. Fiorina, *Congress: Keystone of the Washington Establishment,* 2nd ed. (New Haven, CT: Yale University Press, 1989).

17. For a discussion of the presidential nominating process, see David A. Yalof, *Pursuit of Justices* (Chicago: University of Chicago Press, 2001).

18. Richard F. Fenno Jr., *Home Style: House Members in Their Districts* (Boston: Little, Brown, 1978).

Chapter 7

1. Joseph Ellis, *His Excellency: George Washington* (New York: Knopf, 2004).

2. Dates provided after a president's name refers to year(s) of service as president of the United States.

3. H. W. Brands, *Andrew Jackson: His Life and Times* (New York: Random House, 2005).

4. John Seigenthaler, *James K. Polk, 1845–1849* (New York: Times Books, 2003).

5. See *Ex Parte Merryman,* 17 Fed. Cas. 144 (1961).

6. Edmund Morris, *Theodore Rex* (New York: Random House, 2001).

7. See Clinton Rossiter, *The American Presidency* (Baltimore: Johns Hopkins University Press, 1987).

8. See John Locke, *Two Treatises of Government and a Letter Concerning Toleration,* ed. Peter Laslett (Cambridge: Cambridge University Press, 1963).

9. Baron de Montesquieu, *The Spirit of the Laws* (Anne M. Cohler et al., eds.) (Cambridge: Cambridge University Press, 1989).

10. Michael J. Gerhardt, *The Federal Appointments Process: A Constitutional and Historical Analysis* (Durham, NC: Duke University Press, 2003).

11. Robert F. Kennedy Jr., *Thirteen Days: A Memoir of the Cuban Missile Crisis* (New York: W. W. Norton, 1999).

12. Mark Peterson, *Legislating Together: The White House and Capitol Hill from Eisenhower to Reagan* (Cambridge, MA: Harvard University Press, 1990).

13. Paul Light, *The President's Agenda: Domestic Policy Choice from Kennedy to Clinton* (Baltimore: Johns Hopkins University Press, 1999).

14. Lee Hamilton and Jordan Tama, *A Creative Tension: The Foreign Policy Roles of the President and Congress* (Washington, DC: Woodrow Wilson Press, 2003).

15. Kenneth Mayer, *With the Stroke of a Pen: Executive Orders and Presidential Power* (Princeton, NJ: Princeton University Press, 2001).

16. The updated version of this work is Richard Neustadt, *Presidential Power and the Modern Presidents: The Politics of Leadership from Roosevelt Through Reagan* (New York: Free Press, 1991).

17. Jules Witcover, *Crapshoot: Rolling the Dice on the Vice Presidency* (New York: Crown, 1991).

18. Bob Woodward, *Plan of Attack* (New York: Simon & Schuster, 2004).

19. For a comprehensive discussion of the various ways that modern presidents have organized the White House, see Stephen Hess, *Organizing the Presidency* (Washington, DC: Brookings Institution Press, 1988).

20. Bill Adler, *America's First Ladies* (New York: Taylor, 2002).

21. Samuel Kernell, *Going Public: New Strategies of Presidential Leadership* (Washington, DC: CQ Press, 1992).

22. Elizabeth Drew, *On the Edge: The Clinton Presidency* (New York: Touchstone, 1995).

23. See Kathleen Hall Jamieson and Paul Waldman, *The Press Effect: Politicians, Journalists, and the Stories That Shape the Political World* (New York: Oxford University Press, 2002).

24. John A. Maltese, *Spin Control: The White House Office of Communications and the Management of Presidential News* (Chapel Hill: University of North Carolina Press, 1992).

25. Ted Rueter, *The 267 Stupidest Things Republicans Ever Said/The 267 Stupidest Things Democrats Ever Said* (New York: Three Rivers Press, 2000).

Chapter 8

1. For a good discussion of the themes of the 1980 Reagan campaign, see Theodore H. White, *America in Search of Itself: The Making of the Presidency, 1956-1980* (New York: Harper & Row, 1982).

2. See James P. P. Horn, *The Revolution of 1800: Democracy, Race and the New Republic* (Charlottesville: University Press of Virginia, 2002).

3. See William Earl Weeks, "Louisiana Purchase" in *The Oxford Companion to United States History* (New York: Oxford University Press, 2001), p. 463.

4. See *Washington Monthly,* a periodical that regularly reports on the excesses and waste in the federal bureaucracy.

5. For a comprehensive discussion of the virtues of contemporary bureaucracy, see Charles T. Goodsell, *The Case for Bureaucracy* (Chatham, NJ: Chatham House Publishers, 1994).

6. Max Weber, chapters 11 and 12 in *Economy and Society,* ed. Guenther Roth and Claus Wittich (New York: Bedminster Press, 1968).

7. For a good discussion of organizational issues in the federal bureaucracy, see James Q. Wilson, *Bureaucracy: What Government Agencies Do and Why They Do It* (New York: Basic Books, 1989).

8. See Joel Aberbach, *Keeping a Watchful Eye: The Politics of Congressional Oversight* (Washington, DC: Brookings Institution Press, 1990).

9. Beverly Cigler, "The Paradox of Professionalization," in *Democracy, Bureaucracy and the Study of Administration,* ed. Camilla Stivers (Boulder, CO: Westview Press, 2001).

10. For a good discussion of the growth of the federal bureaucracy during the FDR years, see Brian J. Cook, "Serving the Liberal State," chapter 5 in *Bureaucracy and Self-Government: Reconsidering the Role of Public Administration in American Politics* (Baltimore: Johns Hopkins University Press, 1996).

11. David Osborne and Ted Gaebler, *Reinventing Government: How the Entrepreneurial Spirit Is Transforming the Public Sector* (New York: Penguin Books, 1993).

12. Harold S. Stanley and Richard G. Niemi, *Vital Statistics on American Politics, 2005–2006* (Washington, DC: CQ Press, 2006), 266.

13. Robert H. Wiebe, *The Search for Order: 1877–1920* (New York: Hill and Wang, 1967).

14. Data from the U.S. Bureau of Labor Statistics Website: www.bls.gov/oco/cg/cgs041.htm.

15. See Ari Hoogenboom, *Outlawing the Spoils: A History of the Civil Service Reform Movement, 1865–1883* (Champaign: University of Illinois Press, 1961).

16. Bruce Maxwell, *Insider's Guide to Finding a Job in Washington* (Washington, DC: CQ Press, 2000), 74–75.

Chapter 9

1. For an account of the ways in which the Supreme Court's methods contribute to its image and status as an institution, see John Brigham, *The Cult of the Court* (Philadelphia: Temple University Press, 1987).

2. John Merryman, *The Civil Law Tradition* (Palo Alto, CA: Stanford University Press, 1985).

3. G. Alan Tarr and Mary Cornelius Porter, *State Supreme Courts in State and Nation* (New Haven, CT: Yale University Press, 1988).

4. 1 Cranch (5 U.S.) 137 (1803).

5. Arthur Hellman, *Restructuring Justice: The Innovations of the Ninth Circuit and the Future of the Federal Courts* (Ithaca, NY: Cornell University Press, 1991).

6. One rare exception to the strict use of the adversarial approach in the American legal system comes in the form of "structural reform litigation," a term that describes certain types of lawsuits brought against bureaucracies such as prisons, school systems, or welfare systems. Judges in these types of cases often assume a more active "managerial approach" in the process, overseeing the implementation of remedies and occasionally taking a proactive role to ensure that the lawyers are properly representing their client's interests. For comprehensive analysis of one example of structural reform litigation in action, see Malcolm Feeley and Edward Rubin, *Judicial Policymaking and the Modern State: How the Court Reformed America's Prisons* (Cambridge: Cambridge University Press, 2000). Of course, the more traditional adversarial system still tends to predominate in most other forms of civil litigation.

7. See George Fisher, *Plea Bargaining's Triumph: A History of Plea Bargaining in America* (Palo Alto, CA: Stanford University Press, 2003); Milton Heumann, *Plea Bargaining: The Experiences of Prosecutors, Judges, and Defense Attorneys* (Chicago: University of Chicago Press, 1981).

8. James Eisenstein, Roy Flemming, and Peter Nardulli, *The Contours of Justice* (New York: Addison-Wesley Publishing, 1988).

9. R. Kent Newmyer, *The Supreme Court Under Marshall and Taney* (Arlington Heights, IL: Harlan Davison, 1968).

10. 17 U.S. 316 (1819).

11. 1 Wheat (14 U.S.) 304 (1816).

12. 358 U.S. 1 (1958).

13. 60 U.S. 393 (1857).

14. 347 U.S. 483 (1954).

15. 418 U.S. 683 (1974).

16. 506 U.S. 224 (1993).

17. 6 Pet. (31 U.S.) 515 (1832).

18. See Bob Woodward and Carl Bernstein, *The Final Days* (New York: Simon & Schuster, 1994).

19. Bradley Canon and Charles Johnson, *Judicial Policies: Implementation and Impact,* 2nd ed. (Washington, DC: CQ Press, 1999).

20. 347 U.S. 483 (1954).

21. 370 U.S. 421 (1962).

22. Robert Dahl, "Decisionmaking in a Democracy: The Supreme Court as a National Policy-Maker." *Journal of Public Law*, vol. 6 (1957): 279–295.

23. Philip DuBois, *From Ballot to Bench: Judicial Elections and the Quest for Accountability* (Austin: University of Texas Press, 1980).

24. Sheldon Goldman, *Picking Federal Judges* (New Haven, CT: Yale University Press, 1997).

25. Barbara Perry, *A Representative Supreme Court* (Westport, CT: Greenwood Press, 1991).

26. John Maltese, *The Selling of Supreme Court Nominees* (Baltimore: Johns Hopkins University Press, 1995).

27. Ethan Bronner, *Battle for Justice: How the Bork Nomination Shook America* (New York: W. W. Norton, 1989).

28. 410 U.S. 113 (1973).

29. Richard Pacelle, *Between Law and Politics: The Solicitor General and the Structuring of Race, Gender, and Reproductive Rights Litigation* (College Station: Texas A & M University Press, 2003).

30. 376 U.S. 254 (1964).

31. 478 U.S. 186 (1986).

32. 539 U.S. 558 (2003).

33. 384 U,S. 436 (1966).

34. Jeffrey Segal and Harold Spaeth, *The Supreme Court and The Attitudinal Model* (Cambridge: Cambridge University Press, 1993), 246.

35. See, for example, Sheldon M. Novick, *Honorable Justice: The Life of Oliver Wendell Holmes, Jr.* (Boston: Little, Brown & Co., 1989).

36. 531 U.S. 98 (2000).

37. Justice Antonin Scalia, Interview with CNBC, October 10, 2005.

Chapter 10

1. Vincent Price, *Public Opinion* (Newbury Park, CA: Sage Publications, 1992), 5–22.

2. E. E. Schattschneider, *The Semi-sovereign People: A Realist's View of Democracy in America* (New York: Holt, Rinehart and Winston, 1960).

3. V. O. Key Jr., *Public Opinion and American Democracy* (New York: Knopf, 1961).

4. Samuel P. Huntington, *American Politics: The Promise of Disharmony* (Cambridge, MA: Harvard University Press, 1981).

5. For a good discussion of the value of individualism in the American culture, see Herbert McCloskey and John Zaller, *The American Ethos* (Cambridge, MA: Harvard University Press, 1984).

6. The concept of partisanship and controversies surrounding it over the years are presented in Warren E. Miller and Merrill Shanks, *The New American Voter* (Cambridge, MA: Harvard University Press, 1996).

7. See M. Kent Jennings and Richard G. Niemi, *Generations and Politics: A Panel Study of Young Adults and Their Parents* (Princeton, NJ: Princeton University Press, 1981).

8. James Madison, Alexander Hamilton, and John Jay, *The Federalist Papers*, Federalist No. 51 (New York: Doubleday, 1966, originally published in 1788).

9. Walter Lippman, *Public Opinion* (New York: Harcourt Brace Jovanovich, 1922).

10. Angus Campbell, Phillip E. Converse, Warren E. Miller, and Donald E. Stokes, *The American Voter* (New York: John Wiley and Sons, 1960).

11. This survey was commissioned by the Intercollegiate Studies Institute and included a national adult sample of 2,500 respondents, conducted by telephone.

12. V. O. Key Jr., *The Responsible Electorate* (Cambridge, MA: Belknap Harvard, 1966).

13. Benjamin I. Page and Robert Y. Shapiro, *The Rational Public: Fifty Years of Trends in Americans' Policy Preferences* (Chicago: University of Chicago Press, 1992).

14. Samuel Kernell, *Going Public: New Strategies of Presidential Leadership* (Washington, DC: CQ Press, 1997).

15. Jack Dennis, ed., *Socialization to Politics* (New York: John Wiley and Sons, 1973).

16. See, generally, David Easton, *A Systems Analysis of Political Life* (New York: John Wiley and Sons, 1965).

17. Michael X. Delli Carpini and Scott Keeter, *What Americans Know About Politics and Why It Matters* (New Haven, CT: Yale University Press, 1996).

18. Herb Asher, *Polling and the Public*, 6th ed. (Washington, DC: CQ Press, 2004).

19. Charles W. Roll and Albert H. Cantril, *Polls: Their Use and Misuse in Politics* (New York: Basic Books, 1972).

20. An important book spelling out the variety of problems and issues with the wording of survey questions is Howard Schuman and Stanley Press, *Questions and Answers in Attitude Surveys* (New York: John Wiley and Sons, 1981).

21. For a more detailed discussion of these concepts, see W. Lance Bennett, *Public Opinion in American Politics* (New York: Harcourt Brace Jovanovich, 1980).

Chapter 11

1. James Madison, Federalist No. 10, in *The Federalist Papers* (reprinted by Mentor Books, 1961), 77.

2. Alexis de Tocqueville, *Democracy in America* (New York: Mentor Books, reprint edition, 1956).

3. Robert Dahl, *A Preface to Democratic Theory* (Cambridge: Cambridge University Press, 1956).

4. David B. Truman, *The Governmental Process* (New York: Alfred Knopf, 1951).

5. C. Wright Mills, *The Power Elite* (New York: Oxford University Press, 1956).

6. John P. Heinz, Edward O. Laumann, Robert L. Nelson, and Robert H. Salisbury, *The Hollow Core* (Cambridge, MA: Harvard University Press, 1993).

7. David Lowery and Holly Brasher, *Organized Interests and American Government* (New York: McGraw-Hill, 2004), 8.

8. See http://www.opensecrets.org/lobbyists/index.asp.

9. See Theodore J. Lowi, *The End of Liberalism* (New York: W. W. Norton, 1979).

10. See William Gormley, "Regulatory Issue Networks in a Federal System," in *Polity*, vol. 18 (1986): 595–620.

11. See http://www.uschamber.com.

12. Mancur Olson, *The Logic of Collective Action: Public Goods and the Theory of Groups* (Cambridge, MA: Harvard University Press, 1971), 22–35.

13. Robert Salisbury, "An Exchange Theory of Interest Groups" in *Midwest Journal of Political Science*, vol. 13 (1969): 1–32.

14. Peter B. Clark and James Q. Wilson, "Incentives Systems: A Theory of Organization" in *Administrative Science Quarterly*, vol. 6 (1961): 129–166.
15. For a good discussion of the influence of group member dedication to group effectiveness, see Olson, *The Logic of Collective Action: Public Goods and the Theory of Groups*, op. cit.
16. Olson, *The Logic of Collective Action: Public Goods and the Theory of Groups*, op. cit.
17. See http://www.commoncause.org.
18. David Lowery and Holly Brasher, *Organized Interests and American Government* (New York: McGraw-Hill, 2004), 247.

Chapter 12
1. 438 U.S. 726 (1978).
2. See Philip Meyer, *Precision Journalism: A Reporter's Introduction to Social Science Methods* (Lanham, MD: Rowman & Littlefield, 2002).
3. The word *muckrakers* is derived from the idea that this group was "raking up the mud" from scandals and corruption of government and industry.
4. For a chronicle of the Watergate story, see Bob Woodward and Carl Bernstein, *All the President's Men* (New York: Simon & Schuster, 1974).
5. Richard A. Clarke, *Against All Enemies* (New York: Free Press, 2004).
6. For a thorough review of the history of news, see Mitchell Stephens, *A History of News: From the Drum to the Satellite* (New York: Viking, 1989).
7. Kurt Lang and Gladys Lang, *Television and Politics* (Edison, NJ: Transaction Publishers, 2001).
8. Marshall McLuhan, *Understanding Media: The Extensions of Man* (New York: McGraw-Hill, 1964).
9. For a good review of the process and impact of presidential debates, see Alan Schroeder, *Presidential Debates* (New York: Columbia University Press, 2000).
10. See Doris Graber, *Processing Politics: Learning from Television in the Internet Age* (Chicago: University of Chicago Press, 2001).
11. Mass communications researcher Joseph Klapper was a pioneer of the minimal effects (or limited effects) theory. He introduced the theory in a book titled *The Effects of Mass Communication* (New York: Free Press, 1960).

12. For a good discussion of selection retention, see D. Sears and J. Freeman, "Selective Exposure to Information: A Critical Review," in *The Process and Effects of Mass Communication,* ed. Wilbur Lang Schramm (Chicago: University of Illinois Press, 1972).
13. For a good discussion of social learning theory, see Albert Bandura, *Social Foundations of Thought and Action* (Englewood Cliffs, NJ: Prentice-Hall, 1986).
14. See L. Berkowitz, "Some Effects of Thought on Anti- and Pro- Social Influences of Media Effects," in *Psychological Bulletin* 95 (1984): 410–427.
15. A pioneer in developing cultivation theory was George Gerbner. See George Gerbner et al., "Growing Up with Television: The Cultivation Perspective," in *Media Effects: Advances in Theory and Research,* ed. Jennings Bryant and Dolf Zillman (Hillsdale, NJ: Lawrence Erlbaum, 1994), 17–41.
16. A number of studies have demonstrated the agenda-setting power of the media, including Maxwell E. McCombs, "The Agenda-Setting Approach," in *Handbook of Political Communication,* ed. Dan D. Nimmo and Keith Sanders (Thousand Oaks, CA: Sage, 1981), 121–140; Shanto Iyengar and Donald R. Kinder, *News That Matters* (Chicago: University of Chicago Press, 1987).
17. Doris A. Graber, Mass Media and American Politics (Washington, DC: CQ Press, 2002), 207.
18. Kenneth Dautrich and Thomas H. Hartley, *How the News Media Fail American Voters* (New York: Columbia University Press, 1999), 92–95.

Chapter 13
1. "Toward a More Responsible Party System: A Report of the Committee on Political Parties, American Political Science Association," *American Political Science Review*, vol. 44, no. 3 (September 1950).
2. E. E. Schattschneider, *Party Government* (New York: Farrar and Rinehart, 1942).
3. See chapter 2 in John F. Bibby, *Politics, Parties and Elections in America,* 5th ed. (Belmont, CA: Wadsworth, 2002).
4. See Paul Finkelman and John Moore, "Political Parties," in *The Encyclopedia*

of American Political History, ed. Peter Wallenstein and Paul Finkelman (Washington, DC: CQ Press, 2001).
5. See chapter 2 in Bibby, *Politics, Parties and Elections in America,* op. cit.
6. V. O. Key Jr., "A Theory of Critical Elections," *Journal of Politics*, vol. 16, no. 1 (1955): 13–18.
7. See Walter Dean Burnham, *Critical Elections and the Mainsprings of American Politics* (New York: W. W. Norton, 1970).
8. For a thorough analysis of how the American party system has changed since the New Deal, see Sidney M. Milkus, *The President and the Parties: The Transformation of the American Party System Since the New Deal* (New York: Oxford University Press, 1993).
9. Paul Allen Beck, "The Dealignment Era in America," in *Electoral Change in Advanced Industrial Democracies: Realignment or Dealignment,* ed. M. N. Dalton, T. T. Flanagan, and H. Beck (Princeton, NJ: Princeton University Press, 1984).
10. Angus Campbell, Philip E. Converse, Warren E. Miller, and Donald E. Stokes, *The American Voter* (New York: Wiley, 1960).
11. For a thorough discussion of the concept of party identification, see Warren E. Miller and J. Merrill Shanks, *The New American Voter* (Cambridge, MA: Harvard University Press, 1996).
12. Philip E. Converse, "The Concept of the Normal Vote," in *Elections and the Political Order,* ed. Angus Campbell, Philip E. Converse, Warren E. Miller, and Donald E. Stokes (New York: Wiley, 1966).
13. For a discussion of governance and the parties, see John H. Aldrich, *Why Parties? The Origin and Transformation of Political Parties in America* (Chicago: University of Chicago Press, 1995), chapter 7.
14. See Richard S. Conley, *The Presidency, Congress and Divided Government* (College Station: Texas A&M University Press, 2002).
15. For a good discussion of the rationale for America's two-party system, see Frank J. Sorauf, *Party Politics in America,* 5th ed. (Boston: Little, Brown, 1984).
16. For a good discussion of nineteenth- and twentieth-century

third-party candidacies, see Steven J. Rosenstone, Roy L. Behr, and Edward H. Lazarus, *Third Parties in America,* 2nd ed. (Princeton, NJ: Princeton University Press, 1996).

17. Martin Wattenberg, *The Decline of American Political Parties* (Cambridge, MA: Harvard University Press, 1998).

18. See, for example, Jeff Cohen, Richard Fleisher, and Paul Kantor, eds., *American Political Parties: Decline or Resurgence?* (Washington, DC: CQ Press, 2001).

Chapter 14

1. For a comprehensive discussion of political participation, see M. Margaret Conway, *Political Participation in the United States,* 3rd ed. (Washington, DC: CQ Press, 2000).

2. For a discussion of the struggle for suffrage, see William H. Flanigan and Nancy H. Zingale, *Political Behavior of the American Electorate* (Washington, DC: CQ Press, 1998), chapter 2.

3. See Margaret M. Conway, *Political Participation in the United States* (Washington, DC: CQ Press, 2000), chapter 5.

4. Some southern states continued to use the poll tax in state elections after passage of the Twenty-fourth Amendment. In 1966, the U.S. Supreme Court in *Harper v. Virginia State Board of Elections* outlawed the use of the poll tax in state elections as well as federal elections.

5. See Nancy McGlen and Karen O'Connor, *Women, Politics and American Society,* 2nd ed. (Upper Saddle River, NJ: Prentice-Hall, 1998).

6. A thorough discussion of the development of states' voter registration systems can be found in Joseph P. Harris, *Registration of Voters in the United States* (Washington, DC: Brookings Institution Press, 1929).

7. A federal statute requires that the waiting period from becoming a state resident to being eligible to vote may not exceed thirty days.

8. Michael D. Martinez and David B. Hill, "Did Motor Voter Work?" *American Politics Quarterly* 27 (1999): 296–315.

9. See Lee Sigelman et al., "Voting and Non-voting: A Multi-Election Perspective," *American Journal of Political Science* 29 (November 1985), 749–765.

10. See Raymond E. Wolfinger and Steven J. Rosenstone, *Who Votes?* (New Haven, CT: Yale University Press, 1980), 44–46.

11. Norman H. Nie, Jane Junn, and Kenneth Stehlik-Barry, *Education and Democratic Citizenship in America* (Chicago: University of Chicago Press, 1996).

12. Todd G. Shields and Robert K. Goidel, "Participation Rates, Socioeconomic Class Biases and Congressional Elections: A Cross Validation," *American Journal of Political Science* 41 (1997), 683–691.

13. Anthony Downs, *An Economic Theory of Democracy* (New York: Harper and Brothers, 1957).

14. Angus Campbell, Philip E. Converse, Warren E. Miller, and Donald E. Stokes, *Elections and the Political Order* (New York: Wiley, 1966).

15. For a comprehensive examination of the trends in voter turnout, see Thomas E. Patterson, *The Vanishing American Voter: Public Involvement in an Age of Uncertainty* (New York: Alfred A. Knopf, 2002).

16. See Ivor Crewe, "As the World Turns Out," *Public Opinion* 4 (February–March 1981).

17. For a discussion of trends in political efficacy, see also M. Margaret Conway, *Political Participation in the United States,* 3rd ed. (Washington, DC: CQ Press, 2000), 51–53.

18. Robert Putnam, *Bowling Alone* (New York: Simon & Schuster, 2000).

19. The psychological concept of party identification is developed in Angus Campbell, Philip E. Converse, Warren E. Miller, and Donald E. Stokes, *The American Voter* (New York: Wiley, 1960).

20. For discussion of the role of party identification in forming vote choices, see Warren E. Miller and J. Merrill Shanks, *The New American Voter* (Cambridge, MA: Harvard University Press, 1996), and William H. Flanigan and Nancy H. Zingale, *Political Behavior of the American Electorate,* 9th ed. (Washington, DC: CQ Press, 1998).

21. See Martin P. Wattenberg, *The Decline of Political Parties 1952–1996* (Cambridge, MA: Harvard University Press, 1998).

22. Warren E. Miller and J. Merrill Shanks, *The New American Voter* (Cam-

bridge, MA: Harvard University Press, 1996), chapter 12.

23. See Norman Nie, Sidney Verba, and John Petrocik, *The Changing American Voter* (Cambridge, MA: Harvard University Press, 1979).

24. Morris P. Fiorina, *Retrospective Voting in American National Elections* (New Haven, CT: Yale University Press, 1981).

Chapter 15

1. See Ari Hoogenboom, *The Presidency of Rutherford B. Hayes* (Lawrence: University Press of Kansas, 1988).

2. See Lawrence D. Longley and Neal R. Pierce, *The Electoral College Primer* (New Haven, CT: Yale University Press, 1996).

3. For a good discussion of the development of parties in the early Republic, see Stanley Elkins and Eric McKitrick, *The Age of Federalism: The Early American Republic 1788–1800* (New York: Oxford University Press, 1993).

4. See Paul Finkelman and John Moore, "The Democratic Party," in *The Encyclopedia of American Political History,* ed. Peter Wallenstein and Paul Finkelman (Washington, DC: CQ Press, 2001).

5. See Tadahisa Kuroda, *The Origins of the Twelfth Amendment: The Electoral College in the Early Republic 1787–1804* (Westport, CT: Greenwood Press, 1994).

6. A thorough discussion of the nomination process as well as other aspects of the presidential campaign can be found in Stephen Wayne, *The Road to the White House 2008,* 8th ed. (Boston: Wadsworth Press, 2008).

7. Larry M. Bartels, *Presidential Primaries and the Dynamics of Public Choice* (Princeton, NJ: Princeton University Press, 1988).

8. See John F. Bibby, *Politics, Parties and Elections in America* (Chicago: Nelson-Hall, 1992), chapter 6.

9. Ibid.

10. For a good discussion of the relevance of the New Hampshire primary, see Dante J. Scala, *Stormy Weather: The New Hampshire Primary and Presidential Politics* (New York: Palgrave Macmillan, 2003).

11. Nevada disrupted this traditional order in 2008 when it scheduled its Republican and Democratic caucuses

for January 19, three days before the New Hampshire primary. New Hampshire then moved its primary to January 8.

12. See William G. Mayer and Andrew Busch, *The Frontloading Problem in Presidential Nominations* (Washington, DC: Brookings Institution Press, 2003).

13. For an excellent preview and discussion of the 2008 presidential contest and some of its leading candidates, see Mark Halperin and John Harris, *The Way to Win: Taking the White House in 2008* (New York: Random House, 2006).

14. For a history of party conventions, see CQ Press's *National Party Conventions 1831–2004* (2005).

15. The supporters of Herbert Hoover, the Republican candidate in 1928, briefly considered putting Dawes on the ticket as vice president once again, but backed down when the move was opposed by President Coolidge.

16. See, for example, James Druckman, "The Power of Television Images: The First Kennedy-Nixon Debate Revisited," *Journal of Politics* vol. 65, no. 2 (2003): 559–571.

17. See Alan Schroeder, *Presidential Debates: 40 Years of High Risk TV* (New York: Columbia University Press, 1997).

18. See Darrell M. West, *Television Advertising in Election Campaigns 1952–1996* (Washington, DC: CQ Press, 1997).

19. For an analysis of the effects of negative ads on voters, see Richard R. Lau and Gerald M. Pomper, *Negative Campaigning: An Analysis of U.S. Senate Elections* (Lanham, MD: Rowman and Littlefield, 2004).

20. For a discussion of why the Electoral College was created and how it has changed, see Lawrence D. Longley and Neal R. Peirce, *The Electoral College Primer 2000* (New Haven, CT: Yale University Press, 1999), chapter 2.

21. See Longley and Peirce, chapter 4.

22. See David B. Magleby and Candice J. Nelson, *The Money Chase* (Washington, DC: Brookings Institution Press, 1990).

23. *Buckley v. Valeo,* 424 U.S. 1 (1976).

24. *McConnell v. F.E.C.,* 540 U.S. 93 (2003).

25. For a thorough discussion of congressional elections, see Paul S. Herrnson, *Congressional Elections: Campaigning at Home and in Washington,* 2nd ed. (Washington, DC: CQ Press, 1998).

26. For a complete discussion of the coattail effect, see Gary C. Jacobson, *Electoral Origins of Divided Government 1946–1988* (Boulder, CO: Westview Press, 1990).

27. See Gary C. Jacobson, *The Politics of Congressional Elections,* 5th ed. (New York: Longman, 2001), chapter 3.

Note: Terms in boldface type are key terms defined in the glossary. Page numbers in italics refer to tables, figures, and boxed features